THE MAGICAL UNIVERSE

Baptism. Juraj Kmet', Slovakia, 1793.

Demon carrying off child promised at birth to the Devil. Woodcut
from Geoffroy de Latour Landry, *Der Ritter vom Turn*
(Basel, 1493).

THE MAGICAL UNIVERSE

*Everyday Ritual and Magic
in Pre-Modern Europe*

STEPHEN WILSON

HAMBLEDON AND LONDON
London and New York

Hambledon and London

102 Gloucester Avenue
London, NW1 8HX

838 Broadway
New York
NY 10003-4812

First Published 2000

ISBN 1 85285 251 8

Typeset by John Saunders Design & Production
Reading, Berkshire

Printed on acid-free paper and bound in
Great Britain by Cambridge University Press

Contents

IV DIVINATION AND SIGNS

V THE ELEMENTS OF MAGIC

Illustrations

Acknowledgements

Acknowledgements are gratefully made to the following institutions for the use of illustrative material: Antwerp Cathedral; Ashmolean Museum, Oxford; Bibliothèque Nationale, Paris; Cambridge and County Folk Museum; Fondazione Scientifica Querini Stampalia, Venice; Galleria Nazionale d'Arte Antica, Palazzo Barberini, Rome; Koninklijk Museum voor Schone Kunsten, Antwerp; Metropolitan Museum of Art, New York; Musée du Cloître André Mazeyrie, Tulle; Musée du Louvre, Paris; Musée National des Arts et Traditions Populaires, Paris; Musées Royaux des Beaux-Arts de Belgique, Brussels; Museum of Fine Arts, Budapest; National Museum, Prague; Santuario d'Oropa; Vatican Picture Gallery, Rome; Wallace Collection, London.

By the Same Author

Ideology and Experience: Antisemitism in France
at the Time of the Dreyfus Affair

Saints and Their Cults:
Studies in Religious Sociology, Folklore and History
(Editor)

Feuding, Conflict and Banditry
in Nineteenth-Century Corsica
(Prix du Livre Corse)

The Means of Naming:
A Social and Cultural History of Personal
Naming in Western Europe

For my teachers and mentors
in memory and gratitude

F.N. SWEET

J.B. HOPE-SIMPSON

J.P.T. BURY

'They say miracles are past; and we have our philosophical persons to make modern and familiar, things supernatural and causeless. Hence is it that we make trifles of terrors, ensconcing ourselves into seeming knowledge when we should submit ourselves to an unknown fear'.

Lafew in Shakespeare, *All's Well That Ends Well*,
Act II, Scene III (*c.* 1600).

'We do not believe; we are afraid.'

Eskimo shaman.

Introduction

'I believe it could be shown that *some* degree of belief in magic is almost universal.'

George Orwell (1943)[1]

Historians have focused attention on the more sensational aspects of magic in the 'early modern' period, that is on the witch trials of the sixteenth and seventeenth centuries. These of course have their fascination and their interest, but it is difficult to understand the witch trials without placing them in the wider context of witchcraft beliefs, and witchcraft beliefs at both the elite and the popular level were in turn part of a much wider system of magical belief and practice. Again, although the witch trials emerged at a particular time and then disappeared, which has led historians to think in terms of a 'rise' and a 'decline' of magic, general magical beliefs and practices existed over a much longer time span, in effect from Ancient times down to the modern era. It is this perennial everyday magic, an important subject in its own right, with which this book is concerned, mainly but not exclusively in Western Europe including the British Isles.

Like most human beings world-wide, pre-modern Europeans (and Americans) inhabited a magical universe. The world about them was not simply a material one, following fixed and complex laws but allowing humans a degree of control over it via technology. It was spiritual in the widest sense and not predictable. There was a force in all things, animate and, to our view, inanimate: water, trees, substances, words; and there was a mutual influence among things. There were also human and supra- or extra-human beings, who exercised power of different kinds and at different levels: saints, witches, ghosts, spirits and less palpable entities. God ruled from on high. He might intervene in this world from time to time, usually to express his anger, but he was generally remote and perhaps indifferent. The significant wielders of power were local, close at hand. They controlled the fertility of fields, livestock and humans, the weather, health and the life-cycle. People lived of course in a state of objective poverty and insecurity that comfortable modern Westerners find hard to imagine. Mainly peasants, they toiled to produce enough to eat and drink, to have clothing and shelter, to keep tolerably well, to produce offspring and have them thrive to perpetuate the race. In order to succeed or in order to stave off the disasters of storm and flood, crop failure, sterility, illness and premature death that constantly threatened them, they had therefore always to try to placate, to cajole, even to manipulate these controlling forces, which were seen as capricious and always potentially hostile. So at all stages of life, public and private rituals were performed to keep away harm and evil and to procure the good, which consisted of prosperity, fertility, health and life.

Though historians, like anthropologists and others, have discriminated clearly between religion and magic in this sphere, and although there are valid distinctions to make between the established official ritual of the Churches and the informal rites of magic, there was in practice an enormous overlap between the two. The ritual of the Catholic Church in particular was brought into play by the clergy to ensure fertility, well-being and health, while magical practitioners used Christian formulae and prayers, and objects and substances blessed by the clergy.

Rituals relating to the production of food, agriculture and animal husbandry are examined in the first part of the book. These were usually public and often collective and were not exclusively magical, though they had an important magical element. The overriding concern of our peasant ancestors was to produce adequate crops. Their ethic was one of fecundity or fertility broadly speaking. The territory of a community was divided into different spheres: the village, the fields and the wild, each having its special characteristics. The boundaries between the different spheres were marked by processions and other rituals, and by indicators such as crosses. Fields were protected in a variety of ways: blessing by the clergy, placing of holy things, burial of the dead. The wild was conceived of as the realm of the spirits, the dead and demons. It was avoided, particularly at night. But the wild was also an important source of power. Cults of trees and of water (wells and springs) were focused here, together with some saints' cults. The agricultural round was accompanied by ritual. Ploughing, sowing, harvesting of all crops had their own rites and would not be undertaken without performing them. It was also believed that the heavenly bodies, and especially the moon, had much influence on crops, and this affected the timing of specific tasks. Other kinds of work had their own rituals, too, for example fishing. The house also had its magical ambience. The foundations might be consecrated by the clergy or via the burial of animals. Once built, houses carried magical protection in the form of decorative devices and images. So did the rooms within the house and the activities taking place within them. Of special significance here was the hearth, where a fire had to be kept burning, and the culinary processes, particularly making bread.

Chiming in with the agricultural round was the cycle of calendar customs, from Christmas and New Year through Rogations and Midsummer to November pig-killing and All Saints. These were expressions of community and provided a time-framework, but they were also magical rituals, aimed specifically at ensuring the fertility of the fields and animals and the success of the harvests. This can be seen very clearly with Carnival, where ritual excess and over-consumption served to bring about good supplies of food and drink in the future. Meshed in with calendar customs were the cults of agrarian saints, guardians of their communities or associated with particular crops or stages in the growing cycle. Other notions relevant in this area are the linking of rulers with the fertility of the crops in their territories (evident in sophisticated form in Elizabethan royal pageants), and the holding of fasts (maintained in Protestant countries) to ensure general well-being or appease divine anger in times of disaster. Among the enemies of general fertility were witches, who were believed to harm crops in a variety of ways and against whom precautions were taken.

The weather was crucial to producing a decent harvest. The crops were very vulnerable always to late frosts, hailstorms, excessive rain, drought, lack of sun. In these circumstances, peasants developed an extensive system of weather lore and weather rituals. The weather was believed to be controlled by forces of different kinds: God, the saints, sometimes the dead, sometimes malevolent witches who could cause damaging and localized storms on land and sea. God and the saints were implored to divert bad weather. In times of drought, various rain-making ceremonies were employed: dipping saints' statues into rivers and fountains, for example, or urinating in ritual fashion.

Though most peasants were dependent on cereal cultivation, they also kept animals, and there were communities of herdsmen in mountain areas. People lived in very close proximity to their animals, which were essential to their economy and sometimes almost part of the household. A wide range of rituals was used to keep livestock healthy and fertile. They were blessed by the clergy, placed under the aegis of saints, guarded from witchcraft and evil forces via amulets and other means. Magical rituals were also used to control animals by their minders but also by malicious persons. Specific rituals were also employed to ward off and control wild predators, such as foxes and wolves, and to destroy and divert vermin.

In all this there was a correspondence, a linkage, between the fertility of the fields and livestock, the well-being of the family and household, and the prosperity, health and fertility of humans. Human fertility was of the highest positive value. Marrying and having a large number of children was the ideal (though not always realized). Contraception, abortion and barrenness were all deplored. Wedding rituals aimed to ensure that the bride was fruitful.

Human fertility was thought to be vulnerable to hostile forces and especially witchcraft. Barrenness and miscarriages in women and impotence in men were attributed to evil magic, and rituals were performed to prevent or reverse them. Love magic was also widespread. It seems to have been more an urban than a rural practice and to have been most prevalent in spheres outside the norms of marriage. Love magic was often adduced to explain extreme passions and ill-matched couplings, such as that of Othello and Desdemona in Shakespeare's play.

Rites of passage, and especially those relating to birth and death, are described and analysed in the second part. Given the ethic of fecundity, conception and pregnancy were much desired (within marriage), and measures were taken to bring them about: visits to shrines and to standing stones for instance. Pregnant women were subject to all kinds of precautions in order to make sure that they did not miscarry. It was also believed that events experienced by a pregnant woman had a direct influence on the baby she was carrying. So birth marks or defects were attributed to creatures seen or food eaten by the woman, often as a result of a special craving. Childbirth was both painful and dangerous, and it was again hedged about by a whole series of rituals and precautions. The birth room was kept closed and darkened. Saints were invoked, prayers recited or displayed, and amulets such as special girdles worn. Once the baby was born, a further series of rites was carried out. The afterbirth and the umbilical cord had special qualities and were carefully disposed of. The new-born was ritually protected, particularly in the period before baptism. This sacrament required by the Churches was genuinely 'popular' and was quickly performed to guarantee the baby's well-being in the next world but also in this one. Special meaning was attached to the birth of twins or deformed babies. The latter might be the fruit of sinful copulation during periods of prescribed abstinence or during the woman's menstruation. Babies that were odd or unusually fretful might be regarded as changelings, the offspring of fairies that had been substituted for the human child, and steps might be taken to reverse this. The time and circumstances of the birth were significant; omens were read and horoscopes might be drawn.

It was believed that babies needed to be 'formed', which was one of the functions of swaddling. Teething, walking and talking all had their own rituals. Mother's milk was the main food source for babies, and breast-feeding had a special symbolic significance which it has now lost. Mothers prayed, visited shrines and took potions to ensure that they had a good supply of milk. Wet-nurses were employed by the elite in some circumstances but there was always a fear that the quality of their milk might adversely affect the nursling. The mother was also vulnerable after giving birth, as well as dangerous or polluting like the menstruating woman. She was 'confined' to the house for a period, usually forty days, after which she went through a religious ceremony of purification or 'churching'.

At the other end of life, death was similarly surrounded by many rituals, some of which were magical. A difficult death might be the result of some material impediment, and dying might be eased by untying knots. For a time after death, the soul hovered between this world and the next, and care had to be taken to propitiate and control it, and to prevent it from taking anyone else with it or becoming trapped between worlds. There was a series of food exchanges with the dead at certain intervals, as well as prayers and other forms of commemoration. Some dead spirits returned as ghosts, *revenants* or vampires, if they had not been properly buried, had unconfessed crimes on their consciences, or if animals had jumped over their corpses. More generally, the dead were buried by preference in or near a church, in consecrated and protected territory, and the orientation of the burial was important, too, usually pointing east.

The third part deals with disease and healing. There were various concepts of disease and its causes before the modern medical era. Illness could be ascribed to God and seen as the punishment for sin or a testing of character. It could be attributed to climatic or astrological influences; or it could be caused by the influence of the dead or of witches or the evil eye. Approaches to healing depended on these notions about the nature of illness, which was often seen also as an alien invader of the body to be expelled. A religious element was commonly present in Catholic and Protestant milieus: prayers, masses or other religious services. The saints were also widely associated with healing. People made vows, visited shrines, touched relics and statues. Self or home medication within the family was universal, and recourse to other human healers only came when this had failed. There were medical practitioners, of course, official and unofficial. The former were expensive and often ineffective, and most people used folk healers of different kinds. These were recognized within communities as having healing powers, which were acquired in various ways: by birth circumstances (seventh sons, for example), or by learning and being handed down. The methods of folk healers included the use of herbs that had magical associations and might be gathered in particular ritual ways; contact via touching, laying on of hands or breathing; the use of magical substances and of animal parts; and the use of words and spells. These methods were often combined. Spells were of different kinds. Often they commanded the disease to depart or sought to transfer it from the patient to some other thing or person.

In the fourth part the universal belief in divination and in omens and signs is explored. In an objectively random world, people sought extra reassurance about the outcome of projects, and they read a meaning into natural phenomena. Questions about the future could be asked of oracles or seers, and odd events could signify good or bad fortune on a grand or small scale. So comets or eclipses signalled the deaths of kings and epidemics or other great disasters; while seeing a priest or a hunchback or hearing an owl meant good or bad luck to an individual: riches, a good day, or death.

Magic is examined in more general terms in the fifth part. Different types of practitioner existed from the learned magician of late medieval and Renaissance times to the local wise-woman. Their powers too were of different kinds and had different origins. Special powers might be gained by initiation or instruction or they might derive from birth. Some special powers inhered in certain conditions, permanent or temporary. Menstruating women, for example, were believed to give off a polluting influence and hence to cause a range of minor misfortunes, such as butter failing to churn, as well as serious illness or death. There were also independent non-human spirits that magic could use or deter: fairies of various kinds and demons. Learned magicians like Shakespeare's Prospero might try to raise and tame spirits and demons, but at the popular level demons were not very important.

Magicians of all kinds operated with a body of paraphernalia: natural and manufactured things, animal parts, bodily fluids. Iron and salt were important magical substances, as were all types of human (and animal) excreta: saliva, blood, urine. Amulets were universally used to protect their wearers, being made from a wide selection of such substances and objects, usually in combination. Representations were also important, and image magic was quite commonly employed for healing as well as for hostile purposes. The sacramentals: holy water, 'palms' blessed on Palm Sunday, church bells, were a very important element in protective magic. Bells were rung to scare off storms, demons and the dead. The host was more rarely used in hostile and love magic. Words of power were also a stock in trade of magicians. Some special nonsense words were employed. Latin phrases were common, often taken from the Catholic liturgy. Blessing and cursing were more generally used and were of special significance among close relatives. Magicians had their 'secrets', special formulae and spells, which often had a high religious content. Numbers were also highly significant in magic, especially three, seven, nine and forty. Colours were less so. Times and places were important too. Calendar customs show the significance of particular times of the year and especially the solstices, when magical powers were believed to be at their height and when protection was most needed. Certain days of the week and times of the day were also lucky or unlucky. Night-time was not only objectively but symbolically dangerous, a time when evil was abroad. Special consequence attached too to the liminal periods between day and night. The magical significance of places relates back to the division of the territory already alluded to. The wild was associated with evil powers. Particular magical rituals were performed at crossroads, where suicides and criminals were buried. Directions and orientations were also symbolically important. For example, the dead should always be moved feet first. The left hand was linked with magic and perhaps evil; hence the connotations of 'sinister'.

Related to this and other aspects, magical ritual comprised a range of gestures and actions. These included protective signs with the fingers, the drawing of circles around people and sites, circumambulation of churches and other places, measuring and weighing, ritual begging and stealing, and making noise. Of special saliency were ritual tying and untying. These were done in relation to impotence, love, childbirth and dying; and the term 'tying' or 'binding' might be used to mean bewitching. Though noise was an element in some rituals, magical rites might also require silence, and they were often surrounded with some secrecy. A sub-category of magic, linked to a particular gesture, was the evil eye, or the belief that certain people could cause harm, especially to children and young animals and usually involuntarily, just by looking at them. This has been interpreted as the projection of feelings of envy that were so prevalent in peasant communities. Someone with something to be admired: a new baby, a fine calf, thriving silkworms, was necessarily the object of envy among his or her fellows who lacked these things, and the feeling might be directly translated into act.

The magical approach to the world operated at different but related levels. It was important always to obtain information about what the French anthropologist Lévy-Bruhl called 'dispositions' of beings and objects surrounding one.[2] As we have noted, events both extraordinary and ordinary could be read as signs. More deliberate divination of future outcomes could be undertaken by examining, say, the entrails of animals or the way that beans fell when they were randomly thrown. Then there was the necessary precaution of associating with what was fortunate and avoiding what was unfortunate. Certain things might be regarded as lucky and thus worn as protective amulets, like coral or moles' feet. People in certain states, menstruating women or corpses, for example, were particularly dangerous, and they were therefore approached only with great care or altogether shunned. Again, some days might be propitious for undertaking certain tasks and others unpropitious. Such precautions shaded off into the performance of a host of rituals on all possible occasions, as we have seen, from building a house and the carrying out of every task of the agricultural year to childbirth, marriage and death. Rituals here are repeated actions in set forms, which have significance beyond themselves. To take a simple example, drinking a glass of liquid to slake one's thirst is not a ritual; drinking another person's health is. As this shows too, rituals could be quite uncomplicated as well as extremely elaborate, and they could express a great variety of intentions, both explicit and more often implicit.

The principles underlying magical thought and ritual were formulated a century ago by two great anthropologists, Frazer and Mauss, whose subsequent reputations have diverged. James George Frazer was the author of *The Golden Bough* (1890–1915), a vast comparative work centred on the myths of divine death and resurrection but also dealing with rituals of fertility worldwide. This work, which appeared in an abridged edition in 1922, was enormously influential in its time in and beyond academic circles. It fell into disrepute from the 1950s, when British anthropologists in particular turned against its grand theory and universalism in favour of specific local studies and contextual explanation. Marcel Mauss (1872–1950) was the nephew and pupil of the French sociologist Emile Durkheim. Though his output was small – essentially a collection of essays or short studies including *The General Theory of Magic* (1904) - he was a dominant figure not least as an editor, reviewer and teacher. His influence remains very great in France and more generally. Little has been added subsequently to what Frazer and Mauss had to say on fundamentals.

The first principle of magic, according to Frazer, is 'that like produces like, or that an effect resembles its cause', and the second 'that things which have once been in contact with each other continue to act on each other at a distance after the physical contact has been severed'. To these laws of similarity and contiguity, Mauss added those of antipathy: opposites work on opposites; and that of the part standing for the whole, so that 'teeth, saliva, sweat . . . represent a total person, in such a way that through these parts one can act directly on the individual concerned'. A striking feature of this sympathy is its vast and all-embracing nature. 'Everything has something in common with everything else and everything is connected with everything else.' This delicate system of interaction, moreover, includes psychological forces. Consciousness, will-power and intention may be attributed to the imagined agents of fortune or misfortune. At the same time, human beings can act on each other not only 'by the use of symbols and signs' but also 'by the mere presence of wishes or fears'. The magical universe is thus huge and amorphous, but in practice the magical believer or practitioner selects from within its range. Certain substances, certain things, certain people have more magical saliency than others. Rituals were usually required to produce magical effects. Here magic does not 'consist entirely of sympathetic rites', though these are dominant. One also finds purifications, sacrifices and other kinds of rite. And though 'sympathy is the route along which magical powers pass, it does not provide magical power itself '. This derives from inherent qualities and again from ritual.[3]

As all this indicates, magic abhors a vacuum and repudiates the notion of chance or coincidence. If misfortune befalls someone, there must be a reason beyond any simple operation of cause and effect. It is a system of over-rationalization, which requires and produces explanations, where most of us would be content to accept things as fortuitous. Magic here gives a sense of control in a situation of actual insecurity and impotence. It places misfortune, as another writer has put it, 'within a cognitive framework' and thus makes some kind of sense of it.[4] Via rituals, people could also act; they could 'do something' rather than remain passively helpless. Magic can also explain success in situations where neither merit nor effort are usually thought of as being rewarded.

So long as the ritual or the formula is correctly performed or uttered, the effects of magic are believed to be automatic. This implies also that 'magical rites act upon their objects directly without any mediation by a spiritual agent' and this is normally believed to be the case. However, as Mauss noted, magic becomes 'contaminated by religion, from which it borrows figures of gods and demons'. Most students, including Frazer and Mauss, distinguish in principle between religion and magic. Religion involves 'a propitiation or conciliation of powers superior to man which are believed to direct and control the course of nature and human life', while magic either operates without the mediation of any gods or spirits or 'treats them in exactly the same fashion as it treats inanimate agents, that is, it constrains and coerces'. Or as the German sociologist Max Weber put it, 'priests superintend the worship of the gods, while magicians seek to compel demons'. Another important distinction contrasts public and private, organized and freelance behaviour. Religions have established priesthoods, administering public cults and attached to important institutions or Churches. By contrast, 'between the magician and the individuals who consult him, as among these individuals themselves, there are no lasting bonds which make them members of the same moral community, comparable to that formed by the believers in the same god or the observers of the same cult. The magician has a clientele and not a church'. To Durkheim's observation, Mauss added that, in contrast to religion, magic tends to be secretive and may be thought to operate on the edges or even beyond the bounds of the established culture.[5]

This public versus private distinction does not always hold good. Collective rituals, clerical and popular, in pre-modern Europe did have a magical aspect. Moreover, it is ultimately 'public opinion which makes the magician and the power he wields'. Magic may not be formally social, but neither is it purely individual. Magical behaviour depends to a greater or lesser extent on social consensus and reflects a social need. Hence of course the coherence and consistency of magical practices across time and space. It may be equally valid and more helpful to see a magico-religious spectrum or a single field embracing religion, magic and much else, including proto-science. For magic is eclectic to an extraordinary degree, taking components from many different cultural levels and locations. This is partly to be explained by the very principle of sympathy, of multiple correspondences; but it derives, too, from the practical bent of magic. Its adherents are not greatly interested in theory, not worried about how magic functions or where its efficacy comes from. On the whole, they are concerned neither with logic nor with legitimacy, but only or primarily with whether magical procedures 'work' or appear to 'work'. This does not mean that magic is wholly chaotic. Indeed, it seeks 'to organize experience into some sort of coherent system in which events are described and classified, and in which the interrelationships between events are either specified or implied'.[6] This is especially obvious if magic in a specific cultural area, such as pre-modern Europe, is considered. Here it was part and parcel of a world-view and a ritual system involving calendar customs, popular religion, healing, rites of passage, all tied in to a particular traditional economy and society.

Looking at the uses of magic makes this clearer. Magic was employed in an extremely wide range of circumstances. It was deployed, for example, to influence chariot-racing in Ancient Rome, in court intrigues in late medieval Europe, to aid those engaged in duels and to bring about favourable outcomes in trade and business in the early modern period, and to ensure 'good numbers' in the conscription lotteries of modern times. But above all it was associated with the problems of everyday living for most people. It was used to try to bring about prosperity, fertility and health and to ward off or undo poverty, barrenness and disease. Contrary to the impression created by some members of the clergy and others, magic was not marginal in pre-modern Europe, nor, despite its penchant for secrecy, really occult. Rather, it was at the centre of things and openly and universally practised.

Another false impression, encouraged by historians' preoccupation with witchcraft, is that magic was pro-active. In fact most European magic was apotropaic, seeking to prevent, to protect, to repel. It did not tend to take initiatives, to intervene on its own behalf, and its practitioners rarely sought to do deliberate harm. Again, in itself magic was amoral or morally neutral. Only the learned and clerical demonological view of magic, developed from the later medieval period, which linked all magic with the Devil, saw it as inherently evil. At the popular level, it was only the ends to which it was put that made magic evil or good, and these were not absolutes; they had to do with the interest and well-being of individuals, and much more families, competing to survive in a hostile world. Here they pursued their own 'good' via magical and other means, and the fact that this implied someone else's 'evil' was often incidental. Within the limited resources available in pre-modern economies, such a see-saw effect was inevitable or felt to be. But to offset this there was always a strong community presence and sense, which also made itself felt via magical rites, such as calendar customs, 'rough music' or charivaris, and those surrounding weddings.

Like most scholars since, Mauss saw European magical systems as rather simple or poorly developed, in contrast say to Hindu systems, which were much more complex. But he recognized that this simplicity might be apparent, 'the result of their being poorly described or poorly observed', which is undoubtedly true. This book seeks to redress this balance, both by drawing attention to the wealth of rituals recorded by folklorists and others and also by extending the boundaries of what previous historians have regarded as magical. Mauss also believed that European magic was 'a shadow of its former self'. While this is also true if one looks back from the perspective of the early twentieth century, the 'remnant' theory of magic has in general terms to be discarded. It assumes that magic comprises scattered survivals of a system of thought and action that was once an integral whole, or, in another formulation, that magic is 'ritual which has lost its theology'.[7] This theory derives from two overlapping sources. First, like other new religions, Christianity dubbed its predecessor 'magical', fuelling the long-standing view that European magic had its origins in paganism. Secondly, the 'remnant' theory of magic was part of the wider 'remnant' theory of folklore, a more recent idea that saw modern folk customs and beliefs less in terms of their own context, past or present, and more as odd bits and pieces mysteriously left over from the distant, even prehistoric, past. The particular theory fails to take account of the perennial nature of magic and its ability to take from and to colonize all religions, including Ancient paganism. The general theory has more to recommend it, as we shall see, though it requires some revision.

Writing of the 'rise' or 'decline' of magic, historians have really been concerned only with the attitude of the elites and particularly the clergy. In reality these fluctuated above a bed-rock of popular belief and practice which changed very little down the centuries. Magic here was a central component of traditional culture, a culture with an unchanging or very slow-changing core, which died out in most of France, for example, only in the last third of the nineteenth century, in Britain earlier perhaps, in much of southern and eastern Europe later. This culture was the correlate of the prevailingly agrarian economy and of a society constituted mainly of peasants. In earlier centuries, it encompassed urban society, too, and much of the elite; later it became restricted to the countryside. As the great French historian Lucien Febvre observed many years ago, until Descartes there was no intellectual alternative to magic and therefore no bar to the acceptance of occult forces and entities,[8] and the new framework of understanding took centuries to establish itself, first among the elite and then among the rest of the population. As peasants belonged to a wider society in terms of government and religion, so traditional culture was contaminated to some extent from these quarters earlier on, but they did not affect its fundamental features. It was anyway an adopting and adapting culture with its own diversities and in-built flexibilities, and all this added to its staying power.

Many historians are uncomfortable with the perspective of the *longue durée*, of deep time; they look at and for what is changing rather than what is permanent and structural. Some of them may therefore regard this picture of European magic as too static, too monolithic, a return to the old survival approach of folklore. To disarm such criticism one can only hope to show that magic was indeed perennial or at least very slow to change, that principles and rituals did persist over the centuries. Take two examples at random from the very many described in the book. The fourteenth-century Belleville breviary has an illustration of sick people passing under a saint's relics as they are being processed, a scene exactly reproduced in a photograph from Brittany taken in 1972 (see Text Figure 14 and Plate 17). Again, Bishop Burchard of Worms in the eleventh century condemned the practice of discarding objects associated with sick animals at crossroads in the hope of transferring the illness to other beasts; variants of the same practice were noted by the sixteenth-century medic and magician Paracelsus and by modern folklorists. This does not mean, of course, that further research may not be able to introduce refinements and add comparative perspectives that this essay, this broad-brushed survey, cannot attempt.

One should admit, too, that over the millennium and a half under consideration, there were significant new developments, to which I have already alluded. First, an important Christian element was introduced into magic or amalgamated with it. This happened during the early medieval period with a degree of encouragement from the Church. The book shows again and again how objects, substances and words used in the Christian liturgy were given magical significance and employed accordingly by lay people but also by clerics. Some important Christian rituals like baptism could be regarded as magical in themselves. The cult of the saints was a particularly fruitful adjunct to the magical repertoire, with relics and shrines becoming the focus for a range of ritual practices intended to ensure the fertility of fields, livestock and humans as well as good weather and good health. Secondly, demonology had some impact on popular magic from the late medieval period onwards. This was a body of mainly clerical opinion which believed that all magic, but especially witchcraft or magic intended to harm, was inspired and activated by the Devil. Witches and other magical practitioners, often not distinguished by demonologists, were the Devil's agents and not people with special intrinsic or acquired powers. One of the first and most influential demonological treatises was the *Malleus Maleficarum* or *Hammer of the Witches* of 1486, written by two German Dominican inquisitors. Demonology is a significant factor in explaining the outbreak of official witch-hunting in the sixteenth and seventeenth centuries, but its effect on everyday magic was slight. It contributed to a divergence between elite and popular views of magic, which should not, however, be exaggerated, and it probably encouraged clandestinity. Thirdly, magic began to die out with the decline and disappearance of Europe's traditional agrarian economy. This process began earlier in some countries than others but was essentially a phenomenon of the later nineteenth and early twentieth centuries. This does not mean that magic is absent from our contemporary 'scientific' culture, but its modern forms are different and it is clearly 'alternative' or ancillary to the dominant modes of explanation and action.

Then there is the problem of documentation for our long-term survey. The further back in time that one goes, the scarcer and less informative the evidence becomes and it is very often indirect, collected and recorded by those who wished to condemn, reform or later patronize the inarticulate practitioners of traditional magic. Ironically, the fullest picture usually exists for the nineteenth and twentieth centuries, when the whole system was in its final phase. But this is less of a problem than it appears. Earlier sources, including penitentials, Visitation records, Inquisition investigations, witch trials, literature, provide a fair and consistent view of magical practices and beliefs in their time; and they chime in with the later and richer accounts by folklorists and social anthropologists. Each confirms the other, indicating that one is dealing with a single phenomenon present over the entire period. Visual material paints the same picture, and it applies all over Europe.

There is currently some vaguely post-modern squeamishness about recognizing that sources, such as those outlined, allow us access to any past 'reality' at all. This is compounded by the 'class' nature of the sources, gathered or brought into being by superior and powerful social groups investigating and supposedly trying to control inferior and weaker ones. Here everything becomes 'mediated', part of a loaded 'discourse'. All this is much too clever, and curiously it takes the side, as it were, of the would-be manipulating elites, treating the 'lower orders' as if they were both malleable and wrong-headed. I believe rather that there was an authentic, quasi-autonomous popular or traditional culture, of which magic was a part, and to which the fragmentary sources do give access if they are read comparatively and with imagination. The controlling mechanisms, the mediations, are a screen which it is the historian's job to see through. Moreover, as we have already noted, magic or concern with magic was by no means confined for much of the time under consideration to the quiet peasantry, to those without a historical voice. One only has to read the classic authors from Dante and Chaucer through Ronsard and Shakespeare to Mistral and Hardy to be convinced of this.

The book was conceived and the writing of it began in the 1970s in an inter-disciplinary milieu where history was seen as one among the human sciences. Its intellectual debts are to the early *Annales* venture of Marc Bloch and Lucien Febvre, to Keith Thomas's *Religion and the Decline of Magic*, to Carlo Ginzburg, and to the French, American and British schools of anthropology. As will be clear, I include in the last the now unfashionable Frazer. Some of the criticism – notably of his excessively eclectic and *pointilliste* methodology and of his neglect of context – was well founded, but Frazer was right about three things. The customs he described are universal in time and space and demand a comparative approach to understand them. Magic operates mainly on the principles of sympathy and contiguity which he outlined. And fertility is a central concern in most human rituals. We may abandon the corn spirit but not the ethic of fecundity which it stood for.[9] Research into the history of traditional culture in Europe has developed considerably since the early 1970s. We now have thorough studies, for example, of English calendar customs and rites of passage and of Venetian magic. With this solid work accomplished, perhaps the time has come again for a return to something of Frazer's grand and dangerous sweep.

Perhaps the time has come, too, to take traditional magic seriously again. Here we have beliefs and practices which were of the greatest importance in the lives of our ancestors. They should not be dismissed lightly or treated condescendingly, as they often continue to be even by historians interested in religion and culture at the popular level. Rather they need to be carefully described and understood in the same way as the official philosophies and the established ceremonies of Church and State. This does not mean that we need to lend them any credence. But, as the arch-sceptic Voltaire suggested, disen-chantment has its cost, and our new verities, scientific and technological, though comforting for now, are sometimes hardly better founded and may prove less enduring:

> On a banni les démons et les fées;
> Sous la raison les grâces étouffées,
> Livrent nos coeurs à l'insipidité;
> Le raisonner tristement s'accrédite;
> On court, hélas, après la vérité:
> Ah! croyez-moi, l'erreur a son mérite.[10]

I

AGRICULTURE

1

House, Work and the Land

Most European people living before the First World War were peasants. They worked the land (which usually did not fully belong to them) with simple tools to provide food for themselves and a surplus to pay taxes, rents and tithes. The main crops which they grew were cereals: rye, oats, buckwheat and millet more often than wheat which required better conditions than most of them had access to. Yields were low since the land was poor. It had to be left fallow every other year or one year in three or more. The land was cultivated until well into the nineteenth century in many parts of the Continent according to very ancient collective systems. Depending on the region, peasants also grew some pulses, plants that could be used to make and dye textiles (hemp, flax, woad), fruit and nut trees and, in the south, olives, vines and mulberries. All were subject to the vagaries of the weather and to attacks from pests and diseases. Peasants also reared livestock. Few were stock farmers as such, though in the uplands sheep and goats were the main resource. But all required some animals to provide labour and transport, for manure and for meat and milk products, though meat was only consumed sparingly and was essentially a festive food. Poultry were also kept. Only the wealthiest had horses. Most had to make do with a pig or perhaps a cow. It was hard to provide enough for these animals to eat especially through the winter, and they were puny and prone to illness.

The life of our peasant ancestors was thus penurious and insecure. Their aim above all was to have enough to eat, which meant fair harvests, fields fertile and free from vermin, and animals that did not fall sick and that reproduced themselves generously. Their ideal, expressed in folk-tales, proverbs and songs, was plenty, the land of Cockagne where food and drink were overflowing. Their religious activity, their rituals, often magical in kind, were centred on ensuring fecundity, or at least on warding off the forces that threatened it. For the rituals were often more negative than positive, 'a symbolic struggle each day and night against a universe of invisible dangers'.[1]

The actual and conceptual division of the territory belonging to peasant communities reflected these magico-religious concerns. There were three spaces: the village where peasants lived, the fields and the wild, each distinct. Within the village, the house was at the heart of the peasant family and its livelihood. Very often house and family were synonymous. This identity was reflected in the fact that in some areas, the Basque region and Alsace, the family took its name from the house. In modern Rumania, when a person dies, not only do the family members mourn, but it is said that 'the house cries', 'the table cries', 'the courtyard cries'.[2] As this implies, houses were inherited and kept in families over long periods of time, but at some stage houses were built, and much ritual surrounded such an undertaking.

The site would be chosen with care, not only from the physical but also from the metaphysical point of view. In Ireland, for example, 'it was at all costs necessary to avoid giving offence to the fairies by building across one of their pads'. In Tyrone, a man stuck a new spade into the earth on the proposed site. 'If the fairies had not removed it overnight, the site was safe. In Cavan ... , a small line of stones was first built on the site; if it was intact next morning, the fairies were not displeased'. Again, the design of the house had to follow traditional lines. A house that was different or too large would arouse envy. In modern Ireland once more, to be lucky, a house could not be more than one room wide. 'Widen the house', they said in Donegal, 'and the family will get smaller.'[3]

Perhaps most emphasis was attached ritually to the foundations of the house. In Rumania and elsewhere, the walls and foundations were blessed by the priest. A range of objects have been found by archeologists deposited in walls, under floors, and especially under thresholds and hearths and in chimney pieces, in order to give 'protection against external dangers'. Such objects include parts of statues, bottles, pots, coins, paper charms and old shoes (see Plate 2). Animal sacrifices were also carried out and the carcase or some part of it buried. In Greece, according to a custom dating from Ancient times, a cock, ram or lamb was sacrificed, and its blood poured on the foundation stone, under which the animal was then buried. A cock was also sacrificed in modern Russia on building a new house and its blood sprinkled. In Ireland and elsewhere horses' skulls were buried under the floors of houses. Dried cats are not infrequently found in old houses all over Britain and Europe, dating from the medieval period onwards. They too were foundation sacrifices, some having been walled up alive. Others, mummified in life-like poses, were probably intended to scare off vermin.[4] Animals or animal parts were also placed under other buildings. Horses' skulls are found under threshing floors in Scandinavia, for example. The practice persisted into the eighteenth and nineteenth centuries – in some surprising places. The first Blackfriars Bridge in London, built in the 1760s, had animal bones placed in its foundations. When the Primitive Methodist chapel was built at Littleport, Cambridgeshire, in 1897, a horse's head was placed in the foundation trench and a glass of beer was poured over it, the rest being drunk by the workmen.

Once built, the house needed continuing protection. Geometric or floral designs in paint or plaster covered the walls in Alsace, East Anglia and elsewhere. Gables, beams and barge-boards were carved with symbolic devices such as circles or swastikas; in Russia phallic forms ensured good luck and prosperity. In Provence, houses were whitewashed in ritual fashion for Easter Sunday every year. Tutelary trees, rowans, elders, yews, were planted by houses or in courtyards. Branches or parts of the same trees might be placed on the roof or elsewhere (see Plate 3). 'On the walls of many of the houses at Montelepre, near Palermo, hang branches of myrtle to bring good fortune.' Herdsmen's huts, even, in the Pyrenees had wooden crosses on the roofs 'to protect them from lightning and all evil influences'.[5]

Most ritual behaviour, however, concerned the interior. In Germany and elsewhere in the early modern period, people asked the priest 'to incense and asperge their houses on the feasts of Christmas, New Year and Epiphany'. In the Franche-Comté, the priest blessed hearths and traced a cross on chimney pieces during Lent and especially on Passion Sunday; he also traced crosses on the external doors and windows. The objects used in foundation rituals were also employed for more general protection. In Ireland, flasks, eggs, sheep's bones, and special stones were kept in walls or cupboards.[6] In Spanish Galicia, amulets, horns and bags of salt were deployed, and there and elsewhere the sacramentals obtained on Palm Sunday or other feasts were used to guard the house. Religious statues were also placed in niches and on mantelpieces. Often attention focused on one particular room. Irish cottages had a 'west room', where religious objects were kept and later photographs of the ancestors. The old people would move into this room after they gave up control of the family holding. In Rumania, there was a special room for the icons, where the branches of willow blessed in church were also kept and the ceiling was decorated in a particular way. Furniture and other things were decorated with symbols to give protection again and to ensure effectiveness. In Provence, flour-bins were embellished with ears of corn or fishes; salt-boxes with bay leaves or samphire. Among the Basques in the early modern period and later, dressers and cupboards were elaborately carved, as were shepherds' crooks, spinning gear, ox-yokes, cheese moulds and so on. A favourite motif here was the Oriphilo sign, a fertility symbol also found on tombs, lintel stones and sheep-folds. Similar magical ornamentation of everyday objects was prominent in Eastern Europe. In Scandinavia, runic inscriptions had been placed on weapons, personal effects and household articles from earliest times, and this tradition continued.

Special care surrounded the threshold, which connected the house to the external and potentially hostile world. In Ancient Rome there had been a special festival on the Calends of June devoted to Carda or the hinge, the god of the door to the house and the threshold. In Galicia, the doors and windows were covered with sharp thistles on Midsummer Eve to keep out evil forces, and bonfires were lit in doorways, customs paralleled elsewhere, for example in Corsica. In the Forest of Dean, a yew stick was nailed behind the door for the same purpose. In Provence, 'the door lintel was sometimes decorated with a shining object, a plate with a glaze, etc., whose reflection was supposed to prevent evil influences entering the house'. Even in an urban environment, like that of early modern Venice, magic relating to the doors, sills and windows of houses was prevalent. Care had also to be taken in crossing the boundary from inside to outside. Like human excreta, waste from inside the house was vulnerable and had to be specially disposed of. In the Limousin, typically, 'when the house was swept in the evening after the meal, the sweepings should not be thrown into the street but burned'.[7]

This relates to the other focus of ritual: the hearth. Households were known officially and unofficially as 'hearths'. European peasants continued the ancient cult of the household fire. The hearth was at the centre of the family's life and in a sense stood for house and family. As a Basque proverb put it: 'A house without fire is a body without blood'. The kitchen was the most important and often the only room. In Ireland, the man and woman of the house had 'their bed near the fire, either in the kitchen or in the bedroom behind the chimney fire'. The fire was kept burning continuously, and it was very bad luck to let it out. It was tended by the women. In parts of Scotland, only exceptionally at the turning of the New Year did men assume the task of keeping the fire. In Celtic lands, there were special terms for covering and uncovering the fire and each was carried out in ritual fashion. In the Hebrides, the names of God, of Light, of Peace and of Grace were solemnly invoked as three peats were laid on the hearth at night before being covered with ashes. 'In Wales, the "seed of the fire" – a glowing ember of peat or wood – was singled out and replaced on the hearth after it had been swept clean. It was then covered with ashes for the night, to become the following morning the nucleus of the new day's fire. When the fire in a new house was lit for the first time, it would be kindled with embers taken from the fire in the old house, symbol of the continuity of family life'. In Ireland, all the paraphernalia to do with the hearth (and cooking) had sacred significance. Even soot from the hearth was carried 'in the pocket to give protection on a journey'. Above all, with its purificatory power, the fire was 'the symbol of the sacred character of the household'. In Portugal, as elsewhere, 'a profound relationship' was held to exist between the members of the household and the fire around which they were united, and membership here included the dead. For this reason, fire should not be taken out of a house where a person had just died, lest the deceased follow the light and become permanently detached from the household.[8] The importance of the fire was manifested in other ways. Throwing salt and other objects and substances on the fire was a typical magical gesture, and in sixteenth-century Venice the hearth chains were used in love magic.

The hearth fire was a symbol of the wider community, too. Very often, as at the May festival of Beltane in parts of Scotland, or on New Year's Eve, the hearth fire was deliberately let out and then rekindled from the communal bonfire, which had been lit from friction. On Lewis, the hearth fire was newly kindled in this way with the ashes from the New Year bonfire; a pot of water was immediately boiled on it and this was sprinkled over people and cattle.

The hearth, of course, is where the food was cooked. We have stressed that in traditional Europe the food supply was problematic. Dearth and famine were always round the corner or believed to be. Normal diet, moreover, was monotonous: bread, gruel, some vegetables, a little fat. But food in these circumstances had sacred significance, whether it was the normal everyday food or, more obviously, the special food associated with festivals. Here the consumption of particular kinds of food was part of the ritual occasion, and an underlying aim of the exceptional consumption of roast meats and other delicacies was to ensure good supplies of food in the future. So, in Provence in modern times, black-wheat crêpes were eaten on Mardi-Gras or Shrove Tuesday; *gigot* of lamb on Easter Sunday with *pastissoun*, little pies filled with beef marrow and citron conserve; and chick peas in a salad on Palm Sunday. On Christmas Eve, 'the meal had to consist of frugal dishes, served in abundance, as a presage of prosperity'. At Arles, people ate mullet in red sauce with black olives and chard or cardoon; snails in garlic sauce; anchovy fillets in oil; blanched celery hearts; and the thirteen desserts, which included raisins, dried figs, pine kernels and pistachios, black nougat with honey, white cheese, and pancakes seasoned with fennel or cumin. At Toulon, people ate fried cod. In the Upper Var valley, they ate ravioli, stuffed with squash and spinach, and squash or pumpkin pie, dressed with a sauce of crushed walnuts and cream.[9] This culinary calendar, with its local variations, was found all over Europe.

Festive and everyday food was ritually prepared by the women. This is very clear with making bread, the essential foodstuff, the 'staff of life', lent further significance by its central role in the mass or Eucharist. In Sicily care was taken never to bake on a Sunday or an important festival, lest the displeasure of God or the saints be incurred. Very generally, ordinary bread was not eaten at festivals but rather crêpes, pancakes or cakes. Getting the bread dough to rise could be difficult. Again, in Sicily, prayer-charms were recited: 'Grow dough, as Jesus did in his swaddling clothes; grow big, dough, as the Holy Father [St Joseph]'s staff grew; St Nicholas, let it come out well'. In the Alto Minho region of Portugal, the dough was always marked with a cross, and a small bottle of vinegar might be stuck in it, or the hat or trousers of the male head of the household placed by the dough-bin or the man might actually sit on the bin. All this underlined the symbolic relationship between cooking, commensality and the reproduction of the household via the proper inter-dependence of male and female. If the dough still would not rise, this was taken to be a sign of impurity: a spider or a rat must have passed under it. In Sicily, further prayers accompanied the risen dough into the oven, and a sign of the cross was made on the oven door. In Provence until quite recently in small towns and villages, 'it was not "done" to eat bread that had not been made with the family's own wheat (or other grain) and certainly not bread that had been kneaded by alien hands'. The dough-bin and the bread cupboard, the latter usually over the former, were salient objects in the house. Together they formed 'a little domestic shrine, accompanied often by a reli-gious image', usually of a local saint or saints. In the Hebrides, 'the quern was rubbed every Saturday evening with a wisp of straw, "for payment" of its benevolent labours'.[10]

Cooking, especially of meat, could be dangerous. This has been empha-sized in a study of making black puddings in south-western France and else-where following pig-killing. While the puddings were cooking, men were excluded from the kitchen and the doors and windows were closed to keep off the evil eye or other women's looks of envy that would make the puddings burst. This is reminiscent of childbirth, as we shall see, another ceremony of blood. The cooking of the puddings also attracted fairies and other spirits, especially the spirits of dead children and these had to be propitiated with food gifts. It was particularly important that the puddings never boiled. If they did, they would spoil. This echoes other beliefs about boiling water. In the Comtat-Venaissin, for example, it was believed that water should never be boiled alone; this made the livestock 'heavy'. Boiling *per se* attracted evil forces and needed to be controlled.[11]

Eating was also hedged about with ritual. Festive and other food might be blessed by a priest before being consumed. Regular meals were preceded and sometimes also followed by graces or blessings. 'May all that we eat and drink be blessed', was the formula enjoined on Corsicans by the bishop of Aleria in his 1565 catechism, together with making a sign of the cross. 'Ask a blessin', Mr Stiggins', Mrs Weller instructs in Dickens' *Pickwick Papers* (1836–37), before they start a 'tea' of hot-buttered toast and pineapple rum at The Marquess of Granby. Again, eating bread had particular significance. 'Before cutting into the bread', in Languedoc, 'whether it was made of black wheat or buckwheat or proper wheat flour, the master of the household made the sign of the cross with the point of his knife on the top of the crust, saying: We do not know if we will finish it'. Wasting food and especially bread was abhorrent. Even the crumbs were carefully collected. In Poland before the First World War, 'it was thought a sin to brush crumbs off the table on to the floor. Whoever chanced on crumbs lying there would gather them and salute them with a kiss, meaning thus to ask divine pardon for the injury done'. The flat spade and the brush used in baking, moreover, were always stored with the head upwards to prevent any bits of dough or flour falling to the ground.[12]

Where possible, it was important to have a well-stocked house and to show hospitality with food. In modern Greece, for example, villagers took a pride in being able to supply unexpected guests with cheese, bread, eggs, wine and so on from their own land and in unlimited quantities and of good quality. The house should be a cornucopia, an image of what nature should be like.

A further supernatural dimension was lent to the house and the activities taking place within it by the belief, found in many parts of Europe, in house spirits of different kinds. Some did domestic chores; some were especially concerned with order and cleanliness in the household; most brought luck and plenty; some could be mischievous, causing minor mishaps. They were therefore placated by keeping the house tidy and by leaving out food and drink for them. 'Indeed your grandam's maids', wrote Reginald Scot in *Discovery of Witchcraft* (1584), 'were wont to set a bowl of milk before him [the house fairy] and his cousin Robin Goodfellow, for grinding malt or mustard and sweeping the house at midnight.'[13]

As this reflects, domestic work was not just domestic work. Like other tasks of everyday life, it had a magical or religious dimension. In the Outer Hebrides down to this century 'the spinning wheel was blessed when it was put away for the night; the cow before she was milked; the horses when put to any new work; the cattle when they were shut up in the byre; the fire when the peats were covered up at bed-time; the door was signed with the cross when closed for the night'. Tools were blessed too, as they were left in the work-shop, and the fishing boats at the start of the season. Among other domestic tasks, we may cite those to do with making and washing clothes. Distaffs and spinning-wheels had symbolic significance, which is reflected in a number of folk-tales like 'Rumpelstiltskin' and 'Sleeping Beauty'. In Languedoc and elsewhere distaffs were often highly decorated in red and blue or with hearts or crosses. Weaving also had magical associations. Texts from the Carolingian period refer to 'incantations pronounced by women when they begin to weave a piece of cloth'. Laundering was particularly prone to ritual attack, since clothes were seen as extensions of the persons who wore them. There were taboos on doing the washing at certain times, which is reflected, as far as the days of the week are concerned, in the English nursery rhyme: 'They that wash on Monday'. In the Nivernais in the nineteenth century, washing clothes was banned in some places on the Feasts of Our Lady and during the end of Holy Week. Elsewhere, washing did not take place during the Twelve Days of Christmas, during the weeks of the Ember Days which were fast days, or during the whole month of May. By contrast 'in the Amognes district washing had to be done at Mardi Gras to ensure that the hens would lay'. In Languedoc, account was taken of the phases of the moon and of the weather before choosing the time for the annual great wash. Other ritual practices existed. In Languedoc again (and elsewhere), washerwomen's beetles or paddles were carved with suns and stars. When the clothes of a dead person were washed at Fours, 'every inhabitant of the village had to put a garment in with them so that the soul of the deceased would be at peace'.[14]

We turn now to the territory outside the village and, before dealing with the cultivated land, to the wild. Set against both village and fields, human spaces, were the forest, heaths, marshes, rivers and lakes, an important resource for pasture, fuel, food, water and so on, but untamed and dangerous. For the elites of the medieval and early modern periods, the wild landscape was an object of fear and reproach, and saints and religious, like the Desert Fathers and the early Cistercians, occupied it to stress their rejection of the secular world and its concerns. Peasants shared this view. 'They dislike mountains and torrents and forests', Norman Douglas wrote of Calabrians in 1915, 'not only as an affront to the eye, but as hindrances to agriculture and enemies of man and his ordered ways.' Both Catholics and heretics at Montaillou in the fourteenth century believed that wild nature was the realm of the Devil and not of God, and all over Europe down to this century isolated and unculti-vated places, woods and streams were thought to be haunted by fantastic animals, by the spirits of the unquiet dead, by fairies, demons and witches. Shrines might be sited in the wild or on the confines of villages precisely to give protection against such beings. So the chapel of St Roch built on the edge of Minot in Burgundy in the seventeenth century 'guarded the village and its boundaries against dangers coming from afar, but also against the wild closer to, the waters, the rocks, the moor, which, unlike the communal forest, have not been domesticated and have kept their evil power'.[15]

But this power in the wild was not always 'evil', something to be avoided. The powers 'out there' might be harnessed, used for good. This can be seen in the near-universal cults of trees and fountains or springs. Tree shrines were important in northern Europe in particular in pre-Christian times and vener-ation of trees survived the suppression of paganism. St Caesarius of Arles referred in the sixth century to people making vows to trees, while a study of modern Rumania evokes peasant belief in these terms: 'The tree speaks; it shelters the living; it can be annoyed or content; it can help, bring good health or misfortune'. As we shall see, trees were frequently involved in healing

rituals all over Europe, and branches and saplings from the forest were gathered and brought into the villages at particular times during the year. Certain
kinds of trees, moreover, had special powers. In the Limousin and elsewhere,
hazel sticks were used to guard flocks; they were also blessed at Christmas and
used to protect against witchcraft. In many places elders were planted by
houses to keep them safe, and in parts of France it was believed that elder
wood should never be burned: it was symbolic of fertility and its destruction
would lead to sterility. By contrast, other trees had evil connotations. In the
Limousin again, according to a popular saying: 'Whoever uses buckthorn to
guard his flocks brings the Devil to his byre'. The shade of a walnut was
'extremely strongly discouraged as a place to sleep or rest'; unless special
precautions were taken, one would become ill or infirm. Similarly in England
sleeping under an apple tree 'rendered one liable to be carried off by the
fairies'.[16]

Springs, fountains and wells were more obvious objects of cult. Votive
offerings had been made at them from the Bronze Age onwards and later
included bread, coins, pins and rags. Well and spring cults were later
Christianized and associated with the saints, especially in the Celtic western
fringes of Europe. They were visited for cures and good luck of various kinds
and to procure fertility. There was also a concern to ensure a good supply of
water itself. In villages in Yorkshire and the Midlands, bottles were filled at
wells on Easter Monday or Palm Sunday and offerings made there, so that
'the lady of the well' would provide clean and abundant water during the
coming year. Wells were also 'dressed' with flowers at certain times of the year
in Derbyshire and elsewhere. If the spring ran dry at Lignane near Aix-en-
Provence, a young virgin was sent into the underground passage to restore
the flow; while at Cap-Couronne, on St John's Day, the parishioners 'made
the priest exorcize the spring, believing that a corpse had once been thrown
into it'. Running water figured in many magical rites and charms. In Anglo-
Saxon magic, for example, it was used against snake bites and 'to clear a
person of the disease-spirit'. Here the direction of the current might be significant. In a recipe for a 'holy drink', 'an immaculate person [had] silently to
fetch half a jar of running water against the current', while in another charm a
girl had to 'go to a spring that runs due east, and ... draw a cupful a water
moving with the current'.[17]

Like houses, fields were sacred. Fields or sections within them were often
identified with particular families or lineages and might even serve as burial
places for the dead. More generally, fields were guarded by landmarks or
crosses and blessed and protected in ways that we will describe. Votive offerings and amulets were placed in the ground from ancient times to make the
soil fertile. A famous Anglo-Saxon charm, the Aecer-Bot, sought to 'improve

the fields', particularly 'if harm had been done to them by sorcery or witch-craft'. Four sods were cut from the four sides of the field, soaked in oil, honey, milk and holy water, and carried to church to have four masses sung over them. Aspen-wood crosses with the names of the four Evangelists written on them were then placed in the holes left by the sods, which were replaced to the accompaniment of elaborate prayers and gestures. Manure for the fields was of course in short supply and was correspondingly prized and granted symbolic status. In modern Ireland, as elsewhere, the dung-heap was kept by the house and seen as a sign of the fertility of the farm. A sprig of rowan might be stuck in it to keep away mischief.[18]

The hero of Guillaumin's *La vie d'un simple*, a sceptical and anticlerical sharecropper from the Allier in the nineteenth century, yet relates that

> I never failed to sprinkle the haylofts with holy water before storing the fodder. On beginning to cut a field of wheat I made the sign of the cross with the first sheaf, and I also made it when vitriolizing the seed corn ... and on the backs of the cows with their first milk after calving.[19]

As this indicates, it was probably the main agricultural tasks which attracted most ritual and which were felt to be most important from ploughing through sowing to harvesting. Ploughs and plough tackle were sacred objects. In many parts of Europe, for example, there was a taboo on burning a yoke. If this were done, the owner would die in agony. Related to this, yokes were put under the mattresses of the moribund in the Sologne in the seventeenth century and later to ease their deaths. Festivities frequently preceded ploughing in both Spring and Autumn. The festival of the plough at Biot in Provence, for instance, took place on 23 October and dates back to at least the sixteenth century. The peasants' ploughs were all taken to the square, where at night to the sound of fifes and drums, two men, one dressed as an angel, the other in a jacket with bells, simulated agricultural work: ploughing, sowing, hoeing, in a kind of dance.

'When you drive forth the plough and cut the first furrow', the Aecer-Bot charm instructed, 'say then: Hail to thee, earth, mother of men, may you be fruitful under God's protection, filled with food for the benefit of men'; and a special loaf had also to be placed under the furrow. In northern France, according to Abbé Thiers who made a vast collection of 'superstitions' in the seventeenth century, peasants would 'turn three times around the plough, holding in their hands bread, oats and a light, before starting to plough a field, so that their work might be successful'. A seventeenth-century print from Bologna shows a peasant on his knees by his pair of oxen and plough, praying to heaven before he begins (see Text Figure 1). Taking food and particularly something made with the expected cereal crop into the field at

1. Peasant praying before starting to plough. Engraving, Bologna, seventeenth century.

ploughing time remained current much later. In modern Aberdeenshire on the first day of ploughing, special oatcakes baked with cream or butter were eaten with cheese and whisky by the ploughman in the field, and a piece of the cake was fed to the horses. The time to start ploughing might also be significant. In some parts of Scotland, for example, Spring ploughing began at Candlemas in February; elsewhere it could not begin till specific dates in March. The direction taken by the plough team was important too. In modern Ireland, 'the ploughman should turn his horses with the sun, from left to right, to invoke its blessing on the work, and when yoking and unyoking his team his horses' heads should be facing south'.[20]

Once the land had been ploughed, the right day had to be chosen for sowing. In the Vosges, for example, in the nineteenth century, 'for haricots to grow well, they had to be planted on a Saturday in May'. In Ireland, the Hebrides and elsewhere, Friday was the best day to begin sowing, and Good Friday the best of all. Saints' days were also significant here. As a modern folklorist has put it, the peasant of the Périgord 'would never begin sowing before the saint marked in the calendar had given him the order which opened the proper season'. In Ireland again 'the countryman liked to have his first ridge of potatoes planted on St Patrick's Day'. Some days were unlucky, for example in parts of France St Leger's, 2 October, for Autumn sowing, because the saint would make the corn grow light (*léger*).[21]

When Dr Johnson was on the island of Col in 1773, he asked the local clergyman if the people 'had any superstitions [and] the cutting peats at the increase of the moon was mentioned as one'. He later added that 'they expect better crops of grain, by sowing their seed in the moon's increase' and noted also that 'it was a precept annually given in one of the English Almanacks, to kill hogs when the moon was increasing, and the bacon would prove the better in the boiling'. Such beliefs and practices were universal and longlasting, being recorded by Pliny and by modern anthropologists. Generally, the association was made between the increase of the crop (or product) and the increase of the moon, but there were variations. In some parts of France and elsewhere, for example, 'plants that developed above the soil should be sown during the waxing moon and those that developed beneath the soil in the period of the waning moon'.[22] The new moon was linked to germination and the rapid growth of leaves and branches, while the old moon gave maturity and fruit. In Languedoc, however, sowing and planting in the new moon was avoided lest the young plants develop too quickly and prove weakly.

The seed to be sown would have been ritually treated to ensure that it would germinate and produce a fine crop. In Wales, corn from the last sheaf harvested the previous year was mixed with the seed corn 'to teach it to grow'. An alternative additive was ash from the Yule log or, in Ireland, ashes from

the Midsummer bonfires. On Eriskay, the seed (and the sower) were sprinkled with salt and water; on Lewis in modern times a nail and an egg were
placed in the sowing basket: 'The nail was emblematical of long, strong
straight stalks of corn; the egg was symbolical of corn as full of substance as
the egg is of meat'. In the Périgord, empty egg-shells were mixed with the
seed-corn to preserve the crops from witchcraft and the evil eye. In many
Catholic places, a sample of seed was blessed by the priest in church and then
mixed in with the rest, often after having been sprinkled too with holy water.
In the Hebrides, the seed was sprinkled with clear water three days before
sowing in the name of the Trinity, 'the person sprinkling walking sunwise the
while'. 'At Angres (near Arras), the peasants had bread blessed on the day of
St Eloi. They then mixed the blessed bread with the grain destined to be used
as seed, in the hope of obtaining a rich harvest.' Ecclesiastical magic was also
employed by Protestants. In the Cévennes in modern times women 'took a
sachet of silk-worm eggs hidden in their corsages to the temple during the
service in order to avoid diseases and be sure of a good harvest'.[23]

The seed was distributed according to similar kinds of rituals. In Sicily, just
before sowing, a sign of the cross was made over the first lot of seed and it was
scattered in the name of the Trinity. 'I will go out to sow the seed', they said in
the Hebrides, 'in the name of Him who gave it growth ... in the name of
Gabriel and the Apostles kind.' In Ireland, 'the sower going forth should
begin his labours with the solemn words: In the name of God, and he should
give the horses a handful of the corn from the seed-bag and throw a handful
of earth over each horse's rump'. More generally, there was a belief in
Languedoc that 'the crops grow better and are more abundant when sowing
and ploughing are done while singing' (see Plate 4).[24]

Again, ritual gestures and prayers were made or said at harvesting and the
first enjoyment of the crops. 'Let no one put his sickle to the ripe corn', Virgil
had advised, 'without first crowning his brow with the oaken wreath of Ceres,
surrendering himself for a moment and pronouncing the sacred words.' By
the medieval period in Europe, this meant making signs of the cross and
saying prayers to God and the saints. A French poet wrote in the sixteenth
century:

> Then the first to start work in the field, he goes with sickle raised,
> Praying the great God who gives all
> That He will grant this boon, that they may harvest their grain,
> Get it safe into the barns,
> And that it will feed them until the next summer comes.

The June grain harvest in nineteenth-century Sicily began with the binder
making the sign of the cross and saying: 'Praised and thanked be the most

holy and most divine Sacraments!', to which the reapers responded: 'Forever be it praised'. And at once they bent to mow, murmuring at the first cut: 'In the name of God!' The reapers sang during their task, usually prayers, lauds and laments, and rarely profane songs, and all closed with the refrain: 'Praised be the Holy Sacrament!' and shouts of 'Viva Maria and Jesus' or vivas to the saints. In the Highlands of Scotland on the day chosen for reaping 'the whole family repaired to the field dressed in their best. The father took his sickle and, facing the sun, cut a handful of corn. Putting it three times sunwise round his head, the Reaping Blessing was sung'.[25]

Often a small part of the crop would be left in the field as a kind of offering. In Brittany, handfuls of buckwheat were thrown around the edges of fields. In Northern Ireland it was customary when digging turf to leave three strips uncut. 'Behind the custom there lies the widespread notion that a task should never be completely finished and that a small portion of anything taken by man should be left for luck or the fairies'. Sometimes land could be more permanently dedicated in propitiation. In a case brought before the church courts in Aberdeenshire in 1650, two farmers

> gave away a field, to the Goodman, as they called him, to make their good stand [prosper] and ... they went to the field and promised to let it lie unlaboured as long as they possessed their tacks, and in testification thereof they did cast some stones over the dyke of the field.[26]

Similar practices are recorded in Scotland in the nineteenth century.

Special attention often focused when bringing in the grain harvest on the last load or last sheaf. The German diarist Hentzner met some country people near Eton around 1600

> celebrating their harvest-home; their last load of corn they crown with flowers, having besides an image richly dressed, by which perhaps they would signify Ceres; this they keep moving about, while men and women, men- and maid-servants, riding through the streets in the cart, shout as loud as they can till they arrive at the barn (see Plate 5).

Ceremonies centred on the last sheaf were widespread in Britain according to nineteenth-century accounts. In Devon, for example, all the harvesters took the last sheaf, made of the best ears and called 'the neck', to the highest part of the farm, where the person with the loudest voice led shouting: 'A neck we have! God save it!' In Scotland, reaping hooks and sickles were thrown into the air, and there, as in England, the sheaf might take the form of a doll that was afterwards placed on one of the ricks. In Pembrokeshire and parts of Carmarthenshire, the last tuft of standing corn was plaited and was then cut by the reapers throwing their hooks at it. Whoever cut it shouted a set formula, referring to the sheaf as 'the harvest mare' or the 'hag'. He then had to get the sheaf into the farmhouse without the women discovering him and would be soaked with water in the process.[27]

Last sheaf ceremonies were also common on the Continent, from Russia to Provence. In the Paris region, the last sheaf was ritually gathered and processed and was then placed at the entrance to the farmyard or barn, where it remained until the next harvest. In Normandy, it was presented by the harvesters to the farmer's wife. Elsewhere it might be fed to the livestock to invigorate them, used to bake special cakes or bread, or put into the seed corn, as we have seen. Sometimes a domestic bird or animal was sacrificed at the gathering of the last sheaf. The last sheaf was often larger than the rest. In parts of Germany the harvesters 'intentionally make the last sheaf as big as possible, and sometimes even tie stones in, so that it, and with it the next harvest, may be heavy'.[28]

The last sheaf ceremonies were once seen as the classic demonstration of Mannhardt's theories about the corn-spirit, annually killed and resurrected, which Frazer and his disciples adopted. In Central and Eastern Europe, explicit references were made to the Corn Mother or the Rye Mother, but in general the rites were more properly magical and did not involve spirits. They also had other functions only indirectly linked to fecundity. There might be competition to get the last sheaf to its destination, or the last sheaf might be handed round ending up with the last group to harvest, sanctions against late starts or slow work.

After the harvest was gathered in, harvest feasts were held in celebration and blessings were invoked. A nineteenth-century English harvest supper song ran:

> Here's a health to our master,
> The lord of the feast;
> God bless his endeavours
> And send him increase;
> May all his crop prosper
> So we reap them next year.

Threshing the grain was also the occasion for ritual. At the threshing in Sicily, the mules were encouraged with songs calling on God, the Virgin, angels and saints. The Provençal poet Mistral recalled the threshing on his father's farm near Maillane in the early nineteenth century: 'In the evening when the grain had been heaped up with shovels, my father measured the heap with great strides and traced there a cross with the handle of a shovel, saying: May God make you grow!' Similarly in Scandinavia 'in the old days, people used to make a cross in their grain after they were done threshing. That way the mound folk would not be able to steal any of it'. In Savoy, according to an account by an eighteenth-century parish priest, he went to everyone's granary in October to the threshing-floor 'and recited there the verses and prayers contained in the Prayerbook under the rubric: Blessing of Seeds, since there is nothing there specifically for the gathered crops and fruit. Then he blessed the sheaves and the whole house and its appurtenances'. In return he was usually given a small cheese or some eggs.[29]

The harvesting of other crops was treated in the same fashion. When the hay harvest was finished in the Franche-Comté, 'the last cart of hay was decorated with flowers and foliage and taken back to the village accompanied by singing'. In parts of Wales anyone entering a hayfield at hay-making time 'was immediately pounced upon by hay-makers of the opposite sex and tossed about on the hay-cocks' in a simulation of sexual intercourse. William Cole, rector of Bletchley, noted in his diary in July 1766 that despite the wet season he had got in all his hay. That done, his hay-makers 'made a sort of procession, with a fiddle and a German flute. Jem dressed out with ribbands and Tom Hearne dancing before the last cart, I giving a good supper to all ... , being above thirty persons in the kitchen, who stayed till one'.[30] Similar and usually more elaborate celebrations took place at the grape harvest or vintage on the Continent. In Provence the last cart of grapes was decorated and the faces of the harvesters smeared with grape juice Everywhere there was music and dancing and much consumption of wine.

In the Ancient world the first fruits had been dedicated to the gods or other spirits and consumed in ritual fashion. So Athena offered the first fruits to the Eumenides or the Fates in Aeschylus' play. 'The first fruits of the turning year are mine', proclaimed the god Vertumnus in Propertius' poem. Such customs continued through the medieval and modern periods with a degree of Christianization depending on the milieu. At Cluny, 'when the grapes were beginning to ripen (in early August), the precentor presented some at the mass, and they were blessed and afterwards eaten as eulogies or unconsecrated elements in the refectory; the new beans, bread and wine were each year blessed and eaten in like manner'. In early modern Corsica the first fruits, grain, wool and cheese, were often given to the local priest. Loaves made from the first grain were offered or blessed in church in England before the Reformation at Lammas (loaf-mass) on 1 August, and related customs survived later. Frazer related that 'in one part of Yorkshire it is still customary for the clergyman to cut the first corn', which was then made into communion bread. On Barra and elsewhere in the Highlands of Scotland, the first ears harvested were made into a bannock called 'Mary's fatling', which was baked on a bonfire and eaten by the family members in rank order. A hymn to the Virgin Mary was then sung and the people walked sun-wise round the fire. It was an 'archaic practice' in Ireland 'for the first sheaves cut to be scutched or lashed, that is the grain was beaten out without using the flail. The winnowed grain was parched over the fire, ground in a quern and boiled in time to make a breakfast for the reapers'. Other first fruits were offered at holy wells. In nineteenth-century Sicily, the first beans were cooked in the field where they grew in communal gatherings of several families, and similar feasts were held for the new watermelons, figs and olives. Special bread was made from the newly-harvested wheat, which was eaten while saying: 'What I eat today, may I eat next year too!' In Mistral's *Mirèio* (1859), a marvellous evocation of rural life in Provence, one woman tells the others collecting silk-worm cocoons from the mulberries:

> Yesterday I took my best branches
> To put on the altar of Our Lady as a tithe.
> I do this every year;
> For after all, it is she who with largesse
> Commands the silkworms to come up, when it pleases her.[31]

In addition to offering the first fruits to tutelary beings to please them and ensure supplies in future, peasants were also seeking to purify their crops of possible evil influence and make them wholesome. As we have seen, these concerns extended to the protection of produce in its storage and processing. The motifs on containers and tools here were not purely decorative. They were designed to avert harm, like the swastikas and rosettes on Transdanubian winepresses, for example, or the animals, plants and stars on dough- and flour-bins in other places.

Crops in store or in the fields were vulnerable to pests, and until recently peasants had little that they could materially do against their ravages. A French peasant remembered that the Autumn of 1926 in the Beauce region was one

> of misery: an invasion of field mice arrived. Nothing but mice all over the plain. They ate our wheat; they stripped the bark from the trees; they nibbled all the grass by the roadsides. Soon, over the whole district there was not a blade of green to be seen. In the evenings, when I came back with the plough, the sound of the mice really scared me. People dug holes hoping that the mice would drown in them; they laid traps; they put down poison; nothing worked. The mice had taken our seed, everything.[32]

But if there were no effective physical remedies in such circumstances, the gap was filled by a great variety of rituals, preventative and reactive. Frazer describes a number of magical procedures used to deter vermin. They could be propitiated by giving them a proportion of the crop in advance. So 'amongst the Saxons of Transylvania, in order to keep sparrows from the corn, the sower begins by throwing the first handful of seed backwards over his head, saying, That is for you, sparrows'. The pests might also be tricked by simulated sowing; or they could be addressed orally or in writing, in a more or less threatening manner. In many parts of France, peasants paraded through the fields and orchards with torches on the First Sunday in Lent, in order to protect them from pests through the coming year. In the Bessin district of Normandy, they shouted: 'Moles and fieldmice, get out of my fields, or I will break your bones!'. Barns and granaries were given similar cover. When the first sheaf was brought into the grange in the Seine-et-Marne, three Paternosters and three Ave Marias were recited, followed by this formula: 'Rats, male and female, ratlings; mice, male and female, and baby mice, I conjure you by the great living God not to touch the grain and straw that I will put here for a year'. In other places, a written notice conveying the same message was put up or stuffed into rat or mouse holes. Rosalind in Shakespeare's *As You Like It* says she must be 'an Irish rat', when Orlando hangs or carves rhymes to her on trees all over the Forest of Arden, a reference to a sixteenth-century English belief that rats were conjured in Ireland with incantations and written charms. At Lamballe, a rat was roasted alive to deter the others. Similar preventative action was taken against insects, worms, caterpillars and so on, and methods were varied. In the Limousin in the nineteenth century shots were fired at Carnival for the destruction of all kinds of vermin. According to a German text published in 1795, 'they make a menstruating woman with no fastening in her clothes, her hair loose, her feet bare, walk around as a protection against canker-worm and other garden pests'.[33]

Once an infestation had occurred, such rites might be repeated or others deployed. In various parts of France, attempts were made to induce caterpillars to leave fields and gardens by putting an odd number of them at a crossroads, by going round the infested area before dawn reciting prayers and charms, or by enticing them to another spot. A sixteenth-century source reports that cockchafers were expelled from an orchard by reciting a verse from the 35th Psalm: 'Let them be turned back and brought to confusion that devise my hurt'. Similar procedures were used in Italy. 'Cursed worm, I speak against you', went one formula from the south,

> I conjure you by the moon and the sun
> And by all the saints that are or were in this world or the next
> And by this red cloth.[34]

Recourse was also had to expert conjurors, but, if the attack were serious, then the power of the saints and the Church was resorted to. There were some specialized pilgrimages. Men attended the '*pardon*' or pilgrimage of the cockchafers at Gouesnou on Ascension Day, for example, with at least one of the dreaded insects pinned to their hats. Many saints were specialists in dealing with vermin. In New Castile, St Augustine was believed from at least the fourteenth century to have special powers against locusts. 'They say in Augsburg', Montaigne related in 1580,

> that they are free, not of mice, but of the large rats with which the rest of Germany is infected ... they attribute this privilege to one of their bishops who is buried there; and they sell little pieces of the earth of his tomb, the size of nuts, which they say can be used to keep off vermin, in whatever region it is taken.

In modern Greece, 'St Serafim is very good for the wheat. The priest has his ikon all in gold and when they put that ikon over the wheat the little fly that goes and spoils the wheat flies away'.[35]

These powers were often indicated in hagiography. St Bernard excommunicated swarms of flies that were pestering the new Cistercian monastery of Foigny near Laon, and they fell dead in heaps. 'This miracle became so well-known that the cursing of the flies of Foigny became proverbial among the people round about'. From the Byzantine cultural area, St Theodore of Sykeon performed several miraculous expulsions of locusts, beetles, mice and other pests. A miracle of this kind in the mid-eighteenth century was reported in the canonization process of St Gerald Majella.

> While the servant of God was crossing some fields sown with crops [near Bari], a peasant came up to him and said: 'Father, the mice are damaging my fields; curse them', to which Gerald replied: 'Do you want them to die or to go elsewhere?' The poor farmer said that unless they died, they might continue to do harm to others. So Gerald raised his right hand towards the fields and made the sign of the cross, and at once all the fields were full of mice, dead on their backs.[36]

This 'miracle' closely follows the pattern of normal exorcisms performed by the clergy, as we shall see.

In early modern Spain and elsewhere, collective vows were made to saints with powers against pests. In a village near Toledo, for example, in the late fifteenth century, the inhabitants

> promised and vowed a chapel to St Barnabas and the entire [population] went out and began to dig the trenches to make the chapel. And the next day when the people went to do their ploughing they found that the trenches which they had dug were full of locusts, and since then they have never suffered from them. So they took the devotion and built a chapel, where they go in procession on that day and give a charity feast for the poor.

Relics or substances associated with the saint were often used. In Savoy, the Dauphiné and the Aosta region, St Grat was invoked from the seventeenth to the twentieth century to get rid of moles, rodents and bugs. Water was blessed in various chapels dedicated to him according to a special formula and was sprinkled on the fields. During a Jesuit mission in the Eifel (Palatinate) in 1736, the peasantry used 'Ignatius-Water' in the same way 'in order to exterminate a plague of caterpillars'.[37] This was holy water blessed with relics of St Ignatius. In the same vein, in many parts of Switzerland in the seventeenth and eighteenth centuries, the crozier of St Magnus from Füssen was used to drive off rodents and insects.

Both the Eastern and the Western Churches provided official ceremonies to get rid of vermin that might be seen as the agents of demons or the result of divine anger. In the diocese of Périgueux, for example, after mass, prayers and blessing of holy water, the congregation went out 'to pray on all the roads' of the parish, stopping at the highest point. There further litanies were recited and the priest blessed all the fields with the cross, scattering holy water to the four quarters. Then the insects or other pests were exorcized with these words:

> We conjure Your Infinite Goodness and Your Mercy, O Lord; know that insects and all kinds of creatures devastate, gnaw and devour our harvests, our grass, our grain and all other products that are born of the earth for the use of men. Deign to repulse, dissolve and exterminate these enemies. May the power of the demons that resides in them melt before Your Face as smoke dissipates in the wind.

Then the priest addressed the 'disgusting spirits who manipulate these insects' themselves, ordering them to go away in the name of Jesus Christ, the Virgin Mary and all the saints. A 1588 Italian formula was even more magical in tone: 'I exorcize you pestilent worms, mice, birds, locusts, and other creatures, cursing you; wherever you are, may you be accursed, shrinking and shrivelling into yourselves from day to day, until none of you remains'. Many specific examples may be cited of such rituals of anathema and exorcism being deployed against pests. In the diocese of Fréjus alone, thirty-five cases occurred between 1647 and 1779.[38]

Most commonly, the pests were dealt with by the parish priest, or sometimes visiting missionaries. But, if they ignored the warnings of the lower clergy, recourse might be had to the bishop or even to Rome, or proceedings might be taken against the offenders in the ecclesiastical courts. Such trials seem to have occurred particularly in the early modern period in Switzerland and the bordering areas.[39] Around 1500, for example, the inhabitants of Beaune in the prime wine-growing area of Burgundy applied for some kind of legal instrument from the tribunal of Autun against certain flies that were attacking their vines. In a better-documented case, villagers from Saint-Julien instituted proceedings in 1545 in the bishop's court at Saint-Jean-de-Maurienne against the weevils ravaging their vines. The court recommended that public prayers and masses be said, and that the villagers repent of their sins and pay their tithes, remedies commonly advocated by the clergy. When the attacks continued, the insects were eventually brought to trial. A ruling was obtained against them, and this was taken in procession around the vine-yards, like a talisman, with singing of psalms and prayers.

We should also mention rituals against snakes and other reptiles. In the Sologne a branch was placed over the doors of houses and farm buildings to keep these away. Saints also offered protection against snakes and snake-bites. The most elaborate ritual here was probably that of the festival of St Domenico at Coccullo in the Abruzzi on the first Wednesday in May. The statue of the saint was processed in the usual way, but it was entwined with living snakes captured for the purpose. It was taken to a hillock overlooking the village where a general blessing on the pasture, and flocks, fields and corn was implored (see Plate 1).

In many instances we have seen that agriculture and the fertility of the land were threatened by witches. This was a general belief at all levels of society from the earliest times. According to the Roman poet Lucan, the witch 'stoops over a fertile cornfield burning the seeds, and her breath poisons air that was wholesome before'. A sixth-century Visigothic Code refers to sorcerers paid by peasants 'for putting curses on their enemies' crops'. Pope Innocent VIII's Bull *Summis desiderantes affectibus* of 1484, which gave the go-ahead to witch-hunting on a new scale, declared that witches by various means 'ruin and cause to perish ... the products of the earth, the grapes of the vines and the fruits of the trees ... orchards, meadows, pastures, harvests, grains and other produce of the earth'. First, they could make the soil infertile, as we have seen in discussing the tenth-century Aecer-Bot charm. A man tried at Vesoul in the early 1600s was accused of 'having by his looks bewitched the field [of another man] so that in that year no plant good or bad would grow in it, though it was sown at the right time and after a soft rain suited to make a crop grow'. When cabbages were planted in the same field later, they immediately shrivelled at the root. Similar effects could be obtained by broadcasting poisonous powders and by polluting the ground with raw meat.[40]

It was also possible to spirit away the seed. Another man tried in the diocese of Lausanne in 1461 confessed that he and his companions sometimes made themselves invisible at sowing time and 'walked in front of the sowers stealing the seed as it was scattered'. At a trial in Livonia in 1692, a man claimed that 'witches carried seed corn into Hell to keep the crops from growing', a kind of inverse replica of the real ritual of taking the seed corn to be blessed in church. Then pests, blights and weeds might be sent to ruin or damage the crop as it grew. Sébillot notes that the mid nineteenth-century potato rot was attributed in some parts of France to spells cast by dissatisfied farm workers. Again, as we shall see in more detail, witches could produce adverse weather conditions to ruin crops. In the Cotentin, they could even do this without raising storms but simply by spells.[41]

If a harvest came to fruition, then witches might steal it. 'Incantation draws the crops from the neighbour's field', wrote Tibullus in the first century BC. Lévi-Strauss refers to an early medieval French law ordering the death penalty for a witch 'who, by reciting the Psalm *Super aspidem ambulabis*, emptied the fields [of others] of their corn to fill her own granary'. When the witches of Auldearn, who were tried in 1661–62, 'desired to secure for their own use the crop of some neighbour, they made a pretence of ploughing it with a yoke of paddocks, praying the Devil to transfer to them the fruit of the ground so traversed, and leave the proprietors nothing but thistles and briars'.[42] In the Limousin, the same effect could be produced by burying a special egg in the field. Finally, a court indictment in Essex in 1587 involved bewitching a wind-mill, that is preventing the production of the flour that was the end-product of the entire agricultural cycle.

According to Foster's concept of the 'limited good', peasants viewed their environment 'as one in which all the desired things of life such as land, wealth health, friendship ... honour ... status, power and influence, security and safety, exist in finite quantity and are always in short supply'.[43] Witchcraft and magic fit neatly into this schema. Not only did they explain failure; above-average success was also attributed not to enterprise or hard work but to the exercise of occult powers. So if crops failed or were damaged by storms, they might well have been transferred to someone else's field or granary. Similarly, as we shall see in more detail, if a cow went dry, her milk might well have been syphoned off by a witch.

It is relevant here too that peasants who worked the land themselves tended to suspect those who did not of witchcraft or the possession of special powers: artisans, especially smiths, shepherds, gypsies, mole-catchers, forest workers. In the Burgundian village of Minot, the 'woodspeople' were believed to 'dabble in sorcery'.[44] This takes us back to the more general symbolic opposition between cultivated land and the wild, the latter being associated nearly always with the forces of evil and death.

2

Calendar Customs and Agrarian Saints

'... these pretty pageants, these now innocent diversions, had their
origin in ignorance and superstition; ... and if they are a record of
human endeavour, they are also a monument of fruitless ingenuity, of wasted labour, and of blighted hopes; and ... for all their gay
trappings – their flowers, their ribbons, and their magic – they
partake more of tragedy than of farce'.[1]

Overlapping and intertwined with agricultural ritual were calendar customs.
Traditional Europe had a complex cycle or cycles of such customs, made up
of various historical and sociological layers. The Ancient world had had a full
panoply of annual rituals associated with both local and general deities, as
had the Germanic peoples who succeeded Rome in the West. They were often
explicitly concerned with fertility. For example, Ovid relates that at the
Roman Sementiva holiday, a movable feast early in the year at sowing time,
'Ceres and Tellus [Earth], mother of the fruits, were propitiated with their
own corn, and the entrails of a pregnant sow', while wishes were made for
good weather, an absence of pests, mildew and weeds, and an abundant crop.
Again, the main purpose of the annual feast of the Ancient Scandinavians
'was to renew the contract with the gods, so that the luck and prosperity of the
land might continue'.[2] In the Spring, images of Freyr and other deities were
drawn on waggons through the fields.

The Christian Church introduced new festivals but within and to a large
extent building on this pagan framework. By the later Middle Ages, if not
earlier, a sacred calendar had been established, which more systematically
meshed the feasts of the Christian year and the days of the saints with the agricultural and pastoral seasonal round. The two solstices were also marked and
given more or less strong Christian colouring. Equally significant, especially
in northern Europe, were the times marking the beginning of Spring or
Summer in May or earlier and of Winter in November. They signalled the
dividing-line between times of scarcity and plenty, and for those living from
flocks and herds in mountainous areas the times when the animals moved to
the upland and then down again to the lowland pastures.

The calendar festivals had many functions. Most obviously, they provided
a calendar, a time-framework in an age before clocks existed or were

common. Involving the whole community, they stressed the obligations of community and collective, coordinated action, without which the traditional economy would not have been viable. Festivities were also seen as 'a guarantee in some way against the threats to the traditional economy presented by the supernatural powers pitted against it'.[3] Ritual consumption and excess exorcized shortage and want. Every festival and holy day, moreover, was an opportunity to call down blessings from on high and to obtain protective material. In this sense, Mannhardt and Frazer were quite right to see calendar customs as primarily fertility rituals of a magical kind. Calendar customs also provided a model for other less public rituals.

There had always been some distinction between official and unofficial rituals here, between what the authorities, mainly clerical, approved and what most people did. The Reformation especially and the Counter-Reformation widened this gap, and new festivals were introduced into the cycle by the State, for example Accession Day ceremonies and Guy Fawkes in England. But, despite all this, the old customs were remarkably resilient and survived into the Industrial Age, and they survived because they were still believed to be necessary or effective.

The year opened or ended with Christmas, which coincided with the older or 'pagan' Winter solstice. Christmas was part of a mini-cycle of twelve days, including New Year's Day. In much of Europe, evergreens – holly, ivy, yew, box – were brought in to deck houses and churches. Their function as expressions of the perpetuity of vegetation through the Winter and its ultimate general renewal seems clear. Other more explicit rituals are reported. In Provence, offerings were made at midnight mass on Christmas Eve of the fruits of the earth and of the sea in order to ensure prosperity for the year to come. Special significance attached to the lighting of the Christmas log. This was accompanied by shouts of joy, and a libation of wine was poured over it by the grandfather who recited this prayer, according to Mistral:

> O fire, o sacred fire, let us have good weather,
> And make my ewes give birth happily;
> Make my sow fruitful;
> Make my cow calve easily;
> And make my daughters and my daughters-in-law have children without trouble!

Much the same ceremony was described by the Swiss Thomas Platter junior, who was studying medicine at the famous School of Montpellier and who spent Christmas Eve in 1597 with a family in Uzès. The log was called by the same term: *cachofiò*, and a prayer for prosperity and fertile livestock was said as it started to burn, though by all members of the household in unison. Then wine, bread, salt and wax or tallow were thrown on to it by the youngest member of the family, each substance in turn and each in three lots. So 'the child threw a pinch of salt on one end of the log, saying, In the name of the Father; a second pinch on the other end, saying, In the name of the Son; and a third pinch in the middle, saying, In the name of the Holy Spirit, and everyone then cried out together, Make us happy, God, make us happy', and so on. Ashes from the log were kept all the year round and used to cure 'any swelling in sick men or animals'.[4]

In other places where this or similar customs were followed, the ashes of the log were mixed with seed corn to make it germinate, while larger chips might be put in the bedding of animals and poultry to make them prosper or lay well. In the Périgord in the seventeenth century, seed corn was placed in the table cloth used on Christmas Day to make it grow better; while in parts of early modern Italy women engaged in a ritual sowing of 'the earth floors of their houses on Twelfth Night to ensure bounty'.[5] (See Text Figure 2.) In Upper Brittany, the Christmas or Yule log ashes were kept to ward off storms. Sometimes, the kind of wood used was significant. In the Limousin care was taken to choose a log from a fruit tree to ensure an abundant fruit crop.

Christmas and New Year libations in northern Europe were done with beer or cider rather than wine, as in the Welsh and English wassailings. These were often concerned with fruit trees, and it is no surprise that one of the earliest references to wassailing comes from the orchards of Kent in 1585. But the custom was not confined to wishing the fruit harvest well. According to an account from 1832, on the eve of the old Christmas Day or Twelfth Night, thirteen fires were lit in the cornfields in the Hereford region. These were said to represent the twelve apostles and the Virgin Mary. While they were burning, the farm 'labourers retired into some shed or outhouse into which they led a cow, on whose horns a plum-cake has been stuck'. A bucket of cider was then thrown in the cow's face with the wish:

> God send thy master a good crop of corn,
> Both wheat, rye and barley, of grains of all sort.[6]

In parts of Wales a plough was placed under the table during the Christmas feast and was wetted with beer during the meal.

In some parts of Europe, bonfires were lit at this season. In the Jura, the Christmas fires were lit by young people who jumped about brandishing torches and shouting: 'Good year, come back, with bread and wine!' When the torches were burned through, they were either put on the fields to ensure a good harvest or taken home and used to cook the omelette eaten on the return from midnight mass. In Herefordshire down to recent times, a hawthorn globe was hung in the farm house from one New Year's Day to the next. Early on the morning of 1 January, 'it was taken down, carried out to the first sown wheat field and there burnt on a large straw fire'. The men made a ring around the fire and chanted. The globe itself and a brand from the fire were sometimes carried across the field. All this was supposed to bring good luck to the crops and make them grow.[7]

Christmas and New Year were also a time for divining how prosperous would be the year to come. Sometimes the twelve days of Christmas indicated the weather for each of the twelve months. There was a saying in the Alto Minho: 'If the moon is in its strength [waxing] during Christmas Eve, there will be a good harvest of wine during the year'. In Provence, grains of wheat were placed in saucers of water by the fire on St Barbara's Day (4 December). By Christmas they had germinated and were put by the crib. 'If the wheat has grown well and is green, this is a sign that the future harvest will be good; but if the sprouts are yellow and unhealthy, there will be a bad harvest.' Elsewhere, New Year's Day itself was the focus for prognostications. According to a tenth-century English text, if New Year's Day fell on a Sunday, 'this meant a good warm Winter and dry Summer with excellent crops'.[8] In modern Wales attention focused on the first visitor coming into the house on New Year's Day, who might bring good or bad luck, depending on gender or certain personal characteristics. This belief was also important and widespread in Scotland, where, for example, a dark young man might be lucky as a 'first-foot' but a red-haired woman unlucky. A youth carrying a sheaf of corn or oats might be contrived to be the first person to cross the threshold, and sometimes grass and water were brought into the house first thing to ensure a plentiful supply of each through the year.

Ritual visitation of houses and begging also occurred at this time in many places, with groups of young men in disguise – 'guisers' in Britain – or children going from house to house to ask for food and drink and delivering blessings or curses in return, depending on how they were received. In the Hebrides in modern times, the guisers approached the house with loud shouts and went 'sunwise round it'. At the door, they blessed the dwelling and its inmates, and once inside they went sunwise again round the fire, and set light to a sheepskin or cow hide, with which they fumigated the room or rooms. They were given special food and drink and repeated their blessing before leaving. A typical Gaelic blessing ran:

> May God bless the dwelling,
> Each stone and beam and stave;
> All food and drink and clothing;
> May health of men be always there.

2. Twelfth Night festivities. Cornelis Dusart, *The Twelve Months of the Year* (January). Mezzotint, Amsterdam, 1680s.

But if the guisers were inhospitably treated, 'they filed round the fire wither-shins and raised a cairn in or near the door', a cairn of malediction. At the same time they wished 'the malison of God and of Hogmanay' on the house-hold and called down on it the 'scath' of a variety of predators, including the raven, the wild cat and the wolf.[9] In parts of South Wales, the guisers took with them the Mari Lwyd or grey Mary, a man under a sheet carrying a horse's skull. Elaborate verses were improvised between the guisers and the people in the house, before the former were let in. These stressed the antiquity of the ritual and the need for generosity and also included blessings.

In England, the first working day after Christmas was Plough Monday. Before the Reformation, ploughs were blessed in church on that day. A prayer preserved at Cawston, Norfolk, indicates the intention behind such blessing:

> God speed the plough
> And send us all corn enow.

Then and later youths dragged ploughs round the villages, collecting for the parish funds. They were known as the Plough Witches in some districts, a hint perhaps of the influences which they 'conjured'.[10] Here one can see a calendar custom merging with the agricultural ritual that we have already described.

The next important festival was Candlemas on 2 February, forty days after Christmas. This was the Feast of the Purification of the Virgin in the West and of the Presentation of Christ in the Temple in the East. From the metaphor used in the *Nunc Dimittis* or Song of Simeon, it had become a festival of lights appropriate to the time of year, and it was extremely popular from the central medieval period onwards. Attention focused on the candles blessed in church. This was done in an elaborate ritual and involved various categories of candle: the great Paschal candle, candles offered to the priest and others blessed and taken away. The prayers used to bless the candles 'unequivocally attribute apotropaic power to the blessed wax, asking that "wherever it shall be lit or set up, the Devil may flee away in fear and trem-bling with all his ministers, out of those dwellings and never presume again to disquiet your servants" '. The candles were made at home, of beeswax if possible, and they were ceremonially lit on the day and taken round the house, the farm buildings and the bee-hives, drops of their wax being left everywhere. In different parts of France, drops were let fall on the heads or shoulders of all in the household and on the horns of cattle, and crosses in wax were traced on the doors and windows or on the floor of the rooms, all with the aim of offering protection from illness and harm. Sometimes crosses were traced on beams and ceilings with the candles' smoke. The candles would be lit again during the year as necessary 'to bless fiancés, to keep off storms, to ensure fat beasts in the byres or to keep away anything that threatened the household'.[11] They were also lit when a person was dying. Other objects could complement or stand in for the candles. In the Limousin, for example, hazel twigs picked at Candlemas with the catkins on them were placed in the house, the cowsheds and the sheep-run to protect them.

Candlemas was ended as an official ceremony in Britain at the Reformation, but it persisted at the popular level into the nineteenth century, an indication of its importance. In Wales, there was ritual visiting of the guising kind on Candlemas Eve down to the eighteenth century. Groups of men went round singing at doors to gain admittance. Once in, a young virgin with a baby was placed in a chair in the middle of the floor and further carols were sung, referring to Mary and to light. On parting, the carollers wished the goodman of the house and his household a happy year, long life and prosperity.[12] Sometimes the ritual activity of Candlemas was transferred or extended to two saints' days which straddled it: St Brigid's (or St Bride's) on 1 and St Blaise's on 3 February. In sixteenth-century Romans, a threshing-dance with flails was performed on St Blaise's day, while in parts of Scotland processions with torches or candles took place and bonfires were lit, and ploughing often began on this day.

Carnival was a more obvious festival of fertility. The Carnival season ran from Christmas to Lent but centred on Shrovetide or the period immediately preceding Lent. As in Brueghel's famous painting of 1559, the main ritual focused on a guy or mannequin representing Carnival. The picture shows a combat between Carnival, a Rabelaisian male figure representing meat-eating, gorging and plenty, and Lent, an old scrawny crone, standing for fasting, abstinence and want. In some parts of Europe, the 'old woman' personified the Old Year or Winter, driven away by the New Year and the Spring. In England, a straw figure, this time male and known as Jack-o'-Lent, was 'dragged about on Ash Wednesday, pelted with stones, abused and derided, and finally shot to pieces, or burnt'. This can be seen as the ritual 'driving out of Winter'. More generally, at Carnival, copious eating, especially of meat and sausages, and drinking, and real or simulated copulation were expressive of the prosperity and fertility that everyone desired. In the Hebrides this was made explicit in a prayer or charm that was recited on 'Ash Eve':

> We shall have flesh:
> We should have that;
> We shall have mead;
> We shall have spruce;

We shall have wine;
We shall have feast;
We shall have sweetness and dairy stuff,
Honey and milk,
Wholesome heavenly food,
Abundance of that,
Abundance of that![13]

In some places there were processions of animals decked and beribboned like sacrificial victims, or dances for general wellbeing or the success of particular crops. At Rochechouart in the Limousin 'they danced in the granges to have plenty of hemp. While everyone leapt about, a youth who was more agile than the others "made the cloth". He lay down full-length on a bench belly-down, then jumped up in the air in a somersault, landing on the bench again on his front'. He carried on until he was tired, when another youth would take over. Dances also took place around the figure of Carnival, after which the guy would be burned, thrown in a river or buried to ensure a good harvest. As Varagnac explains, the Carnival figure brings fecundity and health and when he is got rid of, 'he takes away vices and illnesses in his fat belly'.[14] In many parts of Europe, too, there were visitation rituals at Carnival, tying households again into the community. In Champagne, youths went in disguise and sometimes female dress (see Plate 7). Houses and people were sprayed with mud, clay, flour, ashes or soot. Houses were sometimes fumigated with burning rags, cow horns or resinous woods, a kind of purification against disease and evil influences. The visits were often made to the female *veillées* or work bees, and involved horseplay with the girls and sometimes ritual pairing. There was also publication of imaginary marriage banns between unlikely partners. Another feature of Carnival was ritual violence against animals and birds, for example cock-throwing, reminiscent of animal sacrifice again.

Sacred material associated with Carnival was also kept and used later in the year. In Brueghel's picture, one figure in Carnival's train is wearing a necklace of egg-shells. In the Périgord and the Limousin in this century, eggs eaten at Carnival-time were not cracked open but sucked out of their shells, which were threaded together on strings and hung from the ceiling. They were then taken down at sowing-time, crushed and added to the seed-corn to make it grow well. Sometimes the paraphernalia of Lent itself was paradoxically used in the same way. Pious women at Marval on their return from mass on Ash Wednesday with the penitential ash on their heads used to make a detour on their way home through the fields, so that they could shake some off there to protect the crop.

Though the official Roman Rite ended Carnival on Ash Wednesday, this was not always accepted at the popular level, and Carnival returned on the first Sunday in Lent or in Mid-Lent or Mi-Carême for further celebrations. The first Sunday in Lent or Brandons in France was particularly associated with fire. In many parts of France, Belgium and Germany, people lit bonfires, danced around them and leapt over them when they had died down. The aim was sometimes explicitly to drive off 'the witch' or 'the wicked sower' who is mentioned in the Gospel of the Day. Sometimes a burning wheel was set alight and rolled down a slope. In the same places and elsewhere brands or torches were carried round the houses, fields and orchards. Sometimes this was specifically done to frighten off pests, as we have seen, or to keep weeds from growing in the corn. Carrying round the brands also had a more general purgative and vivifying intention. In the Franche-Comté the young people in the orchards called for 'more fruit than leaves'; while in the Romagna, where fires were lit on the first three days of March, the peasants sang:

> Set light to March, set light to March.
> The burning branch makes a good harvest.[15]

Mass on Palm Sunday in the Périgord around 1920 'attracted far more people even than Easter. It is a question of making sure of the blessing of the box, so fruitful for the land ... The box branches are agitated like a forest swept by the wind when the priest blesses them and again when he incenses them'. In addition to box, the palms were represented in northern Europe by branches of yew, pine, willow and hazel, and in southern Europe by olives and laurels (see Plate 8). In Provence, the olive branches were hung with sweetmeats. In Sicily, the bigger the olive branches were the better and they had to be stolen. After the blessing, the 'palms' were taken back to the farms and placed everywhere in the house and the yard: over beds, on crucifixes and religious pictures, over doors. Often they were taken to the livestock, including the bees, and to the fields before they were brought into the house. Some were 'planted' in the fields, usually already sown, following set rituals. Sometimes holy water was sprinkled at each corner of the field; sometimes the peasant stood or knelt in the middle of the field or vineyard, making the sign of the cross to each corner before driving in the branch. Like the Candlemas candle, the 'palm' was also used in specific situations of potential danger or crisis. A piece might be placed on the cradle of a new-born child or left on a grave, and the branches were used to ward off storms. Often small crosses were made with the blessed branches and used as talismans. In medieval England, such crosses were made up in the church during the reading of the Passion narrative.[16] The hallowing of 'palms' and making palm crosses were banned in England in the 1540s. But people continued to collect branches on Palm Sunday and to use them in the ways described down to the end of the nineteenth century.

Easter, the prime Christian holiday, is a celebration of the Resurrection, but like the Jewish Passover, with which it coincides, it is also an agrarian festival representing and marking the final end of Winter and the revival of vegetation in the Spring. This amalgamation is especially clear in rituals performed in the Sierra Nevada in Spain. The statue of the Risen Christ carried on Easter Sunday 'was represented as a young man in a green dress crowned with leaves, with a bunch of flowers in his right hand and a sheaf of barley in his left'. Elsewhere offerings and blessings were given to the land and to the sea. On the western seaboard of Scotland, mead, ale or gruel was poured into the waves on Maundy Thursday to ensure a good supply of the seaweed that was used to fertilize the land. Among the Greek colonists of western Corsica, the fields were blessed on Easter Monday to the singing of '*Christos anesti!*' and the firing of salvoes in a ritual continued from the seventeenth century to the present; icons of the Risen Christ and the Virgin and Child were also processed. In other parts of the island a spiral dance, called the *granitula* was performed, evoking the cyclical return of life from death. Evoking a similar idea, in parts of Wales people climbed mountains on Easter morning to see the sun 'dancing'. In the Périgord, 'on Easter Monday, the wife goes round the property sprinkling the furrows with water, blessed on Holy Saturday and put at the disposal of the parish in a large wash-tub'.[17] In the Aisne, the apple trees were watered at dawn on Easter Day with holy water.

The house was also cleaned and purified at this time. In Languedoc, for example, 'the priest, dressed in surplice and stole, placed blessed salt over the lintel of the door of the house' on Easter Saturday. He then went inside and blessed all the beds, on which food and provisions were laid out as an offering. New clothes were also worn at Easter. The nineteenth-century Dorset poet William Barnes wrote:

> Last Easter I put on my blue
> Frock coat, the vust time, vier new;
> Wi' yaller buttons aal o' brass,
> That glittered in the zun like glass,
> Bekaze 'twer Easter Zunday.[18]

The link between the Easter period and fertility was expressed in other ways. In many regions, Good Friday, the day on which Christ died, was ill-omened. In the Basses-Alpes, potatoes planted on that day would rot in the ground, 'since the earth was bleeding'. But in some places, for example the Belgian Ardennes and parts of Ireland, it was the best time to sow wheat and later potatoes. The custom of decorating, giving, rolling and eating eggs at Easter dates back to the early medieval period. In the Franche-Comté, coloured hard-boiled eggs were distributed, often having been blessed by the priest after mass. Eggs were given by godparents to godchildren and were begged by youths from girls with whom they had or were about to take First Communion. Eggs are an obvious symbol of fertility, but rituals involving them also reinforced significant ties and marked time and again the advent of Spring. At Trelon in the Nord in the late nineteenth century, an altar boy announced at house doors on Holy Saturday that 'Lent was dead'. He and his companions would be given 'red or blue eggs, and we knew that Spring had been duly inducted and clean houses were ready for brighter days'.[19] In some places, bonfires were lit and rituals for driving out Winter took place.

Easter too provided peasants with talismans, starting with eggs. In France generally it was believed that eggs laid on Good Friday gave protection against disease, accidents, fires, impotence and hostile spells, while in the Limousin the shells of eggs eaten during the week before Easter were kept and stuck on to sticks in the form of crosses. These were planted in the fields on Easter Day to protect the crop and make it more abundant. In the Landes, 'during the office of *Tenebrae* on Good Friday youths took up alder sticks and broke them against the pillars of the church [or a cross outside]; the pieces were carefully collected and put in the soil to help the millet grow'. In Britain it was believed down to modern times that bread, cakes or buns baked on Good Friday 'would never go mouldy'. They were preserved and used as remedies for illnesses in man and beast and 'to protect the house from fire and the granary from rats'. In Wiltshire, more specifically, 'bread baked on Good Friday determined the success of domestic baking throughout the rest of the year'.[20] If the bread was light and good on that day, so it would be over the ensuing period.

Further rituals were performed in early Summer and especially in May. Those on 1 May or May Day were found all over Europe and involved young people gathering greenery in the woods during the night before and engaging in sexual play, and then decking and erecting the familar pole or *mai* and dancing around it. In France, the *mai* was a sapling stripped of all but its topmost leaves. A symbol of fertility, it also figured as a boundary marker and could be used to honour leading persons in the community. In the Franche-Comté and elsewhere, young men gathered their own particular *mais*, which they planted in front of the houses of their sweethearts; *mais* of specific trees might be used to indicate the reputation of the girls. Bay, oak, willow and holly testified to the girl's honour, but fruit trees, hawthorn, black poplar and hazel were signs of 'scorn or derision'. May Day involved nubile girls in other ways. Passing through San Angelo near Urbino in 1581, Montaigne reported: 'We found little queens in the town because it was the eve of the first of May'. Next day at a village past Borgo San Sepolcro, 'several girls stood in front of us and seized the bridles of our horses, singing a special song for the occasion and demanding some donation for the day's festivities'. Similar ritual begging by adolescent girls acting in an independent manner, sometimes led by a 'Queen of the May', was reported in France from at least the fifteenth century onwards. In the Franche-Comté, the ritual was known as 'making wives'.[21] Varagnac has linked it to the general idea that the month of May, otherwise associated with fertility, was also ill-omened. The month was a closed season for weddings; children conceived then were likely to be unfortunate in some way. In the Limousin, plants or crops planted then would be no good; and eggs laid in May would be addled. It was as if fertility could rebound on itself with negative consequences. May Day itself was also widely believed to be a time when witches and evil forces were particularly active and ritual protection was therefore especially necessary.

Like Carnival, May Day also had its symbolic figures: a person acting in the rites or in plays, or a mannequin, processed and destroyed. In England, Robin Hood was sometimes present or 'Jack-in-Green, who wore a heavy wicker cape completely covered in greenery'.[22] Springs were visited too on May Day and bonfires lit.

Some of the most elaborate May Day rituals involving fires occurred in Celtic areas, where the feast was called Beltane. An early medieval Irish text refers to 'the beneficent fire, that is the two fires made with great incantation', between which 'they passed the cattle to protect them each year from epidemics', May Day being the day when the cattle were taken up to the Summer pastures. This and related customs continued in many places down to this century. At Beltane in the Highlands of Scotland, according to an eighteenth-century account, bonfires were lit at dawn and a special caudle, 'a sort of custard of eggs and milk, to which a little oatmeal was added was cooked on the bonfire'. Some of it was consumed by the company, 'and some of it was poured on the ground by way of libation, that the hens might lay plentifully, the cows give abundant milk, and the fields yield a rich harvest'. In another account, knobs were broken off a bannock and thrown over the shoulder with the exclamation: 'This I give to thee, preserve my horses; this to thee, preserve thou my sheep ... After that, they use the same ceremony to the noxious animals: This I give to thee, O Fox! spare thou my lambs; this to thee, O hooded Crow! this to thee, O Eagle!' In Scotland, too, there were often the two Beltane fires through which cattle and people passed 'for purification and safeguarding against mischance and murrain during the year'.[23] Where there was only one fire, cattle were driven sunwise round it and people leapt over the flames; animals and children were passed over the embers. During Beltane in many places all domestic fires were extinguished, the ritual fire or fires were lit by friction, and hearths relit with brands taken from the communal fire. Beltane fires were also regarded in Scotland as affording protection against the witches who were active at that time as we have seen.

Beltane was celebrated in Wales too. In the Vale of Glamorgan, according to an account from the nineteenth century, the fire had to be kindled by nine men who had no contact with any metal; and 'sticks of nine different trees' were used. The flame was kindled in the archaic way by rubbing two bits of oak together. 'Sometimes two fires were set up side by side'. As in Scotland, special oatcakes were baked; and chosen people leaped over the flames. If there was any disease in the herds, a calf would be thrown on the fire and the rest of the cattle driven between the two fires 'to stop the disease spreading.' People carried the ashes left after these fires to their homes, together with the charred brands, all of which were effective talismans against a range of evils. In modern Ireland other rituals to protect the cattle were performed. May Day plants, buttercups, primroses and gorse, were 'gathered before sunrise, scattered on the threshold of the house and ... tied to the cows' tails. In the Antrim glens the May flowers were crushed to provide a juice with which the cows' udders were washed'. Elsewhere milk was poured 'on the threshold, or at the roots of a fairy thorn'.[24] Sometimes the cattle were taken out to places associated with the fairies, old raths and forts, and their blood was drawn and tasted.

May Day was perhaps the least Christianized of all the major calendar rituals, though some attempts were made to link it to religious occasions. May Day itself was the feast of St Philip and St James, though a reference to this fact in Shakespeare's *Measure for Measure* stresses that it was a time of sexual licence not piety. Mistress Overdone explains that 'Mistress Kate Keep-Down was with child by him [Lucio] in the Duke's time, he promised her marriage. His child is a year and a quarter old come Philip and Jacob'. More successful was the clerical institution of the Invention of the Cross on 3 May. In many parts of France, small crosses, usually of hazel, were blessed by the priest on this day and then placed at the doors of houses and byres and among vines and fields 'to guard and defend the future crops and establish protective barriers against external threats'. In the Franche-Comté when the crosses were planted in the fields, people knelt down and recited five Paternosters and five Ave Marias. Each field had its own cross and 'the taller the cross, the more vigorous and abundant the harvest would be'.[25] In the Mâconnais and elsewhere the cross was recovered at harvest-time, crowned with ears of corn and placed on the last harvest cart, decked with flowers and greenery.

Also universal were the Rogations performed on the three days before

Ascension. They were instituted very early in the history of the Church to replace 'the corresponding pagan cultic ceremonies'. They were recorded in France from the sixth century and referred to in the *Anglo-Saxon Chronicle* for 1061. Typically in the early modern and modern periods, the Rogation rituals took the form of processions around all the fields of the village. Crosses, banners, relics, statues and the host were carried, and the priest, followed by his parishioners chanting prayers and litanies, called down a blessing on the crops and freedom 'from baneful insects and intemperance of the air'. As an early sixteenth-century English sermon put it:

> In these Rogation Days, it is to be asked of God, and prayed for, that God of his goodness will defend and save the corn in the field, and that he will vouchsafe to purge the air. For this cause be certain Gospels read in the wide field among the corn and grass, that by the virtue and operation of God's word, the power of the wicked spirits, which keep in the air and infect the same .. may be laid down ... to the intent the corn may remain unharmed, and not infected ... but serve us for our use and bodily sustenance.[26]

In Savoy and the Limousin, the first day's procession was for the hay, the second for the cereal harvest, and the third for the vintage. Sometimes the church bells were rung during the proceedings or muskets were fired, and the priest often blessed livestock as well and the springs and fountains. As on other occasions, crosses might be planted in the fields or hazel, hawthorn and other branches that the priest had blessed. In some parishes in the Franche-Comté,

> the priest collected stones on the road as he went round the village territory, stuck wax crosses to them, and threw them into the fields that had been sown. This was to conjure hail, flooding rains, storms and all bad weather. These blessed stones were popularly called the curé's manure.

In many French towns, including Paris, mock dragons symbols of the fertility of nature – were processed and propitiated by putting offerings of food into their mouths. In Sicily, 'the benediction of Heaven was believed to come down to earth at exactly midnight' on Ascension Day itself in the form of fructifying dew;[27] while in and around Gubbio bonfires were lit at this time on the occasion of the procession of the Ceri or Great Candles. It was significantly at this time also that the *benandanti* of the Friuli region of Italy rode out at night in dreams to fight the witches and thus ensure good harvests and abundance in the coming year. Similar battles for fertility are reported in Rumania and Hungary.

It is indicative of its importance too that Lutherans and Anglicans retained this 'Catholic' practice, albeit with some change of emphasis. In England, the

Elizabethan church settlement did away with the crosses and banners and required the priest to wear secular dress, but the processions themselves were still prescribed and prayers thanking God 'for the increase and abundance of the fruits upon the face of the earth'. One such prayer called on God to send 'such seasonable weather, as may preserve to our use the kindly fruits of the earth' and acknowledged 'that it is from Thy gift that the rain doth fall, the earth is fruitful, beasts increase, and fishes do multiply ... though for our sins we have worthily deserved scarcity and dearth'.[28] In some places, moreover, Rogations continued in the old fashion. At Wolverhampton, for example, long poles decked with flowers were carried and the clergy and choir wore their vestments down to the 1760s. The rituals were also accompanied by eating and drinking and general merriment, and parishioners complained if they were allowed to lapse.

Later Rogation processions did tend to become 'perambulations', 'beating the bounds' of the parish, with the days being known as 'Gang' or 'Ganging Days'. As such, they were taken very seriously to judge by Parson Woodforde's 1780 account. It took this somewhat indolent cleric five hours mostly on foot 'to go the bounds' of Weston Longeville and he was so tired afterwards that he declined an invitation to dine with the squire, not an opportunity that he usually missed.[29] But this had always been an important part of the old rituals: drawing a sacred line of protection around the village territory to keep off evil forces and to induce fertility. Occasionally on the Continent a furrow was ploughed around the village, bringing together both barrier and prime agricultural act and continuing also an Ancient Roman rite.

In some parts of Europe, the fertility rituals with which we are now familiar: sprinkling fields with holy water, planting sacred branches, processions with garlands, effigies and animals, occurred at Whit. One of the most interesting Whitsun rituals was the series of Căluş ceremonies performed in Rumania and parts of Bulgaria. In the week following Whit Sunday, the spirits of the dead returned and malevolent forces were active. Work and ordinary activities like washing were suspended, and the Căluş ritual was performed 'to assure fertility and fecundity for the ensuing year'.[30] Căluş was performed by groups of male dancers, wearing special costumes and bearing a flag on a pole. They trained in secret and they had to be ritually pure or chaste during this time. Grain was placed on the flag with garlic and wormwood and it was never allowed to touch the ground. The herbs were also attached to the dancers' clothes. At the end of the week the flag was buried in a secret place. One of the dancers was a fool or mute who wore or carried a large red phallus. The Căluş dancers went from village to village – not every village had its own group – and danced in the courtyard of each house. People placed salt, water and grains next to the Căluş flag during the dance to ensure rain and good crops, and the salt was later fed to the livestock. During the dance, one of the dancers fell into a trance. In the final dance, the members of the household, especially the women, would join in the dance, and contact with the Căluş dancers was believed to be beneficial. The herbs worn by the dancers or parts of their clothing might be stolen and used as talismans. The Căluş dancers also performed plays on themes of sex, death and resurrection. When different Căluş groups met, they fought, and sometimes men were killed. This parallels the dream fighting of the *benandanti* of the Friuli.

The next near-universal calendar custom was Midsummer. Another solstice, this was loosely Christianized as the Eve of the birthday feast of St John the Baptist. St John was sometimes depicted as a vegetation spirit (like the Risen Christ) or as 'a wild man of the woods'. In Andalusia, he was believed to bless 'everything on the earth (as his day began) – the fields, the crops, the trees, the wild plants and the rivers and springs'.[31] Sometimes, water, linked to baptism, figured in St John's Eve rituals in other ways. In parts of the Limousin, dew was carefully collected before dawn and sprinkled on the fields by the youngest member of the family to protect the crops. But the predominant fertilizing and purifying element associated with St John was fire.

Bonfires were lit from Ireland to Scandinavia, from Orkney to Spain, though not, it seems, in Italy. 'On St John's Day', wrote the bishop of Pamplona in 1544,

> the faithful sound the bells and light great bonfires, having gathered early in the morning special fragrant and medicinal plants that are then at the height of their powers. Some light fires at crossroads and in the fields in order to prevent witches passing these places during the night of St John. Others, having burned the herbs gathered on the day of St John against lightning, thunder and tempest, believe that by their fumigations they will keep off demons and storms.

In some places the fire was blessed by the priest (see Plate 9). The Synodal Constitutions of Geneva recommended this in 1683, though the practice was later condemned by Rome. People danced around the fire, sang songs, and jumped over its embers to bring them luck, spouses or children. Livestock might be driven through the smoke or over the embers. In some places, grain was thrown into the fire and also stones of different sizes to represent turnips and pumpkins. In Provence three stones were thrown into the fire by each person and garlic cloves were roasted in the embers. People and objects were fumigated with the smoke as at Pamplona. In parts of the Limousin, hazel branches were waved in the smoke and people called out:

> Produce, produce, my millet,
> May each ear make up a bushel

and the branches were then planted in the millet field. Brands were plucked from the fire and again waved in the air to make sparks to the incantation:

> As many cartloads of turnips
> As sparks,
> As big as tree stumps,
> As tasty as loaves!

On Orkney, 'a farmer who wanted to ensure a bountiful crop lit a great heather cowe (or faggot) at the communal blaze and took care that it did not burn out before he had completed the sunwise circuit of his fields with it'. Faggots were also 'carried round the cows in the byre to make them thrive, to prevent cows from casting calf and to ensure fertilization in those not yet in calf'. Similarly, in modern Ireland, where St John's Eve fires were still lit in the 1950s, everyone carried home 'a burning stick from the fire', which brought good luck, or else 'a glowing turf from the fire was carried three times sunwise around the dwelling house',[32] while others were thrown over the growing crops. Scatterings the remains and ashes from the fires in the fields and elsewhere to improve and protect the crops was a very general practice.

In some places in France, Germany and Britain, burning wheels were rolled down hills. If the wheel kept alight all the way down and reached a certain destination, sometimes a river, this was an augury of a good harvest or vintage. In some places, too, animals were burned in the fires: in Savoy, for example, a fox or a cat; in Languedoc, a cat, a snake or a mole. It has been suggested that moles 'were offered as expiatory victims, because, deprived of organs of sight and living underground, they symbolized somehow the antithesis of light'.[33]

Light of course was represented in the fires. As we have seen, fires were at the centre of many calendar customs. Some places had bonfires on more than one occasion during the year. In parts of France, for example, fires were lit at the Kings or Epiphany, during Lent and at Midsummer; but it was more usual, at least in the early modern and modern periods, for particular places to have their fires on one main occasion, which was often Midsummer. At Long Melford in the early sixteenth century, fires were lit on four occasions, but they were all concentrated in the period from mid June to mid July. Scholars have argued over the meaning of bonfires. Were they essentially purifying, exorcizing the land and community of evil influences and witchcraft, or were they evocative of the sun, of warmth and light, the life forces for crops and men, something expressed most obviously in fire wheels? In fact, both functions are compatible, and others were also present. Contemporaries saw the fires as expressions of community – in some places each family supplied a faggot for the collective fire – and of harmony within the community. 'These were called bonfires', explained John Stow writing of medieval London, 'as well of good amity amongst neighbours, that being before at controversy, were there, by the labour of others, reconciled, and made of bitter enemies loving friends.' Fire was also the double-edged agent of civilization or the mediating symbol between nature and culture.[34] Fire was the main means of clearing land and thus of making new fields and the wherewithal to grow crops. Fire was used in cooking and provided in the hearth the focus and emblem of the household. But fire was also dangerous and destructive and needed to be tamed via regular rituals. To all this was added the Christian notion – from the central medieval period onwards – of the Souls in Purgatory being purged by fire. Here the bonfires recalled the dead and their progress towards Paradise.

Along with the brands and ashes of the fires, the St John's herbs figured as important talismans, as at Pamplona. These varied enormously from place to place, including vervain or verbena, yarrow, St John's wort, maywort and fennel. The circumstances in which they had to be gathered also varied. Sometimes they had to be picked during the night before the Eve, sometimes at dawn, sometimes at noon on the day. Sometimes they had to be picked by a particular person; sometimes anyone could do it. The herbs were dried in bunches and hung up to protect and purify the house, to stop meat from going bad, to prevent and cure illnesses, to keep off storms, and to bring general good fortune and good harvests. As at Christmas and May Day, witches and other supernatural influences were believed to be especially powerful on St John's Eve, an idea expressed in Shakespeare's *A Midsummer Night's Dream*. The rituals aimed to ward off the harm that this power might do, but also to attract it for the peasants' benefit.

We have discussed the rituals that accompanied harvest. The harvesting of the different crops came at different times in different parts of Europe and was not so closely tied to the Christian or calendar year, though there was some linkage. The four Sacrament Sundays in the Church of England were 'on the three great festivals of the Church (Christmas, Easter and Whit) and in the Autumn after the ingathering of harvest'. In France, the Assumption of the Virgin Mary on 15 August often became a harvest festival, with the standing corn being blessed by the priest before reaping in a Rogation-style procession.[35]

Early November is the start of Winter. This was marked by two related Christian festivals: All Saints or All Hallows on 1 November and All Souls, linked to the belief in Purgatory, on 2 November. The dead were remembered with gifts and visits to graves. Ritual begging on behalf of the dead or 'souling' continued in Wales long after the Reformation had removed the official standing of Purgatory. The dead were also believed to return or 'walk' on Hallowe'en, along with other dangerous forces. Breaking pots or plates was 'one of the elements in Hallowe'en rites' in Ireland and elsewhere: breaking the pot broke its spirit and thus by extension the power of the dead to do harm.[36] Ringing the church bells through the night also gave protection against harmful forces, including witches who were active at this time. Hallowe'en was also a special time for divination – of spouses, but particularly of imminent deaths in the community. There were also taboos on performing certain activities on the Day of the Dead, as on other ritual occasions: in Languedoc, for example, washing was proscribed.

There were also clear links between All Saints/All Souls rituals and fertility. In Ireland, all crops and fruits had to be gathered by this time or they would rot. At Moray, 'the festivity of this night was a thanksgiving for the safe ingathering of the produce of the fields'. All over Europe, too, fires were lit at this time, as an alternative usually to Lent or Midsummer and accompanied by the rituals which took place on those occasions. In Lancashire and Westmorland, farmers would light fires in the fields and take a piece of burning straw on a pitch-fork and throw it over the land 'to purify the soil and guard it against evil, and to make the crops grow in due course. Meanwhile their families knelt round the bonfire and remembered the dead of their kin.' In England, the November bonfire became attached to State-sponsored celebration of the discovery of the Gunpowder Plot in 1603, but, as Thomas Hardy emphasized in *The Return of the Native* (1878), the new festival, which quickly became popular, almost certainly did so because it took over an established and ancient ceremony. Dancing and singing round the fire, leaping over the flames, as well as burning an effigy and making a loud noise, were all traditional features. Swift wrote to Stella in 1711 of the festivities in London: 'Twas a terrible windy day, and we had processions in carts of the Pope and the Devil, and the butchers rang their cleavers; you know this is the fifth of November, popery and gun-powder'. At Olney, according to Cowper in 1785, the boys engaged in a sport, which they called 'Hockey; and [which] consists in dashing each other with mud', a typical Carnivalesque activity.[37]

Bede called November 'Blood Month', and it was also the time for the annual slaughter of livestock that could not be fed through the Winter. 'A slaughtering feast' inevitably followed the butchery, which continued in Europe until the end of the traditional system of animal husbandry.[38] It often centred on killing the pig and was associated especially with 11 November, the feast of St Martin or Martinmas. St Martin's Day was also the date in many regions when farm servants were hired, and when the annual provision of wine was bought. This necessitated the consumption of all the old wine to make room for the new.

Cults of local agrarian and guardian saints were inserted into or added to this calendar. In their Lives and legends, saints were always planting sticks that grew into trees, producing water from the ground or from rocks, making the desert produce flourishing plants, diverting rivers that eroded the soil, causing grain to last or multiply through famines. One of the Fathers in the Egyptian desert explained why the peasants whose land bordered on his hermitage came every year to 'trouble us for sand'. The peasants' land was infertile and infested with worms, and, when they had been instructed by the Fathers

> and had become Christians, they asked us to pray for the harvest. I said to them: If you have faith in God, even this desert sand will bear fruit for you. Without a moment's hesitation they filled the folds of their tunics with the sand which had been trodden by us, and bringing it to me, asked me to bless it.

He did so, and 'they sowed the sand together with the corn in their fields, and at once their land became extremely fertile, more than anywhere else in Egypt'. Much later, according to a witness at the canonization process of St Thomas Cantilupe in the early fourteenth century, 'people say that since the bones of Lord Thomas have been brought to the cathedral of Hereford, the harvests have been better, the rivers and ponds fuller of fish, and the livestock has been more prolific'. Again in a modern and in a popular rather then a learned Life, that of St Edern of Lannedon in Brittany, sung by a driver of a public coach, the saint's cow strayed on to cultivated land, a common threat to crops, but instead of causing any harm the sacred cow's incursion only made them grow better.[39]

Saints were associated with the seasons. In Rumania, for example, St George was the patron of Spring, the Virgin Mary of Summer, St Demetrius of Autumn and St Nicholas of Winter. As such they were often involved in seasonal festivals: in Provence, in Brittany, in Portugal, in Italy with the Rogations. There was a particular 'concentration of processions and vows' in early modern Spain in the period around late April and early May when the vines were especially vulnerable to pests, late frosts and hail, and similar concentrations are found elsewhere. Particular saints' days were propitious, we have seen, for doing certain agricultural tasks, and saints were invoked against pests. Some saints' days were full-blown festivals associated with fertility. In the Hebrides and elsewhere in the Highlands of Scotland, a sheaf of corn 'in the likeness of a woman' was processed by girls on St Bride's Eve on 1 February; while in the Franche-Comté, gleanings of all the crops: wheat, oats, barley, peas and lentils were taken to the church and blessed on St Bartholomew's Day, 24 August.[40]

Many examples can be cited of important local cults devoted to agrarian saints. At her shrine at the abbey of Faremoutiers in the seventeenth century, St Fare was 'always represented with an ear of wheat, which she received out of season from heaven. This symbol, pagan rather than Christian, designates her as the patron of the grain-growing region of Brie'. The *pardon* or pilgrimage of Saint-Servais attracted pilgrims in their thousands from all over Brittany. Pilgrims 'made the voyage', according to an eighteenth-century account,

> to ask for an abundant harvest. On entering the chapel, the women take off their *coiffes* and put them on the end of sticks so that they can touch the statue of the saint with them, praying out loud to him to accord them good black wheat, good oats and other cereals.

Later sources indicate that St Servais also furnished protection against frost, and that pilgrims from different regions competed for his favours, shouting: 'Bring oats and wheat to the people from Vannes!' or 'from the Cornouailles!' and so on, which led to regular fighting both inside and outside the chapel. The statue of the saint was always broken and a new one used every year. As a result of this commotion, the civil and ecclesiastical authorities combined to suppress the pilgrimage around 1900, and the subsequent decline of agriculture in the region was blamed on this ban. In similar vein, Stendhal was told in 1837 by the hostess of the inn at Auray, where there was an important shrine of the saint, that 'Brittany owed the few good harvests which it still had in these unfortunate and impious times to the protection of its good patron St Anne, who watched over it from the height of heaven'.[41]

In Spain, south-eastern France and Savoy, St Blaise was invoked to protect the crops. In many parishes seed corn was taken to church on his day, 3 February, to be blessed by the priest. At Romans on the same day a 'threshing' or 'flailing' dance was performed in the general context of Carnival. Among many other saints and madonnas linked with fertility in southern Italy and Sicily was St Anthony of Padua. At his harvest-time feast on 13 June, his image was decorated with flowers and ribbons, and the peasants prayed:

> St Anthony, St Anthony,
> You are close to the great God:
> Let the ears fatten, let the grain whiten,
> And every heart rejoice and be healed!
> St Anthony, St Anthony,
> Lovely the ears, well-filled the grain:
> May every ear fill a measure ...[42]

We may also mention the cult of St Zapito at Loreto Aprutino in the Abruzzi, which dates in its modern form from the early eighteenth century. Here attention focused on a garlanded ox ridden by a male child. The ox was taken into the church, where it knelt. There was a belief that the amount of the ox's excreta during the occasion gave an indication of the fertility of the coming crops. The more dung the better the crops. Cults of Virgins of fecundity, often black, were also popular in southern Italy and Sicily. At Bagnara participants in the procession wore 'wreaths of corn-ears on their heads and necklaces of macaroni', and they laid these as gifts at the feet of the image of the Virgin. At Lucera the statue of the Virgin was 'showered with wheat, corn and other sacrificial offerings on feast days, particularly on those which coincided with the seasons of planting and harvesting'. At Castrogiovanni in Sicily, the Virgin's 'worshippers placed before her statue large sheaves of grain and bunches of wild flowers' and made offerings of grain.[43] In the last, as in other cases, the modern cult occurred in a place where a temple to a pagan fertility goddess had existed in classical times.

Saints and madonnas were thus not only honoured and implored; they were propitiated with appropriate gifts in kind, and other examples of this may be cited from elsewhere in Europe. In 1835 the new priest in a Limousin parish replaced the old statue of St Affre with one of the Virgin. When he asked his housekeeper where his predecessor had obtained his oats, she told him:

> If you had kept the altar of St Affre you would have known. The peasants can no longer make that saint friendly to them by putting little sacks of oats on the steps of her altar. By the end of the year they used to add up to a good provision.

In the Western Isles, the gift was the central element in a quasi-sacramental Michaelmas ritual. A cake called a *struan* was 'made of all the types of cereal grown on the farm during the year' and representing the whole produce of the holding. It was baked by the eldest daughter of the family and at different stages in this process she said prayers to St Michael and the Trinity. On the saint's day, the *struan* was blessed by the mother of the house – on Barra in these words:

> Milk and eggs and butter,
> The good produce of our own flock,
> There shall be no dearth in our land,
> Nor in our dwelling ...
> In the name of Michael.[44]

The *struans* were taken to church for a general service of thanksgiving, at which they were blessed. Then a special meal was prepared in the family house, consisting of the *struans* and lamb. A piece of each was taken like the sacrament at the start of the meal, while a hymn to the saint was sung. *Struans* and lamb were also given to the poor in the neighbourhood, and any meal left over after cooking the *struan* was scattered over the livestock.

Most of the saints so far mentioned were concerned mainly or exclusively with the cereal harvest. Other crops had their own protectors. St Domenico of Muro protected the vines in the Naples region. In Cyprus the same office was fulfilled by St Tychon, and the vintage festival was celebrated on his day. In Spain, St Gregory of Nazanzius was often the special protector of the vines from pests, his feast falling on 9 May when the vulnerable young shoots begin to emerge. In Berry, the patron of winegrowers was St Vincent. His feast was on what seems the unlikely date of 22 January, but this gave him a connection with the frost which he was supposed to control. After a severe and unseasonal frost at Sury-en-Vaux around 1900, which damaged the vines, the peasants removed the statue of St Vincent from its usual place to the draughty bell-tower, and only returned it to its place of honour in the church after a satisfactory vintage. Other kinds of arboriculture were not forgotten. In the Bigorre region in south-west France, St Agatha was the protector of agriculture and fruit trees. On the eve of her feast day, 5 February, 'people hit the trees with sticks to obtain good fruit'. On Monte Amiata at Abbadia San Salvatore in the 1920s 'where chestnuts form a large part of the poor man's diet – a procession used to walk through the streets on St Mark's Day (25 April) singing: St Mark, our advocate! See that no worm enters our chestnuts, and that each kernel bears three nuts; pray for us'.[45]

Fasts were traditional in Catholic Europe, weekly on Fridays and annually during Advent, Lent and at other times, and they were also called in times of crisis for repentance and to avert divine anger. The latter but not the former were retained and even expanded in Protestant countries. In the Netherlands, for example, days of prayer and fasting were ordered as 'propitiatory responses to plague, flood and invasion' through the seventeenth and eighteenth centuries, for example during the floods of 1731 caused by worms eating the piles holding sea dikes. In England, Puritans had introduced their own fasts in times of difficulty, and governments ordered national fast days from the time of the Long Parliament down to the start of the nineteenth century. As in the Netherlands they were called in times of war, civil disturbance, plague and other dangers. Sometimes such general fasts were related to non-political matters. A fast in England had been ordered by the king in January 1662 'to pray for more seasonable weather'. In Scotland in the later seventeenth century fasts were ordered on Sundays immediately preceding seedtime and harvest. More locally later the bishop of London 'ordered that

20 March 1866 should be observed as a day of fasting and humilation in the metropolis' as a response to the rinderpest epidemic among cattle.[46]

Throughout the year the power of which the clergy were the custodians and the agents was being harnessed by the peasants. The priest had to bless the land, the animals, the garnered crops, and he blessed the protective elements during the festivals that were distributed about the houses, cowsheds, barns and fields. But much of the ritual involving these elements was carried out by the peasants themselves, and words and gestures of Christian and clerical derivation were mixed in with others that had nothing to do originally with the Church like the Easter eggs, the May-poles and the Midsummer and other bonfires. The patron saints again were generally authorized by the Church, but the peasants often regarded and treated them as independent sacred entities. Peasants were eclectic, taking bits and pieces from here and there and combining them in a whole which only seemed incoherent to interfering reformers. The whole was aimed to procure fecundity and prosperity and was guided by the principles of magic.

Within peasant culture generally and within particular peasant or allied cultures, one may see a spectrum ranging from the less to the more Christian. At one end, people prayed to the earth or the sun. The Anglo-Saxon Aecer-Bot rituals included a prayer to 'Erce, Mother of Earth' and 'Earth Mother of men'. The Dominican preacher St Vincent Ferrer reported in 1403: 'Among other enormities I came in those parts [the Alps of Savoy, Switzerland and Swabia] upon an error only too common in the feast of Corpus Christi, during which, every year, solemn confraternities are held in the name of the Holy Rising Sun'. The fire wheels which figure in St John's Eve and other festivals may be seen as representations of the sun. Elsewhere the sun might be directly addressed in ritual and prayer. In the Romagna during the Napoleonic period, 'on 1 March, the peasant went to the roof of his house, took down his trousers, and exposed his buttocks to the sun, saying: March sun, burn my arse but don't burn me'. Still later gypsies implored the sun: 'Cast thy glance upon our crop, and on our horses, our tents, our wives and our children. Let thine arrows awaken the earth from its slumber: may she as a mother bring forth fertile gifts'.[47]

There was a general belief in traditional European society in various kinds of fairy, pre- or non-Christian supernatural beings, who had to be propitiated. In the Hautes-Pyrénées, for example, it was thought that the fairies visited people's houses on New Year's Eve, and care was taken to leave out a good meal that night on a well-set table.

> Those who gave them the best meals could hope to see their flocks multiply, their harvests flourish and so on, while those who neglected the fairies would suffer fires

in their houses; wild beasts would attack their flocks, their crops would suffer hail and withering, and their marriages would be unhappy. At dawn on 1 January the master of the house took the bread that had been presented to the fairies, broke it solemnly, and having dipped it in the water or wine in the vessel on the table, gave a piece to each member of the family including servants. Everyone wished each other a good year to come, and they breakfasted with the bread.[48]

In the middle of the spectrum fall the mass of rituals which we have described. Here the priest imbued a range of objects with special power. Statues, relics, the host itself might be processed around the village and the fields. Christ and the saints were decked out and addressed as vegetation spirits; the Virgin Mary, especially in the form of a Black Madonna, became a chthonic earth goddess hung with fruit and flowers and showered with grain. At the other end, perhaps, were the official Catholic rituals to obtain divine blessings on the earth and its creatures; and those of Protestants who attributed all good (and all bad) things to God and who sought only to influence Him by prayers and fasts, eschewing other 'superstitions'.

This is in some ways, however, a misleading schema, suggesting that peasant customs reflect a simple progress of clerical influence. Where Christianity was more obviously present, peasants borrowed more from it, but they continued to incorporate it into their own communal and family rituals. The Roussillon example provides an extreme instance: food and drink left for the fairies is used in a kind of Eucharist. Clerical policy varied too and not in an altogether linear chronological course. For every reformer, Protestant or Catholic, there was Voltaire's or Chaucer's panderer to peasant needs:

> Here is a mitten, look.
> He who puts his hand in this mitten,
> He shall have multiplying of his grain,
> When he has sown, whether it be wheat or oats,
> Providing that he offers pence or groats.

Reformers, too, frequently linked moral and theological issues to the all-pervading concern for material prosperity. A Franciscan preacher at Nancy in 1520 told his congregation: 'If you want to have peace and you do not want your vines and corn to perish, cut out the tongues of the blasphemers'. Dancing was forbidden in pre-Reformation Zurich 'in order that the Lord God will protect us, that our crops may flourish in the fields, and that there may be good weather'.[49] The common Protestant custom of ordering fasts in times of crisis follows the same logic. Much later, the Virgin of La Salette warned in 1846 that the potatoes would rot and the grapes be blighted as a punishment for people's irreligion, and this part of her message was significantly in *patois*, while the more 'clerical' elements were in French. Here clergy and people were meeting in a common culture, where misfortune might equally be attributed to the breaking of a taboo, like cousin marriage, or to witchcraft as to sin.

The cultural influence moreover was by no means one-way, from the clergy to the peasants. Both belonged to a fundamentally agrarian society. It is striking, for instance, how prevalent is the recourse in theological writing, following biblical precedent, to the metaphors of fertility. St Bernard evoked the Virgin's womb flowering with the Son like the flowers of the field, and celebrated the heavenly Jerusalem in these terms: 'I say that you are a good land, the best land; you received in your fertile womb a heavenly seed from the treasury of the Father's heart and have brought forth a great harvest in the celestial progeny of martyrs'. In his Life of St Francis, Giovanni di Ceprano described how the saint 'awakened new life' from 'the earth numbed by the frosts of Winter' like the rising sun. And of the essentially urban communities which he founded, Giovanni exclaimed: 'How marvellous was their fruitfulness! It was like the coming of Spring to the world'. The Eucharist or mass itself was a central and perpetual expression of this link between religion and agriculture. As St Alexander Sauli, who was bishop of Aleria in Corsica from 1570 to 1591, explained in a sermon:

> the wine made from grapes crushed in the press as is customary signifies the blood shed by Our Lord by the press of the Cross. The grain, pounded and milled in the mill, then baked in the oven, shows Christ in His passion pounded by the whips and baked in the oven of the Cross.[50]

3

The Weather

Traditional agriculture was extremely vulnerable to adverse climatic conditions. Late frosts, drought in the growing season, wet weather when the grain should have been ripening, freak storms could all mean crop loss or failure and consequently dearth or famine. Thunder and hail storms were particularly destructive. A contemporary described such a storm in 1692 in Piedmont. On 28 June

> the vigil of the feast of Saints and Apostles Peter and Paul, around four in the afternoon, the weather worsened in such a way that from the heavens, thundering horribly and with much lightning, there fell first a quantity of dry storming [hail] that lasted the time to say three Credos [and] shortly after ... an enormous quantity of rain ... When the skies cleared, from my house I saw the land completely white, as if it had been covered with snow ... The vines were so battered that they were left without leaves, branches, or grapes; and the grain with the rest, so smashed to the ground that it was as if horses had trampled it, so that it was not even worth the trouble to gather it for the straw; and the like happened to what was left of the Spring crops and fruits.

Guillaumin provides a remarkably similar account of a June storm in the Bourbonnais in 1861.

> Right in the middle of a Summer's day it grew suddenly as dark as night, the sky had turned so black. At every moment jagged flashes of lightning pierced the darkness, and after every zig-zag of fire the thunder rumbled more loudly. And then the hailstones came down, first as big as partridges' eggs, then like hens' eggs, battering the roofs and breaking the windows. This was followed by a downpour of rain and the house was flooded.

The house was severely damaged, and after the storm

> the countryside looked bruised beneath the premature defoliation of the hedges and trees ... There were no longer any ears on the corn, the broken stalks leant over in a horrible tangle. The hay, covered with mud and as though flattened with a mallet, lay over the meadows like a dirty, greasy lump of plaster. The clover showed the underside of its riddled leaves. The tops of the potatoes were broken off. Garden vegetables no longer existed.

In an official table of losses in French agriculture in the first two decades of the nineteenth century, over half the total was attributed to hail storms. It was for this reason that peasants resisted the consolidation of holdings. They 'feared the risk of a local hail storm that could ravage a single field, a danger that the traditional dispersed parcels made less'.[1]

In these circumstances, peasants and herdsmen were close observers of the weather. A host of proverbial sayings expressed both their empirical observations and their wish to bring some kind of order and predictability to an otherwise arbitrary situation. It is significant too that almanacs with weather prognostications were among the most popular early printed material. John Clare evokes countrymen in the early nineteenth century reading *Old Moore's* and other almanacs in the tavern in January:

> ... thumb'd pages swarm
> With frost and snow and many a storm
> And wisdom gossip'd from the stars ...
> Bible at once and weather guide.

Some prognostications were related to the aspect of the sun, the moon, the stars, rainbows, as they are still. Others related to features of the local landscape and notably the look of hills and mountains. In different parts of Savoy, it was a sign of bad weather to come if the Thuria mountains, Mont Blanc and other peaks 'were smoking their pipes', that is covered with cloud in a particular way. The behaviour of birds and animals could also be read. In southern France 'the woodpecker had the reputation for announcing wet weather in advance: Listen to the rain bird, people say'.[2] In the Romagna from the medieval period a peasant knew it was going to rain if his ass's ears twitched.

An eighteenth-century French almanac suggested that the weather of the coming week could be predicted from that on the previous Sunday between 7 and 10 am. More common in this style were what we would call long-term forecasts. Often the weather experienced during the twelve days of Christmas or the first twelve days of the New Year provided a guide to the weather over the whole year, each day corresponding to one of the months. Sometimes the linkage was less exact and more complicated. In some parts of France, an onion was taken at midnight on Christmas Eve and cut into twelve pieces designating particular months. These were sprinkled with salt and those that became wet prefigured months that would be wet, and those which remained dry months that would be dry. Again, the weather on a significant day or days could predict conditions for the year ahead and thus whether harvests would be good.

'If it rains at New Year', they said in the Limousin in recent times,

> Much straw, little wheat.
> If the ground is like a drum [frozen],
> We will eat plenty of good hot bread;

or:

> When it rains on Palm Sunday,
> The cow will go hungry [that is, there will be no hay];

or again:

> If it snows in March,
> You will have plenty of bread and lard.

Such sayings were commonplace all over Europe. In Aberdeenshire, the sky was deliberately scanned during the last night of the year. 'If it was cloudless, the year would be bad.' If there were clouds, the largest was examined, and depending on its appearance and on which quarter of the sky it occupied, the prosperity of the coming year could be foretold. For example, 'if it lay toward the north, was densely black, and had a soft appearance, it would be a year of plenty for man and beast'; but if it hung in the west, the year would be unproductive.[3]

Special attention was often focused here, as the importance of Christmas and the New Year shows, on the equinoxes, or other pivots between the seasons. In Savoy, they said: 'At Candlemas, the Winter either ends or takes on new strength'; or 'When the bear comes out at Candlemas, he goes back into his den for forty days', that is it is better for Candlemas to be dark and cold rather than sunny and Spring-like, which will mean that Winter will return. In the Abruzzi: 'By St Donatus' Day [7 August], Winter is already born'.[4]

In general, normal conditions were a good sign and abnormal ones a bad one. So, from the Abruzzi again: 'Great cold in January, fills up the granary'; from Scotland:

> If February gives much snow,
> A fine summer it doth foreshow;

and from the Franche-Comté:

> Snow in February
> Is worth a load of manure;

and

> Better to see a wolf on the dung-heap [near human habitations because of the cold]
> Than a man in shirt sleeves in February [because of the heat].[5]

The weather on saints' days could also provide long- or medium-term predictions. An eighteenth-century version of the much older *Prognostication perpétuelle des laboureurs*, incorporated into many French almanacs, advised:

> Take care on St Vincent's Day [22 January],
> For if you see and feel on that day
> That the sun is fine and clear,
> We will have more wine than water.

Apart from its connection with viticulture, St Vincent's Day was another pivotal day, at which 'the Winter rose or fell'. Elsewhere in Europe the Day of the Conversion of St Paul (25 January) fulfilled a similar role. According to a Scottish rhyme, probably dating from the fifteenth century:

> If St Paul's Day be fair and clear,
> Then shall it be a happy year.
> If it chance to snow and rain,
> Then shall there be all kinds of pain.[6]

Especially common was the idea that if it rained or remained fine on a given saint's day, it would rain or keep fine for twenty, thirty, or forty days after. In England, the most popular day here was St Swithun's (15 July); in France, St Médard's (8 June). Such predictions were related to the tasks proper to those seasons and for which the saints' days provided markers. 'If you want good silkworms', they said in the Abruzzi, 'they should be on the tray by St Mark's Day (25 April)'; or

> By St Urban's Day [25 May]
> The corn has made its grain.

In the Puy-de-Dôme, St Barnabas (11 June) could 'cut the feet' or counteract the effects of St Médard's Day, and it was on St Barnabas' Day that peasants were advised to sow their turnips or elsewhere to begin harvesting their wheat.[7]

It will already be evident that peasants did not regard the climate as a purely natural phenomenon. Rather it was governed by mysterious forces, some vague and some more precise. The breaking of taboos could cause adverse weather conditions. In parts of Greece, heating water and washing clothes were avoided on St Trifona's Day (1 April); otherwise hailstorms might damage the crops later in the year. Throwing stones in certain lakes or ponds could cause storms. In the Azores, children were forbidden to play with *rhombos* toys 'at harvest time, on the ground that it was likely to spoil the weather'. The *rhombos* was 'a piece of wood about eight inches long by three wide, sharpened somewhat at the ends', which was attached to a piece of string and whirled rapidly round and round, making 'a loud and peculiar whizzing sound'. It had been used in Ancient Greek mysteries. In a more clerical ambience, unnatural darkness and storms of lightning and thunder occurred when the reliquary of the Holy Foreskin was opened at Calcata in 1559 and the relic was then touched and damaged by a canon trying to test its authenticity. More generally, the fifteenth-century Flemish *Evangile des quenouilles* averred that if those related by godparenthood married, 'there would be terrible storms on land and sea'. There was also a belief that women giving birth on board ship caused storms that could only be stilled if they were thrown into the sea. The pollution was particularly strong where the parturient woman died, as Queen Thaisa appears to do in Shakespeare's *Pericles*. 'Sir', a sailor tells Pericles, 'your queen must overboard; the sea works high, the wind is loud, and will not lie till the ship be cleared of the dead.'[8]

Bad weather could also result from behaviour that was more obviously wicked: quarrels among relatives, incest, murder, infanticide. The night of Duncan's murder in *Macbeth* is strangely stormy and the following morning overcast and dark. 'Thou seest the heavens, as troubled with man's act', Rosse tells the old man. This moral interpretation was often given a clerical slant, guided perhaps by the New Testament model of the eclipse and earthquake that followed Christ's death on the cross. St Francis told the people of Greccio that the 'great storms that devastated their corn and vineyards' were a punishment for their sin; they should repent or 'the wrath of God' would be redoubled against them. According to an account of 1609, a pilgrimage of some kind to the lake of Tabe, in what is now the Ariège, became the occasion for riotous festivities overnight. Fires were lit in and around the chapel and ribald songs were sung. Then there was 'a terrible thunderstorm and flashes of lightning fell on the fires, striking terror into those present; the fire fell from the heavens five or six times in quarter of an hour'. Though the lake had a reputation for producing storms if it was agitated, this one, it was suggested, was more probably 'a punishment from God of those people who were profaning religion by their stinking and disordered excesses'. In similar but inflated vein, a chapbook produced in Württemberg during the Thirty Years War and retailing the prophecies of a local rural visionary threatened that, as a result of the people's sinfulness, swearing, and avarice, 'the Lord will send such a terrible storm' that cities would be destroyed and 'many people and animals will perish'.[9] A homily by an Angers priest in the later eighteenth century told, less apocalyptically, how peasants were struck by lightning for working their fields on a Sunday.

Bad behaviour could also anger the ancestors or the dead. In a Corsican folk-tale, a severe storm took place on the Day of the Dead, because a man had failed to leave out the customary water for the visiting dead to slake their thirst with. In Brittany winds were often said to be lost or damned souls, and ghosts were associated with wind and thunder in northern and Germanic folklore.

In this ambience, the weather mirrored and could affect human behaviour, individual and collective. Battles and other great events were accompanied by spectacular storms, as were religious conversions, like that in which Luther first vowed to become a monk. King Lear's conversion in the famous storm scene in Shakespeare's play brings these together: his abdication of kingship, the general catastrophe which that provoked, and his personal arrival at self-knowledge. Illness of all kinds, from epidemics to head-aches, was attributed to the wind and the weather. In the Périgord a specific condition, called the 'encounter of air' was 'produced by a sudden chilling or a gust of wind', and had to be 'lifted' like a spell by a charmer. In fifteenth-century Florence more prosaically worms in infants were put down to 'cold air and strong winds'. The influence of climate on disease had been emphasized by Hippocrates and his disciples and remained an axiom of medieval and later official or upper-class medicine. Joseph Greene, a Stratford-on-Avon clergyman and school-master, for example was a firm believer. He wrote to his brother, an apothecary, in 1779: 'The late strangely diversified weather has at times much affected our Sister Coleman, as to pain in her breast'; and again in 1782: 'my pains also increase or decrease with the weather and are most acute, when there is most humidity in the atmosphere'.[10] We will return to this topic in Part III.

It was even believed in some villages of the Sierra Nevada in southern Spain that a strong wind could make a woman pregnant, and women either hid from such winds or threw special stones at them, which had been collected on Holy Saturday. The climate had an emotional as well as a physical impact, as Mauriac conveyed as late as 1961.

> During the terrible week in September when so many storms lashed the country-side on the eve of the grape harvest, it was not only the wine-grower in me who suffered; the hail pelted me, it attacked and wounded me. The storm passed, and in stunned silence we leaned over the battered vineyard as if it were a martyred child.[11]

Conversely, very unusual climatic or celestial phenomena, eclipses, comets, meteors as well as unseasonal heat or cold, were read as omens, boding ill for those humans who saw or experienced them. We will discuss these beliefs further below in Part IV.

If the climate was not purely natural, who then controlled it? Sometimes the various phenomena, and especially storms and winds, were conceived of as independent entities, King Lear addresses them directly and calls on them to punish his daughter Regan:

> You nimble lightnings, dart your blinding flames
> Into her scornful eyes! Infect her beauty,
> You fen-sucked fogs, drawn by the pow'rful sun,
> To fall and blister her!

In a modern Greek popular song, a brother and sister about to commit incest unwittingly are warned by a hailstorm. Particular winds were often identified and given names. In Provence, for example, there was the Mistral, known also as 'Jan d'Arle' in the district around Arles. Other winds associated with the tops of mountains were Christianized like Sainte-Ventura or Sainte-Victoire on Mont Ventoux. In Greece, the winds were 'often regarded as persons acting their own will', for example the north wind called 'Lord Boreas'. Clouds could also be personified. Canziani was told by a priest in the Abruzzi in the 1920s that hail was 'made when two clouds join, one [male] being over the top of the other [female]. The male cloud makes the rain wind pass between them, and the female cloud freezes the rain, producing the hail'. Waterspouts at sea were also male and female spirits, while each kind of cloud again had 'a different significance. Black clouds mean pouring rain, lightning and wind. Red mean wind, and white mean hail. The biggest cloud is the king, the next is the queen, the small ones are the captain, sergeant, and troops', and they fought, producing storms.[12]

In the Ancient world this idea was taken further by linking such climatic phenomena to multiple divine beings, all under the general aegis of Zeus or Jupiter, the omnipotent sky-god and 'wielder of the thunderbolt'. Similar characteristics were attributed in Germanic religion to Odin or to Thor, 'associated with storms and wind, but above all with thunder and lightning'. Such ideas could be accommodated quite well with Christian monotheism. 'God is raining' or 'God is throwing water', Greek peasants said, or, when it thundered: 'God is marrying his daughters', because modern Greek weddings were always accompanied by the noise of fireworks and salvoes of firearms. The Bible of course reinforced the association of the Almighty with the skies and the weather, notably in the story of Noah and in the Psalms and the Book of Job:

> He directeth ... his lightning unto the ends of the earth ... he saith to the snow, Be thou on the earth; likewise to the small rain and to the great rain of his strength ... By the breath of God frost is given ... Also by watering he wearieth the thick cloud: he scattereth his bright cloud.[13]

In the New Testament, Christ stills the tempest on the Sea of Galilee.

The Scriptural texts are very frequently echoed in learned and popular literature. God told the fifteenth-century Lynn visionary Margery Kempe:

> Thou seeest how the planets are obedient to My will; that sometimes there come great thunder-cracks, and make the people sore afraid. And sometimes, daughter, thou seeest how I send great lightnings that burn churches and houses ... I send great winds that blow down steeples, houses and trees out of the earth,

all of which was a manifestation of 'the might of My Godhead'. According to Thomas Tusser in 1552, God

> ... sendeth thundering claps, like terrors out of hell,
> That man may know a God there is, that in the heavens doth dwell.

Such ideas were still very much alive in the world of popular non-conformity in seventeenth-century England 'The thunderstrokes of the Almighty have to purpose uttered their voices in me', declared the Ranter Joseph Salmon in 1651; 'heaven and earth have trembled at their dreadful sounds.' George Fox returned by ship from Ireland in 1669 and noted in his journal: 'In the night time a mighty storm arose that was almost ready to rend all to pieces; it rained and blew ... and I saw the power of God went over the winds, he had them in his fist, his power bound them'. Again, on a voyage from Jamaica to Florida in 1671, his ship encountered heavy storms 'that tossed us backwards and forwards, but the great God of the sea and of the land who rideth upon the wings of the wind gave us dominion'. Much later, Kilvert reacted to the Great Storm of December 1872 in very similar terms: 'Dark storms and thick black drifts were hurrying up out of the west, where the Almighty was making the clouds His chariot and walking upon the wings of the wind'.[14]

There was a tendency here to trivialize the divine origin of the climate, by emphasizing extreme conditions and lending them a convenient didactic function. As the late medieval *Dives and Pauper* objected: God 'useth not the thunder as a horn to blow his counsel about the world'. And Montaigne complained in the 1580s: 'If the frost chance to nip the vines about my village, my priest doth presently argue, that the wrath of God hangs over our head'. However, this remained a common mode of explanation, especially but not exclusively among Protestants. An early Protestant pamphlet by Eberlin addressed to the Emperor Charles V in 1521 saw hail, bad weather and pestilence as God's punishment for monasticism and other abuses in the Church. For the Puritan Essex clergyman Ralph Josselin in the mid-seventeenth century, 'God's main weapon was the weather, which he used to threaten, to confuse and often to punish'. Again, in the Protestant Netherlands, floods and other catastrophes were seen as punishments for sins. But God could also manipulate the weather to help the faithful. The siege of Leiden in 1574 was represented by the Dutch 'as the national epic par excellence, when sea, wind and polders had fought on the side of the righteous'. According to a local historian, after prayers and psalms, 'God Almighty sent the great wind from the north to put fear into the hearts of the Midianites [Alba's Spanish troops] who broke camp as the waters rose around them'. Among Catholics, the Dominican reformer Savonarola in Florence in the 1490s presented densely black skies, storms of thunder, lightning, wind and hail and wild weather as signs of the wrath of God and the scourge of sinners.[15] Catholics also saw God intervening in religious wars via the weather. During the 1560s, the Jesuits, among others, attributed the storms and heavy rains which impeded the Huguenot armies to direct divine intervention.

In Catholic and Orthodox cultures there was perhaps a stronger tendency to attribute normal and propitious conditions to God and 'the more striking and irregular phenomena' to other lesser agencies. Indeed Fox and other Protestant pastors and theologians in England and Germany stressed the power of God in storms to counter the common view that they were brought about by witches, spirits or demons. Catholic theologians attempted a compromise here. Aquinas in his *Exposition on Job* explained that 'one must therefore believe that with God's permission demons may disturb the atmosphere, raise up strong winds, and make fire fall from Heaven'. But the Spanish Inquisition classified as 'dangerous' the denial of 'God's power to create good weather, or to produce rain for thirsty crops'.[16]

Popular views often reflect a similar hedging. The weather is after all ambiguous. Destructive winds bring needed rain. Rain that is beneficial can come too hard and quickly, causing erosion and damage, washing away seeds and flooding crops. So a fifteenth-century vernacular Life of St Norbert linked the Devil with 'boisterous storms' as opposed to the 'pipeling wind' of a heavenly visitation. More recently in the Hautes-Alpes, it was said that 'thunder is the work of the Devil, but lightning, which warns that thunder is imminent, is the work of God'. Much more generally, however, adverse weather as a whole was blamed on hostile spirits and demons, if not the Devil. It was a Gaelic belief that 'the storms of Spring' were raised by the Cailleach or 'old woman' of Winter in a final effort to prevent the renewal of growth and life. Similarly among the Basques, the Lady of Anboto (a cave) or of Murumeni (a mountain) was propitiated annually by the peasants of Guipúzcoa on the day of the Holy Cross. They 'climb up to her cave and solemnly pronounce a blessing on her', believing that this will take away her 'power to loose storms upon them for the rest of the year'. In the same vein, Shakespeare's fairies 'control the weather and the seasons, and when they quarrel all Nature goes awry'. A late medieval schoolbook from Exeter reported: 'A general rumour is spreading among the people that the spirits of the air, invoked by necromantic art to find mines of gold ... and other treasures ... have appeared in bodily form, stirring up great tempests in the air'.[17]

Such spirits were sometimes termed demons, especially in clerical sources. According to Bede, for example, when Germanus and Lupus set out for Britain in 429 to counter Pelagianism, 'on a sudden they were obstructed by the malevolence of demons. They raised storms and darkened the sky with clouds' threatening the ship with wreck. At Montaillou in the fourteenth century, the peasants believed that the Devil produced hail, thunder and storms. God could do nothing about the weather, which belonged to the Devil's realm of 'nature'. In the same part of the world, peasants in the nineteenth century described the Pic d'Anie mountain as the place 'where devils, witches and magicians assemble, and from which they launch storms on the inhabitants of the plains'. Such demonological notions were commonplace all over Europe from the medieval to the modern periods. According to Myrc's *Festiall*, demons 'rear winds and blow down houses, bell-towers and trees'. In his hymn 'Les Daimons' (1555), Ronsard followed a common learned-cum-popular schema in placing demons in 'the airs' between the earth inhabited by humans and the heavens inhabited by angels. Here they lived beneath the moon in the midst of clouds and among winds, lightning and storms. Some were good, others bad; and the latter 'brought plagues and fevers, storms and thunder to the earth'.

> They make sounds in the air to affright us.
> They make two suns appear.
> They blacken the moon in a hideous way
> And make the sky rain blood ...
> In brief, all that occurs in the air that is horrible
> Is done by them.

In the Abruzzi and other parts of southern Italy, people recognized spirits or demons in the approach of clouds and thunderstorms. Devils made hail by taking snow from the mountains, while damned souls produced lightnings and hurricanes, or else the Devil did when a soul escaped his clutches.[18]

Demonic responsibility for bad weather overlaps with the idea that special categories of humans, alive or dead, could be involved. Behind some of Canziani's waterspouts were people who assumed spirit-form 'just for mischief'. 'They are born during Christmas Eve', she was also told, 'and from the length of their hair, one can see their sex. Don Giuseppe from Ortona was one of them. A girl from Ancona was another'.[19]

All over Europe and from the earliest times it was believed that witches and sorcerers could control the weather. 'At one time they drench the world with rain and veil the hot sun with clouds', the first-century Roman poet Lucan wrote of the witches of Thessaly, 'and the heavens thunder while Jupiter knows nothing of it; and also by spells they disperse the canopy of watery vapour and the dishevelled tresses of the storm-clouds.' He also attributed to them power over the tides and the heavenly bodies. Later, their ability to raise storms was singled out. Visigothic laws of the sixth and seventh centuries include 'a condemnation of persons who maliciously bring tempests down upon another's property'. 'Conjurors of storms' or '*tempestarii*' were condemned by medieval church councils and in penitentials. The influential demonological treatise *Malleus Maleficarum* (1486) included a chapter on 'How witches raise and stir up hailstorms and tempests, and cause lightning to blast both men and beasts', and its claims were repeated and elaborated by later continental demonologists like Rémy and Guazzo. In Shakespeare's *Macbeth*, the witches meet 'in thunder, lightning or in rain' and cause storms at sea and destructive gales.[20]

Particular accusations of this kind often figure in the witchcraft trials of the fifteenth, sixteenth and seventeenth centuries in all parts of Europe. Barbe Vissot, for example, was convicted of witchcraft at Luxeuil in 1631. One of the charges against her was that

> around St John's Day three years earlier when they had been haymaking in a field on the territory of the village of Anjeux, the sky being without clouds and quite serene, she had addressed another woman who was mowing and, tapping her on the shoulder, had said: You wicked people, you'd better start saying your pater- nosters. Look at that cloud that's coming over. You know every time I have a headache it hails without fail; and in fact, although there had been no sign of it, it then started to rain and to hail so hard that a great quantity of hay was lost.

Similarly, in a case before the Inquisition in the Friuli in 1649, a man was accused of being able to 'evoke storms whenever he chooses, even when the sun is shining and the weather is clear'. The trials at Szeged in Hungary in the 1720s and 1730s centred round accusations of 'destroying vineyards with hail storms' and selling rain to the Turks.[21]

Witches raised all kinds of winds and storms, but above all those that were very local and sudden and peculiarly destructive. As a Welsh folklorist noted generally, witches were believed to 'produce tempests to destroy the produce of the earth', part of their general attack on fertility. This intention was often emphasized in early modern trials. In a seventeenth-century variant from the Cambrésis, a witch sent a 'dense drizzling rain' to rot her neighbours' fruit.

The accusation of witchcraft against Françouneto in Jasmin's nineteenth-century poem came when storms damaged the crops of others but left hers and those of her grandmother standing. Witches, King James explained in his *Daemonologie* (1597), could

> raise storms and tempests in the air ... though not universally, but in such a partic-ular place and prescribed bounds, as God will permit them so to trouble: which likewise is very easy to be discerned from any other natural tempests ... in respect of the sudden and violent raising thereof, together with the short enduring of the same.[22]

In some areas, witches were conceived of as riding the air. Agobard of Lyon in the ninth century referred to belief in airships guided by spirits or sorcerers, which sucked up the grain beaten down by storms. At the start of the sixteenth century, both Dürer and Hans Baldung Grien produced images of witches – some specifically termed 'weather witches' – riding animals in the air (see Text Figure 3). Cyrano de Bergerac in the seventeenth century wrote of witches 'walking the air' and leading storms through the sky. Such notions must be related to the demonologists' belief, frequently found in confessions, that witches travelled or flew through the air to attend the Sabbath. Sébillot points out that in most of Europe witches seem to have been unable to produce snow, though they could cause fog and frost. In a trial at Metz in 1456, a boy claimed that he had been with witches who had destroyed the local vineyards with frost. Rainbows, lightning, the Northern Lights and St Elmo's fire were also beyond their control, though Ariel causes the last on a ship in Shakespeare's *Tempest*.[23]

Unlike poor Barbe Vissot, whose case reversed the usual relationship between climate and human illness, most witches were supposed to employ some ritual to produce the effect they desired, and we will return to these. Nor was supposed witches' control of the weather always malevolent. It was reported that a *tempestarius* was kept on hand at Moissac in the mid fifteenth century to produce rain when it was needed. In a case in Swabia, described in the *Malleus Maleficarum*, a young girl was able to make it rain on her family's fields during a drought, and rain-makers were active in many parts of Europe until quite recently. In sixteenth-century Spain, 'cloud chasers were hired by communities to conjure hail-bearing clouds away or make the hail dissolve into [harmless] rain'. In many villages in the Gironde in the nineteenth century, storm conjurors similarly had 'the power to divert thunder and hail-storms'. And the facility of keeping storms off one's own fields and sending them either into the wilds or out to sea or on to the territory of a rival village or a neighbour is widely reported. Synge wrote in 1907 that two attempts at evicting the inhabitants from the island of Inismaan off the west coast of

3. Witch riding a goat backwards. Albrecht Dürer, engraving, *c.* 1500.

Ireland were prevented, 'for each time a sudden storm rose, by, it is said, the power of a native witch, when the steamer was approaching, and made it impossible to land'.[24] Witches could also produce winds when ships were becalmed.

Saints could also be associated with or held responsible for storms. According to legend, St Maudé used to ride on a storm from Ireland to attend his feast on 26 November in Brittany, returning by the same means. In the Orthodox world, St Elijah or Elias was linked with mountain tops and thunder and he also had power over drought and rain. Elsewhere, other saints assumed the same role, for example, St Barnabas in the Puy-de-Dôme, and St Agatha, 'a sinister and maleficent figure', in Languedoc and Provence. Legends also relate how living saints manipulated the weather. St Daniel the Stylite sited his column on land planted with vines belonging to a certain Gelanius, who objected and arrived at the place to evict him. 'Although it was a calm day and the air was still, yet it came to pass that suddenly the clouds gathered and a storm arose accompanied with hail, so that all the fruit of the vineyards was destroyed and the leaves were stripped from the vines', which convinced Gelanius to allow the saint to stay. Storms could also make known a saint's posthumous wishes. Such a storm legitimized Western Christendom's most important shrine. 'Immediately following the passion of the Apostles [Peter and Paul]', according to Pope Gregory the Great,

> Eastern Christians sought to take the bodies home with them for burial. They carried the corpses as far as the catacombs, but a violent thunderstorm prevented their further removal. The Romans then came out from the city, took up the bodies and carried them to their present burial places.[25]

The proverbial weather prediction associated with St Swithun had its origin in a similar legend. The monks of Winchester tried to move his body from the common burial-ground where he had asked to be buried, 'but they were prevented by fierce rains which lasted forty days and nights'. Saints also sent storms to destroy pagan temples and idols, and if they were angered by insult or neglect. The latter was linked to specific ritual responses or the lack of them.

> When it was flat-calm, the sailors of Tréguier believed that St Anthony, patron of the wind, was annoyed or asleep; they would therefore begin to blaspheme to wake him up, and since it was forbidden to whistle at sea, they whistled too for all they were worth.

Elsewhere in Brittany, it was St Clement who governed the sea and the wind. He was implored to change the wind when needed, 'but the sailors insult him if he does not answer their prayers'. Peasants in early modern Spain 'saw the coincidence of a natural disaster with a certain saint's day as a clear sign'. Hail in particular indicated 'that devotion was not being accorded where it was due. Thus when the villagers of Brea (Madrid) noted that it hailed several years in a row on St Anne's Day, they instituted a vow to observe her vigil'. Again, at Usanos (Guadalajara) St Barbara's Day was observed and a *caridad* (dole) distributed, because 'this same day ... a lightning bolt hit the tower of the church and burned three or four people'. Margery Kempe drew similar conclusions from the storms that occurred at Rome while she was there, though she put a more orthodox gloss on them. On the day of St Bridget of Sweden, 'Our Lord sent such tempests of wind and rain, and divers impressions of airs', she noted, that 'through such tokens this creature supposed that Our Lord wished his holy saint's day to be hallowed, and the saint held in more worship than she was at that time'.[26]

Saints were also associated with other climatic phenomena. In southern France, where late frosts at the end of April and the start of May were a special danger, that period was placed under the patronage of the four saints of the frost or the four horsemen: St George, whose feast occurred on 23 April; St Mark on 25 April; St Eutrope or Tropez on 30 April; and the Holy Cross on 3 May; to which might be added St John at the Latin Gate on 6 May. If the day passed without a frost, 'the saint was thanked, but if there was a frost, he was told off'.[27]

The Virgin Mary was fully included in this association of saints and meteorological phenomena in the popular mind, though her influence was usually only benign. Images often depicted the Virgin in the sky from Velasquez's Immaculate Conception of around 1619 to the cruder ex-voto pictures at Oropa and other shrines (see Plate 30). In Piazzetta's altarpiece of 1744 in the church of the Alpine village of Meduno, the Virgin floats in the clouds over the 'swirling mists' as if part of the local landscape.[28] There was a cult in the Céret region of south-west France to Our Lady of the Rainbow, who had appeared according to legend sitting on a triple rainbow like a throne. In other apparitions, for example at Fátima in 1917, the Virgin appeared in or like a flash of lightning; while in Jasmin's poem, a violent thunderstorm with lightning and hail broke out when Françouneto kissed a statue of the Virgin.

Members of the clergy were also believed to have control over the weather. 'In eleventh-century Denmark, the priests were held responsible for disturbance in the weather in the same way as witches'. A canon from Agen was put on trial at Avignon in 1326, accused among other things of 'having provoked thunder, lightning, tempests and hailstorms'. Again, in a village in the Hautes-Alpes in the nineteenth century, the parishioners drove out their priest because they claimed to have seen him 'going through the air and sowing handfuls of hail over the fields'. The belief that priests could send, ride or direct storms was found in many parts of France, Italy and elsewhere. Sometimes they used 'priestly' formulae from the breviary or other religious texts; sometimes they employed more traditional magical means, such as agitating the water in ponds and lakes. Often they used their powers to punish or to get their own back on enemies. In coastal areas priests might divert and direct winds to help or hinder those at sea. In and around Cancale, for example, it was thought that the priest had a rope with which he could 'turn the winds', and, when sailors lacked a wind they needed, they cursed him, much as those of Tréguier annoyed St Anthony in order to prompt him to action.[29] Though most commonly reported of the Catholic clergy and more consonant with their generally more 'mystical' religious functions, weather-making powers were also ascribed to Protestant ministers. When a seventeenth-century Württemberg pastor was cheated out of his inheritance by his stepmother, a vineyard which she had bought with the money was washed away in a cloudburst.

The rituals engaged in by peasants and others to influence the weather were usually guided by this general belief that it was ultimately controlled by God, by saints, by demons, by human beings with special powers. However, some 'natural magic', without recourse, direct or indirect, to intermediary spirits was used, though such magic was often tinged or mixed with Christian elements. In an Anglo-Saxon addition to an older text, a supplicant addressed a castor-oil plant: 'I pray you to be present at my incantations and to keep off the hail, the lightning and all storms, in the name of the all-powerful God who caused you to be born'.[30]

A variety of means was used here to change the weather. In the twelfth-century Icelandic *Saga of Gisli*, Audbjorg avenges an offence against her son by a man called Berg. She goes outside during a still and cloudless night and walks

> withershins about the house a few times and sniffs in all directions with her nostrils lifted. And as she was doing these things, the weather began to alter, and there came a heavy, drifting snowstorm, and after that a thaw; a flood broke out on the mountainside and an avalanche rolled on to Berg's steading, and twelve men were killed there.

This is the weather witchcraft that we have already encountered, looked at from a different angle. In the French and British navies in the seventeenth and eighteenth centuries, 'it was a religiously observed tradition to oblige the cabin-boys to whip each other', in order to produce a breeze during a calm, and the custom survived on fishing boats into this century. We have seen that whistling was another way of provoking winds, and Sébillot noted in 1904 that special ropes were still being sold to sailors in northern countries, 'tied with knots, that brought about a breeze, a wind or a storm', depending on whether one untied one, two or three of them. On Fielding's voyage to Lisbon in 1754, the captain attributed their long initial becalming to bewitchment, and some of the sailors 'asserted that the drowning a cat was the very surest way of raising a favourable wind'.[31] In Normandy and Brittany, wives burned brooms to make the wind change and bring their husbands home. In the Ille-et-Vilaine, the broom had to be stolen and the ashes were thrown into the air.

On land the commonest rituals had to do with rain- or storm-making, and they are very well attested all over Europe from the Middle Ages onwards. The basic gesture was to beat or agitate water, often in wells or ponds. The *Malleus Maleficarum* mentions several examples. According to Albert the Great rotten sage was thrown into running water; a woman from Waldshut in the diocese of Constance was said to have raised a hailstorm by urinating in a small trench and then stirring it with her finger; others stirred water in a bowl. In a tale in *The Mabinogion*, written down in the fourteenth century but much older, a thunder- and hailstorm of great intensity, which strips the leaves from the trees and kills animals and humans, is brought about by taking a silver bowl from a fountain and 'throwing a bowlful of water over the slab'. A document of 1593 from Swabia refers to a small girl 'stirring water with her little finger'. In a French witchcraft trial in 1618, a woman from Clerval confessed to 'beating the water' at a particular spring frequented by local people, using white sticks and saying: 'Hail, fall on the woods!'. A woman in the Vivarais in 1519 raised a storm which destroyed the harvest by washing her donkey in a river. Another woman from the same region threw a powder supplied by the Devil into a gorge. Sometimes, as the last example suggests, flour and other substances were scattered on the water; and the water might be beaten with shovels, brooms or spoons as well as with sticks and the hands. A woman and her daughter, aged nine, convicted of witchcraft at Huntingdon in 1716, were said to have raised 'a storm by pulling off their stockings, and making a lather of soap'. Sometimes, as this indicates, the water was splashed about or mixed with mud, thereby 'troubling' or polluting a spring or fountain. Stones or other objects might be thrown into the water or taken out of it. A man, tried at Ouchy near Lausanne in 1461, confessed to making hail 'by taking hailstones [pebbles?] from springs and hitting them with a stick'.[32] Some reports say that rain- or storm-makers operated in threes; and they nearly always accompanied their mimetic gestures with certain formulae (see Text Figure 4).

Such rituals were often carried out clandestinely and with malevolent intention, but they could also be benevolent and public. Thomas Platter junior related erroneously but significantly in 1599 that witches were not punished with death in England because one of them had 'held off a tempest' on the water, raised by others to encompass the queen's 'destruction'. Rain-making 'witches', like storm conjurors, might be employed by communities. Lawson met one on the island of Santorini around 1905. She was very old and was muttering incantations on the edge of a cliff. An account of 1661 described how in time of drought people from the Dauphiné

> went in crowds to a spring situated in the parish of L'Espine; there the old men and women chose a young girl, the most virtuous and pure; her clothes were removed, and while everyone prayed, she plunged into the pool by the spring and removed all the rubbish from it.

This is reminiscent of a custom reported by Burchard of Worms in the eleventh century. 'When they have no rain and need it', he wrote,

> then they assemble a number of girls, and they put forward one little maiden as a leader, and strip her, and bring her thus stripped outside the village, where they find the herb henbane ... ; and they make this nude maiden dig up the plant with the little finger of her right hand ... Then while each girl holds a twig in her hands, they bring the aforesaid maiden, dragging the plant behind her, to a nearby river and with these twigs sprinkle her with the water and thus they hope that by their charms they shall have rain.

Similar rituals are reported from southern Italy and from all over the Balkans in the modern period. In Rumania,

> a girl, usually a gypsy ... dressed only in leaves, weeds and flowers, goes through the village. At each doorway people drench her with water, while she dances and sings – together with a whole escort of others – such songs as are purported to bring down the much-needed rain:

> > Come and wet us
> > With water pails,
> > That rain may fall,
> > To make the corn grow
> > As high as the hedges,
> > To increase the crop
> > And fill up the barns.[33]

Similar rituals were practised in Russia and the Ukraine. Here witches might be held responsible for causing droughts by withholding rain, and droughts could be ended by identifying such people and placing them in water. In the Ukraine in the eighteenth and nineteenth centuries, witches were detected via rituals that have features in common with Western rain-

4. Witches making hail. Title page, Ulrich Molitor, *De Ianijs et Phitonicis Mulieribus* (Cologne, 1489).

making: suspected persons had to carry pails of water from a pond or river to a local shrine or cross without spilling the contents. Once detected, they might be 'swum' or drowned to induce rain.[34] It is possible that some Western procedures for ducking witches had analogous connotations. Drought was also attributed to the influence of vampires in Russia and the Balkans, and bodies that had not decomposed were thrown into or sprinkled with water to bring rain.

Sébillot suggests, in connection with the Dauphiné example, that as bad weather may be caused by polluting springs, so purifying them may restore propitious climatic conditions. Hence the stress, too, in this and other cases on the innocence of the actor or actors in the rite. Purification to produce rain could also paradoxically be brought about via fire. In many parts of central and northern Scotland it was believed that burning the heather caused rain.

Similarly important and benevolent was conjuring storms, which was openly practised in many parts of Europe from the Middle Ages onwards. In the Gironde storm-conjurors diverted potentially dangerous storms by blowing or uttering formulae. Aubrey provides several examples of such practices in seventeenth-century England, including the still current: 'Rain, rain, go away', rhyme sung by children. An edition of the *Dragon noir* published in 1896 contained a spell to calm tempests and storms. In Spain, as we have noted, the storm could be sent into the wilds or the sea, or the hail dissolved into rain. At San Stefano in the Abruzzi, Canziani reports how a priest stopped a hail-storm by putting 'the largest hailstone he could find into the palm of a child under seven years old (the most innocent of the family), because he believed the tempest would only last the time the hailstone took to melt'. Elsewhere in southern Italy, storm-conjurors recited formulae taken from the catechism, drew a circle on the ground with a sickle and made the evil being driving the storm come down into the circle. This relates of course to the belief that storms were piloted by malevolent spirits or persons. A similar practice was noted by Abbé Thiers, though it seems to have been a collective one:

> They make a simple circle on the ground with a knife, big enough to contain every-thing they want to protect; then they make a cross in the middle and write on it: *Verbum Caro factum est*, and stick the knife in the middle of the cross, the blade pointing in the direction from which the lightnings, hurricane, storms and rain are likely to come.[35]

This takes us on to general protection against storms via magic. Brandishing an axe, knife or other sharp instrument in the air was practised in many parts of Europe, including the Alps, Provence and Italy. In the Alps this was explained as a means of frightening off the spirits responsible for the storm, who might cut themselves if they came too close. In Sicily, the threads attaching the storm clouds to their manipulators were being cut. Other gestures or procedures included throwing a broom into the courtyard, throwing stones into the air, throwing salt on the fire, lighting the 'family candle' that was otherwise lit only when someone died, and cooking a goose. In Provence, if other measures failed, 'the fire-dogs and the pot-hanger and anything to do with the fire were brought outside and assembled, preferably by a lime tree, and one traced a cross on the ground in T form, which is a magical sign'.[36]

Many protective amulets were also used and worn, in particular to defend against thunder and lightning. These could be special plants, like the house-leeks planted on houses in the Auvergne or the red poppies placed in the rafters by Walloons. 'Reach the bays', says Cornelia in Webster's *The White Devil*,

> I'll tie a garland here about his head;
> 'Twill keep my boy from lightning.

Often the name of the plant had some connection with the weather. The yellow flowers believed to protect against lightning in Béarn were called 'light-nings' in the local dialect. As in other circumstances, the virtue of the plants was often enhanced by their being picked in a special way or their being linked with some religious ceremony. Storm amulets could also be parts of animals, like antlers; old coins; pieces of iron; or faggots from bonfires burned on ritual occasions. An early medieval text castigates as pagans 'those who believe they can prevent hail by means of inscribed lead tablets or charmed horns'. But the most common amulets probably were various stones, fossils or prehistoric objects, usually called thunderstones. These were believed to fall from the air during storms. In the Abruzzi 'the thunder which strikes straight from the sky forms flint arrow-heads', while 'small thunder striking zig-zag' made small round stones called *gocci*.[37] In Portugal, the thunderstones or thunderbolts penetrated the earth when they fell and then gradually rose to the surface. Since such objects fell from the sky, then they must, it was believed, give protection against the same, and they were placed on or in the roofs of houses and farmbuildings, under thresholds, even under livestock, or they might be worn by persons around the neck. Sometimes they were held in the hand during a storm, while a charm was recited.

Some of the procedures which we have outlined involved noise: shouting, whistling, firing shots into the sky, letting off fireworks. In some parts of France, pots and pans were banged and other loud noises made on St John's Eve in order to keep off hail and lightning during the coming year. Elsewhere

reapers would make their sickles resonate in the air at the approach of a
storm, and winegrowers would beat the containers into which they put the
grapes with vine-stakes. The ringing of bells to dissipate storms must be seen
in this context. The practice was reported from the later medieval period, if
not earlier, and continued into this century in many parts of Western Europe.
A witness in the canonization process of Cardinal Peter of Luxemburg in 1390
testified that the putative saint had appeared to him in a dream 'and charged
him to tell the people of Avignon to raise a belfry on his tomb with a large bell
which would ring out at the time of Elevation [during mass] and at the
approach of storms, thunder and lightning, to preserve the fruits of the
earth'. At Sennely-en-Sologne in the seventeenth century, the church bells
were rung incessantly especially in the Spring, sometimes 'three times a day
and for several hours at a time'.[38]

Very often the ringing was official, despite the doubts of some of the clergy.
At Sennely, the churchwardens appointed a man to do the ringing or deputed
children to do so. Such arrangements seem to have been normal. At Spalding,
for example, the churchwardens' accounts list three pence paid in 1519 'for
ringing when the tempest was'. In some places in the Yonne in the eighteenth
century 'the inhabitants were pressed into fulfilling the function of bell-
ringers during storms. At Vézinnes in 1779, eighty-nine persons were
inscribed on the list'. At Vermenton a meeting in 1703 decided that six people
should be available day and night to ring the bells if a storm threatened. No
one was exempt, and fines were imposed on those who failed to turn up when
required. At Guerchy in 1778, all in the village, men and women, were put into
gangs of ten to fourteen people each with a leader. Anyone who failed in his
or her duties was held responsible for any damage done if a storm did occur,
and this system was still in operation in the 1830s. Certain bells had special
reputations. The smallest bell at Fleury, for example, had the reputed power,
when it was rung first at the approach of a storm, of 'cutting the clouds' and
making them 'burst on neighbouring villages'. At Sennely, the bigger the bell,
the more effective it was supposed to be. Many old bells had appropriate
inscriptions, such as: '*Tempestatem fugo, nubes fugo*' (I make the storm and
the clouds flee).[39]

Bells were also 'solemnly baptized and anointed with the holy oils' to
increase their power. As early as 789, a capitulary of Charlemagne forbade the
'baptizing of bells against the threat of hailstorms'. This introduced an ecclesiastical element into their magical function, but also underlined the bells'
association with and representation of the community. Bells, moreover, were
rung on other occasions and notably at the rites of passage and during All
Souls' Night. Bells were rung too as a preventative measure at Rogations, on
St John's Eve and on other occasions. Abbé Thiers said that this was done 'to

chase away the witches' and to 'prevent their *maleficia*', and most commentators link the ringing of bells in storms to the popular belief that they were caused by witches or evil spirits. So Wynkin de Worde explained around 1500 that bells were rung 'during thunderstorms, to the end that fiends and wicked spirits should be abashed and flee and cease the moving of the tempest'. Very occasionally ringing bells was believed to cause storms by agitating the air. During the yellow fever epidemic in Barcelona in 1822, a suggestion was made that the ringing of bells should be forbidden, on the grounds that 'they attract lightning during storms and so might serve as conductors of the poison miasma', which supposedly caused the disease.[40]

While 'natural' or direct magical rituals were thus important and widespread, more rituals concerning the weather probably came under the aegis of the Church and sought the aid of some supernatural intermediary. The old liturgies included prayers and masses for rain, against storms and so on, and these were retained in vestigial form by some Protestant churches. Some of these services were slotted into the sacred calendar and performed on a regular basis. In eighteenth-century Angers, 'special prayers and services for rain' were usually recited in May and 'for fine weather' in July and August. At Combloux in Savoy, the parish priest said the prayers against storms from the Geneva Missal at Rogation time. In many parts of southern Germany, Austria and Switzerland, in the fourteenth and fifteenth centuries and later, the clergy 'blessed the airs' at Ascension, Corpus Christi or on Rogation Days, often processing relics, 'weather crosses' and the host through the fields.[41]

This was sometimes done following a collective vow. At Champs-Romain in the Périgord, a church service was held on the Eve of Corpus Christi, followed by a procession through the fields, in order to keep off hailstorms. By early this century, although they were largely anticlerical and it was a busy time of the year when they could ill afford to take a whole morning off, the villagers remained 'fanatical' about the procession of the vow. When in 1919, in the absence of a resident priest, the procession had to be postponed for a week, very few people attended, and when it did hail the following September, the priest from a neighbouring parish who had officiated was blamed for not performing the ritual on the right day. Complete withdrawal of the normal ecclesiastical rituals was even more serious, leaving the peasants vulnerable. When a district in the diocese of Vienne, for example, was threatened with an interdict in 1742 after a notary and a tax-collector had been murdered, the local clergy were physically attacked by women claiming that, if the threat were carried out, it 'would bring hail to destroy the crops indiscriminately; the priests rejoined that only the guilty need fear'.[42]

Very adverse weather conditions would call for extraordinary services and processions. 'And now see we proved often', Sir Thomas More noted in *The*

Dialogue of Comfort (1534), 'that in sore weather ... by general processions God giveth gracious help.' At Montmélian in the diocese of Grenoble, according to the Visitation report of 1673, 'the confraternity of penitents goes in procession to the Capuchins' convent when the weather is bad and there is danger of storms'. Mme de Sévigné described the great procession of St Genevieve in Paris in July 1675, ordered after two month of incessant rain: 'Monks and nuns, priests from every parish, the canons of Notre-Dame, and finally the archbishop, clad in his pontificals, proceeded on foot' from the saint's church on the Left Bank to the cathedral. The religious, including the abbot of Sainte-Geneviéve and the archbishop, were bare-footed, and the archbishop and the abbot blessed the crowd. The reliquary, encrusted with gems, was carried by twenty men, also barefoot, and dressed in white, and it was followed by the members of the Parlement in their red robes and representatives of the city's trades.[43]

In later centuries, bishops reserved the right to order such processions. The synodal statutes of Périgueux repeated a ban in 1874–75 on parish priests' 'making extraordinary processions in the event of continuous rains, droughts, etc., without our authorization'. In general these services enjoyed popular support, as we have seen, and attempts by reforming clergy to withdraw them were resisted. However, 'townee' bishops could sometimes earn the scorn of countrymen for using thier powers obtusely. When the cardinal-archbishop of Bordeaux ordered public prayers for rain during a severe drought one Autumn in the 1950s, François Mauriac protested: 'One should never ask for rain on the eve of the grape harvest, especially when there has been none since June, for it would be a miracle if it were to come then except as a storm bearing hail'.[44]

Whatever bishops decided, the parish clergy were generally expected to use their powers, official and unofficial, to ensure good meteorological conditions for their parishioners. A reforming Franciscan preacher at Strasbourg in the early sixteenth century criticized lay people for urging 'priests to say masses for secular ends like changing the weather'.[45] And there are many reports of parishioners abusing and attacking priests who failed them in this respect; some refused to pay their tithes. The two main areas in which ritual action was called for were again preventing storms and obtaining rain.

'In case of hail, storm or hurricane', Abbé Thiers reported, 'in order to save the crops, the priest brings the ciborium containing the host to the church door and makes signs of the cross with it in the direction of the storm.' 'The hail has brought great damage to the cereals and the vines' of Vimines, the Visitation report of 1678 related;

> the people are very angry with their priest because he was not in the parish when

the hail fell, believing that, if he had been in his church and had said the customary prayers, then the hail would not have fallen. These popular prejudices in such places about the power of the clergy to chase away or prevent storms mean that they are captives during the Summer months, most not daring to leave their parishes at all, while the crops are still unharvested. Last year the parish priest of Montagnolle was nearly stoned, because hail fell in his parish while he was in Chambéry.[46]

If fully and properly carried out, the usual ritual was a form of exorcism, with prayers imploring the aid of God and his angels against the infernal powers. The Missal of Périgueux, for example, included an 'Exorcism against storms', which was used in villages down to the start of this century. 'O God, chain up by your virtue all the adverse forces', the priest asked, 'all the malice of incantations, all the disobediences of the infernal serpents, all the advances of darkness', held responsible for the storms. And he then

> adjured ... all you angels of darkness, all you evil-doing enchanters and ministers of Satan ... to withdraw, to go to the mountains, to the desert regions, where no one lives and no one works or sows, there where no human habitations exist or can exist!

An additional element of non-ecclesiastical magic was often also present. In modern Spain, the priest performing the exorcism was firmly held by several men, lest 'the demon of the storm' try to blow him away, and in some places he threw a stone sprinkled with holy water into the air. A sixteenth-century French Protestant source cites a case in Savoy, in which a priest went through a gradation of rituals to allay a particularly severe and recalcitrant storm.

> First he used conjurations which he knew by heart; then he brought out his breviary and his missal and chose the strongest texts he could find; but, seeing that all this was without effect, he fetched the holy sacrament, that is his God of dough and told him: If you don't show that you are stronger than the Devil, I'll throw you in the mud!

Similarly in a procession more recently at Mont-Saxonnex in the Alps, someone commented to the person carrying the crucifix in a procession to calm a storm: 'Hold Him up high so He can see all the damage He is doing!'[47] Proximity to the storm-bearing clouds up in the sky was a factor, too. At Bonifacio in southern Corsica, which was particularly prone to storms, a relic of the True Cross was an object of general devotion. It was taken out during bad weather and raised in the air at the porch of the church of St Mary Major as high as the bearer could hold it.

Sometimes the power to control storms seems to have been more purely personal. The 'enlightened' priest of Combloux in Savoy complained that some of his colleagues encouraged the popular error that attributed all storms to witchcraft by 'presenting themselves against the storm clouds with a martial air, waving the cross and the holy water sprinkler like soldiers brandishing their sabres' and then taking all the credit when the hail or storm stopped or passed by without causing harm. In a Corsican lament for a priest killed in the Franco-Prussian War, his mother declared in his praise:

> When you raised your hand,
> You calmed the winds and tempests.

Around 1920, an old women from a village in the Périgord compared the new young priest, who was reluctant to use the rituals against storms and performed them without enthusiasm with his predecessor: 'O, that good gentleman. He took the trouble. He sweated over it'.[48] More generally, there is evidence that the efficacy of priests as storm-conjurors depended on their being good and pure. In parts of Spain, they had to be virgins.

Priests appear to have been less actively engaged in rain-making, though their participation in official rituals was necessary. The inhabitants of Courségoules in the diocese of Vence petitioned the bishop in the early eighteenth century through their consuls for 'permission to go to the shrine at Courmes on Whit Monday in order to ask God for rain for the good of the land', and the bishop agreed so long as a priest led the procession.[49] Such processions were very commonly asked for and ordered in times of drought, as we have already seen. Before the Revolution, the hermitage of Saint-Maurice near Ille-sur-Tet in the Roussillon housed a miraculous crucifix which was appealed to in crises, especially meteorological. During an extreme drought in 1775, the consuls and local clergy, followed by large crowds, carried the crucifix from the hermitage to Ille, where it was taken around half the town to the accompaniment of prayers and placed in the main church. A week later rain came, and the crucifix was taken around the other half of the town and returned gratefully to Saint-Maurice.

In Italy such processions were often more exuberant and less clerical. In Nice a prime role was played by the White Penitents of the Holy Cross. Some carried heavy crosses and iron chains, with which they beat themselves. 'They tore their shoulders with scourges having iron points', an onlooker reported in May 1718, 'and they hit their chests, shouting: My God, rain. Many women followed them in the robes of penitents. The air was full of their cries and howls, and the paving stones ran with blood.' In Apulia, some penitents went naked. Elsewhere there was less stress on the idea that drought was some kind of punishment that needed to be expiated, and a more obviously magical element in the ritual. Frequently the processional cross or crucifix was immersed in water either to induce rain by association or to force the cult object to fulfil its function. Bodin noted in *De la Démonomanie* (1582) that 'the custom of dragging crucifixes and images in the river to have rain is still practised in Gascony, and I have seen this done in Toulouse in full daylight by small children in front of all the people, who called it the *tiremasse*'. A similar custom was still practised in the city in the 1860s during the Rogations. Again, according to a *jota* or popular song from the other side of the Pyrenees, in north-eastern Spain in the 1950s:

> I have never seen people stupider
> Than the people of Alcocer,
> Who throw their Christ in the river,
> Because he has not made it rain![50]

Crosses were also dipped or plunged in pools and lakes, often by chapels, and, at San Fiorenzo in Corsica, in the sea. Another mimetic rite involved the sprinkling of water from sacred springs on to the ground or on to participants in the processions imploring rain. In a number of places in France, it was important to douse the priest himself. Of course all these rituals involving water are versions in a sacred setting of the more direct one that we have already encountered.

The Protestant Churches abolished such procedures, retaining only prayers and fasts, but still the odd piece of ecclesiastical magic survived or crept in. In 1869, Emily Tennyson referred to the 'Lincolnshire clergyman who, praying for rain, said, O my God, send us rain and specially for John Stubbs' field in the Middle Marsh and if thou dost not know it, it has a thorn bush in the midst of it'. Geoffrey Keynes, who was born in 1887, was told as a child by his grandmother of a Congregational minister of her acquaintance who had occasion to offer up a prayer during a drought. 'Lord', he said [in a formula of pure onomatopeoic magic], 'please give us rain – drizzle drozzle, drizzle drozzle, for about week'.[51]

To return to the medieval and Catholic worlds, exorcisms and processions involved sacred objects, like the host or the cross. The Protestant Reformer Guillaume Farel recalled going as a child in the early sixteenth century to the shrine of the Holy Cross at Tallard in the Dauphiné. The cult object was a crucifix containing fragments of the True Cross. The priest told the pilgrims 'Whenever the Devil sends hail and thunder, this crucifix moves so violently that one would think it wanted to get loose from the cross to go running after the Devil ... and all the while it keeps throwing off sparks of fire against the

storm. Were it not for this, the whole country would be swept bare.' In addition
a plethora of minor sacred paraphernalia was used by the peasants themselves,
particularly to keep off storms and lightning. The Ten Articles issued in
England in 1536 noted that 'against tempests of thunder and lightning many run
to the church for holy water to cast about their houses to drive away ill spirits
and devils'. A nineteenth-century Breton poem referred to an old woman using
her broom to calm a storm, sweeping into the air dust collected in the church
from saints' statues, tombs and the floor trodden by clergy and pilgrims.[52]

We have already come across many of these objects or substances in our
account of the calendar festivals at which they received their power. Among the
Basques, for example, the 'Saviour bread' or 'the crust of the bread eaten on
Christmas Eve, over which the sign of the cross has been made ... serves to calm
a rough sea, to make floods go down and to abate rainstorms'. The candles
blessed at Candlemas or at Easter might be lit in time of storms. It was reported
in the late sixteenth century that Huguenots from one village near Montbéliard
used to go to a neighbouring Catholic village to procure these useful articles.
Again, the branches of box, laurel, willow and other trees blessed on Palm
Sunday were put in the fields and elsewhere to keep off hail and lightning and
might be burned when a storm occurred. The prayer of benediction in the
Roman Missal specifically promised that 'wherever the palms are placed
thunder and tempests may do no harm'. In the Puisaye and Normandy as well
as the Vosges, hawthorn was believed to ward off lightning, having been used to
make the Crown of Thorns. Hazel crosses or bundles, gathered and/or blessed
on 1 or 3 May, also preserved fields from hail. Charcoal, ashes or faggots from
the Christmas log or the Easter or Midsummer bonfires gave similar protection. Prosper Mérimée noted around 1840 that he had 'seen a St John's Eve
bonfire solemnly blessed at Jargeau near Orléans by a priest in a stole. The men
and women then rushed forward to get a piece of the embers to carry away.
These I was told kept thunder and lightning from their houses'. The herbs of St
John or the bouquets carried at Corpus Christi might also be brought out and
burned. A sixteenth-century bishop of Pamplona referred to this custom and
explained that the fumigations were supposed to keep off the demons responsible for the storms. Other talismans included eggs laid on Good Friday or
Ascension Day, stones collected as the Gloria bell rang on Holy Saturday, salt,
and, as we have seen, holy water and loaves baked or blessed on holy days. In
Corsica these were the loaves of St Rocco, which were placed on window-sills.
Home-made crosses of wood, sticks, or straw might also be used, or crosses
combining some of the other items. In the Abruzzi, a cross was made at
Candlemas with the remains of the Easter Eve bonfire tied together with a Palm
Sunday palm or taper, and the peasants knelt in front of it 'to avert a tempest'.
Official crosses might be used, too, if access could be had to them. At some

places in the diocese of Vence, little crosses were kept in the tabernacles to be 'used in the prayers that are said against bad weather', and ownership of these was sometimes claimed by the confraternities. When a miraculous crucifix was discovered at Socuellamos in La Mancha in Spain in 1569, the sacristan suppos-edly 'borrowed' it to put in his vineyard to protect it from hail.[53]

In general peasants deployed a combination of these protective objects in some kind of ritual. In an account relating to the Franche-Comté in the early nineteenth century, a man recalled that when lightning struck near the house, his father 'took a glass of holy water, picked off a sprig of box from the blessed branch and sprinkled all the corners of the house; then he lit the family candle and everyone knelt and prayed'. At Viviers (Yonne), according to a slightly later account, 'crosses were made with handfuls of wheat to keep off whirl-winds at harvest-time. These were raised as high as possible into the air to the words: Wicked Esterbeau, Esterbillon whirlwind, I conjure you as Judas conjured Jesus Christ on Good Friday!' In the Limousin, the Candlemas candle was lit and the St John's herbs were burned, while various formulae were recited, for example: 'Come on, my friend, come on [addressed to the storm]', which replied:

> How do you want me to come on?
> The cornflower stops me
> And the St John's wort takes away my breath.[54]

More conventional prayers such as the Paternoster were of course employed as well as the simple recitation of the Name of Jesus. The latter was recommended by St Bernardino of Siena, who normally proscribed 'incanta-tions'. In late medieval England, the Prologue to St John's Gospel was read to quell thunderstorms. The sign of the cross was also much used everywhere. In an interesting variation from the Sierra Nevada region, the stones collected on Holy Saturday were thrown from the roofs of the houses during a storm, 'one stone in the direction of the storm and one to either side of it, thus making the figure of the cross'.[55]

William Christian suggests that in early modern Spain there was a scale of responses to adverse weather and other troubles, from simple conjuration and exorcism by the parish clergy to more elaborate services and proces-sions, and then to vows to saints and recourse to important shrines. Though things were not always so neat elsewhere, there is no doubt that calling on the saints in some form was almost universal throughout Europe, especially when the weather was very bad. This reflected both the view that saints themselves might be responsible for weather conditions and the more general belief that they were best placed to combat the influence of spirits and witches.

The power of the saints and the Virgin Mary could be used to prevent storms and keep off lightning. In an early miracle of St Martin, a piece of wax from his tomb was placed in a field to protect it from hail. The fourteenth-century English cleric Robert Mannyng claimed that Saturday afternoons were kept holy in Italy in honour of the Virgin Mary 'to the great advantage of the vines, which were thus preserved from damage by tempest'. Again, it was believed that a black Virgin at Murat (Cantal) had 'always preserved the town from lightning'. Significant here is the practice of giving saints' names to ships to protect them from storms and wreck, which can be traced back to at least the fifteenth century. Also significant is the building of chapels dedicated to saints on hill-tops and mountains, from where storms were often believed to come. In the West of England, Brittany, Corsica, Italy, these were often dedicated to St Michael, who battled with Satan in the skies and who was associated with thunder and lightning. In the Orthodox world, as we have seen, St Elijah was a favourite patron. In Rumania, glass icons representing the saint going up into heaven in his chariot were very common, and the saint was 'called upon to protect the grain, to bring down the beneficial rain to the parched earth, and to protect from lightning'. Prophylactic processions or pilgrimages might be made to these mountain chapels. In 1714 the parish of Millas in the Roussillon resolved to make an annual procession to the chapel of Our Lady of the Snows on the summit of the Força-Réal mountain 'in order to conjure the storms' that were believed to emanate from there. According to a later account, this laborious and difficult devotion declined from around 1830, 'leaving the district without protection, and Millas, which had always been preserved from storms before, saw its vines and olives devastated by hail in 1854'.[56] There was a belief, too, that some statues or images of saints had dropped from the sky, for example the image of Santa Maria-Celesta in Venice. Cases are reported from all over Europe from the eleventh to the nineteenth centuries. The sky-born saint could naturally be thought to have influence in the skies.

Once a storm occurred, a variety of actions could be taken. Prayers or charms could be said. In Sicily and Otranto, the following was recited by a lighted candle:

> St John was the first
> Of the apostles to be blest ...
> His father was Zaccheus.
> His mother was Elizabeth,
> Who was so old.
> Long live St John!

5. Man and horse saved from lightning following a vow to the Virgin Mary. Ex-voto painting, Notre-Dame-du-Château, Allauch, southern France, 1820. (Ex-voto paintings like this were commissioned from local artists to represent the 'miracle' performed by the saint and were then given to his or her shrine.)

Other prayers to St John were said, while shaking a small bell. Vows could be made, as in early modern Spain. A good proportion of ex-voto pictures at shrines depict the donor and his or her family escaping death or injury in a storm thanks to a vow made to the saint. In a picture at the shrine of Notre-Dame-du-Château at Allauch, for example, dating from 1820, a zig-zag of lightning passes through the legs of a peasant packing a bundle of hay, just misses the head of his horse grazing nearby, but hits and sets fire to a granary (see Text Figure 5). According to an early modern miracle account, St Ubaldo of Gubbio 'preserved from rain on one occasion a plot of ground belonging to a poor woman, who, with a vow, offered him a request to save it from a storm, which threatened and burst upon all the land about it'.[57] Vows could also be collective.

In another collective ritual, the relics of the saint might be deployed. At Villarrubio (Cuenca), the relics of St Sylvester were brought out. 'It has been seen many times', a sixteenth-century account relates, 'that when bad storm clouds are coming and the holy relic is taken outside, the hail has stopped and changed into clear water'. In some circumstances, there might be a special pilgrimage to a shrine. In the late seventeenth century there was one to the shrine of Notre-Dame-de-Mièges in the Jura 'to obtain from God weather suited to harvesting the crops which are being ruined by the rain'. Peasants went in procession in this century to the hermitage of San Bernardino near Seggiano to call on him 'for help after a series of severe hailstorms', and these did not recur. Livings saints or holy people like Margery Kempe were of course also credited with the ability to affect the weather, as we have seen, and the Lives of saints, Catholic and Orthodox, are full of instances in which they did so. St Bernardino's miracles in his lifetime include 'numerous occasions on which his protection saved ripening wheat or vineyards from hailstorms'.[58]

Lives and legends also sometimes explain why one saint rather than another was consulted. St Donato of Arezzo, for example, was invoked against storms over a wide area of northern Italy, northern France and Flanders. Two episodes in the legend of this early martyr may explain the complexion of his cult. According to Voragine's *Golden Legend* of the thirteenth century, he cleansed a spring polluted by a dragon, and, while he was imprisoned by the Emperor Theodosius, no rain fell for three years. He is sometimes represented, moreover, carrying an axe, which we have seen, was an implement used against storms. St Barbara was even more widely invoked, especially against lightning: in Spain, Portugal, Sicily, and many parts of France. Her legend associates her with both fire and water, but popular prayers and charms emphasize rather a connection with the cross, which we have already seen was a powerful, force against storms in its own right. A prayer from the Limousin ran:

> St Barbara, beautiful flower,
> You who carry the Saviour's cross,
> If I say that three times,
> The thunder will never fall
> On me, or my relatives, or my children,
> Or anyone in my family.[59]

She also provided protection appropriately against sudden death in general. Other saints with special powers against storms included St Agatha (Savoy, Provence), St Blaise (Germany, Switzerland), St Mary Magdalene (Limousin, Languedoc) and the Virgin Mary.

A large number of saints were also invoked for rain. Again, this could be a feature in their Lives and legends. According to Bede, when St Wilfrid converted and baptized the South Saxons in 681, he also brought a three-year drought to an end. 'On the very day on which the nation received the baptism of faith, there fell a soft but plentiful rain: the earth revived again, and the verdure [was] restored to the fields'. Again, preaching near Segovia in 1219 during a lengthy drought that prevented the local peasants from sowing their crops, St Dominic 'promised that the Lord would soon give them rain' and a downpour occurred before his sermon had ended.[60]

Many saints could bring either rain or its cessation, depending on the circumstances, like Notre-Dame-de-Mièges, St Genevieve, patroness of Paris, or St Rocco or Roch. At Bazoches in the Morvan, in addition to being the general patron of the village,

> St Roch was considered personally responsible for the climatic conditions. At no matter what date in the calendar, depending on whether moisture was wanted or dryness, a procession might be formed led by the priest. The faithful went up to the chapel [on the edge of the village] after their work in the fields was finished, singing the litanies of the saints. If their wishes were granted, a further procession for St Roch would be made on the following Sunday to give thanks.

At Sulmona in southern Italy, the weather for the year could be divined from the statue of the Madonna processed on Easter Sunday. This statue was covered in a black gauze, which was 'whipped away' at the stroke of noon as the statue was placed on the altar of the Risen Christ. If the veil came off easily, this meant that there would be fine weather to come; if it stuck, this meant that there would be 'much rain and hail'.[61] We have seen, too, that weather sayings were often connected with saints' days.

The same kinds of action were taken against drought as against storms: prayers vows, processions, sometimes of relics or statues. At Valdelaguna (Madrid),

> St Toribio was vowed for water. And in the deposition that was taken on the day of the vow [it says that] there was a great drought, and lots were thrown among the saints, and it fell to this blessed saint, and immediately they vowed to keep his feast and build him a chapel.

A painted ex-voto at the Marian shrine of Oropa in the Italian Alps was presented by the inhabitants of villages in the region following a vow and a procession during a drought in 1685 (see Plate 29). As in the case of storms, there might be an escalation of ritual action from prayers to processions, from pilgrimages to local chapels to ones to more important regional shrines. In the Périgord, as a last resort, villagers went to the chapel of Bedeau, dedicated to the Virgin Mary. The name was a corruption of Vedeau or *Voeu d'eau* (water vow). In the southern Pyrenees, according to a text of 1872, 'Uston used to be famous for the chapel of the Holy Fountain, which legend associated with St Lizier, former bishop of Couserans. In years of drought, people came on pilgrimage from the whole district and even from Catalonia to implore the saint for an end to the affliction'. The same pattern is found in Spain. The penitents carrying a statue of the Virgin Mary, who, Don Quixote thought, were abducting a lady, were villagers visiting a hermitage in the hills: 'The people had wanted rain for a whole year together, wherefore they appointed rogations, processions and disciplines throughout all that country to implore Heaven to open its treasury, and shower down plenty upon them'.[62]

One of the most celebrated rain-making saints was the Madonna of Impruneta near Florence. From the fourteenth to the seventeenth centuries, Florentines turned to her after petition to God and other processions had failed. The city government would decide by vote to call on her aid, and, on a determined day, the clergy and confraternity of the suburban town would take the painted panel in solemn progress from Impruneta to Florence, joined by growing crowds. The Madonna would be met by clergy and officials from the city and her image would be exposed on a special platform by the church of San Felice and beseeched for rain. If this failed to produce results or in the event of some other grave threat or disaster, the Madonna might be taken further into the city and exposed in the main square. In the drought of 1354, the image was taken to the Baptistery and to San Miniato on the edge of the city, and on the day after the procession it became cloudy and on the third and fourth days began to rain. Although rain-making was her primary function, the Madonna was also invoked in other crises and was regarded as a general protector of Florence (see Text Figure 6).[63]

Two further procedures are significant. Sometimes saints might be threatened or punished for not producing the rain that people desired. 'If drought desolates their fields, and no attention is paid to their prayers', Ramage wrote of the peasants of Calabria in 1828,' they proceed to put the statues of their most revered saints in prison, hoping that this humiliation may make their intercession more effective.' Similarly when St Michael did not grant the rain demanded of him at Caltanissetta (Sicily),

> he was covered in a worn-out gown and confined to the Capuchin church to do penance. He was only brought back to the Duomo once it started to rain. St Nicholas suffered a parallel fate at Corigliano-Salentino, when he refused to make rain. His usual red cope was replaced by a penitent's cowl, and a salted sardine was stuck in his mouth, so that he should have a taste of what drought was like.

The Madonna of Impruneta was decked with garlands of flowers in March if the Spring rains had been normal, but if there had been too much rain she was covered in rubbish. Over-reaction was punished elsewhere. In one village in the Abruzzi, 'the people prayed to St Gregorio for rain. It rained so hard

6. Procession, Madonna of Impruneta. Jacques Callot, etching. c. 1620.

that all the crops were destroyed, so the statue of the saint was thrown out of the church by the parishioners'.[64]

More commonly, the saint was dipped or immersed in water, either as a punishment again as some commentators suggest or more plausibly in a ritual of mimetic magic like those more direct ones that we have already met. At Graveson in Provence, for example, the statue of St Anthime was taken on his day (27 April) to a nearby shrine and back. If by the time of the return, it had not rained, the statue was plunged three times in a stream. In case there was too much rain, 'the inhabitants had another saint in reserve, St Aurelle, whose business it was to bring the wind and stop the rain.' At Catanzaro in Calabria, the statue of St Rocco was plunged in a well, until he made it rain. In parts of the Limousin, statues of the same saint were dipped in sacred springs or had water from the springs sprinkled or poured over them. 'When there was a prolonged drought around Perpignan, the inhabitants used to ask the abbot of Saint-Martin-du-Canigou for the relics of St Galderic'. The reliquary bust containing these was taken in procession to the edge of the River Tet and plunged in the water. St Galderic's credit having fallen after several fruitless processions of this kind, the consuls decided in 1612 to use the relics of two other saints, which were also ceremonially dipped in the river. By the nineteenth century, a wooden statue of St Agricola, life-size and gilded, had been substituted for the relics and other sanctions added to the dousing. During a drought in 1818, the saint was processed on a kind of palanquin, preceded by a long file of Black Penitents in their cowls, each carrying a candle. The procession approached the river and the bearers threw the statue into it. 'There then arose a chorus of reproaches and insults of all kinds. The statue was also threatened with being burned if it did not quickly send them water. Once the statue had been recovered, the procession returned to Perpignan in an orderly fashion.'[65] Elsewhere, as at Lumbier in Spanish Navarre, the saint was merely threatened with immersion. Statues of rain-making saints were also immersed or aspersed on their regular festivals, together with the participants.

Why certain saints were selected as rain-makers, for example St Madrona in the Barcelona region or St Tillon in Flanders and the Auvergne, often remains unclear, though the lotteries reported in Spain may have been quite widely practised. Sometimes again the saint's legend was relevant. St Vincent performed climatic miracles in his lifetime. The Virgin Mary was the most common rain-maker, a reflection both of her growing vogue as a general protector and of her association with the fertility of the earth, most obvious in the case of the black Madonnas of the Mediterranean region. In a more particular example, the normal function of the Holy Milk of Evron: to provide milk for nursing women, was extended in periods of drought to providing liquid from the sky.

The Virgin and the saints also helped in other climatic circumstances. An ex-voto picture at Oropa indicates that the Virgin saved the village of Issime from catastrophic floods in 1755 (see Plate 30). In another mountainous region, the County of Foix, Notre-Dame-de-Val-d'Amour, the object of a cult predating the seventeenth century, was credited with saving the village of Belesta from being destroyed by floods in 1890. Again,

> in 1784, during a flood, the inhabitants of Blagnac near Toulouse made their priest lead a procession to the banks of the Garonne, and throw into the river an image of their patron St Exupéry, saying in a loud voice: There you are. Drown yourself, poor fellow.[66]

In other areas, frost was more of a problem. 'In the flowering season (of the olives in Provence) the slightest sharpness in the air sends half the rural population bare-foot upon a pilgrimage to the nearest St Briggitte or St Rossoline.' St Servais, whose *pardon* on 12 May attracted pilgrims from the Vannes region of Brittany and beyond, was supposed to have promised that singing his litanies would always keep off frosts that threatened their crops, and it was the custom at the *pardon* 'to shout and agitate the air with sticks as if to avert and break up the freezing air'.[67] Sanctions might also be taken against saints who failed to fulfil their office of preventing frosts. According to a sixteenth-century source, the people of Villeneuve-Saint-Georges threw a statue of their patron into the Seine after he had allowed a frost to spoil their vines.

4

Livestock

European peasants relied on their domestic animals for food, clothing, manure, draught power, transport and even warmth in the Winter, and the animals' good health and fertility were thus essential to their economy. Peasants lived in very close association with their livestock. Animals were often conveniently housed under the same roof as humans, with the byre either being a continuation of the house on the same level, as in Ireland, Wales or Brittany, or forming a floor beneath it, as in Provence. In many ways, animals were regarded and treated as members of the household. Ford noted that in rural Spain in the 1840s, 'pigs are the pets of the peasants; they are brought up with their children'. In Savoy, cows were given the same pick-me-up after giving birth as women. Animals were present at wedding feasts and wakes in the barns; they were talked to; and they were often specifically informed when people died. Among the Basques, 'the cattle will not be tranquil until they have been told of their master's death'; while in Languedoc, 'the bees must be told immediately when there is a death in the house' and their hives covered with crêpe to stop them leaving. There was a complex vocabulary to describe each category and sub-category of animal by age, sex and appearance, and another to cajole or command each one. In Sicily, for example, a cat was called with 'Muci! Muci!'; a horse or a mule with 'Ve! Ve!'; chicks with 'Pi! Pi!'; a cat was driven off with 'Chissi! Chissi!'; a horse or a mule with 'Acca!'; and poultry with 'Sciù! Sciù!'[1] Usually each beast also had its own individual name, which was sometimes related to its type.

Attitudes towards animals could not be sentimental. The family pet would ultimately be sold or killed to eat. Slaughtering was far from humane and took place in a festive atmosphere. As Flora Thompson, who was born in the Cotswolds in 1876, noted, the annual pig-killing was 'a noisy, bloody business ... country people of that day had little sympathy for the suffering of animals, and men, women, and children would gather round to see the sight'. We have seen, too, that blood sports and animal sacrifice could be features of calendar customs. Nevertheless, real attachment to animals did develop. When Sancho Panza's ass was stolen, he laments the loss with a typical mixture of emotion and realism: 'O dear child of my bowels, born and bred under my roof, my children's play-fellow, the comfort of my wife, the envy of my neighbours, the

ease of my burdens, the staff of my life, and, in a word, half my maintenance!';
and when the animal is recovered, he welcomed him as 'my darling and treasure ... and my dearest companion' and 'stroked and slabbered him with
kisses, as if the beast had been a rational creature'. As a young man before he
became a Franciscan in 1635, St Charles of Sezze wrote that:

> I had some oxen that I used in my work. My affection for them was very great,
> because to me they were wonderful and gentle. One of them was a young one
> which I had trained to the plough. In every way I liked him more than all the others
> and, as we say, he could do everything but talk. Sometimes it happened at night
> that he became separated from the others. All I had to do was to call his name and,
> as soon as he heard me, he would come running to me, lowing.

From a later period, Hélias recalls the close relationship that existed between
his Breton grandfather and his cow, 'that swarthy old dear, that silken girl,
which won first prize at the county agricultural fair'. In the Pyrenees, 'every
shepherd loves his animals; he knows them all, often caressing them, and is
particularly fond of some of them. The lambs especially live close to him,
rarely go far from him, run when he calls, and show that they appreciate his
marks of tenderness, eating from his hand'.[2]

Animals of course were much more prone to disease in the past than now,
and livestock were protected with perhaps even more concern but in the same
kinds of ways as the crops.

The calendar rituals often involved animals. After midnight mass on
Christmas Eve in the Franche-Comté, the peasants visited their livestock.
'They take them pieces of bread seasoned with salt. This is for the animals'
festive supper, and brings them good luck and good health during the coming
year.' In some places there was competition on New Year's morning to have
one's animals be the first ones to drink from the village water fountain, for the
first water of the year, known as the 'flower' or the 'cream' ensured that 'they
would prosper and fatten'. At places in the Yonne, hay was blessed on the day
after Candlemas and given to the livestock to eat. In the Limousin, the livestock
were sprinkled with Carnival broth. The cattle and sheep were 'sained' in the
Highlands and Islands of Scotland at Shrovetide, Beltane or Lammas. 'In parts
of Ireland the pig was driven into the house for luck on May morning'.[3] In
many parts of Europe, the animals were driven through the ashes and/or the
smoke of the St John's Eve and other bonfires to keep them well and make
them fat. In some places, animals were ritually washed or dipped at the same
times. Again, the material made sacred on all these occasions was used to give
protection to the livestock. 'Palms' and crosses were placed in byres, stables
and poultry-houses and on bee-hives, and they were sprinkled with holy water.

Some calendar customs were focused more exclusively on the livestock. In some parts of Europe, blood was taken from cattle as food by poorer people. In Wales, this was done on St Stephen's Day; in the Highlands of Scotland in mid-April on the so-called 'Borrowing Days'. In Scotland, the blood was mixed with oatmeal and made into cakes that were eaten by the family, like other first fruits. We have mentioned pig-killing, which was a more important and widespread festive occasion, occurring before Christmas or early in the New Year. In Gascony the victim was called 'sacred out of respect'; and special ritual precautions surrounded the preparation and preservation of the pig products there and elsewhere. Both suggest the need to placate the familiar animal and excuse its death.[4]

Other occasions had to do with pasturing. In Spring in Poland before 1914,

> when the cattle were let out to pasture for the first time, the women would place on the door-sill of the stable a hatchet, a broom, a palm from Palm Sunday, some green branches for the week of Corpus Christi and for Our Lady of the Ascension. The cows walked over these, and they would remain until the animals came back again.[5]

In the Alps, the Pyrenees and other upland districts the journey of the animals up to the Summer pastures was a festive occasion, on which they were groomed and specially decked out. In some places, the clergy went up into the mountains in July to bless the flocks and herds and the shielings, and they were given cheeses in return. Sheep-shearing was also a ritual occasion.

Animals might be blessed by the priest at the calendar festivals, or a special day might be set aside during the year for this purpose. In Sicily the general blessing of livestock took place on Ascension Day. Sheep, oxen, cows, goats, mules and asses were taken to chapels and churches situated near the sea-shore, where the priest blessed them and they were sprinkled with holy water. They were then led into the sea 'to cleanse and heal them of real or imagined ills, and to preserve them from all harm that could possibly occur to them during the coming year'. The animals were festively decked for the occasion with ribbons, papers and bells, and, where appropriate, wore their best harnesses and had their manes and tails braided. In the valley of the Tet in the Pyrenees on a similar occasion, the mules were blessed and then 'ridden furiously' round the village square to particular tune. If they were not blessed, it was believed that they would get weak and be unable to work.[6]

Animals were also taken to regional shrines to be blessed. At Montclard in the Auvergne, the pilgrimage was on Trinity Sunday. After early morning mass, salt, seed and bread were blessed 'to keep the animals from all harm during the coming year', the blessing being done with a cow's tail rather than the usual water-sprinkler. At the Basque pilgrimage church of Urquiola, cattle-bells were blessed by the priests and were 'thought to be a protection against the evil eye'.[7]

Many of the old liturgies had services offering protection to animals, especially during epidemics. A prayer from the Roman Ritual for Assumption Day (15 August), for example, asked God to 'pour on our pastures the abundance of your graces. Grant that they may be remedy for men, for the flocks and herds and for beasts of burden ... against diseases, plagues, scourges, evil spells, incantations, poisonous snakes and the bites of other wild beasts'.[8]

But most religious rituals to protect livestock were associated with the saints. Most simply prayers were said invoking the saint's protection, usually at some significant point in the year, as we have already seen. In the Outer Hebrides, St Columba was petitioned as the herds went out to pasture in the summer:

> May the herding of Columba
> Encompass your going and returning ...
> May it keep you from pit and mire,
> Keep you from hill and crag,
> Keep you from loch and downfall,
> Each evening ...
> May it keep you from the mean destroyer ...
> And from the untoward fairies.

In many regions, animals were never worked on their saint's day. In the Allier, if oxen were even taken outside on St Blaise's Day (3 February), they would be likely to suffer an accident. Usually such a day was a festival, however, in which the animals played their part. 'In the Basque country, on the day of St Blaise, one made a cross on the back of each animal with the blessed Candlemas candle; after having let several drops of hot wax fall along the spine, one burned three hairs on the tail of each head of cattle'.[9]

In addition to ritual carried out in the village on the saint's day, there were visits to shrines. 'Until the Reformation, an annual pilgrimage was made to Bawburgh (near Norwich) by farmers and herdsmen who sought a blessing on their stock' from St Walstan. At Llansaintffraid (Denbighshire), it was customary down to the latter half of the seventeenth century 'to make offerings to St Fraid to invoke a blessing on cattle and sheep'. Similar gifts were still being made at the shrine of St Beuno at Clynnog (Caernarvonshire) in the nineteenth century 'for the prosperity of the cattle'. The Breton *pardon* of St Cornély in September again offered protection to cattle:

Then decked with flowers, greenery and ears of corn,
The oxen with their heavy necks, the cows with their long udders
Arrive in their thousands, and the whole week
Their procession turns around the holy spring.

In Moscow in the 1890s, Pasternak remembered,

in the Autumn, horses were blessed in Yushkov Lane which ran between the
College [of Arts] and the church of St Florus and St Laurus, who were regarded as
patrons of horse-breeders; the horses and the grooms and coachmen who brought
them crowded the church precincts and the Lane as if it were a horse fair.[10]

Some saints had a general reputation in this sphere. St Anthony of Egypt or
St Anthony Abbot (sometimes confused with St Anthony of Padua) is probably the best-known, and he was invoked all over Europe. Boccaccio's Frate
Cipolla (Brother Onion), going round the villages of Tuscany to collect alms
for his order, tells people:

You know, Ladies and Gentlemen, that it is the custom amongst you to give every
year to the poor Friars of St Anthony, both wheat and oats, some a little, some a
lot, according to your means and your piety, so that the blessed St Anthony will
take care of your cattle, your asses, your pigs and your poultry.

Iris Origo indicated that the cult was still alive in the same region in the 1920s.
'On St Anthony's Day ... the farmers would bring an armful of hay to church
to be blessed by the saint, so that for the whole year their beasts might not lack
fodder.' Similarly in the Franche-Comté all the animal feed-stuffs were
blessed on St Anthony's Day (17 January). 'A vessel full of oats and other
grains and slices of bread spinkled with salt was taken to mass; and afterwards
this food was given to the livestock, which ensured that no animal would be ill
during the year to come.' Often a more elaborate ceremony was carried out.
At a small town in Lucania around 1960, the June festival of St Anthony
Abbot was still going strong. It was held at a chapel outside the town, used
only on that occasion. While mass was said inside the chapel,

herds of sheep mixed with goats are driven around and around through crowds of
donkeys and mules resplendent in plumes, harness and bells. Each animal must
make three full circuits around the building – no more, no less. And, to follow the
magic of numbers, each human being must bow nine times to the Cross.

A similar ritual took place in Rome on 17 January at the church of Sant'
Antonio Abate. 'The priest stands at the [church] door, and with a broom

dipped in holy water sprinkles the animals [horses, mules and donkeys], as they pass in procession before him, and gives them his benediction.' In Aragón, bonfires were lit at the January feast, brushwood being 'contributed by all those who have animals to guarantee their health'.[11]

Although St Anthony was commonly invoked to protect all kinds of animals, he was especially associated with pigs, the pig being one of his emblems. At Sennely-en-Sologne in the seventeenth century, there was an established devotion focused on an altar in the church, on which a statue of St Anthony was installed with his pig by his side. The bishop of Orléans decided that the pig 'was ridiculous and unworthy of such a great saint' and ordered the parish priest to remove the statue. But as the latter explained, 'it was impossible to carry out this order' in the face of popular resistance. Nor was the priest very happy about the episcopal instruction, despite his general opposition to 'superstitions', 'for no parishioner failed to make a gift to St Anthony or rather perhaps to his pig of some large piece of their own pigs, which turned to the profit of the church and of the priest, since they could be sold for 40 or 50 *livres*.' In late medieval Paris, St Anthony, after whom the Faubourg Saint-Antoine is named, was the patron of pig-slaughterers and of the *languyeurs*, who inspected pigs' tongues before they were killed. 'If you ask a Minho swineherd if those are his own pigs that he is minding', an observer related in 1961, 'he will most probably reply: Yes, after St Anthony, they're mine'. Again, in Spain in the nineteenth century, 'pigs which are dedicated to St Anthony, on whom a sow was in constant attendance ... get the soonest fat; therefore ... young porkers are sprinkled with holy water on his day' (see Plate 10).[12]

Other popular protectors of animals were St Roch and St John. It was on St Roch's Day (16 August) that the priests in the Forez went up into the mountains to bless the flocks, and the same date for blessing them was chosen in the lowland Yonne region. In the Morvan

until the beginning of the twentieth century, the oxen participated directly in the cult of St Roch; integrated into the religious procession, they went up with the men to the chapel. There they circumambulated the building in honour of the saint, and were then blessed collectively by the priest.

In a variant at Saint-Jouvent in the Limousin, women went with small packets of wool, in order to ensure the well-being of their sheep. They walked round a cross on the edge of the village, being sure to touch it with the wool, then went to the church, where they prayed in front of the statue of St Roch and deposited some of the wool by it. St John the Baptist, sometimes confused or conflated with the Evangelist, was the patron primarily of sheep.

Gifts of wool and lambs were taken to his shrines. Before the 1890s, five thousand people used to attend his festival at Sainte-Marie-de-Frugie in the Périgord and up to fifty lambs were offered. In Provence, St John was the patron of horses. 'The peasants made them go over the bonfire embers on St John's Day, as a guarantee of prosperity, and bathed them in pools and streams, following a double rite of fire and water.' Horses, mules and donkeys, all richly harnessed and garlanded, were also blessed at chapels and shrines on that day, after which races took place.[13]

St Eloi, whose feast on 25 June followed St John's, was also linked with horses in parts of Provence. In northern France, England, Spain and parts of Italy, he was the main patron of horses and other beasts of burden. According to a witness born in 1833, in Brittany 'all the horses through all the country far and near were brought to the church of St Eloi [at Loch-ar-Brugg] once a year to be blessed by the *curé*. This was called the Baptism of the Horses'. The animals were ranged in groups of four or six. They were then led around the church row after row seven times, while the priest stood at the west door of the church sprinkling them with holy water as they passed. He then moved to the font, the horses were led into the church, and he marked each of them on the forehead with a sign of the cross with water from the font. 'Finally the tail of each horse was carefully cut off, and all the tails were hung up in the church together, to be sold off'. The ceremony survived until after the First World War, but in its last phase the horses were no longer taken inside the church or baptized. At Paule, the ritual was similar. The horses were led three times round the chapel with a stop each time at the west porch. They were then taken to the nearby spring where water was poured over their foreheads, ears, withers and rumps. In north-eastern France and Normandy, more attention was paid to the legend that St Eloi was a blacksmith. At Arras, Abbeville and Douai before the Revolution, the horses were blessed by the priest with 'hammers of St Eloi', which were also used to cure animals.[14] In Normandy, churches and chapels dedicated to St Eloi were the recipients of ex-voto horseshoes.

Other elements of the rituals in addition to blessing, circumambulation and aspersion should be noted. At the *pardon* of St Herbot at Ploudalmezeau the animals were made to jump over a stream near the chapel, allegedly to make them vigorous and fertile. This recalls leaping over the St John's Eve bonfire. Cows' tails were often given to the saint, too, and hung up in the church like ex-votos. In some cases, as in Tuscany and the Franche-Comté, fodder was symbolically blessed. Elsewhere, water from the saint's fountain was sprinkled on the feed, or bread and salt, blessed on the saint's festival, were given to animals and poultry as a general preservative. In the Alps, people brought back a kind of *brioche* from the pilgrimage of St Guérin at Saint-Jean-d'Aulps and this was fed to the cows. In southern Spain, St Mark was the patron saint of bulls and all grazing animals, and they were blessed on his day. During the ceremonies

> small bracelet-shaped rolls known as *roscos* were distributed, one for each person and animal. They were the gift of a confraternity, whose members drew lots each year as to which of them was to provide the flour and make them. After being blessed by the priest they were hung on the horns of the cows and goats and over the ears of the donkeys ... Other *roscos* were handed round to friends and relatives, to whom they were believed to bring luck, and at the end of the day each of the animals was given a piece [to eat].

In Provence, a similar bread or cake called a *tortillade*, 'perfumed with anise and golden with eggs', was blessed by the priest at the festival of St Eloi, but its consumption seems to have been reserved to the human participants. In Corsica, a piece of the bread blessed at the chapel of St Roch or St Anthony was often put inside a hollow horn, which was attached to the neck of the bell-wether that led the flock.[15]

Many other amulets associated with saints were used. A seventeenth-century source describes how horses taken on pilgrimage to the abbey of St Eloi at Noyon were given scarves or collars made of feathers or beans threaded together. In many parts of France, from the fifteenth to the nineteenth centuries, lead images of St Anthony were placed round the necks of animals. At Orcet in the Puy-de-Dôme stones were collected from a particular quarry on St Roch's Day. 'When they had been blessed by the priest at mass, the stones were crushed and put into sachets that were attached to the cows' horns; each cow had one to protect it from accidents and harm.' In the district north of Cintra in Portugal, St Mamede was 'the local advocate of livestock'. At his August festival, peasants from all around brought their animals to the church at Janas and, after performing rituals of the kind already mentioned, they 'went into the church and bought waxen ex-votos in the form of cattle, which they offered up on the altar, and coloured favours with which they adorned their beasts'. In Ireland and elsewhere in the Celtic world, rushes were 'fashioned into protective charms known as Brigid's crosses' on the eve of the saint's day at the end of January. They took 'the form of either swastikas or lozenges, magic symbols of suns or eyes' and were placed at the doors of the houses and byres.[16]

Not all protective rituals and gestures were associated with the festival of the saint. In the Sologne in the mid nineteenth century cowherds baptized their new calves on the Good Friday following their birth and formally gave them names. Animals were not generally given saints' names, but in Sicily peasants did commonly refer to their animals by the generic name of the saint who was their special patron and protector: so a cat was a Martha, and ox a Luke and so on. In Corsica, from medieval times, people dedicated 'one or more of their beasts to the church or to a saint. So that these could be recognized, one of their horns was sawn off, and they were therefore called *mozzi* or *signati*'; they were used to provide for the clergy. Everywhere the images of protective saints were placed by livestock. In the Roman Campagna and beyond 'a little picture of St Anthony was hung up for luck in every stable': while in Rumania, paintings of St George and St John were put 'in stables and barns to protect the cattle and the gathered crops'.[17]

Despite clerical involvement, or some connection with the ecclesiastical calendar or a canonized saint, many of these protective rituals were in essence magical. Others were exclusively so. In the Highlands of Scotland, animals were sprinkled at Beltane in some places with water or urine into which charm stones had been dipped. 'The people of Strathspey made a hoop of rowan through which all the sheep and lambs were made to pass in the morning and again in the evening'. Elsewhere, tar was put on the tails and ears of cattle at Lammas, red or blue threads were placed on their tails and incantations said at their udders. Also 'in order that the cattle and milk might retain their virtue and substance, a ball of cow's hair, called a *ronag*, was put into the milk pail on Lammas Day and the following Thursday'. Other procedures in Scotland included rubbing earth taken from the first ploughing on the necks and shoulders of horses to save then from 'being injured by an evil eye or witchcraft' during the season; and burning juniper or old leather on New Year's Day to make the cattle cough, which would prevent disease. To stop cows being 'forespoken' in north-east Scotland, they were given to drink water taken from the well on the first day of each quarter that had been poured over a new shilling. On Lewis 'the first night the cattle were brought home and housed for the Winter, fire was carried round them three times sunways'. In the Niolo and the Upper Taravo valley in Corsica, the flocks were 'blessed' after shearing. Water was sprinkled over them and this formula recited:

> White sheep, black sheep,
> Who goes away in the morning and comes back at night,
> Go safely,
> Graze on the good grass and leave the bad plants alone!
> Grow and multiply!
> Fill the country that you pass![18]

The use of particular plants like rowan to give protection was common, Hellebore was hung on pig sties in the Gard to keep off predators. Sticks and crooks used by those guarding sheep or goats were usually of a particular kind of sacred wood, like hazel. In Berry, bundles of hazel twigs, stripped of bark and often decorated with bizarre carvings, were taken to church on White Friday, ten days before Easter, to be blessed by the priest. The sticks in each bundle were of unequal length and odd number and they were kept to protect the sheep from spells and illness.

Salt and iron were other preservatives, and amulets of different kinds were worn, especially in modern times in southern Europe. In central Greece, blue beads repelled the evil eye from cattle. In the Roman Campagna, oxen were 'adorned with scarlet ribbons or bands' as they worked; and on festivals further wreaths, tassels and flowers were added. At Aquila, Canziani noted in the 1920s, the carrier's horse at the station had 'red tassels, metal horns, and badger's hair hung on its harness to keep away the evil eye, and a large *biga* (rein holder) covered with tin and hung with bells [that] glittered in the sun'. In Portugal, 'a cow which had just given birth wore on its forehead a little bag of red cloth containing salt, rue, garlic and a splinter from a broom handle'. Like their mothers, young animals were particularly vulnerable. In the Limousin, anyone going into a building where they were had to wash his hands and say a blessing. John Clare noted that the shepherd took special care of his lambs:

> And round their necks in wary caution ties
> Long shreds of rags in red or purple dyes
> That's meant in danger as a safety spell.

Bells were very common. In nineteenth-century Spain, the leading animal in a mule team was 'furnished with a copper bell sometimes two feet long with a wooden clapper, to give notice of their march and scare away the Evil One'. In the Auvergne, little bells were placed on the ox-yoke 'to preserve the team from lightning'.[19] Nor should we forget the brasses and other ornaments worn by English work horses.

The progress of garlanded animals to sacred places is reminiscent of classical rites in which they were actually sacrificed. There is evidence that horses were killed at St George's Well in Denbighshire, and we shall meet with other examples when we consider rituals to cure sick animals. Carcases or parts of animals and birds were also placed in stables and elsewhere. In modern Ireland, an animal's leg or some other piece of the body might be kept in the roof 'to bring luck to the livestock'; while in modern Provence 'the main entrance to the stable' might be 'blazoned with a barn-owl or an osprey spread out and nailed in the form of a cross, which was called the devil-chaser'.[20]

A special set of rituals protected livestock from predators, mainly foxes and wolves. In the Puisaye

> it was customary to charm the fields around the farms, as they called it, the kind of charm depending on which carnivore was being targeted. For the fox, an omelette with a dozen eggs was prepared in four parts. After making the sign of the cross on each quarter, someone ran round the territory to be protected with the omelette throwing one part at each corner and shouting three times: Fox, here is your share; take it and don't come back! For the wolves, it was a young sheep that was cut up and distributed in the same way. Only one added the prayer: St Mary, king of the wolf, muzzle the wolf; St Agatha, tie up his paws: St Loup [wolf], twist his neck.

In a fifteenth-century text one lamb a year was offered to the wolves. Around Metz, the sacrifice was even more attenuated. 'The youngest boy in the house went up on to the roof at Mardi Gras, holding in his hand the shoulder-blade of a sheep. He shouted:

> O wolf,
> Here is a shoulder-blade for you.
> You will not have more before Easter,

and then threw the bone as far as he could into the street'. Similar rituals were performed in the Highlands and Islands of Scotland, in which special cakes were offered to the wolf, the fox, the eagle, the raven, the marten and the hen-harrier to induce them to spare sheep, lambs, goats, kids and poultry respectively.[21]

As the Puisaye example illustrates, as well as sacrifice the other element in the rituals aimed at excluding the predators with a barrier. This could be done with thread, by sprinkling salt, Carnival broth or some other substance, or by dragging a bone around the premises. These rituals were performed annually at Carnival, Easter, Assumption and All Saints. Abbé Thiers reported, for example, that 'people sprinkled a broth of chitterlings around the house on Shrove Tuesday or Thursday to stop the foxes from eating the chickens'. Charms were also used. In Thiers' example, the sprinkling was accompanied by a charm-prayer conjuring the fox 'not to remove any birds nor eat their nests, nor suck their blood, nor break their eggs' in the name of the Trinity and the Virgin Mary. At Chiaramonte in Sicily, a charm against foxes and wolves was said while tying a knot:

> May this bind the wolf's teeth,
> Over the way, under the way,
> So he may not touch my cattle.

If a shepherdess saw a wolf in the Limousin, she recited a Paternoster back-wards and said a prayer to St Lawrence. The power of experts was also used. In the Pyrenees before the nineteenth century, the clergy would go up to the Summer pastures expressly to bless the flocks and herds, if wolves and bears had been attacking them.[22] Communities had their own wolf-tamers, too, like the old grave-digger whom Carlo Levi met at Gagliano in the 1930s.

As some of these examples show, the saints might also be invoked against predators. In the Vosges, St Genevieve protected the flocks, dogs and herdsmen against wolves. In much of French-speaking France, recourse was had to St Blaise, as Ronsard testifies:

> If the wolf, thirsting for blood,
> Takes a sheep in his teeth
> When he comes slinking out of the wood,
> Raise the hue and cry after the beast:
> May he quickly be rescued,
> I beseech you, Blaise, listen to us.[23]

Sometimes, St Blaise's name was written on a piece of paper which was fixed on a stick like a flag and planted among the flocks in rough pasture. As in other instances, the choice of saint here could be associated with his or her legend. St Genevieve was a shepherdess, as prayers and charmes stressed. In parts of Brittany, butter was given to St Hervé, a blind saint who was guided by a wolf, so that wolves would not harm one. In France, of course, St Loup was an obvious defender against his homonym.

The same kinds of procedures were brought into play more specifically to ensure the fertility of livestock, and to cure them if they did become diseased. An eighteenth-century source relates that special care was taken at a shrine of ʾt Eloi near Saint-Brieuc to sprinkle water from the spring on the genitals of ʋoth stallions and mares. In the Western Isles, the Michaelmas *struan* meal was 'dusted over the flocks to bring them progeny and plenty'. Elsewhere, mares were taken over certain streams to make them fertile. In Sicily, a hen placed on a clutch of eggs at noon on 25 March, the supposed time of the Annunciation, was bound to become broody. More generally, great care was taken over the reproduction of livestock. Sitting hens would be marked with the sign of the cross; clutches should be of odd numbers of eggs; and broods should be started when the moon was waxing. There were similarly good and bad days for the coupling of animals. In parts of Brittany, the first three and last three days of May were unlucky. In the Limousin, sows would not conceive while a particular wind was blowing. Amulets and formulae were used during coupling too. Women taking cows or sows to be mated would often carry salt in their pockets or turn their apron pockets inside out. Salt might be put between the cow's horns or a particular plant in its mouth as it was with the bull to ensure conception. Similar rituals were employed during and after parturition. According to a Norfolk man in 1933, 'when cows calved, the after-birth had to be hung on a white thorn bush ... to prevent milk fever and other ills'.[24]

Official rituals existed, we have seen, to protect livestock against disease. The Périgueux Missal included services 'to bless the food of animals in time of contagion' and 'to bless and exorcize animals in time of pestilence'. Material associated with the calendar rituals might be used if animals fell sick: for example, some of the fodder blessed during the Rogations might be fed to them. Recourse was also had to the aura of the priest. According to a fifteenth-century French source, 'if a horse is lame in leg or foot, ride it to the priest's house and call him out; then, without speaking to him, return home and for certain the horse will be right as before without feeling any pain'. At Belin in the Gironde, the priest recalled in 1912, 'a poor woman with a sick piglet knelt in front of his cassock' as it hung in the vestry. Protestants might use the Bible. In a Welsh parish in 1863, a farmer 'having a cow sick on the Sabbath day, after giving her physic, [and] supposing she was dying, ran into the house to fetch the Bible, and read a chapter to her'.[25]

However, the most frequent response, individual and collective, to ailments in livestock was to call on the saints or on 'natural' magic. Vows were made to saints in the event of illness. In the West of Ireland, a sick cow was 'devoted' to St Martin. 'The ceremony was performed by letting a few drops of blood from the cow in honour of the saint.' Very often visits were paid to shrines, some of which specialized in the cure of livestock. 'There is no illness to which their animals are prone', wrote the priest of Sennely-en-Sologne of his parishioners,

> for which they do not make pilgrimages. To St John the Baptist for sheep because he is represented with a lamb; to St Paxent, whom they call St Paissant, when their beasts lose their appetite and will not graze (*paisser*); to St Yves, whom they call St Yvre [drunk], when their sheep stagger about; to St Firmin, whom they call St Frémin, when their animals tremble and shake (*frémir*).

Medieval miracle books recorded many cures of animals, for example at Norman shrines of the eleventh and twelfth centuries or at the tomb of St Louis of Anjou at Marseille around 1300. At Cazenave near Tarascon in 1637 there 'was a procession to combat an epidemic of epizootic disease' on the feast of the patron saint of the church, St James the Great. Similarly, the parish records of a village in the Limousin relate that 'on 16 August 1738 [the feast of St Roch], the parish went in procession to the collegiate church of Le Dorat for the relief of the livestock, of which great numbers were dying'. More recently, St Diboan at Plévin 'cured animals and humans. As soon as a cow was in pain, one ran quickly to him. If the beast was no better when one got back, it was time to slaughter it'.[26]

Sometimes the animals were touched with an object associated with the saint: the hammer of St Eloi at Arras, the key of St Martin at Tours. 'When disease breaks out among the animals [in that part of Corsica]', Vuillier wrote in 1891, 'the shepherds hurry to Zicavo to obtain the key to the oratory of St Roch, which they throw the in the midst of the flock', and the epidemic was supposed to cease instantly. Ex-votos at shrines and chapels testify to the same belief and practice. In Hungary and Germany, ex-voto figures of cattle and pigs in metal-work were offered to saints. (see Plate 6) Relics might also be used in curing rituals, like that offered by Chaucer's Pardoner:

> Then, framed in metal, I have a shoulder-bone
> That belonged to a holy Jew's sheep.
> When this bone is dipped in any well,
> If cow, or calf, or sheep, or ox should swell
> From eating a worm or being stung by a snake,
> Take water from that well and wash his tongue,
> And it will be better; and furthermore,
> Of pox and scab and every sore
> Shall every sheep be cured that of this well
> Shall drink a draught.[27]

Other modes of cure included feeding sick animals with feed-stuff, cakes or bread made and/or blessed on the saint's day, for example the biscuits of St Anthony baked at Civitella dei Pazzi in Umbria; or washing or watering them in pools or springs associated with a saint, like the pool at Assevilliers in the Somme named after St Martin. Prayer-charms referring to saints' legends were also recited. Once again the power of particular saints in this area was linked to the sound of their names, as we have seen, and also to their legends and miracles. St Martin, for example, was said to have watered his horse at Assevilliers, while his Life records that in his lifetime he stopped a frenzied cow that had gored several people, exorcized the demon that was tormenting her and restored her placidly to her herd.[28]

We turn now to non-ecclesiastical magic. As a young man around 1885, the historian Coulton noted that 'peasants still brought sometimes their sick cattle' to a haunted pool near Llandovery, 'and left bread and cheese on a sacred stone in acknowledgement of the healing they expected form the spirit of the waters'. This was a survival of practices associated with sacred lakes and springs that had usually by this date been Christianized. From earliest medieval times, too, magical formulae had been said over sick or lame beasts to cure them. Burchard of Worms in the eleventh century condemned more elaborate 'enchantments' used by

> swineherds, ploughmen and sometimes hunters ... ; they say diabolical formulae over bread or grass and over certain nefarious bandages, and either hide these in a tree or throw them where two or three roads meet, in order that they may set free their animals or dogs from pestilence or destruction and destroy those of another.

Here the illness was transferred to an animal or animals that found the discarded objects. In other cures something relating more directly to the sick animal was used in a similar way. In a cure for red murrain in the Scottish islands, a wise woman threw urine from the affected animals into running water, while shouting a charm through her hands formed like a trumpet. In a Suffolk cure for a cow that was 'tail-shotten' or had 'gargot' or red water, its urine was boiled with nine nails from nine horseshoes. For a cow with a swollen hoof in Radnorshire, the hoof was imprinted on grass and the sod cut out and placed on a white thorn bush. As the sod dried, the swelling was supposed to disappear. The learned sixteenth-century magician Paracelsus advised the following procedure against sheep diseases: 'Having taken earth and sand from the nearest stream at which the sheep drink, and that at the time of the waning moon, with this same earth and mud you must paint on the folds this incantation.' The formula included Latin and Greek words and a form of the swastika, which was actually painted on Basque sheepfolds in modern times.[29] Recourse might also be had to specialist animals healers.

Two magical procedures deserve special comment. One is the custom of burying the corpse of an animal that died of a disease or part of it in the stable or cowshed to stop the others from catching the complaint; sometimes part of the animal was simply hung up. At Lochbroom (Ross and Cromarty), for example, Margaret Dow was 'summoned for sorcery in 1650 for burying a lamb under the threshold'; she 'acknowledged the fact alleged, affirming that she did it only in simplicity by the information of a poor woman that came to her house, as a preventative against the death of the rest of her beasts'. In North Yorkshire and elsewhere in England down to the nineteenth century, if a calf was aborted, it was buried on its back 'at the threshold of the cow-house' to prevent a recurrence of the event.[30] Similar customs are reported on the Continent.

The other procedure was the actual killing of an animal as a kind of sacrifice. In a case during a livestock epidemic in the Brie in the eighteenth century, a beast was killed and hung upside-down by the feet over the threshold of the byre while formulae were said. Burning animals alive in such circumstances seems to have been not uncommon in early modern Britain. A Welsh text from the 1590s relates that a farmer, whose animals had been attacked by a plague, 'bound a live horse to a post, surrounded it with tinder, and set fire to it until it burned to ashes'. Sir Roger Wilbraham was told at Huntingdon in 1604 of a local farmer who had lost a large number of animals in a few days which had gone 'suddenly sick, crying, grinning and staring'. He 'was advised to burn a sick horse alive and so did, and after had no more die'. At about the same time, John Townsend and his wife were presented before the Essex and Hertfordshire Consistory Court 'for burning a hog for witchery upon the Sabbath day on Bedford Heath' to preserve the rest of the cattle. From Scotland, 'instances are attested of a cow being rubbed over with tar, and driven forth from the stricken herd. The tar is set on fire, and the poor animal is allowed to run till death puts an end to its sufferings'.[31]

Animals were also buried alive. Isobel Young from Dunbar was accused in 1629 of burying a live ox and a cat with salt 'as a sacrifice to the Devil' so that the rest of her 'animals should be freed of sickness and disease'. In a better documented case, the villagers of Beutelsbach in Württemberg, faced with an outbreak of foot-and-mouth disease in 1796, sacrificed their communal bull to the dismay of the 'enlightened' authorities. The animal was killed after it had mounted a cow and, for the ritual to be effective, it had to be stifled to death with no blood shed in a pit at a crossroads.[32]

Magic was also used to control animals. In a modern case, an 'old witch called Priss Morris who lived at Cleobury North (Shropshire) had a grudge against a farmer for having prevented her from gleaning in his fields'; when the farmer's 'waggoner was driving some time later past her cottage, the horses stopped dead' and would not move. Only when the farmer made the 'witch' lift her spell by saying: 'May God bless you and your horses!' could they proceed. This power to 'freeze' animals is attested in many early modern witch trials and in many saints' Lives and miracle books from much earlier. After a group of soldiers had attacked and whipped St Martin, not realizing who he was, the mules drawing their vehicle became 'fixed to the spot like statues' and no amount of beating would shift them. Only once the soldiers had begged the saint for pardon did he restore their movement to them. In Ancient Rome, 'freezing' was apparently used to affect the outcome of chariot races. Magicians designed lead tablets on which the names of horses and their stables were accompanied by special signs and prayers. One such implored a demon to 'hold back certain horses, and get their reins caught up so that they cannot move'. According to Gervase of Tilbury in the twelfth century, similar tactics were employed against opponents in medieval tournaments. More general power to control and tame animals, domestic and wild, was attributed of course to saints like St Martin and St Francis, and others shared this wider power. Bandits in nineteenth-century Corsica were said to have recourse to those with the ability to enchant dogs and stop them from barking, so that they could carry out their raids more easily. More mundanely, this charm was recited to oxen in Germany to keep them docile: 'Oxen, bear the yoke and be patient, as Christ was patient'.[33]

Like other kinds of magic, the control and particularly the 'freezing' of animals could be carried out by the use of such formulae and spells, by innate powers, or by using paraphernalia, and it was performed both by specialists and by regular keepers of animals. In northern Spain, certain people were thought 'to have the ability to immobilize animals ... with their gaze'; in Hungary 'some herdsmen were believed to have magic power in their staffs: by raising them or striking them in the ground, they could make their flocks stop in their tracks'. Such staffs were elaborately carved or decorated with special signs and motifs. In East Anglia, the practice of controlling horses was known as 'jading', and horsemen who had the power were sometimes known as 'horse witches' and sometimes as 'toadmen'. A few 'witches' relied on 'whispering' or breathing into the horse's nostrils, but most used a magical object in conjunction with some malodorous substance like stale urine. The commonest object was a 'frog's' or 'toad's bone'; hence the name 'toadman'. In an example from Norway in the 1920s, a gypsy girl rendered the horses on a farm immobile by sticking rowan twigs into the harness pins.[34]

Similar powers could be used to 'draw' animals, as we have seen in connection with attracting pests to a particular place. Some people could make wolves follow them, others rats, like the Pied Piper of Hamelin. With horses again, 'drawing oils' were used, often together with the 'milt' of a colt. This is a small lump of fibrous matter which forms behind the colt's tongue in the womb. Particular importance attached to preventing bees from leaving their hives. In France, conjuring formulae were used when they began to swarm: for example, 'Bees, that God has created to light the churches, I conjure you by the Holy Spirit to stop'; or 'Bees, stop, the wax is the Virgin's, the honey is mine'. If such words were ineffective, then pots and pans and metal tools were hit with sticks to make a din.[35]

Many of the rituals to protect livestock were specifically directed against witches, as were the sacred objects and substances placed in byres or given to animals to eat. Sir Walter Scott recounted that when a building at Dalkeith 'formerly used as a feeding-house for cattle' was demolished, 'there was found below the threshold-stone the withered heart of some animal full of many scores of pins – a counter-charm, according to tradition against the operations of witchcraft on the cattle which are kept within'. The *Malleus Maleficarum* again has a chapter on 'how witches injure cattle in various ways'. The claims of its authors and of other demonologists who followed them here closely reflect popular views. In the classic case against Janet Macmurdoch of Airds in 1671, we learn that, after Robert Brown had chased her animals off his pasture, she had scolded him and told him 'she hoped he should not have so many cattle as he had then to eat the next grass'. Before the following Beltane, twelve of his oxen and eight of his horses died, and he laid the blame on her. She was also accused of causing the death of nine lambs belonging to another person.[36] Similar accusations blaming witches for infertility, illness and death in livestock figure in the early modern witchcraft trials all over Europe, and they continued to be made long after the trials were over.

A variety of modes of bewitching were employed, some of which we have already encountered. Burying a dead animal in or near a stable or cowshed could cause as well as prevent disease. More common was uttering a formula or curse or simply looking at animals or touching them. As Ronsard wrote of the witch:

> You are the terror of the village.
> Everyone fearing your magic
> Closes their house to you,
> Trembling lest you touch
> Their oxen, sheep and cows
> With the juice of your poison.
> I have often seen your sinister eye
> Staring three times at the leader of the flock
> As he grazes far off,
> And thus bewitching him,
> So that afterwards I have seen him dead
> With worms on his fleece.[37]

In a case in the Cambrésis in 1611, a woman was said to have 'caused the death of cow whose owner refused her milk'. According to the *Malleus Maleficarum*, women also used milk and milk products from a neighbour's cow to bewitch that cow. The *Malleus*, like later demonological treatises, also pointed to the frequent practice of drying up cows' milk by witchcraft and of syphoning it off for one's own benefit. Guazzo referred in 1608 to a recent case at Trier in which 'a very famous witch had inserted a hollow pipe into the wall of her house through which she charmed all the milk of her neighbours' cows'. Once again the demonologists reflected a widespread and long-standing popular obsession. Milk-stealing by magical means was referred to in a ninth-century capitulary of Louis the Pious. A twelfth-century bishop of Exeter prescribed a three-year penance for anyone 'who strives to take away another's supply of milk ... by incantation, or tries by magic to gain it for himself'. The practice is depicted in fifteenth-century Danish wall-paintings. The accusation, moreover, is common in witchcraft trials all over Europe from the later Middle Ages onwards, and it persisted into modern times. According to Goodrich-Freer writing in 1899, 'of all forms of evil influence none is more dreaded [in the Outer Hebrides] than *torradh*, or the charming away of milk from cattle'. 'Most of all in those [pre-1914] days did people believe in the witches who stole the milk from the cows, or spoiled it', a Polish village mayor wrote similarly. In many parts of Germany, north and south, peasants believed in 'a specialized milk witch, *Milchhexe*, who stole milk by magical means or caused cows to milk blood'; while present-day Normandy a specific term: '*baratter les vaches* (churning the cows)', is used to describe the theft of milk by sorcery. Although cows were primarily involved, witches were also believed to interfere with the lactation of mares, ewes, she-asses and nanny-goats. Sometimes, too, fairies or spirits were blamed for the loss or spoiling of milk rather than witches. In northern Greece, the milk of sheep and goats could be sucked out at night by a spirit called Stringlos or by vampires.[38]

Various means were supposedly used to dry up or steal milk. Some were fantastic, like the idea that witches employed animals to suck cows' udders or transformed themselves into animals to do so. But most belonged to the repertoire of rituals that were actually performed, which suggests that they did take place. Sticking a knife, an axe, a stake or some other sharp instrument in the wall of one's house or in a post was mentioned, sometimes in conjuction with sitting down with a pail between one's legs and simulating the act of milking. Elspeth M'Ewen was charged before the Kirk Session at Kirkcudbright in 1698 with 'having a pin in her kipple-foot [the end of the rafters of her house], by means of which she could draw milk from the cows of her neighbours'. These instruments seem to have worked on the same lines as the more obvious pipe used by Guazzo's witch from Trier. In the Hebrides, the milk was charmed down the chimney via the chain that held the cooking pot over the fire. Seaweed or other plants might also be hung in the chimney, spells uttered, or products of the cow used, such as milk or hair. Walking round the cow a certain number of times in a particular way was another method, and also manipulating the tethering-rope. 'We plait the rope the wrong way in the Devil's name', a woman declared at her trial in Aberdeen in 1662, 'and we draw the tether between the cow's hind feet and out between her forward feet ... , and thereby take with us the cow's milk.' In the Auvergne in the modern period, a particular herb 'was put in a vessel full of milk and this was covered with the skin of a white cow; all the beasts around would then lose their milk'.[39]

Many rituals involved dew gathered on 1 May or sometimes St John's Eve. In the Charente, 'it was sufficient to go on the morning of May Day before dawn into the meadow of the person whom you wanted to bewitch and to collect the dew, and then all the milk of their cows passed into yours'. In the Limousin, a woman dragged rags through the grass to soak up the dew, muttering the formula:

> Drag, drag, my rags,
> All my neighbour's milk;
> Jump, jump into my pail!

She then washed her cows' udders with the dew. In parts of western France, women were said to go naked to collect the dew, putting it into a churn or dragging a milk filter behind them. In the Nivernais, the dew was mixed with some of the milk of the neighbour's cows and then given to one's own to drink. Very similar rituals are reported from Scotland. There was also the ceremony of 'creaming the well' performed at midnight of Hogmanay or on the day of the Invention of the Cross (3 May).

> Such as were envious of their neighbours' success, and wished to draw away their prosperity, creamed the well they drew water from. This act was believed to be particularly efficacious in ensuring a rich supply of milk and butter to the one who had cows, and performed the act on the well of those who also owned cows.

The first water from the well was used to wash all one's dairy utensils and give to one's cows to drink, and this effectively transferred luck in the dairy from one's neighbour.[40]

The importance of the belief in milk-stealing is further reflected in the precautions that peasants took against it. In the Highlands of Scotland, a sprig of rowan 'was coiled into a circlet and placed beneath the milk-boyne to prevent the milk from being spirited away'. Ivy and bramble might also be used, and red thread twisted round cows' tails. These amulets were often put in place at Beltane, when incantations were also said at cows' udders, and other rituals performed. In Argyll water from a running brook was put in cog with a piece of silver and the four paws of a cat dipped in it, and the water then sprinkled on a calf or cow to make the milk come back. Similar measures were taken in Brittany, where elder was the preferred preservative. A charm collected on the Faeroes in the mid nineteenth century invoked the Virgin Mary [who] herself milked cows. She heeds the dairymaid and chases away all evil from my animal. I make the sign of the cross on your back, and no envious woman will have power over you. I pour the last drop of milk through the collar that ties you. May witchcraft and demons come to naught![41]

Protection was also obtained by using the same means that were believed to effect the stealing itself. Abbé Thiers referred to rubbing cows' udders with dew collected on May Day, and a fifteenth-century French source recommends feeding the animals with St John's herbs.

There is a significant overlap between procedures specifically aimed against milk-stealing and those simply wishing for a good supply of milk, for the one might be thought to depend on the other. In the latter category are prayers, incantations, calendar-related rituals and libations. The minister of Calder told Boswell and Johnson in 1773 that a woman in the Highlands might commonly pray 'when she milks her cow'. 'Cushy cow, bonny, let down thy milk', ran a nursery rhyme published in 1805,

> And I will give thee a gown of silk;
> A gown of silk and a silver tee [cow-tie],
> If thou wilt let down thy milk to me.

This was a version of a charm that can be traced back to the early seventeenth century. Much more elaborate charms were recited during milking in the Western Isles down to modern times. One for example invoked the Apostles and other saints, Christ and the Virgin Mary; conjured milk into the udders of all animals from badgers and reindeer to the domestic sows, mares, goats, ewes and cows; and called for livestock

> With milk, with cream, with substance,
> With rutting, with begetting, with fruitfulness,
> With female calves excelling,
> With progeny, with joyance, with blessing ...
> Without man of evil wish,
> Without woman of evil eye,
> Without malice, without envy,
> Without any evil.

In both Germany and Ireland, there was a connection between the May bough or pole and the supply of cows' milk and 'a green bough might be fastened on May Day against the house' to produce plenty of milk. In Scotland again, ritual libations of milk were either to placate the fairies or to increase the flow of milk by mimesis. In Ireland, more particularly, 'the first rich milk given by a newly-calved cow should be milked on to a piece of metal placed in the pail. Offerings of the "beastlings" were poured in the raths and at the roots of fairy thorns, to appease the fairies'.[42]

Witchcraft could also be exercised against milk products. It was common all over Europe for witches to be accused of preventing butter 'coming' in the churn. In France, striking the churn three times with a stick and saying Psalm 31 was one way of doing this, and other procedures are mentioned. Once again there were appropriate precautionary measures. The churn and the paddle had to be properly made of the right kinds of wood. In Ireland, one of the hoops of the churn had to be of rowan, while in Brittany the paddle was made of broom or gorse to prevent witches affecting the butter-making. Prayers or incantations were recited during the churning, and objects or plants put in the milk. In Lancashire, Scotland and elsewhere, an iron plough coulter or horseshoe might be heated to red-heat during the churning. In Ireland, a horseshoe might be tied to the churn or nailed to its bottom; a nail from a horseshoe or a coffin be driven into the churn or the paddle; or a ring of salt be placed on the lid. Sometimes, milk from a particular cow would not turn to butter because an evilly-disposed person had looked or 'blinked' at it. 'The cow could be cured by burning under its nose a portion of the blinker's clothes and a handful of thatch taken from above the door of his house.'[43]

These fears and concerns reflected the crucial importance of cows and other milk-producing animals in the domestic economy, especially in northern and upland Europe. The 'white meats', *lacticinia* or *Butterbrief* (the collective name given to milk, milk products and eggs) were 'the food of the poor. The peasant's cow was his "commonwealth", providing him and his family with butter, cheese, whey, curds, cream, sod (boiled) milk, raw milk, sour milk, sweet-milk, and butter-milk'. White meats might also be marketed to obtain the money to pay taxes, and they were not only marketed for food. Goubert notes that 'the bleaching-houses [of seventeenth-century Beauvais] used great quantities of milk'. Cattle, of course, were of poor stock, ill-fed and often sickly, and their lactation was seasonal and erratic. 'My own experience as a farmer', the Polish mayor concluded,

> taught me why in the old days there was no milk, so that folk said the witches came and took it. As long as people tended their cows in the primitive way, the brutes could barely exist, and milk was so scarce that sometimes even four of them scarcely gave enough milk 'to make a mess of soup' – as the saying is.[44]

Poor low-fat milk was also difficult to make into butter; while bloody or discoloured milk, another misfortune blamed on witches, was a sign of mastitis or some other complaint.

Cows and other animals additionally stood for or represented their owners. Thus, as Lisón-Tolosana comments for modern Spanish Galicia, 'any abnormal condition afflicting a cow reveals the force of a neighbour's envy', and neighbours might be expected to attack a family or a household by causing its cow or cows to go berserk, stampede, miscarry, give no milk and so on. The milk itself also bore great symbolic value. It had magical properties in its own right, being used in divinations and cures and to counter spells. In Lorraine, the milk of black cows was believed to be the only liquid capable of extinguishing fires lit by lightning. Spilling milk accidentally was a universal ill omen. Favret-Saada argues that in modern Normandy, the milk stolen from cows is therefore thought of as the 'force' of their owner.[45] Milk could also be used to forge important ties in the community. One of the main divisions within the modern village of Minot in Burgundy was between those who had their own milk from their own cows and those who had to buy or otherwise obtain milk from others. Those without milk of their own always got it from richer relatives and the exchange made for a close and almost unbreakable tie of trust between them. In such circumstances, milk-stealing was a very serious crime.

II

THE LIFE-CYCLE

5

Human Fertility and Marriage

The well-being and fertility of the fields, the livestock and humans went together and formed an ensemble. This is reflected in many ways, starting with vocabulary and metaphor. In Finland, the same word, *äpärä* meant child, the second growth of grass, a lamb born in the Autumn, and a sheaf of corn left in the field. In early modern France, the same terms were used to describe a barren woman and land that would not produce crops. Writers from Aeschylus onwards evoked the production of new vegetable life in the Spring as a marriage or congress between Earth and Heaven. 'Sow timely thy white wheat, sow rye in the dust', Thomas Tusser recommended in 1573. 'Let seed have his longing, let soil have her lust.' At the same time, sexual relations between men and women were described using agricultural imagery. A Rouen author referred in 1612 to the man 'cultivating the human field' of the woman, and to the penis as the plough and seed-holder. A Christmas carol from the Lauragais associated images of harvest with the Nativity

'Take up your sickle, good man.
Your wheat is ready to cut.'
'How can that be, Madam?
I have only just sown it.'
'Go to look at your field,
Go to harvest your wheat!
The straw has sprung up in a quarter of an hour,
And in the same time the ear has ripened.
Take the first sheaf in your arms.'
'Who is carrying that baby?
She passed by at sowing-time!
When I was sowing my wheat.'[1]

The fertility of fields, animals and humans was defended and called for by the same kinds of gesture, if not in common rituals. The pilgrimage to the chapel at Montclard in the Auvergne procured protection for livestock, but sterile women also went there to touch a standing stone inside the chapel as well as young men and women wanting to get married. In Lower Brittany, water from springs reputed to make women fertile was also efficacious for animals. The shrine of

Our Lady of the Eggs at Gréoux-les-Bains was visited by infertile women but was also the object of an annual parish pilgrimage to ensure the fertility of the land. Seed corn was taken into many churches in Savoy to be blessed on St Blaise's Day, and girls asked this same saint for husbands. The cult of St Agatha in Savoy and elsewhere was associated with ensuring a supply of milk to mothers and nurses, but the saint also gave protection against hail and thunder.

Conversely, sterility in women, drought, crop failure all went together and might be explained by the same causes: the neglect of proper ritual and the effects of witchcraft and other hostile forces. In the Pyrenees, as we have seen, it was believed that those who failed to feast the fairies on New Year's Eve would suffer from wild beasts attacking their flocks, 'hail and withering of crops, and unhappy marriages'. In Provence, according to a court case in 1834 spirits 'walked about the fields at night and broadcast their nefarious influence over the crops, the livestock and all living creatures'. In an interesting variant, poorer townspeople during the French Revolution linked the ritual shedding of blood with staving off famine:

> At the time of the Terror, when the guillotine was in full swing, there was plenty of bread; now that there isn't any more guillotining, we're short of bread. To have bread we need the guillotine in constant action. If we don't want to die of hunger, we need blood.[2]

There was a more particular linkage between human fertility and that of the soil expressed in calendar rituals. This is worth stressing, since reaction against the emphasis on fertility rites by an older generation of folklorists has to some extent discredited it. Calendar customs in the Ancient world explicitly linked general and human fecundity, sometimes via ritual copulation in the fields. There is some evidence that this practice survived into later times but generally medieval and modern European customs were less direct. The fertility element in the Spring rituals is obvious and has been well explored. Carnival was not only a time of general sexual licence but it also involved ritual verbal obscenity and transvestism, as well as simulated copulation and childbirth. Among the Sarakatsani of Greece in modern times, a mock marriage was performed with a man acting the part of the bride. Then the couple went to bed, the bride going through several men, before one succeeded in either deflowering or pleasing her. A mock birth and baptism took place next, followed by the death of the child and its resurrection. 'These goings-on (all most explicit) are said to drive away drought and guarantee an abundance of leaves and grass for the flocks.'[3]

May Day rituals were 'plurifunctional' in the same way. Kings and queens and other figures, decked with flowers, leaves and garlands, represented 'the vernal spirit of vegetation'. Queens were given gifts in return for kisses. Phallic maypoles were erected and processed. In parts of Portugal around this time young men and girls went into the flax fields just before the flax was pulled and rolled together on the ground in couples. Further simulated acts of procreation occurred in other places. In the Valais on May Day morning, 'a group of pretty girls between the ages of fifteen and eighteen processed through the meadows around the village, bouquets in hand, and exerted their beneficial powers by trampling upon the grass in order to make it grow high'. In modern Ireland again, 'the May Baby parades linked the festival with the fertility of the family as well as the fields'. According to an account from 1838, a female doll was made, called the May Baby, and decked with flowers and ribbons.

> Around this figure a man and a woman ... of the humble class, dressed fantastically with straw, etc., dance to the sound of a fiddle and entertain the people with indecent shows and postures ... women who have had no children to their husbands also attend to see this figure and performance, which they imagine will promote fruitfulness in them, and cause them to have children.[4]

Harvesting rituals, and the songs that accompanied them, were even more expressive here. The last sheaf of the corn harvest was often cut by a young unmarried woman. Whether a person would marry or not within the year was divined by how his or her reaping-hook fell when it was thrown in the air. There was dancing in the field, and the last sheaf was commonly made in the shape of a woman. At Saligne in the Vendée, the farmer's wife was tied up in a sheet with the last sheaf and was tossed in the sheet, in a familiar gesture, 'as if she were being winnowed'.[5] At Llansilin in Wales, younger female harvest workers were rolled on the barn floor by the young men in the loose corn after harvest.

In the Western Isles and on the western seaboard of Scotland, carrots were gathered on Carrot Sunday, which was the Sunday preceding Michaelmas. The women alone took part and they competed hard to get the most and the biggest roots. To pull a cleft carrot was considered to be very lucky. As they sang:

> Cleft fruitful, fruitful, fruitful,
> Joy of carrots surpassing upon me,
> Michael the brave [St Michael] endowing me,
> Bride the fair [St Bride] be aiding me.
> Progeny preeminent over every progeny,
> Progeny on my womb,
> Progeny preeminent over every progeny,
> Progeny on my progeny.[6]

Sicilian harvest rituals and songs are even more sexually explicit. The grape harvest began with a religious invocation but continued with insults, teasing and horseplay between the sexes, and songs such as this:

> Tiny little girl,
> Sugar-sweet grape,
> Who picks you, who squeezes you,
> Who eats you ... will die!
> My little 'nzolia grape!
> Oh sweet, oh sweet! oh sweet!
> Oh love, I take you!
> And like a snail
> I suck you, suck you!'

When the figs ripened, whole families went out into the country to gather them. They camped out and all kinds of games, amusements and festivities took place in the groves and fields. It was believed that figs, which were symbols of both male and female genitals, increased mother's milk for suckling babies, made the sterile pregnant, the skinny fat, and gave everyone vigour. Another song underlined these connections:

> Come, come, young women,
> For your milk grows with the figs,
> And with the milk we make cheese,
> Which is sweeter made with figs.
> If you sleep there [by the fig trees] one night,
> Even your thighs fatten ...
> In the month of August we have fun;
> The camps are nests of love.
> Always you see your love,
> Because he's after you at all hours;
> At dawn he picks figs in the branches.[7]

Rites of passage and calendar customs were complementary. Both were concerned with reproduction but in different spheres. 'The individual life-cycle customs are directed towards natural reproduction; women are the executives of this domain. Conversely, the public calendar customs address the necessity for social production, supervised by men.' However, like calendar customs rites of passage also directly expressed the linkage between the two. This is clear in wedding rituals, as we shall see shortly. It can also be seen in customs relating to birth and death. In modern Ireland, as in many other places, child-bearing was 'widely regarded as part of the ritual necessary to bring success with the stock and the crops'. More specifically, a pregnancy test recommended by *The Expert Midwife* (1637) required 'a woman's urine [to be] poured over barley seed and if it sprouted after ten days, she had conceived'. Later, in Tolosa in Spain, the *cedazo* used to sieve maize was kept under the bed of a woman giving birth and was then used as a tray to carry the baby to be washed and dressed once it was born. In many Spanish villages, the umbilical cord was cut with agricultural tools. St Augustine refers to a Roman ritual in which 'three divinities are brought in as guards for a woman after childbirth to prevent Silvanus the god of the forest from entering [the house] and tormenting her'. They were named after and represented by three agricultural emblems: an axe used to prune trees, a pestle for grinding corn and a besom for piling it up. Three men carried these round 'the doorways of the house at night. They struck the threshold first with the axe, then with the pestle, and afterwards they swept it with besoms'.[8] As far as death rituals are concerned, we may point to the sickles, hoes, spades and other implements found in Viking graves.

Another expression of the same linkage is the use of the phallus as a general amulet or bringer of luck. At Torco near Naples, an inflated ox intestine with red streamers was put over the lintel of houses, which was seen as a phallic symbol to ensure prosperity. Similar symbols were placed over doors and windows by Yugoslav gypsies, who associated the penis with life and good fortune. A man would touch his penis to avert evil influences, and having a large organ was regarded as an asset to a man and his family. Ritual bread or cakes made for saints' days or the calendar festivals were sometimes shaped like a phallus. The bishop of Limoges made the bakers change the traditional form of the Palm Sunday *brioches* in 1750 because they were judged to be obscene. At Metz, the Holy Foreskin was processed through the town at Rogation time. Male animal and even human genitalia were used in magic of different kinds, including that relating to the cereal crop. It was claimed, for example, at a trial in the Tyrol in 1645 that, advised by an evil spirit of the way to obtain more grist for his mill, a miller went to a gallows where a boy was hanging, took his testicles and buried them 'under the mill, in a cloth with blessed salt and a candle. The result was that many people would bring their grain to grind nowhere else'.[9]

The linkage between agriculture and human fertility was not always straightforward, however. There was some latent antagonism between the two and a need for each to be kept within limits. A new birth made new demands potentially on the food supplied by agriculture, while human sexuality was a threat as well as a blessing. Taboos relating to ploughs are significant in this context. In the canton of Saulxures in the Vosges, 'if anyone bestrides a plough in a field, the harvest will be considered compromised', a folklorist related in 1878. 'Fifty years ago this belief was so general and so strong that ploughing would immediately be stopped and only started again the next day'.[10] Bestriding the plough interferes here with its function of opening the soil. It is a sexual gesture but one that works against and not for the agricultural task.

Apart from all this, a high value was attached independently to the fertility of women, as historical and folkloric sources illustrate. Synge noted of the men of Inishmaan at the turn of this century 'that the greatest merit they see in a woman is that she should be fruitful and bring them many children'. Until recently in parts of Yugoslavia, 'procreation was considered to be the main aim of marriage and children as a divine blessing'. Clerical views concurred here with popular ones. 'The good man should never fear having too many children', instructed the canonist Benedicti, 'for they are a blessing from God'; while the 1598 Protestant Church Ordinance of Strasbourg declared that a woman's 'greatest honour on earth is her fertility'. Having many children was also celebrated in Scripture. 'Happy is the man that hath his quiver full of them', sang Psalm 127; 'thy wife shall be as a fruitful vine', Psalm 128. Theologians taught that, having brought sin into the world, woman redeemed herself in child-bearing, citing I Timothy 2:15 This was sometimes glossed to mean that the more children a woman had, the greater would be her reward in the next world.[11]

It is significant here that the peasants of Montaillou proved unsympathetic towards Cathar anti-populationism, though they admired or adopted other features of the heresy. As Douglas noted for the people of Capri, the premium set on fertility influenced or formed peasants' ideas of beauty or attractiveness, a 'swelling form' being preferred to a pretty face. It also affected marital relations and a woman's status in the family. Among the Sarakatsani, a husband's attitude towards his wife became much more friendly after she had produced her first child, and her standing generally within the family rose. In early medieval societies, the wergild or blood money of women also rose once they began to bear children and remained high during their child-bearing years. Across European peasant cultures it was felt that 'a woman was not complete until she had a child born in legitimate marriage'. The qualification was important. As Pina-Cabral has stressed, 'fertility is desired, but it must be shifted from the disorder of female fertility (*per se*) to the order of household fertility (via marriage)'. Peasants wanted 'a bountiful life' but one that was at the same time 'orderly'.[12]

By contrast, sterility in a woman was everywhere regarded as a misfortune. More, as in Corsica, it was often 'a form of shame if not dishonour'. 'Barrenness for a peasant woman', a late-nineteenth-century Russian ethnographer related, 'is a most painful situation ... it often constitutes a source of moral humiliation'. In Ireland it was 'regarded as an unnatural and disgraceful thing'. In many parts of France a childless married woman was called a 'mule', the most wounding of insults. Sometimes barrenness was seen as a punishment for sin or the breaking of some taboo. Again, one of the worst things one could do to a woman was to wish sterility on her, as King Lear does when he curses his daughter Goneril:

> Hear, Nature, hear! dear Goddess hear!
> Suspend thy purpose, if thou didst intend
> To make this creature fruitful!
> Into her womb convey sterility!
> Dry up her organs of increase,
> And from her derogate body never spring
> A babe to honour her![13]

Behind this cultural imperative lay the facts that actual fertility was low by modern standards, the result of poor diet, ill health and, indirectly, late age at marriage, and that infant mortality was high. At the same time, the demand for children was great. Agriculture and other work were labour intensive, needing large numbers of people. Moreover, in places where State power was weak and where the extended family acted to protect its members and defend its property directly, the larger a family was, the stronger it was. For economic and political reasons therefore great store was set on having as many children as possible and particularly boys not only to work but also to fight. 'Our only wealth is our children', a Corsican told a French enquiry in the 1830s. Support in old age was also an important consideration. ' "Thank God we've got good children" ', one old farm labourer from the Cotswolds would say in the 1890s as he cashed 'some postal order for a tiny amount sent by a daughter in service or a married son'.[14] This was a modern version of an ancient obligation.

In traditional peasant societies this dependency of parents on children was often cast into an ideology of moral and religious survival. The fifteenth-century *Dives et Pauper* taught 'that a man who leaves progeny behind him is not completely dead, since he lives on in his children'. 'When a man dies he is gone', Dilys Powell, herself childless, was told in northern Greece in the 1950s, 'he is forgotten. But if he has children his name does not die with him. For that reason it is good to have children.' In later medieval and then Catholic societies, parents expected children to pray for their souls and have masses said after they had died to ease their way through the pains of Purgatory. According to a recent account, childless persons in southern Italy often left 'their goods to the church on condition that masses be said and a proper funeral provided'.[15] Godchildren could also act as surrogate children to godparents. But these were poor substitutes for the real thing.

It was always most desirable here to have male children. In Montenegro anyone without male children was 'cursed'. When the French peasant Grenadou's wife gave birth to a daughter in 1925, he commented: 'Of course, we wanted a son'. 'When you bore me, mother', ran a Transylvanian song,

> How happy you were.
> You thought you'd make a son ...
> When you saw I was a girl
> Your whole body ached.

To her mother a girl-child was 'more bitter than wormwood'. By contrast, a male child was the source of pride and happiness. As a Florentine noted in his family diary around 1400: 'when he was born ... male, whole, and well-proportioned, what joy!'.[16] The male child of course was an heir, who would carry on the family name, as we have seen, and keep its patrimony intact.

Various magico-religious means were employed to try to produce boys. Greetings or blessings, especially at weddings, expressed this wish. 'May you have a hundred sons!', they said on Capri. Prayers, vows and gifts were made to saints. St Charles of Sezze related that in 1665 St James of Alcala appeared to him 'and he urged me to pray to God for a woman who ... wanted the child that was going to be born to her to be a son. I prayed for this many times and through the intercession of St James Our Lord deigned to grant this favour. At baptism the child was named Paul James, out of devotion to the saint'. At Zaraúz in Spain in the modern period, 'a husband who has not had sons in the first seven years of marriage makes a little dress for a new baby and goes up to the shrine of St Ignatius to offer it to the saint'. Other procedures required the woman to eat a herb 'which looks like male genitals', or both partners to consume appropriate animal parts. In a ritual inversion, a medieval medical guide advised the man to drink wine in which the dried womb and vulva of a hare had been mixed, while the woman was to do the same with the dried testicles. There was also a common belief, deriving from Galen, that the right testicle produced males and the left females. This led to the practice of tying up the left testicle during intercourse in order to conceive a boy, a practice still reported in eighteenth-century France. The woman might also bend to the right, or, in some parts of France, have the right claw of a magpie sewn under her skirt. Other circumstances might be thought relevant. In Santa-Cruz-de-Tenerife, if the bed were oriented towards the sea during copulation, the child would be male; if towards the mountains, female; while intercourse at high tide produced boys and at low tide girls. It was believed very generally, as in fifteenth-century Florence, 'that a girl child was the fruit of a conjugal act stained by some impurity, sickness, debauchery, or broken taboo'.[17] This included intercourse while the woman was menstruating. Couples were also anxious to know the gender of a baby before it was born, and again various divinatory procedures were used, as we shall see.

Contraception and abortion went against the whole fertility ethos. They were condemned by the Church and generally associated with evil and witchcraft. They were not, however, unknown in traditional European societies. A large number of plants were reputed to have contraceptive effects, for example willow, ivy, hazel root, pennyroyal and cannabis, and their use was denounced in penitentials, canons and confessional guides. The herbs were usually made into potions it seems, though they could also be applied to the body as pessaries or ointments. A popular French herbal of 1723 advised that mint 'placed on a woman's belly before she sleeps with her husband prevented her from conceiving'. Other substances and methods were used. An Anglo-Irish collection of remedies dating from around 1300 prescribes taking 'the beestings of a hare'.[18] Other sources refer to wearing knots and amulets during intercourse. The odd shrine was visited, too, by women not wanting children, like that of St Martial at Roussac in the Limousin. But all this was unusual, something resorted to in times of great hardship, and the aim was nearly always it seems simply to space births – that is, as far as married women were concerned. Prolonged lactation, which was universally practised, has a contraceptive effect, but there were other very good reasons for it without invoking the regulation of fertility.

Hostility to conception and having children was also placed beyond the pale on the symbolic level. Thus in a sixteenth-century Breton version of the Bluebeard story the villain invariably put his wives to death when they became pregnant. Discussing ways in which children were given wittingly or unwittingly to the devil, the *Malleus Maleficarum* claimed that God punished, by allowing it to be fulfilled, a 'commendation used angrily by a woman when her husband after copulating with her says: "I hope a child will come of it"; and she answers: "May the child go to the Devil!" ' We may also cite the belief found in Nordic countries but also elsewhere that 'every woman must give birth to her own series [that is] a certain number of children determined in advance'. If such children, who should have been born, are prevented, then they may appear to the mother on her deathbed to torment her.[19]

The first printed manual for midwives, the *Rosengarten* of Eucharius Rösslin, city physician of Frankfurt in the first quarter of the sixteenth century, followed classical medical theory in teaching that the foetus did not receive life and soul until the third month. This view was accepted and propagated by medical opinion in Europe right through the early modern period and it seems to have fitted or influenced lay perceptions. In England so-called 'quickening' was believed to occur at about the fourth month; while in France a period of three months or ninety days was normal, with sometimes a shorter forty days for boys. Important consequences followed as far as the significance and legitimacy of abortion were concerned. Doctors distinguished between 'slipping away' in the first months of pregnancy and loss of an animated foetus in human form. Most women, it seems, felt that deliberate abortion might be justified before quickening but never afterwards.[20]

Even this is probably to present a view too favourable to abortion, at least as far as peasants were concerned. The abortifacient qualities of certain plants (male fern, rue, artemisia, iris, ergot of rye) were apparently known, and other procedures are mentioned. Midwives were believed to help with clandestine abortions, and their oaths included the promise not to do so. But against this was the overwhelmingly negative attitude presented at both clerical and folk levels. The Catholic Church had been hostile from very early times. Penitentials imposed heavy penalties and it was even equated with homicide. In folklore also 'terrible punishments are suffered for abortion'. In a Bavarian tale, a woman who had had more than one abortion was tortured for seven years by a snake; while a midwife who had caused abortions was forced to wander endlessly after her death.[21] The vengeful Scandinavian child spirits included aborted foetuses along with infants killed at birth or dying without baptism. Always too, abortion was associated with witchcraft by demonologists but also by witnesses in witchcraft trials.

The Catholic Church set an ideal of virginity before the peasantry via the cults of the Virgin Mary and other virgin saints. But it is significant that, from the time of St Ambrose, Mary's virginity was not associated at all in clerical discourse with sterility but rather with spiritual fertility. She was even compared to the 'soil' on which Christ the sun shone. More obviously she was, though virgin, the archetypal mother-figure, represented nearly always before the nineteenth century with her child and often giving suck. She was commonly linked too, as we have seen, with vegetation, fruits and the earth, recalling Artemis, virgin and goddess of fertility, in the Ancient world. Where virginity was more directly praised by clerical writers, it was often with an apologetic tone. The Spanish theologian Vives, for example, addressed Christian women in 1542: 'Know that the old malediction of sterility has passed. Now you have another law according to which virginity is preferred to marriage. The Gospel blesses sterility and the breasts which have not given suck'.[22]

Marriage was a privilege in traditional peasant societies, which younger sons and daughters might be denied. Only the married – with children – were regarded as fully adult, and the lot of the unmarried female was particularly undesirable. It was a common belief in modern Portugal even that 'no woman can attain Paradise as a virgin. If she departs from earth in this state, she is deflowered by St Hilary'. According to a Rhineland legend, 'maidens who die without having either married or taken religious vows are condemned to dance [for ever] on a grassless spot' on the island of Oberworth, unless rescued by their lovers.[23] In these circumstances, and whatever the requirements of a family's marriage strategy, girls sought to find partners by all available means.

First, there were rituals associated with the calendar customs. Children begging eggs on Easter Saturday in the Limousin included potential brides in their blessing:

> If there are girls to be married,
> May they find good partners.

The girls themselves consulted water in well-buckets or other vessels during Carnival or sought to find one of the crosses planted in the fields on the Day of the Invention of the Cross. They rolled in the dew on St John's Eve or jumped over the bonfire on his day and tried to catch a spark in their skirts. They tried to cut or obtain the last sheaf. In more detail, on New Year's Eve in Transylvania, girls went into the forest to 'honour' a kind of belladonna plant with wine and cakes. They sang to it, praised it and made this request of it:

> Belladonna, good lady,
> Marry me in this month.
> If not this one,
> Then in the next;
> Only marry me off.
> For if you don't get me married,
> I won't give you brandy or cakes.

At the May festival at Padstow, the hobby horse chases and captures women under his tarpaulin skirt. 'This is supposed to bring her good luck, in the form of a husband within twelve months if she is unmarried.'[24] At the Whitsun Căluş rituals in Rumania, girls who touch the dancers will find husbands, and when the dancers go to a house with an unmarried girl, something belonging to her is put out. Hallowe'en games in Ireland and Wales used beans, twigs and other objects to determine who would marry within the year. In Montgomeryshire, a wedding ring was placed in a mash made of nine vegetables, and the person to whom it was served would be the one to get married first.

Then there were visits to fountains, trees or standing stones. 'To obtain a husband at Montrieux (in Provence) and at the source of the Gapeau, girls floated a leaf or a pin on the water, previously covered in oil; it was a favourable sign if it did not sink.' Throwing pins in springs, often backwards over one's shoulder, drinking the water, dipping in one's left foot and other procedures are all reported by folklorists. Sometimes an expert was involved. According to an 1807 report, St Dwynwen's Well on Anglesey was attended by an old woman who divined whether a girl would marry or not from the movement of the young eels that inhabited the pool. Visits to trees and stones usually involved friction against the phallic object. 'At Carnac, young girls who desired a husband used to undress completely and rub their navels against a menhir'; at another place 'in the Eure-et-Loir, they lifted up their skirts and rubbed their bellies' against a particular place on the standing stone (see Plate 11). Other magical procedures were followed. From Ireland the eighteenth-century Gaelic poet Bryan Merriman lists:

> Up the chimney stuck the flail,
> Slept with a spade without avail,
> Hid my wool in the limekiln late
> And my distaff behind the churchyard gate;
> Flax in the road to halt coach and carriage,
> And haycocks stuffed with heads of cabbage.[25]

Even more common probably was recourse to religion and the saints. A litany published in France in 1832 incorporated elements from the mass:

> Kyrie, I want! Christ, to get married!
> Kyrie, I pray all the saints,
> Christ, that it may be tomorrow

and then implored eighteen saints in turn, starting with Mary, Joseph and Nicholas. On the night of St Theodore in Rumania, unmarried girls went to the forest or up a hill and danced round a fire all night, singing to the saint and asking for their hair to grow. They gathered herbs, which they then used to wash their hair. This anticipation of modern shampoo advertisements was supposed to procure them husbands. Would-be brides also visited saints' shrines, where they might perform reproductive magical gestures. In Provins, for example, they worked the bolt of the door of St Nicholas' chapel, repeating

> St Nicholas, St Nicholas,
> Get you girls married and don't forget me!

At the hermitage of St Gens in the Comtat, girls spent the night, lying, for part of the time head downwards, in 'St Gens' bed', a kind of sloping trough hollowed out in the rock. Another very common procedure was to stick pins into a statue or its clothing, often making a wish at the same time. The Virgin Mary was a favourite patron here. At Laval, according to a late nineteenth-century account, girls wishing to marry within the year stuck pins into the thighs of a large statue of St Christopher. Saints might also be threatened. In a village in the Minervois early in this century, after a wedding the unmarried girls went one by one to the statue of St Sicre under the church porch and threatened it with an axe:

> Great St Sicre, if within one year,
> You have not given us a lover,
> This is what you will feel in your flesh.[26]

Sometimes the desire to have a husband overlapped with simple divination. Who would be one's spouse? What would he or she look like? – real anxieties in the context of arranged marriages. Here again the same kinds of procedure are found. In his *Pandaemonium*, published in London in 1684, Bovet related that his maids had told him that

> if we fasted on Midsummer Eve, and then at 12 o'clock at night laid a cloth on the table, with bread, and cheese, and a cup of the best beer, setting ourselves down, as if we were going to eat, and leaving the door of the room open, we should see the persons whom we should afterwards marry.

Again, in nineteenth-century Spain, 'anxious maidens used to sit at their balconies [on Hallowe'en night] to see the image of their destined husbands pass or not pass by'.[27] A more intermittent calendar ritual occurred on Guernsey on 29 February. The girl stuck twenty-seven pins, three by three, into a tallow candle, which was lit at the wrong end and placed in a candle-stick made from clay from a virgin's grave. This was placed on the left-hand side of the hearth at midnight, and the whole procedure would induce her to see her future husband after she went to bed. Other practices involved looking into springs or pools, addressing the new moon, and manipulating lucky finds such as pods with nine peas in them or clover leaves.

But the commonest divinatory practice involved dreaming on the eve or night of a particular saint's day. According to Aubrey, girls looked under plantain leaves on St John's Day for a coal to put 'under their heads that night and dream of their future husband'. In the Franche-Comté in the nineteenth century, if a girl wanted to see her future husband in a dream, she had to place a mirror under her pillow on the eve of St Andrew's Day. She might also walk round the house with her back to the wall, reciting this formula:

> St Andrew, Maccabeus,
> Who passed over the sea,
> Let me see in my sleep
> The husband I will have.

In England and Scotland, the appropriate saint was St Anne or St Agnes, as Keats reflects in his poem. Divination relating to them is referred to in both elite and popular sources in the seventeenth century. Invocation of saints could also be combined with the phases of the moon. At Mezières in the Limousin, a girl ate a sardine at supper on the first Friday of the new moon and on going to bed invoked two saints:

> St Hubert and St Thomas,
> Make me see in my dreams
> The man I will marry.[28]

The Church banned marriages at certain times of the year. The details are laid out in a rhyme found in the parish register of St Mary's, Beverley, in 1641 and repeated elsewhere:

> When Advent comes do thou refrain,
> Till Hilary set you free again,
> Next Septuagesima saith thee nay,
> But when Low Sunday comes thou may.
> Yet at Rogation thou must tarry,
> Till Trinity shall bid thee marry.

The Council of Trent relaxed these restrictions for Catholics, but they were maintained by the Church of England and generally adhered to into the seventeenth century. On the Continent there was also a strong ban on marriages in May, which enjoyed clerical and popular support. Having broken these taboos might be adduced as the cause for sterility or the death of babies. There is evidence, too, that auspicious times were sought for marriage. Burchard of Worms referred to 'observing the new moon for making marriages'. At Montaillou in the fourteenth century, one man told another: 'When we wanted to give our sister as wife to Bernard Clergue, we went to see Guillaume Authié the heretic to ask his advice on the following question: when will the moon be propitious to marry our sister to Bernard?'[29] And he told them which day to choose for the wedding. Particular days of the week might also be significant.

The main function of the wedding rituals themselves was to transfer the bride from her own to the groom's family and to give publicity to this event; but specific elements in them were also intended to ensure the fertility of the couple. Indeed this might have been tested by some kind of trial. The Tridentine Catholic ritual asked for the bride to be 'fruitful in offspring'; the English Book of Common Prayer called for God's blessing 'on these two persons, that they may both be fruitful in procreation of children'.[30] In medieval and then Catholic Europe, the priest blessed the marriage bed (see Plate 19). The couple, the bed and others present were incensed and/or sprinkled with holy water, and official prayers of protection and sanctification were said. The probably older custom of the father's or patron's blessing also continued. This is reflected, for example, in Oberon's blessing in Shakespeare's *A Midsummer Night's Dream*.

Many other secular components of the wedding had the same function. The bridal canopy or pall, for example, was 'originally intended to deceive demons and to protect the couple from the evil eye'.[31] The crown worn by the bride (and by the groom in the Orthodox world) had the same intention (see Plate 12). In Rumania in modern times, greenery, symbolizing life and fruitfulness, was sewn into the bride's hair with protective red thread. The plants and flowers used in bouquets and garlands, strewn on floors and decked on the walls of churches and houses, had a similar significance.

In addition to simply wishing the couple well, guests scattered rice, wheat, nuts and other tokens of fertility over them and particularly over the bride. Dr Samuel Collins noted that in Russia in the 1660s the clerk showered the bride with hops, 'wishing her children as thick as hops', while another man attended the wedding in a sheepskin coat and prayed 'that she may have as many children as there are hairs in his coat'. In some parts of Corsica, wheat, dried vegetables and chestnuts were poured into the bride's apron, and similar customs are found elsewhere. 'The English', a French traveller related in 1655, 'when the bride comes from church, are wont to cast wheat upon her head; and when the bride and bridegroom return home, one presents them with a pot of butter, as presaging plenty and abundance of all good things.' Elizabethan Puritans referred disparagingly in their Admonition to Parliament of 1572 to women 'carrying wheat sheaves on their heads and casting ... corn at weddings'. In Poland, the father of the groom threw barley corns over the couple when they arrived at the door of his house. These were 'carefully gathered up and sown', and, if they grew, it was considered a good omen.[32] More directly, a child might be carried in the procession, placed on the bride's lap, or even in the marriage bed. Given the preference for males, this was nearly always a boy.

Weddings were always accompanied by feasting, itself conducive to fertility in general (see Plate 20). The particular kinds of food eaten were also significant, together with other features. In modern Rumania, 'on each table, there are grains of wheat, a spindle of wool, and the ritual bread, *colac,* with basil in its centre. These are symbolic magic tokens embodying abundance and fertility (the wheat), prosperity (the wool), and holiness (the ritual bread ... and holy plant)'. At a later stage in the feast, the cook carries in 'a cooked hen bedecked in greenery and necklaces of bread' and sings a song full of sexual connotations. She attests to the bride's virginity and announces her entry into sexual activity. The couple are also given specific items of food and drink to encourage their fertility. On their return from church in the Limousin, they were presented with a kind of punch into which bread or oats had been put 'as a promise of fecundity'. A similar drink given to a couple in the marriage bed in sixteenth-century Foix was supposed to 'ensure the newly-weds ardent mating and a fertile marriage'. In modern Portugal, cakes symbolizing fruitfulness and plenty were thrown at the couple, while at a village 'in the district of Braganza, the bridal pair hold small cakes phallic in form, which other guests try to snatch from them in the belief that if successful they will be married within the year'. Among the Greeks of Salento, 'the bride offers the groom a cake in the form of a wheel, surrounded by hard-boiled eggs, all symbols of fecundity'.[33]

Further ritual accompanied the bedding of the couple. As we have seen, they might be given special drinks. According to a seventeenth-century English ballad, the points of the groom's codpiece and the bride's garters were taken by the young guests and cut in pieces. In modern Ireland, 'a hen which was about the lay an egg was tied to the bed-post on the marriage night'. In La Cabrera in Spain,

> the mother of the bride, the last to leave the bedroom, made a sacred aspersion over the heads of the couple, using as a sprinkler an ear of wheat, symbol of the multiplication of the seed, well soaked in holy water. At the same time, she said this fecundity charm: May it take root, Little Virgin of Carmen, may it take root! Meanwhile, to frighten off the demons of sterility, the father swept the floor outside the room towards the outside with a branch of broom, reciting another magical formula: Evil vermin, get away from here; may the holy water go over you!

Throughout the wedding there was ritual noise, driving off evil influences that might be hostile to the couple's happiness and fecundity: drumming, piping, shouting. Songs, often ribald, were sung. In recent years, crockery was broken; or shots fired. In the Vosges in the mid nineteenth century, a pistol was fired between the legs of the bride. It was common in England until around 1850 for butchers' boys 'in their blue coats to attend the front of houses where weddings had taken place and play on their cleavers with knuckle bones'.[34]

1 Statue of St Domenico, with snakes, being processed at Cocullo, south Italy, mid twentieth century.

2 Objects found in walls of Cambridgeshire houses to protect against witchcraft: bone, bottle, old shoes. (*Cambridge and County Folk Museum*)

3 House in Nairn with protective figure on the roof made from branch of a fir tree, early twentieth century.

4 (*top*) Ritual before sowing in
Ruthenia: prayers are said, candles
burned, and loaves placed between
the seed-corn and the candles,
early twentieth century.

5 (*centre left*) Harvest festival
figure made from the last sheaf.
(*National Museum, Prague*)

6 (*centre right*) Metal ex-voto ox.
Vasvár, Hungary.

7 (*right*) Transvestism and fertility
symbols at Lisbon Carnival,
c. 1930.

8 Taking 'palms' to church to be blessed on Palm Sunday, France, *c.* 1930.

9 Priest blessing the St John's Eve bonfire, Eure-et-Loir, France, *c.* 1930.

10 Blessing the pigs on St Anthony's Day, Corsica, *c.* 1900.

11 Prehistoric stones visited by girls wishing to marry and after betrothal. Barroza, Minho district, Portugal, early twentieth century.

12 Bride wearing crown and dress, Bückeburg, Hanover, Germany, c. 1930.

13 Ritual to protect bridal couple from harmful magic, Karelia, Finland, early twentieth century.

14 Untying the bride's hair, which was left loose for a week following the wedding, Karelia, Finland, early twentieth century.

15 Pilgrims and patients at the well of Sainte-Anne-de-la-Palude, Brittany, c. 1900.

16 Procession of skull of St Yves in its reliquary, Tréguier, Brittany, *c.* 1900.

17 People passing under the procession of the relics St Theliau for protection or cures. Troménie de Landelau, Finistère, Brittany, 1972.

Visits might be paid to shrines or sacred sites as part of the wedding cere-mony. Wedding parties in the Hainaut in the modern period visited a local shrine of Notre-Dame-de-Bon-Secours to ask for offspring for the couple. At the foot of the Pied-de-Cantal in the Auvergne, the newly-weds and some-times the guests danced round a standing stone. In several villages in Poitou, the couple soaked their shoes in certain sacred springs in order to be sure of conceiving. The shoe or clog was associated with the female genital organ. At La Roche-Rufin (Deux-Sèvres), the bride was taken on the wedding day to a particular spring, into which she dipped her foot. Those present then shouted: 'The bride has "booted". She will have a dolly before the year is out'. In many parts of France, brides went on pilgrimage to springs soon after the wedding in order to become mothers. More commonly, the bride's bouquet was presented to the altar of the Virgin 'in the hope by this gesture of obtaining fertility and happiness'.[35] In parts of Normandy, the gift was a distaff decorated with ribbons. Glass paintings of the Virgin and Child or the Nativity often formed part of a girl's trousseau in Rumania, again symbol-izing the wished-for fertility. In Tuscany and southern France, dolls were given to the bride in earnest of babies to come.

Care was taken in all this to protect the couple from forces that might prevent their becoming parents (see Plate 13). The blessing and sprinkling were intended to exorcize as well as to benefit directly. Salt might be sewn into the clothing of the couple and scattered in their bed. We have seen that 'evil vermin' were swept away from the bedroom in Spain. At Salento, the room was roped off with a red ribbon to ward off the evil eye. In modern Greece, it was important 'after the wedding ceremony that the relatives took away the wicks of the candles; otherwise, if some enemy gets a hold of them, he can bewitch the bride so that she may die or not have children'. Omens were read anxiously here. In Portugal there was a 'widespread prejudice in favour of [fructifying] rain falling on the wedding day'; while in the English Fens, a thunderstorm during a wedding was a sign that 'the couple would have no children'.[36]

It is very significant here finally that charivaris were mounted to protest at the marriage of older couples, whose union would not be fruitful. There was something improper and contradictory about such unions.

Some of the rituals to induce conception took place after the wedding. A number of calendar customs specifically involved those married within the last year. In the Franche-Comté, for example, newly-weds had the duty of making the Brandons bonfire, which had a pole on it with a wooden berib-boned cock. At Mesnil-les-Hurlus in Champagne, in a custom well-estab-lished in the eighteenth century and almost certainly much older, the last man to be married had to provide the cart-wheel at Brandons, which was set alight and rolled down a hill, a custom associated with the fertility of the vines. At Couvin in Belgium at Mardi-Gras, the last man to be married had to place a stick with a banner in a lake. Varagnac notes that there was here an element of 'taxation' by the community of those entering the married state, but there is no doubt that the rituals were also connected with the fertility of the new couples, apart from the phallic symbolism often involved. In the Jura, the Brandons rituals were explicitly said 'to assure the fecundity of the young ménage'; while in other parts of France new couples were at once excluded from such rituals when their first child was born. In the Roannais, maypoles were planted in front of the houses of newly-weds after their weddings and removed when the new wife gave birth. Other procedures involved the cult of saints. At Martigues in Provence, the two youngest brides served annually in the confraternity of St Margaret, a saint associated with childbirth. 'Natural' magic was also routinely employed. Among some gypsies, for example, it was believed 'that no woman could become pregnant without the moon's help'; while in northern Mississippi in the late nineteenth century, according to Faulkner, 'the full moon of April [shining on the marriage bed] guaranteed the fertilizing act'.[37]

If the bride failed to conceive within a reasonable period, a wide range of remedies was available. Herbs and herbal potions might be taken. St Bernardino of Siena refers in a sermon to 'eating elder leaves in order to have a child'. Motherwort was prescribed later in Italy on its own or mixed with other plants; and tisanes of hawthorn or mistletoe were used in the Charentes until recently. Tansy, sea-holly and dock figure alongside these in English recipes. Sometimes the power of the plant derived from a religious source. The Swiss Dominican Felix Fabri reported in the 1480s that 'roses from Jericho were said to be of assistance to barren women'. Sometimes bathing rather than drinking was prescribed. Hot baths with decoctions of herbs, above all St John's wort, were employed in eighteenth-century France. Clearly reserved to upper-class women, this procedure still has traditional features. Other practices involved bodily contact, often with the appropriate parts. According to an Andalusian rhyme:

> There is a herb
> Called *borraja*;
> Every woman who walks on it,
> At once becomes pregnant.

The custom is noted in England of a childless wife going naked to pick St John's wort at Midsummer, while in parts of Portugal women rolled naked in a field of flax before dawn on St John's and rubbed their bodies with the dewy stalks. Elsewhere plasters or poultices were applied. A late medieval guide to health advocated plasters of eggs, cloves and saffron put on the belly of the woman, the man or both; while an Anglo-Saxon leechbook included this prescription: 'Bind on her left thigh, up against the kindling limb, the nether-ward part of henbane, or twelve grains of coriander seed' – to be kept there until 'the bairn be kindled'.[38] A Venetian medical book of 1602 referred to placing a bag of herbs in the vagina prior to intercourse.

Other magical procedures involved visiting another woman who had just given birth, sometimes being sure to be the first visitor; wearing clothes or shoes belonging to such a woman or to the father of a large family, or to one's own husband. 'A south Slavonian woman who desired a child put a chemise on a fruitful tree and next morning placed it on her own person.' This practice was found elsewhere, and trees whose fruit had sexual connotations were favoured, for example figs and pomegranates. Other examples of sympathetic magic involved animals and animal parts. In the fifteenth century, a white bull 'suitably festooned with garlands' was led in an annual procession by the monks of Bury St Edmunds from a particular meadow to the abbey gates, and 'women who wanted to conceive would accompany the bull, stroking its sides'. In the Lodève region 'putting on one's head the skin of a ewe that had had lambs' was practised. But most common was contact with or consumption of the reproductive organs of an animal. A French manual on husbandry, published in 1564 and frequently reprinted, gave this recipe 'to make a barren woman fertile: Take a doe big with fawn, remove the womb from her belly, pull out the fawn without washing it, dry it in the oven', from which a potion was made. The late medieval guide already cited had a similar recipe for powder made from the womb and vulva of a hare. 'In the Rioja, in modern times, sterile women applied to their bellies for three days a cow's udder with two teats, indicating the two ovaries.' The testicles of pigs, foxes and other animals were also used. According to an English medical compendium of around 1390, for example, 'for sterility in a woman let her swallow the right-hand testicle of a hare at the end of her menstruation, and she will conceive'.[39]

Touching, encircling, bestriding, but above all rubbing standing stones was a very common procedure to induce fertility all over Europe, and was already being condemned by the clergy in the sixth century. The Great Rollright stones in Oxfordshire, for example, 'could cure barrenness in women if certain ceremonies were performed beside them'. Other accounts are more specific about the nature of the rituals. 'Young wives rubbed their bellies against the stone of Ronan [in Brittany] in the first months of marriage, and sterile women slept on it for three successive nights in the hope of becoming mothers.' Large crowds went on annual pilgrimage on 15 August to 'the most famous standing stone in the Haute-Vienne. Young women who were struck with sterility did not hesitate to lift up their skirts, so as to rub their genitals against the granite', which had the form of a phallus. Quite often as here such cults had been taken under vague clerical aegis by building a church or chapel beside the stone or by placing it inside one. The chapel of St Nicholas at Huez in the diocese of Grenoble, for example, contained 'a phallic stone revered in the seventeenth century by young girls and sterile women'; and Douglas noted a similar object in the church at Positano on which women knelt. Columns might have the same function as stones. In the crypt of the church of Notre-Dame-d'Orcival in the Puy-de-Dôme, 'sterile women went to rub their bellies on the biggest pillar and those who want to marry on the smallest.' At Venosa in Calabria, 'a round Roman pillar near the entrance to the church was worn smooth by the bodies of females who pressed themselves between it and the wall, in order to become mothers'.[40] We should also mention sitting in natural stone niches or 'chairs', or lying in or even copulating in stone 'beds'. These again might be Christianized by associating them with saints.

Image magic was also performed. When Eleanor Cobham, Duchess of Gloucester, was accused in 1441 of trying to procure the king's death by sorcery, human figures in wax and metal were found in her possession. She denied, however, that they were for use against the king; rather 'she did it for to have borne a child by her lord the duke'. Recourse was also had to magical practitioners. In folk-tales, for example 'The Beautiful and the Ugly Twin' or 'Tommelise', barren wives seek the aid of witches or sorcerers. Tom Thumb was born only after his mother had consulted Merlin, 'cunning in all arts and professions, a conjurer, an enchanter, a charmer'.[41] In the Arles district, women invoked the fairy Esterelle to become pregnant.

More direct recourse might be had to the ritual of the Church. The clergy recommended prayers, masses and fasting, and later frequent confession and communion. In the medieval French story of 'King Florus and the Fair Jehane', when the couple remained childless, 'the lady caused masses to be sung and was urgent in prayer for her desire'. In modern Spain, women gave alms or promised to wear a religious habit for a certain period of time. In hard cases, priests might celebrate the special masses included in the old diocesan rites 'to free them from all ligatures, release them from the malign influence of Satan, and give them a holy posterity'. Exorcism was also used where male impotence was ascribed to spells, as we shall see. Religious amulets were also sometimes employed. A 'True Letter from Jesus Christ' was published at Bastia in Corsica in 1858, having supposedly been given to a young girl cured of being deaf and dumb. Among other things, it claimed that 'if any woman cannot have a child, she will conceive if she places this holy letter on her breast and recites three Ave Marias'.[42]

But far more common for infertile women was seeking the aid of the saints. Accounts of miracles in the Lives of saints and at shrines feature this category of favour from earliest times. St Theodore of Sykeon's biographer and disciple Eleusius relates that his own parents 'had been married several years yet had had no children, so they came to the saint who prayed over them and blessed their girdles, and through that prayer I was conceived and born'. In gratitude, Eleusius' parents donated him to St Theodore's monastery, a common reaction in the early medieval period in the East and the West, 'and through the saint's [further] prayer my parents received another son, as a substitute for me, whom they named after the saint', another frequent way of expressing thanks. The first miracle performed by Edward the Confessor was the healing 'of a young woman, married to a man of her own age, who was unable to have a child. After the king touched her, her health returned and within the year she gave birth to twins'. Again, in the later twelfth century, 'a childless couple was finally able to conceive after Gilbert [of Sempringham] slept in their bed'. After the death of the saintly Béranger at Saint-Papoul in 1093, miracles multiplied at his tomb, and, among them, 'a sterile woman who prayed there became pregnant'.[43]

Most regions had a number of shrines which specialized in this area (see Plate 23). They were associated with many different saints, but certain patrons predominated. First of these was the Virgin Mary. The archpriest of Talavera referred in a sermon in 1438 to a couple 'going on a pilgrimage to pray St Mary to give them the son they wanted'. An ex-voto inscription at Notre-Dame-de-Grâce at Gignac dating from the sixteenth century reads:

> Jean Cabanette, of Lodève, was deprived of posterity, when his wife Catherine Pastourel vowed to go for three successive years to Notre-Dame on the day of the Feast of the Assumption. Her wishes were fulfilled and, after twenty-five years of sterility, she brought into the world a son, who became a monk in the Order of St Benedict.

Similarly, St John Eudes claimed that he had been conceived only after his parents had gone around 1600 to the shrine of Notre-Dame-de-Récouvrance at Touailles, where a fourteenth-century statue of the Virgin was reputed to aid sterile couples. More recently, the women of Monterchi in Umbria objected to the suggestion that Piero della Francesca's fresco of the Madonna del Parte be moved from its chapel there to a museum. 'For them it was a potent talisman of fertility and birth.'[44] In a more 'folkloric' cult, existing in the seventeenth century and dying out only in the inter-war period, women wanting children climbed up to the chapel of Notre-Dame-des-Oeufs in Haute-Provence. They had to take two eggs with them, one of which was consumed on the spot at the Spring festival, the other being buried in the ground and eaten the following autumn.

St Anne was another universal maternal saint. A sixteenth-century French prayer to her explained that she was herself 'for a long time sterile, but then you conceived in your old age and beyond the age of conception, by the wish and goodness of God'. Devotees hoped to follow this example. At the end of a fifteenth-century English Life in verse, the author prays to the saint on behalf of the couple who commissioned the poem and who longed for a male heir:

> Provide, lady, even that John Denston
> And Katherine his wife, if it please the grace
> Of God above, by thy merits, may have a son
> Of her body.

Aubrey reported in the 1680s that the chapel dedicated to St Anne in the Temple Church in London 'was [still] much resorted to by barren women; and was of great repute for opening the womb'. St Anne's cult was greatly encouraged, St Charles of Sezze relates, in seventeenth-century Carpineto after a leading votary conceived a child after eighteen years of fruitless marriage. The shrine of St Anne at Auray in Brittany became important at about the same time. Childless men, women or couples made vows to the saint, visited the shrine and left ex-voto gifts if their wishes were granted. In a case in the late nineteenth century a peasant woman went on foot to the shrine over many miles dragging a cradle behind her, thus making clear to the saint and to everyone else what she desired. A cradle was also involved in the cult of St Anne in the cathedral of Apt in Provence: women wanting children came to rock it. Elsewhere in France, 'putting a hat on St Anne' or placing one's coiffe or other headgear on the statue of the saint was the commonest ritual, a gesture signifying a wish to be impregnated, like taking off and offering one's girdle which was also done.[45]

St Catherine of Alexandria was another specialist in ending sterility, perhaps because her emblem, the wheel or sun, was also a symbol of fertility. Her relics in Rouen were credited with this particular power from the central Middle Ages. A rather unlikely addition to the list of female fertility saints was the 'Fair Rosamund', Henry II's mistress. She was at first buried in an elaborate tomb before the high altar of the church of Godstow nunnery, but this was removed to the chapter house on the orders of Bishop Hugh of Lincoln. There it 'was much visited [until the Reformation] ... especially by women seeking the gift of children and young people seeking a happy issue to their love affairs'.[46]

Many male saints had the same faculty: St Martin, St Domenico of Muro, St Edmund, St Hilary. One of the most important was St Leonard. His relics were kept at the monastery which he was supposed to have founded at Noblac in the diocese of Limoges. But his cult there, which flourished from the seventeenth to the end of the nineteenth century, focused on a large bolt on the church door, known popularly as the 'bolt of St Leonard'.[47] Childless or sonless women, including three queens of France, came to pray there and to move the bolt in and out of its socket. Similar bolts existed elsewhere in France. The cult of St Leonard was also particularly followed in southern Germany, Austria and the Tyrol. Twenty-two miracles attributed to him were recorded at Fürstenfeld in Bavaria between 1588 and 1592, all relating to the cure of sterility or easing the pains of childbirth.

Many of the features of saints' cults here have been mentioned. Devotees made vows, visited and touched the tomb, relics or statue, often with bodies bared. Frequently some other object was the centre of attention. This might be a cord, girdle or garment. 'In Paris we have the mantle of St Lewis', John Bale wrote in 1538,

> Which women seek much, for help in their barrenness:
> For be it once laid upon a woman's belly,
> She goes then with child, the miracles are seen there daily.[48]

In 1395 Francesco di Marco Datini's wife was offered a belt associated with St Catherine. As with St Leonard's bolt, the object might have phallic significance, and the gestures simulate sexual intercourse. An ex-voto figure offered to St Leonard at Aigen-am-Inn, in Bavaria, had an erect penis, according to a report in 1913. The statue of St Guénolé or Guignolet in his chapel near Brest also had a prominent genital organ. According to an account in 1820, women unable to have children scraped the saint's penis, infused the powder in water from a nearby fountain and drank it. At other similar shrines in France, women rubbed the statue or lay on the tomb of the saint, sometimes removing some of their clothes and moving their bodies up and down. Following a parallel line of thought, relics of Christ's foreskin were believed to make sterile women fertile, as were the clappers of church bells. In parts of Spain in recent times, the Child Jesus carried by St Anthony of Padua was taken to their houses.

The association of the fructifying cult with a well or spring was common. St Winifred's well (Holywell) in Flintshire was visited in 1686 by James II and Mary of Modena in order that 'they might be blessed with a son'. Often the water was drunk. Sometimes it was naturally red water like blood; sometimes the water was mixed with wine. Women also washed their breasts or other parts of the body, or bathed. Basque couples without children went up to the hermitage of St Elias to petition the saint, and they bathed in a pool there and washed baby clothes in it. 'At Sangenjo (Pontevedra) in Spain, sterile women bathed in the sea on the eve of the Feast of Our Lady of the Lanzada [the thrust of the lance into Christ's side] before dusk, believing that the ninth wave would fertilize them'. At a Breton shrine dedicated to St Berhed or Brigid, women 'dipped one of their chemises in her well and wore it still wet when they got into bed [later with their husbands]'. According to legend, St Berhed was the innkeeper's daughter at Bethlehem, who helped the Virgin Mary during the birth of Christ.[49] At another Spanish shrine near Burgos, the miraculous pool of Santa Casilda, people threw in little stones and tiles, which it was believed would be converted into children, male and female respectively.

Visits to spas might be an extension of such practices. The sulphurous waters of the later spa of Gréoux-les-Bains were reputed to cure sterility like the nearby shrine of Notre-Dame-des-Oeufs. In Perrault's version of 'Sleeping Beauty', the heroine's parents are unable to have a child: 'They went to all the waters in the world; vows, pilgrimages, everything was tried'. The behaviour at spas might echo that at shrines. At Plombières, for example, in the late nineteenth century, the water gushed out of a rock, and women sat on special seats like saddles 'so that they could receive the jet on their genitals'.[50]

Other practices at shrines are reported. In modern Spain

> at Ribavadia (Pontevedra), sterile women went to the shrine at midnight, at full moon, prayed, took oil from the sanctuary lamp and mixed it with communion wine [which they took away] and gave to their husbands to drink, the latter being ignorant of these manoeuvres.[51]

As we have seen, if a child were born through the saint's action, a gift would often be made to the shrine. For the rich, gifts might take the form of babies in gold and silver of the exact weight of the new-born baby concerned. Humbler folk offered swaddled babies in other metals or wax, or candles, rings and other objects. It was also common to give the child the saint's name.

Infertility was blamed more often than not on the woman. 'I planted seeds in her for forty years', Djilas' Uncle Mirko protested, 'and all in vain. No seed can sprout on rock, and out of her you couldn't get even a stone.' But not all made this assumption. A medieval medical guide included a test to discover whether failure to conceive were the fault of the man or the woman. Each urinated in a different pot of wheat bran, which was left for nine days. Worms and a terrible smell would develop in the pot of the responsible partner.[52]

Human infertility was frequently blamed on witchcraft. The Bull *Summis desiderantes affectibus* of 1484 asserted that witches 'hinder men from begetting and women from conceiving'. 'It is witchcraft ... when a woman is prevented from conceiving', declared the *Malleus Maleficarum*, a view echoed by most later demonologists. Specific accusations were made. The Belvoir witches tried in 1618–19 were accused among other things of preventing the earl and countess of Rutland from having any more children. And similar ideas existed at that time and later at the popular level. 'A childless couple in the Abruzzi was regarded as being under an evil spell.' Taven, the witch of Les Baux tells the other women in Mistral's *Mirèio* that 'an evil look [can] tie up a woman's seed'. The notion of 'tying' women by witchcraft also existed in northern France, Italy and Spain. In the Metz region, the number of knots tied in a length of flax during the wedding determined the number of babies which would be 'suppressed'. In Catalonia and elsewhere in Spain in modern times, the supposed witch used a hair-slide or other contraption with a sliding knot or fastener. She chanted: 'Needle, little needle, may the place stay firmly closed', and while the slide remained closed the woman would remain infertile.[53]

Paradoxically, however, much attention was paid to the problem of male impotence. All over Europe from Ancient times to the present, it was believed that a man's ability to perform sexually could be removed or diminished by magic. The *Malleus Maleficarum* distinguished five ways in which men were prevented by witchcraft from copulating, the most important being making their partners loathsome to them, impeding erection and stopping ejaculation, and specific accusations figure in witchcraft trials. Special weight was lent to the charge by the fact that impotence, whether induced by magic or not, could be a reason for annulling a marriage.

Bewitching of this kind was most likely to occur at weddings. Isabeau Cheyné, tried as a witch in the Vivarais in 1656, was asked 'if she had not sometimes by means of spells tied the lace [a means of causing impotence, as we shall see] on newly-weds, to which she replied that the only lace she had tied was that on her own skirt'. Precautions were therefore taken, some of which we have already encountered. In northern France, the fiancés might go a few days before the wedding to the parish church, where they passed in front of the crucifix without saluting it. Sexual intercourse before the wedding or the espousals was wise. In Renaissance Tuscany, the moment of consummation was advanced from the wedding proper to the 'ring day', in order to avoid 'spells and enchantments threatening the couple with impotence'.[54] In early modern England perhaps half of couples had intercourse before the wedding. This consideration was also one of the motives for clandestine weddings.

On the wedding day, the groom put salt, grain or a coin in his pockets and/or his shoes. The bride might also put grain in her shoes or keep the ring in one of them until it was needed, and the ring had then to be knocked out without handling it. In the Perche, it was important for the bride and not the groom to push the ring over the second joint of her finger.

Impotence was brought about by a variety of means, usually during the wedding ceremony. In Languedoc in the 1590s, according to Thomas Platter junior,

> while the priest says: 'What is united by God, let no man put asunder' – 'But let the Devil do it', murmurs the sorceress, throwing a farthing over her shoulder and tying a knot in lace. If the coin disappears without being found, the trick is done: the newly-wed man will be impotent towards his wife as long as the lace remains knotted.

The spell could also be cast at other points in the ceremony. Knotting or tying a lace, string, ribbon or braid, known in French as *le nouement de l'aiguillette* or in German as *Nestelknüpffen* was the commonest method, and the French demonologist Bodin claimed that there were more than fifty ways of doing it. In the Limousin in modern times, a string with knots in it was hidden in the bridal chamber, the number of knots indicating the number of times that the groom would try and fail to consummate the marriage. The French term derives from the *aiguillettes*, or laces that attached the hose to the doublet or that tied the cod-piece, this referring to undressing for sexual activity. It is significant that among the ways of preventing impotence was either unloosing 'every knot in the clothing of the bride and bridegroom before the celebration of the marriage ceremony', as in eighteenth-century Scotland; or preempting the 'tying' by having the bride wear something with knots in it, as in modern Greece (see Plate 14).[55]

Other means were used. The German demonologist Stridtbeckh wrote in 1690 that 'a lock was commonly fastened with conjurations during the wedding ceremony and then thrown with its key into water'. Locking a door and saying magic words was said to be practised in northern Greece in modern times. In the Charente, a wooden peg was driven into the wall of the church during the nuptial mass at the precise time that the *sanctus* bell was rung. The larger the peg, the more effective the ritual; some magic words were also uttered. A defamation trial in Northumberland in 1435 referred to 'planting a stake which tied up men's organs so that they were unable to copulate'. Other methods involved the use of plants or animal parts. According to the late medieval health guide already cited, 'vervain carried or drunk will not permit the penis to go stiff ... and vervain placed under the pillow makes an erection impossible for seven days'. The juice of vervain might also be rubbed on shoe-laces, which were placed against the flesh. Albert the Great in the thirteenth century described another procedure: 'Take the penis of a newly killed wolf, go to the door of him you wish to bind and call him forth by name. As soon as he answers, tie the penis with a length of white thread and immediately the poor man will become impotent.'[56] This method found its way into the popular magical book, the *Petit Albert*, current in France down to the eighteenth century, and was still supposedly practised in the Charente in this century.

As some of these examples show, it was believed that impotence could be brought about in circumstances other than the wedding itself, though the aim was nearly always to prevent marital intercourse. 'Hast thou done what some adulteresses are wont to do?', asked the 'Corrector' of Burchard of Worms. 'When first they learn that their lovers wish to take legitimate wives, they thereupon by some trick of magic extinguish the male desire, so that they are impotent and cannot consummate their union with their wives.' An English-French dictionary of 1611 explained *esguillette nouée* as meaning: 'The charming of a man's codpiece point so, as he shall not be able to use his own wife or woman [though he may use any other]'. Platter noted too that the spell he described left a man's 'virility undiminished for other women, and from this comes adultery and all kinds of disorders'.[57] Though witches were most often linked with such magic, others could perform it: discarded mistresses, as we have seen, disappointed suitors, priests, jealous step-mothers, even children.

There were many 'cures' for impotence. Canon law referred to penitence, prayers, almsgiving and exorcism – standard ecclesiastical remedies. 'Between 1500 and 1790, all French diocesan service books included condemnations of the *aiguillette* rite and prayers to exorcize it'. Martin Guerre and his wife in the County of Foix in 1546 'had four masses said and were given sacred hosts and special cakes to eat' by an old woman. Unorthodox prayers were also said. Abbé Thiers mentions saying certain prayers for seven mornings at sunrise with one's back to the sun. A modern prayer from the diocese of Meaux was addressed to Jesus and the Virgin Mary and also referred to Jacob, Abraham and Sarah, and it had to be said morning and evening for fifty days, while abstaining for the same period from any attempt at intercourse. Visits to shrines were rare, though pilgrimage to Notre-Dame-de-Puy-en-Velay and to the shrine of St Foutin, a phallic saint, in Provence is mentioned. One of the miracles occurring at the tomb of the cardinal of Luxemburg at Avignon in the 1380s involved an older man married to a younger woman, who prayed successfully to the saint 'to be able to accomplish the conjugal act, which he had been prevented from doing through eighteen months of marriage'.[58]

Medieval and early modern herbals recommended eating the flowers of willow or poplar, or taking concoctions of 'hot' plants: ginger, leeks, scallions, wild rocket. Artemisia, mistletoe and orchid bulbs were also prescribed, the last having a resemblance to testicles. But the commonest magical remedy for impotence was some kind of 'untying'. In the Limousin, it was enough to find the knotted cord or thread and undo the knots. The seventeenth-century canonist Bordoni referred to the bridegroom who believed that he had been 'tied' 'making water through the wedding ring to recover his virility', as though it were common practice. And a woman accused before the Inquisition in the Veneto in the 1580s said that she advised this technique among others. In her case, the ring had to be one 'with which a young virgin had been married' and it was dipped in holy water. A variation in seventeenth-century France involved 'pissing into the keyhole of the church where one was married' preferably three or four mornings in a row; or white wine might be poured through the ring. The alternative techniques in the Veneto included placing a ploughshare under the bed, or 'the hoe and the shovel which were used for burying the dead'.[59]

In France again, the couple might strip naked and each kiss the other's left big toe, or they might be put in a barn, once more naked, tied to a post and whipped, untied, and then given food and a flagon of wine and locked in for the night. A Scottish folk-tale seems to reflect a similar kind of sexual therapy. When a young man refuses the advances of a witch, she changes him into a worm; the worm is restored to its proper shape by a queen who 'took it up in her hand and stroked it three times over her knee'.[60]

Love magic was important in the Ancient world and is referred to by writers from Theocritus to Apuleius. Love charms have been preserved in Egyptian papyri of the fourth and fifth centuries. Medieval evidence is also clear. The Penitential of Theodore in the eighth century referred to making 'an unclean mixture of food for the increase of love'. Other texts from the Carolingian period mention potions given by wives to their husbands to make them love them and a philtre, given by a nun to a man to attract him, which was made of the bones of the dead, hairs or pubic hairs, herbs and snails. Burchard of Worms condemned women 'who through certain spells and incantations can turn the minds of men either from hatred to love or from love to hatred'. A later German text explained that 'rue for use in erotic magic should be sprinkled with urine by the interested party, then with salt'.[61] Garlic, leeks and other plants were also believed to be aphrodisiacs.

All of this is greatly amplified and details filled in by the much richer sources from the early modern and modern periods. We are particularly well-informed about early modern Italy, thanks to the work of Ruggiero, Martin, O'Neil and others on cases brought before the Inquisitions. In a case in Venice in 1581, for example, Andriana Savorgnan sought to bind her lover to her. She burned the tips of the olive branches given out in church on Palm Sunday, and tied them together and dipped them in holy water, while she recited this incantation: 'As I bind this wood with this string, so too may be bound the phallus of Nicolo Corner so that he may not be able to go with any woman other than me'. The branches were then planted in the floor of a ground-floor room to the recital of a similar formula. In another case in 1631, a nail or a knife was hammered 'into the chimney-breast or into a piece of bread in the shape of a heart' to the incantation: 'So Christ is nailed to the cross; as the nail wounded Christ, so the heart of [whoever] will be wounded' with love.[62]

All kinds of other or additional procedures were employed. Religious paraphernalia were common. These included the use of holy oil and holy water, invocation of saints, having a priest bless or 'baptize' magical objects, or placing them under the altar cloth during mass, as well as magical use of formulae from the liturgy and of the host itself. Paolina de Rossi in Venice in 1588 tried at first to retain the affections of her lover by giving him sage and her menstrual blood in his food. When this failed, she hired a priest to write the 'secrets' of the mass on the herb: '*Hoc est enim corpus meum*'. When this too failed, she appropriated a piece of the host and placed that in his food.[63] Menstrual blood was regularly used, together with particular herbs. Sage and rue were believed to be especially effective.

Written charms were also common. In Venice and elsewhere these were known as *carta di voler bene* and bound the intended person to love oneself and be unable to eat, drink or sleep otherwise. A wide range of other objects and procedures are reported. The use of *calamita* or magnets, sometimes blessed or baptized by a priest, was frequent, to draw one person to another. St Bernardino in early fifteenth-century Siena referred in a sermon to 'spells and paint or dead men's hair or cork or cotton-wool', which is reminiscent of early medieval procedures already mentioned. Measuring the erect penis was also done, placing semen in food and placing magical objects in the bed. There was also image magic and invocation of the Devil. Matteuccia Francisci, a woman from Todi tried in 1428, specialized in love magic of various kinds. When the mistress of a local priest complained that he was neglecting her, 'Matteuccia took a wax image and placed it on a fire, while the client recited words comparing the wax to the priest's heart; after this ceremony the priest loved the woman passionately and did her bidding'. A young apprentice in Venice made a written pact with the Devil in 1590 to make a particular woman 'be inflamed with love for me'. In another case in the city, a lamp was lit before a tarot card of the Devil; and hammering procedures were sometimes believed to conjure the Devil.[64]

Another mode of love magic was the use of tokens and gifts, knots and hearts being very popular. Italian majolica plates from the fifteenth to the seventeenth centuries were sometimes love gifts of this kind, adorned with the names of the couple and with appropriate devices. A Faenza plate from

1470–80, now in the Victoria and Albert Museum, depicts 'a naked youth bound in the guise of St Sebastian to a tree and exposed to the cruel archery of his mistress; a heart pierced with arrows in a chalice [stands] between the two'.[65]

Love magic was also important in other parts of Europe, south and north. Don Quixote told a man sent to the galleys for being a pimp and a conjuror:

> As for philtres and such-like compositions which some silly women and designing pretenders make, they are nothing but certain mixtures and poisonous preparations, that make those who take them run mad; though the deceivers labour to persuade us they can make one person love another.

St Teresa of Ávila, referring to a real case, was less dismissive. A priest, to whom she went for confession as a young novice, was involved with a woman. Teresa enquired into this

> from members of his household ... and saw that the poor man's fault was not so grave, because the miserable woman had had recourse to enchantments, by giving him a little image made of copper, which she begged him to wear for love of her around his neck; and this no one had influence enough to persuade him to throw away.

St Teresa did, however, persuade him to give up the little image and 'had it at once thrown into a river'. The priest at once came to his senses, lamented 'his ruinous state', became very devout and died within the year.[66]

Similar kinds of evidence exist from most countries. The French *Petit Albert*, published in 1709, includes two examples of 'love secrets'. The first required blood to be drawn on 'Spring Friday' and dried on the stove with two hare's testicles and the liver of a dove. The resultant powder placed in the drink of the victim 'will make that person love you'. The other was more psychological. The would-be lover had 'to live chastely for five or six days leading up to a Friday', then 'eat and drink hot things to excite your love'. Finally, 'a familiar conversation should be sought with the object of your passion, and ensure that you can look at her for the length of an Ave Maria, for the visual rays meeting mutually are very powerful vehicles of love'.[67]

Love magic was also practised extensively in early modern Britain by both men and women. Shakespeare refers to love magic in several of his plays, notably in *A Midsummer Night's Dream*, where it is central to the plot. The juice of the flower Love-in-Idleness placed on Titania's eyes while she sleeps makes her love Bottom, when she sees him first on waking. The same love magic is used to make Lysander love Helena rather than Hermia and later on to make Demetrius reciprocate Helena's love. Again, in *The Merry Wives of*

Windsor, when Mistress Page and Mistress Ford appear to accept Falstaff's advances, Mistress Quickly tells him: 'I think you have charms'. He replies as if she meant the use of magic of some kind: 'Not I, I assure thee; setting aside the attraction of my good parts, I have no other charms'. And fiction here reflected reality. In a case before the church courts in Montgomeryshire in 1579, Gruffydd ap David ap John was accused of practising 'enchantments and witchcraft' to procure the love of a local woman; while in another around the same time in Essex, a woman was said by her accuser to be 'a common whore, who would have gotten loving powder to have made the said Byatt to have loved her'. At the end of the seventeenth century Aubrey noted the custom of 'moulding of cocklebread', in which 'young wenches' kneaded dough with their buttocks, saying:

> My Dame is sick and gone to bed
> And I'le go mould my cockle-bread.

The dough was then baked into bread and given to a favoured male in the belief that he would henceforth adore the girl. Another procedure recorded in a seventeenth-century magic book involved writing magical words on an apple hanging on a tree,

> and then say: I conjure thee Apple of Apples by the name of these devils, which deceitfully deceived Eve in Paradise, that what woman soever it be that doth eat and taste of this apple that she may burn in love of me. Say this four times upon the apple and then give the apple to what woman you will.[68]

Love magic has continued to be practised in the modern period in Europe, especially but not exclusively in the Mediterranean area. 'Love potions have great local currency', Pina-Cabral writes of the Alto Minho. 'They are used extensively by young unmarried and married women alike, both to win the love of young men and to preserve that of their husbands. When men claim that women *enfeitiçam* (bewitch), they mean it both metaphorically and literally.'[69] Much the same situation obtained in southern Italy. In Lucania, De Martino reports the use of incantations and of potions put in wine, coffee or broth in order to bind a lover or detach him from another woman. Menstrual blood and blood drawn from veins, and hairs from the armpits and pubes, were put in the philtres. Sometimes a powder made from such blood and hair was surreptitiously consecrated at mass. Knots were also used. In Sicily, similar charms were used, but also dogs' teeth and bones from human corpses, and incantations were addressed to the saints and to the Devil.

In Provence, 'to inspire love, a potion is boiled up in the open air and full sun, made of bark, sap and honeysuckle; if one wants to induce a hopeless love in an enemy, the potion is made at night at full moon'. In a village in the Deux-Sèvres, 'to make a woman whom he coveted go after him, the caster of spells would shut up a green frog in a box pierced with holes. He left the box for a few days on an ant-hill. Gathering the remains of the frog later, he threw them secretly over the woman he loved'. In a similar procedure from the Confolentaise region around 1880, a youth bewitched a girl who had rejected his advances. 'Following the instructions of a sorcerer, he captured a young corncrake and got the girl to kiss it. Then, he burned it in ritual fashion, collected the ashes and sprinkled them over and under the bed where the girl slept.'[70] The same kinds of procedure are found in modern Britain, Germany and Scandinavia. In Scandinavia, for example, accounts refer to placing urine in a drink and drops of blood in an apple, and also to spitting in a woman's clogs. The use of bodily fluids and hair, especially those associated with the genitals, is an obvious feature of love magic in most places.

Love magic was used by both men and women, but it seems to have been more the province of women than men, both in terms of the magical practitioners involved and their clients, and those acting independently. In early modern Portugal, for example, it seems that love magic was above all the domain of female sorcerers. De Martino notes that in Lucania, men were much freer to pursue women in the real world via courtship, serenades, seduction and so on. 'But women are traditionally expected to be passive in affairs of love, and strict custom prevents them from assuming real initiatives in this domain, which explains why they are more likely to go in for magical procedures to win or hold on to the love of men'.[71]

Love magic was used within the context of marriage, sometimes to win a spouse or to force marriage on a reluctant lover, but usually it seems to bind erring or possibly erring husbands. In an exemplar of Caesarius of Heisterbach from the early thirteenth century, a woman used magic 'to hold on to her husband's love'; while a woman at the Russian court in the 1630s used a herb acquired from a witch 'as a love potion to make her husband love her better'.[72] Here love magic acted as a complement to the arranged marriage, either providing an alternative to parental choice or, more commonly, seeking to overlay and reinforce the arranged relationship with passion.

However, in general, love magic was practised in the different environment of illicit sex outside marriage. Many of the examples from early modern Venice involve prostitutes. Or else love magic was adduced to explain unsuitable matches, licit or illicit. The duchess of Bedford was accused in 1469 'of having contrived the marriage of Edward IV and her daughter, Elizabeth Woodville, by witchcraft'. The marriage had occurred secretly five years earlier. The news of the Yorkist king's wedding to a non-royal widow of a

Lancastrian 'caused general astonishment' and some 'found the whole affair so amazing that sorcery seemed the only possible explanation'. Similarly, when Mario Dandolo, from a leading Venetian family, married a courtesan in 1581, his family accused her and her mother of witchcraft. Relevant here is Brabantio's claim in Shakespeare's *Othello* that the Moor must have 'enchanted' his daughter Desdemona for her to love him:

> She is abus'd, stol'n from me and corrupted,
> By spells and medicines, bought of mountebanks,
> For nature so preposterously to err ...
> Sans witchcraft could not.[73]

Here magic explains a daughter's failure to marry according to her father's wishes and the attraction of a white woman to a black man.

7. Prayer to St Margaret for pregnant women. Broadsheet, Toulouse, early nineteenth century. (*Musée National des Arts et Traditions Populaires, Paris*)

6

Conception and Pregnancy

We have seen what magical and religious means were used to ensure the fertility of couples. Magical and religious beliefs also surrounded the circumstances of conception. The Churches proscribed sexual relations at certain times, and breach of these and other taboos was cited when babies were stillborn or born with deformities, a topic to which we will return. Many other notions and experiences had little to do with Christianity, though they were not necessarily incompatible with it.

The reproductive process was not scientifically understood even among the elite. It was a popular belief, according to a Montpellier doctor in 1775, that illegitimate children were more vigorous and cleverer than legitimate ones, since they were usually 'the fruit of intense love-making' and their parents had had to use great ingenuity to arrange their trysts, 'an ingenuity that was transmitted to their offspring'. By contrast, 'children born in the indolent security of licensed copulation' were characterized by 'a certain inertia of spirit'. This is only one expression of a very general mode of explanation via association. Plutarch, an influential author from his own time down to the nineteenth century, recommended 'people to procreate when they are happy, joyful and relaxed', after festivals but not after funerals.[1]

The state or behaviour of fathers might be the determining factor. Falstaff claimed that serious and demure young men, who do not drink or eat a lot of meat, 'get wenches ... when they marry'. In seventeenth-century England, a man who had intercourse while his stomach was full or when he was drunk, according to a contrary view, would be likely to engender sick or foolish children. Gerald of Wales tells the story of a man who saw someone with a tic on his way home. This 'affected him so much that he could not stop thinking about it' and continued to do so while having intercourse with his wife. They conceived a child, 'and, from the moment of his birth, he was afflicted with the same nervous convulsion'. More directly, Tristram Shandy's weaknesses in Sterne's novel of 1759 stem from the fact that he is 'the child of decrepitude! interruption! mistake!', his old father having been distracted during intercourse by his wife's asking if he had remembered to wind the clock and thus ejaculating, it seems, without the proper degree of concentration.[2]

The comportment of the mother was usually more important. There was some idea that only if she achieved orgasm would she conceive at all, and whatever 'conception' possessed her imagination at the time 'would be imprinted on her foetus'. Infatuations with other men, pictures, anything strange, all might produce their effects. Ambroise Paré recounts a case of a cure that went wrong in early sixteenth-century France. A woman 'had a fever, and a neighbour advised her that to cure it she should take a frog in her hand and hold it until it was dead' (a familiar type of procedure as we shall see). She was holding the frog, presumably because it was still alive, when her husband impregnated her that night; she conceived, and the child was born with a frog's face.[3] It was believed too that conception was possible though undesirable during menstruation. The result would be a child with some kind of deformity, at best freckled or with red hair, at worst a leper in the medieval period.

The same structure may be seen in a favourite motif in saints' Lives, which parallels the Annunciation: that is the presaging of future career and greatness at conception. The mother of St Dominic had a dream shortly before she conceived him, in which she saw a little dog, 'which she was to bear in her womb whence it would issue forth holding in its jaws a flaming torch seeming to set the world on fire'. This was a symbol of course of the Order of Friars Preacher which he would found and which were known by the punning name cani Domini or 'dogs of the Lord'. The mother of St Thomas of Canterbury had a dream at the moment of conception in which 'the water of the Thames entered her womb', which sounds like a commoner fantasy.[4]

Conception was also affected by heavenly and climatic influences. It was a common belief in the early modern period that boys were conceived or born in the increase of the moon. In modern Portugal, on the other hand, children 'born or conceived during the waning moon or the period without moon are said to be ... rickety' or scatter-brained. There was a general belief in modern Provence that certain winds induced conception in women as they fertilized the fields. Winds could also determine gender. Writing particularly of the Low Countries, the Elizabethan traveller Fynes Moryson believed that the 'invigorating north wind' produced males, while 'the humid south wind ... created conditions more favourable to the generation of females'.[5]

Pregnancy in traditional Europe was objectively a difficult and dangerous time for a woman and the foetus she bore. Among the elite, women often 'drew up their wills during their first pregnancies'. Indifferent general health, poor diet, hard physical labour for most, all meant that gynaecological complaints, miscarriages and still-births were more prevalent than they are now in the developed world. A view of pregnancy as a 'hardship', if not actually 'a serious illness', in the words of a seventeenth-century doctor from Languedoc,[6] was thus evident in the culture of all classes, though, given the premium set on reproduction, this only strengthened the desire to bring the period of gestation to a successful conclusion.

The threats, dangers and accidents were often attributed to hostile forces. St Hildegard of Bingen wrote in the twelfth century that 'the evil spirits of the air' were always at work to harm the child in the womb. Blame was more often cast on witchcraft and the evil eye. The *Malleus Maleficarum* referred to 'a most notorious witch' at Reichshofen 'who could at all times and by a mere touch bewitch women and cause a miscarriage'. Many of those tried as witches all over Europe in the early modern period were accused of or confessed to causing miscarriages. De Martino provides a more circumstantial and recent account from Lucania. A woman who was seven months pregnant felt someone pulling at her bedcovers one night.

> I awoke and saw another woman who bent over me and began to pinch my belly. 'You will go back to sleep', she said, 'and your baby will die'. I could not move and stayed where I was for a while. Finally I could move, and I heard a sound of clogs. The next day I miscarried. Everyone told me that someone had bewitched me ...

explaining that it was the result of envy.[7] Such envy, often manifested via the evil eye, was most likely to come from a woman who was herself barren.

Witches could also cause false pregnancies and prevent or delay the termination of normal ones. Marguerite Mathieu from Toulouse claimed in the late 1660s that her pregnancy had dragged on for years after she had refused the services of a particular midwife who had a reputation as a witch. This woman had told her 'that, since she didn't want her help, that of any other midwife would be useless, for she would never be delivered', and she made a sign on Marguerite's belly. In the Scottish ballad 'Willy's Lady', Willy's mother, a 'vile rank witch', binds the child in the womb of her daughter-in-law of whom she disapproves, saying to her son:

> But she shall die and turn to clay,
> And you shall wed another may [maid].[8]

It is hardly surprising therefore that pregnancy was surrounded by a host of religious and magical rituals and precautions. These started with pregnancy tests. As now, interruption of the periods was the essential sign, but it was harder to read given the much less regular menstruation of women in the past and the practice of lengthy breast-feeding. As we have seen, moreover, the role of menstruation in the reproductive cycle was not understood. Recourse was therefore had to other criteria. Medieval and early modern texts refer to changes in the face and especially the eyes, the 'mask of pregnancy'.[9] Other tests included urinating in a pot of grain to see if it germinated or not, and placing a clove of garlic in the vagina: if the woman could taste the garlic in her mouth in the morning she was not pregnant, since there was free passage through her womb.

Although there is evidence that many women worked through their pregnancy, this does not necessarily mean that no account was being taken of their state. The most obvious way to avoid the threats from hostile forces was precisely to ignore or conceal the pregnancy and to behave quite normally, at least in the early stages. When the pregnancy had become common knowledge, which was ultimately difficult to stop in small communities, then it would not be mentioned or alluded to only indirectly and via euphemisms. In many places, pregnant women were accorded special treatment and privileges. They might be shown leniency by the authorities if they committed offences; they might be given special supplies of food; and they might be let off work. According to an account from around 1600, in dividing up carcases among the leading members of Irish communities, certain parts went to the tailor, the harper, the carpenter and so on, and the 'sweetbread to her that is with child'. A medieval Irish legend 'traced the origin of the first watermill to a king's love for a beautiful captive, telling how he would fain spare his mistress the fatigue of turning the millstone [a real female chore] when she was great with child'.[10]

Sometimes pregnant women were secluded from normal social life altogether as if they were impure. In the Limousin, they were not allowed near bee-hives or byres where there were young animals. It was bad luck, moreover, to meet a pregnant woman: a hunter would have no luck; a conscript would draw a bad number. In Languedoc similarly, expectant women were not permitted to make preserves or set hens on their eggs, taboos similar to those which affected menstruating women. In Rumania, pregnant women had to keep away from the Căluş dancers and vice-versa, because they were polluting. The same notion was present much earlier in debates as to whether a pregnant woman could be baptized. According to Bede, St Augustine of Canterbury sought the opinion of Pope Gregory the Great on the subject in 597 and was assured that there was no bar, 'since the fruitfulness of the flesh is no offence in the eyes of Almighty God'. The old anxiety persisted, however, for in the Italian Marches in modern times it was believed that a pregnant woman could not administer emergency baptism. Another reflection of the idea that pregnancy was a polluted state was the belief that milk produced then was 'sullied', an idea found in Renaissance Florence and elsewhere and which was confirmed by elite medical theory.[11]

The Churches provided pregnant women with protection and aid of various kinds. In sixteenth-century Strasbourg 'congregations regularly prayed for expectant mothers. The pastors visited them and devised special prayers to strengthen them'. The Catholic clergy also supplied prayers and blessings, continuing medieval practice. The names of the pregnant women in a parish were traditionally read out at mass, and they were encouraged to attend confession and to receive the Eucharist as the birth approached. More practically, fasting requirements were mitigated in their favour. Belief in the effectiveness of ecclesiastical ritual is again indicated by the development of para-liturgical accretions. Abbé Thiers referred to pregnant women sitting through the Gospel at mass and to the idea that if a mother did receive the Eucharist it would 'sanctify her child so that it would not require immediate baptism'. But the sources also mention acts of individual piety by ordinary women. 'And when the mother feels that the child quickens', an Anglo-Saxon text recommended, 'then let her go to church, and when she comes before the altar, then let her say: "To Christ I have declared this child announced" '. In the fifteenth century Margery Kempe was informed by Jesus that she was pregnant, she related. Though a reluctant mother, she at once asked: 'Ah, Lord, what shall I do for the keeping of my child?', and received an assurance of divine guardianship. Prayers were also said in the household, sometimes it seems by women together. The wife of the Essex parson Ralph Josselin and some women neighbours said prayers together in 1657, when her child 'quickened at about two months'.[12] We have seen that 'quickening' was the time when the foetus became animated.

Particular saints were invoked in pregnancy: St Barbara in Brittany; St Juliana in the Ile-de-France; St Margaret, St Dorothy, St Faith and of course the Virgin Mary in various avatars all over Europe (see Text Figure 7). Most of these patrons were paradoxically virgin women, but there are occasional exceptions. St Mamert, appealed to in the west of France, was a man, but he had a special association with the abdomen and its ills, being 'frequently represented with his belly open, holding his guts in his hands'. Some pictures and statues of the Virgin Mary show her to be pregnant, for example Piero della Francesca's fresco of the Madonna del Parte at Monterchi, and Rubens' 'Visitation' in Antwerp cathedral (see Plate 21). These date mainly from the later Middle Ages and are most common in Spain and Portugal, where they remained objects of popular devotion down to this century despite official ecclesiastical disapproval. They were known as 'Senoras do O' and girls were named after them: 'Maria do O'. In the Nièvre in the nineteenth century and earlier, mothers-to-be went on pilgrimage to a statue of the Virgin at Reclesne. After mass, 'the priest opened the statue to show the Infant Jesus inside his mother, then closed it, reciting prayers'.[13]

Where the saint's statue was the focus of protective influence, women might touch it directly, sometimes with their naked bellies, or indirectly with ribbons or girdles, which then became amulets. They would have votive masses said at shrines and they performed rituals of circumambulation and repeated set numbers of the common prayers. Invoking statues, however potentially helpful, was not without risks, since they were lifeless and dumb and might transmit those qualities to the baby. So mothers in Lucania prayed to statues of the Virgin and Child: 'Let mine be fine like yours, but of flesh and blood like me'; or 'able to speak like me'.[14] Blessing by reputed saints in their lifetimes is also reported. So St Teresa of Ávila was asked in 1582 to bless the pregnant daughter-in-law of the duchess of Alba.

Sacred wells and springs were also much visited, both to treat conditions arising from the pregnancy and to bring it safely to term and ensure an easy birth. Women might drink or immerse themselves in the water, or someone else might dip one of their garments in it, all familiar procedures. Much more unusual was the practice of 'midnight baptism' found in the Minho district of Portugal. A woman with a history of miscarriages would go to a bridge over the River Lima near Ponte da Barca in the middle of the night accompanied by a male relative other than her husband. They stopped in the middle of the bridge and drew up

> a bucket of water from the river. They then await the first man to cross the bridge after midnight and oblige him ... to baptize the unborn child. The woman lowers her garments, and the stranger, dipping his fingers [or an olive branch] in the water, makes the sign of the cross on her bared body

He also said the baptismal formula, but without saying 'Amen' or mentioning a name. The man was then given a meal and later acted as god-father to the child. As Pina-Cabral explains, this is a rite of purification, but, by baptizing the baby in advance, it also preempts any threats to its safe delivery. Some procedures concentrated on trying to secure an easy birth. In Portugal, women walked under the canopy in a religious procession. At Clocnapeacaib in Ireland, women drew some of their clothes through a large holed stone there. Elsewhere clothes were pulled through 'the perforated arms of ancient Irish circular-headed crosses', in an obvious simulation of the birth process.[15]

Relics of saints were also believed to be efficacious in pregnancy. The favoured object here was a holy girdle. Expectant women walked nine times round the girdle and other relics of Sister Iñes of Beniganim in the cathedral of Valencia. In other cases, women might wear the girdle at least for a while. At Angers in the eighteenth century, the girdle of St Lezin was available every Monday in the church of Saint-Julien, for pregnant women 'to wear and pray for a safe delivery'. A fragment of the Virgin Mary's girdle at Quintin in Brittany attracted women from all over the region in the seventeenth century and from even further afield later. Originally the priest carried it to pregnant women 'who put it round their bellies and kept it on during the mass, which they offered for their safe delivery'. Later, in the nineteenth century, the relic was touched with ribbons that were then worn by mothers-to-be round their waists. Particular efficacy was attributed, according to an English folklorist writing in 1893, to those ribbons in white and blue silk provided by the Ursuline nuns of the town.[16] A similar girdle, that of Notre-Dame-de-la-Daurade in Toulouse, is still placed on women when there is special danger of miscarriage.

The girdle or ribbon figures in other more obviously magical practices. In general, expectant women (like newly-weds) avoided strings, ties, ropes and threads of all kinds, and the activities associated with them. In Cracow, a woman 'should not put her legs over a rope, because this would lead to a hard labour'. In the Charentais, a pregnant woman doing any sewing 'had to be careful not to place her thread round her neck as women often do; otherwise her child risked being strangled by the umbilical cord'.[17] In other parts of France, passing under a rope by which an animal was tethered, wringing wet clothes, winding or unwinding yarn, twisting a necklace round the fingers, seeing a priest at the altar put the belt on his alb, all might have the same unhappy effect. In many parts of Europe women did not wear their girdles when they were pregnant. The French term *enceinte* or Latin *incincta* means literally 'without a girdle'. They often also removed scapulars and other religious necklaces, sometimes placing them instead in a bag sewn to their clothing.

But, if they took off their regular girdles, they quite frequently replaced these with others. Some were associated with saints and shrines, as we have seen, but they might have no Christian connection or serve the quasi-practical function of supporting the enlarged belly. Such 'bands' might be of ordinary leather, but wolfskin, dogskin or lead, all with some magical significance, were also used. While normal girdles were worn around and outside the dress, holy girdles and bands were put next to the skin and were invisible. If necklaces (with amulets) continued to be worn, they too were put inside the clothing out of sight. This precaution relates to the belief in the evil eye and also to the idea again that harm would come to pregnant women and their offspring via strings and cords in the wrong place or the wrong hands. The wife in 'Willy's Lady' tried to placate her mother-in-law with the gift of a girdle, which only put her more in the latter's power, and, among the multiple causes of the binding of her womb were the tying of 'nine witch-knots' and doing up her left shoe-lace in a special way. When these were undone, she was delivered of a healthy son. Such 'tying' could be inadvertent.

In Paco [in the Alto Minho], a certain man who had been tying vines the whole
day got up in the middle of the night and undid the whole of his day's work, when
his wife told him that she suspected she was pregnant. He was afraid that the child
would be born with his arms or legs 'tied up'.[18]

Many other taboos were associated with pregnancy. In France, as a rule
mothers-to-be did not prepare the baby's layette, so as not to anticipate a
successful birth; they could not act as godmothers; and they normally avoided
all contact with death, dead persons and dead animals. Healing fountains were
also shunned, in case the baby picked up one of the diseases lurking there. In
southern Italy, women kept away from slaughtered animals and the preparation of fish. Both had little or no blood in them, which might induce a wasting
anaemic illness in the baby. Certain plants or trees could be harmful. In a
modern Danish example, when a baby never made a sound, even at seven
months, people thought the mother 'might have come too close to the elder
tree in the garden or dug the ground near it when she was pregnant'. Yawning
and staring were also dangerous. Linked again to fear of binding or thwarting
the birth were bans on sitting cross-legged, on crossing the hands over the
back of a chair especially in church, and on visiting crossroads. Circular
motions like grinding coffee and cutting and sawing were also often
proscribed. In Poland and parts of Germany 'nothing should be loaned out of
the house of a pregnant woman, because witches could use such objects to
exert an influence'. The same fear underlay concern over the disposal of waste
products. In the Yonne, 'care was taken in a house where a woman was pregnant to empty the washtub the wrong way, and this was supposed to make the
labour easier'. Food taboos included not eating green salad, parsley or
parsnips, not taking the first slice of cheese, and not drinking milk. In Bilbao
this was believed to swell the head of the foetus. In Galicia seafood was
avoided since it would give the baby speckled or hard skin. In the Alto Minho
'the pregnant mother must not eat octopus or lampreys, for otherwise the
child will be born with weak bones or no bones at all'.[19] All over Spain pregnant women would never take food from another person's hand without
saying the name of Jesus from fear of possible evil influence. More generally it
was a common belief that pregnant women should overeat, since they were
'feeding two', or conversely that they should restrain their appetites to keep
the foetus small and thus ensure an easy delivery.

Positively many other protective amulets were worn besides girdles. The
best-known was the eaglestone or aetites. As a twelfth-century writer
explained, 'it contains another stone, as though pregnant: it is therefore
believed to be able to help those with child, lest they should have a miscarriage or give birth laboriously'. One was owned by a canon of Canterbury in

the later seventeenth century. Its power to prevent miscarriages was such, he wrote, 'that my wife can seldom keep it at home, and therefore she has sewed the strings to the knit purse in which the stone is, for the convenience of the tying of it to the patient on occasion'.[20] In modern Greece, lockets were worn with incense and herbs in them. The lockets were made from silver coins that had been begged for and then blessed in church. Commoner examples were pieces of iron, dried toads and a variety of herbs: witch-elm, St John's wort, bistort or snakeweed, medlar, and the so-called 'seeds of St Colette'. Some of these were consumed rather than worn.

More elaborate procedures are recorded. In Gerona in Spain in modern times 'a black hen was sacrificed to cure nausea and sickness [in pregnancy], which was attributed to the evil eye'. According to a nineteenth-century Danish account, 'if a woman crawls naked through the caul of a foal, she will give birth without any pain, but her first born will become a *mare* (nightmare) or a werewolf'. An Anglo-Saxon charm associated the well-being of the child-to-be with the sexual act that had engendered it. 'And when a woman is with child and she goes to her lord to bed, then let her say:

> Up I go, over thee I step;
> With a living child, not with a dying one;
> With a full-time one, not with a doomed one.

Early modern medical opinion discouraged sexual relations during pregnancy, probably in vain. There are indications indeed that at the popular level they were believed to be beneficial, helping to strengthen the child or, in the later months, as John Pechey wrote in an English midwife's manual in 1698, 'to facilitate delivery'. Death, we have seen, was usually avoided from fear of contagion, but the aura of the dead could be harnessed for protection, as the same Anglo-Saxon charm illustrates. A woman, afraid of not being able 'to nourish her child' in the womb and of the other usual dangers, should 'go to the grave of a dead man, and step three times over the grave, and say three times these words':

> Be this my aid against hateful slow birth;
> Be this my aid against dour and dismal birth;
> Be this my aid against hateful miscarriage.[21]

A further range of beliefs and practices relates to the impressionability and cravings of pregnant women. 'Enlightened' and medical as well as general opinion held that the child she was carrying could be 'marked' or otherwise affected by the mother's behaviour and experience in pregnancy. Not only was she extremely receptive to external influences, but her own wishes and thoughts could be translated to the foetus. Montaigne declared that 'we see women transfer divers marks of their fantasies, unto children they bear in their wombs', and he referred to a baby born in Pisa 'all shagged and hairy over and over, which her mother said, to have been conceived so by reason of an image of St John the Baptist, that was painted, and hung over her bed'. In modern Lucania, drinking from a bucket could give the child a mouth as wide as a bucket, while burning the wood of a tree with rough and spiny bark near a pregnant woman could make her child have scaly skin. Having been impressed by the picture of an angel, the wife of a surgeon from Langres in the 1780s gave birth to a baby with exactly the same features and colouring, but within three days he had returned, angel-like, to heaven. Shakespeare's Autolycus mocks the same belief in *The Winter's Tale* with his ballad of 'how a usurer's wife was brought to bed of twenty money-bags at a burden'.[22]

Many of the taboos that we have already encountered derive from the same belief. In a range of others it is even more clearly present. Pregnant women everywhere were advised to avoid shocks, frights and any experience inducing strong emotions. They could not in law be tortured. In Spain they did not attend bullfights. But there was more to this always than practical concern not to bring about a miscarriage. The shock or intense feeling could fix some aspect of what had caused it on the child, in the same way that any experience at the moment of conception could. When a child in Shropshire in the last century was born with a withered arm, this was said to be the result of 'the fright her mother felt when a one-armed beggar cursed her'. When Napoleon was visiting the Low Countries in 1810 with the pregnant Marie-Louise, the grotesque giants of Wetteren paraded in their honour. On seeing them, the Emperor became alarmed and ordered: 'No monsters, no monsters!' The sight of drunkards, epileptics and cripples could all be similarly dangerous, since they could all stamp their deformities on the foetus. Lady Mary Wortley Montagu expressed a view shared by elite and people when she referred in a letter to her daughter in 1759 to a visit she had received from a young man who 'has neither visible nose nor mouth ... which hindered my sleeping all night ... You may imagine such a figure should not be seen by any woman in a possibility of breeding'.[23]

These beliefs often related to animals. There was a woman in Presteigne in 1871, a Miss Sylvester, Kilvert reports in his diary, who was known as the 'woman frog'. Her head, legs and feet were frog-like and instead of walking she hopped.

Shortly before she was born a woman came begging to her mother's door with two or three little children. Her mother was angry and ordered the woman away. 'Get away with your young frogs', she said. And the child she was expecting was born partly in the form of a frog as a punishment and a curse upon her.

A similar idea informs Grimm's tale, 'Hans My Hedgehog', though the wish involved was the father's. A successful peasant had no children and was ridiculed by the other men for this failure. On one occasion this made him so angry that when he got home he said. 'I must have a child, even if it's a hedgehog'. So then his wife had a son, whose upper half was indeed hedgehog with the lower half human.[24]

More often it was the sight of the actual animal which produced the effect. In central France contact with or sight of a hedgehog could cause a woman to produce a litter of small hedgehogs. Another animal with special aura generally and in this field was the hare, which was held responsible for a common defect. In Suffolk, according to a nineteenth-century folklorist, 'if a pregnant woman meets a hare and turns it back, the child will have a hare-lip; but if she allows it to pass, no harm will happen'. On the Welsh Borders, the child would be marked unless the mother 'instantly made a tear in her shift' in substitution. Similar effects were attributed to dogs, frogs, toads, lizards, pigs and rabbits. In a village in Lucania sight of copulating dogs caused the baby to be born with a deformation of the os sacrum, known locally as 'the pair of dogs'.[25]

Some encounters with animals simply caused marks. In a modern English example, a woman 'had been frightened in the third or fourth month of pregnancy by a black and tan dog' and 'was convinced that the child would be marked' as a result, though a doctor assured her to the contrary. When the baby was born it had a giant naevus or birthmark resembling the coat of the dog. In the Saintonge, if a mother were frightened by a toad, the child would have a brown mark on its skin, if by a mouse a small hairy place. All over Europe odd sights could cause birthmarks, and women were advised that if they did see something strange or otherwise experience a shock, they should immediately touch some inconspicuous part of their body so that the mark would be transferred to the same place on the child. Alice Thornton in the late seventeenth century, a gentlewoman, thought that 'a mark of a deep bloody colour' on the chest of her second child was caused by 'a fright which came on me by surprise at the sight of a penknife which was nigh to have hurt me'.[26]

Birthmarks were also explained in other ways. In the Chartres region in the seventeenth century, if a woman went into the room where a person was dying, her child risked being born 'with a white mark over the nose, called the bier', which also signified that it would not live long. Sniffing flowers could cause disfiguring marks in parts of Portugal, where birthmarks are called flores or flowers. In modern Greece, St Simeon was held responsible for 'making marks', and expectant mothers took care not to touch any domestic utensil and above all nothing black on his day or 'a birthmark would inevitably appear on the child'. Blemishes caused by disease were also thought, even among the elite, to be transferable to the foetus. When Lady Burgoyne contracted smallpox during her pregnancy in 1646, it was considered 'a miracle', according to her friend Lady Verney, 'that notwithstanding her being so full of the pox, her child be very clear from the least spot'.[27]

However, birthmarks were more usually associated with the mother's cravings in pregnancy, and in some languages the same word was used for both. Great care was therefore taken either to control a woman's appetites – some plants or berries, like medlars, were supposed to stay 'the longings [of pregnant women] for unusual meats'; touching a dead person's hand had the same effect in the Saintonge – or to ensure that they were satisfied. In Fielding's *Joseph Andrews* (1742) typically, Mr Wilson tells Parson Adams that his lost son 'had a mark on his left breast of a strawberry, which his mother had given him by longing for that fruit'. Raspberries, gooseberries, cherries, grapes produced similar fruit-like marks, if the mother ate them or if she wanted to and they could not be procured. A miracle performed in the fourteenth century in Valencia by St Vincent Ferrer reflects the latter belief. Three pregnant women saw a single fig in a tree and each had a craving to eat it. To prevent a fight and the potentially evil effects of allowing only one of the women to be satisfied, the saint caused the tree to produce two more fruit. Pina-Cabral has argued that strict control of the cravings represents 'a moral indictment against the mother's tendency to oral self-indulgence, and the importance for the formation of the child of the need to control this moral failing'. The reproductive needs of the household overrode the individual needs of the woman. On the other hand, where the cravings or 'envies' had to be satisfied, if the child were not to be harmed, there was an idea that those envies which had no outlet might turn back into the mother causing the harm. As Tristram Shandy's father explained: 'She fumed inwardly ... and that, let me tell you ... was ten times worse for the child'.[28] In Minho, the unsatisfied woman might produce a child with the evil eye, which was an expression of envy. The mother's envy had become permanently attached to the child.

Not all these influences were negative. Some women went to shrines to obtain desirable features in their offspring, such as curly hair. Drinking wine, brandy, tea or coffee, that is luxury drinks for most women before the end of the nineteenth century, could help produce a well-favoured child. When Aeneas Piccolomini, the future Pope Pius II, was returning from a mission to Scotland around 1430, he obtained wine and white bread from a monastery in northern England and brought them out at a farmhouse: 'They excited the liveliest wonder among the barbarians, who had never seen wine or white bread. Pregnant women and their husbands kept coming up to the table, touching the bread and sniffing the wine and asking for some, so that he had to divide it all among them'. Looking at beautiful images could generate beautiful babies, though there was some risk in this as we have seen. Brides in fifteenth-century Florence were sometimes given dolls in wax or plaster modelled on the Christ-child, a practice which stemmed in part from 'the belief that the woman would engender a child analogous to the image she kept before her eyes during her pregnancy'. Visions and dreams in pregnancy like those at conception could also forecast the child's future. Addison related in *The Spectator* in 1711:

> There runs a story in the family that when my mother was gone with child of me about three months, she dreamed that she was brought to bed of a judge ... I am not so vain as to think it presaged any dignity that I should arrive at in my future life, though that was the interpretation which the neighbourhood put upon it.

Aeneas Piccolomini is said to have appeared to his mother with mitre and tiara on his head. St Bernard's mother like St Dominic's 'dreamed that she had within her a barking dog', which was taken as a sign that he would defend the Church against its enemies.[29] Here elements from popular belief provide a motif not uncommon in clerical hagiography. Other saints spoke or cried out in the womb.

Most people are curious to know whether a baby is going to be a boy or a girl. In traditional societies with a strong preference for male children, this concern was particularly pressing and a whole range of signs was scrutinized. According to Laget, three factors were of special importance: 'the position of the child in the womb, the place of the child in the family, and the phases of the moon'. 'Boys sat higher in the womb than girls' – a belief that has persisted in England into this century. Again, the abdomen was usually pointed if it contained a girl and round if it contained a boy, and males tended to the right and females to the left. In many parts of France, the first child was likely to be a girl. In Lucania, odd numbers in the birth order were female and even ones male. Characteristics of one child could predict the gender of the next, for example the way the hair fell on the nape of the neck. The influence of the moon was 'linked sometimes to the date of conception, sometimes to that of birth ... In the Vivarais boys are born when the moon is full and girls at new moon'. Lunar influence also combined with birth order. In the Abruzzi 'if a male is born in a waxing moon, the next born will be male. If a female is born in a waxing moon, the next will be female. If a male is born in a waning moon, the next born will be female. If a female is born in a waning moon, the next born will also be female'.[30] Similar schema are found elsewhere, and there were always exceptions in their application, for instance for babies born on special days like Christmas Day.

Many other indicators existed. Some types of women were thought to be more likely to have boys, notably those who were not too 'feminine'. Psychologically this meant women who were 'alert and dextrous', independently-minded, even domineering, and physically those 'of high colour ... brunettes, not too soft, thin rather than fat, on the small side, with firm breasts', in the words of a seventeenth-century French text. Younger women were paradoxically thought more likely to produce girls than older ones. The circumstances of conception were again important, as we have seen. Another French medical source referred to the popular view that 'young couples who make love madly and without restraint usually produce females', which explains why first children were girls.[31]

There were further signs to be read in pregnancy itself. According to an Anglo-Saxon leechbook, if a woman 'walks slowly and has hollow eyes she will bear a boy; if she walks quickly and has swollen eyes she will bring forth a girl'. More generally, where the mother's face changed aspect or colour, or became blotchy or freckled, this meant she was carrying a girl. According to the most widely read German 'housefather book' of the seventeenth century, by Johannes Coler, 'if the mother's nipples turn dark or black, that is a sign of a boy, if yellow [of] a girl'.[32] Again, a woman carrying a boy would tend to have the right breast firmer than the left and the right eye brighter. She would also have any pains in her right side. In Spain, if a woman felt well during the pregnancy, this indicated a boy; if she were sick, a girl. In France, by contrast, vomiting at least at the start of pregnancy showed a boy, as did a pregnancy that outlasted its expected term. Cravings could also be pointers. In early modern Germany, strange desires to eat coal, live fish, chalk or glue signified girls. In France, a liking for wine, a masculine trait, suggested a boy. The time of quickening could also be significant. As we saw in discussing abortion, the male foetus was sometimes believed to show signs of life well before the female. In all this, reference was being made to a general system of gender differentiation. This associated the male with the right or dexter, with rationality, health, and harmony, and the female with the left or sinister, with irrationality (lust and cravings), illness and disorder.

In addition to interpreting natural phenomena, recourse was had to divinatory rituals. One of the oldest of these, referred to in the eleventh-century Salerno treatise by 'Trotula' and by Coler, consisted of letting a few drops of liquid or 'milk' from the woman's right breast fall into a vessel with fresh water in it. If they sank, she could expect a boy; if they floated and then dissipated, she was carrying a girl. In southern Italy, the woman or someone in the family told a friend, as if on the spur of the moment, that his or her hand was dirty. If, in verifying this, the person first turned the hand palm upwards, the baby would be a boy; if palm downwards, a girl. Another procedure featured a certain kind of macaroni. If it assumed a vertical position, when it was being boiled, the baby would be a boy; if a horizontal position, a girl. De Martino suggests that the symbolism here refers to the normal position in intercourse and to the sexual organs. In France, a knife and a pair of scissors were concealed under handkerchiefs on two chairs, and the pregnant woman was invited to choose one chair to sit on. If she chose the chair with the knife, she was bearing a boy; if she picked the scissors, a girl. Again the symbolism is sexual, but the tools are also gender-specific as tools. In many places, a coin was put in the pregnant woman's bodice and allowed to work its way through her clothing. When it fell to the ground, the side that was uppermost indicated the gender of the baby, depending on the devices found on the coins. In Aragón, use was made of that ancient piece of divining equipment: a sheep's shoulder-blade. This was held in the fire before it was dry. If a large, dark spot appeared in the middle of the blade, this signified a boy; a small spot meant a girl; but if no spot at all was seen, this predicted a miscarriage. In the Fens, a couple slept 'with a piece of horseradish under each of their pillows. If the husband's horseradish turned black before his wife's, then the expected child would be a boy, and vice-versa [for a girl]'.[33] Another expedient was to count the number of letters or syllables in the parents' names. If the number of syllables was uneven in Palma de Mallorca, then their first child would be male. Baby clothes, suited one for a boy, one for a girl, were floated on some French holy wells: the garment which stayed afloat longest showed which gender the child would be.

It was also possible to predict whether a woman's labour would be difficult or not. In the Chartres region in Abbé Thiers' time, it was a sign that a woman would have a long labour 'if she left her washtub empty for a long time', while in Provence and elsewhere roses of Jericho were put in water: if they opened out the birth would be easy; if they remained curled up, it would not.[34]

8. Representations of the birth of the Virgin Mary reflected traditional practice.
Carlo Maratti, etching, Rome, *c.* 1650.

7

Childbirth: Delivery and First Days

Though it was a familiar and frequent experience for them – five or six children would be born to the average couple and a married woman would have a baby roughly every two or three years of her reproductive life –, childbirth was dreaded by women before the modern period and with good reason. Death in childbed or shortly afterwards was a salient feature in general mortality rates. First births were always the most dangerous: one first-time mother in eight died around 1600 in the region south of Paris, which seems to be a typical proportion.[1] Problems attributable to congenital defects or to those arising from malnutrition like rickets were more common than now and more likely to prove fatal. Women were also relatively old when they had their first child: the late twenties was usual, the early thirties not uncommon. Medical understanding of the birth process was limited before the seventeenth century and anyway had little impact on most women's experience.

An abnormal presentation or a narrow pelvic passage meant births going on for hours if not days. Surgeons in eighteenth-century France 'do not seem to have been surprised that women could remain five, six or seven days in labour'. Some mothers simply died from exhaustion, others from injury or infection. The village midwife's equipment consisted of a pair of scissors, none too sharp, or a knife to pierce the placenta and to cut the umbilical cord, thread to bind the cord, vinegar in case of bleeding, lubricant of some kind, and a phial of holy water for emergency baptisms. Even a more 'advanced' practitioner in the Netherlands in the early eighteenth century only added to these some 'hooks to help with turning infants in awkward presenting positions or to extract foetuses that had died *in utero*, and a catheter'.[2] Effective forceps had been invented in the late 1700s but they remained the monopoly of a few town doctors for a century and a half more, and even then there remained much popular hostility to their use. Midwives and doctors relied heavily therefore on manual intervention – with hands that were never of course sterilized. Continuous massage of the thighs and genitals with lard, oil, butter, honey or other substances was normal practice, and the opening to the womb was dilated with the fingers. On top of this, women were kept overheated in dirty bedding; they were made to eat and drink copiously; and they might be purged, induced to vomit, or relieved of blood.

Even where the birth was free from complications, the pain would often have been extreme, albeit in an age when people were inured to suffering. Both doctors and the clergy recognized that this agony was the measure for all others. 'The pain caused by one spark of hell-fire', asserted a sixteenth-century picture catechism from Heidelberg, 'is greater than that caused by a thousand years of a woman's labour in childbirth.' Church services, Protestant and Catholic, referred to 'the great pain and peril of childbirth', linking it to the primary human transgression. 'In my confinement', ran a prayer authorized in Provence in the mid seventeenth century, 'fortify my spirit to support the pains that accompany it, and may I accept them as the effect, Lord, of your justice on our sex, for the sin of the first woman.' The same theme is found in sermons and religious plays. In fiction, pain and maternity were closely associated. 'you ne'er oppress'd me with a mother's groan', the Countess tells Helena in *All's Well That Ends Well*, to stress that she is her adopted and not her natural daughter. 'What, is she crying out?', Henry VIII asks of Anne Boleyn in another of Shakespeare's plays and is told:

> So said her women, and that her suff'rance made
> Almost each pang a death.

Unmarried mothers were questioned about the paternity of their babies during the pangs of labour, as if they were being judicially tortured. Direct testimony is rare, but Alice Thornton cannot have been untypical. Her fifth pregnancy ended with contractions lasting three days, then 'sharp travail' which continued for most of a further day; finally 'I was on the rack for the space of two hours ... with such exquisite torment, as if each limb were [being] divided from the other'.[3] Strong drink and sometimes other drugs were administered to deaden the pain, but effective anaesthetics were not of course available for anyone before the second half of the nineteenth century and for poor women until considerably later.

For this and other reasons it is not surprising to find that childbirth like pregnancy was highly ritualized and hedged about with magical and religious precautions to aid and protect both mother and child. Montaigne referred to 'the painful throes of childbearing which our women pass with so many ceremonies'. First, there was no exact knowledge of when the birth was due, and a variety of signs would be looked for: the phases of the moon, as we have seen, or the cries of birds, particularly owls. As the expected time of birth approached, the woman would go to church, confess, take communion, and masses might be said for her in pre-Reformation and Catholic milieus. Taking the sacrament, fasts, and domestic prayers and religious exercises were common in Protestant England. She might also receive the benefit of non-Christian ritual. In the Corrèze, according to a report from the 1890s, 'a woman would go to the blacksmith on the three last nights of the full moon before delivery was anticipated, and he would stretch her out on his anvil pretending to strike her with his hammer and making terrible noises as he did so'. Another procedure to induce labour, found in modern Portugal, was 'to cut a thread of twisted red silk into fragments and drink these in wine'.[4]

Everywhere in Europe the objective dangers of childbirth tended to be attributed to the agency of hostile forces: fairies, the Devil, the evil eye or witchcraft. A Scottish woman claimed in 1576 to have been visited when she was lying in childbed by 'the Queen of Elfdom', who told her that her baby would die. 'The tongue of the ancient serpent', St Hildegard of Bingen wrote, 'extends itself to the sweat of the infant emerging from the mother's womb, and he lies in wait for both mother and infant at that time.' 'Pastors and preachers', the reforming Brandenburg-Nuremberg Church Order of 1533 laid down, 'ought to instruct women in childbed that they are not under the power of the Devil, as has hitherto been imagined.' Many people prosecuted as witches were accused of causing difficulties in childbirth. A woman testified in a trial at Douai in 1610 that her neighbour 'had come to lean against the door-jamb of her house, while she [the accuser] was giving birth with the result that her labour was far longer and more dangerous than normal'. A man tried in the Tyrol in 1645 was said to have wished 'an evil confinement' on a pregnant woman who had refused to give him some wine, causing her 'to suffer greatly in childbed'. Again, in a case from Estonia in the 1650s, when a woman had lost consciousness while giving birth, remaining in a coma for several days, responsibility was pinned on a cat that had climbed on to the roof just over the spot where she was lying, and which everyone believed to have been a local witch in temporary animal guise. In the west of France, 'people went in pairs to fetch the midwife, so as to be strong enough to offset the power of any witch encountered on the way'.[5] We shall see that midwives themselves could be suspected of harmful magic.

One strategy to ensure a safe and speedy birth in these circumstances was to conceal it as far as possible. According to an account of Macedonian customs in 1903, great care was taken to hide the birth from the neighbours. 'Otherwise it is feared that the confinement will be attended by much suffering, due to the influence of ill-wishers or to the evil eye. For the same reason the midwife is summoned in all secrecy and under a false pretence.' Similar precautions are reported from modern Russia, where 'women preferred to give birth in bath-houses, barns and other secluded places' rather than in their houses. Among gypsies, this secretiveness amounted to a full-scale taboo surrounding the act of birth. Gypsy mothers went off into a field, a barn, a tent away from the main camp, and non-gypsy midwives were sometimes chosen to avoid pollution in the community. The same attitude is reflected in the way women all over Europe neglected to make material preparations for their confinements. The special charities that existed universally to provide for women in childbed may be linked to this same culture trait, which also emphasized reliance on the community and fear of preventing good fortune by counting on it. At Flora Thompson's Lark Rise, a box of baby clothes and food was loaned out by the rector's daughter to all women in the village when they needed it and was 'a popular institution' unlike other charities.[6] An actual box is preserved in the Cambridgeshire Folk Museum. Midwives, we have seen, brought their own equipment.

In most of Western Europe, however, the opposite strategy was adopted. The birth took place within a closed but semi-public environment and was enveloped by a network of exclusively female solidarity. (see Text Figure 8 and Plate 22). Typically, in Aragón earlier this century 'when the time of birth approached, all men (including the husband) leave the house in order to avoid complications. This meant that no doctor could be called in'. In the *Quinze joyes de mariage*, a text from fifteenth-century Burgundy, the house is invaded by a large group of women and the husband is kept out in the rain and the cold. In some noble and royal households a screen or traverse was erected in an anteroom beyond which no man could go. The number of women present was generally smaller than this suggests. Five or more are mentioned in seventeenth-century English sources; four to six in French ones. The women usually had to be married. They obviously had a practical role to play, but they were also witnesses, 'gossips' and guardians. The fifteenth-century legist Nider deplored the fact that mothers in childbed were 'surrounded with old women and serving-maids who are full of superstitions which they practise on them'. More recently in the Fens it was customary to have certain women present at the birth 'to take off any curse or spell'.[7] Isolation at birth was a sign of social rejection or abject poverty. On the other hand, not to be included in a birth or events to do with it could be a serious slight. In a case at Dumfries in 1671, a woman not invited to the birth and baptism of her sister-in-law's baby was accused of witchcraft when she fell ill.

In a few places, husbands were present. Thomas Platter senior followed the custom of his native Valais, where 'husbands have to stay beside their wives during childbirth ... But the women surrounded her so that I did not see what they were doing; but I know that my shirt was dripping with sweat'. In late medieval iconography of the Nativity, St Joseph is quite often in the scene 'but in a subordinate role'. If not in the birth-room, husbands might often stay in the vicinity. They are reported as making vows to saints, and they might be called on in an emergency. 'If a woman faints in labour and cannot be revived', Coler advised in his manual, 'then her husband should go to her, take her hand in his, and give her friendly encouragement.' More frequently the husband was 'symbolically present' in the form of an article of his clothing,[8] which might be used to assist the labour as we shall see.

Some official sources, for example from eighteenth- and nineteenth-century France, report that the birth was an entirely group affair, with no midwife attending; but there are many more indications from all over Europe that one woman did play the leading role. She was rarely externally trained before the eighteenth century in Western Europe. Instead she was a local woman, a repository of popular wisdom and expertise, as her names suggest: *matrone, sage femme, comadre, levatrice*, goodwife, *povitukha, hebamme*. She would usually be in her fifties or older, a widow, having had children of her own. Sometimes the office was hereditary, daughters following mothers for generations. Often a kind of apprenticeship was served. Sometimes and not necessarily as an alternative to these, a midwife was chosen by the women of the community who might assemble formally for the purpose. Although she would be poor – the midwife in *Tristram Shandy* 'had been left ... a widow in great distress' – she had much prestige in the village.[9] When professionals did become available in rural areas in more recent times, most women preferred the village matron.

An important element in the midwife's prestige was the fact that in addition to officiating at births, she had other ritual functions. She took or accompanied the baby to baptism and the mother to churching. In Rumania she formed a relationship akin to godparenthood with all the children she delivered and their parents. She was often also a general healer or 'wise woman'. She laid out the dead and performed other funeral rites, for example, emptying the water jars 'in a bereaved household so that the soul will not be kept in them' in modern Portugal.[10] At Minot in Burgundy she cooked for the wedding feast. Most notable of all, as the phial in her equipment proclaimed, it was her duty to baptize the infant if it were in danger of imminent death.

This was the main reason for the ecclesiastical regulation of midwives from the later medieval period onwards. The Brandenburg-Nuremberg Church Order typically stipulated that 'pastors ought most diligently to instruct and warn midwives, that they take baptism in hand seriously and in the fear of God, but chiefly that they know how to recite the [correct] words ... distinctly and in an orderly fashion'. In eighteenth-century Angers, 'a parish midwife had to be blessed by the church before entering upon her work. The ceremony took place at the main mass of Sunday morning'. The baptismal formula was read out to her, and she took an oath while holding a candle near the font. In post-Reformation England midwives were licensed by the bishops and were also required to take an oath, promising to be diligent, not to 'use any kind of sorcery or incantation in the time of travail of any woman', not to destroy or dismember the child, and to baptize the child in time of 'necessity', afterwards informing the parish priest. Similar systems of licensing and swearing existed elsewhere, but in practice many midwives were unlicensed. And there is some evidence that peasant women again preferred the unlicensed village midwife and thought her powers superior. A modern Transylvanian lament for a midwife was full of praise and thanks:

> You took such good care of them,
> My God, you cared for them well ...
> You were not a midwife with a salary;
> You were not the licensed midwife;
> You had a gift from God ...[11]

The civil authorities were also involved in the attempt to control midwives. Informal regulation existed in Nuremberg from the early sixteenth century. From 1590 in France the law required midwives to be authorized by magistrates (and later intendants) and to have passed a test before medical men. Midwives were supposed to report illegitimate pregnancies and births and suspected abortions and infanticides, and they were called in to examine parties in court cases relating to rape and impotence. Doctors tended to be extremely critical of midwives, especially from the eighteenth century onwards when they themselves entered the realm of obstetrics in a serious way. To some extent this reflected a real divergence of standards and skills, but it chimed in too with a more general hostile stereotyping among the elite.

In the Netherlands in the early modern period midwives were frequently represented in a negative way in both art and literature. They were 'custodians of feminine secrets ... often characterized as prime collaborators in plots to dupe husbands [and] ... suspected of exchanging children or covering up for a wife's infidelities'. They were also associated there and elsewhere with child abandonment and prostitution. The 'wise woman' in an English play published in 1638 dealt in general healing, fortune-telling and finding lost objects: 'Then I keep gentlewomen lodgers, to furnish such chambers as I let out by the night ... I am provided for bringing young wenches to bed: and for a need ... I can play the match-maker'.[12]

Midwives were also accused of witchcraft. The witch-midwife was a commonplace in demonological treatises from the *Malleus Maleficarum* to Guazzo, Boguet and Bodin. The first asserted that midwives

in various ways kill that which has been conceived in the mother's womb; or when they do not do this, offer the children to devils ... midwives surpass all other witches in their crimes. And the number of them is so great that there is scarcely any tiny hamlet in which at least one is not to be found.

Such beliefs were reflected in prosecutions. One of the best-known is that of Walpurga Hausmännin 'a licensed and pledged midwife of the city of Dillingen', who was executed in 1587 following her conviction on numerous charges of witchcraft. These included killing new-born infants, causing still-births and causing mothers to die in childbed. For example,

> she had rubbed Anna Hämännin with her salve on the occasion of her first child-birth and also otherwise damaged her so that mother and child remained together and died ... When the organist's wife was awaiting her confinement, Walpurga touched her naked body with her salve, whereby the child promptly died and came still-born.

A third woman also had a still-birth after taking a drink given her by Walpurga, who then buried the corpse 'under the doorway [of the woman's house] on the pretext that she would then have no further [stillbirths or] miscarriages'. Similar cases are reported from all over Europe. Sometimes midwives were blamed for the loss of baby or mother or both, as we have seen, or for deformed babies or for allowing babies to die without baptism. Quite often the charges related to using magic of various kinds to ease the birth, prevent miscarriage and so on. The stereotype in effect both scape-goated the midwife by making her responsible for any untoward outcomes of the birth and represented a caricature of real folk practices. Midwives were engaged in multifarious ritual activity, as we have seen. They were often believed to have special powers and links with the supernatural. In parts of Spain skill as a midwife went with seventh daughters. In a Somerset village early this century the local midwife was credited with having the evil eye. In folk tales from Wales to Hungary human midwives attended fairy mothers and vice-versa. In Transylvania, the midwife was 'involved with sins' and had to be ritually purified every year by her 'god-daughters' or women she had aided.[13] But most obviously midwives orchestrated the magical ambience of the birth, to which we return.

The birth process followed a local traditional pattern that it was thought dangerous not to observe and which was for this reason very persistent. This can be seen in the attachment to specific birth positions: standing holding a bar or ladder or supported by two chairs or by other women; sitting on the edge of a bed, on the knees of other women, on birth-stools; kneeling; squat-ting, and so on. These were specific to particular localities and very slow to change in the face of medical preference for lying on a bed or birth-table.

Women could not be left alone for a minute and they were plied with a special alcoholic drink or caudle throughout the delivery. The room in which they gave birth, usually the main room of the house, was sealed, and a fire kept burning and candles lit. Cold was believed to be a danger to the woman's health, but the excessive heat of the birth-room had more than practical significance. Women nearly always remained clothed. In Languedoc, it was reported in the sixteenth century, they were warmed or 'cooked' over cauldrons. Sometimes they actually gave birth in or by the hearth, the focus of the family and its well-being. Covering the doors and windows provided a barrier against evil forces as well as draughts. In eighteenth-century Lancashire 'every crevice in the windows and doors is stuffed close', a doctor complained, 'not excepting the keyhole; the windows are guarded not only with shutters and curtains but even with blankets'. In nineteenth-century Cracow, special thick curtains were 'put at the windows to which herbs that had been blessed were fixed and the palms from Palm Sunday'.[14]

The same intention underlies other practices. The house, the room or the bed might be surrounded with a protective circle of string, thread or rope, or defended with other objects.

> In Bavaria, an old broom and a fork are placed behind the door of the house, with the handles on the floor and crossed, to stop any witch from entering. In Hessen, an axe and a broom are used; in Switzerland, a knife and a fork crossed; in Bohemia, a knife with a cross; in many countries a knife is stuck in the door.

In the Highlands of Scotland 'nails in the front of the bed' warded off elves.[15]

Crying and shouting were natural reactions to the pain of birth, but they were also regarded as a means of aid and protection. Noise of course was very commonly used in rituals to scare off evil influences. 'You must shout so loud that the whole village can hear!', mothers were told at Minot. The other women present joined in too. In eighteenth-century Berry 'the first thing that they did on arriving at the house was to make a din'. According to a parish priest from the Auxerrois in 1683, 'it is believed that when one woman cries and shouts while another is in labour, these cries help her delivery and diminish the pain which she feels'.[16] The *Rosengarten*, which was frequently reprinted in several languages to the end of the seventeenth century, also advised yelling – by the mother – to lessen her pain.

Many procedures were followed to try to facilitate delivery. Once labour began, if not before, all knots, strings and ties on the mother or in the room were undone or removed. Doors were unlocked, and those present avoided crossing their legs. Precautions merged here with active rituals. These could be simple gestures like opening the fingers of the hand or letting the hair down. In some parts of Spain in this century, 'a pair of scissors was held open under the bed'; in others 'the key of the door was placed under the pillow to stop the womb being closed up by magical means'. In Lucania, stitches would be unpicked from a petticoat or from the mattress on which the woman was lying. Other rituals were a little more complex. When a birth was proving difficult in Corsica, nine knots would be tied in a rope hung over the woman. These were tied in such a way that they would come undone when the ends of the rope were pulled. As they did so, the womb too would be 'undone'.[17] Roses of Jericho, which were used we have seen to divine whether a birth would be easy or difficult, were also brought into play in Spain and elsewhere during the birth itself. Resembling and representing the female organs, it was hoped that if they opened in water, the latter would also dilate.

Visitation articles and other sources reflecting the clerical and elite desire to suppress such practices refer to the use of charms and incantations. An article from the diocese of Coventry and Lichfield in 1584 for example asked: 'Whether any within your parish be suspected to use sorcery, witchcraft, charms, unlawful prayers, or invocations in Latin or English: namely midwives in time of women's travail with child, and who resort to such for help and counsel'. Isobel Malcolm tried as a witch at Botary in Scotland in 1637 confessed that she had charmed two women 'for the bairn bed'.[18]

Charms or unorthodox prayers might also be written down and attached to the woman or hung over her in order to speed the birth or alleviate the pain or both. An Anglo-Saxon narrative charm was written in Latin on wax and bound to the woman's right foot. It read: 'I conjure thee, infant, whether thou be male or female, by the Father, the Son, and the Holy Ghost, that thou come forth, and draw not back, and that thou do no harm to thy mother'; it then referred to Lazarus coming forth from the tomb. This charm was extant in various forms in England until early this century and it is also found in Scandinavia. In the early fifteenth century, St Bernardino of Siena condemned recourse to *brevi*, pieces of parchment allegedly obtained from witches and inscribed with 'words that cannot be understood' or sometimes with the name of Jesus. They might be 'tied to the big toe of a woman in labour to draw the child down more easily'. Other medieval examples contained esoteric names of God, 'scraps from the liturgy' or anagrams of the Paternoster.[19] Abbé Thiers referred to the custom in seventeenth-century France of a woman holding a special prayer in her right hand during labour. By this time, printed versions were often available.

Such prayers were really a type of amulet and only one of many such employed. Coler 'strongly recommended' the eaglestone, which was also used in pregnancy as we have seen, and which in Germany was 'tied to the mother's right knee at the time of delivery'. In Spain and France, it might be attached to the arm, the belly or the thigh. In England the stone was believed to be so powerful 'that midwives were warned not to leave it in place once the child was born for fear it might cause prolapse of the uterus'. Other amulets might have the same drastic effect. Among other minerals and objects, pumice stone, coral, special sea-shells, axe-heads, horseshoes, magnets and cramp rings were all used in different parts of Europe. Cramp rings were rings originally made from the offerings placed on the altar by English kings on Good Friday and later simply blessed by them, and which were believed to have general healing power. Poor women might not own the rarities included here, but they might be lent out within the community or as a form of charity. Animal parts were probably more generally available. Culpeper favoured 'an ass's or horse's hoof hung near the privities'. 'The skin which a snake has cast off' was mentioned by Trotula in the eleventh century and by modern French folklorists. Its sympathetic magical function is obvious, though the clergy linked it to the serpent of Genesis and hence to the Devil. Jane Sharp's *Midwives' Book*, first published in 1671, which both criticizes and reflects popular practice, advised wrapping a woman in a newly-flayed sheepskin or rubbing her belly with hare's blood in cases of 'sore travail'.[20]

Another type of amulet was the birth sachet, placed usually on the woman's belly and reported from the Middle Ages onwards all over Europe. One that had been in her husband's family for generations was opened by a woman from the Cher in 1955. It contained a ring with the image of a saint; a fragment of wood and two little stones wrapped in paper with the inscription: 'Piece of the True Cross and pebbles on which the blood of Our Lord dropped'. One from Galiera in Corsica from around 1920 had in it an image of St Francis with a prayer on the back, torn into small pieces. A less common talisman was the pincushion presented to expectant mothers in East Anglia. The message of one of these in arranged pins sufficiently indicates their function: 'May God Preserve Them Both From Danger'.[21]

We have seen that girdles were worn in pregnancy, and they also figure prominently among the protective devices employed during the birth. They could be purely secular. A fifteenth-century handbook on women's complaints mentions putting on a girdle of hart's skin when the birth began. Snakeskins were worn as belts in the Angoumois and they 'had to be quickly removed once the baby appeared or it would belong to the Devil'. Specially embroidered girdles were used in the Highlands of Scotland until the start of this century, and ordinary leather belts with iron buckles in modern Dublin. However, most of the girdles employed had some supernatural connection which lent them their power. Bessie Dunlop, accused of witchcraft in Ayrshire in 1576, admitted that she tied lace round women in childbirth to ease their delivery, lace that had been given to her by a ghost. In seventeenth-century England, a piece of the church-bell rope might be tied round a woman's waist. Jewish women used the leather strap from around the Torah scroll.[22] A surviving English medieval prayer-roll girdle measured 180 cm. long, the supposed height of Christ – only one such example.

Most often such girdles, ribbons or sashes were associated with a saint. They might have been taken to a shrine or have been placed in contact with or measured against a statue, like the ribbons used in pregnancy, or they might be actual relics. According to the Life of Brother Christopher, a thirteenth-century Franciscan from Aquitaine, 'a woman in labour was only happily delivered when a cord that had belonged to him was placed on her'. Girdles of St Joseph and St Robert of Newminster were used in medieval England. Better-known examples were linked with female saints who had a particular respons-ibility for childbirth. Parisian women might be allowed to wear the belt of St Margaret kept by the monks of Saint-Germain-des-Prés. Belts or girdles of the Virgin Mary existed in many places: Palermo, Assisi, Prato in Italy; Quintin, Toulouse, Le Puy and Chartres in France; Valencia, Dorthes and Tortosa in Spain and Catalonia; Westminster in England. The Tortosa girdle (used by the Spanish royal family as late as 1822) was supposed to have been woven by the Virgin herself while she was alive and brought to the cathedral by her in person in 1178. These relics too might be lent out like 'Our Lady's girdle of Bruton, red silk', referred to in the dissolution inventory of 1536, 'which is a solemn relic, sent to woman travailing, which shall not miscarry *in partu*'.[23]

Some plants were supposed to speed delivery, if taken or sometimes worn. Culpeper mentioned balm, bay, mugwort, motherwort, lilies and tobacco, which was also prescribed in the Netherlands. Some of these herbs may have been effective in deadening pain or aiding labour, like ergot, a fungus which grows on rye, but many plants were used magically, alone or in elaborate potions. A coriander seed held close to the vagina was supposed to draw out the baby, according to a thirteenth-century text. In another three grains of pepper were swallowed by the woman in a drink. The Paternoster had been said over each grain with the words: 'Deliver this woman from the pangs of childbirth' being substituted for 'Deliver us from evil'. The ingredients of a seventeenth-century New England medicine 'for sharp and difficult travail' were not of vegetable origin, however. 'Take a lock of virgin's hair on any part of her head', the recipe instructed,

> of half the age of the woman in travail. Cut it very small to fine powder; then take twelve ants' eggs dried in an oven after the bread is drawn or otherwise make them dry and make them to powder with the hair. Give this with a quarter of a pint of red cow's milk or for want of it in strong ale.'[24]

Young girls were usually excluded from the birth-room, but in some parts of France they might be brought in if the birth proved difficult. At a village in the Jura, it was reported around 1850, the woman's hand was always held through the birth by a young virgin. These customs should be related to the invocation of virgin saints.

If successful childbirth was thus linked by a principle of opposition to virginity, it could also be more directly associated with the act of reproduction from which it originated. In parts of France and probably elsewhere sexual intercourse took place after the first contractions to lubricate the birth passage and bring good fortune. A specialist performed this function in the Hautes-Cévennes instead of the husband, according to a 1925 report. Procedures involving the husband's clothes, which were much more common, are relevant here. According to Abbé Thiers, it was believed in the Chartres region that a woman 'will be delivered sooner if she puts on the stockings and slippers of her husband'. In Spain and Portugal, a woman might wear her husband's waistcoat or his hat once her pains started. In the modern Languedoc the husband's hat was placed on his wife's belly; in the Limousin his night-cap; and elsewhere in France it was specified that the night-cap should be the one worn during the child's conception and it might be put on the genitals. The hat seems to have had special sexual significance. While the man's hat was taken off and placed on the woman's reproductive organs, the woman usually kept her head covered. In the rare cases where women did give birth in the nude, they did not remove their head-dresses. Clothes belonging to the husband might also be turned inside-out to draw the baby down. In Spain it was the husband above all who had to avoid crossing his legs during the birth, while in Portugal he could 'hasten a slow or difficult birth by lifting or turning over a tile from the church roof'.[25]

In a few parts of Europe the custom of the couvade was practised. In Béarn 'the father lies down and simulates the pains of the mother, then takes her place in the bed at the moment of congratulations'. 'In Léon, the father gets into a wicker or straw basket and cackles [like a hen laying an egg]', while in the Canaries, according to an early nineteenth-century text, 'both parents lay together on the same bed all through the birth, eating and drinking at the same time from the same vessels'. Around the Mediterranean and in France and Britain, husbands suffered from toothaches, backaches and other pains during their wives' pregnancies and while they were giving birth. In parts of Corsica, the husband took to his bed following the birth 'as if sick and worn out'. Elsewhere legends and stories told of men actually themselves giving birth, for example the thirteenth-century French romance *Aucassin and Nicolette*. The couvade has generally been explained as a diversionary exercise taking attention away from the mother in her time of danger and from the child. It was also intended in the European context to mitigate the woman's pain. In the Welsh Borders in modern times, if the husband suffered pains, those of the wife would be correspondingly less severe. The symbolic wearing or coming into contact with articles of the husband's clothing could have the same function, transferring some of the pain to him via his personal belongings. More direct magical or religious transfer of the woman's pain is also found. According to Lady Gregory, writing of the west of Ireland in the 1920s, 'some of the old women are able to put a part of the pain upon the man or any man'. A Scottish woman was indicted in 1661 for causing a man to contract 'the pain of a woman in childbed ... whereof he died'. In a different idiom, St Charles of Sezze 'offered Our Lord to stay in Purgatory' for many years in order to spare women in childbed.[26]

Pain could also be switched to other women and to animals. Allie Nisbet of Hilton in Scotland was accused in 1632 of having taken 'the pains off a woman in travail, by some charms and horrible words ... and laid them on another woman who straightaway died'. Another 'notorious' Scottish witch, Annie Sampson, was charged in 1591 with using various illicit procedures in childbirth. These included putting a paper, presumably a charm, in the woman's hair and placing her husband's shirt under the bed to send the pain into a dog and a cat.[27]

Most procedures of this kind were aimed at relieving the pain or opening the birth passage, but some rituals were intended to turn the foetus from an awkward position. In modern Portugal, people turned a tile on the local church roof or that of the chapel of a shrine. In parts of France, 'if the presentation seemed wrong, they would fetch a man used to putting corn or flour into sacks; he would grip the woman by the feet and shake her as if he were emptying a sack'. Similarly in County Mayo 'a ploughman would be called in to lift and shake a woman in difficult labour'.[28]

Pagan deities, Classical and Germanic, had been called on or linked to childbirth and the saints here took over their role. Many different saints were invoked: St Bride in Scotland and elsewhere in the Celtic world; St Catherine in France; St Coleta in Burgundy and Flanders; St Leocada in Sicily, to name but a few. They were often virgins, which was itself a recommendation as we have seen. Sometimes another rationale was present. St Catherine was resorted to for the 'deliverance' of prisoners and hence was believed to be able to deliver women too. St Bride attended the Virgin Mary in the stable at Bethlehem, according to legend. St Edwige, invoked in the Baugeois district of France, was known locally as St Etanche, which means 'tight' or 'closed up'. Male saints were called on also: St Bartholomew, St Anthony, St Roch, St William of Norwich, St Ignatius Loyola. A significant number of the miracles reported at the shrine of St Leonard at Fürstenfeld in Bavaria in the sixteenth century were ones 'which delivered women from the pains of childbirth'. The saint was also associated with fertility, as we have seen, and with freeing pris-

oners, and similar links usually explain the choice of other patrons. St
Erasmus, invoked in Switzerland, was 'reputed to have met his death by
disembowelment' and was called on 'for intestinal colic as well as labour
pains'.[29] St Gerard Majella, venerated in Basilicata, himself suffered from a
bowel disease. St Ramón, a Catalan saint of the twelfth century, invoked by
women all over Spain to the present day, was supposed to have been born by
Caesarean section. St Raphael had relayed the message of the Annunciation.

Most of these saints had only local cults. A few others were called on all
over Europe. St Margaret of Antioch is one of these, probably because her
legend attributes to her the experience of being swallowed by a dragon, which
subsequently burst open leaving her unharmed and virtually reborn. In the
Mattins for her feast day in the Sarum Breviary she is represented as soliciting
this favour from heaven: 'That if any woman in labour invoke my name, she
will escape imminent danger, and her infant will also escape all ill'. Both
Luther and Rabelais refer to the practice of reading to women in labour from
the Life and legends of St Margaret. From the same period, the Swiss Thomas
Platter senior wrote of his wife's first confinement: 'In her pains, the women
who assisted her ... imposed on her a big wooden rosary in the name of St
Margaret so that she should give birth more easily'. 'Obtain for me, Virgin
and Martyr', ran a prayer to St Margaret published in Narbonne in 1770, 'that
the Lord by His favours, may relieve me in my pains, may keep and comfort
me, with the fruit borne in my womb.'[30] Such prayers and also vows were
common all over Europe from the late medieval period down to this time and
beyond, and girls were frequently named after the saint in both Catholic and
Protestant areas. Girdles of St Margaret were also used and Lives of the saint
in small format were placed on women's bellies.

Equally or perhaps more popular in the late medieval and early modern
period was St Anne. In France written or printed prayers placed on a woman
in labour were often addressed to 'St Anne who gave birth to the Virgin
Mary'. The cult was also strong in Italy, where in some places women dressed
in yellow and green, the colours of the saint, after having been protected by
her in their confinements. The knots that were tied and untied in Corsica to
facilitate delivery were called 'knots of St Anne'.[31]

But none of these saints was so widely called on as the Virgin Mary herself,
who of course gave birth to the Infant Jesus without suffering any pain.
Cacciaguida tells Dante in the Paradiso that 'Mary was called to with great
cries' at his birth in Florence, reflecting a common practice of the day.
Thomas Platter junior noted in 1599 that candles from the shrine of Our Lady
of Montserrat had 'notables virtues, especially for women in childbed, who
light and hold them in their hands at the moment of delivery'.[32] Many
Marian shrines and images reflected the specialism in their appellations: Our

Lady in Jeseyn (childbirth) in late medieval England; Our Lady of Deliverance or Our Lady of the Sorrows in southern France and Spain; Our Lady of the Paridas (women who have just given birth) in Spain; Our Lady of Childbirth in Portugal. Many of the girdles used in childbirth were associated with the Virgin as we have seen, and pictorial and other ex-votos testify to the success of vows made to her.

We can already see that recourse to saints took various familiar forms. Saints might be taken as name-patrons, even as 'godparents'. Votive masses might be offered, and prayers, orthodox and unorthodox, might be said, usually by the midwife who also decided which saint to petition. 'Women giving birth, who suffer great pains', a vernacular prayer from Umbria instructed, 'pray to St Anthony, and he will give succour.' Narrative prayer-charms were also common. According to a Spanish example:

> St Bartholomew ... walked along the road
> And he met the Lord,
> Who greeted him with these words:
> 'Where are you going, Bartholomew?'
> 'In search of you, Lord.'
> 'Then turn round, Bartholomew,
> And I will give you the gift
> That whatever house you enter
> No thunderbolts will fall on it or lightning,
> Nor any woman die in childbirth,
> Or baby from the shock of it.'

We have seen that popular hagiographies might also be read. When a verse from St John is read to Rabelais' Protestantly-inclined Gargamelle as she is giving birth to Gargantua, she says: 'Good, I much prefer to hear something from the Gospels than to have to listen to the Life of St Margaret or some other nonsense.'[33] Prayers to the saints were used as amulets, but images and relics were better suited for this purpose.

Images of Cardinal Peter of Luxemburg were placed on women's bellies in the Avignon region in the fourteenth century. 'There is not a woman in labour to whom I give his picture who does not then give birth in the easiest way', a doctor testified in the canonization process of St Gerard Majella. Pilgrims to his shrine at Ekelsbeke in Flanders from the seventeenth to the nineteenth century brought back small printed triangles with a picture of St Folquin on them and an inscription stating that he 'helps those who are in danger in childbed', and these were used in a similar way.[34] In the Huelva region of Spain, prints of St Ramón and St Vincent Ferrer might be placed at the mouth of the womb to get the foetus in the right position.

Many kinds of relics were used from rosaries, girdles and other articles of clothing to parts of the body. At Ekelsbeke, the stole of St Folquin might be placed on the shoulders of women suffering particular difficulties in labour. At Amberg in the Upper Palatinate in the early eighteenth century, the Society of Jesus kept a piece of the soutane of St Ignatius Loyola, 'which was lent out in cases of difficult childbirth'. St Vincent Ferrer's bonnet was stolen by people at a place in Valencia who believed that it would 'assure women a safe and easy delivery', a belief that would seem to be related to those centred on husbands' hats. Shoes, sandals, sticks and chairs belonging to or otherwise associated with saints were also employed, and water from their wells or fountains was drunk. Other non-bodily relics included a fern which had been put under the bier of St William of Norwich at his first translation in 1145, and reeds from St Catherine's fountain at Sinai. A Swedish charm-prayer recorded in 1722 implored the 'Virgin Mary, gentle mother' to 'loan your keys to me; to open my limbs and my members', referring to special amulets linked with Mary.[35]

Bodily relics were less often used, since most women did not have access to them. However, the bones of the hermit Pedro were placed on the heads of women in labour in a village near Madrid in the sixteenth century, and a much more prestigious relic was available to ordinary women at Nogent-le-Roi. The abbey of Coulombs near the town possessed the Holy Foreskin of Christ, which 'was supposed to have the power to make sterile women fertile and also to facilitate delivery'. It had been borrowed by King Henry V of England in 1422 for the confinement of Queen Catherine. By the later nineteenth century it had come down in the world, being kept in a presbytery, where, according to an account of the time, 'pregnant women still went to benefit from its favours. The priest donned his surplice and stole, while the women knelt and kissed the reliquary'. Other relics of Christ included pieces of the cross. We have seen that a French birth sachet contained these. At Long Melford in the late medieval period, a relic of the True Cross belonging to the Clopton family 'was loaned out to the parish wives when they were in childbed'.[36]

Often a vow was made to the saint or to the Virgin in the midst of the birth and the appropriate shrine was then visited afterwards and an offering made. The Injunctions for the diocese of Salisbury in 1538 referred to women in travail making 'foolish vows to go on pilgrimage to this image or that image' after their deliveries. In one story in the *Quinze Joyes de mariage*, the women attending the mother 'vowed the lady in her pain to go on over twenty pilgrimages, and her husband also vowed her to all the saints'. In another, when the mother's life was despaired of, 'her husband made vows to all the saints, male and female', and she also 'vowed herself to Our Lady of Le Puy in Auvergne, of Rocamadour, and of several other places'; she later visited Le Puy, where she touched the relics and the image of the Virgin and was bought a girdle and a rosary by her husband. In another example, a Maltese woman was cured of puerperal fever in 1890 when 'her mother made a vow to the Virgin Mary and anointed the patient on the forehead and breasts with oil obtained from the sanctuary lamp of Ta Pinu church'. The woman, who was called Maria, 'fell into a calm sleep. Our Lady appeared to her in vision, touched her on the parts smeared with the oil and healed her'. Ex-voto offerings of babies' dresses 'in thanksgiving for an uneventful delivery and the birth of a normal infant' were common in Malta at this time.[37]

Most of the saints invoked were of course dead, but a few of our examples indicate that the sacred power of living people might also be harnessed. Joan of Arc was asked at her trial 'whether midwives did not touch their rings against the ring which she wore?'; to which she replied that 'many women had touched her rings and her hands but she did not know why'. The strength of popular attachment to the help of saints in this as in other extremities is shown by the persistence of the custom of invoking them in Protestant countries. The oath administered to midwives in the diocese of Chester in 1584 specified that they should not use 'any witchcraft, charms, relics or invocation to any saint in time of travail'.[38]

A range of other religious rituals and aids was available. Masses and other services might be said for women in childbed; vigils held; fasts and almsgiving performed or promised. The Périgueux service book contained blessings, special Gospel readings at mass and a liturgy for women in danger of death in childbed, all of which are found in other dioceses. The priest or pastor might visit the house to say prayers just before or during the births, as in Corsica, and relatives often the husband, went to the church to pray. Prayers were said, we have seen, and passages from Scripture read by the women in the birth-room. The latter practice could be a Protestant or 'enlightened' alternative to readings from hagiography or the use of charms, but Biblical and liturgical passages or phrases were also chosen in a magical spirit. So the prologue to St John's Gospel was often recited: 'In the beginning was the Word'; or another opening formula: '*Quincunque vult*' from the Athanasian Creed, which was 'said three times over a woman in labour', according to a fourteenth-century English manuscript.[39]

Religious objects or sacramentals were treated in the same way. Church bells were rung during the birth in England, Spain, Portugal and elsewhere. At Turquel in Portugal, in this century, the husband rang the bell nine times. At Escalho a more complicated procedure was followed. Nine virgins named Maria had to ring nine peals there – 'by pulling the rope with their teeth'. Holy water was used; also water in which the Gospels had been immersed; unconsecrated or blessed hosts; bread, palms and other things blessed at festivals; and, as we have seen, oil from sanctuary lamps. In many places a

crucifix was placed on the woman's breast, and candles of religious prove-
nance were nearly always burned. In early modern Germany, the wax tapers
carried by the women at the Candlemas service 'were used at childbirth
placed by the hands and feet of the woman in labour and by the utensils, to
keep evil spirits from mother and child'.[40] In parts of Mallorca and Galicia,
special candles were made by pouring wax into rolled-up prayer-sheets.
These were lit when labour started and the birth was supposed to be over
before they burned down. If it was not, that was sign of death.

Magical protection continued after the birth had occurred for both mother
and baby. The mother was given food and drink and kept warm and
confined. Sometimes a plug of cloth was placed at the entrance to the womb
and the abdomen was bandaged up to prevent the womb from dropping. In
some parts of modern France, an omelette made with almond oil was placed
on the woman's thighs and genitals. In France and Spain, women were not
allowed to sleep for a period of time following the birth. Sleep symbolized
death and was thought to cause bleeding. Women were also left in their dirty
clothes and bedding, again from the idea that to remove or replace these
would cause bleeding. More specific procedures to prevent this in seventeenth-century Spain included drinking water into which hoes or
ploughshares had been dipped or in which the blacksmith had cooled iron.
Nearly everywhere women stayed in bed for several days at least, and most of
the ritual precautions set around the birth-room remained. Among the
Sarakatsani of Greece, the room was regularly fumigated with smoke for
twelve days to keep off evil powers. 'The fairies ... steal away the good women
that are in the straw', the Welsh maid Winifred Jenkins asserted in Smollett's
Humphry Clinker (1771), 'if so be as how there a'n't a horseshoe nailed to the
door.' New amulets were also attached to new mothers; among modern
Greeks and Macedonians a clove of garlic and a gold ring or a gold coin were
hung in the woman's hair.[41]
     It was thought to be extremely important to expel or extract the after-birth
or placenta as soon as possible, and a variety of methods were used. The
woman's belly could be pressed or she could be made to sneeze, jump or
vomit. In parts of Spain a hair was put in her mouth to achieve the last effect;
elsewhere potions were given, some of which were clearly magical as well as
nauseating. The *Grand Calendrier des bergiers* recommended powder of agate
in wine or an infusion of plantain seeds. Broth made with the after-birth of an
animal or another woman was also given in France; while Rösslin's
Rosengarten advised 'having the stricken mother drink the milk of another
mother whose infant has recently died'.[42] The genitals might also be fumigated by burning chicken feathers, old shoes or donkeys' hooves. In many

Cordoban villages a hoe was passed over the woman's belly, and in the Burgos region the strap of an old sandal was attached to the end of the cord. In the Landes district in south-west France, the husband's beret was placed inside-out on his wife's head, as if to represent the placenta. Most of these practices echo those used to induce the birth itself, and the placenta was indeed regarded as a kind of double of the child, which could not be left too long inside the womb once the former had emerged. In some places, the after-birth was dangerous to the mother: she should not see it or she would die.

Great care was taken over the disposal of the after-birth. There were four main ways, corresponding to the four elements, as Belmont has noted, though they could be combined. In most of Europe, the after-birth was buried, either under the threshold of the house, in the byre or granary, or in the garden or a field, often at the foot of a fruit-tree – in Germany a pear-tree for boys and an apple for girls. In Minho it could be buried 'underneath a pile of wood which is kept in the corner of the kitchen to burn on the hearth'. In parts of Spain it was placed in a pot for burial, and nearly everywhere the father of the child performed the act. In western Sicily the placenta was buried in different places according to the gender of the baby. That of a girl was kept in the house, usually being placed in the latrine, because 'a woman's place is in the home'. But since 'the man's place is to go out into the four corners of the world, they bury the [male] placenta in a hole outside the house, facing the wind and the wide world. The hole must be deep, and then the placenta is covered with stones and earth so that the dogs can't dig it up'.[43] In parts of Norway and Sweden and of the Iberian peninsula burning was traditional, sometimes taking place in the smithy. In parts of northern Portugal and France, the placenta was hung in the chimney to dry and then preserved. In parts of Germany it might be hung in the branches of a tree until the weather and the birds destroyed it. In the Abruzzi it was thrown into a river, a course also recommended by the Rules for Midwives in Würzburg in 1555. In addition, the placenta could in some circumstances be eaten, in whole or in part.

Whatever the mode of disposal traditional in any area, failure to follow it could have dire consequences. If the after-birth were simply thrown away to be eaten by wild animals or taken by demons or other ill-wishers, the infant might suffer correspondingly. If it were burned, where burning was not the established practice as in ancient Iceland, the infant's guardian spirit might be destroyed. In those regions of Scandinavia where burning was the norm, any other procedure might lead to 'haunting'. 'Do not leave the after-birth without attention or bury it in the ground', an early text instructed; 'the unburnt after-birth becomes an *utburd*', that is a supernatural child spirit. In other cases failure to burn after-births properly led to their turning into goblins or 'screaming spirits'.[44]

The fate of the after-birth was clearly linked with that of the child. If the baby were in immediate danger of dying after birth through asphyxiation, cold or whatever, the placenta might be placed over it again, or, before the cord was cut from it, the after-birth might be heated in wine 'in the hope that the heat would be transferred to the baby'.[45] In Iceland, we have seen, the guardian spirit of the child resided in the placenta. If it was eaten by animals, the spirit could enter one of them. In Languedoc, where a new sapling or shrub was planted over the buried placenta, its growth represented and prefigured that of the child. In Catalonia, the placenta was buried at the foot of a rose or an oak, so that the child would have the good colour of the first and the strength of the second.

The fate of the placenta was also linked to the supply of mother's milk, as we shall see. Elsewhere the after-birth had a more general association with fertility. In Minho, Pina-Cabral suggests, it was buried in the kitchen to keep female fertility in the house. In Hungary, placing it under the bed assured that a couple would conceive, while a French medical text of 1683 recommended it as a cure for sterility. In the Balkans, women bathed in water into which a new placenta had been put and would-be fathers consumed three bits of one. By contrast, transgression against the placenta could be a threat to fertility. In the west of France, care had to be taken not to bury the placenta in a place where the mother would walk on it, for, if she did, she would become sterile. In Minho, a nail was 'hammered into the spot [on the floor] where the placenta has fallen ... if this is not done and a drop of wine should fall upon this spot, the mother's blood would lose colour and she would go mad'.[46]

The new-born infant was objectively very vulnerable after the trauma of birth. In pre-industrial Europe at least one child in four died before the age of one, and the proportion of deaths was often locally much higher. In some English parishes in the sixteenth century over half died in the first month and 30 per cent during delivery. French medical writers in the eighteenth century estimated that one tenth of babies died in the first ten days of life. In Rouen one in seven died in the first week. Probably half these infant deaths were the result of the birth itself or of congenital defects and about half the result of external disease. The baby, moreover, was in a liminal state, born materially into the world but not yet incorporated into society. In Corsica a new-born baby was called a *turco*, in Portugal a *mouro*.[47] Until baptism in particular he or she was not a Christian, not a member of the community.

The dangers besetting or lying in wait for babies were often personified as fairies, evil spirits or witches. In the Ancient world, harpies, part birds part hags, 'polluted the bodies of unprotected children at night, tore out the entrails of sucklings' and drank their blood. The Strasbourg Church Order of 1598 referred to the red dragon, the living Devil, gobbling up the poor children at birth 'and damning them for all eternity' unless they were protected by prayers, faith and the intervention of guardian angels. 'If there be any children unbaptized, or not guarded with the sign of the cross, or orisons', wrote Reginald Scot of popular belief in England in the 1580s, 'then the witches may and do catch them from their mothers' sides in the night, or out of their cradles, or otherwise kill them with their ceremonies.'[48] Similar beliefs were found all over Europe, and they became part of the demonological myth of the Witches' Sabbath, at which babies were supposed to be killed, eaten or made into special ointments.

After birth, according to a study of modern Greece, 'the infant is not only exposed to supernatural dangers but is himself a potent source of trouble ... in a sense, still part of the "uncivilized" natural world of powers and spirits ... he may *be* a demon as well as be hurt by demons'. A Russian folklorist noted in 1880 that the new-born baby was 'regarded as unclean', like its mother,[49] another way of indicating its dangerous state. In the Balkans very often mother and child were left alone until the christening for this reason, while in gypsy communities the father never touched or fondled his baby before it was at least three weeks old.

The baby therefore lived its first hours inside a circle of protection, solidarity and ritual. Every gesture was significant. In parts of France, after the birth but before the expulsion of the after-birth, the baby 'was often put between the mother's legs', or sometimes placed for a moment or two on her belly. Sometimes, as we have seen, the placenta would be put on the baby, especially if it were weakly, a custom referred to in sixteenth-century France by Ambroise Paré. The umbilical cord would then be cut. This was an important symbolic act, the final separation of mother and child. Hence the midwife's scissors and thread became her emblems. The operation required some practical skill, but there were also ritual requirements and connotations. The cord was not usually cut until the baby cried. There was an old idea that cutting it with iron was 'of ill omen', but this does not seem to have been heeded in the early modern and modern periods. In parts of Spain, agricultural tools were used to sever the cord. The cord was cut in different ways according to gender, usually long for boys and short for girls. 'For the women think', a sixteenth-century text relating to the Montpellier region explained, 'that the virile member will take its form from this operation and that it will become longer if what hangs from the navel is long.' Girls did not need long penises, but cutting their cords close to their bellies also prevented the entrance to their wombs from being too narrow. Similar beliefs and practices were found elsewhere. In the Toledo region of Spain, a long cord on a boy meant that he would have a strong voice, be brave and learn to speak early; while cords of girls were ideally short to ensure a good figure.

The linkage between length of cord and gender could also be reversed. The aspect of the cord was read too to divine the mother's future fertility. The number of notches in it indicated how many more babies she would have. In France and elsewhere 'the cord was squeezed after being cut to make the blood in it flow back towards the baby to strengthen it', and the mother's breasts might be rubbed with it to induce a good supply of milk and prevent sores. In the Balkans, probably under Turkish influence, some kind of spiritual relationship was created 'between the child and the woman who cut the umbilical cord', whether it was the midwife or someone else.[50]

Since the cord, like the placenta, was so closely associated with the baby, it too had to be carefully disposed of. In Minorca, 'if the cord were to be eaten by a cat or a dog, the child would turn into an animal or go mad'. More generally, the fate of the cord was believed to predict that of the child, so that, if it was burned, the child risked suffering death by fire; if it was thrown into a lake or river, the child would drown. Nevertheless, in some parts of Europe such as Brittany or Portugal, the cord was burned. In the Yonne it was put behind the chimney piece, and in Tuscany the cord of male babies was put under the hearth-stone – to ensure that they would prosper but also to keep them in the house. More often the cord was buried, sometimes like the placenta under a tree, whose qualities would then be transferred to the child. There was no prescription in Europe for disposing of the cord in water. But frequently it was dried, becoming a powerful talisman. Coler urged mothers in early modern Germany 'to save the cord as a kind of magical charm, for times when the child became sick'. Generally its preservation was associated with the health and well-being of the child and then of the adult. In the modern Limousin, a knot was tied in the cord at birth, and this was undone when the child was seven years old in order to make it grow straight. In the Périgord, a girl was given her umbilical cord when she became nubile or as soon as she was able to tie and untie a knot. She then threw it in the fire with her right hand, so that she should have a husband in the future. In modern times too in France and Spain, the cord or a piece of it was sewn into the clothing of youths when they went to pick their conscription numbers, in the hope that they would be lucky and gain exemption. In the Yonne, to gain a 'lucky number', the cord had to be hidden in the highest part of the house.[51] The umbilical cord was also used in love magic and in healing.

The cleaning of the baby followed the cutting of the cord. A fourteenth-century medical work referred to the practice in France 'of placing the new-born child on the straw and rubbing him gently with straw', and straw and flour are mentioned in later French sources. The baby could also be rubbed with oil, wine or cider, or be washed in milk. But from the later Middle Ages onwards, if not before, washing with warm or cold water became the commonest procedure, the water often being mixed with oil, wine, honey or other substances. In modern Portugal, 'the baby's head was washed with water containing white of egg and brandy' and the sign of the cross was made over its first bath. Often herbs were used: St John's wort, rue, myrtle, fenugreek. It was the custom among some gypsies to wash babies 'all over with water in which willow peelings had been boiled so that the fairies should not steal them'. In Rumania, water in which a goose had been boiled gave special protection against witchcraft. In Scandinavia, the baby was bathed in cold water or water into which a live ember had been dropped. In parts of Portugal, needles were placed in the water; in Spain and Portugal coins were thrown into the baby's first bath water in the hope of making it rich in the future. In Transylvania, the crown from the wedding flag was placed in the water to ensure luck. In the Mediterranean region bathing in wine remained common. In the Abruzzi, for example, the baby was washed with wine which had first been boiled with aromatic herbs. 'Among the Greeks and the Macedonians, the child is bathed in lukewarm wine with myrtle leaves, after which it is generally covered with a layer of salt. When the salt is washed off, the relatives and friends throw into the bath money, which becomes the property of the midwife.' In the Scottish Lowlands babies were bathed in salt water, which they were made to taste three times.[52] Salt of course was believed to have powerful protective properties.

As Pina-Cabral notes with reference to Minho, the first bath was 'a rite [both] of purification and separation'. Also 'this first event in a person's life is seen as determining the rest of it'. This is shown in the way in which the water was disposed of, paralleling that of the placenta and the cord. In Portugal the water used to wash a boy was thrown away outside the house and that of a girl inside, indicating their respective spheres of activity. In Transylvania, a boy's water was thrown over 'one patch of flowers so that he will not have to go to more than one place to ask for the hand of someone; the bath water of a baby girl [by contrast] is thrown over many flowers so she will have many suitors'.[53] There was also a danger from hostile or possibly hostile forces. In Rumania great care was taken to dispose of the water within the shade of the house; otherwise the Fates would be offended.

A great range of gestures was employed towards the baby after, during or even before cleaning it. After bathing in Rumania, women danced round and 'a small spot of white ashes' was made on the child's forehead 'to protect it from the evil eye'. Elsewhere spitting on or around the baby, pulling its nose, rubbing or touching its lips with garlic or a coin, or making a circle or the sign of the cross fulfilled the same purpose. Among the Sarakatsani, 'a cross was inscribed on a new-born child' with a brand that had been 'quenched in water'. Gestures could also be incorporating. In Scandinavia in early times a hammer, associated with Thor, 'was raised over a new-born child as a mark of its acceptance in the community'. These rites and gestures were only very slowly Christianized. St Vincent Ferrer complained in a sermon in the fourteenth century: 'And when a child is born, what sign do you make over him in the cradle? Still this same circle that you use when you get up, or when you sit down to table. It is the Devil who puts it in your head'.[54]

The cradle was not always or perhaps commonly the first repository of the baby. In parts of Italy, Germany and the Balkans it was placed 'on the ground as soon as it is washed and swaddled'. In the Berne region, 'immediately after birth the child was placed under the settle or table to preserve it from evil spirits'. In parts of France, it was carried near the hearth. In the Abruzzi, it might be placed for a moment on the hearth-stone and then be tied to the fire-side chair. Until recently in Lucania, the new-born was put in a pot and hung on a nail – to prevent a fleeting existence for the child by 'nailing' it. In early modern England *The Expert Midwife* reported that many advised placing the baby after washing and swaddling

> by his mother, lying in her bed, on the left side near the heart first of all; for they think ... that the mother doth attract and draw to her all the diseases from the child, and that she doth expel and void again by the flux and issue of her womb what evil soever she hath attracted, without any hurt to herself.[55]

Often having been placed on the ground the baby was then 'lifted up' in a ritual fashion. 'There is an extraordinary notion in regard to the birth of children', the *New Suffolk Garland* of 1866 declared.

> As soon as they are born they ought, it is said, to be carried *up* stairs, or they will never *rise* to riches and distinction in their ... life; and accordingly, if there are no attics for the nurse to climb up into, she will sometimes mount upon a chair or stool with the new-born baby in her arms.

The same custom is found elsewhere in the British Isles, and the further explanation is offered that it symbolized the hope that the child would ultimately go to Heaven. There is also evidence from further back in time and from other countries. The German and Italian words for midwife mean 'she who raises up'. An illustration in the ninth-century Utrecht Psalter shows a new-born baby held aloft in the arms of his mother or possibly another woman. The German Jewish custom of Holle Kreisch in which the baby was lifted up three times in the air in its naming ceremony derives from late medieval Gentile usage. When witch-midwives did not kill new-born babies, according to the *Malleus Maleficarum*, 'then, as if for some other purpose, they take them out of the room and raising them up in the air, offer them to devils'. Elsewhere they noted that this was 'done by the kitchen fire ... on the pretext of warming'. Other demonologists repeated such reports and the gloss put on them, and they figure also in witchcraft trials. A Scottish magistrate was accused of handing his new-born baby over to the Devil 'stepping out with it in his arms to the staircase' in order to do so (see Frontispiece).[56]

It seems likely that the rite varied depending on the different designs of houses in northern and southern Europe and the accessibility of the roof. It is also probable that raising the child on a piece of furniture or taking it to the stairs or up a ladder was a substitute for an earlier rite involving the roof itself. All over Europe the roof symbolized the house and was intimately associated with the hearth and the fire which went through it. The roof figured too in a wide range of rituals ensuring the health and fertility of the house and its family, and it was also linked to the dead. It was therefore appropriate to raise the new family member towards the roof or to take him to the roof in a ritual of incorporation. The idea that the child was being offered to the Devil may be a reinterpretation of some offering to a pagan deity. What is clear is that all these raising rituals had the aim of protecting the new-born, and this included protecting them against the Devil and against witches. Holle was an evil spirit who would try to carry off children, and the ritual invoking its name was designed to 'call it off '. An ecclesiastical Visitation in the county of Nassau-Wiesbaden in 1594 referred to the common use of charms and spells 'when a babe is taken up or put down, so that no evil enchantment may befall him'.[57]

But raising the child had another set of connotations. In the Ancient world, the new-born baby was either placed on the ground at its father's feet or handed to him by the midwife from the ground, and he indicated his recognition of its legitimacy and its right to live by raising it in the air and sometimes carrying it round the hearth. In earlier times, if the child was not 'raised' in this way, then it would have been killed or abandoned. Similar rituals existed in the Ancient Celtic and Nordic worlds. At the time of the sagas, the baptismal ceremony included 'the lifting of the child from the floor and placing him in his father's arms'. More generally, the gesture and terminology of raising the child were also transferred to baptismal sponsorship. So the godfather 'raised' the child from the font. In pre-modern Europe, we have seen, the father was absent from the birth as a rule, and the baby was ritually presented to him some time afterwards. In the Netherlands, where 'the arrival of the child occasioned innumerable feasts and celebrations', there was 'a party on the birthday or following day' at which the father wore a special 'tall quilted satin hat', and a further gathering about a week later, at which 'the midwife made an official presentation of the infant' to the father. These festivals figure in the well-known paintings by Jan Steen (see Plate 25).[58]

But this is to anticipate. Nearly always the baby was kept in the house until baptism and often long after, and here it was carefully watched over, some reports note like a corpse at a wake, with a candle constantly burning. The room remained darkened. As in early modern England, sun or moonlight falling directly on the baby was reckoned unlucky. Writers have stressed the wish here to recreate the conditions of the womb for the baby, keeping it warm, well-wrapped and behind curtains. The Franciscan poet Jacopone da Todi imagined his own birth around 1300:

> They washed me and put me in swaddling clothes,
> Wrapped me up again as in the womb.

Behind all this there was also the desire to keep the child hidden and away from the sight of strangers. In Spanish Galicia, babies were not 'displayed' until after baptism, and they were 'carried to church [for the ceremony] completely covered up so that no one could see them'. Similar precautions were taken in Burgundy, where cradles were later draped with tulle to keep out draughts but also hostile looks. In the Scutari region, one of the eggs presented to the new-born baby was 'broken over the child's face to protect it from the evil eye. Presumably this makes the child unrecognizable or hideous'.[59] Concealment here overlaps with ritual neglect.

Cradles seem to have been in fairly general use from the central Middle Ages onwards, though there were local variations. They were often handed down in families. They could be of straw or basket-work as well as of wood, and sometimes babies were suspended in hammocks or placed in *ad hoc* receptacles such as horse-collars, cooking pots, drawers or boxes, though these could also have symbolic significance and served again to conceal the child. Where cradles were used, they were often not the first repositories of the baby and their use was surrounded by some ritual precautions. Sometimes, as we have seen, the baby was put straight after birth in the mother's bed. Very often, the child was not put into the cradle until it had been baptized. Before this one of the other receptacles mentioned would serve. In some parts of Britain, a cock or a hen or a sack of meal had to be put into the cradle before the baby was. Cradles were often decorated with protective designs and they had amulets attached to them.

The baby was surrounded by further taboos and rituals. It was most important not to take anything out of the house during the liminal period after the birth, lest it be used to harm the child. In Germany nothing would be lent to neighbours until the child had been baptized. In Lucania, if a mother of an unbaptized baby gave fire from her hearth to a neighbour, the baby would fall sick with what was called 'pagan fire', becoming red like a pagan or a devil. Nothing in the child's progress, moreover, was anticipated. So the layette was not prepared before the birth, as we have seen; the cradle was not brought in until the child was born alive and well. The child was never referred to by name until after the christening. Later there was great hostility to measuring and weighing babies. It was very dangerous for a new baby to be in the same house as a person who had died. In the Périgord baptism was hastened if someone in the family became ill, in case the person should die and thus threaten the baby. The new-born baby's soul was only tenuously attached to its body and would like all souls be prone to leave the body during sleep, when 'it might be captured by the soul of the deceased' which would also be wandering about.[60] The idea that letting a baby see itself in a mirror might cause its early demise reflects the same view that the baby's hold on life was very tenuous.

Positively, religious rituals were performed. Prayers and blessings were said; masses and intentions at mass promised. Babies were also vowed to saints and to the Church. St Bernard's mother, Aleth, according to his Life, offered all her babies to God 'with her own hands' and she pledged Bernard himself to the religious life.[61] Later, vowing a child to a saint would involve dressing it in a religious habit for a period of years. The protection of saints was also invoked in lullabies. Venetian lullabies call on Sts Lucy, Mary Magdalene and Martha, for example; Greek ones on Sts Marina and Sophia.

There were also secular rituals associated particularly with the hearth, as we have already seen, and with fire. Abbé Thiers referred to new-born babies being 'passed through the fire' to protect them from spells. In the Highlands and Islands of Scotland, baby and mother were 'sained' by having a lighted fir candle or some other flame carried three times round their bed or their heads, a ritual repeated night and morning until baptism and churching. Among the Sarakatsani, 'the powers of darkness are driven off with foul-smelling smoke' from the hearth for twelve days after the birth.[62]

Protective objects and 'a battery of amulets' were placed around the baby. Knives or daggers might be stuck in the cradle, or a something made of iron or steel placed there, for example a key or a pair of open scissors. In Wales, firetongs or a poker were placed 'crossways on the cradle' to stop the baby from being stolen by the fairies. In Minho an ox-yoke might be placed on the cradle. Sulphur, gunpowder and coins were also placed around or on the cradle. Special herbs might also be used: in Lucania juniper was usual; in Portugal rue and rosemary were 'fastened to the bed to protect the child from being carried off by witches'.[63] In parts of Scandinavia, flax seeds were 'sown' around the house. In many parts of Catholic Europe, the 'palms' blessed on Palm Sunday were employed here.

Similarly all kinds of things with the power to ward off evil forces were attached to the baby, sewn into its clothing or placed round its arms or neck. These included eaglestones, coral, jet and amber; red thread; little bells; coins; garlic, peony, dill, mistletoe and other plants and herbs; bread, pretzels and nuts; parts of animals such as a badger's paw, a wolf's tooth or bones of rabbits or hedgehogs; and again salt. If a baby were left at the Florence Foundlings Hospital in the fifteenth century 'with a tiny sack of salt around its neck, the administrators knew that the child had not been baptized'. Corsican mothers who could not afford a coral bracelet for their babies sewed a few lumps of salt into their clothing 'to conjure the evil eye'. Some of these amulets were manufactured for the purpose. In the Mediterranean region, horns, stars and above all the *figa* gave protection to infants. The last was 'an amulet in the shape of a clenched fist with the thumb clasped between the index and the second finger', which was widely believed to be especially effective against the evil eye. The circumstances in which an object had been found could also determine its suitability here. For example in modern Portugal, a goat's horn found on a Tuesday or a Friday 'and twice kicked before being picked up' had the power to protect infants.[64]

Often these preservatives were left on after baptism and after the baby grew into a child, and they were often combined. In the Cévennes in the 1950s sachets used to protect babies comprised a snake's head, salt, a crumb of bread and a peppercorn. In Lucania, the objects inside such sachets varied. One included a piece of a horseshoe from a horse shoed for the first time, three grape pips, three pinches of salt, a hair of a black dog, a thread from a priest's stole, and a statuette of a saint. As this indicates, religious objects often figured as amulets in Catholic countries. Scapulars of different kinds were put on babies: in Lucania, scapulars were 'baptized', and that of the first-born was used to protect later siblings; in Belmonte de Los Caballeros, scapulars of the Virgin of Carmen were supposed to ensure that babies would not suffer the pains of Hell should they die before baptism. Crosses, medals and images of saints; relics such as stones or dust from shrines; miniature versions of the Gospels or extracts from those parts recounting the birth of Christ; and texts of prayers, 'some of them written backwards', are all reported also. Abbé Thiers wrote in 1679 that he had found an image representing the Three Kings with a Latin prayer invoking their aid in 'a tin phylactery around the neck of a baby'. Ironically, given later clerical disapproval, the Christ Child was sometimes represented wearing protective amulets. For example, in Piero della Francesca's Madonna of Senigallia and in his altarpiece, now in the Brera Museum in Milan, the Child is wearing a coral necklace.[65]

The baby might also be placed just after birth in special clothing – often temporarily. In England 'directly after birth, the baby, before being dressed, was wrapped in a cloth called a "receiver" in the seventeenth century, the term surviving into the nineteenth'. In parts of France the baby was received at birth into its mother's wedding shawl or its father's shirt. In Switzerland,

Scotland and elsewhere, it was wrapped in its father's shirt, coat or trousers. In a tale from Selkirkshire, flinging the father's waistcoat over a baby saved it from being taken by the fairies. In parts of France and Germany, the father's breeches or trousers were hung up in the room or a pair of his slippers. Here we may see a direct recognition of the child's paternity being made as well as symbolic incorporation into the family. In north-east Scotland, a boy was 'wrapped in a woman's shirt and a girl in a man's, otherwise they would never marry'.[66] In some places, the baby was placed directly into the skin of a sheep or a lamb that had been skinned during the birth and was still warm. The English lullaby, 'Bye, baby bunting' links this provision of an animal skin with the father.

Rituals were also followed in swaddling or putting on the baby's own proper dress. In the Highlands of Scotland, the baby used to be turned heels over head three times, was blessed, and had its head shaken three times before it was first dressed. Putting a garment on inside-out was common, and there are indications that swaddling could be regarded as a form of concealment.

Ritual neglect may also explain other clothing customs. In England, as far back as the seventeenth century, there was an idea that a new-born baby's first clothing should be old; anything new was unlucky. Often, too, clean linen was thought to be bad for the baby as it was for the mother. So until recently in parts of rural France, the nappies that were put on a new baby were supposed 'to smell of the urine of another baby'. In Portugal, the baby's first shift was kept unwashed.[67] All of this diverted evil forces away from the child. Beliefs about gender also played a part here. In Upper Brittany, if a boy was placed in rags made of old petticoats, he would run after women when he grew up and could not become a priest; while a girl put in nappies made from male clothing would become a tomboy or run after men.

The first nourishment of the baby was also most important. From the medieval period onwards, medical advice and popular views agreed that this should not be human milk. In the British Isles, salt or honey or later sugar with butter, or hot water were given; in France wine or wine with honey. As well as fortifying and purifying the child, one of the aims of the first nourishment was to purge the meconium, and oil of almonds, cooked apple, peony juice and fennel were believed to have this effect. There was also a fear that the vulnerable new-born might take in something hostile to it. In the Highlands of Scotland, according to a mid nineteenth-century report, the baby 'was given ash-sap, because it was a powerful astringent and also a guard against witches'. In Upper Brittany in the early 1900s, babies were sometimes fed with sugared water only between birth and baptism or not fed at all, 'lest the Devil take advantage of the passage of food into the throat, stomach or intestines of the child to cause its death and carry it off '. At the same time there was a

general belief that the mother's initial milk was bad for the baby and especially the colustrum that flowed from her breasts in the first few days after
birth. For this period therefore or longer – in some cases for up to fifteen or
twenty days – the mother might have her milk sucked by a pet animal,
another child or an adult, while her baby was fed as already described or
suckled by another lactating woman. This might be ritualized. The medieval
text attributed to 'Trotula' reported: 'Some men say it is good for the baby to
drink the milk of nine women before he drinks his mother's milk'.[68]

Festivities followed the birth too. Relatives and neighbours would visit, in
most places only women. Mother and child would be surrounded by a kind of
female wake for several days. Those attending brought food and drink both
for festive consumption and to supply and comfort the new mother. In the
Périgord in modern times a cock was killed if the baby was a boy and a hen if
it was a girl, and a broth made which was given to the mother. In Hungary,
the godmothers brought food for the mother a few days after delivery in
specially decorated pots. There were also gifts for the child of specific kinds.
In the Welsh Borders, they comprised bread, salt and silver in recent times,
and an egg was sometimes given too in a basket. In the Balkans in and around
Scutari, 'all the women neighbours go at once to visit the mother and take
offerings of eggs. For a boy, two, four, six, or eight – an even number – are
brought; for a girl, one, three, five or seven'. Eggs, bread and fruit were
universally given, also salt, cheese, special cakes, coins, pins and, more
recently, matches. The gifts were often accompanied by explicit wishes. In
Provence, the traditional offerings were made by the first woman to visit, who
said to the baby, using 'these sacramental words: May you be as good as
bread, as full as an egg, as wise (or as healthy) as salt, and as straight as a match
(or the prop of your parents in old age)'. The matches might also stand for the
fire of the hearth, and matches and salt were preservatives against witchcraft.
Sometimes more expensive presents were given. *Deschi* or birth-salvers were
offered in Renaissance Florence among all social classes, and also elaborately
woven bed-jackets and simple shawls. The *deschi* were displayed prominently
in the house afterwards.[69] Faïence plates were given in France and maternity
pincushions in England.

The birth-feast or 'nursing ale', as it was sometimes called in Britain, could
involve dancing, excessive drinking and the letting-off of guns and fireworks,
and it could become a more general gathering. On Grand Canary, the party
lasted several nights. Young men and girls amused themselves with games,
riddles, singing refrains and making a great deal of noise. In the Netherlands,
as we have seen, a party was held on the birth day or the next. 'A caudle was
prepared and toasts were drunk in honour of the new mother', and a special
role was played by the father. Another party then took place about a week

later, when the mother got up for the first time, a pattern found elsewhere. In Scandinavia, where the custom is attested to from the thirteenth century onwards, the birth-feast was known as the 'women's feast'. Women drank and danced and engaged in ritual aggression against property and against men. There are reports of waggons, gates and haystacks being destroyed, and of men who ventured too close being taunted, having their hats or caps stolen or even being stripped naked. All over Europe reformers tried consistently to curb or abolish these feasts, without much success until the start of the eighteenth century. One argument expressed in the later medieval period was that excessive rejoicing might annoy God 'and cause the death of the child'.[70]

8

Childbirth: Omens and Strange Births

See how a granny, or an auntie, who fears the gods, takes the baby out of his cradle. Skilled in averting the evil eye, she first, with her ... middle finger, applies the charm of lustrous spittle to his forehead and slobbering lips; she then dandles the wizened hopeful in her arms and destines him in her prayers to the domains of Licinus, or the mansion of Crassus [both very rich men]: 'May kings and queens desire him for their daughter! May the maidens scramble for him! May roses bloom wherever he plants his feet!'

So the first-century Roman poet Persius evoked the universal blessing of the new-born baby and attempts to influence its destiny for the good. In nine-teenth-century Rome, 'the "wise women" of the neighbourhood, who are thought to be skilled in divination, are admitted to the chamber of the mother (between birth and baptism), and then, after examining carefully the infant ... they prophesy his future and wish him all sorts of luck'. Similarly in Scandinavia, there are reports of 'local wise women journeying round the farms and uttering words of prophecy concerning the destiny of small child-ren'.[1]

In southern Europe in particular, the role of making such wishes and offering gifts at the same time was often transposed to supernatural women: the fairies, 'house-women' or Fates, who were usually referred to indirectly and euphemistically. A Sicilian lullaby, for example, mentions 'certain ladies whom I dare not name'. In Greece and the Balkans, the three Fates came during the first three nights after the birth, or on the third or fifth night, to determine the 'future' or the 'luck' of the child. The dogs were chained up or sent away to friends and the house door left open or unlatched. The rest of the family went to bed early. A candle was left burning in the main room, where a table by the baby's cot was prepared with eatables, often being placed under the icon and having 'three cushions or low stools around it' for the expected visitors. The fare included bread, wine, and water, fruit and nuts, and honey or a special honey cake prepared by a virgin. The midwife and relatives ate this cake the next day on the spot, taking care that no crumb was removed from the room, since it could be used in spells to harm the child. Other gifts were left out for the Fates, too, in the form of money or the family heirlooms;

the mother's wedding ring might also be put out. The baby's 'destiny' was supposed to be written by the Fates on its forehead, and 'any little mark or abrasion there' was later interpreted. Alternatively, 'people with good souls can eavesdrop and (then) expound their prophecies'.[2]

In the Abruzzi, the Fates visited the baby on the third night after the birth. A table in the room of the mother and child had been covered with a freshly laundered white cloth and a glass of water and a slice of bread had been placed on it. The Fates arrived at midnight.

> If all is to their liking, they drink the water and eat a little bread. They dance round [the table] and then go and look at the baby and assign its fate. To a very poor baby they may say. 'Gentleman, knight, little baron', while to a rich one it may be 'Poor little one'. In the morning the mother looks at her baby's cheeks to see if there is a lucky kiss-mark. If there is this mark, a family feast is given, but should the child's nose be a little pinched, the child will die, and a coffin is prepared. Sometimes, the fates take the baby and throw it either into the middle of the room or into a corner, and this means that it will grow up stupid or unlucky.

More familiar is the scenario in Grimm's 'Sleeping Beauty'. Here eleven of the twelve fairies or wise women invited to the birth-feast endow the child with virtue, beauty, riches and so on, but the uninvited thirteenth, who arrives at the end of the celebrations, prophesies that she will prick her finger with a spindle at the age of fifteen and die. The twelfth fairy of course, is able to commute this sentence to a hundred-year sleep.[3]

The hour, the day, the time of year and other circumstances of the birth all had their significance. 'The owl shriek'd at thy birth', King Henry VI tells Richard of Gloucester in Shakespeare's play,

> ... an evil sign;
> The night-crow cried, a boding luckless time;
> Dogs howl'd and hideous tempests shook down trees;
> The raven rook'd her on the chimney's top,
> And chattering pies in dismal discords sung.

The literate would note more prosaic details down in family record books: 'My daughter Phoebe was christened', Robert Bulkeley of Dronwy on Anglesey wrote on 20 October 1672; 'she was born on Tuesday ... the moon in Taurus' – and from them the future destiny of the child could be told.[4]

In France and elsewhere birth at dawn was a good sign, the child's start in life fitting the start of the day. By contrast, birth during the night was unlucky, and efforts might be made to advance or retard the delivery to avoid this time. Midnight and noon were particularly dangerous times, since evil powers were very active then. In the west of Ireland, a 'child born after midnight was especially vulnerable to being stolen by fairies'. Elsewhere a child born at or after midnight might have special psychic powers. In modern Suffolk babies born at the 'chime hours' had 'the faculty of seeing spirits and cannot be bewitched'.[5]

The significance of days of the week is familiar from the English nursery rhyme 'Monday's child is fair of face', and similar schema exist in other countries. In Catalonia, for example, children born on Mondays will be unfortunate; on Tuesdays, poor and unlucky; on Wednesdays, merchants; on Thursdays, wise; on Fridays, artists and lovers; on Saturdays, small of stature; and on Sundays, lucky and gifted. Sunday was a lucky birthday nearly everywhere. In parts of Germany, 'Sunday children' also had special power to see spirits and so on. On the other hand, Friday, the day of the Passion, was very often unlucky, though birth on that day could also convey extraordinary powers. 'It was declared by the nurse, and by some sage women in the neighbourhood', David Copperfield recounts, '... first that I was destined to be unlucky in life; and secondly, that I was privileged to see ghosts and spirits; both these gifts inevitably attaching, as they believed, to all ... infants of either gender, born towards the small hours of a Friday night.' In Spain those born of Friday 'were gifted with a power of seeing into the earth and of discovering hidden treasures'.[6] In the Haut-Vivarais in southern France, girls born on Saturday would be infertile.

Particular days in the year could have similar significance. Christmas Day was universally a day of good omen. In Catalonia, those born on the first two days of the New Year would enjoy longevity. Again, certain saints' days brought special protections and abilities. On Mallorca, for example, 'those born on St Pablo's Day had the power of curing insect stings and burns with their saliva'. Holy Innocents was generally a day of bad omen for obvious reasons. There were also other generally recognized unpropitious days, often called the 'Egyptian Days'. There were at least two of these each month, and according to St Bernardino, in fifteenth-century Tuscany people believed that 'a child born on one of these days will not live, or if he lives, he will always be poor. And if he takes a wife, he will lose her soon or she will be unfaithful to him, and never will they have peace together'. Individuals could place curses on days too. So Constance, in Shakespeare's *King John*, declares the day of the proposed marriage of Lewis and Blanche, which dashes the hopes of her son Arthur, a 'day of shame, oppression, perjury' and adds:

> ... let wives with child
> Pray that their burdens may not fall this day,
> Lest that their hopes prodigiously be cross'd.[7]

In southern France, May and November were unfortunate months to be born, November being associated with the dead and thus dying. Being born on the Day of the Dead could, however, convey special powers, as it did to the *benandanti* of the Friuli. To these months, August might be added. In the Limousin, children born in December and January, when the days were short, would be small. In much of France, the worst period to be born was 'during the fast of the Four Seasons between Advent and Lent'; this period was associated with evil spirits and the dead, and babies born then would be likely to die prematurely. In Ireland, those born at Whitsuntide 'were supposed to have the evil eye, to be fated to die a violent death, or to take a life. A chicken would sometimes be killed in the hands of a Whitsun child to serve as a substitute slaughter'.[8]

From Ancient times among the well-to-do elaborate horoscopes were cast on the basis of such data about the time of birth, linked to the position of the stars and other heavenly bodies. 'It makes all the difference', Juvenal declared in his Seventh Satire,

> by what conjunction
> Of the stars you utter your first thin squalls,
> Still red from your mother's womb.

Shakespeare's Suffolk says:

> A cunning man did calculate my birth
> And told me that by water I should die.

This was one of the commonest applications of astrology through the medieval and Renaissance periods. In a famous example, the horoscope of Michelangelo 'showed Mercury and Venus in the house of Jupiter, peaceably disposed; in other words, his mind and hands were destined to fashion sublime and magnificent works of art'. Horoscopes were still take seriously among the elite in the seventeenth century – 'Dryden calculated nativities', according to Dr Johnson – ,[9] but they were beginning to be ridiculed by the early to mid eighteenth century, for example in England by Congreve and Sterne.

There were popular handbooks enabling ordinary people to draw up their own horoscopes, but at the popular level most attention seems to have been paid here to the simpler observation of the phases of the moon. In Champagne, infants born on the first, sixth, ninth, thirteenth and sixteenth days of the moon would have long life; those born on the third, fifth and seventh days would not live; those born on the fourth would be treacherous; and so on. St Hildegard of Bingen noted that the twentieth day after a full moon was especially unpropitious: a boy born then would become a robber and a murderer, and a girl a deranged woman and a poisoner. In southern Italy and the English West Country, it was unlucky to be born when there was no moon or a new moon. In Thomas Hardy's *The Return of the Native*, Christian Cantle who is simple-minded and, it is implied, sexually impotent, was born when 'there was no moon'; in discussing his case he and his neighbours refer to the popular saying: 'No moon, no man'. In early modern Germany, however, according to Coler, a child born under a new moon, and especially when this coincided with a Sunday, would develop and prosper as the moon waxed, while a full moon, which would wane as the baby grew older, brought disease and death. In modern Wales, 'children born when the moon was new would be eloquent; those born during the last quarter would have excellent reasoning powers'.[10]

Other natural phenomena could have their influence on the new-born and its fate. 'In coastal areas [of Britain], births are looked for with the incoming tide, for life comes in with the flow and goes out with the ebb'. Importance was also attached to unusual climatic and celestial happenings, such as eclipses, comets and storms. In a well-known example, Shakespeare's Owen Glendower attributes his magical powers and other extraordinary qualities to the fact that

> at my nativity
> The front of heaven was full of fiery shapes,
> The frame and huge foundation of the earth
> Shak'd like a coward.

'The heavens were overcast when I was born', ran a popular song from Calabria in less apocalyptic vein,

> No luck for me, luckless and forlorn,
> Even from my cradle.

Again, for early modern Germany, Coler reported the belief that children born during thunderstorms would turn out to be 'weak and timid'.[11]

All other circumstances of the birth could be read in similar ways: whether the birth was easy or difficult; dreams or visions experienced by the mother at the time; birth order; length of gestation; presentation; how the baby looked. Last-born children were given special names, 'Benjamin', 'runt', 'nestling', and were expected to be weaklings or short-lived. Seventh children had special powers. In Catalonia and Valencia, for example, seventh sons could put out fires with their breath, were immune to gun-shot and could cure rabies. In Eastern Europe they were prone to become *revenants* or ghosts. There was uncertainty, we have seen, about the normal period of gestation and how to calculate it, but estimates were made. Premature babies were obviously at great risk, but, according to the *Grand Calendrier des bergiers*, those born at seven months had a better chance of survival than those born at eight months, since the latter were 'born under Saturn, which is a cold and dry planet, two qualities quite contrary to nature', while the former had the benefit of the warm damp influence of the moon.[12] Children born after the death of their fathers were sometimes credited with healing powers. Rarer and thus more sacred were those born by Caesarean section after or via the death of their mothers. Many folk heroes had been born in this way.

Among foetal positions, being born feet first attracted most concern. In the modern Limousin, such children were lucky. In Brittany, they had healing powers, relating especially to sprains. In Scotland, they could cure rheumatism by treading on the affected part or parts. In most of Europe, however, the sign was negative. In Spain, the baby would be a slow walker. The special powers conveyed might be unwelcome ones. A priest from the Friuli denounced a midwife to the Inquisition in 1587. When one of her patients 'gave birth to an infant who came into the world feet first', he reported, 'this guilty sorceress persuaded the mother that if she did not want her child to become a *benandante* or a witch, she should place him on a spit and turn him over in the fire, I do not know how many times'. But most commonly this presentation was associated with death. As Belmont has argued, the birth axis went normally from head to feet, whereas the opposite orientation was that of death. The dead were carried out of the house feet first, and the expression 'going out feet first' was used to mean dying or 'going to the cemetery'. For a child to be born in the same way therefore either prefigured its own premature death or indicated that it did not belong to this world and hence had special powers linking it with the beyond.[13]

We have seen that birth marks were believed to be caused by the mother's cravings or by events during the pregnancy. They could also be signs, usually of ill omen for the child. For this and other reasons, attempts might be made to efface them. In the Cambrésis in the nineteenth century, the mother was advised to lick the marks first thing in the morning for nine days following the birth. Elsewhere they might be licked by dogs. In France, the worst sign on a baby was a particular 'blue vein' on the temple or forehead. In Alsace this was called the 'sign of the cemetery' or 'artery of death'; in Brittany it was the 'vein of St Vizin', to whose well the baby would be taken to have its head put in the water and the vein 'washed off'.[14]

Being born with teeth was always a bad sign. In different parts of Britain such a child would be 'unlucky for life', 'have an ungovernable temper', 'grow up hard-bitten and grasping', or 'die by violence'. Shakespeare's Richard of Gloucester adverts to this circumstance of his birth after he has stabbed and killed the king:

> The midwife wonder'd, and the women cried
> 'O Jesu bless us, he is born with teeth!'
> And so I was, which plainly signified
> That I should snarl, and bite, and play the dog.

Elsewhere in Europe this might herald a child with special powers. The Hungarian *táltosok*, shaman-like persons, were 'born with teeth',[15] as were *revenants* in Upper Silesia. In other parts of Eastern Europe and in the Balkans, an infant born with teeth would not live, but once it had died it would become a vampire, returning to take its relatives with it to the world of the dead. To prevent this, the baby would be decapitated before burial, or at least the offending teeth or one of them would be drawn from its mouth.

Particular attention has been devoted to beliefs relating to the caul. Babies are occasionally born with part of the amniotic membrane covering the head and shoulders. Various terms were used to describe this membrane in European languages, terms which compared it either to a cap, or a shirt, or a second skin. The belief that to be born with a caul was lucky was proverbial. 'Midwives claim to foretell what will happen to these children born with a caul', wrote Guillaume Bouchet in 1584, 'which is usually happiness and great wealth ... If one sees a rich man, one says: He must have been born with a caul!' Dapper in Ben Jonson's *The Alchemist* (1610) is flattered and has his hopes of riches raised by Face and Subtle who tell him:

> a rare star ... reigned at your birth ...
> Yo' were born with a caul o' your head.

Again, in nineteenth-century Provence, according to Mistral, if the silk-worms tended by a person were doing particularly well, the neighbours would say: 'It's clear you were born with a caul!' This belief is reflected in one of the names given to the caul in northern England: 'sillyhow' or happy hood. More particularly, birth with a caul conveyed invulnerability and immunity from wounds, fire and especially water. Christian Cantle in Hardy's novel reflects the popular view when he says that someone born with a caul 'can be no more ruined than drowned'.[16]

If fifteenth-century Florence, the happy state of such children was indicated by giving them the name 'Santo' or 'Santa', though this may also have

been a precaution, for the fortune which the caul brought with it was not
always unambiguously favourable. In many parts of Europe those born with
the caul were burdened with extraordinary powers. A belief going back to
Ancient times linked the caul with the gift of eloquence and it could also
convey manual skills. But in general it brought psychic gifts. In much of
Western Europe, this was the gift of healing. In Italy, for example, 'when a
boy is born with a caul, the midwife immediately calls the father who chooses
the illness that he wishes his son to be able to cure. He pronounces the name
of the illness and describes its symptoms in front of the infant.' In Iceland and
elsewhere, these children became clairvoyant. In the Netherlands, Denmark
and the Balkans, they had a special connection with the dead, being able to
detect ghosts and foretell deaths in the community. In the Friuli, they became
benandanti, those who rode out at night to ensure the fertility of the crops.
This 'access to the supernatural' might immunize them against the effects of
witchcraft, the evil eye or evil spirits,[17] but in some parts of Europe and in
some circumstances it could make them into witches, werewolves or
vampires or it could prefigure an early death.

Here the colour of the caul might be significant, a white or red caul being
generally a good sign and a black one a bad sign. 'In Herzegovina ... it was
thought that a baby born with a black caul would grow up to be a witch or
sorcerer unless, on the first night after the birth, a woman carried the caul to
the rooftop and announced' that the child had been born with it.[18] In
Dalmatia, a black or a red caul meant a child destined to become a witch,
unless a similar disclaimer were made, sometimes at the threshold of the
house. Whether from the same connection with the supernatural or because
the caul suggested the monk's cowl or the priest's surplice, it was a presage of
a religious vocation in France, England and elsewhere.

Special care was taken of the caul itself. In Iceland it was 'buried by the
midwife under the threshold. In Belgium it was thought that the child would
be lucky if the caul were buried in a field, unlucky if the membrane were
burned or thrown away'. Among the Sarakatsani, it was buried under the
hearth-stone. Where burial was the normal, it might be dangerous to keep the
caul, and some writers specifically proscribed doing so. 'Never keep the coiffe
or caul which covers the head and shoulders of the child', Louise Bourgeois
ordered in her midwives' manual of 1617, 'lest witches make use of it.' Where it
was not normal to bury the caul, it might be dried, and then either kept as an
amulet, or reduced to powder and fed to the child. According to Lemnius in
the mid seventeenth century, the latter procedure was believed to prevent the
evil effects of being born with a black caul, though in Pomerania feeding the
caul to the child caused it to become a vampire. Where the caul was preserved
as an amulet, it was often thought to retain its power only if it were not sold,

and there are examples of cauls being formally passed on from generation to generation like heirlooms. In his will of 1658, for example, Sir John Offley of Madeley in Staffordshire bequeathed 'the caul with which my face and shoulders were covered when I was born', and which he had had mounted in a gold and enamel setting, to his daughter and then to her son and his male heirs after that in perpetuity.[19] The caul was thus treated much like the placenta and the umbilical cord, though there are significant differences.

Often the influence benign or malign of birth with a caul stemmed from the event alone, but the fate of the membrane itself and its relationship to the person could also be decisive. In many places, children born with a caul would only be lucky if it were preserved. In Iceland, it was given to the child to play with. If the child did not harm it, this confirmed and reinforced its beneficent power. Often elsewhere it was attached to the child, being sewn into its clothing or hung round its neck, like other amulets. *Benandanti* continued to wear their cauls round their necks as adults. In parts of Germany and Hungary, where the caul conveyed skill in particular métiers, the relevant part of the child's body, its tongue, its hands, its feet, would be touched by the caul, held sometimes by the mother on her return from churching, sometimes by others or at a later stage. Adults might don their cauls in dangerous or critical situations. In modern Germany, 'the owner carried his caul when he was conscripted, with the hope that this ... would speed his release from military service'.[20] Similarly, in France the caul was worn at the draft selection so as to pick a 'lucky number'. In extreme cases, destruction of the caul meant the death of its owner. In early twentieth-century Somerset, a mother kept her child's caul until it was two years old, when she threw it away; soon afterwards the child drowned.

Underlying all this perhaps was the idea that a 'guardian spirit' or 'outer soul' resided in the caul, or that it was a kind of 'double' of the person. But more simply it was the magical equivalent of its owner, as hair, nail-clippings and other bodily waste might be though to a lesser degree. Indicative of this is the '*peau de chagrin*' phenomenon associated with the caul. In many places the appearance of the caul reflected 'the present health of the owner, even if he were absent; a dry, white crisp caul meant good health, while a damp, limp caul betokened illness'. In an English case from the 1860s, a woman kept her own caul

> stretched out in paper in her chest of drawers, and regularly consulted it ... If all was going well, it remained smooth and unchanged, but whenever danger threatened, it was found to have shrivelled. If she was about to fall ill, it became damp ... When she cut her hair, it changed colour ... She believed it would disappear when she died.

More generally in Britain 'it was thought that a caul must be buried with its owner, otherwise the dead person could not rest in his grave. His ghost would return to search for it'.[21] Much less often, maintaining links with the caul maintained the disadvantages it could bring. In some parts of England, one born with a caul would remain a wanderer, unless he separated himself from the membrane.

The virtues of the caul for the person born with it could extend to others who acquired it, though taking the caul from its rightful owner could destroy its powers. We have seen that midwives were sometimes suspected of stealing cauls either to pass on to witches or to sell. Many advertisements appeared in British newspapers from the mid eighteenth to the early twentieth century offering cauls for sale, mainly as preservatives against drowning and accidents at sea. Prices were high until the end of the nineteenth century, and a clear link was assumed between the good condition of the caul and its efficacy.

This belief in the power of the caul to preserve against water is probably related to the fact that it forms part of the amniotic sac which holds the foetus in fluid, the 'waters' which are broken at the start of birth. Birth in a sense rescues the baby from drowning. It is significant in this context that the caul's power was sometimes reinforced in late medieval and early modern Italy and France by 'baptizing' it, thus establishing another link with water.[22] In some texts, moreover, the term used to designate the caul is also used to describe the chrisom cloth in which the child was placed after the baptismal anointing. However, it should be added that other amulets were 'baptized', and cauls had masses and blessings said over them too. Cauls also provided other kinds of protection: against fire, particularly in Scandinavia, and by extension against fire-damp in mines; and against wounding and gun-shot, which may explain the link with conscription. Cauls were also used all over Europe in love magic, though paradoxically they might also cause impotence or sterility in women. In some parts of Ireland, a girl born with a caul would become rich if she married but she would have no children.

We turn now to other kinds of unusual birth. In many cultures, multiple births are confusing. They are regarded as an animal rather than a human characteristic and as such they arouse fear and horror. Twins, triplets and so on are therefore believed to cause epidemics and other disasters, and often all or at least the superfluous members of such sets used therefore to be exposed or killed at birth. In some cases, however, multiple births might be taken as signs of abundance and prosperity and thus be especially welcomed.

Both negative and positive connotations are found in Europe, with the former prevailing, though twins and other multiples were usually allowed to live. In modern Burgundy, for example, twins were thought to be infertile.

Very widely, multiple births were explained as general signs, or as the sign of some offence committed by the mother, most often unlawful intercourse, or as the effect of a curse. When a woman in the Lyon district gave birth to quintuplets in 1576 and three sets of twins were born in another parish, a local Jesuit reported 'this prodigious fecundity' to his superiors, noting that 'as a result we live in fear'. There are cases in medieval epics and romances of women abandoning one of a pair of twins. This relates to an old idea that a woman could conceive twice consecutively, though not with the same man. In one of the legends of El Cid written around 1480, the Spanish hero 'was a twin who was begotten when a knight forced himself' upon a miller's wife, who 'later lay with her husband, at which time the twin brother was conceived'. Fortune West of Rusper in Sussex was presented before the archdeacon's court in 1621. She had been 'delivered of two [illegitimate] children; and she saith that Henry Smith now of Horsham and William Walter late of Rusper are fathers, and that they lay with her, one night and the other the next night'.[23] Twins could thus be a very specific indication of adultery, which women might seek to conceal.

The association with animals was also present and was manifested in different ways. The mother could be suspected of bestiality. She could herself have animal features, such as more than two breasts. In a tale popular in Norway and Iceland, a barren woman 'longs for a child. She gets advice from a witch, but breaks one of the conditions, and as a result has twins, one of them beautiful, but the other hideously deformed, sometimes with an animal head'. Twins were also widely credited with magical powers. Among Yugoslav gypsies, they had second sight. In Andalusia they might become *sabias* or wisewomen. In Saragossa, they could cure colic in horses, and in Catalonia it was believed that 'a twin's shirt would revive the moribund, preserve one from bullets and put out fires'.[24]

Recent studies have pointed to a convergent interest in monsters and 'monstrous births' in early modern Europe at the popular and elite levels. Among the educated, however, they were coming to be seen by the seventeenth century as natural oddities requiring scientific explanation, a project taken further in the Romantic biology of Goethe, Cuvier and Saint-Etienne.[25] Before this and for a long time afterwards at the popular level, other kinds of interpretation prevailed.

In general terms, babies with serious deformities were viewed from Ancient times onwards as portents along with the climatic signs that we discussed in Chapter 3. The strange events occurring at the time of the murder of King Duff, according to Holinshed's Chronicles of Scotland, included storms and 'monstrous sights ... In Angus there was a gentlewoman brought forth a child without eyes, nose, hand, or foot'. Typically, in the view of an English ballad of 1562, these births foreshadowed great catastrophes, perhaps the advent of the last days:

> The silly infants, void of shape,
> The calves and pigs so strange,
> With other more of such mis-shape,
> Declareth this world's change.[26]

During the Reformation, Protestant leaders had made skilful use of this theme, Melanchthon pointing to a foetus with an ass's head produced in Rome in 1496 as a guide to the real nature of the pope and an indicator that his days were numbered, and Luther using the 'calf-monk', born at Freiberg in Saxony in 1552, to attack monasticism in general and to predict its fall.

However, for Protestants and Catholics monstrous births were also signs from God – in the German-speaking world deformed children were often said to be 'marked by God' – and as such they could provide lessons and deal out punishment for sins and errors, as well as making predictions. A broadside published in 1568 interpreted the birth of a deformed child at Maidstone in Kent in this way:

> This monstrous shape to thee, England,
> Plain shows thy monstrous vice,
> If thou each part wilt understand
> And thereby take advice.

So its 'gasping mouth' signified greed; its hands without fingers, idleness; its leg twisted up to its head, the refusal of subjects to be led by proper authority, and so on. More theologically, John Winthrop, Governor of the Massachusetts Bay Colony in the early seventeenth century, noted that a headless stillborn creature with scales and claws and its body all hideously deformed had been born to a woman suspected of Antinomian opinions as God's 'instruction to parents'. When another suspected heretic, Anne Hutchinson, produced multiple deformed foetuses, he commented: 'And see how the wisdom of God fitted this judgment to her sin every way, for look as she had vented mis-shapen opinions, so she must bring forth deformed monsters'. Another Puritan, in England, traced the birth of deformed offspring to Catholic parents in 1643 to the fact that its grandmother had mocked the 'glorious sufferings' of the 'martyrs' Bastwick, Burton and Prynne by naming her cats after them.[27]

The sins more usually adduced as explanations here were of a grosser, more obvious kind. Parents had wanted children too much; or they had not wanted children at all. Most often, they had ignored sexual rules and restraint. The Fugger newsletters reported from Venice in 1592 that a baby 'covered with cat's hair' had been born to 'a woman of evil repute' and an unknown father. A confessional manual, published in 1596 at Liège, asked: 'Where do they come from, the monsters, the deformities, the abortive fruit ... , if not from the unchecked lechery of their fathers and mothers?' A late medieval medical text attributed deformity to the behaviour of women whose periods were blocked, producing an uncontrollable 'desire to consort with men'.[28] Illegitimate birth was often linked with deformity, though we have seen that it could contrariwise produce lively and vigorous offspring. Incest was another explanation.

The Church had established times when sexual abstinence had to be maintained, for example, for a period before and after birth, sometimes until the child was weaned; and more generally during Lent, on Sundays, on the vigil of important feasts, and for three nights before receiving holy communion. Deformities at birth were frequently attributed to copulation and conception at these forbidden times. A woman from Berry, for example, mentioned by Gregory of Tours, 'confessed that the deformed child to which she had given birth had been conceived on a Sunday night contrary to the prescription of the Church'. In modern Greece, 'you should never have intercourse with your husband on a Wednesday or Friday, on a holy day or Easter, or during the Lenten fasting period. If you do so and conceive, your child will be born handicapped'.[29] More obviously a question of breaking a taboo rather than a moral rule was intercourse while a woman was menstruating. This was very generally believed through the Middle Ages and into the modern period to give rise to the conception of monsters, lepers or children with disfiguring marks on them.

Deformity could also arise from human malice. In Shakespeare's *King Richard III*, Lady Anne curses those who killed Henry VI in these terms:

> If ever he have child, abortive be it:
> Prodigious, and untimely brought to light,
> Whose ugly and unnatural aspect
> May fright the hopeful mother at the view.

From a witchcraft trial in the Franche-Comté in the early seventeenth century, we learn that one woman was supposed to have made another give birth to a crippled and deformed baby following a quarrel over the use of the communal oven, when the one had told the other that 'she would count herself lucky one day if her belly had been empty or full of shit'. Witchcraft was also blamed when a woman in the province of Namur gave birth to twins in 1608, one of whom was 'all deformed and mis-shapen with its legs bent forward and turned over its back and one of its arms interlaced with one of its legs'. The blessing of couples at marriage and on other occasions was sometimes aimed specifically by contrast to obviate deformities. Shakespeare again reflects this popular custom in Oberon's blessing of the marriage partners in *A Midsummer Night's Dream*:

> And the blots of Nature's hand
> Shall not in their issue stand:
> Never mole, hare-lip, nor scar,
> Nor mark prodigious, such as are
> Despised in nativity,
> Shall upon their children be.[30]

Congenital deformities were also attributed to intercourse with demons. Guazzo, for example, related the story of a Scottish girl seduced by an incubus who gave birth to ' a monster of utterly loathsome appearance ... and lest it should be seen and bring disgrace upon her family, the midwives lit a huge fire and quickly burned it'.[31] Other demonologists maintained that such couplings could not bear fruit. Whatever the status of such scholastic debates vis-à-vis popular belief, there is no doubt that the concept of devils' children was widespread in literature, early and late, and in proverbs, and it figures in the evidence from some of the larger witchcraft trials, for example in the Basque country in the mid 1550s and in Sweden in 1670. The demonic origins of such children may have shown themselves more in moral evil than in evil appearance, though in traditional European societies these two usually went together.

A related explanation of monstrous, deformed or unusual babies was that they had been substituted for the mother's real offspring. The publicity and precautions surrounding the birth were aimed in part at preventing such switches from taking place, whether they were natural – a real fear – or supernatural. 'Substitutions of children are, with God's permission possible', wrote the authors of the *Malleus Maleficarum*, who attributed them to the agency of the Devil:

> Such children are always miserable and crying; and, although four or five mothers could hardly supply enough milk for them, they never get fat, yet are heavy beyond the ordinary ... God permits this on account of the sins of the parents, in that sometimes men curse their pregnant wives, saying, 'May you be carrying the Devil!' or some such thing. In the same way impatient women often say something of the sort.

This seems to be a fairly accurate reflection of popular belief, though at the popular level changelings were believed to be substituted after the birth as we have seen, and the deed was done by fairies rather than by the Devil or demons. Stories about changelings are very common all over Europe,[32] and they figure in the folklore of most countries. Often they looked like little adults, with large heads, wrinkled skins, prominent eyes and deep voices, and, as the *Malleus Maleficarum* suggests, they had insatiable appetites.

Opposing strategies were open to parents landed with changelings. They could treat them extremely well, in the hope that the fairies would do the same for their own 'real' child; or, as happened more frequently, they could try to force the fairies to reverse the substitution. This could be done by making the normally impassive or grumpy changeling laugh, or reveal its proper age; or else by mistreating it. Beating the intruder, scalding it, putting it in the oven, or exposing it in some magical location such as the junction of three roads or three rivers, are all reported. In the Hebrides, 'a changeling placed below high-water mark on St Bride's night would be taken away and the original child restored'. Other forms of counter-magic were also employed. In parts of France, oats, milk and other substances were boiled in a pot. The thirteenth-century Dominican, Etienne de Bourbon, referred to the procedure of passing the changeling through a split tree to force it to depart. Shrines were also visited; and the sign of the cross was made. In some places, the baby ceased to be a changeling once it was baptized, suggesting that the changeling concept was a way of expressing the child's liminal and dangerous status before baptism humanized it. Elsewhere, there might be some doubt whether strange and particularly deformed babies should be baptized at all. Icelandic laws of the twelfth and thirteenth centuries required 'that every child be brought to church for baptism, even if severely deformed'.[33] Exposure of supposed changelings reflects the real practice of abandoning deformed babies.

In the urban world, the still-born might be disposed of, as though they were detritus. The Hôtel-Dieu in seventeenth-century Paris controlled a so-called tower of Limbo,

> where they throw still-born children which are brought there from the entire city ... as well as from the *faubourgs* and other surrounding areas, in which they toss a measure or so of quicklime in order to burn them and prevent too great an odour.

A midwife's oath in contemporary England required her not to 'suffer any child [born dead] to be cast into the jakes or other inconvenient place'. Where they were buried, still-born babies were often put in the remoter parts of churchyards away from other graves, or they were not buried in consecrated ground at all. In the Nièvre, where the still-born were not usually registered or declared, they were buried in gardens as late as the second half of the nineteenth century; while in modern Portugal they were buried in the courtyard or inside the house. These mainly rural practices have also been seen as an indication of negligence, but this is far from the case. In Portugal it was felt that the child had not been properly born and so should return into the household. If it was buried in the cemetery, this was done secretly at night by the father, for the same reason. Among the Sarakatsani, one finds the idea that burial of a miscarried foetus in the house and particularly beside the hearth facilitates the reincarnation of the spirit in a new baby that will live. The still-born child was also dangerous. Elsewhere in Greece, the still-born comprised one of the categories of vampire, the restless and aggressive dead, since they had been frustrated in the natural cycle which they had begun. But, only if the dead foetus was disposed of in the wrong place would vampirism ensue. Among the Sarakatsani again, 'they used [sometimes] to stow still-born babies in a goatskin full of salt and hang it on a branch by the hut for forty days, then burn it lest it should take its mother with it'.[34] In the Chartres region in the seventeenth century, the bodies of still-born babies were removed from houses via the window and not the door. If this precaution were not followed, the mother, having to use the same door afterwards, would give birth only to dead babies.

A woman who died in childbed was not buried in the usual way. In the medieval period, she 'could not be buried in church, but only in the church-yard', and then and later even this might be denied her. In seventeenth-century England, according to Misson, the pall was not black but white as for 'a bachelor or maid'. A Berkshire funeral account from the same time mentions the provision of 'necessary cloth fit for a woman dying in travail', as though it were of a special kind. At Skipton in Yorkshire, later, 'it was an invariable custom to bury at midnight a woman who died at the birth of her first child; the coffin was carried under a white sheet, the corners of which were held by four women'. Dr Blondel in 1729 referred to 'pregnant women' acting as the 'pall-bearers of their friends dead in childbed'. In parts of Lancashire, if a mother died 'within a month of the birth of her child, the baby was taken to the funeral and held over her grave'.[35]

Two considerations seem to have been at work here. First, the mother who failed to remain a mother, especially if she had had no children before, was treated as if she were a virgin: she had not fulfilled the purpose of marriage. Secondly, the mother who had not completed her birth was dangerous and required special placation or exclusion from the world of the living. A thirteenth-century text criticizing Corsican bishops for various shortcomings noted that: 'They do not admit women who died either preg-nant or in childbed to be buried in church cemeteries, for they affirm that they are damned in the same way as pagans'.[36] Of course, too, they had not been purified after giving birth. The importance of this is reflected in a practice found in some places by which a dead woman was represented at a proxy churching by the midwife or another woman. Only if this ritual were carried out could she be buried in consecrated ground and would she be able to go to Paradise.

Other special qualities might be attributed to this category of the restless dead. Their presence might raise storms at sea. Their 'relics' might have magical powers. In a case at Nuremberg in 1622, a man was accused of 'taking wood from the coffin-stand of a woman who had died in her first childbed' in order to use it to cure or harm horses. These thwarted mothers might also stay around to watch over their babies. In Alsace, it was believed that they returned to suckle them at least until churching would have taken place, and they might indicate their displeasure if the baby was being neglected. They might also wish to take the child with them. The custom in Lancashire of holding the baby over its dead mother's grave at the burial may have been a way of satisfying this wish symbolically. The same interpretation may be given of upper-class monuments in England showing mothers clasping or even suckling the babies they had not lived to cherish.[37]

Relating to all this was a further horror (found in many cultures) of burying a woman with an unborn child within her. Pregnant women could not by law be executed, and the claim to be pregnant was thus 'a recognized means of avoiding or postponing the death-penalty'.[38] It was quite frequently used, for example, by women accused in the witch trials of the early modern period. In France, pregnant women were not executed even during the Terror, and one of the most damaging charges made after Thermidor against Fouquier-Tinville, former Public Prosecutor of the Revolutionary Tribunal in Paris, was that he had broken this rule.

According to Roman Law (*Lex Caesare*), if a woman died while she was pregnant, the child was immediately to be cut from her abdomen, hence the name Caesarean applied to this operation. Though there are reports of successful Caesarean sections on living women from the sixteenth century, they remained extremely uncommon until the end of the eighteenth. The heroic status conferred on those born in this way in mythology and fiction is an indication of their rarity. The requirements of the *Lex Caesare* were handed down to the Middle Ages via Justinian's Digest, and became a firm prescription on the part of the ecclesiastical authorities lasting into the modern period. The midwife or the priest was obliged 'to make an incision ... and to extract the infant', in case it could be saved alive or at least be baptized. Later, surgeons might perform the operation. A case brought against an officer of health in Rennes in 1837 shows that they were still sometimes doing so, although it had by then become illegal. A comment by the *Gazette des Tribunaux* points to the traditional context:

> In the countryside here, when a woman who is pregnant dies, the clergy, adhering to a very ancient idea, refuse to bury her unless the child still in her womb has been extracted from it; as a result, it is usual for one of the women who has watched over the deathbed ... to rip open the dead woman's belly soon after death in order to get the child out.

Here the concern was not with saving a child who might be alive, but with avoiding the perceived anomaly of burying a mother with an unborn child. In another case in France, at Arras in 1838, a priest discovered during the funeral service that a mother and unborn child had not been separated and insisted that the coffin be opened and the separation effected, before he would proceed.[39]

If a pregnant woman were buried with her child *in utero*, special precautions might be taken, such as were appropriate also to those dying in a state of mortal sin or unbaptized, or to vampires. 'Hast thou done what some women, filled with the boldness of the Devil are wont to do?', asked Burchard of Worms. 'When some woman is to bear a child and is not able, if, when she cannot bear it she dies in her pangs, they transfix the mother and the child in the same grave with a stake driven into the earth.' This was believed to prevent the burial from bringing about disasters in the community. In one Russian village during the 1848 cholera epidemic, the disease was blamed on the fact that a pregnant girl had been buried. The peasants disinterred her body, opened it to find the foetus, and then drove a stake through the corpse. Once the corpse or corpses had been fixed with a stake, or the child had been removed from the womb, or both, the danger ceased And the removal could be temporary, symbolic. In a case in a village near Béziers in 1746, after the surgeon had removed the baby from inside its mother and it had been given emergency baptism, having apparently shown some signs of life, it 'was replaced a few moments later in its mother's belly and was then buried with her'. Elsewhere, in modern times, the fact that a mother and child occupied the same grave would be indicated. In parts of North Wales, where box hedging was grown around graves in the nineteenth century, 'an inner enclosure within an outer enclosure usually denoted a young child and its mother who had died in childbirth'.[40]

9

Baptism, Godparents and Naming

In the early Church, baptism had only been administered to adults, fairly spontaneously at first and later following a lengthy period of testing and instruction, known as the catechumenate. The baptism of infants was not ruled out, but it did not fit the situation of a missionary Church of first-generation converts. By the fourth or fifth centuries, the catechumenate of adults was on the wane, and infant baptism had become common in the West. At the same time, St Augustine elaborated the doctrine of original sin, which provided the theological basis for the custom. By the eighth century, infant baptism had become the rule, save for the newly Christianized.

As we have seen, new-born babies were believed to be especially vulnerable to attack from evil powers before they had been baptized. The *Malleus Maleficarum* asserted that witches 'set their snares chiefly for unbaptized children'; and the idea that witches used the bodies of such infants in their rites and to make magical substances was retailed in a succession of demono-logical treatises and trial evidence. In an early witchcraft case in 1428, a woman from Todi was reported to have 'taught people to cure illness by taking a bone from an unbaptized baby out to a crossroads, burying it there, and saying various prayers and formulae on that spot over nine days'. Much later, a Scottish text from 1811 noted that 'Highlanders regarded the rite of baptism as a means of disarming fairies and other sprites dangerous to newborn babies'. Concern for the fate of the child in the after-world, which we will see was very strong, could be mixed with fears of witchcraft. In Upper Brittany, according to a late nineteenth-century source, 'when a child died without baptism, a rosary was at once placed round its neck, while a sprig of vervain was put in its hand'. Without these precautions, the infant risked being taken by witches and/or tormented until the end of the world.[1]

The unbaptized were denied funeral rites and, like the still-born, they were excluded from burial in churchyards or consecrated ground, or at best given inferior disposal there. In his Injunctions of 1577, the bishop of Durham enjoined burial in the churchyard, but added 'yet without ringing or any divine service or solemnity, because the same was not solemnly professed and received into the church and congregation'. In the Charente in modern times similarly, the unbaptized were 'buried without ceremony in a special corner of the cemetery usually at nightfall'. Where burial occurred in other places – in caves or grottoes, by standing stones, by wayside crosses, at crossroads, and in or by houses are all reported – there are indications that these were not merely convenient destinations. According to Gallop writing in 1930, 'the ground space outside the [Basque] house yet sheltered by the eaves [is] known as the *itchasura*, [and] is regarded as semi-sacred. A laurel is often planted within it, and any children who die without baptism are buried there'.[2] Burial in the other places mentioned almost certainly had a similar ritual intention.

In all this two concerns seem to be present. First, there was a wish to save the infant from the consequences of dying without baptism, a concern that we shall see reflected in other ways. At a village in Alsace in 1880, for example, the parents of a still-born child buried it clandestinely under the eaves of the sanctuary roof of the church, hoping that the water running off the roof would bestow some kind of posthumous baptism. The other concern was a fear of the spirit of the dead child, which closely parallels the fear aroused by the still-born and the unborn child. Burchard of Worms condemned the custom by which 'when an infant dies without baptism, women take the little corpse and bury it in a secret place. They transfix the body of the child with a stake, saying that if they did not do this, it would return and could do harm to the living'. All over Europe from Ancient to modern times, one finds this belief that the spirits of the unbaptized were never at rest and could and did come back to haunt the living and especially their families. In variations of this idea, they could be *folletti* or *feux follets* – spirits waylaying travellers at nightfall, water-spirits, other kinds of fairy, shooting stars, supernatural hounds, werewolves, participants in the Wild Hunt, birds, moths or butter-flies. In Greece, the unbaptized might be represented by a spirit called Stringlos which made crying sounds at night. They might also manifest them-selves as half-animal, half-human creatures who returned to houses during the Twelve Days of Christmas, creating a minor nuisance, putting out the fire, spoiling food and so on, but also reproaching their parents for failing to baptize them and trying to steal any new-born babies who had superseded them. In Rumania, too, they were aggressive, envious spirits seeking to attack and take away babies. Some accounts suggest that these lost souls haunted marginal places especially by rivers and pools, seeking water with which to get baptized. In Norway and west Sweden, there was a belief that the victims of infanticide in particular haunted watery places and screamed until someone baptized them. Once this was done, they were pacified. In Transylvania, if one saw a falling star, this indicated that an unbaptized child was dying, and one should 'baptize' the child by saying: 'If it is a boy, let him be named Ion; if it is a girl, let her be Ioana'.[3]

Always, dead or alive, a firm distinction was drawn between the baptized and the unbaptized. 'The midwife', Mercier wrote of Paris in the 1780s, 'never fails to say to the mother as she bears away the child to the church [for baptism]: Madame, from a pagan we are going to make him into a Christian.' In modern Corsica, two different rituals were used to divine and cure illnesses resulting from the evil eye, one 'Christian' and the other 'Turkish', the former being used for baptized children and the latter for the unbaptized and for animals. A memorial brass at the church of St Cross in Oxford of Elizabeth Franklin who died in childbed shows her 'surrounded by her dead babies. The one who had been baptized' has its face exposed, 'but those who died unbaptized are depicted totally enveloped in shrouds, with no visible human characteristics'. Quite early on, baptism became also a naming ceremony, so the unbaptized were also anonymous. They could not therefore be remembered or commemorated with the other dead of the family. In the Minho in modern times even, 'prior to baptism the child is thought to have no soul'.[4]

This was not the official view and the Church taught that baptism ensured salvation for the individual soul concerned, and death without it could mean damnation. Langland asserted in fourteenth-century England that 'a bairn without baptism may not be saved'; while the *Rosengarten* declared in 1513 that a child dying 'before it receives holy baptism [would] ... thereby be robbed of eternal life'. By this time, Catholic theologians had on the whole abandoned the severe position of St Augustine, according to which such infants were condemned to suffer eternal torments. They might go to Hell but they would not feel its worst pains. They might even go to Limbo, a celestial projection of their marginal state, where a state of natural happiness might be achieved though not the love of God. St Vincent Ferrer referred in a sermon around 1400 to 'the dwelling-place of unbaptized children, where there are neither demons nor sensible suffering but which means the loss of heaven'. Though endorsed by St Thomas Aquinas, the notion of Limbo was never officially formulated by the Church, and with the Counter-Reformation it reverted to a more rigorist stance. The catechism of the Council of Trent taught uncompromisingly in 1566 that 'the law of baptism is that unless they [infants] be regenerated ... through the grace of baptism, [they] are born to eternal misery and perdition'.[5]

There is evidence from down the ages of popular anxiety about or rejection of the doctrine of infant perdition. The thirteenth-century heretical sect, the Poor of Lombardy, 'asserted that infants who died without baptism, far from being condemned to eternal torments, would rejoice in the pleasures of Heaven'. Among the items raised for discussion at the First Zurich Disputation of 1523 were taking interest on money, tithes and the fate of unbaptized children. Richard Baxter relates in his autobiography that he was 'railed at' in the streets of Kidderminster in the 1640s by many of his parish-ioners who had misunderstood his preaching of the doctrine of original sin; 'they vented it abroad ... that I preached that God hated or loathed infants'. In the 1720s, Edward Burt encountered a woman in the street in Edinburgh, 'crying and lamenting as in the utmost despair', because 'the ministers had refused to christen her child, because she did not know who was the father of it ... she talked to it as if it must certainly be damned if it should die without baptism'. He and others arranged for it to be baptized, 'not that we thought the infant in danger, but to relieve the mother from her dreadful apprehens-ions'. Charles Lamb at the start of the nineteenth century referred to St Augustine as 'the consigner of undipped infants to eternal torments, ... whom all mothers hate'. Folklorists at the end of the century reported that people in Brittany believed more positively that, though unbaptized infants might suffer for a period, at the end of the world St John the Baptist would baptize them all and they would enter Paradise.[6]

Original sin was an attractive doctrine to many Protestants and could lead them to emphasize the need for baptism. 'Infants must needs be christened, because they be born in original sin', declared the English *Bishops' Book* of 1537, and drew the corollary that without the sacrament of baptism, they were not 'undoubtedly' saved. Other Protestants, like Zwingli and Calvin, however, rejected the idea that baptism was absolutely necessary for salva-tion. Bishop Barnes of Durham, for example, told his clergy in 1577 that they should teach their parishioners 'that if any infant die without public baptism first to it ministered, that the same is not to be condemned or adjudged as a damned soul, but to be well hoped of'.[7]

Despite these differences, clergy and laity were both very anxious that chil-dren should not die without baptism. Hincmar of Reims in 874 opposed the practice of monks looking after parishes on the grounds that they were apt to be 'careless and let infants die without baptism'. Similar arguments were used against monastic appropriations in fifteenth-century England. Interdicts, like that imposed on England in the reign of King John, banned 'all ecclesiastical offices save the baptism of infants and the confession of the dying'. Laws and ecclesiastical regulations, moreover, laid down ever tighter deadlines for bringing children to be baptized, abandoning the ancient practice of holding group baptisms at Easter and Whitsun. Also abandoned was the assembling of candidates in cathedrals or special baptismal churches, where the rite was administered by the bishop. Instead the ceremony became a purely parochial affair. The ecclesiastical laws of Ine, King of Wessex, laid down as early as 693 that an infant must be baptized within thirty days of birth. A fine of thirty shillings was to be imposed if this was not done, with confiscation of the parents' property if the child died. Similar provisions existed in other early law codes, for example those of Norway, where 'the penalty for leaving a child unbaptized for a year was exile'. In England again, Archbishop Pecham in 1279 required infants to be brought to baptism within a week of birth, referring to the danger of their dying without it. This weekly interval became the norm from the fourteenth century in diocesan regulations all over Europe. According to the *Sarum Manual* only infants born within a week of Easter or Whitsun might be reserved for initiation at those seasons. The Council of Trent required baptism to take place 'as soon as possible', but most local synods and service books were less elastic. The usual rule in France in the seventeenth century, for example, was three days, or a week at most, and severe penalties were threatened for non-compliance: fines, no ringing of bells at the ceremony when it did take place, or, as in the statutes of the diocese of Lodéve in 1745, excommunication of the parents.[8] Penalties were also imposed on clergy and midwives. Special inducements to prompt baptism were also offered. It was believed in Corsica and the Abruzzi in the nineteenth century, perhaps following clerical teaching at some level, that baptism on the day of birth freed a soul – usually that of a deceased relative – from Purgatory.

Despite theological differences, Protestant churches maintained similar rules on the timing of baptism. From 1525 infants had to be baptized within eight days of birth at Zurich; while the Brandenburg-Nuremberg Church Order of 1533 stated 'as soon as possible'. 'The pastors and curates shall oft admonish the people', ran the rubric in the First Prayer Book of Edward VI in 1549, 'that they defer not the baptism of infants any longer than the Sunday, or other holy day, next after the child be born, unless upon a great and reasonable cause declared to the curate and by him approved.' The Book of Common Prayer relaxed this slightly to 'the first or second Sunday'. The Church of England, like other Protestant Churches, preferred baptism on Sundays when the regular congregation was present, but it made provision for private baptism in case of 'necessity'. Protestants also maintained sanctions against delaying baptism. Presentments of parents and clergy before the ecclesiastical courts in Britain were fairly common in the early modern period, where the legal deadline had not been met and especially where the child had died. In 1584, for example, the incumbent of Blackmore in Essex was suspended after 'two children died unchristened by his negligence, for that he would not christen them before Sunday following, and died in the meantime'.[9]

Detailed research indicates that these rules were effectively put into practice. Among the Florentine elite, most children were baptized on their birthdays or at least within two or three days. Similarly at Porrentruy in the Swiss Jura, nearly all infants were baptized on the day of birth. In many parts of

France and Italy, baptism within two or three days was usual by the late sixteenth and seventeenth centuries, though there were always exceptions. In seventeenth-century Nîmes five to six days seems to have been common, while in the Corsican diocese of Aleria an eight-day delay was the norm in the late sixteenth century. The picture is the same later. Typically, in the diocese of Tarbes around 1700, nearly a quarter of babies were being baptized on the same day that they were born, from one half to three-quarters on the next day at least, and only a tiny proportion beyond three days. In the Lodève similarly by the mid eighteenth century, the bulk of baptisms occurred within the first three days, often on day one or two. Still in nineteenth-century France, 'most folklorists' reported that baptism took place within twenty-four or forty-eight hours of birth,[10] and this pattern did not change until right at the end of the century with the decline in infant mortality.

The situation was similar for other countries, with a tendency among Protestants for the delay to stretch over the centuries. A recent study concludes that 'Elizabethan babies were usually baptized two or three days after their birth, but in late Stuart times the median interval was eight days, growing even longer in the following century'. Nelson wrote to Lady Hamilton in 1801 in connection with the baptism of their daughter Horatia: 'It is not usual to christen children till they are a month or six weeks old'. Delays might have special reasons. In parts of Italy, there was a preference for the seventh or eighth day on account of the symbolic significance of these numbers. In the Balkans, baptism and and the forming of godparenthood ties was part of the ritual for ending blood-feuds, which meant that families often kept a child unbaptized for a year or two. Everywhere delays might be caused by the need to make proper preparations for a ceremony felt to be very significant, and private baptism had often already been performed as a precaution. Laget sees the conformity to prompt baptism as 'the clearest sign of the authority of the parish priest over the family',[11] but one should probably rather see it as a manifestation of the convergence of clerical and popular views.

Given the importance of the rite for salvation, the clergy emphasized the need for baptism at or during the birth itself, if the baby was thought unlikely to live. This was known as 'sudden baptism' or 'baptism in necessity', or in French 'petit baptême' or 'ondoiement' or sometimes in English as 'half-baptism' or 'half-christening', at least popularly. The trend towards a clerical monopoly of ritual associated with the rites of passage was tempered here, with stress being laid on the need for lay people to know the correct procedures and formulae.

> For every person, both high and low,
> The points of baptism ought to know,
> To help children in emergency,

Robert of Brunne instructed at the start of the fourteenth century.[12] And there is evidence from all over Europe down to modern times that lay people did perform emergency baptism in the prescribed manner. Western Canon Law even maintained that baptism was valid if performed by pagans or heretics.

Later Catholic texts, unofficial and official, indicated a preference for the priest to be called to officiate, though there was some uneasiness about having him in the birth-room and in intimate contact with the woman's body. The 1745 Lodève statutes stated that a cleric was to be preferred to a lay person, and a man to a woman, and stipulated that there were to be two witnesses wherever possible. Once again the practice of Protestant Churches was not very different, despite their promotion of initiation at the regular public services in line with what was seen as primitive custom. 'The pastors shall in their sermons instruct the people that they shall not lightly have recourse to emergency baptism', ran the Saxon Church Order of 1539, 'but, when the gravest need shall require that baptism should and must be given.' Many Elizabethan and Stuart bishops discouraged private baptism, and several specifically banned midwives and other women from baptizing. And Puritans and Calvinists generally were averse to the practice whoever officiated. But such rigorists were in the minority and they were not in tune with popular sentiment. In ruling in 1675 that the practice of summoning pastors at all hours to administer baptism to dangerously ill babies was 'superstitious and contrary to the Word of God', the Synod of Nîmes was clearly seeking to control a countervailing movement.[13]

By the eighteenth century, if not before, the Church of England had adopted a more relaxed stance, if the diarists among the ranks of the clergy are typical, though it seems that lay baptism had been discontinued entirely. William Cole, rector of Bletchley, baptized as a rule in church on Sundays, but he always, it seems, made exceptions where the baby was sick. 'Baptized a girl, Mary, in Brickhill Church', he wrote typically on 27 April 1766, a Sunday, 'and William, the son of Farmer Coleman at his house, being just born and in fits, fearing lest he should die.' Parson Woodforde in Norfolk followed a similar practice. He nearly always privately baptized the offspring of the squire in the latter's house, and he baptized or 'named' weak and illegitimate babies at the rectory; but he did not like performing baptisms otherwise in private houses, even of local notables. The demand for private baptism remained strong in England among all classes into the nineteenth century. Among the poor of Cook's Court, for example in Dickens' *Bleak House* (1851–53) 'half-baptizing' was always done 'where a child was not ... expected to live'.[14]

From the time of Aquinas, the Church added the further prescription that babies should be baptized in the womb, if a birth was not going to be completed and at least part of the body had emerged. Usually the head had to be visible, and it was sprinkled or later a syringe might be used. The person best placed to perform this and other types of emergency baptism was the midwife, and a concern that she should do so and do so correctly lay behind the clerical supervision of midwives, to which we have referred. Robert of Brunne again, who instructed priests to teach and examine midwives about baptism, told the cautionary tale of 'a midwife who christened a child wrongly', using the formula:

> God and St John
> Christened be the child, both flesh and bone.

She had lost a soul thereby and was deprived of her position.[15] In addition, the Catholic Church required, as we have seen, that pregnant women dying before their term or during childbirth should be opened up by the midwife or a surgeon, so that the child might if possible be baptized. This provision remained in force until Vatican II.

It is repeatedly stressed, however, in both Catholic and Protestant sources that private baptism must be completed by bringing the child to church if it survived, in order to check that the ritual had been properly performed – midwives and other officiants were questioned – and that it might 'gain the virtue bestowed by the prayers of the Church', as St Vincent Ferrer put it in a sermon around 1400. The same point is reiterated in Protestant Church Orders and Visitation Articles, and by clerical diarists. Woodforde refused private baptism to a child in 1777, whose father had had a previous baby privately baptized and had 'never brought it to church afterwards'. The Somerset rector, John Skinner, had similar problems in the early nineteenth century. Very often, parents of bastards, and also poor people, expressed great reluctance to attend the regular services at which baptisms were usually performed and might pretend that their babies were dying to get him to give them private baptism. On the other hand, there was a popular view that complete baptism was absolutely necessary and a fear lest some part of the ritual had been omitted. 'Behold how narrowly people look on the ceremony', William Tyndale complained in 1527.

> If aught be left out, or if the child be not altogether dipped in the water, or if, because the child is sick, the priest does not plunge him into the water, but pour water on his head, how tremble they! How quake they! 'How say ye, Sir John', say they [to the priest], 'is this child christened enough? Hath it full christendom?' They believe verily that the child is not christened'.[16]

We shall see later that such fears might induce some parents to have children baptized more than once, and that incomplete baptism might be believed to convey special magical powers.

There is no doubt therefore that, at an early stage, baptism had become accepted at the popular level as an essential protective rite. It ensured well-being in the world to come, and conveyed Christian identity. Sir Hugh Tabarie in a thirteenth-century French romance tells Saladin that his body 'is but an empty vessel ... empty of Christianity and baptism'. On being asked his age in Hardy's *The Return of the Native*, Christian Cantle says that he is 'thirty-one last tatie-digging ... That's my age by baptism, because that's put down in the great book of Judgment – that they keep down in the church vestry'.[17] Baptism also ensured material well-being, life and health in this world, though the two can hardly be distinguished.

As early as the fifth century there is evidence of parents 'bringing their children to baptism because they thought that with this remedy they would retain or receive temporary health'. In the County of Foix in the fourteenth century, the investigations of the bishop of Pamiers make clear that 'baptism was almost universally practised, not only because of its religious value but also because it was believed to act as a protection'; in particular it prevented a person 'from being drowned or ... eaten by wolves'. This belief that baptism gave protection in the here-and-now and might even act as a remedy transcended denominational differences and is found through the early modern and modern periods. 'It is generally believed by East Anglian nurses', wrote Forby in 1830' that a child never thrives well until it is named; and this is one cause of the earnest desire, frequently expressed, to have children privately baptized. If the child is sick, it is even supposed to promote the cure.' Such ideas were widespread and led again to requests for repeating baptism and to keeping the water a child had been baptized with as a future 'medicine'. The pious Lutheran doctor Lehndorff baptized some children in East Prussia in October 1945 in the circumstances of chaos and famine following German defeat and the Russian occupation. 'On these occasions', he wrote in his diary, 'I often pondered over the nature of baptism as a sacrament and over our strange attitude towards it. Very characteristic was the answer of a woman to my question whether her two-year-old child had been baptized: "No", she said, "he's been vaccinated but not baptized".' It is significant here that baptism persisted in the face of dechristianization and the abandonment of other Christian rituals. In France in 1958, for example, over 90 per cent of babies were still being baptized in a country where barely a quarter of the population went regularly to mass. As Aldous Huxley observed in another but not entirely different context, 'the salt, the water, the Latin words – these constitute, for the Indians [of Guatemala], the essential opening gambit in their lifelong game against the powers of evil. They can do without the magic rites of burial and marriage ... But christening remains indispensable.'[18]

Another and very important dimension to the safety or protection procured by baptism was stressed by De Martino with reference to southern Italy. Together with other non-clerical rituals, examples of which we have already encountered, it gave immunity from spells and 'fascination'. Among many gypsy communities even, baptism might be adopted for this and related reasons. Christian baptism acted for them 'to protect the baby from the multitude of evil forces who would try to destroy him' and also to 'cleanse him from being taboo'. The desire to mitigate or overcome the polluting influence of the new-born, most powerful we have seen when the child died without the purifying rite, was also present among full Christian communities. 'Sicilian women', we learn, 'are loth to kiss a child before its christening, because they consider it a pagan or a Turk', while some Tyrolean mothers would not suckle 'their babies until the rite has been performed'.[19]

There are other direct indications of the importance attached to baptism by ordinary people for whatever reasons. This concern might be expressed in prayers during pregnancy. A prayer invoking the aid of St Margaret for women in labour, published at Narbonne in 1770, also included this supplication:

> May my child be born on the proper day,
> And as soon as he is born ...
> May he receive Holy Baptism.

A supposed 'letter from Jesus Christ', discovered at Paimpol in 1771 and endorsed by the bishop of Tréguier, encouraged pregnant women to say nine Paternosters and nine Ave Marias for the Souls in Purgatory, 'so that their babies should be fortunate enough to receive the sacrament of baptism'. Pregnant women also visited or promised to visit shrines. Over 1000 women went to the tomb of Father Honoré at Chaumont-en-Bassigny in the seventeenth century to touch the border of his robe preserved there; this was again supposed to ensure the grace of baptism for their babies. In northern Greece in modern times, women vowed to take their babies to the shrine of the Panaghia at Tenos, where they were 'baptized' again by touching the icon there.[20]

Parents were also prepared to undergo real danger and difficulty to have their children baptized in what they regarded as the proper way. Catholic parents from Strasbourg in the sixteenth centiry took their babies out into the surrounding villages that had not become Protestant or had them baptized secretly at home. Anglicans behaved in the same way during the Civil War and Interregnum. Collinson suggests that English Puritans in the late sixteenth century were often held back from separation from the established

Church by a reluctance 'to deprive their children of baptism in the font of a parish church'. And a non-sectarian view of baptism continued in otherwise non-conformist circles for at least two centuries. Physical obstacles were also overcome and social penalties braved. Martinengo-Cesaresco tells of a grand-mother from a remote mining settlement in the Tyrol in the nineteenth century carrying a baby many miles over the mountains in winter for baptism in the nearest town. We have seen that English parents of illegitimate children might seek to avoid publicity and shame by having them privately baptized, but not all behaved this way. In a not untypical case in Languedoc in 1755, a young woman gave birth to an illegitimate boy and her employer, who was almost certainly his father, 'took him to church the same day to be baptized'.[21]

Even where such openness was shirked, there was the same concern to have bastards baptized. In a case in Poitou in 1477, when an unmarried girl had a baby, her parents and brother 'baptized it in a pan in their house', before taking it to the local poorhouse. As this shows, the concern to baptize extended to unwanted and abandoned children. A major motive for estab-lishing foundling hospitals from the later medieval period onwards was to prevent infants dying without baptism, but those who abandoned children often shared this preoccupation. In Paris from the late medieval period down to the eighteenth century, 'so that they would not die without baptism, unwanted new-born babies were abandoned on the threshold of the church of St John the Baptist to the north of Notre-Dame, in the expectation that they would be baptized there, it being a baptismal church'. In England, France and Italy 'it was customary to tie around the neck of an abandoned infant a bag of salt as a sign that it had not yet been baptized'. The salt was both a message that baptism was required and gave interim protection, as we have seen. Many children left at foundling hospitals later had notes attached, 'testifying that the sacrament had been administered to them'.[22] In seven-teenth-century Madrid they comprised around half those abandoned.

There is also evidence from the medieval period onwards of mothers driven to infanticide who baptized their babies before killing them or leaving them to die. Denisette Bierart, aged fourteen, from northern France, whose request for clemency was considered in 1457, had been seduced by her step-father. Then, having given birth on a heap of stones in the courtyard of their house, ' she went up to the privies and took the baby in one arm and sprinkled water on its head [while saying the baptismal formula]; then she kissed the child, recommended it to God and threw it into the privies'. In a much later case, Maria-Judith Pietri from Portovecchio in Corsica became pregnant in 1864, while her husband was away doing his military service. She was reported to the authorities by his relatives and fled to another village with her lover.

The body of a baby was subsequently found buried close to their house, and she was arrested on suspicion of infanticide. She confessed to having given birth to a live baby, which she said 'she had been careful to baptize' before it died.[23] Some laws against infanticide made a distinction between killing baptized and unbaptized infants, setting the penalties accordingly.

But perhaps the most striking expression of the overriding importance attached to baptism lies in the efforts made to revive or resuscitate the still-born and babies dying during the birth process for long enough to perform the crucial rite. It could not legally be administered to babies unless they showed signs of life. Many practical procedures are reported: massage, hanging the baby upside-down, breathing into its mouth or other orifices, bathing in aromatic preparations or alternately in hot and cold water, pouring wine or spirits into its mouth or placing a piece of heated onion or garlic there. Some of these methods would have been effective in bringing about genuine and permanent resuscitation. Breathing into the lungs via the mouth was used by both Elijah and Elisha in the Old Testament to revive older children, and seems to have been used by midwives and others to revive babies down to the start of the nineteenth century, when it fell out of favour. Other procedures were clearly magical, relating to notions that we have already discussed. Ambroise Paré had recommended not cutting the umbil-ical cord of a child born inanimate and placing the after-birth on its belly 'until it lost its heat', thus communicating it to the baby. Again, in eight-eenth-century France, boiling the cord or after-birth in hot wine or vinegar was believed 'to transmit life into the infant'.[24]

However recourse was had here above all to religious means. First, vows were made to saints. 'If a baby was still-born, one invoked different saints to reanimate it', Benoît writes of Provence, 'at Avignon, St Peter of Luxemburg; at Venasque, Our Lady of Life; at Moustiers, Our Lady of Beauvoir'.[25] In the Franche-Comté, St Claude was called on; in the diocese of Digne, St Ours; in Savoie, St François de Sales. Often the selection of saint related to a miracle or miracles performed in his or her lifetime or posthumously.

Resuscitations figure in hagiography, in sculptural and pictorial represent-ations of saints' lives, in miracle accounts, and in canonization procedures. The list of saints who performed them is long and ranges in time from St Stephen in the first to St François de Sales in the seventeenth century. Resuscitations are also attributed to saints in the Eastern Church, and they figure in the miracles of the Virgin Mary. A capital in the narthex of the abbey church at Vézelay shows St Benedict, for example, reviving a dead baby, while his grief-stricken father looks on. Another early medieval example is a miracle of St Wilfrid, bishop of York, who died in 709. On a visit to baptize and confirm in the villages, Wilfrid was confronted by a woman 'bitterly distressed, moaning with grief ', who was carrying her dead baby boy 'wrapped in rags and hidden in her bosom. She uncovered its face for the bishop to baptize it with the rest, hoping that it might be brought back to life. Our holy bishop saw that it was dead and stopped, at a loss what to do about it. The woman realized that she was found out' and wept and implored Wilfrid 'to deliver her son from the lion's mouth'. Reluctantly he 'prayed and laid his hand on the corpse. The breath of life returned and the boy breathed again' and was then baptized, so, the hagiographer comments, that 'he might inherit a life of unending happiness in Heaven'.[26]

By the early modern period taking the infants to shrines that specialized in resuscitation had become the commonest recourse. These shrines existed in Switzerland, Germany, Austria, Italy, the Low Countries and elsewhere, but seem to have been most common in France, particularly in the eastern half of the country. They were known in France as 'respite shrines', that is giving respite from death, and some were also associated with getting spouses, pregnancy and childbirth. Most were dedicated to the Virgin Mary. 260 respite shrines have been identified in France in the period from the fourteenth to the nineteenth century. There were fifty at least in Burgundy. And the shrines were well-frequented. A register kept at the shrine of Notre-Dame-la-Blanche at Faverney in the later Haute-Saône recorded 489 resuscit-ations in a twenty-five-year period in the sixteenth century. Sixty-three resuscitations were recorded at Notre-Dame-du-Noyer at Cuiseaux in the Saône-et-Loire in the eighteenth and nineteenth centuries, when it was already on the decline. The abbey of Ursberg in Swabia, another reputed shrine, attracted over 1000 infants per decade in the later seventeenth and early eighteenth centuries.[27]

An early reference to the practice is found in the trial of Joan of Arc and relates to an incident at the abbey church at Lagny-sur-Marne, where there was a much-venerated statue of the Virgin known as Notre-Dame-des-Ardents.

> She was asked what age the child was at Lagny ... and she replied: The child was three days old and was brought [to the shrine]; and she was told that young women of the town were in front of Our Lady, and she wanted to go to pray to God and Our Lady to give life to the child; and she went and prayed with the others. And finally signs of life appeared and the baby yawned three times, and was baptized and buried in holy ground. And the child had given no sign of life for three days, and was as black as her [Joan's] tunic, but when it yawned, the colour began to return.[28]

Later sources indicate the same pattern of events but provide much more detail. The decision to take the baby to the shrine was usually prompted by the mother and often followed a vow. The baby was usually taken to the shrine by the father, according to Gélis, but many accounts, like that cited above, refer to groups of women. In a few cases, the baby had actually been buried and had to be disinterred. In 1516 it was reported that a dead baby was taken to the shrine at Cuiseaux in the skin of a hare.[29] At the shrine, the baby was deposited in front of the statue, on the altar or altar step or on the tomb supposed to have the reviving power – sometimes for a period of days. In some cases, the holy place was a fountain or well, and here the baby was plunged in its water. Prayers were said invoking the aid of the saint, and sometimes a more formal service was performed with a priest and congregation present; sometimes masses were said. If and when the baby gave signs of life, by some movement, change of colour, heat or ejection of liquid, it was at once given emergency baptism either by a lay person or a priest. Then a *Te Deum* might be sung and bells rung to proclaim the little miracle. If the baby then died, which was usually the outcome, it was very often buried at the shrine. Those who could afford it might raise an ex-voto to thank the shrine's patron for the grace procured.

As this indicates, members of the clergy were often involved in the resuscitation rituals, and they recorded the 'miracles'. Often the shrines belonged to religious orders, the Mendicants being particularly prominent, perhaps because they were more in tune with popular religious feeling than the secular hierarchy. From the start, the latter had been hostile. 'We condemn and detest in every way', the bishop of Langres declared in 1479,

> the recent abuse relating to children suffocated in coming into the world and commonly called still-born. They are brought to the church [an indication that this could occur in parish churches as well as shrines], where they are laid out for a certain number of days and nights in front of the images of the saints. These infants, cold and stiff as posts, when they arrived, have baptism conferred on them and are then accorded ecclesiastical burial, on the pretext that, softened for a while by the heat of a few coals, or even by the candles and lights lit, they take on a reddish colour for a while, blood flows from their nostrils, their lower orifices appear to sweat, the veins on their temples, foreheads or around their necks appear to have some movement; they open and shut their eyes, even utter a few breaths strong enough to agitate feathers placed under their noses.[30]

Such an abuse was forbidden under pain of excommunication and fines. There were repeated condemnations of this kind in the sixteenth and seventeenth centuries in many dioceses in northern and eastern France, and Pope Benedict XIV issued a general ban in 1729. But, as we have seen, the practice survived this torrent of attacks and still existed at the end of the nineteenth and into this century. This is testimony to the importance attached by local clergy to baptism, but more to the inveterate popular attitudes to which they were responding.

Protestants of course were thoroughly opposed to these procedures. It is significant that an important stage in the establishment of the Reform in Geneva in 1535 centred on resuscitation 'miracles' supposed to have taken place at the Augustinian convent through the action of an image of Our Lady of Grace. The city syndics decided that the 'miracles' were fraudulently produced by 'several old matrons'.[31]

We turn now to the baptismal rite itself. As we have seen, baptism was originally part of the initiation of adults into the Christian Church. It followed lengthy preparation and the teaching of arcane knowledge; it assumed the free conversion of individuals; the set of rituals involved included what later became confirmation and incorporation via participation in the Eucharist. Many of these features persisted in some shape or form into later centuries – confirmation and communion were not separated from baptism until the central Middle Ages – but changes were also introduced. Most importantly, by altering the context of the ritual, emphasis on baptism soon after birth also altered its meaning: it became a ritual for purifying, protecting and incorporating the new-born. But there was no Catholic liturgy specifically designed for this purpose until 1969; the old one was just adapted. For this and other reasons, the rite became more complex, new elements incrustating rather than replacing old ones, and a magical automatic rather than an expressive view of the ceremony coming to the fore.

This can be seen in several important areas. First, the baptismal water was not originally blessed at all (as it was conceded still that it need not be for private or emergency baptism), but in the public rite it was signed with the cross and blessed from around the fourth century, and this blessing was progressively amplified into a lengthy series of prayers and acts, including the admixture of the two consecrated oils. Similarly, we have seen the enormous significance attached in texts from the later Middle Ages onwards to uttering the correct Trinitarian baptismal formula, but no reference to this can be found in any source before the fifth century and in the West before the eight century. Again, during the ninth and tenth century in the West, sponsors came to play a crucial role in the liturgy, carrying or holding the child and speaking on its behalf. There was also a tendency, evident from the Carolingian period if not before, for 'the exorcisms to take a preponderant position' in the liturgy.[32]

For our further analysis of the official Catholic ritual, we will focus on the Sarum Manual which remained current in England until the mid sixteenth century, and which differs little from other contemporary and later Western rites. The liturgy falls into two stages: rites of separation and preparation; and rites of incorporation. First, the child was brought to the church door or parvis, carried by the midwife and accompanied by the godparents. The priest's first gesture was to make the sign of the cross on its forehead and breast with his thumb. After prayers, the godparents were invited to name the child, a point to which we will return, and the priest again signed the child, which he frequently did thereafter. Salt was then exorcized and signed and some placed in the child's mouth, a practice first mentioned by St Augustine and confined to the West. This was the first of a series of exorcisms, in which 'Satan' or the 'unclean spirit' was ordered to 'come out and depart from' the child. 'I accost you, damned and most impure spirit', the priest declared in the ancient Gallican liturgy, 'cause of malice, essence of crimes, origin of sins ... I adjure you in Christ's name that, in whatever part of the body you are hiding ... you flee from it'.[33] Then, to return to the Sarum Manual, the Gospel was said, and the priest touched the child's nose and ears with saliva (spitting in the face of the child and hence of the Devil inside it occurs in some early rituals, for example that of Milan). Next, the godparents said the Paternoster, Ave Maria and Creed; and the child was signed and blessed again and finally brought into the church for the second stage of the rites. In some places in southern Europe, the entire baptismal rite took place outside the church. In continental rituals, too, the exorcisms were accompanied by the laying on of hands and by blowing.

Inside the church, the child was taken to the font (see Text Figure 9). The water in it would have been consecrated either at Easter or Whit in a distinct ritual, including litanies and exorcizing by signing and breathing on the water and by dropping wax from a candle into it. The holy oils would also have been mixed with it. Some fonts in northern Europe had dragons or monsters carved on their bases to symbolize the overcoming of the Devil by baptism. The child, held usually by its godmother, was called on via its godparents to renounce the Devil and all his works and was asked to make a profession of faith. The child was next anointed on the forehead, between the shoulders and on the breast with the oil of the catechumens using a stylus. Having often been undressed, the child was then baptized, by being dipped three times into the water by the priest, for the Father, the Son and the Holy Ghost, and each time being pointed in a different cardinal direction. The early Church had practised total immersion, and this was not everywhere abandoned for dipping, affusion (pouring water over the head) or sprinkling until the later Middle Ages or after. 'In France affusion would appear to have been widespread by the fourteenth century; in Italy by the fifteenth; in England, however, it did not become the norm until well into the sixteenth century.'[34] The discontinuance of submersion was reflected in a reduction in the size of

9. Baby held by sponsors at bath-shaped font for affusion. *The Art of Good Lyvinge*, England, *c.* 1500.

the font. After the baptism, the child was handed to one of the godparents and anointed on the head with the chrism with the appropriate prayer. It was again named, and dressed in a white chrismal robe as a sign of purity, and a candle was placed in its hand by the priest. The ceremony closed with the priest reciting further extracts from the Gospels over the child, who was sometimes placed under his stole. One of the passages was that relating to the exorcism of the demoniac boy in St Mark's Gospel.

The Byzantine or Eastern Orthodox rite followed a similar pattern with blessing the baptismal water, exorcisms, insufflation and spitting, anointing with the two oils and laying on of hands; but triple immersion was maintained and the sprinkling practised in the modern West was disdained. Anointing with the chrism was done on all parts of the body: forehead, eyes, nostrils, mouth, ears, breast, hands and feet.

Some Protestants like Calvin and the New England Puritans 'attached small importance to baptism, for belief in its necessity contradicted the doctrine of justification by faith'. By the same token, some like the Anabaptists and the Mennonites rejected the practice of infant baptism, since new-born infants clearly had no 'conscious faith' and could not express it. Most of the Reformers remained attached to the rite, however, given its Scriptural basis and its popularity. Zwingli, for example, who rejected the idea that it was a sacrament with any automatic ritual effect, yet saw baptism as 'a public demonstration of a covenant and a public promise of a Christian upbringing', and hence supported infant baptism.[35] Luther and the Church of England retained baptism as one of the two sacraments and administered it to infants.

Protestant liturgies cut down radically, however, on the elaborate and ritualistic features of the old rite, which they saw as specifically magical excrescences. Thomas Becon, chaplain to Archbishop Cranmer ridiculed them in these terms:

> For Baal's priest, before the child can be baptized, bewitcheth the water, shutteth the church-door, conjureth the Devil out of the poor young infant, bespueth the child with his vile spittle and stinking slavering, putteth salt in the child's mouth [and] smeareth it with greasy and unsavoury oil.

Luther's second *Taufbüchlein* (1526), which was widely used in Germany, omitted the use of blowing, spittle, salt and unctions but retained some part of the old exorcisms. It opened with the minister saying: 'Come out, thou unclean spirit', and included a short prayer of exorcism accompanied by three signs of the cross just before the baptism itself. But the Bucerian Strasbourg Order excluded exorcism altogether, as did the Scottish Book of Discipline of 1560, both retaining water as the only ritual substance and stressing that it had only symbolic value. The same is true of the English Book of Common Prayer, though it does refer to 'renouncing the Devil and all his works' and keeps the use of the sign of the cross, to which Puritans later objected. Protestants, moreover, as we have seen, were unfriendly towards private baptism, which they believed encouraged a magical view of the rite. 'It is evident that the sacraments are not ordained of God to be used in private corners, as charms or sorceries', John Knox's Order of Baptism declared. Some Protestants also had specific views about fonts and the mode of baptism, which were related again to their concern that baptism be a part of public worship and that it shed its 'magical' elements. Calvin's Draft Ecclesiastical Ordinances of 1547 ruled that the font should 'be near the pulpit that there be better hearing for the recitation of this mystery and practice of baptism', and in many Protestant churches the font was removed from the west end of churches into the nave.[36] Later in the sixteenth century, Calvinists and others expressed a hostility to fonts as such. They were regarded as articles of 'papist superstition' and were often replaced by basins and other vessels. This in turn reflects the Reformed Churches' minimalist preference for sprinkling. Protestants also brought the entire baptismal ceremony inside the church.

Traditional baptism thus constituted an elaborate and impressive ritual, which stressed both exorcism and sacral gestures and elements, not all of which were abandoned by Protestants. It used acts and elements found in popular magic, such as blowing, spitting, salt and water. It could easily therefore be incorporated into popular culture. This explains its attraction, and also the way in which a further para-liturgy could become attached to it. Some of these features preceded or followed the official ritual; others ran parallel to or elaborated on it.

The baby was carried to the church for baptism in a particular way and with special precautions. Depending on local custom it was held by the midwife, the 'milk-mother' or woman who had first suckled the child, a grandmother, or one of the godparents. In Savoy, the godfather carried a boy baby and the godmother a girl. In the Abruzzi and elsewhere, 'when taken to baptism, a boy is carried by the nurse on her right arm, and a girl on her left'. In some places, where the journey was long, the baby was taken in a special basket or cradle. Baptismal cradles in the French Alps were decorated with protective symbols: stars, circles, painted in red. In Burgundy, the procession was discreet so as to avoid attention. Nearly always the child's face was kept covered. But some show might be made. In Brittany, Hélias says that the milk-mother wore 'her best clothes and her most beautiful *coiffe*'.[37] Sometimes the procession moved with deliberate slowness. In parts of France, if a stream had to be crossed, the child was held over it, its head upstream.

Persons met on the way by the christening party were given gifts. In the North of England in modern times, these were bread and cheese or a piece of the cake served at the birth-feast; in the Asturias, the 'bread of tears'. 'To decline the present from the christening party was tantamount in Scotland to wishing evil on the child.' In England, the recipient had to 'walk a short distance with the party', which was called 'blessing the baby' in Cornwall. In the Asturias, similarly, such an encounter brought good luck. In England, it was more propitious to meet a woman, if the baby was a boy, and a man, if it was a girl.[38]

Information on what babies wore in earlier centuries is sparse. Synodal decrees and reformers like Abbé Thiers in seventeenth-century France condemned the wearing of expensive costumes among the rich, but poor babies must have been taken in their ordinary swaddling bands, perhaps with some element of decoration-cum-protection, or in clothing that had some magico-religious significance. St Bernardino of Siena referred to the use of the monogram YHS from the name of Jesus 'on swaddling bands of babies, on the day of their christening'. In early modern England, babies might wear 'christening-palls' or be carried in 'bearing cloths', which were passed down in families, like christening robes later or among the well-to-do. A Corsican service book from the late sixteenth century laid down that a child should be baptized in 'a white cloth to signify the robe of innocence', and this would be kept by the individual in later life. At Arles in modern times, a baby was 'wrapped in a cloth of red velvet embroidered with gold lent by the priest or in its mother's cashmere shawl, one of her wedding-gifts'. The custom of wrapping the child in its mother's wedding-shawl or some equivalent was found elsewhere in nineteenth-century France. This represented the absent mother and her protective influence. Colours were significant here, too. Red gave protection again; it could also signify a male child, with blue by contrast for females. Ribbons in these colours were attached to babies in nineteenth-century Rome. Protection could also be provided by sewing or placing things in the child's dress – in County Antrim, a piece of bread and cheese, for example.[39] In the Abruzzi, an egg might be placed in the baby's armpit to assure future prosperity. Such protective items could also be placed on or near the child during the ceremony. In the Abruzzi again, amulets, a missal and breadcrumbs or corn were placed on the child. A similar custom is referred to by Robert Brunne in late medieval England.

The procession to the church and the ceremony itself were accompanied by the ringing of bells, a specific number of peals for each gender. Having no bells might be a punishment for a late baptism, as we have seen, or an indication of illegitimacy. In some parts of France, illegitimate children were known as a result as *sansonnets* (without ringing). Particular importance was attached in modern France to having a good peal of bells among the 'popular classes'.[40] Bells were also rung after the baptism and, in southern Europe in modern times, shots were fired. Noise here provided publicity and security.

In earlier times, when the rite had taken place at a greater interval after birth, both parents seem to have been present, offering their own children for baptism and representing them. But by the eleventh century, if not before, they had been 'evicted' from the rituals, being replaced by godparents. From the sixteenth century onwards in Catholic Europe, the father might attend, but, if he did, his role was generally unimportant. In nineteenth-century Rome, it was noted, he cut an awkward figure on the outskirts of the group of women. Mothers almost never attended, being confined to their houses and regarded as impure till their churching, as we shall see. This tradition was maintained until very recently in some parts of Europe, with popular resistance to clerical attempts to change it. In Minho 'in the past to further the distance between the child's impure origins [in sexual congress] and its membership in [Christian] society, its parents were not allowed to attend the baptism', and mothers continued to stay away in the 1980s, 'in spite of the priest's injunctions to the contrary'.[41] By contrast, Protestants required the father to be present.

To return to the ceremony itself, in some medieval liturgies, the child was placed on the floor of the church and then lifted up, an echo of the raising-up rituals that we have already discussed. In a similar gesture, the baby might be placed or rolled on the altar during or just after baptism. This custom was banned by the bishop of Périgueux in 1680 but remained current in that diocese and elsewhere in France down to this century. In some places it was supposed to prevent difficulties in walking. Similar specific effects were attributed to other official parts of the liturgy. According to a rubric in the Sarum Manual, the reading from St Mark's Gospel placed at the end of the liturgy 'was a good protection according to doctors against falling sickness [or epilepsy]'.[42]

We have seen that the child might be dressed in a particular fashion on being brought to church. Further significance was attached to articles of clothing placed on it during the ceremony. A white robe or cloth was placed on the child after anointing with the chrism, and this survived the dropping of anointing in Protestant liturgies. It was seen as symbolic of the child's new purity from original sin. 'Take this white vesture for a token of innocence', the priest said in the First Prayer-Book of Edward VI. The robe might be kept on for a period ranging from a week to a month. 'Dying in white clothes' in medieval Sweden meant dying in this state of innocence, a notion more familiar to English-speaking people from Falstaff's death like 'a christom child' in Shakespeare's *King Henry V*. In fact, in early modern England, the term 'chrissom' or 'christom' from chrism was used to designate both the robe or cloth and the child itself during the period between baptism and the mother's churching. If the child lived, the cloth was returned to the priest or minister at this latter ceremony, 'but if he died within a month of his baptism, he was buried in it [in lieu of a shroud] and was remembered thereafter as a "chrism-child" '.[43]

Medieval liturgies refer to the bandaging of foreheads after anointing with white linen bands or fillets, which were kept on for three or seven days. They were to be removed in church by the priest, 'who was instructed to wash the foreheads of the confirmed, and to pour the water into the font'. These bands were replaced at some stage in some countries by caps or bonnets. The christening bonnet, often called by a special local name, was of particular importance in modern France. It was provided by the godmother. 'So as the better to secure the beneficial magico-religious effects of contact with the holy oils', wrote Gennep,

> the bonnet was kept on the baby's head for nine days and nights, or nine days for a boy and three for a girl (or sometimes until the umbilical cord dropped off) ... It was subsequently very carefully looked after by families, especially that of the first-born which was used for the following children, and because, being seen as a kind of receptacle of the life of the first-born, to lose or spoil it would have brought the child bad luck. If it did have to be disposed of, it was burned, to prevent witches making use of it in their spells.

Where an elaborate christening bonnet was worn, this was put over the 'real' or under-bonnet. The bonnet was never washed and seems to have had a special link with gender development and later fertility. If the bonnet was not worn by a girl for the right length of time, she would have painful periods. Belmont has pointed, too, to the link between the bonnet and the caul, which were sometimes designated by the same term. In the Chartres region in the seventeenth century, it was the bonnet rather than the chrism robe which was returned to the priest at churching – with a coin in it to pay for the chrism. The bonnet was later set aside and burned to make the ashes used liturgically on Ash Wednesday. At Riposto in Sicily, the christening bonnet was presented two days after the baptism to a woman, who thereby became an additional godmother, known as the 'godmother of the cap'.[44]

Similar ideas were associated with the christening bonnet in Britain, it seems, despite the Reformation. Bishop Middleton of St Davids banned the practice of placing a bonnet on the child's head after baptism, which he said was still done 'in sundry places ... wherein hath been great superstition'.[45] In England and elsewhere a similar effect might be achieved by not washing the baby's head for a set number of days, usually seven or nine, after baptism.

Paraliturgical elements reinforced other parts of the official ritual. Water from particular wells or springs or from the Holy Land might be used for baptism. In a church near Morwenstow in Cornwall down to modern times, 'a door known as the Devil's door, was opened during the baptismal service to allow the Devil to depart from the child', not a unique example. A number of customs involved the godparents. In Greece, infants were anointed by god-parents, who also sometimes blew or spat on the child, echoing the gestures of the priest. In a village in the Auvergne at the start of the nineteenth century, the godparents took the child after the church ceremony to a nearby chapel, dedicated to St John. There they said five Paternosters and five Aves over the child, while other children made a din with rattles and hammers. This was supposed to give the baby a good voice and other skills. Elsewhere in France, the godparents kissed each other in the church porch or under the belfry, while the bells were ringing, to prevent speech difficulties for the child. Among other gestures required of the godparents, mention must be made of the distribution of sweets, nuts or seeds outside the church after the baptism, which is found all over Europe. Some have seen these as symbols of abund-ance, like the grain thrown at weddings; others as a kind of tribute paid for the new-born's admission into the community of other children. A godparent who was mean in this respect might be insulted, and his meanness might affect his godchild. There was a saying in Upper Provence: 'Stingy godfather, humpbacked child!'. In Antrona in Piedmont, godparents lit 'candles after the baptismal ceremony to ensure the health of their godchild, but if the candle goes out before the baby is returned to his home, he will die'.[46]

Much divination of this kind or reading of omens was attached to baptism as to other ceremonies. Certain days were to be avoided: Fridays generally and even for emergency baptisms in Burgundy. Tuesdays and Thursdays were preferred in Alsace, and these were also propitious days for ploughing and sowing. In the Sologne in the seventeenth century, 'they believe that their children will die during the year, if they are baptized on the Saturdays before Easter and Whit', a local priest wrote, 'and it is impossible to disabuse them of this crazy opinion'.[47] In the Touraine, girls baptized on Easter Sunday would be infertile.

Risks were involved in having more than one child baptized on the same day. The first child done was believed to take all the goodness out of the baptismal water, leaving subsequent candidates disadvantaged. This was particularly related again to sexual characteristics. In some parts of Britain, if a boy and a girl were to be baptized at the same time, the girl had to go first, in case the boy 'left his beard in the water' for her to acquire. In France, the same concern was expressed slightly differently. If a boy was baptized after a girl, he would never grow a beard, while a girl done after a boy would never marry. It was important, too, for the child to remain alert, with its eyes open, and particularly that it should cry at some stage. In East Anglia, babies that did not cry when actually dipped or sprinkled were thought unlikely to live long. In

Italy and Scotland, screaming during the exorcism was taken as a sign of the
Devil's departure. In many places, a child that remained quiet or that slept
through the ritual was marked to die. There was a close link, as we have seen,
between some elements in the baptismal ceremony and the child's speech. In
the Aude in modern times, the godparents had to speak clearly or the child
would be likely to have some speech impediment; and 'the louder the godfather speaks in pronouncing the child's name the stronger and more
successful the child will be'.[48] Godparents hesitating in saying the required
responses and especially the Creed in the affirmation of faith could cause the
child to stutter in later life, or there might be even more serious consequences, as we shall see.

The baptismal ceremonies were concluded with a christening feast at the
parents' house, which sometimes replaced the birth-feast already described or
formed the high point in a series of festivities. There are references to this in
medieval and later texts and a humble version is depicted by the Le Nain in their
picture *Le Retour du Baptême*, now in the Louvre (see Plate 26). A group of
three sit round a table, while two children stand. The father lifts a glass of red
wine, while the mother holds the swaddled and bonnetted baby, and an older
woman, midwife or grandmother, holds the jug on her knee by a large round
loaf. Such simple celebrations were the rule in many places, for example
nineteenth-century Burgundy. Elsewhere, gatherings were more elaborate.
Special food was consumed; gifts presented to the child; and much drinking and
dancing took place. In modern Catalonia and the Balearics, the godfather had to
lead the godmother in the dance. In the Charente, dancing on the evening of the
baptism was believed to preserve the baby from skin trouble. In many places a
long and boisterous celebration provided protection for the child.

We have noted clerical concern that midwives perform the baptismal rite
correctly, and there were wider fears on this score. St Boniface in the eighth
century had to be reassured by two popes that the Trinitarian formula was
valid even if the Latin endings were wrong and even if it were said in the
vernacular. The ecclesiastical authorities did not shift from this specific
ruling, but they did tend to become stricter about other matters. The '*Ego te
baptizo*' wording was required from the later twelfth century, and Myrc's
Instructions in fifteenth-century England laid down that the sacrament was
invalid if the persons of the Trinity were not placed in the right order.[49] Some
later theologians were even more pedantic. Infants defectively baptized by
using the wrong formulae risked eternal damnation, but more immediate
consequences might follow from these and other mistakes, notably in the
recitation of the Creed by the godparents. In modern Liguria and elsewhere
in Italy, this might simply bring bad luck to the child, but elsewhere it
conveyed supernatural powers. In modern Greece the *mal baptisés* had

second sight; in Rumania, they might become *revenants*; in Corsica, they were recruited into the ranks of the *mazzeri*, announcers and dealers of death in their communities; among the Basques and elsewhere, they might become witches. This relates to the common notion retailed by demonologists and reflected in confessions at witchcraft trails that witches renounced their baptism as part of their supposed pact with the Devil.

In doubtful cases, individuals would be baptized again conditionally. Always the Churches, Catholic and then Protestant, were concerned that baptism proper should not be repeated. 'St Augustine showed that the sacrament of baptism, if validly administered, could not be repeated precisely because it endowed the Christian who received it with an indelible character.'[50] Hostility to rebaptism was reinforced by its association with heresy, first that of the Donatists in St Augustine's time, then of several medieval non-conformists, and finally of the Anabaptists. These denied the validity of orthodox infant baptism on a variety of grounds and wished therefore to reinitiate their adherents. Rebaptism was a specific and serious offence in inquisitors' manuals therefore and was viewed with equal fear and loathing by most Protestants. The Zurich authorities decreed in 1526 that those who rebaptized should be punished by drowning, the penalty echoing the abused rite. The Catholic Church, of course, recognized the validity of Protestant baptism. The rebaptism of Protestants, for example during the French Wars of Religion in the late sixteenth century, was both unusual and unorthodox.

Nevertheless, at the popular level there was a belief that, since baptism was so powerful a rite, its repetition in certain circumstances could only be of further benefit. Notker the Stammerer reported that Northmen in the ninth century went through repeated baptismal rites as a way of paying homage to the Emperor Louis the Pious. This was at a time when mass baptisms signalled submission to conquering Christian rulers. Much later, a manual in Occitan in 1703 stressed that 'a single baptism alone is necessary', suggesting that second baptisms were not uncommon. Confusion may have been caused here by the requirement that privately baptized children be brought to church later. Rebaptism was also used as a healing ritual. The wife of a Herefordshire rector in the 1880s noted that parishioners brought sick babies to her husband for 'christening', regarding it as a last desperate remedy. It is clear from reference to potatoes and pork fat as alternative and unsuccessful medicine that these were not new-born infants and had almost certainly been baptized once already.[51]

A further indication of how well established the notion if not the practice of rebaptism was in later centuries is provided by a folksong from Palermo. A man sings that his love for a woman has prevented him from saying his prayers properly or going to mass:

> I need to be baptized again,
> For I have become a Turk through loving you.

This relates to the idea that witches renounced their baptisms or had not been baptized properly. It followed that rebaptism could be a 'cure' for being a witch. Rémy referred to an example of this in 1590.

> When Agathe, the wife of François Tailleur of Pittelange grew weary of her harsh servitude [to the Devil], she at last decided to have recourse to a remedy which many have impiously thought to be most efficacious. Therefore she went to the neighbouring town ... and caused the priest to rebaptize her.[52]

By extension, rebaptism could also be seen as a remedy for bewitchment. The *Malleus Maleficarum* mentions it.

There was a range of other forms of 'superstitious baptism'. De Martino observed that the first bathing of the new-born baby in wine or a water and wine mixture, a south Italian ritual with many parallels elsewhere, as we have seen, was in effect a kind of baptism. Moreover, the official baptismal ceremony was often completed by unofficial rituals, often performed in the house on the same day. At one village in Lucania, a bowl of water and a towel were placed by the cradle ready for the visit of the Fates or fairies. In parts of Scotland in the eighteenth and nineteenth centuries, on the return from baptism, the baby was passed three times round the chimney hook or vibrated 'three or four times gently over a flame' to protect it from fire and from evil influences. Children were also taken to holy wells. They were 'baptized' at a well at Llanfairfechan, Caernarvonshire, until it was filled up in 1874, either, it seems, to prevent or to undo bewitching. St Bernardino of Siena denounced a similar practice in the early fifteenth century: babies were being taken to a spring for a 'kind of baptism'. It has been pointed out, too, that popular healing or dewitching rituals often borrowed elements from baptism, such as the use of salt, oil and water, touching the parts of the body in turn and especially those associated with the five senses, and the use of formulae with baptismal affinities. A charm from Venezia-Giulia, for example, used holy water, which was referred to as 'the holy water of Jordan with which St John baptized', that would take away all evils as baptismal water took away all sins. In the Lancashire trials in 1612, Janet Device told the court of a prayer taught her by her mother to 'cure one bewitched', which included the words:

> Let chrisom child
> Go to it, Mother mild.

More generally, both the oils and the water used in baptism were employed in magical rituals and were specially guarded by the ecclesiastical authorities against this event. 'Both the holy oil and the chrism must be kept carefully under lock and key', ordered the rubric of the Sarum Manual, 'lest a sacrilegious hand be able to reach them to do wicked things.' Regulations also ordered the covering of fonts for the same reason. A council at Durham, in 1220, for example, called for 'the font to be kept locked on account of sorcery'.[53]

Thomas refers to cases in England where animals were baptized either to mock the ceremony or in all seriousness, and continental folklore yields equivalent instances. In the Sologne in the nineteenth century, cowherds baptized new-born calves on the Good Friday following their birth, giving them a name and praying formally for their protection, especially against wolves. In Lucania, if a sow did not fatten properly, it might be 'baptized' with salt and water. Sometimes even, the clergy were involved. We have referred to the ceremony called the 'baptism of the horses' at Loch-ar-Brug in Brittany, in which the priest made the sign of the cross on the animals' foreheads 'with holy water from the font'.[54] Other intentions besides the wish to protect and heal are recorded. In a case of prosecution for witchcraft at Soissons in 1460, a priest had been asked by a sorcerer to baptize a toad to be used in making a poisonous potion, a practice also referred to by demonologists.

Other things were also 'baptized' to produce good and bad effects. The scapulars worn by babies in parts of southern Italy for their baptisms were themselves 'baptized', as were cauls in the Friuli. A bishop of Vercelli in the tenth century condemned the practice of 'baptizing' herbs of St John in dew to give them healing powers, a custom very widespread throughout Europe down to modern times, as we have seen. 'Baptizing' images of wax and other materials for magical purposes is frequently mentioned in instructions for inquisitors and other judges, penitentials and sorcery trials from the Middle Ages onwards. In the early modern period, the Venetian Inquisition uncovered divers cases of 'baptizing' charms, playing cards and cauls; while in eighteenth-century Auvergne, people asked priests to 'baptize' magic books.[55]

The Catholic Church regarded some other forms of 'baptism' of objects as harmless or even participated in and encouraged them. 'Baptism' of boats, for example, was practised in many countries. In the Boulogne-sur-Mer district in the nineteenth century typically, 'the baptismal ceremony took place on the quayside, the priest wearing his white surplice and stole. The boat was named by godparents. After prayers and signing of the cross, the priest sprinkled the boat thoroughly with holy water', and the proceedings were concluded with a feast. It was believed that only boats that had been baptized in this way were safe from capsizing and would catch fish, and many men refused to serve as crew on boats that had not been through the ceremony, which was specifically called 'baptism'. In England and Scotland, there were no Christian elements in the ritual, which involved breaking a bottle of alcoholic drink on the boat, but the lustration was regarded as equally necessary.[56]

The custom of blessing or 'baptizing' bells seems to have been common already in the eighth century, since a capitulary of Charlemagne forbade it. Such bans were ineffective, however, since the custom spread and persisted and gained clerical sponsorship. The rites involved exorcism, blessing, unction, sprinkling and godparenthood. At Minot in modern times, new or recast church bells were 'solemnly, baptized, anointed with the holy oils and given prestigious godparents'. Such 'baptism' of bells is also reported in other parts of France (Angers, Reims, the Limousin) and in Switzerland. Protestants rejected such rituals. The city clerk of Constance, for example, in a pamphlet in 1524 attacked the 'special abomination [of] the baptism of bells by suffragan bishops, which [he felt] made a mockery of true baptism'.[57]

Godparents were religious sponsors, proxies and guardians for the child. Depending on time and place, they were chosen either from kin following fairly strict rules about which relative should sponsor which child,or from non-kin who were usually patrons of a higher class. Godparenthood formed a close link between the godparent and the godchild, but also between the godparents and the parents. As social anthropologists have stressed, this ritual or spiritual kinship was an important form of social bonding, insurance and patronage, and the value of godparents could lead to their multiplication, despite the Churches' desire to limit numbers. Godparent or godparent-like ties were also formed on occasions other than baptism, notably at confirmation and marriage. Relations within the 'godparenthood complex' were on a different level from either relations with real kin and affines or with other members of the community. They were spiritual rather than natural, based on friendship rather than calculation. This could mean a free-and-easy relationship, where favours could not be refused and gifts flowed, or it could be one hedged about because of its special quality with formality, honour and respect. If god- or co-parenthood ties ceased to be honourable and amicable, trouble would follow, especially for the child. Among the Sarakatsani, for example, conflict, gossip, sexual scandal among spiritual kin was believed to 'destroy the oil' with which the child had been anointed, thus jeopardizing its relations with God and those of everyone else concerned.[58]

One reflection of the ambience created by spiritual kinship and in some ways its most important manifestation was the notion that those involved in the complex formed a group among whose members sexual relations and marriage could not occur. This incest prohibition was drawn in different places at different times and in different countries. It began in Eastern

Christendom with a pronouncement of the Emperor Justinian in 530 simply banning marriage between a godfather and his goddaughter. Later legislation in the East extended the ban to marriages between godfathers and the mothers of their godchildren, spiritual siblings (children and godchildren of the same person), relatives of both godfather and godchild to the third and fourth degrees, and the priest and his relatives. Only from the eighth century were similar rules laid down by Church Councils and other authorities in the West, though they soon proliferated in the same way. Myrc assumed in the mid fifteenth century that marriage relations were ruled out, not only between the child and its kin and the child's godparents and their kin, but also between the priest and his kin and any of the parties and theirs and between any of the godparents and their kin. The multiplicity of godparents meant the creation of a huge network of spiritual 'cousins', none of whom could intermarry. The Sarum Manual even raised the fear that, if parents baptized their child themselves in an emergency, this could prejudice their conjugal bond, and parental sponsorship had been raised as possible grounds for divorce or annulment of marriage in the early medieval period. It was a popular belief still in seventeenth-century France that, if a father baptized his own child, this would create a tie of 'spiritual affinity' with his own wife.[59]

Not surprisingly perhaps, reformers in the sixteenth century began to dismantle this structure of bans. 'The nonsense about compaternity, commaternity, confraternity, consorority, and confileality', Luther declared in *The Babylonian Captivity of the Church* in 1520, 'ought to be completely blotted out' and marriages contracted accordingly. The Council of Trent restricted the wide exogamous network of the medieval period by removing relations between sponsors themselves and their kin from it, and later Canon Law went further. By the time of Vatican II, the impediment to marriage existed only 'between the minister of the sacrament of baptism and the recipient, and between the sponsor and the baptized'. Moreover, it was a minor impediment only and one from which dispensation could fairly easily be obtained.[60]

Meanwhile the idea that spiritual kin should not intermarry had become deeply embedded among the laity and in popular culture. Robert of Brunne related a tale in which a 'bad burgher lay with his goddaughter and was killed for it' and carried off by the Devil. According to the *Evangile des quenouilles*, we have seen, marriage between those related by godparenthood led to storms. 'In northern Portugal it was believed that a child born of a relationship between a godparent and a godchild became a werewolf'. In Provence, Burgundy and elsewhere, it was still believed in modern times that godparents should not marry between themselves, and that if they did it would bring bad luck. In Spain, godparents had to be married or engaged already at the time of baptism to prevent this. In the Mediterranean area generally, the extended incest ban was maintained, despite clerical relaxation of it, and it included godparents of 'folk sacraments' like ear-piercing and hair-cutting as well as of baptism.[61]

But all this represents only one side of the story. There is also evidence from many parts of Europe linking godparenthood with sexual activity and marriage. This was in part a consequence of the familiarity that existed between co-parents. Lovers, who also visited freely, could be ironically or jokingly referred to as *compadri*, and real co-parents could be subject to ribaldry at weddings and so on. In modern Italy, often 'an attempt was made at a love-match between baptismal godparents', while some forms of *comparaggio*, for example those related to St John's Night could be the equivalent of betrothals.[62] In Spain similarly the term *comadre* could be used in some circumstances to mean mistress or fiancée, and a *comadre de carnaval* particularly might become a marriage partner. It was believed in parts of France that becoming a godparent, and especially a godmother, was a presage of marriage for that person, and we have seen that godparents kissed at the end of the baptismal rite.

Whatever the explanation for their existence, the incest prohibitions indicated and mapped out a network of friendship and solidarity, a 'security network', centred primarily on the godchild at its baptism. 'The essential aim [of the whole system], according to Gennep, 'was to obtain psychic, social and economic support for that quintessentially feeble creature, the new-born child'.[63] An examination of the duties and responsibilities beyond the official religious ones of godparents vis-à-vis their godchildren will make this point clearer. The particular relationship could be closer or more distant, life-long or shorter-lived, but certain elements were usually present.

The godparent/godchild relationship was manifested in the first place in and by a series of gift-exchanges. These prestations might begin at the birth but more often they started at the baptism itself and were usually of a ceremonial nature. We have seen that the christening bonnet might be provided by the godmother. She might also give the dress. In parts of Tuscany, she made the goddaughter's entire layette, and the child wore her wedding veil during the ceremony. In northern Portugal in modern times, the godfather provided the warm flannel wrap for the baby and the godmother the christening dress. Such gifts of clothing were traditional. Garments are recorded among baptismal gifts in early Frankish society, along with coins and cattle. And clothes were also given at significant stages later in the godchild's life. In both Spain and Greece, godparents often presented their godchildren with the first long trousers, long dress or pair of shoes, all of which marked their move into a new stage of human life. In the Landes, the child was put into new clothes at the age of seven, a boy by his godfather and a girl by her godmother.

Where money or produce was given, it had a clear symbolic significance. In parts of Austria, among other presents, 'the godparents gave the child a bag containing one silver coin and three copper ones, which was carried by the baby during baptism'. In seventeenth-century England among the well-to-do, plate in the form of spoons and cups was given, while in modern France and elsewhere a christening mug and a set of silver cutlery was presented by the godparents. Where coins in specific numbers and relationship are harbingers of a general wished-for prosperity, the mug or cup and cutlery stand directly for festive and abundant food and drink. Food and drink were also given directly, often in special ritual form. In Le-Puy-en-Velay, for example, godparents gave their godchildren a particular kind of cake, called a *pompe*. In the province of Salamanca, the godmother provided the chickens for the birth or baptismal feast. In parts of Italy it was the godfather who provided the baptismal feast, sometimes drinks and a meal in a tavern, sometimes a more elaborate banquet. We have already mentioned the distribution of sweetmeats to the other children in the community at the completion of the baptismal ceremonies. Sometimes there was a more general dole to the poor, as in seventeenth-century England. Both may be seen as means of forestalling envy directed at the new-born. Ritual exchanges of food continued to be part of the ongoing relationship between godparent and godchild and among others in the spiritual kinship complex. Among the Sarakatsani, on the Easter following a child's baptism, its parents gave the godfather 'the gift of a lamb with fleece dyed red, a round of bread, and a new shirt', while every subsequent Easter, the godfather had to send 'to his godchild a candle to take to church for the service on Easter Saturday, and a red egg'. In Provence, the godparents or grandparents gave ritual gifts on Palm Sunday: 'sticks of light wood garlanded with paper, crystallized fruit and sweets'. These were hung on olive branches and blessed before being eaten.[64]

Often the gift to the child was specifically protective. At Minot and elsewhere in modern France, where the godfather gave the ritual mug and cutlery, the godmother gave a pious medal on a chain. In sixteenth-century Russia, according to Jenkinson, 'the godfather hangs a cross round the baby's neck', which he wore for the rest of his life. In modern Spain, the godparents often gave 'a religious medallion to protect the child from the evil eye'. In southern Italy, the godmother was 'the chief giver of amulets'. In Piedmont, these included medals of the saints, it seems probably those on whose day the child had been born or baptized, 'and annually throughout the life of the child the feast-day of this patron saint was the occasion on which the bond of *comparaggio* was reaffirmed between them by further gift-giving and social festivities'.[65] The Alsatian 'godfather's letter' was at first used to wrap round a coin or a medal. Later the wrapping became more and more elaborate and a gift in itself. Good wishes of different kinds were worked into it, and it became an amulet especially beneficial against illness and convulsions, in which circumstances it was placed in the child's hand.

As some of these examples indicate, gift-giving was not restricted to godparent and godchild, though that was the most significant channel. In Renaissance Florence, the priority given to co-parenthood was indicated by the fact that the baptismal gifts, candles, sweetmeats, sometimes silver or textiles, were given not to the child but to its mother. In Venice, the godfather presented specific gifts to the mother. Godparents also exchanged gifts. At Minot, for example, in the late nineteenth century, the godfather gave a box of sweets or a pair of gloves to the godmother, and she embroidered or bought for him a handkerchief of fine *baptiste* decorated with lace.[66]

Godparents could also play a crucial role on other ritual occasions in the lives of their godchildren. These ranged from cutting the nails of a child for the first time when it was one year old in Provence, or cutting its hair for the first time among the Southern Slavs, to involvement in the child's wedding. At Dinan the request in marriage was made to the godfather of a boy and not to his father. In Cornouaille, the godfather made a speech before the departure to the church, and in most places in France, the godparents had a special place in the wedding procession. In parts of the Limousin, the godfather led his goddaughter to the altar. At Minot, the godparents sat at the wedding banquet between the young people in attendance on the couple and their natural parents. In Transylvania, 'it was the responsibility of the godparents to usher their godchildren through marriage'. They stood by them in the church and sat next to them at the feast. Godparents also provided wedding gifts, presenting furniture for example in Greece, contributing to the dowry in parts of Italy and elsewhere, or giving other presents. At Colognora di Compito in Tuscany, 'the bridal trousseau was entirely the concern' of the godmother, who carried it on her head to the bride's house and was 'the first person to be welcomed at the new home of the couple'.[67] In western France, the godparents might pay for the wedding-feast and supply the straw of the nuptial bed. In the Orthodox world and parts of the West, distinct wedding sponsors were appointed, but these were often the baptismal godparents.

Those linked by godparenthood also officiated at each others' funerals. 'In Catalonia, when a godchild was dying, the godfather was called to give his blessing before he or she died and to close his or her eyes'. 'In many parts of Germany, the godmother carried holy water to the dying godchild and placed its baptismal gifts in its hands'. The blessing of the godparents or even their simple presence was widely believed to shorten or ease the agony. If the child died as a baby in Segovia, the godfather carried it to the cemetery on a cushion. At Antrona (Piedmont), the baby was carried in its cradle, by the godfather to the church and by the godmother to the cemetery. Such pract-ices are found all over Europe. In Liguria, the godparents made paper garlands to put on the child's hearse. In Spain, the godfather often cast the first earth into its grave. Godparents might also pay for their godchild's funeral. Similarly, godchildren played a special role at the death of their godparents. A charitable bequest in late medieval London left fruit to be distributed 'among young children which can speak and say: God have mercy on my godfather's soul'. At Minot, a godson might act as a pall-bearer and would attend the funeral meal. In Alsace and the Valais, godchildren led the funeral procession. In Transylvania 'female godchildren lamented for a deceased godparent'.[68]

This stress on godparenthood links at death has been elucidated in a comparative study by Agnès Fine. The mediation of godparents at birth is mirrored by a mediation at death. 'Passing over to the next world assumed a mutual assistance – between the living and the dead – which spiritual kinship ordered and brought into focus.' So the privileged intercessor for the deceased godparent was his or her godchild, who frequently shared his or her name. In the Abruzzi there was a belief that a dead person had to cross the Jordan river or 'Josephat' valley. 'A godchild is the guide across this river or valley, and, if the child dies before the godfather, it waits to lead him across. Should the godfather die first, the child's guardian angel will guide the god-father.'[69] It was common elsewhere from the later Middle Ages onwards for godparents to leave specific pious legacies to their godchildren for masses and prayers to aid their passage through Purgatory. Legacies to godchildren remained important in Catholic and Protestant countries, suggesting that they were not purely secular arrangements. The dead godchild was widely believed to be of particular assistance to its godparents in this life and after-wards, particularly if it were a baby dying immediately after baptism, since such an innocent would have gone straight to Paradise.

But the intercession also operated the other way. 'The essential function of the godparent was to assure the rest of the godchild in the afterlife.' Among the Sarakatsani, the godfather handed the child back to its mother after baptism with these words: 'I return the child to you in this life, but I shall ask it back from you in the next'. Hence the presence at the death-bed and the funeral. This reflected the basic religious function of baptism, which was to save the infant's soul, but the interdependence also took other forms. 'In very many tales and legends, the deceased godparent figures as a friendly ghost, charged with protecting his or her godchild from other dead spirits and with initiating him or her into the mysteries of the Other World.'[70] In areas where co-parenthood was important or of primary importance, this was reflected in tales of intercession across the great divide between co-parents.

Fine points to two important corollaries of these beliefs. First, in many places, it was thought that a person who was not a godparent was in danger of not being able to cross the divide between life and death. A sixteenth-century book on popular customs in Toulouse related that 'a woman [or a man] who has died without having had a godchild cannot have her hands crossed over her chest after death, nor can one ring the bell for her either'. And there is similar evidence from nineteenth-century France that non-godparents were not buried in the proper pious posture with arms folded over the chest and might thus remain restless and return to haunt the living. Secondly, children without godparents were in like danger, even if they had been baptized. The child's need for godparents is reflected in French ideas about *feux-follets*, unbaptized babies trying to trap passers-by and make them become godparents. In a Hungarian folk tale, St Peter and God refuse to allow an infant who had received only emergency baptism from its natural parents into Paradise. This was, Fine suggests, because it lacked 'godparents to place it in a relationship that was necessary for its salvation in the other world'. 'In rural areas of Portugal, moreover, when an unbaptized child was dying and no human sponsor was available, a saint might be selected as godparent. As elsewhere in the Catholic world, it is considered undesirable to let a child die without supernatural protection.'[71] A folk-tale from the Limousin suggests that an infant was regarded as 'baptized' so long as a godparent had been chosen for it. Here a child was condemned to join the Wild Hunt, having died without baptism, but was rescued by a man who had been selected as its godfather. Similar anxieties underlay concerns that children should have full and complete baptisms. In other words, the provision of godparents was sometimes regarded at the popular level as just as important as administering the sacrament, though the Church, as we have seen, did not require sponsors or naming at emergency baptism.

The supernatural protection afforded by godparents also operated in the here and now. In southern Italy, it was a child's godmother who diagnosed ailments in a child and decided what course of action to take. In a medieval saint's Life, godmother and mother made a vow together for a handicapped child and together visited the appropriate shrine. In Renaissance Tuscany, while godfathers were picked from notables with a view to increasing the influence and honour of the family, godmothers were often poor women, midwives, nurses and so on. 'Choosing these women was to conjure their secret power to the benefit of the child.'[72] In modern Italy again, both godparents were seen as primary shields for their godchild against hostile powers. Often the evil eye could not 'prevail against a child without a preliminary and successful attack against one of the godparents'. Similarly, it was believed in some places that all a godmother's 'luck' passed to her godchild, especially the first godchild of the same sex. This closeness, even identity, was most obviously expressed in the sharing of the same name, which was a custom followed in much of Europe from the later medieval period down to modern times. Godchildren could also take over moral qualities from their godparents, as sucklings did from their nurses.

Negatively, therefore, the wrong kind of godparent or an offence of the godparent could harm the child, bringing it bad luck or even premature death. A court case in the mid seventeenth century in the Pays de Quingey revealed that a woman had refused to allow a suspected witch to hold her child at the font, though it appears that otherwise she was qualified. A godparent's curse was 'dangerous in the extreme', but involuntary effects were also feared. The godparent of a baby who died prematurely might not be asked to sponsor another child. When Alexandre Dumas' father asked his old friend General Brune to be his godfather in 1802, the latter at first refused, explaining: 'I have been a godfather on five separate occasions, and all my godsons have died. When the last of them went, I registered a vow never again to stand sponsor'. In Greece, if the godchild is sickly, 'the godfather himself may suggest a change, or else the father may request permission from the godfather to ask another person to take his place'. Bad luck could also take the form of a succession of children of the same gender. In Portugal the fifth or seventh consecutive child of the same sex was in danger of becoming a witch or a werewolf 'unless the eldest became his godfather or godmother or pricked blood from his little finger', or the child might be baptized with a special protective name.[73]

Babies' names and naming were influenced by notions of protective magic. Children might be given a temporary pre-baptismal name to guard them. In the Algarve district of Portugal in modern times this was Inácio or Inácia. In some places, a secret name might be given to the child in a domestic cere-mony, or the name might be chosen but not divulged. Elsewhere, however, feeling was very much the other way. In the Pays de Sault until around 1940 the child was deliberately not named until formal baptism, which took place about a week after birth. 'In the interval, the child had no name' and was not referred to by one. Similarly 'in Scotland it was thought unlucky to name a child before its baptism; if anyone inquired the baby's name, the answer was: It has not been out yet'. Once a child was named, its name might still be concealed or used with caution. 'In the Confolentais and the Ruffecois, from fear of spells, one should never before a stranger utter the name, or uncover the feet or head of a baby'.[74]

Another ploy was the giving of happy or augurative names. These had been quite common in Ancient Roman society: Felix, Fortunatus, Faustus and so on; and they enjoyed a considerable vogue in medieval Italy. Benvenutus,

Bonaguida, Dietiguardi and similar names were popular in Florence, for example, in the twelfth and thirteenth centuries. 'In Siena around 1270, augu-ratives were paramount; Bonaventura was the commonest male and Benvenuta the commonest female name, and there were a host of others.' Unlucky categories of child would be especially in need of such names. In Portugal, seventh and fifth consecutive sons and daughters had to be saved, we have seen, from becoming werewolves by a variety of ritual precautions, including naming them Adam, Eve, Jeronyma or Bento. Among the Venetian lower classes in the nineteenth century and earlier, 'Nane and Marieta were the commonest names which is explained by the impression that persons so-called cannot be bewitched'. Evil influences could be diverted in other ways. In some societies, precious boys were given girls' names. More common was the giving of pejorative or opprobrious names to avoid malicious influence or envy. This practice, too, was found in Ancient Rome. Byzantine children were called Aporicto or Evreto: 'rejected' or 'foundling'. From twelfth-century Ravenna, we have Nontevoluit and from Lucca Maloncontro. Special onomastic precautions were also taken when a child was sickly. In the Balkans, where baptism was delayed, weak babies were given temporary names like Lively or Wolf, indicating strength. Quite common too was the practice of changing the name of an ill child, 'so as to confuse or deceive the spirit of the disease' or other reponsible agent. In Hungary, 'one of the simplest methods of healing for the new-born' was to remove the name origi-nally entered in the birth register and replace it with another.[75]

The clearest example of the protective name in European societies is the saint's name. Saints' names were not greatly used in Ancient or early medieval times, but they became predominant in the course of the twelfth and thirteenth centuries. This movement was popular rather than clerical, and the commonest names were those of the great New Testament saints, led by Peter and John. The vogue for Mary was post-medieval. These names retained their popularity down to modern times. There is little doubt that saints' names were originally given with the idea of 'celestial patronage' in mind, and this idea continued to fuel and inform the practice.[76]

The notion that a dead person was reincarnated in a living successor who took or was given the same name is found in different parts of the world. Among the Eskimo, for example, the name of the last person to die in a settle-ment was given to the next child to be born: 'The child inherited the dead namesake's qualities, or it may even be considered to be the reborn person itself '. In other cases, the replacement may be an adult, who changes his name for the purpose. 'Among the Lozi [of Zambia] ... when a man [or woman] dies, an heir is selected who "eats the name" of his predecessor' and who is then known by that name.[77]

Though rarely so explicit in Europe, such ideas are present. Naming after relatives, dead or alive, was the rule, and it sometimes implied a kind of reincarnation. This could involve older deceased relatives or baby siblings. In Renaissance Florence, the requirement to 'replace' or 'remake' relatives was compelling.

> Palla di Bernardo Rucellai wrote in 1521 to his brother, for example to announce the birth of a son who had been named Bernardo: 'And thus we have remade our father and God willing we hope to do the same for Madonna Nannina and Cosimo and Piero and the others'. Here it was a paternal grandfather who was being remade, but others would have their chance.

In Potamia and elsewhere in modern Greece,

> the first son in a family regularly receives the name of his father's father. This is done 'so that the name [of the grandfather] will not disappear, so that the name will be heard ... When a man hears his son called by his father's name, he feels joy. When people hear the dead person's name applied to a young child, the deceased is remembered. He is brought back to life ... It is as if the child were the dead person himself'.[78]

Children who died in infancy were also very generally replaced by giving their names to subsequent siblings This guaranteed the preservation of the family's set of first names but also repaired the loss, social and emotional, by 'remaking' the child. There were other strategies in the face of the very high rate of infant mortality. The name of a dead sibling could be specifically avoided, as it was in the Hebrides, or a special name could be given to its successor. In Corsica, a baby of either sex born after its elder sibling had died was called Orso, 'the bear being considered a protective animal'.[79]

10. Joos van Cleve, *The Holy Family*, Flemish, *c.* 1530. (*Metropolitan Museum of Art, New York*)

10

Mother and Child

In all parts of Europe, a woman's confinement continued for a specific period of time following her delivery. This was a kind of ritual seclusion, with special terms to describe it. In early modern England, the woman was known during this time as a 'green woman' and the period as her 'gander month'. In modern Greece, the woman was a *lechona*. Sometimes she had to stay in bed for a set number of days (and significance attached to the day on which she did first get up). In Catholic parts of Hungary, the bed was curtained off and dedicated to the Virgin Mary. Usually a woman could not leave the house; always she was banned from normal life and society, including visiting the church. If she did go out, trouble would ensue. In Transylvania, she could 'pollute the entire village'. On the earthquake-torn island of Thera in northern Greece, there was a saying: 'When the *lechona* ventures outside ... , the earth trembles'. At Lequeito y Arrona in the Vizcaya district of Spain, 'if it was absolutely necessary to go out, a woman would put a tile on her head to make the spirits think that she was still in the house'.[1]

Childbirth in effect rendered a woman impure like menstruation. Hence more precise bans against sexual relations and involvement in work, and especially food preparation and fetching water. It was believed in Poland before the First World War that, if a woman went to a well too soon after childbearing, 'at once worms would breed there'. An older text from twelfth-century Touraine suggests that it was dangerous not only to move but also to touch a woman immediately after childbirth (a taboo applying perhaps only or mainly to men) or to let her touch the ground. A knight left his wife inside a tower that was under siege, because she had just given birth, and, when the tower was captured by the followers of the Lord of Amboise, 'they carefully carried the young woman on a pallet', refusing to let her walk. In early modern Wales, women were said to believe 'that grass will hardly ever grow where they tread before they are churched'. Very generally, a 'green' woman would bring bad luck to any house that she entered, and things from her house were dangerous. Latimer referred in a sermon in 1552 to the popular idea that 'they may not fetch fire nor anything in the house where there is a green woman'. This special power which things could derive from contact with the forbidden woman could be exploited for more deliberate magical ends. According to a witness in a witchcraft trial in Luxeuil in 1529, the accused woman Desle La Mansenée approached another woman, 'while she was in her childbed and made her spin three threads from the curtain around her bed on the lower end of a spindle'. Desle took the threads away, it was believed 'in order to do some sorcery with them', and she confessed that she had indeed used them to divine whether her proposed marriage would come off. Dangerous, women after childbirth were also in danger and particularly vulnerable to attacks from witches, the evil eye and so on. In the Nivernais in the modern period, witches might 'tie the knot' against them. In northern Greece, a *lechona* might be tempted outside by the Devil or some other spirit, in which case she might die or lose her right mind.[2]

The length of a woman's liminal period of confinement sometimes followed and sometimes varied either side of the biblical norm of forty days (though strictly Leviticus, chapter 12, doubles this period for female babies). Also relevant was the physiological period of the lochia or post-partum bleeding which lasted from four to six weeks. In parts of France in the nineteenth century, the confinement might last only a few days. In Corsica around 1600, it varied from three days in one village to two weeks or more in others. In Paris in the 1780s, it was around three weeks. In England, for much of the early modern and modern periods, it was a month; in Nordic countries, six weeks for better-off but not poorer women. The Orthodox world kept quite strictly to the forty days. Very occasionally, the confinement was ended or was mitigated with the baptism of the child, presumably where this was late, but generally it was terminated by a special church ritual, known in England as 'churching', in France as *les relevailles*, in Germany as *Muttersegen*. This of course explains why mothers did not attend the baptism of their children.

A fairly standard description of churching is provided by the eighteenth-century parish priest of Combloux in Savoy.

> On her first time out after giving birth, every woman is obliged to present herself at the door of the church in the morning at the time of mass, with her head covered by a large white veil and accompanied by the midwife. The priest blesses her according to the formula in the service-book, after having given her a lighted candle which she holds until the offertory. Then she presents herself to kiss the relics [of the altar] and gives six sols for the priest and six for the clerk.[3]

The ritual dates back in the West to the late eleventh century at least – women carrying lights at churching are mentioned by William of Malmesbury – and this and other parts of it derive from or relate to those performed on the feast of the Purification of the Virgin or Candlemas, which became popular at about the same time. There was also the precedent of the purification ceremony in Leviticus, chapter 12.

In other French accounts, the priest led the woman into church by the hand or clutching one end of his stole, which was sometimes first placed on her head, and it was noted that she held the candle in her left hand. In the Roman Ritual of 1614, 'the priest wore a reversible stole of purple and white with the purple side uppermost', when he met the woman at the church door. During the service in the church later, however, the stole was 'reversed to reveal its white side'. Here the purple signified the woman's penitential state following the birth, and the white her restored purity. Wearing white by the woman, which was very common, also reflected the notion of purification. Sometimes, the woman held the actual Candlemas candle. In Catalonia in modern times, the midwife carried the woman's child and held the candle that was used at the baptism. More generally, the woman herself was sprinkled with holy water at the start and the end of the service. In the Sarum Rite, hyssop was also used, 'a herb commonly used to cleanse sacramental vessels'.[4] The mother and the midwife often sat in a special seat near the altar, from which the priest eventually conducted the woman to her normal place. Mass might be said for her, and bread was presented and dedicated. In the Périgord, this was then broken by the midwife, who ate a piece and gave one to the mother, the rest being retained as a talisman. In eastern Provence, the bread was distributed to the poor. A further link with baptism is reflected in the custom found in England and elsewhere of giving the priest the chrism-cloth or a substitute for it, together with the money offering.

Some medieval dissidents and Protestants objected to the whole idea of a post-partum ritual. The Brandenburg-Nuremberg Church Order of 1533, for example, abolished it, declaring that 'the benediction after childbed is unnecessary; for it springs from mere superstition, as if women were desecrated by the birth, which comes rather from God's blessing'; and some English Puritans later refused to perform the rite. The First Prayerbook of Edward VI (1549) retained what was still called an 'Order of the Purification of Women' but stressed that its purpose was to give thanks for the woman's delivery 'from the great pain and peril of childbirth'; and in subsequent Church of England books it became 'The Thanksgiving of Women after Childbirth, commonly called the Churching of Women', dropping the idea of a 'penitential cleansing'. The Church of England also abandoned the ritual at the church door and the use of holy water and candles, but the tradition of wearing veils and presenting the chrism-cloth seems to have been maintained in most places into the seventeenth century or later. Puritan opposition within the Church focused on these old Catholic trappings, and especially the wearing of the veil, and not so much on the ritual itself, and the notion of purification was rejected primarily because it was seen as Jewish or Roman Catholic and not *per se*.[5]

This reflects a more general divergence and development of opinion among the clergy, both Catholic and Protestant. A letter attributed to Pope Gregory the Great ruled that women 'who have just given birth are not to be prevented from entering churches'; but penitentials and later ecclesiastical pronouncements and steering proscribed the practice, it seems very effectively. In Corsica, some priests would not allow women inside churches before they had been 'sanctified', as it was called, and the churching ceremony was customarily performed at the woman's house, something which the bishops sought to stop from the end of the sixteenth century. The Roman Ritual of 1614, like the later prayer books of the Church of England, emphasized thanksgiving and divine blessing in churching rather than the need for purification; but it was only gradually adopted and local diocesan rituals retained the stress on 'purification from blemish and sin', sometimes down to the twentieth century. The idea that women were unclean until they had been churched was also encouraged by the name of the rite as well as by features of it that we have described. The threshold location of the first part of the rite indicated that the woman was separated from the congregation 'because of pollution'. The veils worn by the new mothers can be seen as symbols of regained purity – the clerical poet Herrick called them 'holy fillitings' – or as further indicators of the need for seclusion up to the moment that the rite produced its effect. The white hand-kerchief offered in many English country parishes in the seventeenth and eighteenth centuries derived, as we have suggested, from the chrism-cloth and was again a symbol of purity. The special seating also manifested a need to keep the woman apart and at a distance until she had been purified. Some English churches had churching or 'childwife' pews, high-walled, box-like and reminiscent of the criminal dock. One at Sedgefield in County Durham was described in 1663 as 'the sick wife's pew'.[6]

There was some popular resistance to attending churching rituals. The Visitation Articles of 1586 for the diocese of London, for example, referred to ministers 'winking ... at such fantastical women as condemn to come to church' after childbirth as required; while churchwardens were still presenting women in Anglesey around 1750 for 'not coming to be churched'.[7] These may sometimes have been militant Protestants, as the London text suggests, but more often perhaps they were unmarried or premature mothers anxious to avoid the additional humiliations they would have to undergo or poor women unable to afford the dress and the offering required, though the latter might be waived by generous or well-endowed clergy.

In general, however, women made use of the ecclesiastical ceremony, which provided purification via fire and water, clerical blessing and thanksgiving, and a mode of reintegration into the community. 'For rite of churching soon she made her way', Crabbe, another clerical poet could write therefore in 1807, 'In dread of scandal, should she miss the day.' Neglect of churching was 'insignificant' in England down to the seventeenth century and attachment to the rite continued in later centuries, particularly at the popular level. Charles Booth's researches showed that it was almost universal among the London working classes in the 1890s; and it remained a firmly adhered-to tradition at Bethnal Green in the 1950s. There seems little doubt that such adherence came from below and from women. The rule, maintained in England from the late sixteenth to the early nineteenth century, which banned unmarried mothers from being churched, would have made no sense unless the mothers wanted to have the rite performed; and we have seen that the rule was not always followed.[8] There is also evidence that dissenters and gypsies sought churching, and that its recent abandonment by clergy and elites has not enjoyed popular approval.

Popular involvement is indicated too by the paraliturgical accretions which the rite attracted. In the Scottish Borders in the 1840s, a woman went to her churching 'accompanied by her husband who took with him a portion of bread and cheese, and bestowed it on the first person whom they met on the road', in order to ensure good luck. In nineteenth-century Brittany, women went to their *relevailles* with mourning-hoods over their heads and climbed the churchyard wall rather than going through the main gate, all to avoid being seen. A taboo on the woman touching the holy water stoup herself is reported by Abbé Thiers. The midwife or another woman, or in the Périgord a child, would take the water for her and place it on her forehead. In some parts of France, too, a woman risked having no more children if she was churched on a Friday or on a day on which a wedding had taken place in the church. In Provence, churching did not take place on a Friday or a thirteenth of the month. Various divinations about the future of the new-born child or the next one were linked to the ceremony. Other practices reported and condemned in early modern France were for the midwife or another woman to be churched in the place of a mother who had died in child-bed, or having the priest say a so-called 'dry mass', that is, one without consecration or communion. In the Périgord, this was supposed to make the husband temporarily infertile. Writing of early modern Wales, moreover, Edward Lhwyd expressed the view that for most women the entire churching ritual was only 'a charm to prevent witchcraft'.[9] All over Europe, too, churching was followed by festivities, at which special ritual food was eaten. Once again, it was incorporated into popular culture.

Most babies were fed at the maternal breast, which lent breast-feeding a cultural significance which it has lost and helps to explain the magical beliefs and practices which surrounded it. Breast-feeding by the mother and the fact that it had occurred was taken to be the most obvious expression of the maternal bond, which indeed it must have powerfully established.

> I have often heard her say she gave me suck,
> And it should seem by that she dearly lov'd me,

Giovanni says of his mother in Webster's *The White Devil* (1612). The best way for a mother to show her love for her child, according to the Puritan William Gouge in 1622, was 'by letting it suck her own breasts ... for daily experience showeth that mothers love those children best to whom they themselves gave suck'. As we have mentioned, in Ancient Roman and Germanic law, once a child had been suckled, it could not be abandoned. The tie had been formed. Mother and sucking child were also linked across the divide of death. According to a belief in modern Denmark, if a child of a mother who has died cries, 'the mother cannot rest in her grave but hurries to put it to her breast again'. In a Sicilian song, an adult prisoner addresses his dead mother:

> Mother, I weep for you here hour by hour,
> [For] all the milk which you gave me.[10]

The same physical bond between mother and child was also a central element in traditional blessings. The New Testament provided a model here with the woman who addressed Jesus in the Gospel according to St Luke: 'Blessed is the womb that bare thee, and the paps which thou hast sucked'. An incident in the twelfth-century miracles of St Rictrude, for example, tells how a knight got rid of an unjust judge; the local population did him honour and 'blessed the breasts full of milk which he had sucked'. Much later, Carlo Levi and his sister were greeted by the peasants of Gagliano with the familiar words: 'Blessed is the womb that bore you! ... Blessed the breasts that suckled you!'[11]

This tie was adverted too again in crises and used in appeals to grown sons. Clytemnestra in Aeschylus' *Oresteia* pleads with Orestes, when he is about to kill her to avenge his father Agamemnon. She uncovers her breasts and asks:

> Wait, my son; [have you] no respect for this, my child?
> The breast you held, drowsing away the hours,
> Soft gums tugging the milk that made you grow?

In a letter to Heliodorus, St Jerome in 374 urged him to follow the ascetic life, despite the pleadings of his relatives: 'Though your mother with dishevelled hair and torn raiment show you the breasts that gave you suck', a text cited by a French Jansenist in the early eighteenth century with approval. Lamenting the death of offspring was accompanied by the same gesture. In the Life of St Alexis in Caxton's *Golden Legend*, the saint's mother keens over her son's dead body. She scratches 'her paps with her nails, saying: These paps have given thee suck ...'. The Virgin Mary was supposed to have lamented her crucified son in the same way. In the Chester Mystery Plays, for example, Mary declares at the foot of the cross: 'I fostered thee and gave thee suck upon my knee'; while the classic Pietà represents the Virgin with the adult Christ on her lap like a baby.[12]

Before the general introduction of milk concentrates and sterile bottles with rubber teats from around 1900, there was no effective substitute for human milk. Animal milk was used, especially for orphans, from Classical times onwards. Goats', cows' and asses' milk are all referred to in the sources, the last being preferred by the well-to-do probably because it was most like human milk. But feeding with animal milk was always rare and was discouraged by the belief that children might imbibe animal characteristics with the milk. Jean l'Ourson, the hero of a tale from French Flanders, goes on all fours and has the appearance of a bear, 'because he was suckled by such an animal'.[13] Paps or gruels, made with cereals, flour or bread, sometimes premasticated by the mother, were given alongside milk from an early age, often at a few weeks old, and these and similar substances might be given alone where milk was not available. But again this procedure of 'bringing up by hand' was a makeshift and not normal, reserved for orphans, foundlings and babies whose mothers had little or no milk.

As all this shows, there were a few exceptions to the rule of maternal breast-feeding. First, the mother might be prevented. This would obviously be the case if she died, as we have seen, or if she were ill. Direct evidence of this is rare among peasants and workers, but one has occasional glimpses. The medical writer Ramazzini from Modena observed in 1700 'that among the common people mothers always nurse their infants, unless prevented by some accident'. When a yeoman's daughter from Pilkington in Lancashire, Susan Barloe, had a second child in 1630, her father persuaded a man to marry her, but he insisted that the father provide for the child. So, when Susan proved unable to suckle the baby, her father took the child first to his sister-in-law Dorothy, 'a young fresh woman and full of suck' and then for some reason shortly afterwards to his sister, who was pregnant and anyway, according to her husband a woman 'scarce able to give [any of her own children] suck'. She brought the baby up by hand, but it very quickly died. Among the elite, Lady Fanshawe wrote in her memoirs that 'my mother being sick to death of a fever three months after I was born [in 1625] ... , she gave me suck no longer'. Again, the London clergyman Thomas Wilson recited a familiar story when he wrote in his diary in 1735: 'My dear wife tried to suckle her little one but her nipples were so sore and so small that the child could not get hold of them and so, I hope, it will be pardoned, for I know that it is every woman's duty to nurse her own child'. It is likely that peasant women's poor diet, poor general health and need to resume work were further factors reducing their milk supply. A doctor from Tarbes in the late eighteenth century reported that 'very few countrywomen are nourished as well as they should be to produce good milk with which to breast-feed their babies'. As late as 1904 a review in Britain found 'that many [working-class] women were too unhealthy even to produce milk'.[14]

Some women may also have been discouraged from breast-feeding by pressure from their spouses. Some historians have made this claim, and there is evidence to support it. Two considerations would influence husbands here: the desire to resume sexual relations, which were thought to spoil the milk; and fashion or snobbery, for using wet-nurses was an upper-class custom. This idea is lent verisimilitude by the fact that in early modern England, eighteenth- and nineteenth-century France and Renaissance Tuscany, it was husbands who very often arranged wet-nursing rather than female relatives, as might be expected. Trying to discourage a junior partner from having a live-in nurse, Francesco di Marco Datini wrote that 'in Prato and Florence there are few men who keep a child at the breast in the house, even among the very rich'. Another reason for not breast-feeding was erotic or aesthetic: the belief that suckling would impair the shape of the breasts and make them sag, thus losing their attractiveness. According to a Spanish saying: 'Giving birth makes a woman beautiful; giving suck makes her old'.[15]

Against all this was the heavy weight of clerical and medical advocacy of maternal breast-feeding, to which Thomas Wilson alludes, and, much more significant, the force of circumstance. Reflecting this was the belief that it was bad for a child to be fed with anything other than its mother's milk. At Montaillou in the early fourteenth century, the illegitimate Brune Pourcel only agreed very reluctantly 'to the urgings of her neighbour to bring her infant to be nursed' by another woman. She feared 'that the milk of a strange woman would harm her child'. In modern Poland, all women but the mother could affect the child with the evil eye, if they nursed it. In sixteenth-century Scotland, according to Holinshed, 'it was a cause of suspicion of the mother's fidelity toward her husband to seek a strange nurse for her children [although her milk failed, and] each woman would take intolerable pains to bring up and nourish her own children'.[16]

Wet-nursing by other women nevertheless took place. Breast-feeding might be shared, especially in the first days of the baby's life, as we have seen. Hélias, who was born in the Pays Bigouden in Brittany in 1913, notes that he was carried at baptism by 'the woman who had given me milk until my mother's came in', and he remarks more generally that infants whose mothers died were suckled by relatives and neighbours. This could occur, too, without the mother's death. In George Sand's *La Petite Fadette* (1848), set in Berry, when the mature Mère Barbeau has yet another child following twins, 'she could not have managed, if her eldest daughter, who had her first child then, had not helped out from time to time by giving her breast to her little sister'. In a court case in Gascony in 1752, a woman was suspected of having made a baby ill, having suckled it as 'the nearest neighbour'. Mutual or communal breast-feeding was not uncommon in nineteenth-century Italy, where it was blamed for spreading syphilis. Breast-feeding was also shared with hired nurses. In late medieval Italian cities, babies sometimes had 'a brief period of maternal nursing' (two weeks to one month) before being sent out to nurse. A French provincial doctor, writing in 1806, assumed that a baby would be passed 'from his mother's breast to that of a nurse, and from her to yet another woman'. Mother and nurse could also feed the child concurrently. The first son of the president of the Parlement of Dôle was nursed, his father wrote in 1574, 'by my wife and by a woman ... who was hired as a servant in the house, to help my wife'.[17]

This brings us to the subject of wet-nursing proper. It was an elite custom from Roman times onwards, though there were always mothers who did not follow its demands and moralists opposed it. It continued as an elite practice through the medieval and modern periods, when its influence spread lower down the social scale. By the late medieval and Renaissance periods, the offspring of the urban patriciates and bourgeoisies of Europe's great cities were being wet-nursed. A royal ordinance of 1350 sought to regulate the remuneration of 'the servants and ... nurses who serve the bourgeois of Paris'. London's merchant class also 'entrusted babies to the care of live-in and village nurses', though on a lesser scale. The custom is best-known for this period in Renaissance Florence, where it was the rule among the upper and middle classes. It continued among the elites of most countries into the nineteenth century and beyond. It seems to have been particularly prevalent in France. Not general among the sixteenth-century elite, it is well attested in the seventeenth century and it spread to other sections of society subsequently: the urban and rural bourgeoisie, the artisan class of older cities, like Paris and Lyon, and even the peasantry. Bernadette Soubirous, the future saint, for example, born in 1844 in the poor and remote department of the Hautes-Pyrénées, whose father was a miller and then a day labourer, had a wet-nurse, and wet-nursing was reported at around the same time among the rural population of Savoie. Well before this time, wet-nursing had become 'an organized enterprise' in France, 'a major cottage industry', providing complementary work on a sedentary or migratory basis for thousands of women from rural areas with links to cities, as well as providing a living for a network of agents.[18]

It was generally believed that babies imbibed physical and moral qualities with their milk. In the late eleventh century, St Bernard's mother, Aleth, an aristocrat from Burgundy, 'refused to allow her children to be suckled by anyone else: for it almost seemed as though the babies were fed with the qualities of their mother's goodness as they drew the milk from her breast'. Coler's secular manual declared that God had provided mothers with breasts to feed their offspring: 'He has further placed those breasts near the heart so that the child may also gain from its mother true childlike love, fear of God, wisdom and understanding, discipline and a sense of honour'. And what was proverbially absorbed with the mother's or nurse's milk extended to beliefs and traditions. King James I announced on opening his first English Parliament in 1604 that, though he had a Catholic mother, his nurse had been a Protestant and 'I thank God I sucked the milk of God's truth with the milk of my nurse'.[19]

The association of qualities and milk could also be expressed in a negative way. 'For children by drinking in strange milk, drink in also strange manners and another nature', wrote Thomas Becon around 1560. In a panegyric Life, written in 1130, Ide, the sainted countess of Boulogne, determined, like Aleth, to suckle her sons herself to prevent them being 'led into wicked ways by another woman's milk'. In a later anecdote, 'she discovers that a nurse has given suck to her hungry baby. Overcome with righteous anger, she shakes the child, causing it to vomit up the substitute nourishment, and then she feeds it with her own milk'. This belief, this fear was most obvious where wet-nurses were concerned. 'Often times the child sucketh the vice of his nurse with the milk of her pap', wrote Elyot in 1531; while Lyly referred in 1579 to 'the common bye word of the common people ... which is "This fellow hath sucked mischief even from the teat of his nurse" '. Alberti wrote in *The Book of the Family* that 'a dishonest and immoral nurse will corrupt a child, predispose him to vice and fill his spirit with bestial and wild passions, such as wrath, fear and similar evils'. The Hamburg *Patriot* reiterated the same view in 1724: 'A child sucks poor health, coarse habits, and vices with the milk of a nurse, [faults] which stick with it through life'. And specific examples were cited. According to a convent biography of the seventeenth century, the noble Marie Le Demour, who became a nun at Guingamp, had had her character spoiled by the milk of her nurse, who was a woman of loose morals, 'for one sucks in one's inclinations with the milk of one's nurse'. Careful choice of a nurse was therefore crucial. The wet-nurse, a Tuscan merchant wrote in the late fourteenth century 'should be prudent, well-mannered, honest, not a drinker or a drunkard, because very often children draw from and resemble the nature of the milk they suck; and therefore be careful the wet-nurses of your children are not proud and do not have other evil traits'. Similar advice was repeated down the centuries. And wet-nurses, of course, as King James believed, could have a positive effect on their nurslings. Michelangelo, who had a stonemason's wife as a wet-nurse, used to say later jokingly that 'with my nurse's milk, I sucked in the hammer and chisels I use for my statues'. Much later, Mircea Eliade, born in Rumania in 1907, wrote that he once liked to think that he became an Orientalist thanks to the 'exotic breast' of the gypsy wet-nurse who fed him.[20]

There was a related belief, analogous to that about shocks and impressions in pregnancy, that strong feelings in a nursing woman could be communicated to the milk making it harmful to the child. An English *Treatise on the Diseases of Children* of 1784 retailed the story of a nursing mother who had a visitor who suddenly dropped dead, causing her a shock. She 'nevertheless went ahead to nurse a six-month old, who then fell into convulsions and a coma for thirty-six hours'. There was also the idea that the loss of a baby would have an adverse effect on the milk. In a Greek lullaby, the grieving mother 'would weep and fall sick, and her milk would turn bitter'. This was another argument against employing wet-nurses, many of whom had lost their own babies. Magical beliefs also linked a child's gender with nursing. In Languedoc in the late sixteenth century, a male child was put to nurse with a woman who had given birth to a female child, and vice-versa. Reversing this principle, an English manual of the same date laid down that 'a female child must suck the breast of a nurse that had a girl the last child she had, and a boy must suck her that lately had a boy'.[21]

In many parts of the Middle East, 'the relationship of wet-nurse to child created a relationship of brotherhood and sisterhood between the nursed child and the nurse's children, and an impediment to marriage'. Milk siblings were not so recognized in European societies either in law or convention, though the tie did have some significance. Marie de Médicis made her milk-sister Leonora Dori called Galigai her first lady-in-waiting and accorded her other favours; while the duchesse de Créqui obtained a position for her grandson by reminding Louis XIV that 'she had had the honour of sucking the same milk as His Majesty'. Much later and among the peasantry, the narrator in Gérard de Nerval's *Sylvie* (1853) meets up again with his 'milk-brother' in the Valois. The relationship between nursling and nurse could, of course, be one that was deep and lasting, at all social levels, and it is significant that this bond focused on the actual provision of milk. 'For so it is arranged by nature', as a medieval saint's Life put it, 'that nurses always bestow the affection of the spirit on those to whom they provide the milk of their flesh.'[22]

Given this importance of breast-feeding, measures were taken to make sure that mothers had an abundant supply of milk and to protect nursing women and their breasts. Certain of the rituals performed at weddings were intended to procure a good milk supply in the future, for example kissing a particular walnut tree on the wedding-day at Grancey near Niort, or firing guns at the ceremony in nineteenth-century Lorraine: without the latter, it was believed that the bride 'would not be good for milk'.[23]

Once the baby had arrived, the mother should avoid certain foods. Some plants and herbs might diminish or stop lactation: in France parsley and periwinkle especially, but also lettuce, cabbage and other green vegetables and carrots. These were used deliberately to stop the milk should this be necessary. Hitting the breasts with parsley was also reported in France. Medical opinion concurred to some extent with popular views here, a French treatise on infancy advising in 1799 against 'all bitter, salty, astringent and above all acid foods, such as leeks, radishes, garlic, salt pork, [also] cheeses, raw fruit, wines and spirits', though here the concern was with the quality of the milk rather than its volume.[24] Positively, in the Limousin and elsewhere, floury and white food, like crêpes, were supposed to encourage lactation.

Certain actions should also be avoided. There was 'no false modesty in the past over the exposure of the breasts for the fulfilment of their natural function', but in many places suckling in front of strangers risked the effects of the evil eye and was avoided. In Corsica, mothers suckled their babies in church, but this was regarded as a safe environment. In Lucania, touching the breast, wiping milk from it and other minor actions could take away the supply. In Portugal, a mother should not eat or drink while actually suckling. Should this taboo be broken, mothers should attend mass on the festival of St Gregory and 'suckle their children facing the altar at the elevation of the host'. At Grottola in Lucania, if a woman visited another who had just given birth and left the house with her own baby at her breast, she would take away the first woman's milk with her. To prevent this, 'the first woman had to call back the second and explicitly ask her to give back the milk'. Similarly, in the Limousin, visitors had to leave gifts of money or food, so as not 'to take away the milk'.[25]

Women often wore amulets to procure a good supply of milk or to prevent threats to it. Among substances and objects used here, we may note bags of salt, boars' tusks, keys, sea-horses, esparto grass and various kinds of stone. In nineteenth-century Crete, women wore ancient Minoan seal stones as 'milkstones', but the commonest stone generally was white agate, which directly evoked milk by its appearance. In the Périgord, agate necklaces were passed around within and beyond parishes, and at Saint-Saud, a necklace of 'tiles of milk', light blue, dark blue and red, was worn. The amulets or necklaces were hung between or against the breasts themselves, and the shape and design of the stones and other objects often recalled the breasts or other female organs. In Andalusia, necklaces of 'milk counters' were used. When mothers wanted the milk to come, the necklace was placed on the breasts; but when they wanted the milk to stop, it was thrown over the shoulder.[26]

In southern Italy, the supply of milk was linked to the disposal of the placenta. In places in Lucania,

> the placenta was immersed several times in a river, accompanied by this formula, repeated three times: As this bag fills with water, so may these breasts fill with milk ... At Pisticci, the umbilical cord and the placenta were placed under a stone in the middle of a stream so that the water ran over them and the placenta overflowed with water.

Alternatively, the placenta might be ingested. 'If the mother had been dry with her first-born [in the Abruzzi], she should eat a piece of the second-born's placenta in broth to stimulate the flow of milk.'[27]

A whole range of other similar procedures was undertaken if a woman's milk failed. First, herbs were employed. An Anglo-Norman rhymed book of physic included a drink made with fennel, lettuce, vervain, rue and hawthorn flowers: 'If this be given to the woman, she will have plenty of milk'. Some of these plants had been recommended by Pliny and they remained in popular pharmacopoeias down to the modern period. Culpeper additionally listed borage, bugloss, common mallows and sow thistle as 'good to increase milk in women's breasts'. The choice of sow-thistle, also found elsewhere, is explained by the white 'milk' which the stems contain. A modern remedy from the Ariège comprised a tisane of rue, walnut leaves and carrot tops and a plaster to be placed on the breasts made of wall-pellitory and parsley.[28]

Magical charms and rituals might also be used. An Anglo-Saxon charm for 'the woman who cannot nourish her child' required her to 'take in her hand milk of a cow of one colour, and then sip it up with her mouth, and then go to running water and swallow it'. She had also to recite a formula and to be careful not to look round. A fifteenth-century leechbook had a drink 'for woman's milk that faileth', made up of pounded crystal and the milk of another woman. In Forlì around 1700, 'a mother having lost her milk, milk is taken from her who has suckled the child and ... is placed on the shoulders of the mother so that she may again have milk', or animal milk might be used in the same way.[29] These remedies relied on like producing like.

Other procedures were aimed at undoing the effects of envy or the evil eye. In the Périgord, 'if, despite precautions, the milk dried up, one had to go from door to door begging haricot beans, for a boy at three widowers' and for a girl at three widows' houses. These were then cooked and served to the mother, eating alone'. In Lucania, full breasts were the objects of envy on the part of other women. A woman short of milk might be tempted to try to steal another's milk, which she might do by going to visit with her baby, as we have seen, or by inducing a neighbour to take a bag of salt there that had been in the clothes of the baby at risk. The salt was then used in a soup eaten by the woman short of milk, whose breasts would then flow. If a woman believed that she had been robbed of milk in this way and discovered the culprit, she would call for reparation. The two women would meet, uncover their breasts in front of each other and make a little milk spirt out, while the robbed one said: 'I do not want yours and I do not want to give you mine', which undid the spell. Men and animals could also steal milk by envious looks.[30]

A variety of other magical practices are reported. Obstruction of the breasts was sometimes attributed in southern Italy to the nipples being blocked by hairs which had to be magically removed. In the Vosges in the nineteenth century, a woman 'who wants her milk to flow should place her husband's night-cap over her breast'; the same gesture could also be used to stop her milk. This relates to the use of husbands' clothing in pregnancy and childbirth. Recourse was also had to folk-healers and cunning persons. A Sicilian folk-healer, for example, in recent times, used leeches, charms and massage to make the milk flow again in women's breasts when it had stopped and to prevent it from 'curdling'.[31]

Visits were also paid to natural and religious shrines. Fountains and springs were an obvious recourse. In France, their water was drunk and used in potions but most often it was used to wash or sprinkle on the breasts. At Gouezec in Brittany, for example, 'women had to go three times round the chapel of Notre-Dame-de-Tréguron with their breasts bared, stopping each time at the fountain to bathe their breasts, then returning to the chapel to say five Paters and five Aves and leave a coin as a gift'. At Notre-Dame-de-Kergonet-en-Gestel near Lorient, in order to have milk, women let the water from the spring 'run down their sleeves on to their breasts, which they then rub with pebbles'. Some holy wells in Wales were especially reputed to bring milk to nursing mothers. According to a late-nineteenth-century writer, at St Anne's well near Llanfihangel (Glamorgan), 'the water flowed through the breasts of a female bust sculptured upon a stone slab, which was believed to represent' the saint.[32] Analogy was also important elsewhere. At the fountain of Sainte-Pupette near Tarbes, the water made the stones into teat-like or breast-shaped objects.

Similar effects were found in caves. Rocks dripping milk-like water were resorted to, for example near Verona, while stalactites attracted dry mothers for the same reason. In a cave, significantly calles La Mamès at Bostens in the Landes, 'women sucked the breast-like stalactites to obtain milk for themselves'. Similarly, stalactites in a cave in the Val d'Orcia were known locally as 'the *poccie lattaie* (literally, milk-bearing udders)'. They were so shaped,

> each gently dripping a few drops of water. Here [down to the time of the Second World War] ... came nursing mothers who were losing their milk – and after they had tasted the water, their wish was granted. They brought with them, as gifts, seven fruits of the earth: a handful of wheat, barley, corn, rye, vetch, dried peas, and sometimes a saucer of milk.[33]

Many of these natural shrines were associated with the saints and the Virgin Mary. As we have seen, many fountains in Brittany (and elsewhere) were linked to the Virgin. Until the mid nineteenth century, for example,

> there was not a mother or a nurse in the district, who did not feel obliged to go every year to invoke or to thank the 'Virgin of the Milk' or 'Mother of the Springs' at Frout near Carhaix. There they recited a short prayer in Breton:
>
> > Madame of Frout, mother and virgin,
> > Give us health for the child and milk to me.[34]

The Virgin Mary was clearly associated with milk in official iconography and writings. Her own milk was 'a favourite relic in the West' from the Middle Ages onwards. Examples were found at Walsingham, Cologne, Bruges, Antwerp, Clermont-Ferrand and many other places. The milk derived either directly from the Virgin herself, or from pictures and statues. In 1690, for example, 'a painted image of the Madonna, not far from the city of Carinola [in Calabria], was observed to diffuse abundant milk'. Another source of Virgin's milk was the church of St Nicholas in Bethlehem, where she had supposedly expressed her milk against a column and let some fall to the floor. The column sweated perpetually, 'and in all places where her worthy milk fell, the earth is soft and white and has the appearance of curded milk, and whoever likes, takes of it, out of devotion'. According to a modern study, sixty-nine shrines in Europe had Virgin's milk from this source, which was 'reputed to encourage an abundant lactation'.[35]

The image of the Virgin nursing the Infant Jesus was even more common from the time of the Catacombs to that of the Baroque and beyond (see Text Figure 10). The lactating Virgin or the Virgin exposing her breasts to God represented the Incarnation: Christ sucked his mother's milk like a human child, and stressed her mediating role. In a window at Beauvais, the Virgin shows her son her breast, saying to him: 'My son, to whom my breast gave milk, I appeal to you for this sinner'. Luther wrote of Catholic practice: 'They taught us to pray to the dear mother of Christ and reminded us of the breasts which she had given to her son, so that she might ask him to temper his wrath towards us'. Mary also played a special part vis-à-vis the souls in Purgatory, being shown in pictures down to the eighteenth century, 'quenching the thirsty souls [in the Purgatorial fire] with her milk'.[36]

Devotional writings referred also to the *Virgo lactans* or Virgin providing milk, for example the Hymn to the Virgin by Jacopone da Todi, written in popular idiom. Ballads, carols and lullabies employed the theme, too. 'Now suck the milk from my breast, Holiest, best ...', ran a lullaby collected in the Ligurian Alps in the nineteenth century; while in the English carol 'The Twelve Good Joys':

> The first good joy our Mary had,
> It was the joy of one,
> To see her own son Jesus,
> To suck at her breast bone.[37]

All of this must have encouraged the popular association of the Virgin Mary with breast-feeding, on top of her general efficacy.

A number of other saints, male but more often female, were also invoked by mothers and nurses needing milk. Two of the miracles of St Catherine of Siena performed in her lifetime in the fourteenth century 'restored breast milk to women whose breasts had gone dry'; while the posthumous miracles of St Elizabeth of Portugal, canonized in 1742, included two more cases of this kind. In one, the woman's milk, having dried up, came again after the woman had drunk wine 'prepared according to the saint's prescription'; in the other the woman's husband prayed to the saint unbeknown to his wife. Many saints' shrines were visited and ex-votos donated, sometimes in the shape of breasts. Usually there was something about the saint that linked him or her with breast-feeding. The name of St Mammès or Mammard evoked breasts in France, for example. By far the most frequently invoked saint in this area, at least in Western Europe, was St Agatha, sometimes referred to as the patron saint of nursing mothers. According to her legend, she had had her breasts ripped off as part of her martyrdom, and she was sometimes represented holding a dish with the breasts in it. Her cult remained active down to the nineteenth century. 'At Queige, which was one of the centres of her cult in Savoie, little bread rolls in the shape of breasts' were blessed by the priest; while in the Nièvre, women 'attended masses of St Agatha to procure milk'.[38]

Invocation of saints overlaps here with more formal clerical procedures, such as blessings and masses. A miracle reported at Mauguio in 1779 involved a mother who had been dry for thirty-three days; her milk began to come during the baptism of her child, which had clearly been delayed, and then more abundantly during a subsequent mass. The Old Ritual of Périgord, in use still in 1827, provided a 'blessing of seeds for nurses who lack milk'. The woman brought grains or seeds to the church and

> it was asked of Jesus Christ by the merits of Mary and of the saint whose name the woman bore, to fix his attention on the mother to swell her breasts by the virtue of the grains, which were dedicated to the Blessed Virgin and sprinkled with holy water.

In a more folkloric ritual at the church of Clermont-d'Excideuil, also in the Périgord, a woman without milk 'placed a soft cheese on her naked breasts and held it there while the priest read the Gospel over her'. The cheese was then presented to the priest.[39]

Like other misfortunes, the drying-up of milk was attributed to witchcraft or other agencies, such as the evil eye. In Corsica, for example, it was believed that an evil look, especially from a stranger, could dry up a woman's milk, and an amulet known as the 'knot of St Anne' was used to protect her. 'It is a well-known fact', Cornelisen wrote of a southern Italian village, 'that if a stranger's hair falls on the breast, it clogs the tit', an idea we have already encountered. In the Fens in recent times, a mother 'would never suckle her child during a thunderstorm; she would draw off the milk, which was thought to be tainted with brimstone and sulphur, and throw it away', a taboo which seems to be related to the belief that storms were raised by demons or witches.[40] We have seen too that a woman's milk supply might be threatened by the envy of other women.

In addition to these modern examples, a number of historical sources can be cited which link the drying-up of milk more directly with witchcraft. In his *Treatise of Witchcraft* (1616), Alexander Roberts starts his discussion of the harm done by witches by referring to a report that the breasts of nurses had only to be touched by witches hands 'for those sacred fountains of human nourishment [to become] so dried up that they could yield no milk', a comment quoted in other texts. In a case tried at Stirling in 1633, Margaret Chapman was 'accused of taking away a woman's milk', which was a not uncommon charge. On the Continent, the demonologist Rémy claimed that witches' powders or other means were widely used to 'diminish, draw off and dry up the milk in the breasts', and he quoted several cases in which this had allegedly occurred. For example, 'Catharina Latomia of Haraucourt in 1587 ... put a herb given her by the Demon upon the threshold of the house of Jean Antoine, with the result that, after his wife had come out that way, the milk in her breasts was dried up and, in consequence, the child whom she was suckling died'. According to the evidence at a trial at Quingey in 1657, a young mother called Pierrotte, accompanied by the midwife, was returning from her churching wearing her veil, when a third woman came up, lifted

Pierrotte's veil and made an ironically complimentary remark. Pierrotte then found herself unable to suckle her baby.[41]

In a number of cases, witches harmed the breasts of women rather than drying up their milk directly. Whatever their supposed cause, all the same procedures were used to seek cures for ailments of the breast, associated very often with nursing. Comfrey, for example, according to Culpeper was 'good to be applied unto women's breasts that grow sore by the abundance of milk coming into them', while parsley was recommended to soften breasts 'that are hard through the curdling of their milk'. A seventeenth-century French herbal advised the use of geranium leaves for chafed breasts. Groundsel was also prescribed, along with infusions of reed or chervil for sore nipples, a common complaint.[42] Port wine, used as a lotion, was another remedy mentioned in *The Lancet* in the 1840s. Nipple shields of all kinds of material, some of magical significance, were also employed. The skin of a grass snake was a remedy for breast abcesses in the Ariège in modern times; while in Cambridgeshire toads were rubbed on the breasts to cure cancer.

Charms were used too. One collected in the Hebrides went:

> Look thou, O Christ, at the breast,
> How painful it is.
> Tell it to gentle Mary,
> Since it is she who bore the son.
> Whole may the breast be,
> Small may the swelling be.
> Run away, O disease.

Recourse was also had to healers of different kinds. Ointment made by a female healer for nipple soreness was distributed all over south-eastern France in the sixteenth century. In an Andalusian village in the middle of the twentieth century, a woman whose milk was stopped by a swelling was cured by having her breasts 'stroked three times a day for three days' by a ninth son, a boy of twelve. Sucking the breasts was another common remedy. John Winthrop referred in 1646 to the case of a Boston woman, the wife of a sailor, who developed a sore on her breast, following the birth of a child, which was a symptom it transpired of venereal disease: 'Divers neighbours resorted to her; some of them drew her breast and others let their children suck them (no such disease being suspected by any), by occasion whereof about sixteen persons, men, women, and children were infected'.[43]

Visits were also paid to fountains and shrines, and saints were invoked. A healing well in Caron Uwch Clawdd parish in Cardiganshire was 'especially good for the sore breasts of women'. St Agatha, the Virgin Mary and other saints were called on in France and elsewhere 'to cure illnesses of the breasts'.

Ex-votos and miracle accounts testify to successful cures at shrines. In the twelfth century, for example, a certain Matilda of Swafield was cured of 'an intolerable swelling and pain in her right breast' after making a vow to St William of Norwich; while in the nineteenth century a small piece broken off one of the statues on the front of Exeter cathedral was 'pounded up with lard to form an ointment which was applied to a woman's sore breast'.[44]

According to classical medical theory deriving from Aristotle and Galen, milk was a kind of blood. 'After the birth', wrote Isidore of Seville in the seventh century, 'whatever blood has not yet been spent in the nourishing of the womb flows by a natural passage to the breasts, and whitening by their virtue, receives the quality of milk.' An English advice book of 1693 repeated this view exactly: 'The milk by which the infant is nourished is but the blood of which it was framed in the womb, further concocted in thy breast and turned white there'. This belief in the equivalence of milk and blood also existed at the popular level and was manifested in other ways. In medieval thinking, the blood of Christ could be regarded as milk and the milk of the Virgin Mary as blood. According to legend, when St Catherine of Alexandria's head was cut off milk flowed from her neck instead of blood. When an angel appeared to St Pachomius, according to a Russian religious fable warning against fast-breaking, it killed a lamb, whose blood turned to milk. 'Tell the people', said the angel, 'what you have seen; they partake of milk and eggs on Wednesday and Friday [fast days], but in truth they are curdled blood.' In Balkan and gypsy belief, vampires were as fond of milk as of blood. Relating again to female physiology, the combination of red and white substances in women's amulets may be seen as an expression of 'an intimate connection between blood and lactation'. According to a popular view collected in France in 1836, cupping or bleeding the breasts was a way of stopping a woman's periods; while an eighteenth-century medical text saw milk as an emanation from a woman's whole body: 'Our women sweat milk, urinate milk, spit and sneeze milk, and they pass it in their stools'.[45]

Further notions flow from this equation of milk with blood. The categorization of milk as a kind of dirty excreta in the last quotation was not typical of popular or earlier learned views. Blood was polluting, and especially the blood of the womb, which was menstrual blood – the menses stopped during pregnancy and the blood was used to form the child – but this blood was purified by passing through the breasts. Hence, among other reasons, the magical and healing powers of human milk.

Human milk was used as a remedy for eye diseases in particular. A man going blind was told by Sts Cosmas and Damian, according to an early miracle account, to rub his eyes with the milk of a chaste woman. 'For aching of a man's eyes', a fifteenth-century English leechbook recommended anointing 'the eyes with milk of two women, that is to say of the mother and of the daughter', a requirement found in other prescriptions. A Cambridge practitioner of the early seventeenth century advised 'for preserving your sight' a mixture made up of 'woman's milk that bore and nurseth a man child' and 'the urine of the same child' mixed with a new-laid egg and camphor. Human milk continued to be prescribed for eye complaints in France and elsewhere down to the twentieth century. It was also used for earache and deafness, lung-disease, head wounds, coughs and fevers. More significantly and expectedly, it figured in cures for infantile convulsions and gynaecological complaints: in a Middle English text, woman's milk figures among other ingredients in a potion for sores and tumours of the womb. Milk was also used in attempts to remove dead foetuses. It was employed, too, to rejuvenate the old and as an invalid food of last resort. In northern Corsica in recent times, 'for a patient about to die, the supreme hope ... was to procure a woman's milk for him to drink, for, since this food was the first to be given, it was thought to have a resuscitating effect'.[46] Human milk also figured in a variety of other magical procedures: attempts to raise the spirits of the dead, divining the gender of unborn children, and love magic.

Another related idea was that sexual intercourse during lactation interfered with that activity. 'A husband should not approach his wife after her confinement until the child is weaned', Pope Gregory the Great had advised in the sixth century. Though there was not a categorical proscription in the medieval period or later, sexual relations at this time were disapproved of by both clerical and medical writers. According to Guillemeau in 1612, 'carnal copulation ... troubleth the blood, and so by consequence the milk; also it diminisheth the quantity thereof, by provoking the natural purgations', that is the periods.[47] Many writers echoed this view that intercourse spoiled the milk, and wet-nurses were urged to refrain. Suckling during pregnancy was also discouraged. There is little evidence, however, that peasants accepted such views or heeded such advice.

The equivalence of milk and blood reinforced the idea that qualities were conveyed from the nurse to the child via the milk. 'There was no rupture', as Laget puts it,' between gestation and suckling: the baby was given life and had its personality modelled first by blood and then by milk.'[48] We shall see that the modelling continued in other ways.

In a further extension to this idea, the sucking child imbibed the life-blood of its mother or nurse and hence could take away her strength or even prey on her life. This notion was manifested in the image of the baby as a greedy and voracious beast, found in fiction. In Gaelic legend, 'the son of the king of Lochlainn ... as a suckling babe sipped the heart and breast out of his mother and fifty nurses in a row, each with one suck'. Rabelais' Pantagruel is a projection of the same image: he sucked the milk of 4600 cows at each feeding and on one occasion seized a cow, 'chewed off the udder and half the stomach, as well as the liver and kidneys' and later swallowed the rest.[49] Generally, however, the unusually greedy baby was characterized as a changeling or a diabolical substitute or else was believed to be bewitched, and special rituals were employed to calm their appetites, such as boiling the child in modern Hungary.

The kinds of protection afforded the new-born baby were continued into the subsequent period of its life. 'Early infancy', Gennep wrote,

> is accompanied by many rites of magical protection of the normal kind, although the sacrament of baptism was believed to have rendered the child less sensitive to dangerous influences. People continued to make it wear talismans; certain acts were avoided; but, additionally, active procedures were used, most of which had the object of ensuring a regular growth.[50]

When nurslings were sent out in Renaissance Tuscany, they were 'covered with talismans: little crosses or *agnusdei*, pious medals, coral, (wolves' teeth)'.

> Let the superstitious wife
> Near the child's heart lay a knife,

Herrick advised in 1648,

> Point be up, and haft be down;
> (While she gossips in the town)
> This 'mongst other mystic charms
> Keeps the sleeping child from harms.[51]

Other historical sources and a plethora of observations by folklorists in the nineteenth and twentieth centuries confirm that babies and children, sometimes until puberty, retained the armoury of amulets with which they were provided at or soon after birth.

Once they were able to leave the house and once others were able to enter the house where they were, children became more vulnerable to the effects of the evil eye and of witchcraft, and the amulets were often specifically intended to counter these. All writers interested in the subject from the demonologists of the late medieval and early modern periods to modern anthropologists agree that young children – all over Europe, but especially more recently in the South – were particularly at risk from the evil eye. 'The glances of envy and malice do shoot also subtly; the eye of the malicious person does really infect (and make sick) the spirit of the other', Aubrey declared fairly typically in 1696.

> Infants are very sensible of these irradiations of the eyes. In Spain, France, etc., southern countries, the nurses and parents are very shy to let people look upon

their very young children, for fear of fascination. In Spain they take it ill if one looks on a child, and make one say, God bless it. They talk of *mal de ojos.*

Reginald Scot noted earlier the widespread belief that 'the coral preserveth such as bear it from fascination or bewitching, and in this respect they are hanged about children's necks'.[52]

Amulets were only one weapon available. Many rituals were performed to protect infants, to ensure them luck, to make them grow and to cure their ailments. 'We nowadays have no objection to pulling children through fires', a Welsh text of the 1590s observed, 'or to turn them on the anvil of the smith, or to put them on the edge or mouth of the mill.' Passing infants through stones and rock formations, through trees, under tables or between the legs of adults is also recorded for other parts of Europe. In Scotland, France and Italy, babies might be kept in niches by the fire-place or popped for a moment in the bread-oven, particularly when it was thought they might have been bewitched. A Renaissance song from Tuscany refers to taking a child suffering from the evil eye to a healer in the country: 'She wants us to hold him for days on end, practically naked, behind the bread-oven'. In Florence, according to a seventeenth-century account, babies were also protected against epilepsy and other ills by having them scalded or cauterized by a barber immediately after baptism.[53] At Tarascon, mothers had their children touched by the local ritual dragon, the Tarasque.

These practices were often linked to calendar customs and the 'magic' of the Church associated with them. In parts of France at Candlemas, the father 'let fall a few drops of wax from the Candlemas candle on to the hair of each of his children, to protect them'. In the Confolentais, infants were blessed in church on Ash Wednesday, and in the Limousin on the first Palm Sunday or Holy Thursday following their birth. In the latter case, 'the ceremony consisted of exposing them for an instant in front of the altar where the Adoration was'. More dramatically, among the Sarakatsani, 'at Easter, a bloody cross from the Paschal Lamb was dabbed on the shoulders of child-en'. In Rumania at Whit, young children were given to the Căluş dancers to hold or have their hats put on them – to ensure good health and growth. Children might also be danced over as they lay on a blanket. In many parts of France again in modern times, mothers took their babies at Corpus Christi to places on the processional route where the host on its litter was from time to time deposited. Then, when the procession resumed, 'they rushed up and rolled their infants on the cloth where the body of God had rested', especially if they were ailing, or they might assemble at the final station, where the priest would bless all the children.[54] Even more widespread were the rituals linked with St John's Eve or Day. Then, babies might be put in the bonfire smoke until they coughed, laid in the ashes of the fire, or blessed by the priest and sprinkled with holy water.

Many other religious elements were used in the protective magic with which young children were surrounded. The fifteenth-century legist Nider noted that witches could attack even baptized children, causing them to languish and preventing them from growing, 'if they were not guarded by the sign of the cross and prayers', a view echoed by demonologists like Guazzo. There is no doubt that this reflects popular practice. One of the Lancashire witches tried in 1612, confessed that she had been visited by her familiar with her child on her knee. She had at once exclaimed: 'Jesus save my child'. As Aubrey notes, the invocation of God's blessing was the obvious and standard way to counter any possibility of fascination by the evil eye. In the Basque country, an ambivalent kind of fairy known as *Laminak* had the power 'to make away with young babies when they sneezed unless there was somebody present to say *Dominichtekun* (*Dominus tecum*)'.[55]

Religious objects and substances were also used to protect infants. The *Malleus Maleficarum* referred to a case at Speyer in which a devout woman had had a quarrel with a reputed witch.

> In the night she wished to put her little sucking child in its cradle, and remembered her encounter that day with the suspected witch. So, fearing some danger to the child, she placed consecrated herbs under it, sprinkled it with holy water, put a little blessed salt to its lips, signed it with the sign of the cross, and diligently secured the cradle.

Walpurga Hausmännin declared at Dillingen in 1587, according to the Fugger newsletter, that she was unable to harm children, 'if they were protected by holy water'. We have seen that sacramentals and objects associated with saints were used as protective amulets, also that children might be dressed in religious clothes. Richard Ford saw little children in Franciscan garb in early nineteenth-century Spain, 'whose parents had vowed to clothe them in the robes of this order, provided its sainted founder preserved their darlings during measles or dentition'.[56]

The aid of saints was harnessed in other ways. Being named after a saint implied being placed under his or her guardianship. In modern Greece, St Andrew is implored to make weakly children 'strong', a typical example. Infants were touched against relics and statues or passed through or under them, especially during processions. An English anti-Catholic tract of 1633 referred to Catholic parents 'kissing their babies and kneeling to wooden ladies'. In Aragón, babies were handed through the cloak of the Virgin of La Pilarica. A piece of the child's clothing might be placed under the altar cloth on which mass was celebrated, and babies themselves were presented at altars. 'In some areas of England in the late medieval period, babies might be placed on the altar at their mothers' churching and their lips and tongue cleansed with communion wine.' In the Abruzzi and elsewhere, infants were 'passed over the altar of the village church' in pairs or groups. This formed a godparenthood-like bond between the children and their mothers.[57] Many shrines specialized in children's ailments or were resorted to when difficulties arose at any stage of the child's development, and we will return to these.

We should also mention lullabies here. Their primary function was to soothe babies and to make them sleep, though more specific reference might be made to teething and other troubles. Many commentators have noted the spell-like nature of lullabies. Where sleep was being invoked, it was personified and wished on the child in a mode similar to charms used to remove illnesses or counter other dangers or to the supposed spells of witches. Mother 'knows the counter-charm for every spell', ran a Rumanian lullaby quite specifically: 'Sleep, my baby, in thy bed'. English and Sicilian lullabies, to go no further, refer to coral and bells, amulets used we have seen to protect the baby, and everywhere the well-being of the child was invoked both in the present and the future. The function of the singer here was much like that of the imaginary Fates, and the destiny of the child varied of course according to its gender. In two typical examples from Corsica, courage was wished for a boy, and beauty and a good marriage for a girl. 'When you grow up', the boy was told,

> You will bear arms.
> Neither *voltigeurs* nor *gendarmes*
> Will frighten you.
> If you are provoked,
> You will become a proud bandit ...

The girl was assured by contrast:

> When you grow up,
> We will make your trousseau,
> The chemise and the skirt,
> Your blouse made
> Of finely woven cloth ...
> We will give you in marriage
> To a man of standing,
> A fine catch ...[58]

Lullabies often invoked religious protectors for the child. A Russian example appealed to an angel to save the baby 'from all sorrow, from all misfortune, from distress, from bloodshed, from the evil of hostile men'. A Spanish example refers to the Christ Child being rocked by Sts Anne and Joachim, its grandparents:

Then sleep, thou too, my baby,
My little heart, so dear;
The Virgin is beside thee,
The Son of God is near.[59]

Many lullabies from all over Europe called on the saints as protectors.

Beyond such positive actions, there were many negative taboos to be adhered to in relation to infants. The nails were not to be cut until a specific period had elapsed, often six months or a year. In the Yonne in the late nineteenth century, the nails were not cut until the child had begun to talk and above all until it could say: 'Salt'. In parts of southern Europe in modern times, the first nail-cutting was a ritual event, at which godparent-type relationships could again be formed. In some places, the nails were not cut but bitten by the mother or another woman. If this course were not followed in Minho, the child might 'become mute'. Similar notions attached to the hair, though in the Charente boys' hair had to be cut early, because long hair would 'draw the strength out of them'. In Provence, the first hair-cutting had ideally to take place 'on a particular saint's day, St Mary Magdalene's if possible, to ensure strong hair'.[60] In Sicily, knots were left in babies' hair in the belief that the 'house-women' or Fates had tied them and that the child would be adversely affected if they were removed. Behind both kinds of taboo, lay the fear that nails and hair, being in some way part of the person from which they came, might be used in hostile magic against them. As with the cord and the placenta, special care was taken over their disposal. Infants might also be protected, cured or harmed via their clothes. Leaving a baby's clothes out at night, for example, was dangerous.

Special precautions surrounded the infant's sleeping arrangements. Sicilian mothers would say: 'In God's Name', as they lifted their babies from their cradles, but also: 'By your leave, ladies', referring to the 'house-women' again. One had to be careful, too, in Corsica and elsewhere not to lay babies down with their feet towards the door, for this was the way that corpses left the house. Again, it was very risky to rock the cradle when it was empty, and there were special shrines to which children were taken in Portugal to cure them of the effects of such carelessness or malice. Since it made children wild and ungovernable (hyperactive, we might say), one of these shrines was that of Sao Marcos da Serra in the Algarve, where the saint's image had a bull, the Evangelist's symbol, under its feet. The child's head was knocked against the bull, while the mother recited this formula:

> My Lord St Mark
> Who tamest wild bulls,
> Tame me this son,
> Who is worse than all the devils.[61]

More general was ritual concealment or neglect aimed to deflect the envy associated with the evil eye. We have seen that babies were often kept out of sight at least until they had been baptized. The custom was continued in a Fenland village until recently of keeping babies in veils and away from daylight until they were three months old. For the same reasons much-desired boys were not distinguished from girls until fairly late on as a rule. They both had long hair and they wore the same clothes. In pre-Famine Ireland, boys were dressed in long frocks like girls until they were about ten years old, it was said to deceive the fairies. Often, too, babies of both genders were dressed in old clothes and kept in a dirty and unattractive state.

Some medical writers in Germany and the Netherlands advocated regular bathing of babies in the sixteenth and seventeenth centuries. Overcoming the idea that contact between the human skin and water was actually harmful, French doctors did the same from the eighteenth century. In criticizing current practice, both provided some scandalized historians with a catalogue of parental 'neglect'. In fact both doctors and historians were misled here, as they were intended to be. As more empathetic scholars have emphasized, such 'neglect' stemmed from a belief that 'one of the best protectors of the baby was its dirt'. 'The child passes its first years in filth, rashes and lice', a French folklorist noted in 1900, 'which even educated people regard as the natural conduits of the humours and as preservers against the diseases that lie in wait for it.' Particular importance was attached to leaving a crust of dirt on top of the baby's head, and this was retained even when more general bathing had been introduced, for example in Poland before the First World War or Salazar's Portugal. In Portugal, 'washing the baby's head was delayed until it had learned to say the name of Jesus, and when it was washed, the sign of the cross was made on its shoulders'. Elsewhere, as in parts of Britain in the modern period, the palms of the child's hands, or sometimes just of the right hand, would be left unwashed, in order to preserve its 'luck'. There was a belief, too, in the protective effect of parasites. Sébillot wrote of Upper Brittany in the late nineteenth century: 'I have known farmers who were very clean and who regularly combed their children's hair, but who always took care to leave two or three lice on their heads', in the belief that they 'would eat up their bad blood' and keep them healthy. In the Charente similarly, lice were a sign of health and 'sucked the bad blood'.[62]

Besides general protection, magico-religious ritual was associated with the different stages in the infant's progress. The Ancient Romans had deities linked to these stages: one who guarded the cradle, one who put the child on its legs, and so on. Things were not quite so schematic in pre-modern Europe, but the crucial phases were marked.

A lot of nonsense has been written about swaddling by historians guided by their own twentieth-century views about child-rearing and by eighteenth- and nineteenth-century 'enlightened' critiques of a practice 'no longer fashionable'. The practice of wrapping new-born babies in bands is found all over the world and was normal in Europe for all classes from Roman times onwards (see Plate 24). Abandoned in 'developed' areas by the nineteenth century, it survived in remoter places – the Balkans, the Alps, the Massif Central of France, central and southern Italy – and among the poor into the twentieth century. Its purpose was multiple. It was convenient, allowing the baby to be moved and carried easily. It kept the child warm and well-sheltered – everyone tended to wear a great deal of clothing by modern standards; it also kept the child safe from animals and hazards, especially since a swaddled baby could be suspended away from the ground. 'I was nursed with care in swaddling cloths', declared a verse of The Wisdom of Solomon, expressing the conventional wisdom too.[63] There is little evidence that swaddling was seen as a means of deliberate restraint, though in Greater Russia it was aimed at preventing the baby from harming itself by scratching and so on. Positively and related to our specific concerns, swaddling was regarded as an important means of forming the baby and ensuring that it developed properly.

It was often felt that the soft flesh of the baby needed to be 'hardened'. There was also a stress on producing erectness and straightness. The baby must be swaddled, a French doctor wrote in 1675, when medical opinion still accorded with popular views on the subject, 'in order to give his little body the upright form that is most decent and which suits a man, and to accustom him to walk on his two feet; for without it, he would perhaps go on all-fours like most other animals'. Jane Sharp's manual for midwives of 1671 also advocated swaddling: 'For infants are tender twigs and, as you use them, so they will grow straight or crooked', a common view. Mistral, who was born in Provence in 1830, recalled that he had been tightly bound as a baby at his grandmother's insistence, and she later quoted a proverbial saying to justify this: 'Babies who are well-swaddled are neither bandy-legged nor knock-kneed'. Similarly Hélias in early twentieth-century Brittany had been 'tightly swaddled ... in order that my legs and back would be strengthened. Everyone dreaded lameness'.[64] In Provence and elsewhere, the removal of swaddling bands coincided with the baby's first stage of walking, a point to which we will return.

It should also be noted that there was considerable variety in styles of swaddling across Europe. In some places (and for some time), the new-born were tightly bound all over. 'Even my arms were so tightly bound to my hips', Hélias wrote, 'that I looked like a miniature mummy or ... like the baby in La Tour's painting of the Nativity ... in the Rennes museum.' Indeed, in medieval and some early modern sculpture and painting in the East and the West, the Christ Child and other babies appear cocoon-like, only their faces showing. But other sources refer to 'light' swaddling, and Margery Kempe promised in her meditation on the Nativity: 'Lord ... I will not bind You tight'. Sometimes, the baby's arms were left free, as in Della Robbia's medallions on the Ospedale degli Innocenti in Florence, dating from 1487, where the bands are more a means of securing an under-robe than a covering in their own right. Elaborate swaddling was everywhere only within the means of the well-to-do anyway, the poor making do with rags and bits of old clothing. It is also clear that total swaddling was associated particularly with the period immediately after birth and almost certainly with the need for special protection then, if not concealment. In Lucania in modern times, where babies were totally swaddled and where they were kept swaddled for a year at least, they were unswaddled and reswaddled twice daily in ritual fashion. The 'yards and yards of swaddling', moreover, were intended to distract hostile spirits, and amulets were carefully bound into the bands to give full protection.[65] In many places, the bands were either progressively removed or changed for a robe, usually well before the baby was a year old.

Teething was recognized as a time of particular danger and difficulty. 'Fine baby until the teeth came', said a French proverb. Many of the amulets with which infants were guarded had a particular link with teething. This is most obvious where the protective object was actually a tooth. In the modern Limousin, 'to facilitate teething, the general custom was to catch a live mole (sometimes a male for boys and a female for girls) and to pull out one of its teeth, which was then put in a sachet around the child's neck'. Elsewhere in France, the whole skull of the mole, with its sharp teeth, was used, and the mole was killed slowly, 'its suffering, in some way, acting as a substitute for the child, who would teethe painlessly as a result'. Wolves' teeth, vipers' heads and bones cut in the shape of teeth are mentioned in other sources. In Flanders a key that had touched the stole of St Hubert was used as a teething amulet, St Hubert being associated particularly with the prevention and cure of rabies, a disease caused by biting. Sometimes amulets became teething necklaces, on which babies were encouraged to rub their gums. Coral was often used as a teething ring or dummy, because of its apotropaic qualities. Babies' gums were also rubbed with coral, and with other symbolic substances or objects: salt, herbs, seeds, wine, hare's brains, a cock's crest.

Quite often it was believed that dentition had to be deliberately provoked. Leproux refers to the reputation of coral in the Charente 'for bringing out the teeth'. Thomas Phaire wrote in his *Book of Children* of 1544 of the same quality of coral and other things 'to cause an easy breeding of teeth'.[66] Lancing the gums was common practice in eighteenth-century England, and doubtless at other times and places, at least among those who could afford the surgeon's fees.

The appearance of the first tooth was frequently the occasion for celebration, and further ritual. The pattern of teething could be significant. Early teething was an omen of death in Scotland and northern England, and the appearance of the first tooth in the lower jaw could also be taken as a bad sign for the child. As with other bodily discards, great care was taken over the disposal of the first tooth to fall and often of all milk teeth. In different parts of France, they might be buried, burned or retained in the family. The first tooth lost might be treated as an amulet. In Spain and Portugal, it might be thrown away by the child over its shoulder or on to the roof of the house, while a special formula was recited, for example:

> Tooth away,
> A better one in its place;
> In praise of St John;
> May he give me another better one,
> Wherewith to eat bread.

In parts of Britain and Germany, there was a fear that if an animal got hold of milk teeth, the child's adult teeth would resemble those of that animal. Aubrey related that German children threw their milk teeth into a dark corner of the house, as if to the mice, but saying: 'Mouse! Here I give thee a tooth of bone, but give thou me an iron one'.[67] The tooth fairy seems to be a modern invention.

We have seen that babies might be taken out of their swaddling bands when it was judged time for them to walk, and any intermediate stage seems to have been discouraged. Crawling, as the French doctor cited and many other authors noted, was a beast-like means of locomotion that humans of any age ought to avoid. It is significant that child-walkers were employed among most social classes and that very young babies might use them, if Bosch's picture of the Christ Child with the pinwheel and the walker of around 1490 is to be believed. Swaddling was thought again to strengthen the back and limbs for walking, and some of the other rituals that we have described had the same aim. Babies were placed on the Corpus Christi stations in the Vosges in the nineteenth century, 'in the hope that they would acquire strength from this and walk sooner'.[68]

The child's first steps were often taken in a very specific ritual context. Mistral relates that, when he was about six months old, 'my mother carried me to church on St Joseph's Day, according to Provençal custom; and then, on the saint's altar, holding me with reins and while my godmother sang: "Come, come, come", they made me take my first steps'. Elsewhere in Provence, the ceremony of 'the first step' or 'giving the child its feet' took place at Easter. Shoes were sometimes put on babies for the first time then in church, and they were made to take their first steps at the Elevation or when the bells were rung for the Gloria. First steps might also be taken on altars of the Virgin or in anticlerical areas of France during the Third Republic in front of the statue of Marianne in the vestibule of the town hall. Another venue was the cemetery, which linked the child with the ancestors buried there. Symbolic gifts were given on these occasions: salt, bread and so on. In Provence, a boy was sometimes presented with a 'St Joseph's stick', perhaps to represent the male member.[69]

Given the distaste for crawling, delay in learning to walk could be a serious practical problem as well as a source of anxiety and shame for a family. Special relics or shrines might be resorted to in these circumstances, the relevant saint having some connection very often with feet or walking. In Provence in modern times, the child 'might be taken to the chapel of Saint-Symphorien at Vernègues or of Saint-Pancrace at Puyloubier, both saints being curers of lameness; at both there was a stone with a hole in it, into which the baby's feet were placed'. At Donchéry in Champagne, the relics of St Onesimus, a Roman martyr who had his legs broken, were exposed and processed annually. 'If there were infants who could not walk because of weakness in their limbs', an account of 1833 reported, 'two women walking each side of the *châsse* passed them from one to the other under the relics three or four times, convinced that this would cure them of their infirmity.' In Provence again, a more elaborate ritual took place at La Roquebrusanne near Brignoles. According to a writer in 1896,

> a dance called the dance of the Child Jesus is performed [in the church], in aid of infants slow in walking. On the day of the patron saint, after mass, the mothers take their babies in their arms and form a group in front of the altar of the Child Jesus, where one of them begins to sing these words:
>
> > Jump on the right foot,
> > Jump on the left foot,
> > My good little Jesus!
> > Jump on both feet!
>
> The singer makes the appropriate gestures to accompany the words and the others follow her.[70]

Talking was regarded in a similar way, marking a decisive turning-point that could be expressed in ritual. In parts of France, we have seen, the child's nails were not cut until it had learned to talk. Often great importance was attached to the first word itself. This could be a religious word like 'Jesus', or the name of some protective substance. In modern Spain the first word taught to babies was often *ajo* or garlic, that is an amulet effective against the evil eye, and the word was repeated around babies for this reason; it was also believed to prevent speech defects. These or an unusual delay in learning to talk might be attributed to the breaking of taboos, like cutting the nails. In Portugal it was believed that a child would remain dumb if it saw itself in a mirror or had its hair cut before it learned to speak. In the Abruzzi stammering was 'caused by the wet-nurse (or mother) not having touched the infant's tongue, or because the godmother or godfather made a mistake in saying the Creed at the baptism'. Talking could be induced by a variety of means: rubbing the child's tongue with magical and religious substances including salt and frankincense; cutting the flap beneath the tongue – which was *de rigueur* in many parts of Europe until recently and was done at birth or baptism; ringing bells; or carrying out more complex ritual. In modern Portugal, to make a dumb or backward child speak, his godmother carries him in a sack on her back to three (or seven or nine) houses. At each of these she begs on his behalf:

> Alms for the child of the bag
> Which would speak but cannot.

She is given food, some of which she eats herself, giving the rest to the child, and she must leave from a different door than the one she came in by. The word for 'bag' also means 'lungs'.[71] The aid of saints was also invoked, and many shrines from the medieval period onwards specialized in speech therapy.

Weaning came late as a rule, though, as we have seen, solid foods might be given alongside breast milk from within a few weeks of birth. There was no fixed rule as there was among Muslims and Jews laying down how long breast-feeding should last, but anywhere between eighteen months and two years seems to have been usual in Christian Europe in the medieval and early modern periods. Elites tended to wean earlier than peasants and the poor, a pattern maintained into modern times. Quite often among peasants, weaning might be delayed even later to two and a half or three years, for example in Montenegro, in the Limousin and in the Tyrol in this century, and cases are reported of children still taking the breast at the age of six or seven. A natural time to wean was with the appearance of teeth, and this seems quite often to have been a guiding factor, though there were also firm contrary views. According to the marquise de Bombelles in 1781, it was thought by some that 'nothing was so dangerous as weaning a baby at the moment that its teeth are coming out'. Early weaning signalled a crisis. Hermann von Weinsberg, born in 1518, 'was weaned prematurely, within five months of his birth, after a spring plague rendered his mother too ill to nurse him'. Orphans, foundlings and babies of prospective wet-nurses might also be weaned sooner than normal. There is some evidence, too, that girls were weaned earlier than boys. A child would also be weaned if its mother became pregnant, an eventuality that was discouraged for nursing women, as we have seen. Popular and medical opinion agreed that it was highly undesirable for a pregnant woman to suckle. One child would be competing with the other, the milk versus the blood of the womb. As a saying from the Charente put it: 'The first child sucks the feet of the next'.[72]

There were two strategies in weaning: either to do it gradually or to make a sudden break from the breast. In the latter case, the nursling might be discouraged by smearing some bitter substance on the breast, such as aloes or mustard. 'He draws his mouth away from the nipple, *tpu, tpu*', as St Bernardino of Siena described it in a sermon, 'and spits.' Juliet's nurse recalled the occasion when she had been weaned, 'for I had then laid worm-wood to my dug'.[73] The child and the mother or nurse could also be separated for a period.

Whenever and however done, weaning was a significant step, which could affect the temper and the health of the baby. Magical and religious precautions therefore surrounded it. At Arles, for example, in modern times 'a snake-skin was put around an infant at the time of weaning according to an old belief in the apotropaic qualities of the snake'. Care was also taken about the time or season for weaning. Abbé Thiers noted that weaning on Good Friday was believed in northern France to be unlucky; while in Scotland May was to be avoided. Jane Sharp's *Midwives' Book* of 1671 advised positively that 'the best time to wean the child is either Spring or the fall of the leaf, the moon increasing'.[74] In Russia, wet-nurses had often weaned their own infants after three major fasts, in practice a period of around eighteen months. In the American South in the early nineteenth century, Fanny Kemble found that many mothers wished to avoid weaning in the summer heat and so nursed through two summers as a rule. Some French mothers, on the contrary, believed that they should not nurse through some dates or festivals twice. For example, a baby suckled through two Good Fridays would become a cretin. Weaning was nearly always regarded as irreversible. In northern Germany, children who started to suckle again after having been weaned were in danger of becoming vampires.

Behind many of these practices and procedures lay the idea that the child had to be 'formed', that its growth was not a simple natural process to be taken for granted. So straight limbs had to be made by swaddling, teeth encouraged to 'breed', walking upright specifically brought about. 'In every matter we know what to do', wet-nurses boasted in a Carnival song from Tuscany in the Renaissance period,

> So that the baby grows up quickly;
> As long as he stays straight and firm,
> We don't mind getting tired.

Many of the rituals we have described were intended simply to make the child grow, and failure to grow or to grow straight might be attributed to breaking taboos. In modern Portugal, for example, if a child's 'clothes are wrung out in the wash, his growth will be twisted. If another child jumps over him at play, he will never grow any taller'. In the sixteenth and seventeenth centuries such ideas were shared by the elite and informed pedagogical theory and practice. Erasmus declared that 'human beings are not born but formed'. 'Listen, fathers of the house', went one of Jacob Cats' emblematic verses in seventeenth-century Holland, 'the tender youth',

> Must from the start be bent toward virtue.

The metaphor of 'licking' or 'beating' a child into shape was also very commonly employed, the former being based on supposed animal practice.[75]

More particular and on the practical level again was the practice of moulding parts of babies' bodies to a desired shape. If a baby girl's 'nose should appear misshapen' at birth, according to Jacopone da Todi, her mother will

> push and tug and pull at it,
> So utterly reshape it,
> That the girl will have no trouble
> Competing with her sisters [in the marriage stakes].

Writers on child-care from that time down to the seventeenth century, if not later, also advised pulling the nose as well as flattening the ears, moulding the head and altering other parts of the body, and this reflected actual practice. Thomas Pennant commented with surprise in 1769 on seeing a boy on Skye 'with erect ears [that] had never been swaddled down'. Gélis has drawn attention to the custom of binding babies' heads to make them longer or rounder, found in many parts of Europe in the past and which survived in a few areas of south-western and western France until the end of the nineteenth century.

Such binding could permanently deform the skull and distinct local variations in style existed.[76] In seventeenth-century France, midwives massaged
and pulled female babies' nipples to make them bigger.

We will deal with the healing of children along with that of adults in Part
III, but it is worth broaching the subject briefly here, since some historians
have misguidedly stated or suggested that parents in the past were indifferent
towards their offspring and their health. Nothing could be further from the
case. Children and often young infants figured significantly in the various
kinds of general healing to be discussed. What is more, there were specific
diagnoses and cures for particular childhood ailments, and there were healers
and shrines that specialized in them.

There were specific treatments, magical and religious, for infantile worms,
for example. In southern France, according to an account of 1754, the infested
child was laid out by women on a table surrounded by nine candles. One said:
'This little Job has nine worms; he has nine too many; may they be reduced to
eight'; and one of the candles was extinguished. The formula was repeated
until all the candles had been blown out, and this diminishing charm was
supposed to get rid of the worms. Two charms found in the Ain in 1886
invoked religious powers. One commanded the parasite: 'Worm, I forbid you
to do further harm to this child than to Our Lord Jesus Christ when he was
inside his mother, the Blessed Virgin Mary's womb, and I will say five Paters
and five Aves'. The other commanded a saint: 'You, St Médard, who has every
power, remove the worms from this child. They are in league to strangle
babies. They come from nothing; you can make them return there'.[77] Similar
remedies existed in other countries.

There were also specific cures for convulsions, associated often with
worms, rickets, impetigo, thrush, whooping-cough and chickenpox, to name
but a few. Aubrey in late seventeenth-century England referred to a cure for
'the thrush', which involved placing the heads of live frogs inside the child's
mouth and holding them there until they died. The same cure (for
whooping-cough) is reported in nineteenth-century Suffolk. Both transferred the illness from the child's throat to the frogs.

Many childhood complaints (like those of adults) were more vaguely
described and are less easy to identify with modern diseases. One such was
'the shrivelled child' syndrome, apparently known all over Hungary down to
recent times. 'This sickness according to a modern healer, Mrs Palkó, attacks
only infants, or they contract it even before birth because their mother kicked
a dog'; or the pregnant mother is bewitched 'without ... noticing anything,
and the spell goes into the bones, into the stomach, and that causes her to
have a shrivelled child'. The remedy was 'to boil the shrivelled child'. Mrs
Palkó's boiling spell involved stealing water from three different springs or

wells and three splinters from three different wooden blocks. Then the water was boiled, using the splinters as kindling. The child was held naked over the boiling water; and two other children were required to walk round the house and one to sprinkle the water on the baby. This child asked the woman in charge: 'What are you boiling, Godmother?' 'Old man and old flesh!', she replied. 'Boil it! Boil it! until it gets thick like fat', said the child. The process was repeated three times. Mrs Palkó commented of a particular baby, cured in this way: 'I boiled her three times. And you should see what a nice girl she has become! As if one had packed meat on to her bones'.[78] This sufficiently explains the ritual involved in the cure, and is another illustration of the need felt to make rather than let the child grow.

A range of similar ailments was attributed to the evil eye, against which special precautions were taken, as we have seen. In the Condado region of Spain, for example, in modern times, the symptoms of suffering from the evil eye included emaciation and listlessness, as well as loose bowels, vomiting and cold sweats. The first recourse was to diagnose the complaint correctly, for which the child would be taken to an expert woman.

> At Cabanas de Yepes, the woman cuts some hairs from the child, and, holding them in her hands, one over the other, says: Three, you have the evil eye, and four, I hold you to be un-witched. Jesus, Joseph, Mary and the Holy Trinity. If, on sepa-rating the hands, the hairs jump up, it is certain that the child is suffering from the effects of the evil eye; if not, the doctor is called, since the baby must be ill for some other reason.

Elsewhere in Spain, three women are consulted, and divination with drops of oil in a vessel of water is practised, a procedure also followed in Corsica down to recent times. Treatment was of various kinds, sometimes involving the same practioner, sometimes not. A typical prayer-charm from Spanish Galicia went:

> God gave you,
> God made you,
> And God will take off the evil eye,
> If anyone has cast it on you.

'A famous undoer of the evil eye of Guadalajara in the sixteenth century, Maria de Medina, placed on the head of the victim one empty dish and another full of water. Then she asked the name of the child and poured off the water.' In recent times in the Salamanca district, 'the affected child was passed three times through smoke produced by burning the feathers of a particular bird, various flowers and herbs, the teeth of a hedgehog, straw and a piece of a priest's stole'. A Danish cure, reported in 1880, carried out on the advice of an itinerant beggar woman, involved burying the child alive for a while, a kind of 'symbolic death', from which it was resurrected.[79]

Children were important among patients at shrines. Among the votive offerings found by papal commissioners at the shrine of St Thomas Cantilupe at Hereford in 1307, for example, were ninety-five silk and linen children's shifts, and cures of children were also reported in medieval England at the shrines of St Thomas at Canterbury, St Frideswide at Oxford and St Wulfstan at Worcester. The same picture is found on the Continent.

Some shrines specialized in infant cures. A few examples may be cited from the many described by Leproux in the Charentes in modern times. Lichères was one.

> When a child was languishing or peaky in a particular way, the mother went to the fountain of St Denis just outside the town; she said a few Paters on her knees, and then threw into the fountain the bonnet or vest of the little patient. If the garment sank at once to the bottom, the illness was incurable; but if it floated for a while, the child would recover. In this case, the mother took some water from the fountain and went to the church to pray in front of the banner of St Denis. Sometimes she had a mass said and left a piece of bread and a lump of lard on the altar. The water from the fountain was used as a drink and to bathe the child.

Similarly, the chapel and fountain of St Sulpice at Montrollet were visited for infant diseases generally but particularly for stomach trouble and convulsions. Of the modern devotions in the department of the Charente 13 per cent and in the department of the Charente-Maritime 18 per cent were specially concerned with the illnesses of children.[80]

A similar situation is found in the diocese of Meaux. For example, at the chapel of St Lié at Savins, which was demolished in 1793, though the cross and fountain remained, 'people implored the saint for children who were *liés* or knotted and for those with rickets or illnesses of the head. St Lié was believed to "stiffen" the children'. At Saint-Loup-de-Naud, the saint was invoked against 'fear' (quite a common condition), fevers, convulsions and all infantile maladies. The child or clothing belonging to it was plunged in the water of a large pool and also placed in contact with the relics of the saint. In the diocese as a whole, the second largest category of illnesses catered for at local shrines was that concerning children. It is fair to conclude that 'children and their illnesses were the objects in traditional European societies of a great deal of anxiety and of a constant vigilance'.[81]

11

Death and the Dead

In pre-modern Europe death loomed larger in people's lives, given the high mortality rate, than it does today. Death was frequent, public, inescapable. As in other traditional societies, too, 'death was never considered as a purely natural event'.[1] It always had religious and magical dimensions. Given the ultimate mystery of death, moreover, death rites and beliefs were less completely Christianized than most others.

In all parts of Europe, deaths were announced by signs. Very common was the howling of a dog, especially at an unusual time, or the cry or just the appearance of a bird. 'It is observed', wrote Richard Gough in 1701,

> that if the chief person of the family that inhabits this farm [of Kayhowell] do fall sick, if his sickness be to death, there comes a pair of pigeons to the house about a fortnight or a week before the person's death, and continue there until the person's death.

Certain birds or certain kinds of cry were particularly significant, for example, a cock crowing unusually in the night or a chicken or a hen crowing like a rooster, or the call of a crow, a magpie or an owl, the bird of the night. While Macbeth is killing Duncan in Shakespeare's play, Lady Macbeth hears a sound:

> It was the owl that shriek'd, the fatal bellman,
> Which gives the stern'st good-night.

Tapping on windows by magpies or robins was also noted as an omen of death in England and Ireland. The behaviour of animals could also indicate an imminent death. Dogs or cows sensed the death and might stand unnaturally still or run about wildly.

> Other omens are drawn from household occurrences: [for example, in the Welsh Border country] if one of the family portraits or photographs falls from the wall; if the furniture emits loud raps; if a glass, or a glass bowl or vase, shatters for no reason; if candle wax drags to form a 'winding-sheet'; if someone brings a spade or axe into the house; if a badly folded sheet or table-cloth has a coffin-shaped crease at the centre.[2]

Other signs had to do with ritual, including that of death itself. In Anjou and the Vosges in the nineteenth century, if 'the church clock rang the hour just as the host was being elevated', this meant that someone in the parish would die within the week. In Rumania, if the shadow of the Căluş flag paraded at Whit fell on someone, he or she would soon die. In Russia and elsewhere, simply to encounter a funeral cortège might be a presage of death for oneself. People also had visions or dreams of death-bed scenes or wakes or ghosts. Iorwerth Peate recalled that his father and grandfather were both carpenters in a Welsh village and therefore made coffins. His father used to hear the sound of sawing, planing and hammering, that is the symbolic preparation of a coffin during the night before a death. Later, when the family house had ceased to be a carpenter's shop, the inhabitants still used to hear the same sound. The premonition could also take the form of seeing a spirit. The person about to die appeared to a close relative. For example, 'a woman in the Swedish village of Vik saw her father, whom she knew was at sea at the time, standing by her bed dripping wet and the very same night her father drowned at sea'. In another case, from Norway, a woman saw her mother walking along a path, although she was not fit enough to go out: 'two days later she was dead'. Here one might be warned of one's own death by seeing or meeting one's own spirit or 'double', as in parts of Corsica. Certain people were much more likely to have knowledge of deaths than others: those with second sight and holy persons or saints. St Severinus of Cologne, for example, 'saw' and 'heard' St Martin of Tours being carried to heaven by angels, though his priestly companion, 'not of great enough merit', did not.[3]

It was also believed in many parts of Europe that insight into deaths in the community could be gained on certain ritual occasions, usually in or by the church and on performing particular acts. In Scotland, if a person sat in the church porch on St Martin's Day (11 November) until one o'clock in the morning, 'he or she would see the ghosts pass of all the neighbours who were to die within the year'. Similar beliefs were found in northern England in the early modern and modern periods, sometimes attached to St Mark's Eve in April or Midsummer Eve. In Wales, down to modern times, 'one might see who was going to die in the parish in the forthcoming year, if one looked through the keyhole of the church door at midnight' at Hallowe'en. In the Morbihan, 'a person, who fasted on Christmas Eve from daybreak until that moment in the evening when he could count nine stars, saw Death at the Midnight Mass touch those he would take during the following year'.[4]

Here the insight was voluntarily gained, but in other cases, the role of seer or predicter of deaths was not chosen. This is the case with the 'watcher of the churchyard' found in many parts of Britain and the Breton *ankou*. The

DEATH AND THE DEAD

'watcher of the churchyard' was a role taken on by any person buried there 'until such time as he [or she] was relieved of his [or her] task by the interment of another corpse'. The watcher did not 'go to his [or her] rest' but 'was compelled to guard the graves in the churchyard and to summon all those in the parish who were about to die'. This was done by the watcher travelling 'by night through the countryside in a cart, the sound of which was a sure omen of death', and stopping outside the house of the person summoned. The role of the *ankou* was very similar. The *ankou* was the last person to die in a parish during the year. He also travelled about at night in a cart, whose sound was an omen of death. But the *ankou* touched his victims or sometimes struck them with a scythe made of human bones, and some accounts make it clear that the *ankou* did not simply announce deaths that had been pre-ordained; he actually caused them. Moreover, the *ankou* was sometimes regarded as an independent supernatural being rather than the ghost of a particular deceased person.[5]

In many areas in Corsica, it was believed that all deaths in the community were brought about by a person or persons who had this specific role to fulfil. They were known most commonly as *mazzeri*, that is 'strikers' or 'killers'. Actual people in the village, men or women, knew themselves to be and were generally recognized as *mazzeri*. They went hunting at night, in dreams or as 'doubles', since their bodies did not usually leave their beds. They hunted alone or in groups, and their hunting grounds were the wildest part of the *maquis* or scrubland and especially near rivers and springs. They found and killed the first animal which they saw. This was often a wild boar, but it might be another wild, or even a domestic, animal, or a bird. As they slung their quarry on to their backs, the *mazzeri* recognized by its face or its voice that it was the 'double' or 'spirit' of someone in the village, The person so recognized would die shortly after the hunt and always within the year. Illness might be caused by simply wounding the animal. Male *mazzeri* usually killed their victims with guns, and women with sticks or knives, or even with their own teeth like hunting dogs. Some sources refer to *mazzeri* actually turning themselves into dogs or other animals; others to their killing people 'by drinking up their souls', if they encountered them at noonday in a solitary place. Whatever the means, *mazzeri* only killed members of their own community. In some parts of Corsica, it was believed further that on one night in the year, usually the night of 31 July, the *mazzeri* from different villages met to fight each other. Those killed in this dream-conflict would themselves die during the coming year. Some *mazzeri* were 'odd' and were regarded with hostility, but most seem to have led normal lives, at least during the day, working, marrying, having children, though they were treated 'with a certain respect'. There is some uncertainty about how people became

11. Priest anointing the foot of a dying man. *Art or Craft to Lyve Well*, English, c. 1500.

mazzeri, though most commonly they were said to be persons who had not been properly baptized or whose godparents were *mazzeri*. Most accounts stress that the role of the *mazzeri* was involuntary and implied no hostility and incurred no blame: they were simply the agents of a mysterious power. There is some evidence which links them with the spirits of the dead. It is also reported that some *mazzeri* sought to be 'cured' or exorcized by undergoing special rituals of penance in the church, sometimes on Good Friday.[6]

When a person seemed to be moribund, action might be taken to divine whether he or she would survive or not. In many parts of France, this took the familiar form of placing an article of clothing belonging to the person in a sacred spring and seeing whether it sank or floated. The last rites were nearly always regarded in Catholic countries as essential to a proper death (see Text Figure 11 and Plate 31). Sometimes, they had magical accompaniments. In the

Sologne in the seventeenth century, for example, 'they were scrupulous to do the washing during the time that a sick person received extreme unction', presumably with a purificatory aim.[7]

Then there were procedures to ease the death and shorten the agony. A late medieval text, *Omne Bonum*, refers to 'the practice of singing the requiem mass to cause someone to die faster'. In Burgundy, Poitou and Lorraine in the nineteenth century, removing the feathers from the pillow of a dying person 'allowed the soul to depart more easily'. Elsewhere, this might be effected 'by placing the bed parallel to the beams of the house, by removing a tile from the roof, by lighting a candle in church, or by making a pilgrimage to a shrine whose saint specialized in relieving the moribund'.

> If a dying person [in Scandinavia] expresses the wish to die, a friend or relative climbs up on the roof of the house and calls out in a loud voice: Come up! – thereby calling [off] the evil spirit which is supposed to prevent the sufferer from departing this life in peace.

'In Dalmatia, the caul was placed under the owner's head when he lay on his death bed so that his passing would be easy.'[8] In the Périgord in modern times, the agony might be prolonged because a particular person was absent whom the dying person wanted to say goodbye to; while in Greece long death agonies were attributed to the fact that the person had failed to confess some crime or offence; once a confession had been elicited, then death came.

In *Le Moulin du Frau*, a fictional account of peasant life in the Périgord in the mid nineteenth century, Eugène Le Roy described a more elaborate non-clerical ritual for the dying. A 'sorcerer' visits Old Jardon on his death-bed after the priest has been. 'So as to keep away the Devil, he takes a pinch of salt from the salt-container hanging by the chimney and throws it into the fire, where it crackles.' He then uncovered the chest of the dying man, recited a prayer-charm, blew three times and placed a little bag with magical items in it on his chest. He put bowls of water in the four corners of the room, 'so that the soul of Old Jardon could wash itself before going up to heaven'. Later, when the man was actually dying, the sorcerer recited the White Paternoster, making signs with his left hand. When Jardon had died, the sorcerer closed his eyes and emptied the water bowls into the garden.[9]

The circumstances of the death might be significant. In the Sologne in the seventeenth century, a person dying turned towards the wall was in danger of being seized by the Devil. According to Transylvanian belief, certain people ascended directly to heaven: children under seven, nuns, and those who die between Easter and Pentecost. The explanation for the last category is that the gates of heaven are left open at this time 'for the Resurrection of Christ and his

Ascension'. There was a widespread belief that people were more likely to die at liminal times. This might be related to the tides or to day and night as well as seasons. Falstaff, according to Mistress Quickly, 'parted ev'n just between twelve and one, ev'n at the turning o' th' tide'. The idea that death occurs at ebb-tide was frequently found in coastal areas of Italy, France, Portugal, Britain, and it persisted into later centuries. 'People can't die, along the coast', said Mr Peggotty in Dickens' *David Copperfield*, 'except when the tide's pretty nigh out.' Emily Tennyson noted in 1867, when her father was dying in Lincolnshire: 'I sleep but little, but at the first glimmering of light I cannot rest having heard that the spirit so often departs as night and morning meet'.[10]

The corpse was both extremely vulnerable and extremely dangerous at or just after the moment of death. It had to be carefully watched over but also guarded against. Hence the importance of the ritual wake. Magical substances and herbs were also used to keep evil influences at bay, but the most important means of defence was light. In modern Translylvania, for example, once a person had died, candles were 'lit to protect the body from evil spirits and other dangers as well as to illuminate the deceased's journey to the other world. It is considered a great misfortune if someone dies "without light" ', for instance soldiers during war or those dying away from home in other circumstances. 'In addition to lighting candles in the house, a special wax candle is made; it is the length of the deceased's body and wound into a circular shape. This candle ... must be kept burning until the body is buried.' It again 'provides light for the deceased's journey; [and] it is considered dangerous for the soul if the light goes out'. In the past, it was also believed that this candle 'burned the sins of the newly deceased'. The candle was only extinguished when the body was taken from the house, and this was done by dipping it in holy water.[11] A similar candle or succession of candles was lit by the corpse in the Limousin. These belonged to the corpse and the candle ends were buried with it. Another very common custom was to cover all polished surfaces or mirrors or to turn them to the wall. This has variously been explained as a means of preventing the spirit of the dead person from seeing its own reflection and refusing to leave, and as a precaution lest the spirit take the reflection or double of any other person caught in the glass or other surface.

Church bells announced the death to the community. Numbers and types of peals indicated the gender and age of the deceased: nine strokes for a man, six for a woman, and three for a child, for example, in much of early modern England, though there were many variations. The bells were also believed to help the passage of the deceased's soul and to lend it protection. John Donne noted that in seventeenth-century England 'ringing hath been said to drive away evil spirits'. Bells also accompanied the funeral cortège. In parts of

Wales in the eighteenth and nineteenth centuries, 'a corpse-bell, or small hand-bell, was rung by the parish clerk who walked a short distance in advance of the funeral procession'.[12] Calvinists and some other Protestants did away with bells, part of a general scaling-down of funeral ritual, but there was popular resistance to this tendency.

In many parts of Europe, earth and/or salt were placed on or near the corpse, sometimes on a plate. In medieval Germany and elsewhere, earth was put in the mouth of the corpse, in lieu, it was said, of the viaticum. A similar practice is referred to in the English Robin Hood legends. In the Highlands of Scotland in the mid eighteenth century, the salt and earth were placed separately on a wooden platter on the breast of the deceased, the earth being seen as 'an emblem of the corruptible body; the salt of the immortal spirit'. Besides its association with purity, salt was a general apotropaic and was supposed in early modern England and elsewhere, as we have seen, 'to ward off evil spirits [from the dead and] to stop the deceased's ghost from walking'.[13] Salt protected the corpse but also countered the potential harm that it might cause.

Water had an important role in its own right in purifying the corpse. The bodies of the dead were nearly always washed in ritual fashion. This was a procedure akin to baptism, and was often carried out by midwives, who also laid out the dead. Care had to be taken over the disposal of the water used to wash the corpse. In Transylvania, it had to be poured away, 'where no one will tread'.[14] In the Périgord, we have seen, there was a symbolic washing ritual with again careful disposal of the water used in it. Things which had been in contact with the dead were also polluted and had to be treated accordingly. It was a widespread custom to wash or burn the bedding and clothing on or in which a person had died. In County Sligo in the nineteenth century, the whole bed of a dead person was taken out to high ground and burned. Failure to do this could lead to another death in the family. The house was also purified following a death. In Transylvania, house and outbuildings were sprinkled with holy water and marked with signs of the cross.

Mention should also be made here of the custom of 'sin-eating', found in early modern and modern England and Wales, though some later reports have been disputed. According to Aubrey,

> in the county of Hereford was an old custom at funerals to have poor people, who were to take upon them all the sins of the party deceased ... The manner was that when the corpse was brought out of the house and laid on the bier, a loaf of bread was brought out and delivered to the Sin-Eater over the corpse, as also a mazer-bowl of maple full of beer, which he was to drink up, and six pence in money whereof he took upon him *ipso facto* all the sins of the defunct, and freed him [or her] from walking after they were dead.

This sounds like a Christianization of an anti-pollution ritual, with sin being treated as some kind of taboo substance represented by food and drink. In Spanish Galicia, the dead gave off an 'air' or 'breath'. To escape its baleful influence, one should go at midnight to the relevant grave and recite three times:

> Take away the breath of the dead
> From living men and women.
> The breath of the dead will not comfort you,
> But the living will comfort you.[15]

The pollution of the dead extended to animals and humans. In some parts of the Highlands, according to Pennant in the later eighteenth century, it was 'reckoned so ominous for a dog or cat to pass over [a corpse] that the poor animal is killed without mercy'. In all countries, too, executioners were regarded with horror and were shunned. In nineteenth-century Spain, Ford reported, 'all whose profession is to put living creatures to death, are socially excommunicated: the butcher, the bullfighter, and the public executioner, for example'. If the dead body was contaminating, moreover, this meant that death itself was infectious. Another death could be caused by one relative 'calling' or taking another, as we have noted in connection with mirrors. Shakespeare's Pistol referred for this reason to 'doting death'. From this point of view, some mourning customs, long, dark, concealing dresses and veils for women, letting the hair and beard grow for men, were disguises, so that the dead would not recognize their close relatives and potential companions in death.[16]

Related to this, some practices were concerned to ensure the passage of the spirit of the dead person from this life on to at least a stage of the next. In modern Norway, 'when life had fled from the body, one opened the door just a crack. That way the soul would be free to go'. Opening of doors and windows at this juncture or later was common. In Hampshire in the 1890s, 'the outer door of the house, through which the corpse [had] been carried' to church was left open, 'until the mourners return, and in some places the custom extends also to the windows'. The custom stemmed from the belief that it would induce the spirit to leave the body more easily, and, if it was not followed, 'there would certainly be another death in the house within the year'. In Transylvania, once the coffin had left the house, the door was shut, but this was done in ritual manner three times. It is significant in this context that the soul was often conceptualized as a flying creature: a moth, a butterfly, a bird; or as a puff of smoke, all rising and, it was hoped, disappearing into the air. In many places, the corpse had to be removed from the house feet first, so that it would not find its way back. Occasionally, the body was taken through a window, avoiding the normal entrance of the house. In eighteenth-century Pembrokeshire, 'it was a custom to draw the corpse up through the chimney of the house during the wake before replacing it in the coffin'.[17]

The route taken by the corpse from the house to the church and then to the burial place was of great significance, too. In Wales, France and elsewhere, 'there was a traditional route which was invariably taken ... by funeral processions', and trouble would ensue if it were not followed. Sometimes a deliberately roundabout route was chosen to confuse the spirit. This was done, for example at Pembridge in Herefordshire, where the coffin was also 'carried sunwise round the church before entering', a procedure that brought good fortune. There were also required stopping-places on the route. In many places in France these were crossroads, dangerous but numinous places, where crosses were placed. In Transylvania, the procession made several halts, where prayers were said for the deceased.

> These pauses occur at specific locations: rivers or streams, a crossroads, or a threshold (for example, the courtyard gates to the house, the entrance to the cemetery). These places share the characteristic of ambiguity; they are between one possibility and another. Prayers assist the dead in manoeuvring safely across these obstacles.

The route to the cemetery here represented 'the passage of the deceased from this world to the next'.[18]

The corpse was provided, too, with provisions and a fare for its longer journey. Food and drink were traditionally presented to the dead and left at graves, as we shall see. Aubrey reported that in Wales and England in the seventeenth century a coin was placed in the mouth of the corpse 'to give to St Peter', a continuation of old Catholic practice. In modern Transylvania, the corpse was given a small ritual loaf with a coin in it 'to pay the gatekeeper'. Archaeological evidence shows that money was buried with the dead in France through the early modern period, and the custom was still being followed at the time of the Second World War. Mourning customs again expressed the wish to ensure the soul's passage. As in other places, mourning women in Transylvania wore their hair loose and unbraided; this was said 'to prevent obstacles in the path of the deceased' (see Text Figure 12).[19]

There were other magical beliefs associated with burial. Through most of the Christian era until sanitary concerns began to be raised in the later eighteenth century, there was a strong preference for burial in or near the parish church or the church of a religious order (see Plate 32). In this way, the dead were physically close to the relics of the saints and the performance of the liturgy and especially the mass. We have seen that unbaptized children were usually buried in an undesirable part of the churchyard or cemetery, or even outside consecrated ground altogether. Suicides, the excommunicate, male-factors and the very poor might be treated in the same way. They were placed beyond the symbolic community of the dead and outside the protection afforded by the the church. The north of the churchyard was the area usually designated for this purpose: to the left of the altar, in the cold and away from the sun. The orientation of the body in the grave might be important, too. Burial with the feet towards the east was usual in England and elsewhere, and the body was 'buried face up to greet the angel of the resurrection'.[20] At Minot, tombs were orientated toward the west to face the rising sun, with the feet of the bodies pointing towards the tombstone or cross.

Paradoxically, given the desire to allow the dead spirit to depart freely, links were not entirely or not suddenly severed between the living and the dead. In France, death was frequently conceptualized, according to Varagnac, as 'a kind of paralysis of the body in which the soul is dislocated, in pain', rather like some states of bewitchment. In Greece and the Balkans, the soul left the body at death but remained in its vicinity for at least forty days. In Scandinavia, the dead 'continued to "live" in the grave until they finally faded from memory'. They were 'often feared, but relations with them could be [perhaps normally were] friendly'. Churchyards were usually in the middle of villages and from there the dead could easily visit their old residences. 'In Brittany, the tripod in the fireplace had to be carefully folded and hung [up]; otherwise the dead, seeking the warmth of the hearth, might sit on it and burn themselves'. In Scandinavia and elsewhere, dead mothers might return to see and care for their children; and dead spouses went back 'to share the comforts of ... bed and board'. Among the Southern Slavs, the dead continued to participate in social life, being invited to Easter celebra-tions and weddings.[21]

As Flint writes of the early medieval period, though the observation applies much more widely, 'dead members of a family still needed, and deserved, the services of the living'.[22] This was partly an expression of affection and family solidarity, but also a propitiation, a way of satisfying the dead and keeping them in their proper sphere. Provision of food and drink was probably the commonest manifestation of this obligation.

Such provision began at the wake and the funeral. Eating and drinking took place at the wake of course and before and after the funeral, and often specifically involved the dead. In modern Transylvania, an extra cup of liquor was drunk for the dead and special ritual loaves were presented 'for the soul of the deceased', some of which were then given to the priest, the sexton, the grave-diggers and the pall-bearers. The funeral feast in early modern England could take place in the church or churchyard, and bread might be doled out

12. Lamenting at a death-bed in Corsica – note woman with loosened hair. After Gaston Vuillier, watercolour, 1893.

there to the poor on behalf of the dead. Similar feasts took place in Burgundy and Normandy. In Corsica, the post-burial feast was held in honour of the dead, who was supposed to attend. In one lament, a cousin tells a dead man:

> When you leave the church,
> You know what you have to do:
> Come back with me to the house,
> Where the meal will be ready.[23]

Rituals were held at intervals after a death to express continuing, though diminishing, ties, a kind of funeral in stages. Among the Southern Slavs, rites took place on the second, third, ninth and fortieth days and then at three months, six months and at one, three and seven years, as well as at Easter and at weddings. In Transylvania, they were held on the third day, the ninth day, at six months and after a year as well as on All Souls' Day. In much of Western Europe, including post-Reformation England and Wales, commemoration came at the end of a month and a year and at All Souls. The Injunctions for the diocese of Durham in 1577 ordered

> that no communion or commemorations (as some call them) be said for the dead, or at the burials of the dead; or anniversary of month's minds be used for the dead; nor superfluous ringing on All Saints' Day at night, or on the day following, of old superstitiously called All Souls' Day.

But such bans were in many places inneffective. In Radnorshire, for example, the traditional 'month's mind', which had become the 'month's end' was still being marked in the 1950s. There and elsewhere, moreover, it was believed to be unlucky to leave a house where a death had occurred before the 'month's end'.[24]

These commemorative times were again marked by offerings of food and other gifts. These were particularly elaborate in Eastern Europe and the Orthodox world, where they were referred to as 'banquets for souls'. In Transylvania on the ninth day, nine widows gathered at the deceased's house and ate a special fasting meal, comprising bean soup and stuffed cabbage without meat. Commemorative meals were also provided on the other memorial occasions, and passers-by were invited to partake of them 'for the soul of the dead'. In other parts of Rumania similarly, 'offerings of drink and food, chiefly a dish of boiled grain', were made at All Souls or Whit, and in Macedonia 'a special cake covered with walnut and rose leaves' was laid on the graves. In Russia, peasants left food for their dead parents after ceremonial meals, 'invited' them to come and join them at their table and gave them *bliny* (pancakes) at Easter. Among the Southern Slavs, when the dead were invited to family weddings, a gourd of wine and special food (chick peas and sweetmeats) were consecrated and then poured three times over the grave.[25]

Similar customs existed elsewhere from Roman times onwards. Wax, cakes, bread and wine were placed on graves in Castile in the sixteenth century. In seventeenth-century Shropshire, according to Aubrey, on All Souls' Day, a heap of soul-cakes was set on a board and 'every visitor that day takes one; and there is an old rhyme or saying,

> A soul-cake, a soul-cake,
> Have mercy on all Christian souls for a soul-cake.

This custom survived in Wales and the Midlands into the nineteenth century. In Languedoc similarly, a special meal was eaten on All Souls in commemoration of the dead, at which 'bread of the dead' was served. In the Ariège and the Roussillon, chestnuts were placed on the stairs, so that the dead would eat them and not trouble those living in the house and sleeping upstairs. In other places, for example the Abruzzi, food was left out at Christmas. And other customs involved providing food for the dead or enabling them to eat and drink. A penitential from Carolingian times referred to 'burning grain where a man died'; while in the Creuse in the 1890s, 'people still buried a bowl and spoon with a deceased person to eat with if he was hungry'.[26]

Other gifts were offered to the dead. Gloves, rings or ribbons were vicariously presented at English funerals. Flowers, palms from Palm Sunday and pins are also mentioned in the sources. At Grantham in the 1850s, for example, where the crypt was still full of bones, girls went there and threw in pins to prevent bad luck, thus making an offering to the dead. Pins were also thrown at funeral processions in nineteenth-century England. In Burgundy and elsewhere in France, Palm Sunday was one of the occasions on which the dead were commemorated: 'Each family visits the cemetery to place a piece of blessed palm on the tombs of the dead'.[27] The general protection of the family and its property afforded by these sacramentals is thus extended to include the dead.

Religious benefits were also provided for the dead on these memorial and other occasions: prayers, masses and indulgences, which might require survivors to go on pilgrimages or to wear particular medals and scapulars. This provision very often followed stipulations made in the wills of the deceased. Although in the Catholic context these were all intended to reduce the time spent in Purgatory by the soul of the dead person, they also probably had more general functions. They were 'a kind of prophylactic magic', which kept the dead happy and prevented their return.[28]

For failure to supply these services and gifts could lead to retribution. The dead might simply return to remind their kin of their obligations. Gregory the Great referred to souls being temporarily released from Purgatory in order 'to solicit suffrages', and many stories exemplify this. Other factors might take away the peace of the dead and make them restless and dangerous: unexpiated crimes, wishes unfulfilled, funeral services or burial not properly carried out, lives cut short. A classic example is the ghost of Hamlet's father in Shakespeare's play. Hamlet asks it why it has left the sepulchre in which it was quietly buried, and the ghost tells him that it is

> Doom'd for a certain term to walk the night,
> And for the day confin'd to fast in fires,
> Till the foul crimes done in my days of nature
> Are burnt and purg'd away.

In other words, it is suffering in Purgatory for its sins, but the punishment or purging also includes being required 'to walk the night' as a ghost. At the same time, the ghost has returned specifically to tell Hamlet that his father was poisoned by Claudius and to enjoin upon him revenge. This is an evil done *to* the dead person and not *by* him. In another Shakespearean example, the ghost of Julius Caesar appears to Brutus, who had betrayed him and shared in his assassination, 'to tell thee thou shalt see me at Philippi'. Here the ghost prophesies Brutus' defeat and death at the battle of Philippi and announces Caesar's revenge. Thomas has shown that such fictional examples are fairly typical of ghosts seen by English people in the early modern period. 'The essential task of ghosts', he concluded, 'was to ensure reverence for the dead and to deter those who sought to molest their bones or frustrate their dying wishes.'[29] Most continental ghosts fit the same pattern.

An extreme example of the *revenant* or returning dead, not found in Britain, was the vampire, which also has some of the characteristics of 'the blood-sucking *stryx* of Antiquity' as well as of other witches and supernatural beings. Vampire beliefs are recorded from Silesia and Bohemia around 1600 and are later characteristic of Slavic and Greek-speaking peoples. Vampires were often dead people who had died 'in irregular circumstances': suicides, the unbaptized, the excommunicate, victims of violence. There might also be something 'wrong' with their birth, such as being born with a caul; or they might have been cursed; or an animal or a bird might have passed over their corpse. Most important, unlike those of the normal dead, their bodies did not rot in their graves but remained intact. It is significant that vampire beliefs are mainly found in the Orthodox world, where double burial was practised, the bones of a dead person being disinterred after a period, usually a year. 'For the soul to depart this world, the body must not only be returned to the earth, but must be accepted by the earth', that is it must fully decompose. Similar ideas are found in the West, though regular disinterment there was uncommon and intact corpses were more often found by chance. As in modern Burgundy this eventuality was 'a sign that the funeral ritual has not been properly carried out, or the mark of an extraordinary destiny: the deceased is either a saint or damned'.[30]

Beyond troubling their relatives and others by their simple reappearance, the unquiet dead could cause more extensive harm, even disasters. The Greek *vrikolax* or vampire 'returns home to pollute everything – the plates, the olive oil, and the casseroles'. Other vampires killed humans and animals and, in the Southern Slav region, they also caused epidemics and storms and harmed crops. In the Asturias, the unsatisfied dead might cause livestock to abort, harvests to fail, fires to break out. As Catedra points out, they were desocialized, like animals, whose form they could take. In different parts of Europe, the souls of the deceased appeared in the form of all kinds of creatures from bees and beetles to crows and ravens, from toads and mice to wolves. Southern Swedish 'ghost-pigs wandered around in the twilight or at night trying to get between people's legs, in order to split them open with their razor-sharp backs'. Here again there is an overlap, if not identity, between the spirits of the dead and other malignant forces, such as witches or fairies. In the Friuli, 'the sorcerers who are the enemies of the fertility of the fields' were related to or derived from 'the unappeased dead'. Everywhere beliefs about fairies and the dead were 'curiously entangled'. In Scotland, for example, fairies could be 'people who had died ... in twilight, or cut off in some way before their allotted span, or unbaptized', and they were believed to eat funeral food; while 'fairyland' was underground like the habitation of the dead.[31]

Sometimes ghosts returned with benign intentions: to be near children, spouses or lovers and to bring them comfort and messages, as we have seen. In a Danish narrative, a wife returns to tell her husband that his name and that of a neighbour are written in the Book of Life. In a Norwegian one, a mother returned to offer her daughter the more mundane advice that she and her husband should not sell a lot for building but let one of the children inherit it. In Lucania, *revenants* could be like helpful domestic spirits, waking people by ringing a bell, for example, when animals were straying into their crops.

We have seen that preventative measures were taken to ensure that the dead would not 'walk'. Runes were cut on early Scandinavian gravestones 'to protect the grave and its occupant', but also 'perhaps to bind the dead to his new home, to prevent his returning to upset and interfere with the lives of the living'. If ghosts did walk, they could normally be laid by satisfying their wishes and/or by providing prayers and masses. Sometimes exorcism was required; sometimes unorthodox prayers were used. Sir Walter Scott referred in 1803 to a popular Scottish story in which a corpse starts up because a door was left ajar and is settled by a Catholic priest saying the Paternoster backwards. In more extreme cases, the unquiet dead or vampire might be rekilled, by having a stake driven through the corpse or by some other means. This happened in Scandinavia, south-eastern Europe and elsewhere. The Greek *vrikolax* was overcome by pouring boiling water or wine and water over the grave, while 'the priest reads something', or by burning the corpse. Vampires were 'exhumed and pierced by a pole, or beheaded or had the heart extracted and burnt'.[32]

Though the spirits of the dead usually operated under their own or the influence of a higher supernatural power, they might also be summoned or voluntarily consulted by the living. Certain people had the power to communicate with the dead, and there were certain procedures that might be followed. Both had precedents in the Old Testament and the Ancient world. Isidore of Seville around 600 condemned necromancers 'who conjure up the dead with blood and water [and charms] to ask them questions', and both condemnation and practice continued over the next millennium or more. Until the sixteenth century, the term 'necromancy' retained its literal meaning of consulting and manipulating the spirits of the dead rather than meaning 'high' or learned magic generally. In 1578, for example, a pious widow from Modena testified to the Inquisition 'that she was regularly visited by an apparition that took the form of various deceased relatives [whom] she was accustomed to consult ... on issues of importance, such as sickness in the family or possible bewitchments'; while the first 'witch' sentenced to death at the stake in Iceland in 1625 'had woken up a ghost and caused malignity through him'.[33]

The fact that ghosts could harm crops was only one example of the many ways in which the dead were associated with the well-being and prosperity of the community and more particularly with fertility. This link was expressed first in funeral rituals. Wakes featured obscene jokes and games. Greenery was carried by mourners in Stuart England. Flowers and wreaths were placed on graves; and tombstones later often depicted vines and cereals, the staple and symbolic crops. The spirits of the dead, moreover, were thought of as entering the plants and trees planted at their graves. Death was personified as a figure carrying a scythe, the grim reaper.

Death obtruded also on the other rites of passage. In many European societies from Ancient times onwards, analogies were drawn between funerals and weddings. Antigone in Sophocles' play was 'married with death'. In modern Transylvania, a symbolic wedding was performed for an unmarried person who died, 'because otherwise the most important aspect of life would not have been realized'. At the 'death-wedding', the deceased 'bride' was dressed in 'wedding attire'; there would be bridesmaids and a marriage flag, an important emblem in normal weddings, though it would be black and not the usual white. The ritual was similar for dead bachelors. The death-wedding was performed from 'love and compassion for the deceased', but also from fear, since the unsatisfied dead could trouble and harm their survivors. At regular funerals, moreover, the male pall-bearers had to be married lest they be seduced by death, who was thought of as female. There was also a more general parallel between the ritual function of the wedding separating a woman from her own family and joining her to another, and the funeral separating the deceased from kin. In early modern England, there was also a special funeral ritual for unmarried girls. They were carried by maidens who were like bridesmaids and they were mourned in white not black. Publicly executed criminals, moreover, could be dressed like bridegrooms, while girls among the spectators dressed as bridesmaids. Ariès and others have pointed to the erotic aspects of death which existed in the Baroque period and were intensified in tomb sculpture and in literature in the Romantic era. These, too, could take magical form, as when the duchess of Richmond instructed in the 1620s that her corpse should be wound in 'those sheets wherein my Lord [her late husband] and I first slept that night when we were married'.[34]

There are vestiges in the folklore of many countries of the idea that new-born babies are invested with the souls of the recently deceased. It was said in modern Alsace, for example, that 'there would be a birth in a family because there had been a death'; while in Lower Normandy people believed that a baby would not live unless an old person in the family died at about the same time.[35] In Renaissance Florence and elsewhere this idea was reflected in naming practices.

Calendar festivals most obviously expressed the notion that the dead had responsibility for fertility. At the Ancient Athenian festival of the Anthesteria in February, when the spirits of the dead emerged from the underworld and revisited their old homes, 'a dish of gruel made of all the crops of the year' or *panspermia*, was offered to them; for, as a writer of the fourth century BC put it: 'From the dead come growth and increase and seeds'. The custom survived down to modern times, the *panspermia* being 'still offered in churchyards at the beginning of Lent'. Death implied resurrection and in due course renewal of life. In Provence and elsewhere, Winter and Summer both began with 'festivals of the dead: 1st November and 1st May which opens the month of the souls, an unlucky month when souls migrate'. All Souls, we have seen, had features associated with fertility: offerings of wheat, feasts with special food, and ritual begging. Offerings of food were also made to the dead at Christmas. These connections were even clearer in the Spring festivals. Carnival, according to Varagnac was a 'visit to this lower world from the fertilizing army of the dead', with the masked revellers representing the ancestors. One of the functions of the box branches blessed on Palm Sunday in the Périgord was 'to draw the water from the poor dead'. In other parts of France, the maypole brought from the woods and planted in the fields was sometimes thought of as a temporary residence for the spirits of the dead. During the Rogation Days in parts of Spain, prayers were said for those who had died during the previous year, and salt water was sprinkled over the fields to procure their fertility. The linkage is found again when the crops were harvested. In modern Ireland, Lammas or the festival of first fruits was also held 'in honour of the dead', associating the 'ancestral spirits with the fertility of farm and family';[36] while the Michaelmas rituals in western Scotland ended with processions round the burial-grounds.

Those whose role it was to obtain the fertility of their community, like the *benandanti* of the Friuli, often had some link with the dead. A man tried as a witch in Hesse in 1630 claimed that 'whoever had the power to travel during the Ember seasons to the world populated by the dead became a guarantor of fertility'; and other texts associate the spirits of the dead or ghosts with these days. The souls of the dead also figured in other rituals. In charivaris in France and Italy from the late medieval period onwards, youths wore masks and disguises representing them as the spirits of the dead, defending in particular the interests of dead spouses but also community order and marriage. On the Blasket Islands off the Kerry coast, the mackerel fishing was accompanied by women on the shore shouting encouragement to the men in the boats and invoking the souls of the dead.[37]

We have seen that the spirits of the dead might cause bad weather and crop failure if they were neglected or displeased. The earth itself might also show its anger directly if presented with certain categories of corpse. In East Slavic folklore, the earth was believed to reject 'unclean corpses', that is those that were likely to be ghosts or vampires. 'The earth [also] shows its anger with cold and frost in the Spring, which have a destructive influence on the thriving of the grain in the fields.' For this reason, 'unclean corpses' were not in the past buried but were left in wild places such as caves and ravines. Similarly in nineteenth-century Spain there was great hostility to the burial of heretics and Protestants in regular burial places, because it was believed that 'no corn would grow near them'. Sometimes they were buried on the sea-shore or put in the sea, but again the fishermen thought that this would stop them from catching fish.[38]

Since such power emanated from the dead, their remains and anything in contact with them had power by association. This was the basis of the Christian cult of saints' relics. Anything to do with the dead might also be used in other forms of magic. In modern Greece and elsewhere earth from tombs and cemeteries was scattered to harm neighbours. The 'oils of the dead', oil from the lights burned during the services for the dead, might be used similarly. Burial equipment was also employed. A hoe and a shovel used in burying the dead figured in an anti-impotence rite in sixteenth-century Venice. 'At Sévignac in the Côtes-du-Nord in the 1890s, when a child is ill, it is rolled, to obtain a cure, in a bed sheet on which a corpse has been laid out'. Contact with those who had been executed provided special power. The rope that a criminal had been hanged with or parts of the gallows were common magical agents in many parts of Europe. More directly, parts of corpses themselves were deployed, exactly paralleling the use of relics. In a case in 1326, for example, a priest from Agen procured 'the heads and arms of those who had been hanged', in order to raise storms and perform other acts of hostile magic. A friar was brought before the Inquisition in Venice in 1584 for taking three skulls from the convent cemetery for use in a ritual to gain special powers. In a case in 1894 in Bavaria, a man was accused of exhuming a body in order to take one of its eyes, which he thought would make him invisible and thus aid him in robberies. In modern Ireland, 'a long strip of skin removed from a corpse' and wrapped round a person while asleep was 'a potent love charm'; while 'a dead man's hand, thrust into milk, was as a last resort, a sure way of getting the cream to rise'. The commonest body part to be used was probably the hand or finger, especially of an executed person. It was often used in protective magic. In England it was known as the 'Hand of Glory' which seems to be a corruption of *main-de-gloire* or *mandragora*, a magical plant whose roots were shaped like a hand.[39]

13. The onset of syphilis related to the conjunction of
Saturn and Jupiter in the house of Scorpio. Print after
Albrecht Dürer woodcut, 1496.

III

DISEASE AND HEALING

12

Illness, Doctors and Religion

The populations of traditional Europe were unhealthy by modern Western standards. Undernourished, poorly housed, they were prey to a myriad of everyday endemic illnesses, especially in the first months of life, while every so often they were hit by regional and general epidemics: typhoid, influenza, plague. Very often these diseases were fatal. Demographic historians have established that the normal death-rate then was three or four times greater than it is now and that of infants much higher, while average life-expectancy was around thirty. How did people explain the illnesses that so frequently assailed them and what recourse did they have against them?

In some cultures the idea that illness like death has natural causes is quite alien. All ailments are sent by or are manifestations of angry ancestors, evil or neglected spirits, witchcraft and so on. Pre-modern Europe does not entirely fit into this category. Beier writes that in seventeenth-century England 'it was considered natural for infants and the very old to die of almost any illness', and belonging to either age-group might be given as a cause of death. What we would call psychosomatic illness was also under-stood in some quarters, even in the Middle Ages. In his Life of the saint written about 1175, Garnier noted that Thomas Becket became ill at Northampton after further disagreement with the king: 'The pain in his side attacked him, and lasted all day and night. He was subject to it, and it often distressed him; it came back now because of the anxiety he was suffering'. Alessandra Strozzi wrote in a letter in 1465 after a brief visit to Florence from her exiled son: 'I have not felt well, and I've only eaten some eggs. I haven't any fever, but my head is very weak ... Lorenzo's departure has shaken me badly, and just as I felt alive while he was here, so I felt lifeless and dead when he left'.[1] Such ideas fitted well, of course, into the general framework of magical influences.

In this pre-Pasteurian era there could be no realization that most diseases were caused by micro-organisms entering the body, and alternative patho-logical theories, though they existed, were vaguer and their explanatory force was less commanding. One idea present at the popular and 'scientific' levels saw disease as an invader, 'an active force, which enters and advances through the body', as a student of early modern Naples has put it. The notion of contagion was also current and lay behind the practice of isolating lepers in the Middle Ages, and using both isolation and quarantine to contain plague from the fifteenth century onwards. We have also seen that death itself was sometimes felt to be contagious. The environment was believed to affect people's health, too, as we have noted in the case of the weather. Certain winds brought 'health and cleanliness'; others 'dirt and disease', as Albert the Great noted in the thirteenth century. 'Altitude, the lie of the land, the composition and porosity of the soil, landscape features such as rivers, forests, lakes and mountains, proximity to the sea', all might be relevant. Especially dangerous to health were low-lying areas, atmospheric extremes and urban congestion.[2]

To all of this should be added the influence of the moon, the stars and the planets. According to medieval astrological teaching, the moon was wet, cold and female and 'would predispose anyone born under its sway towards worry, irritability ... and in extreme cases, insanity'. In modern Greece sickness in babies was often attributed to being 'hit by the moon' or 'affected by the moon'. In one case, a baby's clothes 'had been left outside before the forty days had passed; they were seen by the moon and that caused sickness'. But the moon could bring good health and prosperity. A Sicilian children's rhyme went:

> New moon, old moon,
> Find me healthy, leave me healthy,
> With money in my purse
> And grain in my basket.

As with other matters, much would depend here on the exact phase of the moon. A fifteenth-century English text warned: 'When thou takest a cure, be it of physic or of surgery, take notice of the moon, and of the time when the sickness took and in what sign it began'. A woman accused in Venice in 1555 of blaspheming against the host was said to suffer from 'alienation and weakness of the brain, to a greater or lesser extent according to the waxing and waning of the moon'. The sun was also a powerful influence, especially when it behaved strangely. 'Dangerous diseases breed in bodies natural', wrote an early seventeenth-century English writer, 'by putrefaction springing out of the sun's eclipse.'[3]

Some scholars, like Marsilio Ficino in fifteenth-century Florence, elaborated much more systematic and comprehensive connections between the body and its health and the heavenly constellations, which had some impact on formal medical education. But astrological explanations tended to be adduced mainly to explain epidemics and the advent of new and unusual afflictions. The Black Death of the mid fourteenth century, for example, was attributed to heavenly conjunctions that 'led to putrefaction of air, food and water in the sublunary world'. And physicians around 1500 'invoked the baleful conjunction of Saturn and Mars to account for the origin and the ravages of syphilis' (see Text Figure 13). Related to all such theories was the ancient but long-lived and pervasive view that the body was host to four vital fluids or humours: blood, phlegm, yellow bile and black bile, linked to the four elements of air, water, fire and earth. Good health depended upon maintaining the right balance among these, and 'sickness was the result when the balance was disturbed'.[4]

Despite the adherence of some of the elite to such theories, their sway was limited. Having studied seventeenth-century Visitation reports from southern dioceses, an Italian historian has concluded that illness there 'was never regarded as a natural event'.[5] Humoralism and environmentalism could easily be accommodated to religious and magical explanations and therapeutics. And among elites and populace supernatural always outweighed 'scientific' notions.

Medieval thinking from Sulpicius Severus and Gregory of Tours onwards 'linked illness closely with sin, as it had been in the Gospels: if one was ill it was because one had some fault on one's conscience'. Pilgrims at healing shrines frequently referred to their sins in their prayers. This general idea remained pervasive and may even have been strengthened by the Reformation. The first lay catechism printed in German, Coelde's *Mirror of a Christian Man*, firmly stated that physical illness 'generally came from sins'. Recent studies have shown how strong this conviction was in seventeenth-century England, especially among Puritans and the pious like Alice Thornton and Ralph Josselin. In Milton's *Paradise Lost*, diseases were visited upon mankind as a result of the Fall of Adam and Eve and as a punishment for their original sin. Punishment here could be individual, familial or collective, and certain ailments were particularly likely to be selected by the divine wrath, sometimes for specific failings. These included epilepsy, blindness and universal scourges like the plague. 'Oh, woe is me', a blind woman cried to St Martin in Gregory of Tours' collection of his miracles, 'for I am blinded by my sins.' Leprosy was everywhere regarded in the Middle Ages as the consequence of sexual depravity either in the sufferer or his or her parents, and venereal diseases were later explained in the same way with more reason. On the epidemic level, 'the so-called English Sweat which broke out in 1486 was interpreted as the scourge of God to punish the sins of primping and lewdness'. The general association between sinfulness and epidemics was obvious in most reactions to plague, whether in Florence in the mid fifteenth century or in London in 1665 for example, and it was prevalent again during the cholera outbreaks of the nineteenth century.[6]

Epidemics here might be reactions to attacks on or defection from the Church. An outbreak of plague at Lyon in 1564 was presented by a Jesuit as punishment for the abandonment of Catholicism for Protestantism; while 'the clergy of Barcelona claimed that God had sent the yellow fever outbreak there in 1821 to punish the Spanish people for their revolutions and anticlerical tendencies'.[7] The idea that certain diseases or complaints were punishments for misbehaviour also took a more direct and local form. It was believed in many German-speaking areas in the modern period, for example, that styes in the eye were an indication that the sufferer had urinated or defecated in an improper place, especially the public highway. Styes were also seen as a punishment for voyeurism or sins with the eyes: looking at a naked person or at a person performing the natural functions, or witnessing sexual acts by humans or animals.

If 'God sent diseases in order to punish' sinners, he also sent them with a more positive intention: to warn, to convert, to test a believer's faith, or as a means of spiritual perfection or expiation, or a reminder of death. Here disease was 'the finger of Providence', and cures could be signs of grace. This way of thinking was common among medieval Christians and among both Catholics and Protestants later. According to the thirteenth-century *Nun's Rule*, some 'sickness maketh man to understand what he is, and to know himself; and, like a good master, it corrects a man, to teach him how powerful God is, and how frail is the happiness of the world'. 'If his wife or any of his children were sick or diseased', Sir Thomas More would tell them: 'Be of good comfort, and be patient, for this sickness is sent you of God to purchase you heaven'. St Alexander Sauli, bishop of Aleria in the late sixteenth century, instructed his clergy that they should visit any parishioner who fell ill 'to console him gently and invite him to accept his illness as coming from the hand of God for the reparation of his sins'. The Puritan divine Richard Baxter believed that his wife's fatal illness in 1681 was God's way of calling 'my sin to remembrance', and he saw his own afflictions as admonitions if not encouragements: 'For being in expectation of death by a violent cough, with spitting of blood, etc., of two years' continuance, supposed to be a deep degree of consumption, I was yet more awakened to be serious and solicitous about my soul's everlasting state'.[8] Particular diseases might be regarded as peculiarly 'sacred' here, like epilepsy or scrofula, which required special religious or quasi-religious cures.

Again, in this kind of religious perspective, an illness might be an indication of a struggle between good and evil forces within a person, of a contest between God and the Devil for his or her body and soul. Psychic troubles were attributed to the Devil at medieval and modern shrines, usually via the concept of possession, but the diabolical origin of illnesses was also a broader alternative to ascribing them to God. 'Some early liturgies explicitly indicated that illness was a manifestation of the Devil's oppression', and the Devil was there referred to as 'plague-bearer'.[9] Later on, too, plague was sometimes thought to be caused by evil spirits, for example by Luther. Finally, under the religious aegis, diseases might be sent by saints, something to which we will return.

It was generally believed too that some diseases were caused by the ill-will of other people, operating by spells or other means. One of the largest categories of alleged bewitchment in early modern witchcraft trials in all countries involved human sickness. Illness might also be the result of the involuntary effects of the evil eye or of some other 'natural' magical effect. 'In 1655 the notion that blue plums, damsons and black cherries had been responsible for a particularly severe outbreak of the plague (presumably because of their analogous resemblance to buboes) led to their being temporarily banned from market stalls in Holland.' In modern Provence and elsewhere, there was a taboo against mentioning illness or death. 'One never says that someone "is ill" but rather "is tired" – even if the person is dying.' Mentioning the disease might bring it about or make it worse if it was already present. Illnesses were also attributed to the spirits of the dead, to vampires and to fairies and other spirits. Among the Anglo-Saxons, for example, elves were 'a cause of illness and gave their name to various complaints'. Some of these, in animals and humans, were brought about by 'elf-shot', or elves shooting the disease into their victims.[10]

Explanations of disease in pre-modern Europe were thus multifarious: natural and supernatural, religious and magical, social and personal. To aid diagnosis and hence cure, distinctions were made among different kinds of illness, again in different ways in different communities, regions and classes. A line was usually drawn, as now, between slight and serious illnesses, only the latter requiring treatment outside the family. For the peasants of the Vosges in the nineteenth century, there were three types of complaint: those dealt with at home like colic or sore throats; those that doctors could cure like chest disease and typhoid; and 'the illnesses of the saints'. In modern Minho, there were 'sicknesses of here' or 'sicknesses of the doctor', and 'sicknesses of there' or 'sicknesses which are not for the doctor', which 'require supernatural intervention'. In southern Italy, illnesses that were felt to be 'natural', however serious, were contrasted with those where the victim felt himself or herself to be dominated by a supernatural force. Similarly in medieval and early modern Russia, some diseases 'were attributable to material causes; others, more numerous by far, were believed to possess a magical pathogenesis'.[11]

Conditions that fell into this latter category took a form that was sooner or later recognizable. In nineteenth-century Sicily, if a sick man, in spite of remedies and cures, of invocations of divine help, continued to be sick, even worsening, and presented new symptoms that seemed unusual and strange, the female neighbours began to look at him with expressions of doubt and preoccupation; and then one of them (usually the oldest) expressed the dominant thought: 'Listen, this is not natural: there is witchcraft here in our midst!'

This stress on the failure of normal diagnoses or remedies and on the strangeness of the illness is found all over Europe in earlier centuries. In a case at Dumfries in 1671, for example, an accused witch, Janet MacMurdoch, was said to have caused the death of a child 'of an extraordinary sickness, sweating to death' and then of a man who took 'an extraordinary sickness and disease and continued therein by the space of seventeen days and thereafter grew stupid and senseless'. Languishing and a slow decline and death, something like modern ME, were also typical of witchcraft-derived illnesses. In *The Tempest*, Prospero declares that his magic can cause 'lingering perdition'; while two alleged victims of witchcraft at Singhem, in what was later Belgium, in 1657 died 'after long and terrible torments'.[12]

Partly as a result of this eclectic pathology, people relied on self-diagnosis and self-medication in the first instance, when they fell ill. Among the elite, and particularly its more introspective members like Samuel Pepys, this might be done on an individual basis, but among peasants the collective element was more obvious. At first, as in nineteenth-century Sicily, the sick peasant would try to carry on working as usual, hoping the illness would go away by itself. Then home remedies would be tried, herbal potions most likely, passed on from generation to generation and prepared and administered by the women, or perhaps some magical rite. Then neighbours or kin would come in with advice. In a trial at Modena in 1582 a woman testified that

> Thomaso, the little son of my brother was sick. He was so distressed and screamed so loudly that he was judged by various people to be *maleficato* (bewitched). So it was suggested by his grandmother that we call in Don Teofilo [official exorcist at the cathedral] to exorcize Thomaso.

As this shows, family and neighbourly diagnosis might be confirmed or tested by consulting someone with recognized healing powers, and/or it might act as a kind of referral mechanism. Once a patient had been referred, more elaborate diagnostic ritual might be employed to discover whether the illness stemmed from withcraft or the evil eye, whether it could be cured at a particular shrine, and so on. Various methods would be used here: in early modern Russia, for example, 'casting of wax on cold water, looking into water, ashes and mirrors'; in modern Corsica and elsewhere in the Mediterranean region, dropping oil on to plates of water.

> In Poitou, when people did not know which saint exactly to address [on behalf of a sick child], they cut several pieces from its chemise; each piece represented a locally well-known saint; and the pieces were placed in a dish full of water. Whichever saint has 'touched' the child, the corresponding piece of its chemise will go to the bottom of the dish.[13]

Barbers, empirics or herbalists might also be consulted.

Only as a last resort and in the modern period might a doctor be called, and his visit would be associated more with imminent death than any hope of recovery. The elite in earlier centuries showed a similar reluctance. The family of Ralph Josselin in the seventeenth century 'almost never consulted physicians and surgeons' even when children were dying. Instead they relied on prayer, herbal remedies and the occasional advice and skills of neighbours and friends, and in this they were fairly typical. When Mozart's mother was seriously ill in Paris in 1768 with 'shivering and feverishness accompanied by diarrhoea and headache', she was treated at first only with home remedies and powders. Only when 'she could hardly speak and had lost her hearing' did a doctor see her. And even if and when doctors were consulted, their advice was not necessarily or exclusively followed. In Minho in modern times, parents might take a child to the doctor, but his prescription would be modified by the pharmacist, and they would also 'promise an ex-voto to a saint' and visit a wise woman.[14]

The inadequacies of medical practitioners in the pre-modern period were highlighted by lampoonists such as Ben Jonson, Molière and Sterne. Addison in the *Spectator* presented them as military men killing their patients in a variety of ways and concluded: 'We may lay it down for a maxim, that when a nation abounds in physicians, it grows thin of people'. Historians have largely confirmed such writers' picture of greed, brutality and pedantry, and of the prescription of complicated and useless medicines and debilitating purging and bleeding to restore the humoral balance. Blood-letting or phlebotomy continued on the Continent well into the nineteenth century and in some places like Calabria till the time of the First World War. The training of physicians was highly academic and their skills owed more to Ancient Greek theory than clinical practice. The less prestigious surgeons were more practical in orientation, but the limits to successful surgical intervention were great, not the least being the lack of any anaesthetics other than spirits and then opium. Also among licensed healers in most countries were apothecaries and midwives. Alongside these were 'irregulars' or unlicensed practitioners. Some had real skills and were able to draw teeth and set bones, but more were mountebanks and charlatans, selling patent remedies at fairs and markets that were supposed to cure every imaginable complaint. One Gosset who arrived in Troyes in 1791 claimed, according to his hand-bill, to cure

> all eye disorders in general including cataract ... by applying a new invention ... He treats and cures hernias in both sexes. He cures scrofula, anal fistulas, and ulcers on the legs. He works on ruptures, fractures, dislocations, and makes malignant ringworm go away, without causing the hair to fall out ... He cures epilepsy ... and jaundice. He makes the menses appear when the reproductive organs are barren. He is familiar with ... all venereal diseases ... He cures prolapse of the uterus, whether caused by effort or by childbirth. He causes all sorts of malignant fevers to go away in less than six days, using a remedy that is very easy to take. He cures internal and external haemorrhoids ... He has a remedy for those who urinate involuntarily. He cures deafness ... in the space of three minutes

and so on.[15]

Though 'irregulars' outnumbered 'regulars', all taken together were very thin on the ground. Around 1600, there were 250 licensed doctors and apothecaries practising in London, and slightly more unlicensed healers, in a population of around 300,000. In France at the end of the Old Régime, there were less than 5000 physicians and about 40,000 surgeons in the whole country of 26 million. Where doctors could be found – and they were always scarcer in rural areas – their services were expensive, confining them to the well-off and placing them beyond the reach of most peasants and workers even at the start of the nineteenth century. In the Périgord in the 1920s, doctors charged five francs for a visit, but it only cost ten centimes to have a candle lit at a shrine and five centimes to have a short extract from the Gospels read. Although they charged less than doctors, empirics and itinerant charlatans also required patients to pay for their services and remedies. It is hardly surprising therefore, as the Cambridge divine William Perkins wrote in 1608, that 'charming is in as great request as physic, and charmers more sought unto than physicians in time of need'. In Rome in the eighteenth century most of the population had recourse to popular remedies, *rimedi simpatiche*.[16] And this remained the picture in many rural areas of Europe until the Second World War. Folk healers did not have to be paid, or not in cash, and they belonged to the same mental universe as their patients.

Doctors and unofficial healers were seen and saw themselves as rivals, and bureaucratic controls over medical practice were introduced from the late medieval period onwards. William Clowes, surgeon to Queen Elizabeth I, for example, denounced his unauthorized colleagues in a litany of abuse as 'tinkers, tooth-drawers ... , horse gelders and horse leeches ... apple squires, broom-men, bawds, witches, conjurors, soothsayers [and] rat-catchers'. The accusation of witchcraft was commonplace. Inger Skraedder was charged with sorcery at Malmø in Sweden in 1590 and was induced to confess to having a familiar spirit which she used to rob the barber-surgeons of both Malmø and Helsingfors of their livings. On the other side, Mammon in Ben Jonson's play of 1610 puffs the alchemist's elixir, which

> Cures all diseases, coming of all causes,
> A month's grief, in a day; a year's, in twelve:
> And of what age soever, in a month,
> Past all the doses of your drugging doctors.[17]

But official medicine had its magical side. The 'elaborate polypharmacy' of learned physicians included a range of magical substances and involved ritual behaviour. A prescription such as this for measles from a doctor in Uzerche in 1742 does not seem far removed from the mixture in the witches' cauldron in *Macbeth*:

> Take two ounces of knapweed water and borage water with water of scabious in which you have dissolved on the stove two drachms of confection of hyacinth: mix in powdered whale sperm, one drachm of diaphoretic antimony, the eyes of a crayfish, and viper powder, all well pulverized; ... add an ounce and a half of white poppy syrup, and give the patient a spoonful every two hours after shaking the phial.

A Huntingdon physician who died in 1662 'used powder of toads to stop bleeding'; while a Cambridge practitioner active a little earlier in the century prescribed a powder made from drying a hare in an oven as a remedy for the stone. Also found in the latter's casebook is the eye remedy described in Chapter 10, involving woman's milk and baby's urine. As late as 1771, Richard Brookes, a regular practitioner, advised readers of his health care book, 'when there is a pain in the head with delirium, cut open a live chicken or pigeon, and apply it to the head'.[18]

Before the eighteenth century, doctors frequently recommended the use of medals and talismans; and they paid attention, as we have seen, to astrological conjunctures. Phlebotomy had to take account of 'the qualities of the seasons and the course of the moon'. Wilhelm Grimm, the folklorist, consulted the famous Professor Reil at Halle in 1809 for a heart condition. He was given a powder to take 'every month when the moon was on the wane' and was also advised to wear a magnetic amulet on his chest.[19]

Unofficial healers, moreover, preserved modes of diagnosis and cure, like uroscopy or astrology, after doctors had abandoned them, largely because of

the aura which they had acquired. Later on, too, despite the scepticism about
doctors that we have noted, peasants often adapted their paraphernalia to
their own conceptions, attributing magical powers to them. A French physician 'at the end of the nineteenth century found that his patients took chips
from his carriage benches and waiting room furniture to use as talismans'. In
Calabria more recently, rather than get a doctor's prescription made up at the
pharmacist's, peasants would

> place it under the patient's pillow. The evil one would then be so preoccupied with
> trying to decipher the doctor's hieroglyphics that he would forget to torment the
> sick person. Alternatively, the prescription might be put under a holy image (as a
> kind of offering), and everyone would wait for its effects to be manifested.[20]

In a way religious conceptions of disease and healing were opposed both to
official medicine and to magic, at least from the point of view of the stricter
clergy, whose opposition to magical healing has often been emphasized. In
the tenth century Aelfric warned those who were sick

> against buying their bodies' health with their souls' through the use of any Devil's
> craft ... It is not allowed to any Christian to fetch his health from any stone, nor
> from any tree nor from any place, unless it be the holy house of God; he who does
> otherwise undoubtedly commits idolatry

Bishop Stafford of Bath and Wells had it proclaimed in all the churches of
his diocese in 1431 'that magic arts, sorceries and incantations can bring no
remedies to the illnesses of men nor cure sick animals, but are the snares and
wiles of the ancient enemy'. 'Many in great distress have been relieved by
sending unto ... wisemen or wisewomen', George Malden, vicar of Maldon
in the 1580s conceded: 'Yet ... they cannot say that the Lord is their health
and salvation, [for] their physician is the Devil'. A Carmelite who died in
Milan in 1622, Fra Simone di San Paolo, had been a doctor before he became
a friar. He then 'became so sworn an enemy of medicine, because it favours
the flesh, that Galen – whom he had previously so esteemed and revered as a
master – he subsequently named the "devil Galen" '.[21] But things were not so
clear-cut in practice, as we have seen with official medicine itself.

Clearly where one believed that disease had religious causes, then religious
remedies were appropriate, though simple resignation might be enjoined as a
Christian duty. Diabolical illnesses could be cured by baptism and exorcism
proper. Where sin was to blame, confession, penance, attendance at mass or
the Eucharist, and anointing were advocated. The priest of Cysoing in
Flanders told his parishioners around 1500: 'Very often illnesses are sent to us

by God for our sins. You must, therefore, cast them out of you through the confessional, in order to please Him and regain His love'. Much earlier the seventh-century Life of Eligius of Noyon instructed: 'The one who is ill should trust in God's mercy alone and receive the sacrament of the body and blood of Christ in faith and reverence. He should also ask some holy oil of his church and have his body anointed in the name of Christ'. Similar advice was being given to Catholics down to modern times. Simple prayer was also enjoined. In his letters of direction to Heloise in the 1130s, Abelard cited Ecclesiasticus: 'My son, if you have an illness, do not neglect it but pray to the Lord, and He will heal you'.[22] This again was typical and perennial advice.

Ministering to the sick was equally important to Protestants. 'All the Church Ordinances of the sixteenth century attach great significance to visits to the sick by the clergy'. Protestants placed special emphasis on prayer. Ralph Josselin 'felt that the best remedy [for disease] was prayer and the best preventative medicine ... a sinless life ... [He and his family] prayed as individuals, in family groups and with friends and neighbours to heal sickness, survive childbirth [and] avoid epidemics'. Richard Baxter presents many instances in his autobiographical writings of sickness being cured by prayer – his own and others'. 'Many a time have I been brought very low and received the sentence of death in myself', he wrote of the Commonwealth period, 'when my poor, honest praying neighbours have met, and upon their fasting and earnest prayers I have recovered.'[23]

But, as this also indicates, Protestants also employed more mechanical and charismatic means. 'Agreed that a public day of humiliation be kept at Manchester upon Wednesday next, the 22 August', the minutes of the town's Presbyterian Classis recorded in 1649, '... in regard that the hand of God is thus fully gone out against us in a violent fever and the small pox.' Such 'humiliations' and fasts were common in such circles and were ordered on a more general basis, we have seen, in the event of unseasonable weather, wars and national crises as well as epidemics. Faith-healing was practised by some Protestant sects like the English Quakers and the Camisards of Languedoc. Interpreting illness in religious terms did not necessarily imply exclusive recourse to religious healing, however. Although the Puritan Lady Hoby in the early seventeenth century 'was convinced that God caused illnesses, she did not expect Him to cure them without human aid', and she herself devoted much time and energy to nursing and dosing her family and dependents. More generally religious and medical language were merged in Puritan writers, and this eclectic approach could include magic. We have seen that Richard Baxter believed that diseases were sent by God to try and test mortals and that prayer was the best recourse for sufferers, but he also employed self-prescribed remedies and those recommended by doctors, which included moss from a dead man's skull to stop nose-bleeding and a gold bullet, which he swallowed, for consumption. The Methodist leader John Wesley was the author of a popular manual *Primitive Physic* (1747), in which pills made from a dried toad were recommended for convulsions, while for consumption the patient was advised: 'Every morning cut a little turf of fresh earth and, lying down, breathe into the hole for a quarter of an hour'.[24]

Medical practitioners worked, too, in a religious ambience. An anonymous treatise of 1392 by a London practitioner laid down that before difficult surgery both surgeon and patient should be 'clean shriven', and the former should 'say three Paternosters and three Aves, in worship of the Trinity' and then proceed again in the name of the Trinity. Much later, images of the Virgin and the saints, 'stoups for holy water, and little cups in which lighted wicks burn floating on green oil' were common in barbers' shops in nineteenth-century Spain, 'and no barber prepared for an operation, whether on veins, teeth or beards, without first making the sign of a cross'.[25]

Epidemics produced special collective religious measures. During the 1580 plague in Corsica, for example, the bishop of Aleria, 'ordered three days of fast and three solemn processions in which he participated, dressed in black, bare-footed, carrying a crucifix'. In similar circumstances in June 1630, the Chapter of Tréguier in Brittany ordered processions on three days of the week after Compline with recitation of the litanies of the Virgin 'that it may please God by his intercession to keep away from this town the plague with which it is threatened'. In 1708 and 1721 further such processions were prescribed 'to supplicate His Divine Majesty to suspend the just rigour of His vengeance irritated by the excess of our iniquity, and preserve us from the plagues with which He is afflicting much of France'. Other remedies against the plague were vows, the celebration of masses, the building of chapels and the founding of confraternities.[26]

At the popular level in Catholic countries, and to some extent also in Protestant ones, religious recourse in illness meant recourse to the saints. The diagnostic process involved determining whether complaints fell into the category for which the saints were responsible and then pin-pointing which particular supernatural helper should be addressed. Various rituals were employed. French examples are recorded from the sixteenth century to modern times and seem to be fairly typical.

They could sometimes be carried out by anyone, but experts were usually consulted, most often old women – in central France those who also laid out the dead. In the Périgord early in the twentieth century, a fresh bucket of water was drawn and some of the water was put in a glass. The woman then burned some hazel twigs about three centimetres long and dropped them on

18 Pilgrims at the shrine of St Sebastian, Rome. Josse Lieferinxe (?), Flemish, *c.* 1500. (*Galleria Nazionale d'Arte Antica, Palazzo Barberini, Rome*)

19 Priest sprinkling marriage bed with holy water. Maarten van Cleve, *Peasant Wedding*, Flemish, 1576. (*Museum of Fine Arts, Budapest*)

20 Pieter Brueghel the Younger, *Wedding Dance*, c. 1600. (*Musées Royaux des Beaux-Arts de Belgique, Brussels*)

21. Pregnancy displayed and protected. Peter Paul Rubens, *The Visitation*, 1612–14. (*Antwerp Cathedral*)

22. Gentile da Fabriano, *Birth of St Nicholas*, early fifteenth century. (*Vatican Picture Gallery, Rome*)

23 Mother giving thanks for child. Ex-voto painting, 1790,
Saint-Jean de Garguier, near Marseille.

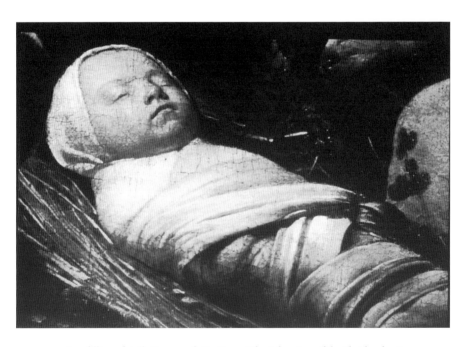

24 Swaddling, detail. Georges de La Tour, *The Adoration of the Shepherds*, 1643.
(*Musée du Louvre, Paris*)

25 Jan Steen, *The Christening Feast*, 1664. (*Wallace Collection, London*)

26 The Brothers Le Nain, *Le Retour du Baptême*, 1642. (*Musée du Louvre, Paris*)

27 Ritual to determine which saint's help to seek to heal baby. Gaston Vuillier, watercolour, c. 1900. (*Musée du Cloître André-Mazeyrie, Tulle, France*)

28 Cure following a vow to the Virgin of Oropa. Ex-voto painting, 1685, Oropa, northern Italy.

29 Pilgrimage and procession to the shrine of Oropa following the ending of a drought. Ex-voto painting, 1685, Oropa, northern Italy.

30 Virgin of Oropa saving a village from floods. Ex-voto painting, 1755, Oropa, northern Italy.

31 Pietro Longhi, *Extreme Unction*, c. 1750. (*Fondazione Scientifica Querini Stampalia, Venice*)

32 Burial in the vaults of a Protestant church. Hendrik Cornelisz van Vliet, *Interior of the New Church at Delft*, mid seventeenth century. (*Koninklijk Museum voor Schone Kunsten, Antwerp*)

the water, muttering secret formulae or prayers. Each twig represented a saint, and the one that sunk first indicated which saint was to be called on to effect a cure.

> At Nontron the operation was done in the bucket. Having said some prayers the diviner drops in one charcoal stick, asking: 'The saint of Abjat?'. No response. So she takes the same stick and successively goes through the names of the patrons of all the churches of the district. 'The saint of Brantôme? The saint of Pluviers? of Villars? of Champ-Romain?' To do this requires a very good knowledge of local devotional geography ... Eventually the stick sinks,

and the saint is revealed. In parts of the Limousin, four candles were lit around the cradle of a sick child, each standing for a likely saint, and the first to burn down indicated the right one (see Plate 27). In other parts of the region, a twig of spindle or other wood was lit and a litany of the saints recited; 'when the fire went out or the twig was burned up, the saint whose name was being pronounced at that moment was the one to whose shrine or fountain a pilgrimage should be made'. In parts of Brittany, an earthworm, whole or cut in pieces, was

> placed on the affected part of the body, while the names of the saints believed to be able to cure the trouble were called out. The name of the saint being pronounced when the worm or its parts finally ceased to wriggle would be the one to be effective.

Lotteries by burning candles were used in sixteenth-century Spain to determine which saints to invoke against outbreaks of plague. A practice found in the late medieval and early modern periods in Britain and the Continent involved all twelve Apostles. In Venice in the 1580s, the names of the Apostles were written on pieces of paper, which were then folded. The sick person opened one each day, 'burning it if his fever persisted; but if the fever abated, he had to vow to fast on the Vigil of the Apostle named and should not burn the paper'.[27]

Many medieval and later saints' shrines were non-specialist, their clerical guardians not wishing to restrict their clientele, they and their clients measuring the importance of a saint by his or her breadth of competence. Here the Virgin Mary was most important and most versatile. Le Braz was told around 1900 at the aptly-named shrine of Notre-Dame-de-Tout-Remède at Rumengol: 'There is no favour that Rumengol does not dispense'. But specialization was ingrained in popular hagiolatry, and the divination rituals we have described must often have confirmed or applied pre-existing associations, or made fine choices within established fields. As Maraspini has written for southern Italy in recent times, 'each saint has a particular power attributed to him, and, though no two lists are the same, the principle whereby each individual saint is concerned with a specific human activity is accepted by nearly all the peasants. In the same way, each saint can effectively cure one particular disease or type of misfortune'. One such list, far from complete, must stand for thousands. In seventeenth-century Flanders, Sts Deodatus and Winoc cured jaundice; Sts Thomas of Camaldoli and Mary of Oignies cured hernias and fractures; Sts Ursmar, Ingelmunde and Ediltrude were invoked for toothache; Sts Gerard and William for mental illness; Sts Adus and Juliana Abbess for headaches; St Reynard healed falling sickness; St Pont lymphatic illnesses; St Leger eye troubles; St Fiacre piles and polyps; St Lambert epilepsy; St Tithon Abbot fevers; Sts Benedict and Syria gravel; and St Eligius the plague. These associations were often indicated for the better-known saints in their iconography. Statues of St Roch from the early modern period display or point to buboes on their legs, while those of St Agatha sometimes hold out one of their breasts.[28] Less permanently, cakes or loaves baked at festivals might take the shape of the part of the body with which the saint was concerned: breasts for St Agatha again in Savoy, Sicily and else-where; eyes or spectacles for St Lucy.

Though there might be disagreement or uncertainty about which saint to consult in any given instance – hence the need for divination – and though there were many local variations, the attributions of some saints were very well-established – in a few cases all over Europe. St Sebastian's reputation as a protector against the plague dated from the earliest Middle Ages, legend linking his cult to an epidemic at Rome at the end of the seventh century. He was to some extent superseded by St Roch in the sixteenth century, though both saints were being invoked still in the seventeenth century, for example in Corsica, the Dauphiné and the Sologne. St Roch's powers were switched later after the demise of the plague to other epidemic diseases. He was invoked, for example, in 1782 during an outbreak of sweating sickness at Pamiers; and he was called on much more generally in the cholera outbreaks of the nineteenth century. St Apollonia was the chief recognized healer of toothache in many parts of Europe. 'The orison of St Apollonia?', asks Don Quixote's house-keeper. 'That might do something if my master's distemper lay in his teeth, but alas! it lies in his brain'.[29] St Apollonia was still being invoked in nineteenth-century France, where henbane, whose seeds were used as a specific against toothache, was known as St Apollonia's herb. We have seen that St Agatha was invoked by nursing women and for all diseases and disorders of the breasts.

These last two examples illustrate one rationale behind saints' specialisms: episodes from their martyrdom related to the part of the body in question. As we have noted, St Agatha had her breasts torn off and they were specifically represented in her iconography. Similarly, St Appolonia had her teeth and jaws removed in her martyrdom and she was represented with a pair of pincers holding a tooth. Miracles and legends also supplied associations. In the early Middle Ages and later, St Blaise was invoked against sore throats. Not only was a collar involved in the saint's martyrdom, but he once 'miraculously healed a child that had a thorn in its throat'. Again, 'St Veronica wiped Christ's bloody face on His way to Calvary and her name is repeatedly mentioned in charms to staunch bleeding'. Another magical kind of association explains why St Domenico is invoked in the Cocullo region of the Abruzzi against both snakes and snake-bite and against rabies. The saint's power focuses on a relic: one of his teeth; and there is a symmetrical opposition, it has been suggested, 'by which the harmful tooth of the snake or the dog is countered by the beneficent tooth of the saint'.[30] The statue of the saint who protected against snakes, moreover, was processed with live snakes fixed to it. More frequently perhaps the specialism derived from a resemblance between the saint's name and the complaint, for example St Cloud and *clous* or carbuncles, or St Aignan and *teigne* or ringworm in France. In Provence, St Eutrope or Tropez, known locally as St Estropi cured *estropiés* or lame people. Sometimes the saint had suffered from the illness he cured. A well, dedicated to St Job, near Namur offered a cure for the skin ulcers with which this Old Testament saint had been afflicted. The Blessed Bonaventure of Potenza, who died in 1711, had suffered from bowel disease, which became his posthumous healing specialism.

Once a suitable saint had been selected, a visit would usually be paid to his or her shrine often following a vow to do so (see Plates 18 and 28). To take the example of the Périgord again, the patient went first to the designated saint's church. Here

> a short reading from the Gospels was obtained, being recited while the patient's head was under the priest's stole. The patron saint was invoked: 'St Sicaire, pray for us!'. Sometimes a sum of money, begged very often from houses in the village, was left to pay for a mass to be said. A small candle was burned.

At some churches, effigies in wax of the diseased member were offered. The commerce in wax dolls, torsos, arms and heads continued in some places until the First World War. After the visit to the church or chapel came that to the saint's fountain or well. This might be in or by the church or at a consider-able distance in the woods or the wild. Pilgrims might walk round the well. Gifts would be deposited. In recent times coins would be thrown into the water, sometimes scratched first with a cross. And the patient would bathe or be dipped in it.[31] In all this, a proxy might stand in for the patient, as we shall see (see Plate 15).

Many variations and elaborations of the ritual are recorded all over Europe, though the exact form required in any particular instance had to be carefully followed. Sometimes, as we have seen in the case of sick babies, the ritual at the shrine entailed an element of divination, a prognosis as to whether the patient would recover. Clerical involvement could be greater. At Montgéard in the Haute-Garonne, 'the priest blessed the water in St Prim's well on the saint's day and dipped his relics in it', and the water, which cured styes and other eye complaints, could be 'procured in the sacristy by ordering a votive mass'. Or secular water might be drawn into the religious framework. 'The saint of Sarrazac', Rocal noted, 'who attracts mothers of babies with twisted limbs, has the whim of not being happy with the still water of a holy fountain or well; he demands running, working water, so the women go for their cures to the Betoul mill-stream.' Some holy springs were only effective when their water moved, often a natural phenomenon, but supposedly induced by the saint or by clerical intervention. In a few cases the Classical procedure of incubation was followed. In some medieval accounts of miracles, we learn that patients spent the night in shrines where they slept and had visions of the healing saint. For example, according to a ninth-century text, a Spaniard, 'who for his sins was so afflicted that he twitched most horribly in all his limbs', went to Fulda in hope of a cure. There he lay down and appeared to sleep in the crypt below 'the body of the holy martyr Boniface'. When he awoke, he was cured and he told the attendant priest 'that he had had an ecstasy', in which the saint 'had made the sign of the cross on his breast'; the disease had then come out of him in the form of a black bird that changed into a devil. Much later in the nineteenth century at the chapel of St Beuno at Clynnoy, Caernarvonshire, 'his votaries afflicted by any malady were laid [there] for the night, in full confidence of receiving a cure'.[32]

Rituals might focus on objects associated with the saint and appropriate perhaps to the complaint, though the connection of some with the saint was remote or obscure. At Meaux in the later Middle Ages, sufferers from piles, known as 'St Fiacre's evil', sat in a chair in the cathedral in which the saint had allegedly placed his bottom, too. At Arles later, the collar used in the martyrdom of St Blaise was kept in a local convent, and it was placed by a priest on the neck of those suffering from goitres or troubles of the throat and neck. St Fillan or Faolan's stones were preserved in modern times at his mill in Killin in Scotland. Sick people would select the stone suited to their ailment and rub against it, one skull-like stone for the head, another for the back, another for the belly and so on, with small 'socket-stones' being placed over the nipples of women's breasts. The virtue of the stones was renewed annually by placing them in the bed of the river on the saint's day.[33]

Pilgrims to the larger shrines all hoped that contact with the saint's relics would bring them relief. These were housed in reliquaries, usually behind the main altar, with provision for pilgrims to file by them to touch and kiss.

14. Sick people passing under relics that are being processed. Bréviare de Belleville, fourteenth century. (*Bibliothèque Nationale, Paris*)

Two unusual rituals at important specialist shrines highlight the principles more generally involved. The shrine of St Hubert in the Belgian Ardennes was associated with the cure and prevention of rabies from medieval times. The relevant relic here was the saint's stole, which had been brought down from heaven by angels, and the ritual procedures connected with it are attested from the sixteenth to the nineteenth centuries. The person bitten by a rabid dog was placed in a chair. After saying a few prayers, a priest made a small vertical incision in his or her forehead and placed in it a thread from the stole. The wound was bandaged up for nine days during which the patient followed a strict regime: daily confession and communion, sexual abstinence, a special diet, no shaving or brushing the hair. Children who had been bitten or adults who had been bitten without blood being drawn were simply touched with the relic. In the eleventh century, according to legend, the bodily remains of St Anthony of Egypt were brought to the Dauphiné, and the shrine which received them quickly acquired the reputation for curing ergotism and other 'burning' diseases, including later the plague. The cure, well-attested from the twelfth to the sixteenth century, involved applying to or giving patients to drink 'a few drops of a peculiar liquid called the holy cordial'. This was made not by the more common dipping of relics in water but by pouring a special wine every Ascension Day through the reliquary that contained the saint's bones.[34] Relics were also processed, which provided further opportunities for gaining across to their power (see Text Figure 14 and Plates 16 and 17).

Contact with the statue of the saint later came to have the same significance as contact with the tomb or relic. In *Jacquou le croquant* (1899), Eugène Le Roy describes the pilgrimage of St Rémy at Auriac in the Dordogne earlier in the century. Men, women and children came from all around with complaints ranging from skin diseases and fevers to rheumatism and hernias. They attended the service in the church and had the Gospel read over them under one of the priest stoles.

> After the Gospel, they went to rub themselves on the saint: for the Gospel was nothing compared to St Rémy himself; what is more, the Gospel cost something while the saint was free. And the saint in question was not the one in the choir, newly-painted, that no one ever looked at. The real saint was a little stone figure that had been demoted from his niche and that everyone picked up to rub the sore part of them, or got someone else to do it, if their pains were in their backs. People rubbed their stomachs with him, their arms, their legs, their thighs, directly on the skin if they could,

lifting or removing their clothes if necessary. And the statue had been so rubbed over the ages that it had lost all its features and was like a smooth and formless doll. When the chapel was closed, pilgrims rubbed themselves against the external wall closest to it. In other cases, material might be scraped from the statue, the tomb, the chapel or its furnishings. One of the miracles of St Martin at Tours in the early medieval period was the cure of a woman who had had dysentery for five months after she 'drained a cup of dust scraped from the blessed tomb'. Other miraculous cures of St Martin were attributed to hangings from his shrine and the rope 'by which the statue of the saint was moved'. Much later in Spain, pulverized stones from the cave at Manresa, in which St Ignatius Loyola spent a year's retreat, were used for cures; while at Noves in Provence infants with impetigo were passed under the canopy of St Baudile.[35]

In some cases, saints' cures converged with or invaded the sphere of secular healing or borrowed from it. Spas, hot and cold, were frequented by the elite from medieval times. Montaigne, for example, was a great believer in them and visited many on his travels through Germany and Italy in the 1580s. Though spas were generally distinct from the springs and fountains frequented by the general population, there was some overlap between them. The latter were pre-Christian healing sites that had been more or less Christianized through association with the saints. And spas might have some religious connection. The bath-house of Villa near Lucca was inscribed with this invocation in Latin in the sixteenth century: 'O Holy Virgin, by your power make everyone who enters this bath, leave it sound in both body and mind'.[36]

We have seen in the case of St Apollonia that certain herbs were linked with or named after saints. In Normandy in modern times, forty-nine plants were named after saints and thirty-two after the Virgin Mary, and this was not unusual. And saints' herbs were linked again to their patrons' specialism. Agrimony or St William's herb was helpful in many situations but was especially efficacious against diseases of the liver and the eyes. St John's wort strengthened the womb and dissipated bladder stones, among other things. St Fiacre's herb or Aaron's Rod was used to settle stomach and bowel upsets and against fevers and, again, piles. It was not uncommon for medieval sufferers to imagine or to dream, sometimes while spending the night at the shrine, that the saint had administered some kind of regular treatment to them. The Virgin Mary appeared, for example, to one of the early Dominicans, Brother Reginald, 'amid the fire of a fever, and rubbed him with a healing ointment which she brought with her. She anointed his eyes, nostrils, ears, mouth, navel, hands and feet'. It would be surprising if such beliefs had not survived into later centuries. There seems to be an echo of them in a custom noted in the Abruzzi before the First World War. During the festival of St Vincent de Paul at Villamagna, a stage was erected outside one of the village gates with beds on it, arranged as in a hospital. Peasants pretending to be ill lay on the beds, imploring help from the saint. Others dressed and acted as nurses and a doctor, who could offer the patients no hope, however. A priest then came on to say the prayers for the dying, and the rattling of chains was heard from the Devil under the stage waiting to have their souls. But then a sheet, behind which the statue of the saint was hidden, was dropped, the Devil was vanquished, and the patients began to recover.[37]

The magical aspects of these cures by saints are often very clear. As with some of the examples involving children, the patient could be represented by a proxy. A woman whom Le Braz met at Rumengol told him that she had been there fifty-six times and always on behalf of a different person. Very often in modern France, the women who divined which saints to consult also performed the necessary pilgrimages. Ernest Dimnet recalled another itinerant in the Nord in the 1860s, 'a sturdy elderly woman' then, called Ninie Lambret. She 'could tell all the varieties of *maux de saints* ... only cured through the intercession of specialists in heaven and she decided which remote chapel was to be visited and prayed in'. Her whole life had been 'spent trudging on road or lane, going on pilgrimages and "serving saints" for people who gave her a little money' to do so.[38]

Proxies usually took something belonging to the patient, most often a garment. Like other gifts, this might be left at the shrine and/or exchanged for another offering. A statue of St Anthony, dating from the seventeenth century in a chapel near Saint-Sernin in the Charente, was reputed to cure diseases in small infants. After prayers, touching the statue and the performance of other standard ritual gestures, a piece of the child's clothing was hung on or by the statue and one already there was taken instead. Ribbons were another common offering and could be used in various rituals. The church at Saint-Didier in the Eure had a well in it covered by a grill. 'Pilgrims affected by fevers come to draw water from it; they burn a candle in front of the statue of the saint; and they cut a ribbon in two parts, giving one to the saint and taking the other away with them.' At another chapel in the same district, resorted to by those with stomach pains, the ribbon taken away was first put in contact with the statue, this time of St Martin; it was then 'worn by the patient for nine days; after which it was burned or buried in the ground'.[39] This is an example of a rite magically transferring a disease from a patient, something very common in the repertoire of folk-healers, as we shall see.

Other kinds of ritual could be attached to saints' cults. The healing water of St Prim at Montgéard received its powers in part from the saint's relics but there was a further complication. Both Montgéard and a neighbouring village had fountains dedicated to St Prim, and the villagers from each place went annually to pay homage to him and ensure the continuation of his cures, but they had to go to the fountain in the other village and *not* their own, for the ritual to be effective. There might be a correspondence, too, between the part of the body to be cured and the part of the statue touched, and this might have to be expressed in a particular way. At Darnac in the Limousin, for example, 'if one had a pain in the arm or the leg or the head, one had to touch the arm, the leg or the head of the statue of St John there with a ball of wool thrown at it from a distance', and one had to keep trying until the right part was hit. The operation was particularly efficacious if performed during mass. In the same region of France, 'at Saint-Junien, a woman wanted her child to touch the nose of the saint, but the statue was too high, so she put her hand-kerchief on the end of her umbrella, rubbed the nose of the saint with it and then that of the snivelling infant'. A better example of contagious magic could not be found. We should also mention the practice of measuring patients, which seems to have been particularly common in the medieval period. At St Frideswide's shrine at Oxford in the twelfth century, a father typically 'measured his daughter with a thread and surrounded the thread with wax and offered it as a candle to the blessed virgin saint'. The girl, who had a tumour, also drank water blessed at the shrine and was cured.[40]

Some gods of the Ancient world, like those of the Hindu pantheon, were generally responsible for the disease with which they were associated; they were able to cure it because they had sent it in the first place. This quasi-personification of the illness is found among gypsies in the Balkans. Bibi is identified with cholera and typhoid; particularly she kills children. But she is honoured and worshipped in order 'to avoid her illnesses' as well as to be cured of them.[41]

The same pattern may be found in the cults of saints. In the Haute-Vienne in the modern period, the diviner of saints declared by which saint a sick person was 'marked'. Many diseases were named after saints. The designation of ergotism as 'St Anthony's fire' or 'St Anthony's evil' is attested from the twelfth century onwards. The thirteenth-century miracle book at Savigny in Normandy refers to the *morbus sancti Laurentii*, a kind of gangrenous erysipelas similar to ergotism, and to the *morbus sancti Eligii*, a kind of fistula. Among 'the illnesses of the saints' recorded by a folklorist in the Vosges in the 1870s were St Golbert's or St Valber's gout, the *mal Saint-Quirin*, the *mal Saint-Gengoult*, the *mal Saint-Hubert*, and so on. Nor is there any doubt that people often believed that the saint had caused the disease which bore his name and which he could cure.

> St Anthony sells me his evil all too dear;
> He stokes the fire in my body.

wrote the fourteenth-century poet Etienne Deschamps. Similarly, the pilgrims questioned in Rabelais' *Gargantua and Pantagruel* of the mid sixteenth century believed that 'St Sebastian brings plague, St Anthony puts fire in the limbs, St Eutropius makes dropsicals, St Gildas lunatics, St Genou those with gout'. St Valentine 'the falling sickness sends, and helps the man that to him cries' a Protestant writer echoed in 1570, in an attack on Catholic 'superstition'. Such beliefs were still present in the twentieth century. In the Périgord, 'St Simeon of Ligueux was believed to send and cure epilepsy; St Eutropius was responsible for crippling the limbs. "Fear" in infants was called "St Paul's evil"... Rheumatisms were attributed to St Avit'. More generally, if a child died after the performance of the proper rituals at a saint's shrine, it was said to have died from 'the saints'.[42]

Saints sent their diseases as punishments or if they had been slighted or vows to them unfulfilled. The aim of Rabelais' pilgrims was 'to turn away the anger of the saint who had produced their trouble rather than to implore the assistance of one who was primarily a healer'. Henri Estienne satirized Catholic belief here in his *Apology for Herodotus* of 1566: 'Some saints are more angry and dangerous than others, and notably St Anthony. If any injury is done to his servants, either human or porcine, they immediately pray to him to carry out vengeance'. (St Anthony was especially associated with pigs and a mendicant order had been founded in 1095 to maintain his shrine and cult.) This assimilation of saints to other persons of ill-will was taken a stage further in nineteenth-century Périgord. There illness might be specifically attributed to the 'malefice or evil spells of the saints', using the same term found in accusations of witchcraft. In the Charente, where the notion of 'saints' illnesses' was also well-established in the modern period, infants might be dedicated to wearing a particular colour for a specified time, usually white for the first year, blue for the second, and grey for the third, 'in order to avoid the evil power of the saints'. Children were also dedicated to and named after particular saints with the same intention. Those born on the festivals of powerful saints were either especially well-protected against disease and other misfortunes or in special danger – unless the saint concerned was very carefully placated.[43]

13

Folk-Healers and Magical Cures

The main alternative to recourse to saints for cures was recourse to folk-healers, though the two were not always distinct. Those who divined the saints were sometimes also healers. Some healers had reputations as 'saints' or holy people. Others claimed to be the descendants of saints, like those of St Marcoul in France, who touched for scrofula. In modern Portugal, the local wise women were considered to be 'mere officiants' and any cures which they achieved were attributed to saints.[1]

Healers existed under different names all over Europe. John Cotta, a Northampton physician, referred in 1612 to

> a sort of practitioners, whom our custom and country doth call wise men and wise women, reputed a kind of good and honest harmless witches or wizards, who by good words, by hallowed herbs and salves, and other superstitious ceremonies, promise to allay and calm ... the forces of many diseases.

'What commune does not have its healer, its bone-setter, its sorcerer, its well-known wise woman, one reputed for his or her water for eye complaints, another for an ointment against bruises, falls, aches or ulcers?', asked a French pamphlet of 1851 rhetorically. Mère Fadet was one such in George Sand's *La Petite Fadette*. A poor widow who owned no land, people came to consult her from far and wide. She cured wounds, sprains and other aches and pains by means of the 'secret' she had. She could also take off other illnesses like fevers and make milk go from one cow to another, and she was a midwife. Although their role was special, such healers were part of the community. In Devon between the wars,

> the herbalist was an honoured figure in the villages. She was more accessible than the doctor. In the case of Mrs Trigg of Kingskerswell you just opened the back door and shouted. She was more like one of us. She lived in the same sort of house, spoke with the same accent and used the same vocabulary. Her diagnosis and prescriptions were chatty rather than bleakly authoritative.[2]

Healers could be male or female. There could, however, be local gender emphases and specialities. In pre-Petrine Russia, for example, most healers seem to have been women, as they were in early modern Modena and Venice; but in the Gironde at the start of the nineteenth century charlatans and empirics were nearly always men.

Folk-healers had a 'gift' or power, which they acquired in a number of ways. It might be 'specially conferred', 'innate in the healer', or the result of 'some condition or acquired status'. In the modern Cévennes, the healer usually received the gift from an older person by touching with the hand, sometimes accompanied by the revelation of a secret formula.[3] This transmission often occurred when the old healer was near death and might take place on a specific date or at a significant time: in Corsica, for example, on Christmas Eve at midnight. The gift was an obligation and, to a certain extent, a burden, and cases are reported of healers trying to pass it on and finding no takers. Most frequently, the gift was handed down within families, from father to son but also from mother to daughter. The royal touch for scrofula of course went via primogeniture, though its exercise also depended on proper inauguration. Other kinship links could be utilized. Little Fadette learned her secrets from her grandmother; while a healer in the Gironde claimed to have inherited his powers from his maternal uncle and godfather.

Birth order might also be significant. Everywhere seventh sons and daughters were believed to have special powers, which were redoubled when the father or mother was also a seventh child.

> In the Ozark country [and elsewhere in the USA] ... a seventh son of a seventh son is thought to be a physician in spite of himself, endowed with healing powers that cannot be denied. Even if such a man does not study or practice medicine, he is very often called 'Doc' or 'Doctor'.

In Andalusia, the ninth son in a succession of boys had 'a special grace' for healing. Other circumstances might convey the gift: birth on a certain day, Good Friday, Christmas Day, certain saints' days; being born after one's father had died; being born with a caul or with teeth. In modern Portugal, the healers called *bento* or *benta* 'derive their reputed powers from the fact that they have cried aloud in the mother's womb'. The anomaly of breech birth might also confer a healing gift. In the British Isles, the healing power here resided in the feet, which were used to 'tread' those suffering from lumbago, rheumatism and sprains.[4] The survivor of twins also often had the gift, presumably acquiring the vitality of his or her dead sibling.

Linked to the hereditary idea was that attributing the healing power to certain occupations. In 1658, a certain Wakefield consulted a healer at Edmonton when his children and servants contracted 'the new disease' or influenza. Wakefield wrote afterwards:

Some people would have scrupled to make use of his physic, he being by profession a horse-smith, and keeps a shop in our town. But he having practised upon many others about us, before we made use of him, the success his physic hath had in our family, hath much increased his fame.

Elsewhere the healing power of blacksmiths was less ambiguously recognized. In Minho, for example, 'before the Second World War, blacksmiths were held to have a special ability to cure wounds'. Besides blacksmiths and farriers, weavers, carpenters and shepherds are frequently mentioned in the sources. Conrad Stöcklin, a shepherd, tried at Oberstorf in Bavaria in 1586, 'asserted that he could cure men and beasts stricken by witches, and that he had done so many times through the grace of God, by imposing prayers and fasts'.[5]

Stöcklin also claimed that his power came from nocturnal journeys to the other world. Religious and magical experiences like this were another general source of healing power. Many healers in France during the early nineteenth century seem to have been given their powers as a reward for saving or restoring statues of saints and other religious objects during the Revolutionary period. The *sabia* in Andalusia might have been visited by the Virgin Mary in dreams. Parallel magical events often involved living creatures, whose power was thereby acquired. In Radnorshire and other parts of Wales, those who had drunk eagle's blood or eaten its flesh could charm for shingles, which was called *eryri* from the Welsh for eagle. This power was inherited by the person's descendants for nine generations. All over northern Europe and in the USA, healing power was conveyed to a child by getting it to throttle or otherwise kill a particular kind of creature: a snake, a toad, very often a mole. An old female healer in the Pays de Baugé in 1903, for example, who cured colics by laying on of hands, derived her power 'from the fact that she had crushed a toad in her hands while she was still a nursling'.[6] The power here was conveyed very specifically and directly to the hands, or even to a particular finger. In Maine, if an innocent boy took a live mole, opened its belly and kept his finger in it all night, then that finger would have the power to dissipate colic in horses by rubbing their bellies.

As some of these examples indicate, healers were more often than not specialists, their speciality being related sometimes to the way in which they acquired their gift. In parts of Brittany, for example, those born on 25 January, the Day of the Conversion of St Paul, partook of that saint's powers and could cure snake bites.[7] Peasant distrust of doctors in nineteenth-century France stemmed in part from their not being specialists. Distinctions were made, too, by peasants and others among different kinds of healer. Alongside the *bento* or *benta* in Portugal, for instance, were the *feiticeiro* and the *bruxo*, whose powers were more extensive. One may even detect a hierarchy. In the

Cévennes, there were conjurors of warts, burns and snake-bites whose clientele was limited to a single hamlet or at best one village; above them were the
healers whose clients came from a whole valley; and above them one or two
famous healers to whom people came from the whole region and beyond.

One of the functions of healers was to diagnose illnesses caused by witchcraft and to cure them by counter-magic. The more important healers
engaged in other magical and related activities beyond simple healing. The
artist and folklorist Vuillier met 'a kind of sorceress' from Corte in Corsica
around 1890, 'who was skilled in making decoctions to ward off the fever of
malaria or induce the less obnoxious fever of love'. The *sabia* of Andalusia
could find lost property and perform love magic as well as curing illnesses. In
many places, female healers were midwives; and they attended death-beds
and dressed corpses. As weavers, healers could make shrouds. Everywhere
powerful healers could lift spells and challenge witches. Their status was thus
ambiguous. In gypsy societies, *chovihanis* could 'find anything which is lost
or cause anything they wish to disappear; they can start fires or stop them;
they can unite lovers or separate them; they can cause disease or cure it'.
Though the Andalusian *sabia* was generally reckoned to be 'good', some
people believed that her power could be used for evil purposes. 'The *magarà*,
masciara or *maàra* [of southern Italy] are healers, magicians, controllers of
the forces of good and evil'. Not surprisingly folk-healers were frequently
prosecuted during the early modern witch-craze for practising witchcraft. In
the 1570s, for example, Janet Pereson was brought before the Durham church
courts on a witchcraft charge for 'measuring belts' and advising that a sick
child be washed in a south-running stream. Madeleine Brotte was accused at
Vesoul of acts of *maleficia* and attending a witches' sabbath and also of curing
by means of herbs and spells. In south-western France in the eighteenth and
nineteenth centuries, 'unofficial healers were still often regarded as witches',
and a number of them sued their detractors for defamation.[8]

No sharp line can be drawn between healing within the family and community and the further recourse to experts. Methods might coincide. Peasants, for
example, used herbal remedies in the form of infusions, poultices and ointments, that were part empirical, part magical. There was a lore about these
going back to Classical and early medieval times and to some extent preserved
in herbal books that were extremely popular in the early modern and modern
periods. Culpeper's *Herbal*, dating from the mid seventeenth century, has
gone through over a hundred editions since; while herbals figure prominently
among French chapbooks of the *Bibliothèque bleue*. People grew or gathered
their own plants, but there were also professionals who collected and sold
herbs in season. As with saints, the aid of experts was sought when self-help
had failed and/or there was a suspicion of hostile magic. As William Perkins

noted in a sermon published in 1608: 'For let a man's child, friend, or cattle be taken with some sore sickness, or strangely tormented with some rare and unknown disease, the first thing he doth, is to bethink himself and inquire after some wise man or wise woman, and thither sends and goes for help'.[9]

Visits to or from folk-healers for cures are often referred to in early sources, though for detailed descriptions we must rely on later material. Salomone-Marino witnessed an operation to cure malaria in Sicily in 1875. A well-known healer called Ticchi-Ticchi had been summoned by the family. Having 'explored the patient's body', she announced that the illness was caused by 'strong witchcraft'.

> From a small packet, she took a few dried herbs, some incense, some little crosses made of palm leaves (that had been blessed in church on Palm Sunday), and a thread of virgin flax. She dissolved some salt in water and sprinkled it on the floor, mumbling unintelligible words and tracing crosses in the air with both hands. Then she approached the patient and with scissors cut up a cross of palm leaves on to his chest; then she put her hands on his head and recited a Credo, most of which was inaudible. She passed at once to his feet and, standing with arms outstretched, let fall on them seven pieces of the thread, while reciting these words:

> > I greet you, bread and *tassu* [a plant believed to combat malaria];
> > Heat and cold I hereby free:
> > Better the head and worse the feet;
> > Health come back again!

> Then she recited half an Ave Maria, which the other women present finished. Returning to the middle of the room, she burned some of the herbs, scattering incense on them; then, when the smoke had spread throughout the room, she prostrated herself, imitated by the other women, and, touching the floor with her bare breasts, recited this powerful spell:

> > I touch and I do not touch! I see and I do not see you!
> > *Furcu* [pitchfork or gallows], *Befurcu* [bifurcated tongue of a serpent],
> > *Lurcu* [vampire], *Cataturcu* [arch-Turk or devil]!
> > I put you to bed, I wrench you, I hang you on the gallows.
> > With water and salt and incense, which all have power!
> > By the wounds of Jesus which none can resist,
> > With incense, salt and water at every moment!
> > Into the ditch with the horrible worms; let them be strangled,
> > Let their bones be chewed away![10]

Most of these elements, together or separately, are found in other accounts. First, there was an empirical element, sometimes more obvious than in the Sicilian example. Rocal mentions a conjuror from the Périgord who 'took off a malingering illness in infants called the *béchou* by saying a special prayer over them, accompanied by massages of the body'. Compresses, lotions, infusions, ointments and fumigations, made of herbs and other substances, figured as in household remedies. Drugger recounts in Ben Jonson's *The Alchemist* that 'a good old woman' cured him of headaches and the effects of overeating 'with sodden ale, and pellitory o' the wall'.[11]

Herbal remedies were very important, as we have already indicated. Some plants were chosen to be used in cures (and for other purposes) for religious reasons. Rue, for example,was associated with 'the bitter sorrow of Christ'. Many plants we have seen were linked with saints. Official herbal medicine depended on two theories. First, according to humoral postulates, particular plants had humoral qualities. Lettuce, for example, was cold and moist and hence a means of cooling and soothing overheated skin. Celandine was 'hot and dry ... Its virtue is to dissolve and consume and draw out ... both choler, phlegm and melancholy, and also rotten blood'.[12]

Secondly, there was the theory of 'signatures', abandoned by doctors in the later seventeenth century but maintained at the popular level. According to this theory, all plants

> bore outward signs to indicate the organs to which they corresponded and the diseases of those organs for which they were the proper medicine. So lungwort was regarded as a remedy for consumption, because its leaves, flecked with white, resembled a tubercular lung. Figwort was prescribed for scrofula (and piles) because of its knotty roots. Gromwell was considered likely to dissolve bladder-stones, because the look and hardness of its seeds recalled these concretions. Liverworts were suited to combat liver disease, because the shape of their leaves was analogous to that organ.

'When the daffodil was first introduced into England by the Romans, the flower was called *healswyrt*, neckwort, from its long stem or neck, and the similarity in appearance and name led to its being used against diseases of the neck.' Again, snake-bites were treated with viper's bugloss because its seeds resembled a snake's head, or because it grew in places where snakes were likely to be found; while a range of yellow-flowered plants (celandine, gorse, etc.) were believed to cure yellow jaundice. As some of these examples show, the popular name for a plant might indicate its curing property. In the Ariège in modern times, centaury was known as the 'herb of fevers'; lesser camomile as the 'herb of the womb'; Solomon's Seal as the 'herb of the whitlow'; gromwell as the 'herb of pissing'; burdock and others as the 'herb of ringworm' or 'of scab'.[13]

Where plants were used in cures, there was usually an insistence that they be gathered at a specific time, in a specific way, and sometimes at a specific place. Such notions went back to Classical times. Medea, for example, in Ovid's *Metamorphoses* gathers the plants to revive Jason's father Eson at night, during a full moon, alone, naked, with triple gyrations. Behind such rituals lay a concern to ensure that the plant's qualities were at their optimum state or even to augment them. There was also a fear that picking the plant might cause offence to it or to some divine or demonic being that had therefore to be outwitted and/or propitiated.

Certain days were prescribed for picking different herbs. So, according to different medieval texts, vervain should be picked on a Tuesday or Thursday; periwinkle on a Wednesday or Thursday; and chicory on a Monday or Friday. Sometimes gathering the plant was spread over several days. In a medieval German text, for example, vervain was located on the Saturday evening nearest to Assumption but was picked on the Sunday morning at dawn. In an Anglo-Saxon treatise, picking knot-grasses stretched over three days. Certain months or seasons were also propitious. A salve in the fifteenth-century leechbook, cited already, comprised forty odd herbs, all of which had to be gathered in May before St John's Day, that is St John the Evangelist's on 6 May. According to the *Maison Rustique* (1597), 'the people believed and affirmed that bracken spores [which had a variety of protective uses] should only be gathered on the Eve of St John's', this time St John the Baptist's, on 23 June.[14] This St John's, the Summer solstice, when the sun was at its height, was generally a favourable time to gather beneficent herbs, and we saw in Chapter 2 that particular plants were picked at this time. These included St John's wort, hyssop, thyme, artemisia, vervain and walnut leaves. Other Christian festivals also came to be used for plant gathering, presumably lending some sacred power to the plants concerned. Delatte's comprehensive study mentions Christmas Eve, Epiphany, Mardi Gras, Good Friday, Easter Day, Ascension, Whit, All Saints, Ember Days and Assumption besides the festivals of major saints.

The time of day was also most significant. The herbs of St John were frequently gathered at noon. Times when bells were being rung for liturgical purposes might also be chosen or during mass, Matins or Vespers, or when the angelus sounded. The virtue of a plant might vary depending on the time when it was picked. In the early medieval herbal, known as Pseudo-Apuleius, groundsel gathered at 6 am opened and purged wounds, but, if picked in the afternoon, it closed and sealed them. There were two especially favoured times for picking herbs: at dawn or during the night. A German medieval text advised picking vervain just before sunrise on a Sunday morning. The three sage leaves prescribed to cure the double tertian fever suffered by Francesco di Marco Datini's wife in 1396 had to 'be picked at morn before sunrise'. Similarly, according to an Anglo-Saxon text, sea-holly should be picked just before dawn, 'since the sun shining on it destroyed its virtue'. In other cases, the new sunlight was thought to be beneficial, as was the early morning dew. Sometimes the herbalist began operations at dusk, slept by the plant through the night, and picked it at dawn. At night, it was often important to pick the plant by moonlight. 'The moon shines bright', Jessica recalled in *The Merchant of Venice*:

> ... In such a night
> Medea gathered the enchanted herbs
> That did renew old Aeson.

It was also significant, as we have seen in other circumstances, whether the moon was waxing or waning. In Morayshire in the 1770s, woodbine wreaths used in cures of 'hectic fevers' and consumptions – patients pissed through them – were gathered 'in the increase of the March moon'. In Wallonia, rue for the cure of quinsy was picked during a waxing moon; but to procure an abortion while the moon was waning. In contrast to plants gathered in the moonlight, which were beneficent, those gathered in the dark were 'evil and death-dealing', as Shakespeare again illustrates. The hemlock root that the witches in *Macbeth* place in their cauldron is not only poisonous in its own right but also 'digged in the dark'; and the potion used to murder the duke in the players' scene in *Hamlet* is a 'mixture rank of midnight weeds collected'.[15]

Medea gathered her herbs in particular places and later herb gatherers did the same. In Provence, for example, Mont-Ventoux was 'reputed for the magical quality of the herbs gathered there', as was the hill of Cordes near Arles. Often the location was wild and isolated. In modern Greece a herb used to cure facial erysipelas grew in 'places where a rooster does not crow'. More generally, plants growing in consecrated places or burial grounds had special powers. In Anglo-Saxon leechbooks, lichen growing on a church or on a cross had its power enhanced thereby. In 'Church Going' (1955). Philip Larkin imagines 'dubious women' coming to the churchyard to 'pick simples for cancer'.[16]

The person gathering the herbs had often to be in a particular state either of preparedness or purity or both. Bathing and washing frequently preceded picking, though, in a few cases, it was laid down that the hands should not be washed. Sexual abstinence was often prescribed in Classical times and in the Christian era being in a state of grace. Sometimes only virgins or the celibate could pick the plants. 'In the Dauphiné [in modern times], it was old women and pre-adolescent girls who were charged with gathering the herbs of St John. In the centre of France, the so-called *herbe au pic* only possessed its virtues if picked by a virgin girl.'[17] Sometimes clothing or the lack of it was prescribed. A Carolingian text referred to women covering their heads to pick fennel, a plant with diabolical associations. In Ancient and modern times, nudity was sometimes required, or at least going barefoot, with loose hair and clothing. Fasting and silence were also very often necessary, and it might be important not to look or to turn back when the plant was approached or taken. Usually herb-gathering was done alone, but assistance was sometimes called for, as with collecting mandrakes or peonies in Ancient and medieval times, both dangerous plants.

In addition to these observances were a range of other ritual gestures often with formulae to accompany them. The gatherer might kneel to pick the plant or prostrate himself or herself. Extremely common was encirclement. The gatherer might walk round the plant or trace or make a circle round it with a knife or some other instrument or with a series of marks. In an Anglo-Saxon text, the healer left the church singing litanies, 'went to the fields and then around the plants to be gathered three times, still singing'. 'In the modern Tyrol, the trace of a circle was indicated [round the plant] by seven crosses made of branches of green elder.'[18]

It was also important to pick the herb with a particular hand or even finger. Most frequently the left hand was used, as was often the case in magical procedures which were to some extent regarded as being in opposition to religious and social acts in which the right hand was employed. Again, where particular fingers were prescribed, 'the dominant aim was to use the fingers least "profaned" by the usage of everyday life'. Occasionally gloves were worn; or the plant was picked with the teeth – to avoid touching it. According to an eleventh-century text, the mandrake should be jerked quickly out of the ground by means of a cord tied round its root and attached to a dog, which would incur the anger of the plant rather than its human picker. Usually plants were simply picked by hand, but instruments might sometimes be used, with the same precautionary aims. Sophocles' Medea and Virgil's Dido cut their magical herbs with bronze sickles; bronze was an ancient metal believed to repel demons. Iron and steel might be prescribed later. In a French remedy from the seventeenth century, vervain had to be cut and uprooted with a new iron or steel knife. But more often iron was banned. It was thought that plants lost their virtue through contact with iron and might even be rendered noxious. Hence the use of coins of bronze, gold and silver to cut or dig up or encircle plants in modern Europe, or the less frequent use of animal bones. In some cases the number of strikes used to gather a plant was laid down, three being the favourite number. Extraordinary plants were collected in even more strange ways. In modern Switzerland, mistletoe had to be shot or knocked out of the tree in which it was growing, during a waning moon, and caught in the left hand as it fell.[19]

An offering might be left at the site. In modern Hungary, for example, 'the picking of belladonna is accompanied by an offering of bread, salt and spices;

while for black hellebore, bread alone is given'. In Béarn, seven roots of mint were collected to cure fevers. 'One knelt before each plant and threw on it seven or nine crumbs of bread and five, seven or nine grains of salt, saying: Good day, mint; I bring you bread and salt, so that you will cure my illness'. In other cases, Ancient and modern, money might be left. Originally, Delatte suggests, the gifts may have been made to the Earth rather than the plant, and, in any event, they had the character of a sacrifice of reparation and compensation for taking the plant.[20]

The *Maison Rustique* mentions 'grand ceremonies and words muttered between the teeth' as herbs were gathered, and these are referred to in many other sources down the centuries. 'Hast thou collected medicinal herbs with evil incantations?' inquired Burchard of Worms. The Anglo-Saxon Leechbook of Bald, of around the same date, advocated picking mugwort before sunrise and after 'saying first these words (in Latin): I pick you, mugwort, so that I may not get tired on journeys'. Incantations could be addressed to the plant itself, hailing, conjuring, threatening or imploring it, or to a spirit in or in charge of the plant, with the former being much more common in the medieval and modern periods. A Classical text went: 'Good day, O sacred peony, you are the queen of plenty'. The Anglo-Saxon 'Nine Herbs Charm' addressed each of the herbs in turn, as if they were persons, for example:

> And you, Plantain, mother of herbs,
> Open from the east, mighty inside ...
> This is the herb that fought against the snake;
> It has power against poison; it has power against infection;
> It has power against the loathsome foe roving through the land.

Again, in a modern Hungarian example, the gatherer declared: 'I salute you and venerate you, elder tree', before asking it to cure jaundice.[21]

Burchard and the Leechbook of Bald both advised substituting Christian formulae or blessings for pagan ones, and this was frequently done. A late medieval English medical text included 'a good eye medicine' made from red honeysuckle, 'and when you shall gather this herb set yourself down on your knees and say nine Paternosters in worship of the Holy Trinity, and nine Aves to greet Our Lady, and a Credo'. Similar advice was given in connection with the sage leaves to be picked for Monna Margherita Datini's fever: 'Let the man who picks them do so on his bended knee, saying three Paternosters and three Ave Marias in honour of God and the Holy Trinity'. In modern Wallonia, 'in gathering *fleur de lys*, a Paternoster is recited to the pistil and an Ave to each of the stamens; and chives are only cut for medicinal purposes after a recital of part of the Gospel of St John'. Religious formulae were also mixed with non-religious elements. A charm to be said when vervain was gathered, found in many sixteenth- and seventeenth-century books of magic and other collections in Britain, is typical of this genre:

> All hail, thou holy herb vervain,
> Growing in the ground;
> In the mount of Calvary
> There wast thou found;
> Thou helpest many a grief,
> And staunchest many a wound.
> In the name of sweet Jesus,
> I take thee from the ground.
> O Lord, effect the same
> That I do go about.[22]

The medicinal plant might also be treated in particular ritual ways after being picked or uprooted. Usually the plant could not touch the ground. Sometimes it was raised to the sky. Often it was washed or purified by being exposed to sunlight or moonlight. Sometimes it received additional consecration. Certain medieval and modern recipes prescribe placing plants on the altar and having one or several masses said over them. In other cases, simple blessing by a priest or sprinkling with holy water was deemed sufficient. The power of plants could also be augmented by other means. Garlic and wormwood, for example, were worn by the Rumanian Căluş dancers, and pieces that had been 'danced' were believed to be especially potent and were 'preserved to be used throughout the year for curing purposes'.[23]

A few plants had extraordinary magical powers and were especially prized. One was vervain, which we have already encountered. In addition to stopping bleeding, it was supposed, according to Culpeper, to strengthen the womb, help jaundice, the dropsy and gout, expel worms from the belly and stones from the kidneys and bladder, and cure ulcers in the mouth and the private parts. It was also used as a talisman against witchcraft and in love and other magic. Ana Gonzalez from Cuenca told the Spanish Inquisition in 1615 'that one was supposed to pick vervain [on Midsummer's Eve] and place it under the altar cloth so that it would be blessed the next morning at mass. Then the plant could be used to ask Our Lady for riches'. Other plants with even greater magical reputations were mistletoe, the Druids' 'all-healer', which also extinguished fires and opened locks,[24] and the mandrake, *atropa mandragora*, both of which we have seen had to be gathered in extraordinary ways.

Another element in folk cures involved bodily contact between healer and patient or some operation on the body of the patient. Like herbal remedies, these may have had some empirical content, but they were mainly magical. Most simply, the healer 'touched', 'stroked' or laid hands (or occasionally feet) on the sufferer. In parts of France, the folk-healer was called a *toucheur*, while in sixteenth-century Venice a woman was said to have 'good hands for signing', that is healing. Massage, rubbing and anointing, often with saliva, were also common. Saliva had been used in cures from Classical and Biblical times, and New Testament precedents were probably influential. In 'The Healing of the Blind Man' in the Chester cycle of mystery plays, for example, Jesus spits on the ground and makes a paste, which he rubs on the man's eyes, as he did in the Gospel account. In Anglo-Saxon magical cures, spitting into salves or on to wounds was recommended, also chewing herbs before applying them to the patient. Saliva is also a feature in modern healing procedures. King Francis I of France was reported to have moistened his thumb with saliva as he administered the royal touch. In the modern Limousin, making the sign of the cross or marking round the affected part of a sick person with the healer's saliva was a common procedure. In a Norwegian narrative from the inter-war period, a healer spat three times on a woman's back, while uttering incantations in order to conjure her back pain into a stone. Oral contact might be more direct. In nineteenth-century Montgomeryshire, healers cured certain kinds of skin disease by breathing and spitting on the rash; while in southwestern France and Catalonia in the eighteenth century insufflation or blowing was used against rabies and eye complaints. A wise woman in early modern Northumberland was said to have put her lips to a sick child's mouth 'and made such chirping and sucking that the mother of the said child thought that she had sucked the heart out of it, and was sore affrighted'. Again, 'the old noble family of the counts of Habsburg was reputed to heal stammering children by a mouth-kiss'. An animal or bird might be substituted here for the healer. Two women were presented before the church courts in Durham in 1604 for being charmers 'of sick folks ... and they use to bring white ducks or drakes and to set the bill thereof to the mouths of the sick person and mumble up their charms'.[25]

Some cures simulated violence against the sufferer and/or the complaint, for example the ritual called 'hammering the spleen' that was practised in central and northern France in modern times. This took place at night; the patient was placed on the blacksmith's anvil, naked or with the midriff bared. The forge was lit and, when the fire was red, the blacksmith wielded his biggest hammer, striking the forge with two blows and stopping the third just above the patient's body. In similar procedures, carpenters used their axes to reduce swellings in the neck or restore displaced nerves or veins. Organs might be magically removed and replaced, as in some African cures. A healer from the Limousin in the 1920s cured female troubles by taking all of a woman's insides out and putting them in pots ... She has a pot for every part, depending on its form and volume, one for the intestines, one for the bladder, one for the pancreas and so on. Then, with prayers and charms, everything was put back in place again, and the patient was better.

We have seen that in modern Hungary, babies born 'shrivelled' as a result of witchcraft or some breach of taboo by their mothers during the pregnancy were filled out via an elaborate 'boiling' ritual. Among 'real' as against simulated operations on the body, we may cite the insertion of the threads of St Hubert, and the scarification of the wrists, hands and legs of sufferers from *les hunes* in Brittany that was practised well into the nineteenth century. Combining heat treatment and magical cooking, the 'sorcerer' of Premilhac in Le Roy's *Le Moulin du Frau* cured old Gustou's rheumatism by tying him up naked in a blanket with some herbs and putting him in the bread oven for half an hour or so.[26]

A range of objects and substances was used in cures. Some were substances produced by the body, like saliva and the milk of women, which we saw in Chapter 10 was a specific for eye complaints in particular. Indeed, as an Italian doctor put it at the end of the sixteenth century, there was 'no part of the human body, no residue which comes forth from it', which could not be used 'on behalf of the sick'. Human fat, ear-wax and faeces and urine, animal and human, are all reported. An Anglo-Saxon recipe for an ointment for pain in the shoulder, side, loin or breast involved 'mingling a turd of an old swine, which be a fieldgoer, with old lard'. In a later medieval guide to women's health, 'man's excrement burnt' and 'the dung of a goat mixed with honey' figure as cures for breast cancer. In the modern Limousin, cow manure was put on burns and a poultice of pig muck was supposed to stop wounds from bleeding. A modern Portuguese cure for a tumour on a boy's leg required that it be anointed with some of his urine, in which a dead lizard had been steeped for three days; while freckles were treated in the Limousin by washing them with urine on the first Friday of the new moon. It has been suggested that employing such excreta, 'as well as putrid or rotten things, in the composition of medicinal charms' was based on the idea that the spirit responsible for the disease would thereby be made to feel uncomfortable and would be induced to withdraw.[27] But other notions entered into it.

Reading a patient's urine was an orthodox medical procedure down to the early modern period, as we have mentioned, and was taken over by folk-healers when doctors gave it up. When Maria, Sir Toby and the others in *Twelfth Night* try to convince Malvolio that he is possessed or bewitched, Fabian says: 'Carry his water to th' wise woman', as if this will clinch the matter. A modern Suffolk cure for jaundice uses the patient's urine as a symbol of the disease itself. A bottle filled with the urine is placed 'in a running stream, uncorked with the neck of the bottle facing upstream against the current'. As the water in the bottle gradually clears, so the jaundice will leave the sufferer. Sympathetic magic also lies behind cures involving urination. According to a sixteenth-century French remedy for dropsy, one should 'piss for nine mornings in a row on a hoarhound plant before the sun has touched it; and as the plant dies, so will the belly subside'. Again, Catharine Oswald, indicted for witchcraft at Edinburgh in 1629, was alleged to have cured a boy of a severe case of 'the trembling fevers' by getting him 'to pluck up a nettle by the root and to lay it down upon the high gate and to piss upon the crop thereof three several mornings before the sunrising and to be back again in his house before the sunrising'.[28]

Natural mineral substances also figure in folk medicine. As our original Sicilian example illustrates, salt was universally believed to have great prophylactic, healing and other magical power. Often such substances were given extra or more obvious supernatural significance, like the water of saints' wells. For example, grains were scraped from the 'alluring stone' of Carmarthen and given to those who had been bitten by dogs to prevent them from contracting rabies. The stone was 'said to have fallen from heaven on the farm of Dysgwylfa about twelve miles from the town' and, despite continuous erosion over the centuries, it always remained the same size, that of a man's head. De Martino explains why soot from the iron chain used to suspend the cooking-pot over the fire should have been given to sick infants in Lucania.[29] Iron has special power in itself, as we have seen, and the hearth is sacred, centre of the house and family, symbol of its life and well-being. The dirty soot, moreover, absorbs the 'dirt' of the disease, another explanation perhaps for the use of excreta.

Other objects used in cures were manufactured. Those that came into contact with the body were especially prominent. Pins were thrown into wells or stuck in statues. Rings were worn or touched. Even the Church in the medieval period recognized the belief in the curative power of rings. The statutes of the Hôtel-Dieu of Troyes, drawn up in 1263, declared: 'No nun should wear rings or precious stones, save in the case of illness'. Healing 'cramp rings' were made from the Maundy money distributed by English monarchs. In Marseille and the Comtat in modern times, people thought that wearing a gold ear-ring was beneficial to the health and especially prevented eye complaints Sometimes making the ring involved complicated ritual. In Suffolk, a person suffering from epilepsy had to procure ten or twelve pieces of silver (coins, broken pieces of cutlery, etc.) from the same number of people of the opposite gender without telling them why and have the pieces made into a ring to be worn on the fourth finger of the left hand. Touching the rings of bishops,. rulers and others could also be therapeutic.

> One of your eyes is bloodshot; use my ring to't,
> They say 'tis very sovereign,

the Duchess tells Antonio in Webster's *The Duchess of Malfi*.[30]

Then there were the universal ribbons and threads. When a child was born in Pisticci in Basilicata with its cranial suture wide open, an unmeasured red ribbon was tied around its head, while formulae and prayers were said, and it was kept on for thirteen days, each day being tightened. Ribbons were often given or exchanged at shrines. Measuring was significant in itself, as we saw with saints' cults. A patient's whole body might be measured 'from head to toe and fingertip to fingertip', or round the waist, or merely the affected parts of it, in order to diagnose illness, to cure it or to ensure good health in the future. In some parts of Europe and the USA measuring a young child was thought to stunt its growth or to bring about its early death, but elsewhere regular measuring 'was believed to ensure health and well-being, particularly if the child were frail or sickly'.[31]

Frequently clothes belonging to the patient or having some mystique were central to the cure. In another south Italian village, the cranial suture was treated by making the baby wear a special cap that had been fumigated with incense. This is analogous to the christening-cap. Most commonly, clothing was substituted for ill people unable to visit shrines or folk-healers themselves. Alice Hancock, accused before the bishop of Bath and Wells in 1438, used to send sick persons 'a health remedy by blessing the girdle, shirt or garment of the diseased, though she never saw or touched the patient'.

> There was a very efficent witch at Campiglia d'Orcia [in the 1920s] to whom one could take a garment or a hair of anyone suffering from some affliction that the doctor had been unable to heal and which was presumed to be caused by the evil eye, and she – with the help of some card-reading and some potions – would cure him.[32]

In some cases it appears that the proxy element, which we encountered also in connection with saints' shrines, derives not from the patient's incapacity but rather from a deliberate choice: the cure depended on someone else going to the source of healing power and not the patient. This is akin to other categories of cure in which something anomalous is believed to produce a special effect. The most obvious example perhaps is the use of inversion. A cure for toothache in the Limousin involved attending mass but doing everything the opposite way to normal, standing when everyone else was sitting and so on. Similarly, sufferers from many diseases were advised to wear their own or someone else's clothes inside out, to walk backwards from shrines. We have come across some references to the ritual theft of ingredients in cures already, and this element was often most important. In a German instance, sore throat and hoarseness could be combated by wrapping around the ailing part a scarf made from 'a flour sack stolen from the miller'.[33] Other examples of anomalies include rubbing warts against the father of an adulterous child (in Scotland) or a cuckolded husband (in Portugal) to get rid of them, and the insistence in Suffolk that the words 'please' and 'thank you' should never be used in dealings with the folk–healer.

In practice, the things used in magical cures cannot be separated from the rituals in which they figure. These took many forms and were based on a variety of assumptions, but a number of categories or significant patterns in them may be isolated.

First, most rituals included a command to the disease to stop its action and depart. In a modern Portuguese example, fevers were told:

> Go hence,
> Take bread to eat and
> Straw for your bed,
> Farewell, and never let me see you more.

In the Limousin, this formula was recited by the healer over a sufferer from rheumatism:

> Ache from cold,
> Ache of Anthony,
> Go away to the sea
> Where you will find
> Plenty of stones and rocks
> To rub against!

Similarly, the blood flowing from a wound could be ordered to stop; or the command could be made to the medicinal agents, as in Tom Sawyer's cure for warts in Mark Twain's novel of 1876:

> Barley-corn, barley-corn, Injun-meal shorts,
> Spunk water, spunk water, swaller these warts.

Such instructions were frequently enhanced by religious invocations. Goodwife Veazy, recommended to Robert Cecil in 1604 for her ability to expel worms, for example ordered them: 'Thou tetter-worm [or Thou canker-worm] begone hence in the name of the Father, of the Son and of the Holy Ghost'.[34]

A modern Cornish charm elaborated on this command and introduces a further feature:

Tetter, tetter, thou hast nine brothers,
God bless the flesh and preserve the bone,
Perish thou tetter and be thou gone.
In the name of the Father ...
Tetter, tetter, thou hast eight brothers ...

and so on, until the worm has no brothers and is ordered to go itself. Such numerical charms are found in Classical and medieval as well as modern texts and are preserved in children's counting-out rhymes. They operate on the principle of making the parasite or illness diminish and then disappear as the numbers are counted down. The same effect could be achieved with letters and in other ways. In a Swedish charm against frostbite, collected in 1926, the word 'Kulumaris' was written on a series of strips of paper, one letter being dropped each time, i.e. 'Kulumaris', 'Kulumari', 'Kulumar' ... These strips were fed to the patient each day, and the frostbite decreased as did the word. Diminishing word charms could also take the form of amulets. According to Defoe, the magic word ABRACADABRA written in triangular form and missing off a letter on every line, was worn round the neck during the Great Plague in London. Other forms employed metaphors. An Anglo-Saxon charm for a cyst addressed it: 'May you be consumed as coal upon the hearth. May you shrink as dung upon a wall. And may you dry up as water in a pail. May you become as small as a linseed grain, and much smaller than the hipbone of an itch-mite, and may you become so small that you become nothing'. A modern example from Savoie conjured atrophy of the limbs 'to go away in twenty-four hours as completely as the dew of St John goes away with the first rays of the sun'.[35]

Such sympathetic magic could also operate via plants or animals. Marcellus of Bordeaux, court physician to Emperor Theodosius I in the late fourth century, recorded this cure for a tumour: 'Take a root of vervain, cut it across, and hang one end of it round the patient's neck, and the other in the smoke of the fire. As the vervain dries up in the smoke, so the tumour will also dry up and disappear'. A cure for warts in the *Evangile des quenouilles* instructed: 'Rub the wart on the Eve of St John's with a cabbage leaf, and then bury the leaf in the earth; as the leaf rots, so will the wart shrivel'. This procedure with variations is found all over Europe down to modern times. In late nineteenth-century Brittany, warts were rubbed with slug's slime. The slug had then to be pierced 'through with a stick that you planted in the ground. When the slug dried out, the wart was gone. Or so they said'. Other creatures were sacrificed to cure other complaints. Aubrey referred to holding live frogs inside the mouths of children suffering from 'the thrush' until the frogs died. In modern Suffolk, a live flat-fish was placed on the bare chest of a child suffering from whooping-cough and kept there till it died. Alternatively, spiders, frogs or snails might be passed through the child's hands and then suspended in the chimney or elsewhere on a string, in the belief that as they died the illness too would disappear. 'In Sussex a snake is drawn along a man's neck if it be swollen, and afterwards the snake is put in a bottle, which is tightly corked. The bottle is buried in the ground, and, as the snake decays, the swelling goes'.[36]

Sometimes the spell or charm to expel the disease or poison or whatever had invaded the body showed it the way to go in detail. An incantation against snake-bite was collected in 1934 among the Huculs of the eastern Carpathians. It followed the injection of the poison from the hair, the skin, the veins and so on and then symbolically reversed the process:

> From the heart you are called out into the blood,
> From the blood into the veins,
> From the veins into the flesh,
> From the flesh into the lining [of the skin],
> From the lining into the skin,
> From the skin into the hair.

The same pattern is found in a medieval Saxon charm, which conjures worms 'from the marrow to the bone, from the bone to the flesh, from the flesh to the blood, from the blood to the skin, and from the skin into this arrow'.[37]

As this shows, rituals of this kind frequently aimed to transfer the complaint elsewhere, as other magical procedures sent pests or storms to other places. Most simply an object representing the disease would be thrown 'over one's head or shoulders, over a gate, over a wall, over a tree limb, over the roof'. An Anglo-Saxon charm against 'flying venom' ordered: 'Make four strokes with an oaken brand towards the four quarters of heaven. Make the brand bloody, throw it away and sing three times this prayer', the prayer being an invocation of the Four Evangelists. Another charm found among the Rumanians of Hungary ran: 'Headache caused by eating, headache caused by drinking, ninety-nine kinds of headache, go away to the mountains, there where the cock does not crow and no one cooks pancakes'. A complicated ritual to cure a bewitched child in Venice in the sixteenth century concluded with it being anointed and washed. When the sea-water in the *rio* (canal) went down, the female healer told the Inquisition, 'I throw the water from bathing him in the *rio*, saying: Just as this water goes away to the sea, so all your illness will run off and go away'.[38]

The disease was more commonly transferred to some other entity. This could be another person, and the transfer could be direct or indirect. Direct transfer could be quasi-natural or more obviously magical. New York Italians at the time of the First World War believed that syphilis could be cured by passing on the disease via sexual intercourse with a virgin or a sexually immature girl. Elizabeth Wryte from Somerset, who consulted a wise woman about her sick daughter in 1555, was told that 'she must cause herself to be in as ill a case as the said child', which should be brought about by taking the daughter into the mother's bed at midnight. Montaigne recounted an experience of his own, which is relevant here. An old man from Toulouse, 'troubled with the cough of the lungs' had become acquainted with the young Montaigne, and he declared that

> fixing his eyes upon the liveliness and freshness of my face, and setting his thought upon the jollity and vigour wherewith my youthful age did then flourish, and then filling all his senses with my flourishing estate, his habitude might thereby be amended, and his health recovered. But he forgot to say, that mine might also be impaired and infected.[39]

Healers might also take their patients' diseases on themselves, at least temporarily, as in modern Greece.

Diseases could also be wished on other people. There was a belief in the Middle Ages that leprosy could only be caught from a leper who bore one ill-will. Folk-healers and witches were quite generally credited with the power of switching illnesses from one person to another. Isobel Youngs of Eastbarns near Dunbar was accused in 1629 of taking 'a sickness off her own husband' and putting it on her nephew instead. Again, Agnes Sampson, tried for witchcraft in 1590, had been called in to cure Robert Kerr of a disease 'laid on him by a warlock when he was at Dumfries, which sickness she took upon herself, and kept the same with great grieving and torment till the morning'. She then tried to pass the disease on again to an animal, but it went instead to another man who 'pined away and died', while Robert Kerr 'was made hale'.[40]

As this indicates, the process of transfer could be and probably was most often indirect. Isobel Youngs put the illness on her nephew via grain in a barn; Agnes Sampson tried to put her illness on to an animal via a cloth. Stones, nails, pieces of paper, coins, eggs and other objects might be used, too. In a Norwegian charm, collected in 1923, a sprain was conjured out of the victim's knee into two juniper branches placed crosswise over it. In a ritual found all over Europe from Classical times to the present, a sufferer or someone acting on his or her behalf went to a particular place, often a cross-roads, a tree or a spring, and deposited there either a garment, nail parings or some other object: the next person to pass the place would pick up the complaint. A French traveller to Italy, for example, noted this cure for a cold in the mid-seventeenth century: 'One should wipe one's nose on a paper, place in the paper a small coin, throw it away, and whoever picks it up will catch the cold and you will be cured'. In north-eastern Scotland in the nineteenth century, an individual with warts 'might go to a crossroads, pick up a stone, rub his warts with dust from under the stone, and say:

> A'm ane, the wart's twa,
> The first ane it comes by
> Take the warts awa'

Related to this were the belief that itinerants could cure certain conditions, especially warts, by taking them away with them, and the practice of transferring illnesses to the dead. A nineteenth-century account of a wake in Donegal relates how an old man crippled with rheumatism took 'the hand of the corpse, applied it to his arm, to his shoulder, and to his leg, saying, Take my pains with you, Thady, in the name of God!' He uttered the same words when the body was lifted out over the threshold and threw a stone after it. The magical transmission of diseases to the dead was commonly effected in modern Germany by placing clothes and other things that had been in contact with the sick person in the coffin or grave.[41]

Agnes Sampson tried to transfer Robert Kerr's illness to a cat or a dog, and other 'witches' all over Europe were accused of manoeuvres of this kind. Marguerite Touret, a healer and child-minder from Lavans near Quingey, was accused of witchcraft in 1657; among the charges against her was one that she had switched an illness to a calf which subsequently died. The 'disappearing' cures to do with animals that we have discussed often involved an implicit or explicit transfer of the complaint. A cure for asthma among gypsies was 'to catch a trout alive, breathe into its mouth three times and then throw it back in the water', in the hope that it would absorb the illness.[42] The cures for whooping cough and other throat diseases in which frogs or other creatures were put inside the child's mouth and sometimes held there until they died were based on the same idea. In several parts of Britain, a hair from the child was fed to a dog in a slice of bread and butter; if the animal coughed in eating it, this was a sign that the transfer had taken place.

Many other examples may be cited. It was believed in Marseille in the 1640s that, 'if one urinates before a quartian fever "takes" and kneads a loaf with this urine, and gives this bread to a male dog, he will get the fever and the sick person will be cured'. Epileptics carried out an elaborate series of rituals at St Degla's well in Denbighshire, which the local clergy tried to suppress in the mid eighteenth century. These included taking a cock (or a hen for a woman) to the well, pricking the bird with a pin, and putting its beak into one's mouth and blowing into it; this was supposed to transfer the disease. The birds were left behind at the church, and, if they died, the patients were cured. The use of guinea-pigs in the prevention and cure of human disease was anticipated by peasants in Central and Eastern Europe, where these and other pets were kept to absorb illnesses from the sick, often being put to sleep in the same bed as the patients in order to effect this. It was also possible to use a part of the animal in such rituals. Among gypsies, an animal brain was rubbed against a person suffering from mental illness, and the brain was then ritually disposed of with the aim of transferring the affliction to it.[43]

Transfer to trees was also very common. In seventeenth-century France

it was customary to tie oneself to the trunk with a rope or some other tie and to remain there for some time to be cured of a fever. Sometimes this had to be done at first light, fasting, and one had to bite the bark of the tree before leaving and abandon the rope or tie to rot.

Such customs were often noted in nineteenth- and twentieth-century France. In the Ariège, a fever sufferer took gifts to a hawthorn tree, saying: 'Good day, hawthorn, I bring you bread and salt, and fever for tomorrow'. The salt was scattered at the foot of the tree and the bread was put in one of its branches, and the patient had to be careful not to follow the same route on the way home and to reenter the house by a different door from the one he left by, or, if there was none, by the window, to ensure that the fever stayed in or with the tree. In the Ille-et-Vilaine, an itinerant healer told patients with fevers to climb an aspen, cut the bark with a knife and suck the sap, telling the tree: 'Aspen, aspen, may you quiver more than I do'. The patient's shaking (and thus the fever of which it was the symptom) would be passed to the tree. A more elaborate version of the same charm was found in seventeenth-century Lincolnshire:

Ague, ague, I thee defy,
Three days shiver,
Three days shake,
Make me well for Jesus' sake;
Pass on the disease by means of this charm:
I tie my hair to the aspen-tree,
Dither and shake instead of me.

According to the Grimm brothers, sufferers from gout in many parts of Germany had to go on three successive Fridays after sunset to a fir-tree, where they recited a formula, which caused the fir to wither and the gout to disappear. Similarly, in Sicily, those with goitres or other throat and neck troubles were advised to bite 'the twigs of a young peach tree, removing a bit of the bark. If the tree decays and dies, the ill is certain to go away because it has gone from the person into the tree'.[44]

Hand has catalogued a number of other modes of transfer found in the USA. These include driving nails into the bark of a tree, making holes in it and 'plugging' them with bits of the patient's hair, nail clippings or the expectoration of consumptives, making incisions and wedging in certain objects, and hanging clothes and threads on the branches. Most of these practices are also found in Europe. In Germany, for example, there was a special name *Lappenbäume* (rag-trees), for the trees on which clothes and rags belonging to the sick were hung.[45] Diseases were also transferred to fruit and vegetables: figs in southern Italy, for example; onions or potatoes in northern countries.

Throwing a symbol of one's disease over one's shoulder or the roof of the house was casting it into the air, and the other elements could also be recipients. We have noted cases of sending diseases into rivers or the sea. Well-cults must also frequently have fallen into this category. In parts of Lorraine, people afflicted with abscesses or ulcers, pricked themselves with pins which they later threw into the well of Saint-Sabine. In the Nièvre to get rid of a fever, one went, a little before dawn, to the appropriate spring. There, kneeling beside it, one said: 'Spring, I bring you my misfortune; give me your good fortune'. The exchange was completed by throwing a coin into the spring over the left shoulder, though oakum, cheese or eggs might also be given. In a much older example, Anglo-Saxon sufferers from a skin-disease called *blaece*, probably psoriasis, were advised to treat it with an ointment made from herbs and old soap but also to perform this ritual: 'Scarify the neck after the setting of the sun, pour the blood silently into running water; after that spit three times, then say, Have thou this evil and depart away with it. Go again by a clean way to the house, and go either way in silence'.[46]

We have also come across instances of burying objects belonging to patients in healing rituals. This can be seen, and often was, as a transfer of the illness to the earth. Toothache was 'disposed of in Saxony by cutting one's nails at a crossroads on a Friday, and burying the clippings there'. A spell to send an illness into the earth is preserved in the work of the Roman scholar Varro, and the Sicilian healing ritual which we described in detail involved a direct contact with the earth that is found more generally. Similar spells from southern Italy sought to pass the illness into part of a building. In Lucania, where jaundice was known as the *male dell'arco*, or illness of the arch, victims sought to pass or give back the disease to an arch in a house or church. One formula used here was this: 'Good day, brother arch, I have brought you my jaundice'. Another ploy was to transfer the *male dell'arco* to a rainbow or *arcobaleno*. Other things might be recipients. A seventeenth-century English doctor, for example, who wrote a treatise on scrofula, believed that the disease could be transferred to certain flasks of medicinal water, scabs appearing on the sides of the flask and cracking the glaze. When this happened the patient became better, but if the excrescences were scraped off the flask, then the disease reappeared on the sufferer's skin.[47]

One possible mode of transfer was to pass the sick person through a hole of some kind, though this procedure had a wider range of meanings. A well-known example of this practice appears in Gilbert White's *Natural History of Selborne* (1789).

> In a farmyard near the middle of ... Tring in Hertfordshire ... stands at this day, a row of pollard ashes, which, by the seams and long cicatrices down their sides, manifestly show that, in former times, they have been cleft asunder. These trees, when young and flexible, were severed and held open by wedges, while ruptured children, stripped naked, were pushed through the apertures, under a persuasion that, by such a process, the poor babes would be cured of their infirmity. As soon as the operation was over, the tree, in the suffering part, was plastered with loam, and carefully swathed up. If the parts coalesced and soldered together, as usually fell out ... , the party was cured; but, where the cleft continued to gape, the operation, it was supposed, would prove ineffectual.

Similar procedures are reported from other parts of Britain, France, Spain, Italy, Germany, Poland and Scandinavia, usually for the treatment of hernias and rickets but also of epilepsy. The Dominican Etienne de Bourbon described the operation being used in the thirteenth century to treat 'black and malingering babies', believed to be changelings. Often the patient had to be passed through the tree a specific number of times, to the accompaniment of special formulae and at particular times. The ritual of an elderly male healer at Modena in the 1590s required the child with the hernia to be passed three times through the tree, 'while a young boy read aloud from the Gospel of St John'; and the rite was 'performed at sun-rise, either on the feast of St John the Baptist or on Good Friday'. Among the Pasiegos of northern Spain, children or adults could be cured, and they were passed through the split sapling 'on the Eve of St John's, at midnight, naked, by two men named Juan Bautista'.[48] In England, the ash was the usual tree chosen; on the Continent the oak.

Sick children and adults might also be passed or go through other kinds of aperture. A widespread cure for whooping cough in the Welsh Border country was to get the afflicted child to crawl nine times under a bramble that had 'formed an arch by rooting itself at the tip'. 'In Belgium and Luxemburg a child ... slow in learning to walk was [similarly] made to crawl under a rerooted bramble, in silence, on a Friday.' The 'Corrector' of Burchard of Worms and other early medieval penitentials imposed special penances for pulling infants through holes in the ground to cure them or to stop them crying; and the custom of pulling sick children through tunnels made of sods persisted in Scandinavia and the Baltic region until recently. This practice is clearly linked to that of burying symbols of disease in the earth, as well as to the notion that the earth itself is the source of supernatural power. Sick people also crawled through natural apertures in rocks or stones. 'At St Declan's Sacred Stone at Ardmore, County Waterford, people with back ailments crawled through the stone in a partial state of undress'.[49] Sufferers with back trouble had similar recourse at places in Austria and Lower Bavaria.

The range of further variations on passing through would include going under the bellies of animals, through horse collars, under the host or statues and relics of saints carried in procession, through clothes, under or through ladders and through loops and rings of all kinds. Presumably the English expression: 'You'll pull through', said to a sick person, is a now unconscious reference to this once universal practice. Some variants seek to discard or transfer the disease via the passage; others obtain a power against the disease. The rituals may also be seen as rites of passage *per se*, from sickness to health, perhaps via a rebirth from a symbolic vagina.

Magical transfer in cures could operate both ways. Diseases could be passed on, but health and vitality could also be absorbed or acquired from the proper sources. The parents of a child born sickly in the Confolentais before the First World War 'would beg on the territory of the three neighbouring villages for clothes belonging to babies of the same age as theirs but healthy and robust. By using the outfit thus collected, the sick baby would acquire a vigour equal to that of his donors'. The new-born and the innocent could convey healing power *ipso facto*. In the Abruzzi, for example, a woman with toothache could be cured if she kissed a new-born baby before it was washed. In parts of modern Germany, 'yarn spun by a girl under seven years of age is worn to prevent gout and arthritic diseases, and sick children suffering from various kinds of ailment are wrapped in the apron of a virgin bride to cure them'. In Kentucky, the saliva of a baby or a virgin was supposed to neutralize snake bites.[50] The vitality of the young combined here with the power of purity.

Paradoxically contact with the dead might have a similar effect. The dead, of course were feared, as we have seen, and communication with them might be dangerous and even produce disease, but they also had an inherent healing power. The touch of the dead cured scrofula, goitres and boils among other things. Earth, dew, grass and other plants, water, from churchyards were all used in cures as were shrouds, the bed linen of the dead and even bones, sometimes ground to powder and consumed. This all reflects the general aura of the dead, but it is significant that especial power was attached to 'premature decease',[51] as if the vitality thus cut off continued to operate, at least until the dead person's normal life-span had run. It also provides an additional explanation for the extraordinary power believed to reside in objects associated with executed criminals.

We have seen that some healers gained their power from animals. Animals have figured, too, in the kinds of medical cure that we have already discussed, notably in 'disappearing' cures. Sufferers were also breathed on and licked by animals, plastered with their dung, passed under them, touched by them, or fed with them. In modern Shropshire, for example, children with measles were treated 'by being passed three times over the back and under the belly of a dancing bear', a procedure used in Rumania for stomach complaints. Parson Woodforde had a stye on his eye in March 1791 and reported:

> As it is commonly said that the eye-lid being rubbed by the tail of a black cat would do it much good, if not entirely cure it, and, having a black cat, a little before dinner I made trial of it, and very soon after dinner I found my eye-lid much abated the swelling and almost free from pain.

In January 1667–8, Pepys was informed that the husband of his cousin Kate Joyce was dying: 'So I to him, and find his breath rattled in the throat; and they did lay pigeons to his feet, and all despair of him' – reference to a common last resource. In Calabria, where 'nearly every animal has been discovered to possess some medicinal property', rickets and scrofula in children were treated by feeding them with puppies, cooked in a saucepan, but they had to be puppies used to draw off milk from women who had lost their babies.[52]

Belief in the efficacy of such contacts or ingestions could derive from some relevant quality in the creature concerned. So snakes, eels or their skins were used in many places to ease rheumatism, sprains or stiff joints, because they were so supple. In a similar way, a cure for jaundice in the fifteenth-century leechbook involved braying nine or ten earthworms in stale ale with yellow saffron, and the worms had to be the kind 'that have yellow knots'. In modern Provence, the powder of a dried mouse was given to a child to stop it from wetting the bed, because the mouse smelled like the wet bed. In Calabria, 'the blood of tortoises was used for strengthening the backs of children – the tortoise being a *hard* animal'.[53]

The principle: 'Take a hair of the dog that bit you' might also apply, sometimes quite literally. In Cervantes' 'La Gitanilla' (1613), a young man was bitten by dogs on approaching a gypsy camp.

> The old gypsy who undertook his cure took some hairs from the dogs, and, after washing the bites … with wine, applied the hairs, which she had fried in oil, with the oil, and covered them with a little chewed rosemary. She then bound up the wounds with clean cloths, and made the sign of the cross over them.[54]

Snake bites were treated in a similar way by killing the snake and putting it on the wound it had caused. In a variation in Thomas Hardy's *The Return of the Native*, after Mrs Yeobright has been bitten by an adder, three other adders are caught to get their oil to put on the bite.

Very often the cure required that the animal be killed, as in these cases. Frequently, this was in order to acquire parts of the animal to be used as remedies or talismans. Animal parts figure prominently in healing from Roman to modern times. St Hildegard of Bingen, for example, in the twelfth century recommended the lung of a tunny fish for fever, and the gall of a nightingale, caught before daybreak and mixed with dew and anointed on the eyebrows and lashes to improve dim sight. The fifteenth-century English leechbook, a collection of mainly herbal remedies, yet included beheading a cat and laying it on the side of a woman with 'cake in her belly' (dysmenor-rhoea); a potion with the gall of a hare and woman's milk for deafness; and hare's blood and swallows' eyes to remove freckles. Sometimes the part required was obviously related to the complaint. An Anglo-Saxon cure for a man who 'cannot retain his water' required him to eat the roast bladder of a pig or a goat or to drink it as powder in wine. Another advocated placing crabs' eyes on the neck for swollen eyes.[55] Again, a seventeenth-century English health manual advised 'that dried hare's liver was good was for those that be liver sick'; while lungs of foxes and other animals were specifics for lung disease. Where an animal had brought about the condition, consuming part of it might be thought to restore the *status quo*. So in a nineteenth-century English example, a mother recovered the drowned body of the dog that had bitten her child, extracted its liver and fed this to the child, who nevertheless died of hydrophobia.

Frequently the animal's curative power derived directly from its death, which was brought about in quasi-ritual fashion. Swollen glands in Calabria were treated with a liniment of snakes' blood. The snakes were 'pricked with needles; and the greater their pain, the more beneficial their blood'. The lizard killed in order to cure a tumour in a boy's leg in Portugal had to be 'killed with the index finger with slow regular blows'. A seventeenth-century English cure for consumption required that a cock be flayed alive and then beaten into pieces. The ritual element is even more obvious in an Anglo-Saxon treatise on the medicinal properties of animals. For example, badgers were to be trapped and many of their useful parts taken while they were still alive. 'Do off the teeth from him, while yet quick [or alive] ... and thus say: In the name of God I thee slay, and beat the teeth off thee ... Then take the right fore foot with these words ... : In the name of the Lord I take thee for a leechdom'.[56] The hunting and mode of killing of badgers and other animals in later centuries is almost certainly related to such ideas.

Often in such cases, the animal's blood was the prime medicine being sought. In parts of the USA, the blood of freshly killed pigs and cows was administered directly to the skin of eczema sufferers. Blood from a cat's ear was rubbed on the same or similar skin rashes in Mid-Wales. In an older example from Scotland, a woman accused of witchcraft at Dalkeith in 1661 cured a sick child in a secret procedure that involved beheading a dog and using some of its blood. In addition or alternatively, the flesh of a dead animal might be applied to a sick person, while that flesh was still warm. A fifteenth-century remedy for a blow to or swelling of the head instructed: 'Take a sucking-whelp, and cleave it [open] and lay it to the head for a night'. This was supposed to draw out the swelling and clean the wound. In 1615, Gervase Markham recommended applying a live pigeon cut in two parts as a treatment for the plague,[57] and the same remedy was used against meningitis in the Limousin in the nineteenth century. Fresh hares' lungs applied to the part cured sore eyes or feet in the Anglo-Saxon leechbooks. Perhaps more common was the use of fowl's entrails which were supposed to ease snake bites and insect stings, to reduce swellings and inflammations, and to cure a range of other complaints from epilepsy to shingles.

Some creatures were reckoned to have special healing (and other) powers and recur in remedies. The toad, for example, was poisonous and associated with evil, but it therefore had the quality of drawing poison and disease into itself and away from the sufferer. Similarly, from Classical times, the mole was considered to be demonic and chthonic, of the earth. A hand in which a mole had been killed acquired the power to cure nearly all diseases, and moles or parts of them figure in many remedies. In a French medical handbook of 1758, for example, convulsions in a baby could be prevented with the aid of a necklace of peony seeds threaded on silk that had been passed through a live mole. The skin of the mole could also be removed and placed over the baby's head, while its paws and snout could be hung round its neck additionally in a bag.[58]

We have mentioned in passing some of the principles upon which magical healing was based. Some may be made clearer here. Perhaps the most obvious is the basic magical idea of sympathy or similarity. A connection was assumed, for example, between things of the same shape or colour. Since jaundice gave sufferers a yellow colour, anything yellow might be used to treat the illness: a gold coin, a yellow rag, a piece of amber, or a yellow flower. In the same way, red objects and flowers were used for disorders of the blood and for other complaints where red inflammation was evident. So red flannel was a specific against sore throats; and red coral eased the sore gums of teething infants. Red was also generally believed to be a colour 'obnoxious to evil spirits'. A further example would be the use of written charms, commonly hung round the necks of human and animal patients, but also ingested. An eighteenth-century healer from the Sologne cured people with fever by getting them to swallow a piece of paper with magic words on it every three days. We have seen that Calabrian peasants treated doctors' prescriptions in a similar way, as if the paper and the words on it in themselves possessed a power that could be absorbed. Another instance of sympathetic magic was 'the idea that one could cure a wound by anointing the weapon which had caused it', a common notion among the seventeenth-century English elite. Again, in the nineteenth century, when a Northumbrian reaper was cut by his sickle, he not uncommonly cleaned and polished it, in order to keep the wound clean.[59]

As we have seen in connection with gathering herbs and more generally, the success of a healing procedure depended, too, on its being carried out at the right time. Some times of the day or night were more suitable than others: before dawn, at midnight. Some days of the week were more propitious than others, notably Sundays and Fridays, though Fridays could also be unlucky. Some days in the year had special significance. The water of many holy wells and fountains was only efficacious on particular days, often St John's Eve, while most saints' shrines achieved their maximum power on the day of the patron's feast. It was generally believed, too, as we have seen, that the weather and the heavens had an important influence on health and its maintenance and recovery. Among the heavenly bodies, the moon was the most powerful. The influence of the sun was less often acknowledged, though a cure for a headache caused by working in the sun from Lucania is explicit. The sufferer went to work in the fields next day as usual and at sun-rise lifted his arm and said:

> Good morning, holy sun;
> At the feet of the Lord;
> From my breast lift the torment;
> From my head take the awful pain.[60]

The left/right contrast was used in magical healing. Some rituals depended on one or the other hand, foot, etc. being used, but there was no general preference for one or the other side. A cure for colic from the Sologne in the seventeenth century, for example, required the recitation of a formula, while the middle finger of the left hand was placed on the navel; but another remedy offered by the same healer involved pushing back piles with the middle finger of the right hand. In modern Sussex, toothache might be prevented by always putting on the right stocking and placing 'the right leg into the trousers before the left. But in Shropshire and elsewhere, exactly the contrary was enjoined'.[61]

Repetition was very important. The Hungarian boiling ritual was repeated three times. Goodwife Veazy repeated her formula against tetter-worms three times. Here the numbers were themselves significant. In many cases, poultices, animal parts and so on had to be left in place for three days and nights. We have noted the healing power acquired by seventh children. The Welsh Borders cure for whooping cough required the child to crawl under the bramble nine times. A Welsh healer ordered his patient's skin disease:

> I send you
> Over nine seas and over nine mountains,
> And over nine acres of unprofitable land.

In modern Portugal folk-healers always did their 'blessings' a given number of times, and the number was always uneven.[62] There is more to say about magic numbers and we will return to the topic.

Though many rituals and formulae used in healing have been recorded, enabling such a study as this to be made, most involved an element of secrecy. The healer had his or her 'secret', which was jealously guarded and carefully transmitted. A Gloucestershire woman, tried in 1563, 'taketh upon her to help by the way of charming, and in such ways that she will have nobody privy of her sayings'.[63] Many accounts stress that part at least of the formula used by a healer had to remain secret or the cure would not work or even the gift itself might be lost. In practice, most 'secrets' seem to have been fairly standard and are found widely across space and time.

Like us, traditional Europeans conceived of disease as an invasion of the body by some 'alien entity'. The Reverend Joseph Greene of Stratford-upon Avon told his brother in June 1760 that 'an ugly dispiriting nervous fever that lurked within me' had prevented him from writing sooner. The most notorious example of this notion was the attribution of certain forms of mental illness and especially epilepsy to demonic possession. The idea that diseases could be sent into victims by organized ill-will fits into the same pattern. In such cases and more generally, the disease or complaint might be conveyed or embodied in animal form. The belief that toothache, for example, was caused by animals or 'toothworms' is found in many countries from the early Middle Ages onwards. In Manx, the plural form of the word for beast is used to mean toothache, 'from the opinion that the pain arose from an animal in the tooth'. A wide range of diseases in adults and children was attributed to worms. In fifteenth-century Florence, for example, many kinds of infant death were officially recorded as being caused by 'worms'. These were believed to be generated in the stomach by eating the wrong foods or by exposure to bad weather among other things. The creatures most likely to intrude themselves into the body were creeping ones like snakes, lizards and worms, and they entered often through the victim's mouth while he or she was asleep. In modern Mayenne, it was thought that grass-snakes got into the bodies of people sleeping in the fields 'and especially those of infants left alone while their mothers are working'. There are parallels here with the notion of animal familiars, used by witches to cause their harm. The idea that disease was a foreign agent in the body might also explain changes in and the odd variety of symptoms in any particular case. In Piedmont in the 1690s a baby, constipated and unable to suckle, was exorcised by a priest and temporarily improved, but then the spirits believed to be responsible for the illness moved elsewhere in his body and he lost the use of his left arm.[64]

It followed that, if some diseases took the form of animals or other agents conjured or otherwise intruded into people, then a cure could be effected by expulsion. A shepherd from the Eure was said to have received 200 francs in the early nineteenth century 'for extracting a beast from the stomach of an epileptic farmer using drugs and spells'. Of course, as we have noted, official medicine before the late nineteenth century placed 'the accent of its therapeutics on expelling toxic substances from the body – by purging, sweating, vomiting and blood-letting'. This may have influenced popular belief and practice or the two may simply have converged. From early in the medieval period, excretion or vomiting was a component of cures by saints. In one attributed to St Thomas Becket in his lifetime, the saint massaged the swollen abdomen of a lay brother at Pontigny, who was suffering from dropsy, and gave him 'something to drink ... and almost at once the brother fell down; he vomited an astonishing quantity of poison and filth and then lay still for a long time' and was cured. In the early modern period, 'unnatural voiding and vomiting of worms, knives, pins, nails, and other things was often taken to be a sign of an illness caused by witchcraft',[65] and alleged victims of demonic possession usually evacuated strange things.

Ritual expulsion or exorcism was a feature of popular charms. An Anglo-Saxon example recommended: 'Against a strange swelling, sing upon thy leech finger [the third] a Paternoster, and draw a line about the sore place and say, *Fuge diabolus* ...'. Clerical exorcism, moreover, could enjoy great popular support, as in the case of those performed in Piedmont in the 1690s by Father Chiesa of Santena. About half of those whom he treated were said to be suffering 'under a witch's curse' or were 'invaded by foul spirits', but almost as many had specific physical ailments: crippled limbs, gout, blindness, tumours, which they also thought he could expel.[66]

Another ploy where disorders were supposedly caused by witchcraft was to return them to their senders, if possible in aggravated form. In an example of this magical retaliation from southern England in the 1870s, a bottle containing water, thorns, and a written charm was buried upside-down in the victim's garden. The charm stated:

> As long as the paper and thorns remain in the bottle I hope Satan, the angel of darkness, will pour out his wrath on the person who is the cause of the illness, and will throw him on a bed of sickness which nobody can cure; and as this water is tormented by the thorns, so may he be tormented by the illness, and as the water dries up in the bottle, so might his flesh dry up on his bones, and he shall not live over nineteen days, when he shall be taken into hell by Satan and his angels.[67]

Only the demonological references are unusual here.

Some cures did invoke supernatural beings in this way, but they were fairly rare. In the early medieval period, these beings might be pagan gods. A Gaulish incantation, recorded by Marcellus of Bordeaux, went: 'Rub out of the throat, out of the gullet, Aisus; remove thou thyself my evil out of the throat, out of the gorge'. A Carolingian charm against pustules and tumours adjured 'Doctor Apollo' to remove them. With progressive Christianization, such direct allusions to pagan divinities became uncommon, but they did survive. In a cure for fever, recorded in Lincolnshire in the nineteenth century, three used horseshoes were nailed to the patient's bed, and when he began to shake, he had to take a hammer in his left hand and tap the horse-shoes, saying: 'One for God, and one for Wod [Wodin], and one for Lok or luck [Loki]', almost certainly a reference to the old Norse gods. Lesser spirits might also be appealed to, though again this seems to have been rare. In the nineteenth century again, children with whooping cough were taken to caves at Runswick Bay on the North Yorkshire coast to be cured by Hob. The parents would call: 'Hobhole Hob! Hobhole Hob! My bairn's got kincough. Tak't off! Tak't off!' The later practice of taking children with whooping cough into railway tunnels to breathe the fumes may have echoes of this belief in a curing earth or ground spirit. Angels and devils were also called into service, as we have seen. Richard Parkyn of Rotherham, prosecuted before a church court in 1481 for conjuring, summoned an angel who told him what was wrong with patients and helped to cure them.[68] In the later medieval and early modern periods the authorities frequently suspected that folk-healers had demonic assistance. This was very rarely the case from the latter's point of view, though the odd example may be cited.

We should also mention a type of ritual healing that does not fall into previous categories: healing by trance or dance, which has often been associated in other cultures with spirit possession. A modern gypsy healer was reported to have gone into 'a species of frenzy, flinging her arms about and muttering a kind of incantation or prayer, until her voice ascended into a wild scream', after which she lay exhausted in a faint.[69] The Căluş dancers in

Rumania cured a particular kind of possession linked with breaking Whitsun taboos or caused by the fairies, and this involved the dancers working themselves into trances. Patients might also approach or achieve such states. Abbé Thiers referred to a case, in which people danced day and night in a church to preserve themselves from falling sickness or epilepsy. This took place at the two August festivals of Assumption and St Bartholomew's, and great care had to be taken not to fall over or one would fall prey to the illness. In southern Italy, complaints associated with the bite of the tarantula were also cured by dancing and trance experience.

All through our discussion of magical cures performed by folk-healers and others we have encountered examples of the use or adaptation of 'orthodox' religious features. First, members of the clergy and of the religious orders often acted as healers themselves, despite the fact that the exercise of medicine and surgery was officially forbidden to clerics – a ban reiterated by the Council of Trent and by bishops later. An official counted fifty irregular practitioners in one district of the Gironde in 1790s, 'not counting the clergy'. Often a parish priest acted rather like a district nurse. In a funeral lament for a Corsican priest, collected around 1850, the singer emphasized that Father Santucci had been

> A doctor of medicine,
> A doctor for poor people,
> Without asking for a sou! ...
> How many came to him
> With dislocated bones,
> And the parish priest healed them
> With his charmed hands!

Even here, however, there is reference to the priest's special aura, and frequently the services expected from the clergy did reflect their sacred and reputedly magical powers. In Modena in the sixteenth century, 'people went to priests with many of the same expectations that they brought to magical healers, creating pressures that these men were often ill-equipped to resist'. As a result, the clergy were often 'induced to expand their healing activities well beyond orthodox boundaries' – into counter-magic, charms, conjurations, dubious exorcisms and abuse of the liturgy. To take a superlative example, the Franciscan Fra Girolamo Azzolini made 'a profession of exorcizing and of telling who had been bewitched' in the 1590s. When a woman brought him a sick child, he told her: 'You must take her to a witch [*strega*], so that she can look at her and free her'. When the woman said that she did not know any witches, he recommended one.[70]

Medicine was practised by monks and nuns from the medieval period onwards both within and without the monastery or convent. Most religious foundations in eighteenth-century France had dispensaries which were 'often the best local source of routine medical care'. Religious also manufactured and marketed 'secret remedies like the True Ointment of the Abbey of Bec in Normandy', which, it was claimed, was 'suitable for the cure of all sorts of wounds'.[71] Everywhere, too, religious acted as the guardians and promoters of the more important shrines. The Protestant clergy also acted as physicians to their flocks. In the Church of England, for example, this was recommended by the conservative George Herbert in *The Temple* (1652) as well as by Puritan reformers, and the practice persisted into the nineteenth century.

Alongside clerical healers with empirical skills but also magical traits were folk-healers who operated within a marked spiritual or sacred ambience. Pierre Richard, an ex-shepherd known as 'the saint of Savières', was seeing five to six hundred patients a day in Champagne in the 1760s, mainly people with rheumatism, sciatica, nervous disorders, cancers, ulcers, epilepsy and defective vision. He used holy water and prayers in his cures, which he said depended entirely on the faith of the sufferers. Again, there were healers in France down to the early nineteenth century who claimed descent from or some other link with a powerful healing saint. One of these, a woman called Marie-Joseph Hué, was arrested near Boulogne in 1808 as a vagrant. She claimed that after fasting and doing penance at the abbey of Saint-Hubert in the recognized way, she had had a vision of the saint and had received directly from him or from a former monk of the abbey, 'the gift of curing rabies and conferring protection against the disease for ninety-seven years'. In exercising this gift, she used prayers and an object representing the stole and the key of the saint. Some cures too involved a degree of asceticism. Children were cured of rickets in Denmark, for example, in an elaborate 'passing through' ritual, carried out in 'strict silence'.[72] Fasting was also commonly required.

Relevant here is the idea, not always adhered to in practice, that healing should be an act of charity that the sufferer should not have to pay for. Like Father Santucci, Pierre Richard never asked directly for a fee, though both men and others like them undoubtedly received gifts from patients and their families. Such gifts were usually in kind. In northern Greece in modern times, folk-healers would not accept money payment, but they would take cheese, coffee and so on. Wine, oil, cheese and poultry were offered in modern Portugal. This aspect of folk-healing as against official medicine was a cause of its continuing popularity, for even when healers did charge their fees were always much lower than doctors'. When her bailiff learns, in Mauriac's *Les Chemins de la Mer* (1939), that old Lucienne Revolou has a tumour in her womb, for which she refuses to have expensive surgery, he advises her to 'go to see the wise woman over at Gazinet. She'll put you to rights, mark my words, and it'll only cost five francs'.[73]

We are familiar with the general apotropaic use made of consecrated objects and substances, and these also had power to combat disease. Statues, amulets and relics associated with Christ might be used in cures, in a way analogous to those associated with the saints. The fifteenth-century statue of the Santissimo Bambino, kept in the church of Santa Maria in Aracoeli in Rome, for example, was carried to the sickbed of all people, but especially of children. Popular belief was that it reddened if the child was to recover, but turned pale if the child was to die. Scrolls measuring the length of Christ's adult body were used as amulets in the central medieval period against all forms of disease as well as against sudden death. But the commonest object of power here was the crucifix or the cross. Simply 'viewing the Crucifix or Christ figure as it was raised from the Holy Sepulchre in the Easter morning ceremonies' had preventative and curative effects, it was believed in late medieval Germany and elsewhere. Fragments of the True Cross and of many replicas had similar power. Bede relates that small chips were cut off a wooden cross erected by King Oswald of Northumbria in 635, 'which being put into water, men or cattle drinking thereof, or sprinkled with that water, are immediately restored to health'. Much more common, even universal was the sign of the cross. As Marc Bloch noted, in making the sign of the cross on or over scrofula sufferers, English and French kings were only employing a ritual gesture that was in very general used in the Middle Ages both therapeutically and 'as a rite of benediction and exorcism in all the ordinary actions of daily life'. It was equally prominent in later centuries, as many of our accounts illustrate. In Venice and the Veneto in the early modern period, the sign of the cross was particularly important in healing rituals; so much so, that the term '*segnare*' (to sign) was employed to mean 'to heal'.[74]

Holy water was another important element in several of the cures that we have described. An Anglo-Saxon medicine for ague was made by boiling a collection of herbs in ale and holy water. In nineteenth-century Gloucestershire the midwife washed out the mouth of new-born babies with 'sanctified water' as a safeguard against teething troubles. Other sacramentals, such as 'palms' were also often used. Anything to do with the clergy or the church might be brought into play here. In Norway and elsewhere the sick might be pulled through clerical vestments. Ailred of Rievaulx in the twelfth century cured a monk with a twisted hand by passing his abbot's staff three times in a circle about the affected part. In Lucania mouth ulcers were touched with the church key; in eighteenth-century Wales soil from the unpaved church floors was used as a medicine. Above all, healing power was attributed to the altar and to the vessels used in the Eucharist. Cures were sought by going round or under altars or communion tables or by placing cloths and other things on them, that were later placed in contact with the sufferers. A cure for whooping cough in late medieval England involved 'getting the priest to give one a threefold draught of water or wine from his chalice after mass'. In Germany, the priest stroked the eyes and mouths of the sick after washing out the chalice. Water used to clean the paten figured in an Anglo-Saxon exorcism of fever.[75]

The regular ceremonies of the church were also harnessed for magical healing, starting with the mass or Eucharist. Objects placed on or near altars were often intended to have mass said over them. Herbs employed in cures had masses sung over them. Baptism, as we have seen, and confirmation were widely believed to have prophylatic and therapeutic effects and might for this reason be undergone more than once. 'A second confirmation is sometimes resorted to in West Sussex', Black reported in 1883, 'in the belief that the bishop's blessing will cure any ailment from which the person may be suffering', and he mentions the case of an old woman elsewhere, 'who was confirmed several times, because she thought it was good for her rheumatism'.[76]

Religious words were also much used in healing as in other magical rites. Here it is significant that formulae from the Latin liturgy were frequently employed and that these and other expressions deriving from Catholic usage remained current in regions which became officially Protestant.

Many folk healers used the standard prayers and recommended them to their patients, as did the clergy indeed. But with the healers there is perhaps a mechanical emphasis and a taking of the prayers out of their context. Margaret Hunt, a London healer, questioned by the authorities in 1528, for example, told her patients 'to say for nine consecutive nights five Paternosters, five Aves and a Credo, followed by three more Paternosters, three Aves and three Credos' and so on. When Don Quixote was boiling up the ingredients for his special balsam to heal wounds, 'he mumbled over the pot above fourscore Paternosters and as many Ave Marias, Salve Reginas and Credos, making the sign of the cross at every word, by way of benediction'. A typical modern cure at Pisticci for a cyst under a baby's tongue involved tracing the sign of the cross on the tongue and the mouth three times followed by the recitation of an Ave and a Paternoster. The whole procedure was then repeated and the cure was terminated by saying the last few letters of the alphabet, bringing a sequence to an end in this way being supposed 'magically to induce the end of the child's malign condition'. Other liturgical formulae very commonly used by folk-healers at all times and in all places were the invocation of the Trinity: 'In the name of the Father and of the Son and of the Holy Spirit', and the opening verses of St John's Gospel. The latter were believed to have particular power. They were commonly employed in late medieval England. Reginald Scot noted in the late sixteenth century that they could be written 'in small letters, consecrated at mass and hung about one's neck as a cure for ague'. A lay healer at Modena in the 1590s sought to cure fevers 'by reciting the opening verses of St John's Gospel over the sick person on a hill-top at sun-rise on Good Friday or on the feast of St John the Baptist'. The same verses were constantly recommended in popular handbooks of magic through the early modern and modern periods.[77]

In addition to having a mechanical quality, religious formulae could be used by folk-healers to adjure or command the disease and not as prayers proper or blessings. Thus a charm to remove a speck from the eye in a fifteenth-century handbook from the Tyrol ordered: 'I adjure you, O speck, by the living God and the holy God, to disappear from the eyes of the servant of God, N. ... May Christ make you go away'. Isobel Gowdie, tried in Edinburgh for witchcraft in 1662, told the court that, for fevers,

> we say thrice over: 'I forbid the quaking fevers the sea fevers, the land fevers, and all the fevers that ever God ordained, out of the head, out of the heart, out of the back, out of the side, out of the knees, out of the thighs ... In St Peter's name, St Paul's name and all the saints in heaven; in the name of the Father, of the Son and of the Holy Ghost!'

A modern charm against burns from the Ariège, similarly instructed the fire in them to be stopped 'in the name of God and the Holy Trinity'.[78]

Moreover, the incantations including religious formulae were often regarded as 'secrets', particular to the healers concerned and having effect for that reason. As we have seen, too, healers used sacred words in unorthodox ways and they mixed sacred and profane elements. Werner of Friedberg, for example, confessed in 1405 to using a 'superstitious' blessing: 'Christ was born, Christ was lost, Christ was found again, may he bless these wounds in the name of the Father, and of the Son, and of the Holy Ghost'. In early modern Russia, water used in healing was 'consecrated' by having a prayer recited over it and a cross dipped in it, but the water had also to be fetched before sunrise from the river with the current and carried without looking back.[79]

Illiterate or semi-literate people often have an awe of the written word *per se*, which must be increased when the words are religious. It is not surprising therefore that written religious formulae were used as protective and healing amulets worn on the body. 'For febrile attacks at any time', an Anglo-Saxon leechbook advised, 'write on parchment and tie about the sick man's neck at sleeping time: In the name of the Lord who was crucified under Pilate, FLEE

YE FEVERS!' The otherwise practical English surgeon John of Arderne recommended another such charm in the fourteenth century – against spasms and cramp. A Latin formula, including the Trinitarian invocation, the name of Jesus, Mary and St John and of the archangels Michael, Gabriel and Raphael, and some magical words, was to 'be closed in the manner of a letter so that it cannot be opened easily, and for this reason I used to write it in Greek letters that it might not be understood of the people'. The charm was then worn around the neck again. An example from *The Pathway to Health* (1664), referring to the cult of the Three Kings of Cologne, indicates the continuing popularity of Latin charms of medieval origin in later Protestant England. 'For all manner of falling evils', blood should be taken from the little finger of the sufferer and the following lines written with it and then hung round his neck:

> Jasper fert Mirrham, Thus Melchior, Balthazar Aurum,
> Haec quicumque secum portat tria nomina regum,
> Salvitur a morbo, Domini pietate, caduco.[80]

In the early medieval period, such verbal charms were infused in water that was given to patients to drink.

As the continued practice of taking the oath in court shows, in Protestant countries the Bible might be lent the kind of magical aura attached in Catholic ones to saints and to formulae from the liturgy, and this too could generate therapeutic power. Asthma sufferers, in modern Wales, for example, were told to place the Bible under their bolsters for three successive nights and they would be cured.[81]

In a distinct category are the many popular, often rhyming, narrative charms that invoke God, Jesus or the saints, and frequently refer to some episode, authentic or not, in sacred history. In a typical example from the Veneto, styes in the eye are induced to transfer themselves to some figs by threatening them with Jesus, Mary and the cross:

> Stye, stye ...
> I take one fig,
> I take two,
> I take three,
> Jesus Christ our King.
> Stye, stye,
> The Lord does not want you;
> Mary does not want you.
> Escape into these three figs.
> This cross means: 'Off you march!'

More obviously, a number of English charms used the analogy of the Crown of Thorns to prevent a prick from a thorn from causing poisoning or 'gathering', as in this example from modern Suffolk:

> Christ was of a Virgin born,
> And crowned was with a crown of thorns;
> He did neither swell nor rebel,
> And I hope this never will.

Episodes from the Passion of Christ were often invoked. A fifteenth-century English charm to staunch bleeding referred to Longinus' wounding of Christ on the cross:

> A soldier of old thrust a lance into the side of the Saviour; immediately there flowed thence blood and water – the blood of Redemption and the water of Baptism. In the name of the Father ... , may the blood cease. In the name of the Son ... , may the blood remain. In the name of the Holy Ghost ... , may no more blood flow from the mouth, the vein or the nose[82]

All kinds of other references were also made. Burns were conjured in the Limousin with:

> Fire, lose your heat,
> As Judas lost his colour,
> When he betrayed our Saviour!

and cuts with:

> May this cut not be poisoned,
> As the sacred Host
> Is not in the body
> Of Our Lord Jesus Christ![83]

Many of these quasi-religious charms had a more developed narrative content. Janet Brown, a Scottish healer accused of witchcraft in 1643, healed injuries with this widely-used charm:

> Our Lord forth rode;
> His foal's foot slipped;
> Our Lord down lighted;
> His foal's foot righted;
> Saying flesh to flesh, blood to blood, bone to bone
> In our Lord his name.

This charm for fevers was collected in the Pays de Baugé in the 1920s:

When Jesus carried his cross, a Jew called Mark Antony came up to him and said:

Jesus, you are trembling. Jesus replied: I am not trembling, nor am I shivering, and whoever pronounces these words in his heart will never have fever or shivering. God commands tertian, quartian, intermittent and puerperal fevers all to leave the body of this person[84]

Two final example are better-known. The first was used to stop bleeding and is found in different versions from the ninth to the early twentieth centuries all over Europe. This one comes from an English book of magic dated 1622:

> God that was born in the borough of Bethlehem
> And baptized in the water of Jordan,
> The water was both wild and wode,
> The child was both meek and good.
> He blessed the flood,
> And still it stood.
> With the same blessing that he blessed the flood,
> I do bless the blood
> By virtue of the child so good.

The second is found in Anglo-Saxon and later medieval collections of charms and remedies in England and on the Continent, and was still in use in Wales and England in the nineteenth century:

> Peter was sitting on a marble-stone,
> And Jesus passed by;
> Peter said, My Lord, my God,
> How my tooth doth ache!
> Jesus said, Peter, thou art whole!
> And whoever keeps these words for my sake
> Shall never have toothache![85]

In a version found among the Rumanians of Hungary in the nineteenth century, St Peter suffers from a sprained foot; while a version from the Pays de Baugé in 1929 substituted St Paul for St Peter and cured ringworm or scalp disease.

IV

DIVINATION AND SIGNS

14

Divination and Signs

Another and very popular form of magic was divination or the discovery by supernatural means of hidden knowledge, including knowledge of the future. Two main categories are involved here: the reading of natural 'signs' and deliberate enquiry, though there is some overlap between them.

In most pre-modern societies abnormal and anomalous natural events have been a cause for concern. 'The unusual happening has the value of a sign that it would at the least be imprudent to ignore. It must be interpreted at once if possible, for it indicates an intervention of the invisible world into the ordinary course of events.'[1] The sign may also be regarded as a cause of the disastrous events which may follow it: the death of a king or leader, an epidemic, a defeat in war.

Natural signs and omens, major and minor, were of great importance to both the Ancient Greeks and the Romans. Aeschylus noted, for example, in *Agamemnon* that two eagles had 'swooped down on a pregnant hare and devoured it with its unborn young', as the Argives prepared to set out for Troy. This was read to mean that they would defeat the Trojans but also that an innocent child would be killed in the process with dire results, a reference to Agamemnon's sacrifice of his own daughter Iphigeneia.[2] Among the Romans, reporting such signs was commonplace in historical and other writing. 'This year the heavens were seen to blaze', wrote Livy of 461 BC,

> and the earth was shaken with a prodigious quake. That a cow had spoken – a thing which had found no credence the year before – was now believed. Among other portents there was even a rain of flesh, which is said to have been intercepted by vast numbers of birds flying round in the midst of it ... The two commissioners for sacred rites consulted the Sibylline Books, where it was predicted that there was danger to come from a concourse of foreigners, lest they attack the highest places of the City, and blood be shed.

Writing of a much later period, Tacitus also recorded marvels and attributed significance to them. So in 54 AD, 'a series of prodigies indicated changes for the worse. Standards and soldiers' tents were set on fire from the sky. A swarm of bees settled on the pediment of the Capitoline temple. Half-bestial children were born, and a pig with a hawk's claws'. Again in 64 AD there occurred 'unprecedently frequent lightning; a comet', and monstrous births, all seen as 'omens of impending misfortune' at the time of Nero's Terror. Juvenal satirized the belief in signs and portents, but other poets took it quite seriously. 'These told that a comet should appear the evil sign of war, and how that thick on earth should fall the stony shower', wrote Tibullus, for example. 'And they say that trumpets and the clash of arms were heard in heaven, and sacred groves rang with the coming rout. From the image of the gods poured the warm tears; and kine found tongue and spoke of the coming doom.'[3]

Of course, these Ancient beliefs were shared and passed on by the early Christians, especially via the New Testament. The Crucifixion was accompanied by an eclipse of the sun and an earthquake, while Christ and the Apostles foretold that natural signs would bring in 'the last days'. In Jerusalem, St Peter retailed God's declaration: 'And I will show portents in the sky above, and signs on the earth below – blood and fire and drifting smoke. The sun shall be turned to darkness and the moon to blood'.[4] Similar beliefs were held in early Celtic and Germanic societies, prior to Christianization, and Greek and Roman notions were preserved and transmitted via Classical texts.

It is not surprising that belief in signs and portents remained very much alive through the medieval period, at all cultural levels. In the sixth century, for example, Gregory of Tours' *History of the Franks* records portents regularly, often explaining their meaning. One year in December,

> new shoots appeared on the vine-stocks, misshapen grapes formed and the trees blossomed a second time. A great beacon traversed the heavens, lighting up the land far and wide. Rays of light shone in the sky, and in the north a column of fire was seen to hang from on high with an immense star perched on top of it. There was an earthquake in the district of Angers and many other portents appeared. In my opinion all this announced the coming death of King Gundovald.

In another year, Gregory himself saw bright rays of light in the sky over several nights – apparently the Aurora Borealis:

> The clouds were blood-red on both sides, to the east and to the west. In between the rays of light there were other clouds flashing vividly as if they were being struck by lightning. This extraordinary phenomenon filled me with foreboding, for it was clear that some disaster was about to be sent from heaven.

Another source covering the period from the sixth to the twelfth century, the *Anglo-Saxon Chronicle*, noted signs and odd climatic events in an even more systematic way, and offered implicit or explicit explanations. 'In this year (734) the moon was as if suffused with blood, and Archbishop Tatwine passed away, and also Bede.' In 793

> terrible portents appeared in Northumbria, and miserably afflicted the inhabitants: these were exceptional flashes of lightning, and fiery dragons were seen flying through the air, and soon followed a great famine; and after that in the same year the harrying of the heathen miserably destroyed God's church at Lindisfarne by rapine and slaughter.

Much later, in 1131, an appearance of blazing fire in the northern sky terrified the population and was accompanied by an unprecedented 'murrain among cattle and pigs'; while the death of King Henry I in Normandy was presaged by a solar eclipse: 'The sun looked like a moon three nights old, and there were stars around it at midday'.[5]

It was common in this period to interpret signs in an apocalyptic way, following Scriptural precedent. In France during the battle of Roncesvalles, according to the eleventh-century *Song of Roland*:

> There is a most terrible storm,
> A tempest with thunder and strong winds,
> Rain and hail in great quantity,
> Lightning strikes again and again
> And the whole earth begins to quake ...
> At high noon a great darkness gathers.
> No one could see it without a feeling of dread.
> Many say: 'It is all over with us;
> The end of the world is upon us'.

Such ideas were particularly associated with the Millennium. Raoul Glaber, for example, recorded the meteors, monsters, violent storms, eclipses, volcanic eruptions and so on, which occurred around the year 1000 and commented: 'People believed that the orderly pattern of the seasons and the elements which had reigned since the beginning of time had reverted to chaos once and for all and that the end of mankind had come'.[6]

Belief in portents continued into the early modern period. 'How it comes about I know not', Machiavelli wrote in his *Discorsi*, 'but it is clear from both Ancient and modern cases that no serious misfortune ever befalls a city or a province that has not been predicted either by divination or revelation or by prodigies or other heavenly signs.' So, for example, Matarazzo recorded in his Chronicles of Perugia that there was a terrible storm during the marriage festivities of Astorre degli Baglioni in 1500: 'And this was held to be an omen of most evil presage; and it followed on other ones [including a comet] that had before portended evil'. Later, in June 1502, 'four signs were sent down from heaven on our city and suburbs'. First, 'there fell a rain like unto blood'; then, in succession, there arrived huge numbers of grasshoppers, caterpillars, and crows; and soon afterwards Perugia fell to Cesare Borgia. Niccoli has shown that elite belief in such signs was waning in Italy by the late sixteenth century. Matarazzo conceded in 1506 that 'many mock and give no credence to these omens'. But they continued to find elite following elsewhere. Signs and evil portents were discerned, for example, in France at the time of the murder of Henry IV in 1610; and St Teresa wrote more generally in mid sixteenth-century Spain, addressing God: 'Thou showest signs in the heavens when Thou takest any of them [kings] away'.[7]

The interpretation of prodigies as signs from God, and especially of His wrath, had always been common among the clergy, and they held on to what was a powerful admonitory and apologetic argument. Many examples could be cited, continuing into the modern period, and they cut across denominational divisions. Jesuits in France and elsewhere in the sixteenth century noted 'extraordinary natural events that could be interpreted as omens', such as comets, swords and spears in the sky, blood-like rain, or earthquakes. As late as 1721, 'strange lights [seen] in the sky' were taken 'to be a God-sent portent of the success' of a mission in Bavaria. In Protestant Strasbourg through the sixteenth century 'bad weather, disease and invasion struck ... people as proof of God's anger ... Whenever natural or human disaster threatened the city, the pastors and preachers attributed it to the obstinacy and backsliding of the [people] ... Famine, plague, and war were the fruits of disobedience', punishments sent by God. According to Richard Baxter, the Great Plague of 1665 was the effect of the wrath of God and had been announced by 'strange comets' the previous Winter and Spring. The Royal Proclamation after the Great Fire of London the following year called for 'due humiliation since it hath pleased God to lay this heavy Judgment upon us all in this time, as an evidence of His displeasure for our sins'.[8]

Signs and omens are frequently referred to in Shakespeare's plays. The many portents of Caesar's death reported by Suetonius and others are retailed in *Julius Caesar*, and also the behaviour of birds which signalled the outcome of the battle of Philippi. This is to be expected given the subject of the play and its Roman setting, but portents also figure in the Tragedies and Histories. 'These late eclipses in the sun and moon', says Gloucester in *King Lear*, 'portend no good to us. Love cools, friendship falls off, brothers divide: in cities, mutinies; in countries, discord; in palaces, treason; and the bond crack'd 'twixt son and father'. In *Macbeth*, a series of portents surrounds the night that Duncan is murdered: an eclipse of unusual darkness early the following morning, a storm, an earthquake, continuous cries from a strange bird, a falcon killed by an owl a few days before, and cannibalism among horses. The Welsh Captain tells the Earl of Salisbury in *King Richard II*:

> 'Tis thought the King is dead ...
> The bay-trees in our country are all wither'd,
> And meteors fright the fixèd stars of heaven,
> The pale-fac'd moon looks bloody on the earth,
> And lean-look'd prophets whisper fearful change.

In both *King John* and *King Richard III* omens and portents are used to underline the wickedness of the kings and popular feeling against them. In *King John*, Cardinal Pandulph explains that the people in England are interpreting all kinds of natural events as

> ... prodigies and signs,
> Abortives, presages and tongues of heaven,
> Plainly denouncing vengeance upon John.

And later Hubert tells the king that five moons have been seen, with one circling the other four:

> Old men and beldames in the streets
> Do prophesy upon it dangerously.[9]

Such notions were also by this time the object of satire, as in Nashe's *A Wonderful Astrological Prognostication* of 1591, which warned that a July eclipse of the sun 'would cause such abundance of fleas that women shall not go to bed before twelve o'clock at night, for the great murders and stratagems they are like to commit upon these little animals'. But intellectuals were here sending up what remained a popular belief in both senses of the word. Gloucester's speech in *King Lear* echoed a 'straight' pamphlet published in 1606. Ralph Josselin, believed that earthquakes reported in several places in Essex in 1650 must 'portend something'; he also noted monstrous births, human and animal, in that year, and in August 1656, 'a remarkable cross' seen in the air and 'two armies [that] were seen in the air fighting', a sign often associated with war. Much later, Gilbert White reported that 'the Summer of the year 1783 was an amazing and portentous one, and full of horrible phenomena; for, besides the alarming meteors and tremendous thunderstorms that affrighted and distressed the different counties of this kingdom', there was a peculiar smoky fog or haze in Britain and Europe; then there was a strange blood-coloured sun that shone for over a month, together with earthquakes and volcanic eruptions in Calabria, Sicily and Norway. White commented that the country people were affected by 'a superstitious kind of dread, with which the minds of men are always impressed by such strange and unusual phenomena ... and indeed there was reason for the most enlightened person to be apprehensive'.[10]

Belief in signs and portents was equally persistent on the Continent, again especially among country people. In the Dauphiné, the sighting of a comet in 1577 and heavy snows and severe frosts that lasted into April 1578 were seen as omens of future wars, famines and unrest. Among the persecuted Protestants in the Cévennes in the 1690s, there were 'numerous stories of earthquakes and lights from heaven; a rain of blood had fallen on the Vivarais ... ; a child of nine months had sung psalms'. These were taken to be signs of 'supernatural interference' on their behalf. In A Sportsman's Notebook of 1852, Turgenev evoked the response of Russian serfs to a solar eclipse. In the village, 'they were saying that white wolves would run about the earth and eat people up, and birds of prey would fly about, and that we would see Trishka himself [a kind of superman]'; while 'in the servants' quarters [of the manor house], as soon as it got dark, the cook went and broke all the pots in the oven with the oven-fork: Who's going to eat now, she says, now the end of the world has come?' Among the peasantry of the Limousin, the sun setting in blood heralded the wars of 1870 and 1914, while an eclipse or a comet continued to strike terror: 'They barricaded themselves into the house, lit the Candlemas candle, and the women went on their knees to pray as if a catastrophe were imminent'.[11]

An important distinction should be made between large-scale natural events, which announced national disasters, like the deaths of kings, epidemics and wars, and minor events of significance for individuals and families.

A prime example in the first category was the appearance of a comet, 'the sad world's ill-boding book', in the words of Henry Vaughan the Silurist in 1655. From earliest times, comets were believed to announce disasters, and particularly the deaths of rulers. As Calpurnia says in Shakespeare's *Julius Caesar*:

> When beggars die, there are no comets seen;
> The heavens themselves blaze forth the death of princes.

A comet had in fact appeared soon after the death of Caesar, and his heir and successor Augustus himself noted 'that the people believed that this star indicated that the soul of Caesar had been taken among the number of the immortal gods'. Again in 60 AD the arrival of a comet was taken to be a sign that Nero was about to be replaced as emperor. Christian writers retained the association with royal deaths, though not of course with divinization. In 729, according to Bede, two comets appeared about the sun, to the great terror of the beholders. One of them went before the rising sun in the morning, the other followed him when he set at night ... ; one was the forerunner of the day, and the other of the night, to signify that mortals were threatened with calamities at both times. They carried their flaming tails towards the north, as it were ready to set the world on fire ... and continued nearly a fortnight. At which time a dreadful plague of Saracens ravaged France ...

while some months later King Osric of Northumbria died.[12]

Comets continued to evoke similar awe and speculation over the next millennium and longer. A comet in 1368, for example, provoked much discussion and was generally taken to portend 'widespread disease, warfare, death of cattle, conflagrations, frost ... , violent thunderstorms and ... hot winds that would destroy crops'. Similar ideas were associated with the comet seen in 1527. In the words of a French almanac in the following century: 'Comets never appear unless they presage disasters to come, that is wars, plagues, famines, earthquakes, mortalities, fires, floods or extreme ravages and desolations ... And in the event this comet was followed by several disasters': invasions by the Turks, other wars in Europe, food shortage and epidemics. In more recent times, the 1864 comet was taken afterwards to have been a sign of the war between Denmark and Prussia over Schleswig-Holstein and of Danish defeat; while the comet of 1905, according to Canetti, was generally believed in the small Bulgarian town, where he was brought up, to herald the end of the world.[13]

Other phenomena might be read in similar ways. The parhelia or appearance of three suns could presage a triumvirate or might be read as a precursor of Christian or Catholic victory, that is the triumph of the Trinity, as well as having more general import. The parhelia were seen before the sack of Rome in 1527 and again in the Netherlands in 1586. The Aurora Borealis, which we have already encountered in Gregory of Tours, was especially associated with warfare, according to a French book published in the 1580s. Another widely reported apparition from Classical times onwards was of armed men and horses in the sky. There were sights of battling celestial armies in Italy in the early sixteenth century, which were taken to be signs of an imminent attack on Christendom by the Turks. In 1529, Michael Behaim reported, 'a most terrifying sign has been seen by many people in the sky over Breslau': an enormous star, with figures of a man and an old woman. There was also 'the appearance of a great multitude of armoured soldiers bearing bloody swords in the sky over Liegnitz. What this portends one must leave to God'.[14] Similar figures were reported from time to time at other times and places.

'Let the astrologers be dismayed at the portentous blaze of comets and impressions in the air, as foretelling troubles and changes to states', Milton declared dismissively in 1641. As this indicates, the obvious phenomena such as comets and eclipses were lent more detailed interpretation by experts, and astrologers added to them more esoteric signs.

> Decisive historical crises such as changes in the leadership of peoples and cultures, the advent or demise of religions, the establishment and the fall of kingdoms and empires: all this was ordered by the movements of the heavenly system. The epochs of man's history could be seen in the skies, in the 'dances' of the stars, in their meetings. The celestial configurations were both signs and causes.

More particularly

> the appearance in the same constellation of the three major planets – Saturn, Mars, and Jupiter – could precipitate illness, war, famine and religious upheavals. The birth of Mohammed, long ago, had actually coincided with such a conjunction, and the Black Death of 1348 again confirmed the same terrible portent.

From early on, Christianity was opposed to astrology. 'The fatalism astrology encouraged was perhaps the main reason for the dislike it aroused among Christians concerned to emphasize the reality of active divine grace and free will.' St Augustine devoted nine chapters in *The City of God* to arguments against astrology. By the high medieval period, however, the attitude of the official religion changed. 'From being bowed almost to extinction by the heavy weight of patristic condemnation, astrology became a perfectly acceptable, indeed encouraged, object of learned enquiry.' Seznec refers to 'an extraordinary increase in the prestige of astrology ... between the twelfth and fourteenth centuries'. At this time, 'the greatest princes took astrologers into their service as intimate counsellors ... In Italy, astrologers directed the life of cities, *condottieri*, and prelates'. In subsequent centuries, astrology became discredited among theologians and intellectuals, but it retained or gained prestige at the vulgar level, as Thomas and Capp have shown for early modern England. The Venetian diviner Fra Aurelio used astrology in his predictions in the 1570s, although he was careful to explain to the Inquisition that celestial configurations simply provided information on the conditions in which events occurred; they did not determine them absolutely.[15]

We have seen that omens surrounded births, marriages and deaths, and there was a host of minor signs that guided everyday behaviour. 'How superstitiously we mind our evils', Delio declares in Webster's *The Duchess of Malfi*,

> The throwing down salt, or crossing of a hare,
> Bleeding at nose, the stumbling of a horse,
> Or singing of a cricket, are of power
> To daunt whole man in us.

The American artist William Wetmore Story provides a good account of such popular beliefs in Rome in the second half of the nineteenth century:

> Every dream has its meaning, every path its stumbling-stone. If you meet a hunch-back or a monk first on going out in the morning, return at once and set out again on your errand. [Elsewhere in Italy seeing a hunchback was lucky.] If you break a mirror, or spill oil, death is imminent in your house. If three candles are accident-ally placed on the table, some one of those sitting round it must make his will ... If any two things fall together in the shape of a cross, stoop and kiss them and then take them up, unless you wish for ill luck. Never sit seven or thirteen at table, if you do not wish to tempt fate ...

And much more.[16]

Such beliefs were universal in the past, and they were not confined to the lower orders or the peasantry. In England, for example, Archbishop Laud reported minor items in his diary in the mid seventeenth century. On one occasion, 'two robins flew into his study. On another his barge sank in the Thames. On another his picture fell from the wall. Such incidents he recorded but always with apprehension as presages of graver events'. Much later another clerical diarist recorded similar or even more trivial incidents. 'As I was going to shave myself this morning as usual on Sundays', Parson Woodforde noted in March 1769, 'my razor broke in my hand as I was setting it on the strop without any violence. May it always be a warning to me not to shave on the Lord's Day, or do any other work to profane it.' Two years later, when his brother Jack saw a strange light in the orchards, he commented: 'I hope it is no omen of death in the family'; while in September 1796 he had an odd dream and then 'a raven fled over my house this morning. All which tokens are said to bode no good'.[17] Of course, such 'superstitions' had long been the object of satire (for example, by Congreve and Swift), but one does not satirize what is not also taken seriously.

Reading the flight of birds had been an important feature in Ancient Roman divination, and the sight and sound of birds remained important signs in later times, as Laud and Woodforde illustrate. Burchard of Worms had referred to those who 'when they make a journey, if a crow croaks from their left side to their right, they hope on this account to have a prosperous journey', while if a kind of owl 'flies in front of them across the road' towards the end of the day, this indicates that they will find a lodging place, and 'they trust more to this augury and omen than to God'. Similarly, a Franciscan preacher at Nancy in 1520 declared 'from flights of birds, people will say it is a sign that you will lose your goods or property'. Strange birds, birds behaving strangely and combinations of numbers were always significant. So the Essex hermit Jimmie Mason in the 1890s saw 'a strange green bird ... flying over so slow; coming out of the clouds from Hatfield forest, going to Dunmow. It was bigger than a duck. Bill such a length, and a large gap in the right wing. Whatever could that mean?' John Clare noted in *The Shepherd's Calendar* of 1827 that seeing an owl in the day-time caused dismay in the superstitious. According to a marginal comment in the parish register of Brailes, Warwickshire, fifty people died there during the great plague of 1603 'and fifty ravens flew about the steeple till the fifty was dead'. In the modern Limousin, 'seeing a single woodpecker was a sign of bad luck: someone in the family would die. But the sight of two such birds announced a marriage; and of three at once a baptism in the house'. Similar signs relating to seeing particular birds or numbers of birds are common in other folklore collections. In many places in England, for example, it was unlucky to see a magpie, 'and when it is seen, it is customary to raise the hat in salutation, sign the cross on the breast or make the sign by crossing the thumbs and then spitting on them'.[18] There is also the rhyme relating to magpies: 'One for sorrow, two for joy; three for a girl, four for a boy'. In France and elsewhere, black creatures were unlucky, while white ones were lucky. The magpie, which is black and white, was therefore ambiguous in its meaning.

We have mentioned the role of bird cries as death omens, but they also had more general significance. In the Limousin, the barn-owl had two cries: one which announced a death, the other a birth. Anomalous cries were especially significant. In the Hebrides, it was a bad omen if a cock crowed at an unwonted hour. Gough relates that two ravens followed a child murderer from Shropshire and 'made a hideous and unusual noise', leading to his arrest. Or a bird might emit the wrong sound. In Verga's *I Malavoglia* (1881), set in Sicily, a woman hears 'the black hen crowing' during the night, before a further disaster strikes the family.[19]

Sights of particular animals might also be portents, especially if the beasts were unusual or behaved unusually. Whales beached on the Dutch coast in the late sixteenth century aroused a great deal of interest among the common people and the elite. They were linked with the other kinds of signs that we have discussed: eclipses, earthquakes and plagues; and they were interpreted both as 'portents of disaster' and as indications that 'the Hollanders [engaged in their bid for independence] would triumph over their enemies'. Here the bulk of the animal was important and its displacement from its proper environment. But whales were also anomalous in a general way, both fish and

15. Monstrous Sow of Landser. Albrecht Dürer, etching, 1496.

mammals – like porpoises. Shakespeare's fisherman in *Pericles* relates the common view that porpoises were harbingers of storms and shipwreck: 'They say they're half fish, half flesh; a plague on them, they ne'er come but I look to be wash'd'.[20]

Meeting some land animals was a good augury; meeting others was bad. In many places, for example, seeing or encountering a hare was a bad omen. According to the *Evangile des quenouilles*, 'if anyone is setting out and a hare runs in front of him, it is a very bad sign. And, to avoid all dangers, he should return three times back to where he started and then begin his journey again'. The weasel was also unlucky. In the Pyrenees, to prevent a mishap following sight of one, a person should say: 'Weasel, what a pretty lady you are!' The time at which a creature was sighted was often significant. In modern Greece, for example, seeing a snake in the morning meant good luck, but seeing one at dusk or later indicated bad luck and probably a death. Again, it was a bad sign if an animal appeared in the wrong place or at the wrong time. It was noted, for example, that, when Richard I was crowned in Westminster Abbey in 1189, 'a bat flittered round the throne in broad daylight', which was taken to be an evil omen.[21]

We have discussed monsters in connection with unusual births. All freaks of nature caused fascination and fear, and they were read as signs. For example, the monstrous sow of Landser, born in 1496, which had one head, two bodies, and eight feet and which Dürer illustrated in a print, was generally taken to be an omen (see Text Figure 15). In France and elsewhere, there was a belief in the malevolent effects of a supposed serpent born of a cock's egg. This creature hid in some corner, and those who saw it immediately died. One was reported in the cemetery at Ardon in the Sologne in 1790, and the ossuary was burned to destroy it.

Deliberate divination was widely practised in the Ancient world, forming a recognized part of official Greek, Etruscan and Roman religion. Methods of divination included consulting oracular temples and shrines, of which the best known is the oracle of Apollo at Delphi; interpreting dreams; observing the behaviour of animals and especially birds; scrying or looking in water and other surfaces; and examining the entrails of sacrificial animals and particularly the liver. Divination took place on public occasions, such as the designation of consuls at Rome. It was also resorted to at times of crisis for the State, but most often it occurred in a range of everyday situations relating to individuals and families. Questions put to an Egyptian oracle about 300 included: 'Shall I receive an allowance? ... Am I to be sold [as a slave]? ... Am I to be reconciled with my offspring? Am I to profit by the transaction? Is my property to be put up for auction? ... Am I to become a senator? ... Will I be divorced from my wife? ... Have I been poisoned?' 'Your wife ... is for ever consulting diviners', Juvenal mocked in his Sixth Satire in the second century;

> Why does her jaundice-ridden
> Mother take so long dying? When will she see off
> Her sister or her uncles ... ?
> Will her present lover survive her?[22]

Deliberate divination continued to flourish in medieval and modern times, and took many of the ancient forms. First, dreams provided insight, warnings and prediction. For example, in 1407, according to Vespasiano da Bisticci, the mother of the future Pope Nicholas V, a woman of humble status from Pisa, received an assurance in a dream that he would recover from a childhood illness and that he would become pope. The Franciscan in Nancy in 1520 noted: 'A goodwife will say, I dreamed last night that I was at a wedding, and I believe it is a sign that my husband is ill'; or again, 'when one dreams of a hare, they say it is a sign that one will be ill'. Molly Dade, the sister of Parson Woodforde's maid Betty, died in January 1785 soon after he had dreamt of corpses. In February, he related: 'I dreamt a good deal about Jenny Woodforde, Frank Woodforde's wife, of her being dressed all in white, looked exceeding pale ... I hope my dream portends no ill to her'. Often the meaning of dreams was more precise than this suggests. In northern Greece in modern times,

> if you dream of smoke or darkness, it means death; if you dream of a ring, it means worry; if you see a house burn down, it means death ... If you are chased by a cow, it means illness will come; if you dream you are naked, it means someone will soon insult you; ... and if you dream you are in the sea, poverty will come.[23]

Freud in *The Interpretation of Dreams* (1900) was in some ways revamping a popular tradition.

The behaviour of animals and birds continued to be read by experts and others. A Burgundian penitential of the eighth century condemned those who 'took auguries by birds'. The 'taking of auspices from entrails' probably also persisted into the early medieval period. Many other techniques were employed. La Bruyère in the 1690s referred to 'palmists and soothsayers, those who cast horoscopes and read the configuration of the stars, those who discover past events by the movements of a sieve, those who reveal the truth in a mirror or a bowl of water'. Plants and other objects might be 'read'. In Calabria in modern times, a herb, called Fortune's Grass, was hung from the ceiling beams. If the leaves curled upwards, this meant good luck; if downwards, bad luck. 'The oracle is chiefly consulted on Ascension Day, when it is asked to tell the secrets confided by Christ when He walked upon the earth.' In Corsica, similar divination was practised via the colour and texture of eggs laid by poultry. Cooking and other processes were also exploited. In Lanarkshire in modern times, a special oat bannock was baked for each child in a family on Hogmanay evening. If the bannock broke in the baking, this was 'a very unlucky omen for the child ... It denoted illness or death during the year'. Elsewhere in Scotland, attention was paid to the 'wort' or malt used in brewing the New Year ale: 'If the wort boiled up in the middle of the pot, there was a fey (doomed) person's drink in the pot'. Another means depended on the behaviour of grains. 'Hast thou done what many do?' enquired Burchard of Worms. 'They scrape the place where they are accustomed to make the fire in their house and put grains of barley there in the warm spot; and, if the grains jump [they believe], there will be danger, but if they remain, things will go well.'[24] We have seen too that the weather for the coming year could be divined from that occurring at Christmas or the New Year.

Casting lots was practised down the ages, too. Ongendus, King of the Danes, is said to have 'cast lots three times every day for three days to find out who should die', after Willibrord and his companions had killed some of the sacred cattle of the pagan god Fosite around 700. Burchard of Worms again laid down penances for 'those who practise lots or expect lots to foreknow the future'. Bean-casting was a very popular procedure in the early modern period in Venice and elsewhere in the Mediterranean region. A handful of beans was counted to a formula such as 'He loves me; he loves me not'; or a fixed number of beans was thrown, sometimes along with other objects, and the configuration on the ground or a table was then 'read'. Similar procedures were followed with ashes from the fire, smoke, oil, molten lead, shears and other instruments in different parts of Europe. We should also mention reading the shoulder-blade of an animal, usually a sheep or a goat, which was practised in Greece and the Balkans, in Corsica, Scotland and elsewhere. The holes and marks on the bones had particular meanings, indicating the gender of the unborn, as we have seen, and health or illness, prosperity or death more generally. Pennant met a woman on Rum in the 1760s, for example, 'who has the power of foreseeing events [including death] through a well scraped blade bone of mutton'.[25]

Though, as we have seen, the Church condemned pagan forms of divination and many clerics were unhappy about the general principle involved, others allowed or favoured the introduction of new Christian forms. The early eighth-century penitential ascribed to Bede banned the use of 'the oracles which are falsely called *sortes sanctorum*'. This was a procedure, clearly practised by members of the clergy, and which involved opening the Bible, or often particular books in it such as the Psalms or the Gospels, 'usually upon the high altar of a church ... and the first passage on which the eye alighted was taken as a divine oracle'. Later, worry about the legitimacy of the practice seems to have abated. According to Giovanni di Ceprano, for example, St Francis and his early companions 'prayed God very devoutly to show them His will by the first words they should find on opening the book'. St Francis then opened the Bible in front of the altar of the church of San Niccolo in Assisi, and 'the first thing he found was the advice of the Lord: If thou wilt be perfect, go and sell that thou hast, and give to the poor, and thou shalt have treasure in heaven (St Matthew, 19, 21)'. Then, 'as his devotion to the Holy Trinity was so great, he wished to receive a threefold sign, so he opened the book a second and a third time', finding similarly appropriate verses. 'Each time that he opened the book, Blessed Francis thanked the Lord for having thus confirmed the resolution he had held in his heart for so long', and he took the oracular verses as the justification for founding his new community in complete poverty. Such Scriptural divination was widely practised by later Christians, especially but not exclusively Protestants. For example, the eighteenth-century English evangelist, Berridge of Everton, recounted how he consulted the Lord, when he had the momentary weakness to think of getting married: 'So falling down on my knees before a table, with a Bible between my hands, I besought the Lord to give me direction ... This method of procuring divine intelligence', he commented, 'is much flouted by flimsy professors who walk at large, and desire not that sweet and secret access to the mercy-seat which babes of the kingdom do find'.[26]

Other forms of Christian divination are reported. The papal legate, Cardinal Cajetan, for example, *en route* from Dijon to Paris in 1590, received news of a possible ambush to his party. According to Roberto Bellarmino,

> his Lordship being unable to discover the truth by any human means, secretly dropped two little pieces of paper into the chalice when he had finished mass. On one was the word 'Go', and on the other 'Do not go'. Then, commending the whole affair to God, he drew out one of the folded notes, and opening it, saw that it bore the words 'Do not go'. A short time afterwards we learned that the story of the ambush was true in every detail.

Bellarmino, of course, was one of the leading churchmen and theologians of the Counter-Reformation. He was canonized in 1930 and declared a Doctor of the Church the following year.[27]

This brings us to the circumstances in which divination was resorted to, and here again the situation in medieval and modern times was little different from that found in Antiquity. Some divination involved public events. The shoemaker prophet called Asdente was consulted on public affairs at Parma in the thirteenth century; while in sixteenth-century Venice Fra Aurelio, a renegade friar, and other diviners gave advice about elections to civic office, though their clients may have been more interested in betting on these rather than on their outcome itself. Niccoli has shown that prophecies relating to public matters, either in printed form, sermons or other oral forms, were very common in Italy through the Renaissance period to around 1530, when they went into decline. After that 'the prophetic culture' became devalued and broken up. Its procedures became 'tied to purely private concerns; they are powerless to read the supernatural world, the world of nature, or human society (thus politics and history) in any sort of unified manner'.[28] This is too dismissive, certainly re the natural world, as we have shown. And, as Niccoli admits, in France, England and elsewhere popular prophecy involving public events continued into the sixteenth, the seventeenth and even the eighteenth centuries.

Prophecies and divination moreover, had always mainly involved purely private concerns, the difficulties and anxieties of everyday life, and continued to do so. Fra Aurelio again was consulted in connection with marriage negotiations and trading ventures. La Bruyère noted that diviners 'predict to men that they will make their fortunes, to girls that they will marry their suitors'; they also 'console sons whose fathers refuse to die and pacify young women who have old husbands'. Illness and wondering whether oneself or one's relatives would recover from it was a perennial preoccupation, as we have seen. 'Hast thou done what some do when they are visiting any sick person?', asked Burchard of Worms.

> When they approach the house where the sick person lies, if they find a stone lying nearby, they turn the stone over and look in the place where it was lying [to see] if there is anything living under it, and if they find there a worm or a fly or an ant or anything that moves, then they aver that the sick person will recover. But, if they find nothing there that moves, they say he will die.

Many springs and fountains were used in a similar way, clothing of the patient being floated in the water. Fountains were also consulted in coastal regions to learn whether sailors would return from sea. Information was also sought about the gender of unborn children, about the weather, and in connection with State lotteries. In Chaucer's *Miller's Tale*, Nicholas, a clerk at Oxford and a student of astrology, forecast

> When that men should have drought or else showers
> Or, if men asked him, what should befall
> Of everything.

In early nineteenth-century Naples books explaining signs for the lottery were very widely distributed: 'Every dream, encounter, incident, or accident has its own particular sign and number'.[29]

As Thomas has shown for early modern England, one of the commonest forms of divinatory magic related to stolen or lost property. A number of Anglo-Saxon charms against theft have been preserved. Gregory of Tours mentioned thief divining with a chalice, and in the Carolingian period in France the back of a suspected thief might be touched with blessed wax containing mercury, on which a formula had been written. In a late medieval Norfolk school book again a formula was written on wax, which was placed under the head of the victim during the night, 'and he shall appear in thy sleep that hath thy goods'. The formula consisted of a series of letters and Latin words. A fourteenth-century Flemish manuscript evoked the analogy of the 'invention' or discovery of the true cross by St Helen: 'The diviner lies four times on the ground, once in each of the compass directions, with arms outstretched in the form of a cross, and each times recites a formula commanding the cross of Christ to fetch back the thief and the stolen goods'.[30]

The eclectic means used in thief divining: formulae, sympathy, religious objects and power, continued into the early modern and modern periods. In sixteenth-century Modena, we hear of drawing lots to discover who had stolen a stock of sausages; and of 'balancing a sieve on a pair of scissors and saying, By St Peter and St Paul, tell me who has taken my money', where the sieve was expected to rotate at the mention of the thief's name. In a more elaborate ritual, supposedly widely used in sixteenth-century Venice, a pregnant woman and two virgin girls were put in

> a well closed room. Then in a hand-washing basin in which there is a wedding ring of a true and legitimate marriage you put a flask full of holy water on the top of the ring. Then the ... woman and ... girls kneel with a blessed candle in their hands, calling upon the Devil in the name of the White Angel, calling him Saintly Angel. [Then they] look in the flask [to see the thief or to see where the stolen goods were hidden].

Similar procedures continued to be used all over Europe in the modern period. At a fountain near Plestin in Brittany, for example, several pieces of bread were thrown into the water, to each of which the name of a suspect had been attached. The actual thief was indicated by the piece which fell to the bottom of the pool and stayed there. Several instances are reported in nineteenth-century England, in which thieves were detected by using a Bible and a key. In a case at Ludlow in 1879, a woman who had lost a sheet, placed the key at Ruth 1, verse 16, and crossed her fingers, 'and when the thief was named, the key would spontaneously move'. Then, when she went to the culprit's house, the Bible fell out of her hand.[31]

V

THE ELEMENTS OF MAGIC

15

Magical Power:
Persons, Spirits and Animals

We have seen that much magic was part and parcel of everyday life and was practised or performed by ordinary people in the communal or religious or family context. But there were those who had or could manipulate magical power in a special way, and magical power belonged to certain human statuses and conditions as well as to supernatural beings and animals.

There were various types of specialist magician. One important distinction lay between the learned magician and the popular practitioner. Perhaps the best-known example of the first is Prospero in Shakespeare's *The Tempest*, with his book, staff and robe, controller of the weather and raiser of spirits who do his bidding. Such magicians were still operating in Europe around 1600 and later, though they were mainly a phenomenon of the medieval and Renaissance periods. Some of their practices and habits rubbed off on later popular practitioners, and they retained a vicarious prestige and influence via early modern and modern almanacs and chap-books.

Among the popular magicians, across all periods, one may distinguish various categories: fortune tellers and those with second sight; folk healers; diviners; animal tamers and healers; witch doctors or undoers of spells; exorcists. In the Ancient world, there were also interpreters of dreams, sellers of oracles and those who could communicate with the dead, all of whom were less important later. There were also shamanistic people, who left their bodies in sleep or trance to accomplish a variety of tasks: ensuring fertility, regulating deaths and so on, like the *benandanti* of the Friuli, the Corsican *mazzeri*, or the Hungarian *táltosok*. Then there were witches, known under a variety of names, who specialized in harmful or malevolent magic; and there were those who did tricks, conjurors in the modern sense. Webster refers in *The White Devil* to 'some that use to juggle upon cards [and] show juggling tricks'.[1]

Many popular magicians, however, seem to have been generalists, wise or cunning women or men able to prognosticate, heal, find lost property, raise spells and so on. Skelton described such a person in the early 1500s in England:

> She seemed half a leech,
> And began to preach
> Of the Tuesday in the week
> When the mare doth kick,
> Of the virtue of an unset leek,
> Of her husband's breek;
> With the feathers of a quail
> She could to Bordeaux sail;
> And with good ale barme
> She could make a charm
> To help withal a stitch:
> She seemed to be a witch.

The peasant Kalinick in Turgenev's *Sportsman's Notebook* similarly 'knew spells to cure fear, frenzy or bleeding; he could drive out worms; his bees did well'; and he was asked 'to lead a newly-bought horse into the stable, for luck!' In Calabria in the early twentieth century, the many wise men and women 'mostly occupied themselves with the manufacture of charms for gaining lucky lottery tickets, and for deluding fond women who wish to change their lovers'. In modern Portugal, the *bruxa* was 'a person endowed with supernatural powers to annul the effects of antisocial forces, and, at times, to counterattack these. This person may be a diviner, a sorcerer, a faith-healer, a medium, an exorcist, or even a certain type of priest'.[2]

As we saw with folk healers, magical powers were acquired in a variety of ways: from birth (which sometimes conveyed an inner 'mana' or 'grace'), from a knowledge of 'secrets', derived sometimes from a formal initiation, or from a special event or revelation.[3]

In some societies, castes of magicians exist. The closest one comes to this in Europe is the association of magical powers by the majority population with certain ethnic groups or people from particular places. In Ancient Greece and also Rome, 'witches came from Thessaly or the Black Sea, that is, from countries at the end of the world'. The Persians or Chaldeans and the Jews were also thought of as potential magicians. In Scandinavia down to modern times, the Lapps and the Finns, again people living on the frontiers of known lands, were believed to have magical powers. In the medieval period and afterwards in Calabria, the Saracens and their descendants came into this category. All over Europe, gypsies had 'a considerable reputation' as fortune tellers, healers and makers of 'efficacious and sometimes noxious' magic. Other outsiders or strangers were also credited with special powers: vagrants, peddlars, bandits, shepherds. Among vagrants reported in Salisbury in the 1630s, for example, were a fortune teller, a minstrel, a morris-dancer and two conjurors. In the Commingeois in south-western France typically, shepherds knew 'how to talk to animals ... could foretell the weather by the sky and heal by means of plants'; they also had second sight and could make contact with the dead. Like shepherds, members of other professions were outside the community and might be classified in the same way. Mauss notes that 'doctors, barbers, blacksmiths, ... actors and gravediggers' all might be thought to possess magical faculties.[4] He might have added members of the clergy. Their ordination and their involvement in 'high' rituals and especially the Eucharist, their learning and especially their access to esoteric knowledge via Latin, and for Catholics their celibacy, all lent clerics an aura that both they and more often others could translate into the powers of the magician.

Magical powers might be inherited. Healing and other powers were passed on in the sixteenth-century Veneto, for example, from mother to daughter or aunt to niece, while in modern Greece they were often transmitted 'in a "zig zag" chain from one sex to another through the generations; father to daughter to daughter's son to son's daughter, and so on'. Imparting the skills by instruction was often as important as bloodline here. A woman charged with heretical magic at Latisana in the 1590s admitted: 'I taught this signing to my children'.[5] In Greece, the secrets had to be deliberately handed on in a face-to-face encounter, but they did not become operative until the existing holder of them died. The mother-daughter tie was often a prominent feature in north European witch trials in the early modern period. We have also noted the significance of birth circumstances: being born on a particular day or with a caul or as a seventh child, for example.

Formal initiation into being a magician, perhaps by joining a group, was not important in Europe, where magic did not enjoy the established status that it did in some societies. At most there was the teaching of secrets to descendants that we have mentioned or the passing of them to a chosen successor often at death. In a case before an ecclesiastical court at St Albans in the early sixteenth century, a man learned a Latin spell to cure horses from his father; while at Colchester in 1597, a woman acquired a similar charm 'from Goodwife George of Much Tey'. More generally in modern Normandy, 'the most traditional way' of acquiring healing power was via 'its transmission to a person showing particular aptitude', but written prayer charms were often given to the first takers.[6] Some magic was learned from books, but this only became an important means of transmission in the modern period. Even with the advent of a culture of literacy at the popular level, magic belonged essentially to the pre-literate era.

Acquiring magical powers through a revelatory experience was also not much in evidence in traditional Europe, though some examples may be cited from early sources. In twelfth-century Denmark, Saxo Grammaticus referred to a hero standing 'in the bitter Winter sea till his wolf-skins freeze upon him', in order to gain 'magic power to repel the venom of dragons'. This parallels a well-established Japanese custom of procuring special powers by enduring cold water. Nor was spirit possession an avenue to magicianship in Europe, having an almost entirely negative connotation there. People were possessed by malevolent demons which were exorcized from them. Only very occasionally is trance mentioned in the sources. We have cited examples in connection with healing, and Pennant noted in 1769 that 'pretenders to second sight [in the Scottish Highlands] fall into trances, foam at the mouth, grow pale and feign to abstain from food for a month, so over-powered are they by the visions imparted to them during their paroxysms'.[7] However, short-term preparation for magical activity via fasting, sexual abstinence and general purity was more common. The Rumanian Căluş dancers, for example, refrained from all sexual contact for a period before and during the rituals.

Virgins had a general role in ritual, religion and magic. Their purity and innocence gave them invulnerability and a force for good. As Milton noted in *Comus*, no spirits, witches or ghosts had 'hurtful power o'er true virginity'. In practice, this most often meant children. Children played an important part in calendar customs – most obviously in the Boy Bishop ceremonies held on and around Holy Innocents –, in civic pageantry, and at funerals. Always here they had a special quality that adults wished to exploit. Michel Yvard, a Parisian surgeon, for example, called in his will for as little ceremony as possible at his funeral, which occurred in 1555, but 'he did nevertheless wish to have children present (as was customary) ... those privileged intercessors who have natural access to the Kingdom of God'.[8]

Children were used in magic in Ancient times. Apuleius was accused, for example, of bewitching a boy and thereby getting him to 'utter prophecies'. Boys were also used to 'scry' for lost objects and for other purposes. Children continued to figure in a variety of magical rituals through the medieval and modern periods. The sixteenth-century learned magician Cornelius Agrippa wrote that elemental demons were especially likely to come to those of 'innocency of mind ... wherefore they do often meet children, women and poor and mean men'. And children do figure in reported attempts to raise or communicate with spirits. John of Salisbury recalled that he and another boy had been used by a priest in the early twelfth century in 'the art of crystal gazing'. Eymeric's handbook for Inquisitors of 1376 referred specifically to the invocation of demons by placing a child in a circle with a mirror, a sword and an amphora. In several cases brought before the Inquisition in Venice in the early modern period young boys and girls were employed in a similar way 'to enquire of the spirits'. Children also play a role in more everyday procedures. An Anglo-Saxon ritual to procure rapid childbirth required a boy or a girl, 'still virginal' to hold a linen cloth, on to which coriander seeds had been sewn, on the woman's left thigh. Fifteenth-century remedies for facial lupus and deafness required 'the urine of a man-child that is a pure maid' and 'of a young child'. In the Abruzzi in the modern period, to conjure a storm, a baby 'was exposed to the storm cloud with the thought that at the sight of such an innocent one the anger of the spirits inhabiting the cloud would be softened'. In the same way, 'the Austrian peasants believed that the house in which a child sleeps is safe from being struck by lightning. During a thunderstorm they therefore put to bed the youngest child'. Children could also protect livestock. At Gebruth in the Protestant Rhineland around 1600 the flocks were led in procession by three naked children, supposedly representing the Trinity, in order to save them from a cattle epidemic. In the Cévennes, another Protestant region, more recently, an analogous ritual was performed to keep foxes away from the poultry run. A sorcerer led the youngest girl of the family, completely naked, round the property on a moonless night, uttering various formulae.[9] Here, as in other cases, nudity emphasized purity.

Belief in the polluting influence of menstruating women is found universally, together with consequent prohibitions and taboos. These centre on the menstrual blood. Menstruation's relation to conception was not fully understood before the end of the nineteenth century. In elite theory, the monthly flow of blood was seen as a natural purgation necessary to keeping the humoral balance, and/or as a punishment for and mark of Eve's original sin. The purgation idea meant that it was important to regulate menstruation, and a number of herbal and other remedies were used to do this. Culpeper, for example, lists twenty-two herbs for 'provoking the terms' or 'bringing down women's menses', and five for stopping or preventing an excessive flow.[10]

The Early Church did not allow menstruating women to be baptized, and the early medieval clergy had doubts as to whether they should be admitted to churches or receive communion. When St Augustine of Canterbury put these questions to Pope Gregory the Great in 597, the pope ruled that they should have access to both, but he added in relation to receiving communion: 'But, if anyone out of profound respect does not presume to do it, she is to be commended'. Nor was papal guidance always followed. The eighth-century Penitential of Theodore laid down that 'women shall not in the time of impurity enter a church or communicate – neither nuns nor laywomen; if they presume [to do this] they shall fast for three weeks'.[11] The Catholic Church seems later to have followed the tolerant line here, but some Protestant sects and the Orthodox Church maintained what was effectively an excommunication.

Debate took place in the Middle Ages as to whether the Virgin Mary menstruated or not, and again opinion was divided. The feeling that there was a discrepancy between holiness and menstruation was also manifested in accounts of female saints and holy women who had ceased to menstruate, like St Colette of Corbie.

More generally, menstruating women produced a range of negative effects by their looks, touch or mere presence. Here medieval and later writers repeated and elaborated on the claims made by Pliny the Elder, all reflecting popular belief. According to Pliny, 'the touch of a menstruous woman turned wine to vinegar, blighted crops, killed seedlings, blasted gardens, brought fruit down from trees, dimmed mirrors, blunted razors, rusted iron and brass, ... killed bees', and caused animals to miscarry. Later evidence stresses the deleterious effects of menstruation on tasks that had to do with provisioning and the production of food. In nineteenth-century France, for example, the presence of a menstruating woman would 'corrupt meat, make milk go sour, prevent bread from rising, interfere with wine-making' and stop butter 'coming'. For this reason, they might be kept away from all the relevant processes. Victor Hugo noted in 1846 that no woman was allowed in the part of the Paris catacombs, where mushrooms were grown: 'They say that the presence of a woman at a certain time of the month is enough to turn and rot a whole batch'. In modern Rumania 'menstruating women are discouraged from approaching the sheep fold. It is believed their blood will curdle the sheep's milk'.[12] Fear of the polluting effects of women here was so strong among gypsies, that they did not eat the same foot as men and their clothes were washed separately.

Sexual intercourse with a menstruating woman was dangerous both for the man and for any offspring. Contact with the menstrual blood might 'burn' the penis. There was a medieval idea that 'a child conceived as a result of relations with a menstruating woman would be born a leper'. Later, as we have seen, monstrous births might be associated with the same cause. Another angle on such beliefs is provided by evidence gathered by the Inquisition in Venice in 1563. 'A boy in the house of Jewish converts is alleged to have said "that Christ was a bastard born of carnal sin, when the Virgin Mary had the menstrual blood upon her"'.[13]

Menstruating women in effect possessed special powers akin to those of witches or people with the evil eye. Menstrual power was mainly involuntary, but it could be manipulated for evil and for good. A woman in the Friuli in 1618 asserted that witches used menstrual blood 'to injure people, make them fall sick, become stunted and even die'; while in modern Greece it was strewn on the path up to a house along with 'oils of the dead' in order to break up an engagement. Positively, menstrual power, often in the form of blood, was used to protect houses from evil forces, to break or undo spells, to avert plague and storms, to put out fires, to cure illnesses and the bites of mad dogs and to frighten off pests. The last was done, according to a sixteenth-century bishop of Grasse by 'women walking through the fields with their skirt raised to expose their private parts'; in some places in Italy they wore no clothes at all. In seventeenth-century Venice, it is reported that women made omelettes with their own blood to alleviate menstrual pains.[14]

But the most common use of menstrual blood, especially in the Mediterranean area, was in love magic. At Montaillou in the fourteenth century, 'Beatrice de Planissoles kept the first menstrual blood of her daughter to use as a love-potion to bewitch some future son-in-law' and ensure that he had eyes for no other woman. A woman called Giovanna, condemned for witchcraft in Florence in 1427, had tried in various ways to infatuate Giovanni Ceresani and to strengthen his virility 'to satisfy ... her insatiable lust'. Finally,

> she took a little of her menses ... and placed it in a small beaker ... and then poured it into another flask filled with wine ... and gave it to Giovanni to drink. And on account of this [and other procedures] Giovanni no longer has time for his affairs as he did in the past, and he has left home and his wife and son ... and does only what pleases Giovanna.[15]

Similar practices were current in early modern Venice.

This brings us to the question of gender and magic power, for menstruation concentrated a dangerous quality that some thought belonged to women generally. There was a long-standing assumption that linked women with magical activity rather than men. It is found in Ancient literature. The early medieval penitentials presume that magic would be practised by laywomen or clerics and not by laymen. In the fourth circle of the Inferno, Virgil shows Dante 'the wretched women who left the needle, the shuttle and the spindle to become diviners and to work evil with herbs and images'. The authors of the *Malleus Maleficarum* devoted a chapter early on in their treatise to explaining 'why it is that women are chiefly addicted to evil superstitions', and later demonologists elaborated indefatigably on the same theme. Witchcraft prosecutions in the early modern period show the same gender bias. Trials can be cited in which men were the main suspects or where men and women were equally important. But the bulk of those accused and convicted from all countries save Estonia, Finland and Russia were women, often in the proportion of 70 to 90 per cent. This of course reflects an elite view and, in the case of the witch trials, an elite view of malevolent magic. The position on the ground for all magical practitioners was far less clear. In some regions in the past and more recently, healers, lifters of spells, those engaged in love magic might tend to be women, but male practitioners were always found in these roles too. They were not exclusively or inherently female. Again, women predominated, this time more exclusively, in magic relating to childbirth and infancy, but this was because childbirth and infancy were the domains of women, like most things to do with the house.[16] By contrast, magic relating to the crops and the livestock was usually performed by men, since these belonged to the male sphere of activity. This is not to say that notions relating to gender did not become engaged in magical ritual and thinking – we have shown that they did – but magic always transcended gender, always came first. Very significant here is the degree to which magical powers depended in European popular culture on the manipulation of things, words and gestures rather than on any inherent quality in persons, the degree that is, in the terminology of social anthropologists, that one is concerned with 'sorcery' rather than 'witchcraft'. Both were present, but sorcery predominated in everyday protective magic, which was often directed against more charismatic evil powers.

Another stereotype presented the witch as an old woman. Samuel Harsnet, archbishop of York, wrote typically in 1603 that the witch was 'an old weather-beaten crone, having the chin and her knees meeting for age, walking like a bow, leaning on a staff; hollow-eyed, untoothed, furrowed on her face, having her limbs trembling with palsy, going mumbling in the streets'. And again a high proportion of those accused of witchcraft all over Europe in the early modern period were women aged over fifty.[17] This age-bias does not seem to be reflected in those actually practising magic.

One important example of inherent magical power was the evil eye. The look of another person here was thought to have a harmful effect, almost like a physical force. A Portuguese medical treatise of 1680 wrote of 'a thin spirit that emanates from the eyes like an ... arrow and pierces the victim's body'. A visitor to Corsica in the 1860s described the look as 'like a fluid' or a 'magnetic force'; and it was later said to be 'like electricity'. Belief in the evil eye is found all over the world and has existed from earliest times. It is referred to in the Old Testament and figures in a number of Classical texts. In Europe in more recent times, the belief was most pronounced in the Mediterranean countries, but in earlier times it was also important in northern Europe. 'The mythical Irish giant Balor of the Evil Eye, for instance, was celebrated for his lethal gaze which could strike whole armies dead. There is also mention of the "glance of the eye" in *Beowulf* (*c.* 1000) ... as one of the dark and evil forces to confront the warrior'.[18] Both Burchard of Worms in the early eleventh and Gerald of Wales in the early thirteenth century refer to the belief; while further testimony is provided by the existence of by-names such as Malregard or Malreward in the same period in England and elsewhere. Evidence of the existence of the belief in the modern period is much fuller, and comes from all countries.

Many accounts stress that the evil eye is involuntary. The person who has the power to harm in this way cannot help it and wishes no evil to his or her victims. Occasionally, as in parts of Corsica, 'people believed that everyone could cast malediction by a certain manner of looking'. In northern Greece 'anyone *can* have the evil eye, but a few are outstanding with regard to the strength of their eye'. But in general the evil eye was restricted to certain persons. Here possessing the evil eye might be related to birth cicumstances like other magical powers, or to some physical oddity relating specifically to the eyes. Elizabeth Device, tried as a witch in Lancashire in 1612, 'was branded with a preposterous mark in nature, even from her birth, which was her left eye standing lower than the other; the one looking down, the other looking up, so strangely deformed'. Other early modern sources refer to 'blinking eyes', 'oblique looks', and to eyes of different colours. In modern Poitou, where most people had dark eyes, those with blue eyes were suspected. There might also be marks in the eyes – in the Basque country in the sixteenth century in the left eyes. In modern Normandy 'the location of magical force was recognized in bleary, glazed, globulous or bulging eyes'. In the Périgord, people with bloodshot eyes or with squints were avoided. Among the Sarakatsani, too, 'a powerful eye' was 'attributed to a prosperous villager who had a squint' – and a club-foot.[19] Elsewhere in Greece and in other places, having eyes that were very close together or set deep in the head might be a sign of the evil eye. But such indicators were by no means always found.

Moreover, the evil eye could sometimes be used voluntarily, when it became a kind of witchcraft. 'Witches may kill with their looks', a seventeenth-century Scottish writer noted, 'which looks, being full of venomous spirits, may infect the person upon whom they look'; and the term 'overlooking' was frequently used to mean 'bewitching' in early modern Britain, with the implication that a look or glance was the means employed. Trial evidence provides many examples of such bewitching via the eyes. A woman who had quarrelled with another at Wearmouth in 1601, for example, alleged that she had caused her cow to abort and blamed her 'glowing eyes'. In the Salem trials in Massachusetts in 1692, Bridget Bishop was accused of 'overlooking a sow'; she was also said to affect the possessed girls with her eyes: 'If she did but cast her eyes on them, they were presently struck down'. And another of the accused, Elizabeth How, was reported to have the same influence: the afflicted people 'were not able to bear her look'. In another seventeenth-century case from the Bourbonnais, a groom supposedly bewitched a woman by looking at her 'with a terrifying eye and an extremely penetrating look'. Whether the evil eye was deemed involuntary or not could depend on the relationship of those involved. With the Sarakatsani for example, the power was involuntary among kinsfolk, but ill-will might have been involved where bewitcher and victim were unrelated.[20]

Both men and women could posses the evil eye, though women were sometimes thought to be more likely to have it. This bias was sometimes explained in a physiological way, by linking it to menstruation or the onset of the menopause. Though usually restricted to humans, it was sometimes ascribed to animals and, in particular, to snakes, wolves and toads. Mythical beasts also had harmful eyes, notably dragons, basilisks and cockatrices. In *King Richard III*, Richard is compared by the Duchess of York to 'a cockatrice, Whose unavoided eye is murderous'.[21]

Evil eye beliefs are related to more general ideas about the eyes and psychic powers. According to Buffon, writing in the eighteenth century, 'the eye belongs to the soul more than any other organ; it seems to touch and participate in all its movements; it expresses the liveliest passions and the most tumultuous emotions but also the softest and most delicate sentiments'. The same idea was expressed in the proverbial saying that 'the eyes are the mirror of the soul' (or the heart), extant in the medieval and modern periods in Eastern and Western Europe. The eye thus indicated both character and status. 'Burning and shining eyes signify a great heart and power', asserted the French *Calendrier des bergiers*; 'little eyes, reddish and narrow signify melancholy and persons who are bold, scheming and cruel'. Such detailed analysis of types of eyes in relation to character and temperament is also found in humanist writers like Bartolomeo Fazio:

> The eyes are the windows of the soul: almost everyone knows what their colour, what their restlessness, what their sharpness indicates ... people with long eyes are malicious and immoral. And if the white of the eye is widely extended and visible all round, this shows shamelessness; if it is concealed, not visible at all, this shows unreliability.

Such 'popular physiognomics' relating to the eyes (and to the body generally) were the stock in trade of Renaissance and later painters. Hazlitt explained in the early nineteenth century what had become rules for painting different looks in different circumstances:

> Thus the eye turned round to look at you without turning the head indicates generally slyness or suspicion: but if this is combined with large expanded eye-lids or fixed eye-brows, as we see it in Titian's paintings it will denote calm contemplation or piercing sagacity, without any thing of meanness or fear being observed. In other cases, it may imply merely indolent enticing voluptuousness, as in Lely's portraits of women.

Character was often believed to go with rank here. In *Hrólfs Saga Kraka*, for example, 'a man observes that another has "not thrall's eyes" – suggesting that the difference between lofty and ignoble ancestry was evident in the eyes'. Much later in the American Old South, 'the eyes witnessed honour and looked down in deference or shame. Thus a steady gaze from a slave signalled impudence'.[22]

In this tradition, the eyes were often associated with power. Kings had looks that inspired fear but were also effective instruments of government. In the eleventh century, Widukind wrote of Otto I's 'fiery glowing eyes which sent forth a gleam like a flash of lightning', a sign of royal charisma and a cause of terror. Much later the Protestant historian Crespin wrote that the French king Francis I, after the Placards Affair in 1534, 'belched forth' his anger through his mouth but also through his eyes. In the early medieval period again, Notker the Stammerer wrote of King Lewis the German that a single glance of his eyes was enough to repair anything evil or stupid which occurred, and he cited Proverbs, chapter 20, verse 8: 'A king that sitteth on the throne of judgment scattereth away all evil with his eyes'.[23]

The power of the eyes could also manifest itself in the context of sexual passion and attraction. In the strict religious perspective, 'the eyes are the arrows and the first arms of lechery's stings'. According to the Franciscan Jacopone da Todi, 'sight was the Devil's pimp', and a woman's glances were like 'poison'. More positively, in the lay literature of the Middle Ages 'the fire of love is transmitted by an exchange of glances. In the lyrics of the troubadours in the thirteenth century, the loving spark received by the eye descends to kindle the heart'. The same idea is expressed in later texts. In *The Book of the Courtier* (1516), Castiglione echoes and elaborates on medieval themes: 'Those vital spirits that come forth from the eyes, being generated near the heart, enter in through other eyes (at which they are aimed as an arrow at a target) and penetrate naturally to the heart'. Even without the specific intervention of magic, there was something out of the ordinary in such phenomena, a kind of magic *sui generis*. Love was associated with 'fascination through the eyes'. The idea of 'bewitching eyes' was a commonplace of love songs. Here it is significant that Oberon's love potion in *A Midsummer Night's Dream* is applied to the eye-lids and makes the person fall in love with whoever he or she sees on first waking and opening the eyes. In Mistral's *Mirèio* again one finds this same idea of falling in love via some ocular fascination. Vincen asks Mirèio:

> Are you a magician then? ...
> For your look to thus overcome me ...
> And render me mad like a man drunk with wine?[24]

All of this places evil eye beliefs in context and helps to explain their impact and operation. The evil eye could have a wide range of effects. In the Highlands of Scotland, 'it causes sickness among men and beasts, prevents butter coming, and promotes general mischief'. In Corsica, 'the evil eye acts against persons, large and small, against animals, and even against crops'. In the Cévennes around 1900,

> the person with the evil eye stopped the milk of cows and goats or made them abort by coming into the byre; the animals stopped eating or became agitated or mad; the hens stopped laying or hid their eggs; in the cocoonery, the silk worms became unproductive, and in the drying lofts the chestnuts would not dry.

There were even reports of a forest fire being caused by a woman's glance in Norway in 1661, and of a tramcar coming off the rails when a man looked at it in modern Greece. In Greece, too, the evil eye caused specific kinds of illness: nausea, vomiting, headache and sluggishness.[25] Similarly in Portugal and southern Italy, strange illnesses involving loss of strength or paralysis were ascribed to the evil eye. Impotence could be another consequence.

In many places the evil eye acted particularly against the young, whether animal or human. The *Malleus Maleficarum* referred to 'those who have singularly fiery and baleful eyes, who by a mere look can harm others, especially young children'. This was explained by the fact that children were 'extremely impressionable' and of 'tender complexion'. Similar claims were made by later demonologists, but other writers, even critics of demonology, made the same observation. In a chapter entitled 'Of Enchanting or Bewitching Eyes', Reginald Scot retailed various Classical and other references to women with 'witching eyes [who] with their angry looks do bewitch and hurt not only young lambs, but young children'. We have seen, moreover, that harm from the evil eye was one of the main dangers against which babies and young children were protected. Ramage on his travels in Calabria in 1828, for example, noted that fear of children being fascinated by 'a particular squint of the eyes called *jettatura* ... is a subject of constant dread to the inhabitants of this country', and babies were defended against it from birth.[26]

A specific and apparently very common way in which infants fell victim to the evil eye was by being admired or praised, without any countervailing precaution being taken. In a trial at Douai in 1708, Marie Lespagnol was accused of killing fifteen children by witchcraft. The mother of one of them testified that Marie had looked at her son and said: 'There's a fine boy', and the next day he had fallen seriously ill.

Take care, in seeing a child, not to omit, if you have said: 'How handsome he is! How big! How intelligent!', those other words, which act as a corrective to the first: 'May God bless him!' It would be ideal, if, at the same time, you put on him a bit of saliva; people would be grateful for it.

Abbe Bartoli's advice from later nineteenth-century Corsica explains what was crucially missing from Marie Lespagnol's tribute, and it could be repeated for most Mediterranean countries and beyond. Dilys Powell recalled the same precautions in Greece after the Second World War. 'She is pretty, I said (praising a child); then, remembering the necessary ritual phrase, May she live! or, on another occasion, May he not suffer the evil eye, I said, and spat.' In a similar vein, in Hungary, 'the one who admires a small child must say, My, you ugly one!'[27]

As social anthropologists have argued, this connection between the evil eye, admiration and harm caused to newly-acquired and highly-prized assets reveals perhaps the prime motive behind the whole complex of beliefs and behaviour: envy and the fear of envy. Aubrey in 1696 referred to the looks of the evil eye as 'the glances of envy and malice'; and, etymologically 'envy' derives from the Latin *invidia*, meaning to look maliciously or askance upon. As Campbell explains for the Sarakatsani, 'it is significant that the two things most important for social prestige, children and sheep, are the two things most prone to attack' from the evil eye. There, and more generally, 'it is men who are prosperous, or more especially men, in a sense, too prosperous, or lucky, who stand in particular danger'. This reflects an essential characteristic of peasant societies with an egalitarian, communitarian ethos and the firm conviction that resources were finite, the idea of the limited good. As the nineteenth-century Corsican writer Viale observed, any sign of wealth, the acquisition of land, even the minor improvement of a house could arouse hostile feelings: 'The man who, through natural talent or good fortune, thinks that he can raise himself above others is destined to become the object of the envy of those others'. Here we find an explanation, too, for the scope and the targets of the evil eye. In the modern Friuli, evil looks were exchanged by female in-laws; in the Alto Minho, most accusations of casting the evil eye were directed at neighbours especially in the same hamlet. In-laws, close neighbours were immediate competitors. 'The evil eye [here] symbolizes the intensity of community interaction; it indicates that each person is under observation by others. Everyone is measured from moment to moment and regarded with admiration or envy, with approbation or censure'. And, if envy was directed against neighbours and their property, their general prosperity, it was particularly 'attracted at certain critical moments': at births, engagements, weddings, or when livestock was acquired or reproduced, or at harvests.[28]

A specific modern example of the last is provided in Mistral's *Mirèio*, which also shows that the mechanism involved was explicitly understood at the popular level. During the silkworm harvest, some cocoons belonging to Ieu are spoiled, she thinks at first by the wind. But Taven, the sorceress of Les Baux, tells her that the cause is actually envy and the evil eye:

> You, thoughtless women;
> If the harvest seems fine,
> Quickly you run out to the street, shouting:
> 'My silk worms, it is incredible
> How good they are. Come and look at them!'
> Envy does not wait:
> Behind you, in the room, she gets up, grumbling.
>
> 'They are a pleasure to see!',
> The neighbours will tell you;
> 'It's clear you were born with a caul'.
> But, as soon as you turn around,
> The envious woman shoots
> An envious glance at them,
> Which burns and twists them for you.[29]

Among the forces at work in the magical universe were non-human spirits. Though some of the clergy tended to assimilate them with demons or fallen angels, they were in fact distinct at the popular level: pre- or non-Christian beings, akin to the nymphs and fauns of Antiquity. These spirits or fairies went under a variety of names in different parts of Europe but fall generally into two broad categories. There were spirits associated with the house and farm, and there were those associated with wild places: woods, rivers, marshes and lakes, or more broadly with earth, water and air.

In Calabria, the house spirit was called the *auguriellu*. He was 'harmless and even beneficent if kindly treated', and he took special care to watch over babies in their cradles. In Scandinavia, the house spirit was the *tomte* or *nisse*. Again, these were helpful to the householder, stealing produce to give to him, baking bread, looking after the animals. Similarly, the browny of the Scottish Highlands worked for people, if 'kindly treated'. As we have seen, the kind treatment usually consisted of leaving out food and drink, often milk. In Milton's 'L'Allegro' (1631–32), the country girl

> Tells how the drudging goblin sweat
> To earn his cream-bowl duly set,
> When in one night, ere glimpse of morn,
> His shadowy flail hath threshed the corn.

In Savoie around 1900, people again used to leave milk for the fairies, so that they would bring them good luck. Burchard of Worms referred to more particular offerings:

> Hast thou made little, boys' size bows and boys' shoes, and cast them into thy storeroom or thy barn so that satyrs or goblins might sport with them, in order that they might bring thee the goods of others, so that thou shouldst become richer?

In some cases, fairies vouchsafed secret information or magical lore. Appolonia Madizza of Latisana in the 1580s, for example, had dreams in which a fairy 'told me certain prayers'.[30] Very often, as this suggests, only people with special powers could communicate with fairies or even see them.

But the disposition of fairies was not always benevolent. They could be 'capricious, vindictive, and irritable', mischievous or downright hostile, causing all kinds of minor trouble, similar to that caused by witchcraft. We are familiar with this from Shakespeare, Ben Jonson and others, who were in turn familiar with popular culture. Puck or Robin Goodfellow in *A Midsummer Night's Dream*,

> frights the maidens of the villagery;
> Skim milk, and sometimes labour in the quern
> And bootless make the breathless housewife churn;
> And sometime make the drink to bear no barm.

Ben Jonson's Mab similarly

> doth nightly rob the dairy,
> And can hurt, or help, the churning,
> As she please.

She also takes babies out of their cradles and gives girls sights of their lovers in their sleep on St Anne's night. In Clare's *Shepherd's Calendar*, the fairies, who are 'tiny things', steal food during the night like mice; while the hairy Greek *kallikantzari* steal food and urinate on the hearth, especially at Christmas time. In the Limousin, horses were taken during the night and worn out with riding, and in Scandinavia and Wales, objects and tools were borrowed or mislaid, for example scissors, knives or gridirons.[31]

Generally, as commentators have noted, the behaviour of house fairies provided a kind of sanction against bad housekeeping. Ben Jonson's Mab again

> pinches country wenches
> If they rub not clean their benches,
> And with sharper nails remembers
> When they rake not up their embers.

In Wales in the nineteenth century,

> old people often told their children and servant girls that one condition of the fairy
> visits to their houses was cleanliness. They were always instructed to keep the fire-
> place tidy and the floor well swept, the pails filled with water, and to make every-
> thing nice and bright before going to bed, and that then perhaps the fairies would
> come into the house to dance and sing until morning, and leave on the hearth
> stone a piece of money as a reward.[32]

In a few cases, more serious consequences arose from fairy activity or
displeasure. In *A Midsummer Night's Dream* again, after the quarrel between
Oberon and Titania, their ritual dances are suspended, which brings about
bad weather, crop failure and animal and human disease. We have seen, too,
that fairies might be a threat to babies and young children, causing their
illness or death or substituting their own offspring for them.

The distinction between kinds of fairy was often blurred, but broadly
fairies of the wild were different from those of house and home and they were
more likely to do serious harm of these kinds. One example is provided by
Anglo-Saxon and Germanic elves, 'capable of causing serious disease by
shooting arrows into men and animals'. Another was the female siren type.
These looked like beautiful women, though they sometimes also had animal
or snake features; they sang and danced usually by water; and they enticed or
led astray humans, mainly males. In Rumania, for example, they were mostly
malevolent and were especially active at certain times, including Whit. They
caused strange states or possession. Sexual relations or even marriage could
take place between humans and such fairies, female and male. There are also
stories of human women serving as midwives to fairy mothers. In general,
'wild' fairies were a threat to humans, and precautions were taken against
them, as we have seen. A charm, collected in Moldavia in 1870, ran:

> You fairies, enemies of man, mistresses of the wind, princesses of the earth, who fly
> through the air and slide through the grass, tread the waves, go to places far away,
> isolated marshes, reed-beds, where the priest doesn't sound the bells, where a girl
> doesn't dance; go into the mouth of the wind, strike the bowels of the earth, but
> leave the hand, body, leg, and disappear into a cloud; give man his health, other-
> wise you will be beaten by a sword of fire.[33]

The sacrifice of domestic animals was an important part of official religion
in the Ancient world. Sacrifices took place during calendar customs, after

victories in war and so on, and were seen as offerings to the gods. Animals, including horses this time, were also sacrificed by the ancient Scandinavians and the Anglo-Saxons. The name of the eleventh month in the old Anglo-Saxon year was Blotmonath, which arose, according to Bede 'because they devoted to their gods the animals which they were about to kill'. Here the annual killing-off of superfluous stock before the Winter was ritualized. The Christian Church obviously opposed the sacrifice of animals to pagan gods, but, mindful perhaps of Old Testament precedent, permitted sacrifice to continue under its aegis. In his letter to Abbot Mellitus in 601 on the general need to accommodate Christianity to existing circumstances, Pope Gregory the Great advised: 'And because they have been used to slaughter many oxen in the sacrifice to devils, some solemnities must be exchanged for them on this account'. He suggested that, at the festivities associated with the dedicatees of churches and other saints, people be allowed to 'kill cattle to the praise of God in their eating, and return thanks to the Giver of all good things'.[34] With this encouragement and for other reasons, animal sacrifices of various kinds did survive into later centuries.

Most obvious were those associated, like the Ancient ones, with special dates in the calendar. In modern Provence a lamb, often dressed with ribbons, was offered in church at Midnight Mass at Christmas along with other fruits of the earth. In some places before the Revolution an ox was offered. In modern times the animals were not actually killed. An exception was at Barjols, where an ox or a cow was sacrificed 'no longer in the church but on the square outside'. The ritual was performed on the Eve of St Anthony (16 January), every four or five years. 'An ox garlanded with ribbons and greenery was paraded through the street blessed by the clergy, then killed and roasted', and pieces of meat were distributed among the crowd. One part of the ritual did still take place in church, the 'tripe dance'. Also in Provence at Christmas in the nineteenth and twentieth centuries, a bird might be released in the church, usually a wren, sometimes a pigeon, and it was then chased, and the person catching it became 'king'.[35] The custom was banned without much effect by the archbishop of Arles in 1661. Hunting the wren took place in Britain and Ireland down to the twentieth century. In Wales a wren was captured, alive or dead, and carried from house to house on Twelfth Night by guisers. On the Isle of Man, a wren was killed on Christmas Day and buried with great solemnity. In parts of Scotland on New Year's Day, an animal, usually a cat or a dog, was ritually driven out of the community, like the ancient scapegoat. On Barra, the dog had a bunch of straw tied to its tail which was set alight.

Also in Scotland, sheep were sacrificed on Lewis on May Eve to secure luck through the year; while elsewhere in the Highlands a spotless lamb was killed on 1 May, when the migration to the Summer shielings began. We have seen that cats and other animals were burned in bonfires at Midsummer and other times in France and elsewhere. Animals were also sacrificed at harvest time. A pig was carried in triumph through Bologna on St Bartholomew's Day (24 August) and was then slaughtered. Frazer lists many examples in which the last sheaf was named after an animal: wolf, dog, cock, hare, cat, etc., and noted that sometimes the relevant creature was killed, for example a cock in parts of Germany and Hungary, and a cat in parts of France. 'At Pouilly, near Dijon, when the last ears of corn are about to be cut, an ox adorned with ribbons, flowers, and ears of corn is led all round the field, followed by a whole troop of dancers.' The animal was then killed by a man, disguised as a devil. 'Part of the flesh of the animal is eaten at the harvest-supper; part is pickled and kept till the first day of sowing in the Spring.'[36]

Animals were also sacrificed on saints' days, following Pope Gregory's advice. We have referred to the pig-killing on St Bartholomew's Day in Bologna. In Wales, bullocks were still offered to St Beuno at Clynnos Fawr on the Lleyn peninsula in 1589; while 'on the festival of St Cuthbert a bull was offered in sacrifice at his church in Kirkcudbright', according to a twelfth-century account. In the Orthodox world, sacrifices were performed inside saints' chapels in 'isolated Greek communities in Cappadocia well into the twentieth century';[37] while bulls or lambs were given to the Panaghia on the island of Tenos.

Blood sports, such as throwing at cocks or bull-baiting, which occurred at festivals almost certainly had a ritual origin and function. The bull sacrificed to St Cuthbert at Kirkcudbright was baited first. In parts of Wales in modern times, hens which did not lay before noon on Shrove Tuesday (when there was a great demand for eggs for pancakes) were ritually killed or 'threshed'. We have also noted in previous chapters the placing of animals, dead or alive, in the foundations or other parts of buildings to bring good fortune, and the sacrifice of animals in times of crisis, and notably livestock epidemics. We have glimpses too of animal sacrifice in other circumstances. In *Kormak's Saga*, probably of the tenth century, 'a man who had been wounded in a duel and whose wounds healed very slowly was advised to smear the blood of a slaughtered bull on a knoll, in which the *álfar* (elves) lived and to offer them the flesh of the bull. He did so and was soon healed'. Much later, a woman tried for witchcraft in the Pays de Waas near Antwerp in 1684, was said to have 'had a dog killed and disembowelled and to have scattered the pieces around a field ... to make the wheat grow'.[38]

Animal masks and skins were worn at festivals. Those of sheep, deer, stags, bulls and cows or calves are commonly mentioned in the sources. Clerical authorities from the fourth century to the central medieval period condemned dressing up in animal skins, particularly at Christmas and the New Year. In the English play *Wily Beguiled* of the early seventeenth century, Robin Goodfellow dons a calf-skin suit at Christmas. Dr Johnson noted of the Hebrides in the 1760s:

> At New Year's Eve, in the hall or castle of the Laird, where, at festal seasons, there may be supposed a very numerous company, one man dresses himself in a cow's hide, upon which other men beat with sticks. He runs with all this noise round the house, which all the company quits in a counterfeit fright.

Guisers and others wore sheepskins and bull- or cow-hides in the Hebrides into the nineteenth and twentieth centuries. In Ireland, the 'wren boys' occasionally wore animal skins or horns. Skins and masks were also worn at Carnival time in much of Europe, when, as at Romans, men might be organized into companies associated with totemic animals. Fools and jesters might also wear calf-skins as signs of their office. As this suggests, wearing skins could be linked to ritual status which lasted beyond the festive period or to belonging to specific groups. In ancient Scandinavia, members of special warrior societies, devoted to Odin, 'dressed in the skins of wolves and bears'.[39]

Sometimes animal heads were the focus in such calendar rituals. Dances with real or simulated horses' heads are reported in many parts of Europe: the Basque country, Provence, Scandinavia, Rumania, Britain. In Rumania, the hobby-horse dance was 'closely connected with the Feast of All Souls'. The Padstow hobby-horse rituals in Cornwall occurred on May Day; while the Welsh Mari Lwyd ceremonies took place at Christmas. Similar dances involved bulls' heads, stags' horns and so on. In Rumania, ritual begging at Christmas was done by groups, which included a man with the head of a goat or bull. The dances and other ceremonies had various aims and functions. 'In the Bourbonnais, the dance terminated in the church in front of the altar, where the "horses" ate hay, and in the Norman *bocage* it accompanied marriages'. According to Benoît, the dances, especially when they took place at Carnival or Rogationtide, aimed 'to favour the prosperity of the crops'. Among the ancient Scandinavians, for whom the horse was the object of religious cult, 'the horse-head was ... used in maleficent magic. The worst affront a man could inflict on another was to raise a horse's head on a pole with the opened mouth turned towards his house. This ... was thought to drive away the [victim's] *voettir* [or soul]'. Egil, in the saga bearing his name, does this 'to bring down a curse on the king [Erik Bloodaxe] and his wife'.[40]

Animal skins had other sacred and magical significance in European societies. Important men were buried in bull-hides in pre-historic Denmark and Scotland, and bull-hides were used in divination in Celtic and especially Old

Irish tradition. A diviner slept in a sacrificed bull's hide before choosing the King of Tara. Burchard of Worms referred to sitting on a bull's hide at a crossroads at the Kalends of January in order to foresee the future, and a similar custom was reported in the Hebrides in the early eighteenth century. Animal skins were also involved in witchcraft beliefs. In a nineteenth-century Finnish account, a young girl was initiated as a witch by being carried on a calf-skin; while some descriptions of the Witches' Sabbath have the Devil 'clothed in fearful goat- or dog-skins'.[41]

An actual ritual, in which an animal, usually an ox, was killed and then symbolically regenerated is reported to have taken place over the centuries in different parts of Europe from Ancient to modern times. An ox was sacrificed at the Bouphonia in Athens, a Midsummer festival devoted to Zeus. According to Porphyry, writing in the third century AD but citing an earlier text, after the ox's meat had been eaten and the bones burned on the altar, 'they then sew up the ox-hide [which had been deliberately retained], stuff it with straw, and stand it up again, in the same form as it had when alive, and they yoke it to a plough as if it is working'. Those responsible for killing the ox were then tried, and the knife was found guilty. This ritual and others like it have been seen as attempts to ensure a continuing supply of domesticated livestock, perhaps adapting a myth originally concerned to procure good hunting. Similar rituals and legends existed among ancient Germanic peoples. In the *Prose Edda* of Snorri Sturluson, written in the thirteenth century, for example, Thor, lodging with a farmer, 'sacrificed his goats for dinner and cooked them in his cauldron and after the meal he collected the bones and skins, and restored them to life by raising his hammer over them'. All were fit but one, which had a lame leg, because the farmer had cracked one of its leg-bones while eating it. Archeological finds of skulls, hooves and skins from the prehistoric and medieval periods in Scandinavia, southern Russia, Germany and elsewhere indicate that actual rituals enacting such regeneration must have been fairly common.[42]

There is other evidence of these rituals in medieval saints' Lives and in late medieval and early modern Inquisition records. In a case in Milan in the fourteenth century, two women confessed to visiting nocturnal gatherings at which animals were eaten, their bones put back into their skins, and the beasts then resuscitated. Similar cases were reported in various parts of Italy in the fifteenth and sixteenth centuries; and in Hungary in the eighteenth, where they became assimilated with the demonological Witches' Sabbath. More modern accounts are also found. In a late nineteenth-century Life of Fra Egidio of Taranto, who died in 1812, a cow was stolen from the saint's monastery and cut up into joints by a butcher.

The saint discovered the beast's remains, ordered that they should be laid together on the floor in the shape of a living cow, with the entrails, head and so forth in their natural positions; then, having made the sign of the cross with his cord upon the slaughtered beast,

he ordered it to arise in the name of the Trinity, which it did.[43]

Such rituals involved mainly domesticated animals. We turn now to procedures using animal parts, where the creatures concerned were nearly always wild. The paraphernalia of magicians often included parts of animals. Gregory of Tours referred to an 'impostor', who attracted crowds of peasants in 580. He had 'a big bag filled with the roots of various plants [and] moles' teeth, the bones of mice, bears' claws and bears' fat', all used in magic.[44] Modern practitioners had similar collections. We have seen, too, that animal parts could be important agents in healing. They were also used in divination and in a range of other rituals.

First, animals or bits and pieces of them could be employed to convey their qualities to humans. In a vernacular magical handbook from the Tyrol in the fifteen century, anointing the eyes with bats' blood ensured keen eyesight, since bats could find their way in the dark. In modern Calabria

to take away the dread of the sea from young boys, they mix into their food small fishes which have been devoured by larger ones and taken from their stomachs – the underlying idea being that these half-digested fry are thoroughly familiar with the storms and perils of the deep, and will communicate these virtues to the boys who eat them. It is the same principle as that of giving chamois blood to the goat-boys of the Alps to strengthen their nerves against giddiness.

In this connection, Pliny the Elder mentioned a traditional lie-detector or lie-preventer: 'The tongue of a live frog, set over the heart of a woman while she sleeps, will compel her to answer all questions truthfully'.[45] The use of the tongue is appropriate here, but why the frog should be associated with honesty is not clear.

Animal parts or fluids also offered protection in a variety of circumstances 'A fox's head was nailed to the stable door in some parts of Scotland to ban the entrance to witches.' In many areas of Ireland,

on St Martin's Eve the blood of a farm animal or fowl was spilled and sprinkled in the corners of the house, on the doorposts and windows and in the byre and stable. In some places, the blood was also used to make the mark of a cross on the forehead of each member of the household.

They were also used in other kinds of magic. In modern Sweden, 'a needle or awl that had pierced through a black toad and the blood of a white hen' figured in a ritual to find buried treasure. A fourteenth-century German text advised placing the testicles of a stag or bull, or the tail of a fox, close to a woman that a man wished to induce to love him, for example under her pillow; putting ants' eggs in her bath was also recommended. Another love talisman current from Roman times was the *hippomane* or 'fleshy mass sometimes found on the head of a new-born foal'. In sixteenth-century Venetian love magic, procedures using live animal hearts are reported, and a ritual that involved skinning a bird backwards and sticking pins in it. A similar ritual was used in order to destroy a love relationship. 'Elisabeth Catron ... impaled three young birds with skewers and boiled them alive so that as these birds were consumed ... so the love between Giorgio and Chiara should disappear'.[46]

Animal parts were familiar ingredients in other forms of hostile magic, as the potion boiled in the witches' cauldron in *Macbeth* indicates:

> Fillet of fenny snake ...
> Eye of newt, and toe of frog,
> Wool of bat, and tongue of dog,
> Adder's fork, and blind worm's sting,
> Lizard's leg, and howlet's wing,
> For a charm of powerful trouble.

In an actual modern example from Switzerland, a person was believed to have been bewitched by another burying the heart of an animal in the ground, while it was still warm; the effect of the spell would last until the heart putrefied away. Animal excretions were also powerful here. The Latin poet Propertius referred to a charm, 'gathered for my destruction ... that drips from the pregnant mare'; while a poison supposedly used by the Borgia in sixteenth-century Italy was made with the 'saliva of a mad pig, hung upside down and beaten to death'.[47]

We have seen that the sight or sound of certain birds or animals boded good or ill. Killing certain creatures was also considered particularly unlucky, for example, in Shropshire a bat; in the West of Ireland a magpie; in the English Midlands and elsewhere a robin; and in Sussex a swallow. There was also in some places a taboo on uttering the names of some creatures. In north-east Scotland, the words for hare, pig and salmon should never be uttered at sea, but circumlocutions used. Among Cornish fishermen, similarly, rabbits were never mentioned. Swedes, Lapps, Finns and Estonians never called a bear by its proper name but rather 'the old man', 'the honey-eater' or some other indirect term, a way of placating an animal which they hunted. In Sweden, cats, cuckoos, owls, magpies, foxes and seals, all associated with sorcery, were also referred to via euphemisms.[48]

As our detailed examples indicate, all animals had some special significance that could be exploited magically, but a few animals had very unusual
or powerful properties. The hare, for example, was an especially magical
animal. Parts of the animal were used, we have seen, in folk medicine.
Dreaming about a hare or encountering one was usually felt to be unlucky,
and hare-lips in children were caused by their mothers seeing one in pregnancy. The hare also figures in seasonal customs. Hares were specifically
hunted on Shrove Tuesday in Ireland and at Easter in England. In Ireland, 'a
portion of the meat was not eaten but hung in the rafters' as some kind of
protection; in parts of England, the captured hare was presented to the local
clergyman in return for other gifts. 'Old Hare' was one of the names, too,
given to the last sheaf in harvest rituals. Gerald of Wales referred to witches
changing into hares. This belief surfaces again in witchcraft trials, together
with hares as witches' familiars, and is found in Welsh, Irish and English
folklore. In an Ulster folk-tale a couple are involuntarily changed into hares
by looking in a mirror and are made to attend a 'hares' parliament', which
has features in common with a Witches' Sabbath. On the Continent, the
hare as an incarnation of the Devil seems to have been a more popular idea,
and hares were also believed to have the power to 'fascinate' or bewitch. A
woman tried in the Vivarais in 1519 said that the Devil first appeared to her in
the form of a hare, while another woman confessed to having sexual relations with a devil, who 'appeared now in the form of a man, now in that of a
hare'. Yet another woman, who met a black man on the road near Fribourg
in 1477, knew that he was the Devil because he was accompanied 'by six or
seven hares'.[49] The hare's reputation must owe much to its mysterious
behaviour, which includes the human characteristics of meeting in
nocturnal gatherings and standing on its hind-legs.

No creature suffered a worse reputation in European popular culture than
the toad. Toads were associated with the Devil and were a favourite form
taken by both witches and their familiars. A woman tried as a witch at
Noville-les-Bois in 1607 said that she had been ordered to profane the host. So
she 'spat it into her handkerchief [after mass], took it to her house, split it
into four pieces, which she fed to a large black toad that she kept by her fire-
side'. In north Cambridgeshire the old word for bewitching was 'tudding,
probably a corruption of toading'. Toads were used in Christian iconography
to represent sin and impurity. The statue of the Virgin Mary at Walsingham
described by Erasmus trampled on a toad, 'in token of her victory over evil';
the fallen woman in Hell on the sculptures of the porch at Moissac has her
genitals devoured by a toad. Toads also symbolized avarice, treachery and
envy and were again involved in their particular punishments. Lazarus
explains in the late medieval St Genevieve Passion that 'those who have

performed works of envy ... the dragon often gnaws their heart and bowels and toads hang from their ears'. These imaginary punishments had their parallels in reality. According to the chronicler Salimbene, people were kidnapped in the Romagna in the thirteenth century 'to gain their ransoms ... And, if the prisoners would not pay, they hung them up by the feet or hands and pulled out their teeth, and to force them to pay, put toads in their mouths, and this of all forms of torture was most cruel and detested'.[50]

There was a belief that toads and frogs were generated from corrupt matter or from menstrual blood. Diseases were also represented by toads. Patients at early Christian shrines were said to have swallowed toads or frogs, which they evacuated as they were cured by the saints. In Bayonne in 1733, a surgeon cured a Spanish woman, who thought she was possessed by ten devils in the form of frogs. Toad ex-votos were presented to Bavarian and Austrian shrines. In the same part of the world, the souls of the dead were believed to appear as toads, 'condemned to find salvation by undertaking long pilgrimages' in that form.[51]

More directly and at the popular level, toads were believed to be dangerous. In Brittany, a toad could kill a person if it jumped on him or her while asleep; and Gerald of Wales related how a youth in Cardiganshire had been killed and eaten by toads. More generally, it was a commonplace that toads were venomous, squirting poison at people to blind or otherwise injure them. Shakespeare included in the mixture in the witches' cauldron:

> Toad, that under cold stone
> Days and nights has thirty-one
> Sweltered venom.

Topsell in his *History of Serpents* (1658) noted that land toads were especially 'venomous ... which do descend into the marshes, and so live in both elements', adding that 'the women-witches of ancient time did much use toads in their confections'. In a 1599 witchcraft trial in the Cambrésis, a woman kept a number of toads, allegedly using them to make toxic rain. Seeing a toad was therefore a bad omen and a real threat. Precautions were often taken to keep toads away from farms and livestock, and, if they were seen, they were usually killed. Leproux refers to 'the systematic destruction' of toads in the Charentais, which followed their evil reputation. He also notes that toads were killed with deliberate and sometimes ritual cruelty.[52]

As we have seen, toads were used in many kinds of magic. They were placed or buried in stables, in order to bewitch livestock. They were also extensively used in cures of animals and humans and in love and thief magic. In parts of the Limousin, if a cow failed to give milk and bewitching was suspected, a live toad was attached to the cow's neck and, as the toad dried up, so the effect of the spell was removed. A toad cut in two and applied to the sick organ cured cancer; toads were also believed to draw off fevers. In various French regions, a man wishing to attract a woman to him would place a live toad in an ant-heap, collect the remains after a while and throw them over her. A procedure to detect a thief, noted by the diarist Kilvert in Radnorshire in 1871, involved boiling or baking a toad in a ball of clay. The toad was 'expected to scratch the name of the thief upon a piece of paper put into the clay ball along with him'.[53]

Special procedures focused on a particular bone found in the toad's body. This bone from a toad's head was believed to give protection against plague and other diseases in the late medieval period. In East Anglia into the modern period, a similar bone was used to control or 'freeze' horses. A natterjack or 'walking toad' was caught and killed (or in some cases a special kind of frog). Its body was dried on a whitethorn bush for twenty-four hours, and was then buried in an ant-hill 'for a full month, till the moon is full' or until the ants had picked the skeleton clean. This was put in a running stream, again when the moon was full, and the small bone which left the rest and floated against the current was the one required. Sometimes this bone was kept whole; sometimes it was ground to a powder and mixed with oils. In either form, it could be used by a man to make a horse do what he wanted.[54] We have seen that he might be known as a 'toadman'. The notion that toads had a jewel in the heads would seem to be related to the belief in the efficacy of this 'toad's bone'.

All this suggests a more positive view of the toad's powers. In Languedoc, a toad might be placed by a hen sitting on eggs to protect her and keep off other pests. In parts of the Limousin, a toad might be dipped into milk to make it creamy. On a grander scale, it is reported that a toad was placed in the walls of Le Mans, when it was rebuilt after a fire in 1145, in order to protect the city from any repetition of the disaster. Abbé Thiers noted that seeing a toad was a good omen, and this remained true for many regions of France down to the twentieth century. According to Arthur Randell, born in 1901,

> toads were highly respected in the Fens ... no true Fenman would ever dream of hurting one for fear of bringing ill-luck on himself. We always had two or three at home in the glass frame to eat slugs, and every day my father would look to see if 'Toby', as he called each one, was all right.[55]

Amulets in the shape of frogs were believed to be effective against the evil eye in Italy and elsewhere.

There are indications too that toads (and frogs) were symbols of fertility in European traditional culture. Johanna St John in 1680 recommended a dried toad hung about the waist to prevent miscarriages.[56] In Central Europe, toads were sometimes identified in folk belief with the womb, and toad-shaped votive offerings were presented at shrines in north-eastern France and southern Germany for the cure of venereal disease but also of sterility. In folk-tales like 'The Frog Prince' or 'The Three Feathers', it has been suggested that the frog or toad represents sexuality or the id.

16

Magical Power:
Things, Words and Gestures

A range of objects and substances were used in magic. Some were manufact-ured; more were natural. 'Greco-Latin magicians had a veritable arsenal of bowls, rings, knives, ladders, discs, rattles, bobbins, keys, mirrors, etc'. We have also come across sieves, scissors, rope and string, coins, nails and pins and candles. Sometimes magical paraphernalia had inherent qualities, like iron, salt or body fluids. Sometimes their power derived from religious or magical rituals, like sacramentals or herbs picked in a particular way. In the Hebrides in modern times, stones placed in the thatch of a house were supposed to cause the death of cattle, but some 'evil words' must have been said while placing them there.[1]

Iron often had apotropaic power. It was used, for example, to give protect-ion against the fairies in the Highlands of Scotland; while in modern Greece, 'one touches iron when one sees a priest in order to ward off the bad luck he brings'. The power in iron might also be dangerous and thus avoided. We have seen that cutting medicinal plants with iron was sometimes proscribed. The archon at Ancient Thebes, a sacred magistrate, was not allowed 'to carry any iron object upon his person'. Pilgrims to the shrine of St Marcoul at Corbeny in the diocese of Laon 'were forbidden during their stay to touch any object' made of iron or any other metal, and some wore gloves to prevent this. Metal workers and especially blacksmiths were often credited with special powers in traditional Europe, as sorcerers, as healers via hammering and in other ways; and things to do with the forge, like the anvil, the hammer and the water used to cool the metal, also had magical qualities. Blacksmiths were anomalous in peasant society, and they fashioned an essential commodity in mysterious and sometimes ritual ways. Joe Gargery in Dickens' *Great Expectations* (1860–61) used to hum or sing fragments of a song, while beating out the iron. This was addressed to 'Old Clem', supposedly the patron saint of smiths but not far removed from 'Old Nick' or the Devil himself.[2]

Salt was another precious commodity in pre-industrial societies, a crucial flavourer and preservative of food. It was 'the prophylactic remedy *par excel-lence*' against evil of all kinds, including witchcraft. It was used in baptismal liturgies from earliest times as an exorcising agent to drive away the Devil. It was commonly placed on or by corpses, and we have encountered its deployment in a gamut of other circumstances: to treat seed-corn and fertilize fields, to preserve livestock, to protect newly-weds, new-born babies and lactating mothers, and in healing and love magic. Salt was also one of the ritual gifts offered at births and on other occasions. Salt was also commonly thrown on the fire or over one's left shoulder if spilt in a gesture of protection again, or possibly propitiation.[3] The purifying and protective functions of salt are also found in rituals in the Ancient world and surely derive from its actual qualities.

As we have seen in discussing childbirth, the dead and healing, all human remnants and bodily secretions could be used in magic. Some, as in the case of the placenta or the umbilical cord, were the objects or potential objects of hostile magic. As Dromio of Syracuse remarks in Shakespeare's *The Comedy of Errors*: 'Some devils ask but the parings of one's nails, a rush, a hair, a drop of blood'. In modern Greece, the ill-wisher needed to procure 'the sweat of the person you want to harm – for example, a handkerchief that he has wiped his face with, or the collar, or cuff from his shirt'. Agnes Sampson of North Berwick confessed in 1591 to having intended to bewitch the Scottish king to death by obtaining 'any one piece of linen cloth which the king had worn and fouled'. Clothing represented the person but was also marked by his or her excretions. Hair and nail-cuttings were another obvious target here. A tuft of hair discovered under the mattress of a widow accused of witchcraft at Noville-les-Bois in 1607 was supposed to have been used to cause the death of another woman, from whom it had been taken. Great care was therefore shown over their disposal. In Greece, hair and nails were always burned, lest they might be used in sorcery. At Montaillou, the hair and nails of the dead were specially preserved – to make the house 'fortunate'.[4] As this shows, these remnants were also used in positive magic, to protect and heal. Hair was placed in witch-bottles used to undo spells, together with urine – to represent the victim. In parts of France in the seventeenth century and later, the hair of a person or animal that had been wounded was put in an incision in the bark of an aspen tree to prevent the wound from becoming infected. A cure for ague reported in Suffolk in the nineteenth century involved burying the patient's nail clippings and a lock of his hair in a pot in the ground.

The remnants in all this stood for the person, as Mauss supposed. Anthropologists have emphasized the ambiguity of discarded bodily bits and pieces and excreta. They were both part of the body and not part of it, and they were associated with margins and boundaries, which made them *ipso facto* dangerous. More recently, Lincoln has underlined the link between hair in particular and vegetation in Indian and Roman rituals and belief. The proper disposal of hair, often by burial, ensured the fertility of crops and of trees and plants generally, while failure to do this led by contrast to infertility and disease. Weight is lent to this idea by later European practices, found even among the elite. Emily Tennyson noted, for example, in April 1857: 'We put the cuttings of our hair and the children's in the ground round the cabbage roses'.[5]

We have also encountered the use of bodily fluids in healing and other magic. Washing one's hands with urine was a way to undo a spell, according to Abbé Thiers.[6] Passing water through a ring was a cure for impotence in sixteenth-century Venice and elsewhere. And cures employing urine were recorded from early medieval to modern times.

A person's saliva could be used like hair and nail-clippings in hostile magic against that person, but more often saliva played a more positive role. The Ancient Greeks and Romans 'used to spit, symbolically, to keep off any evil'. The effectiveness of incantations was increased by spitting; and on boasting or noting one's good fortune one would spit to avert the approach of Nemesis. We have seen that saliva and spitting figured in the Christian baptismal ritual. In modern times, spitting for luck was common in all kinds of situations, including bargains or sales, when a coin might be spat on. Abbé Thiers notes that people in the Chartres region around 1700 'spat on the shoes of their right feet, before doing up the laces'. In the twentieth century, 'the long-line fishermen of Carrickfergus would always spit on the first and last hook they baited, and in the mouth of the first fresh fish taken off the hook'. More specifically, 'spittle was esteemed a charm against all kinds of fascination'.[7] Toads, serpents and other malevolent creatures were spat on. Nurses protected children from the evil eye or witchcraft by spitting when strangers approached and we have seen that those admiring infants were often expected to spit to counter the evil eye. In a Swedish narrative, a whirlwind raised by a witch was made to subside by throwing a knife into it, a knife that had been spat on.

Spitting and saliva were also used in cures, as we have seen. Spittle was sometimes conceived of here as akin to water quenching the fire of disease. In a cure for scrofula retailed by Reginald Scot, 'a virgin fasting' had to lay her hand on the sore and say: 'Apollo denieth that the heat of the plague can increase where a naked virgin quencheth it'; and spit three times upon it. But saliva could also have a hot or corrosive quality.

> With spittle from mouth
> And ashes from hearth,
> I will burn you up,

a Portuguese healer recited in a cure for impetigo, while applying a mixture of the two substances around the children's mouths.[8] As the quotation from Scot illustrates, there was a very old view that fasting increased the power of saliva.

Spitting was also a general gesture of contempt, as it still is. Pope Pius II, for example, retailed this anecdote about the cardinal of Arras in 1463.

A Florentine woman who had been his mistress, the daughter of a peasant, angry with him for some unknown reasons, waited for the time when the cardinal on his way from the Curia should pass her house and then, as he was going by, she spat out on his hat saliva that she had held a long time in her mouth and mixed with phlegm, marking him as an adulterer by that vilest of all brands.

Spitting could also be a token of sacrilege. One of the most serious accusations made against the Templars in the early fourteenth century was that of 'spitting on the cross during the reception ceremony'. Again, in the course of the iconoclastic campaign in Geneva in 1534, a Protestant washed his hands in a holy water stoup and afterwards spat in it 'in great ridicule, scorn and mockery'.[9] This all underlines the great symbolic power of the gesture, which could also be used in hostile magic.

Milk, whether animal or human, had a sacred quality. It 'was regarded as an elixir in Celtic lands in pre-Christian times', and holy wells were believed to give forth healing milk. Milk was used by some early Christian sects at the Eucharist instead of wine, and it remained a symbol of the Eucharist in the Orthodox world. Milk was also offered at shrines. At Monte Gargano in southern Italy, for example, jars of milk were left at the sanctuary of St Michael as a ritual offering on Ascension Day, and milk was also given to neighbours and to the poor. There were legends, too, in which saints and holy people had been cured or nourished by the milk of the Virgin Mary. The best-known example is probably that of St Bernard. 'In response to his prayer, the Madonna pressed her breast to squirt out a few drops of milk into the saint's mouth.' This privilege symbolized the close ties between the Virgin and the Cistercian saint and the Order to which he belonged. The story originated a long while after his death and was only represented in images from around 1300. These then became quite common, especially in the Low Countries and Spain from the fifteenth to the eighteenth centuries. The theme of 'miracles operated by the milk of the Virgin [in relic-form] was also very common in the Middle Ages'. We saw too in Chapter 10 that human milk was believed to have healing properties and was used in remedies. It was also used in other kinds of magic, as was animal milk. The combined milks 'of a mother and her daughter when both are nursing their own babies at the same time' was particularly powerful here, and they were used in a sixteenth-century recipe for mitigating the pain of torture, and in modern Greek love magic.[10]

Blood was the bodily fluid above all that represented life and the person. It was used extensively in both religion and magic, in reality and symbolically. Blood was shed copiously in Ancient religious sacrifices, Greek, Roman and

Hebrew, as an offering to the gods, but blood shed outside the religious aegis was taboo, dangerous, terrible but powerful. Medea, for example, used her own 'sacred blood' and that of other humans to make her poisons, and blood was used to call up the dead.[11] Blood-vengeance was a widespread quasi-judicial system, which survived in the Mediterranean region down to modern times. According to its principles, blood shed demanded blood in return, while blood thus spilled in revenge washed away stains to a family's honour. Some of the same ideas informed the related but more restricted institution of duelling.

Christianity lent special significance to blood. Christ's blood had been shed on the Cross to save mankind. As Christ declared in 'The Ascension Play' in the Chester cycle:

> These bloody drops that ye now see
> All they fresh shall reserved be
> Till I come in majesty
> To deem the last day.
> This blood shall witness bear to me.
> I died for Man on the rood-tree.

Wine changed into Christ's blood was one of the two elements in the miracle of transubstantiation performed at the mass, and the element reserved among Catholics to the clergy. Legends in which the host bled in order to indicate that it was Christ's flesh were common in the late medieval period and later. One Sunday in 1571 St Teresa of Ávila went into a trance at communion and could not swallow the host. When she came to, she believed 'that my mouth was all filled with blood; my face and my whole body seemed covered with it, as if Our Lord had been shedding it at that moment'. Drinking or washing in Christ's blood was a feature in other saints' visionary experience, particularly, it seems, female saints of the later medieval period. Special devotion to Christ's blood also focused on relics like that of the Holy Blood at Bruges, and it entered into the later cult of the Sacred Heart. Whipping to produce blood was a Christian penitential practice, followed for example by the Flagellants of the fourteenth century, some of whom 'replaced baptism with water by baptism with blood',[12] and by many zealous religious down the centuries. One should also mention the belief that Jews used Christian blood in their rituals, which fuelled the Ritual Murder legends originating in the twelfth century but still current in Germany in the sixteenth and in parts of Eastern Europe until much later.

Blood, animal and human, was used in a wide variety of magical practices and was associated with witchcraft and other beliefs. Special power was inherent in menstrual blood, as we have seen. Blood was put on doorposts to protect houses from witches and evil spirits. Blood was used germinate seeds, prevent ageing and in love magic and cures. When Cardinal Albergati was gravely ill in 1443, for example, with a bad attack of the stone, the physicians recommended that 'he drink a beaker of the blood of a he-goat', which as a good Carthusian he refused to do.[13] There was a widespread belief that drawing the blood of a witch took away her power, while vampires and were-wolves sucked the blood of their victims.

Magical objects and substances, including parts of animals and plants, were universally worn as amulets to give magical protection and security. They were placed, we have seen, on babies at birth, and most people continued to wear them through their lives, usually round the neck, perhaps acquiring new ones or donning them in special circumstances such as leaving the community, going on a journey, marriage, childbirth, sickness or death. Many kinds of amulet are found down the ages, singly or in combina-tion. St Caesarius of Arles in the sixth century condemned the wearing of 'devilish phylacteries, magic letters, amber charms and herbs'. In modern Portugal,

> children are defended against *quebranto* (general weakness), *luada* (influence of the moon) and the malefices of witchcraft by wearing a half-moon in silver or copper, a *figa* (finger gesture) in silver, marble, coral or jet, a wolf's paw, a perfor-ated coin, or the horn of a goat found unsought on a Tuesday or Friday ... In teething they will be soothed by wearing a wolf's tooth and lily roots or garlic.

In the Abruzzi

> children wear badgers' hair and a little bunch of tin or silver charms all hanging from a circle with the number thirteen in it. The most common charms are a cornucopia, a horn, a frog, a pope's head with mitre and crozier, a closed hand with the forefinger extended, a horseshoe, a boot, a duck, cross-keys, a hunchback, ... a heart, a broom, a bottle ... and a basket.[14]

All these types and others were found elsewhere.

Coral was used to protect babies in the medieval and Renaissance periods, and it continued to be common in later centuries, often in the form of horns or hands. 'The coral preserves such as bear it from fascination or bewitching', Reginald Scot noted in 1584, 'and in this respect they are hanged about child-ren's necks.' Adults also wore coral amulets, mainly to give protection against the evil eye. Queen Victoria and Prince Albert wore them, for example, and 'nearly everyone' wore red coral 'in some form or other' in the Abruzzi. Other stones were also believed to have special powers. Scot again provides a list of these and their qualities. Alectorius, for example, supposedly 'taken out of a cock's belly ... maketh the husband to love the wife, and the bearer invincible ... A topaz healeth the lunatic person ... A sapphire helpeth agues and gouts, and suffereth not the bearer to be afraid'.[15] Milky agate was worn by nursing mothers. More common generally at the popular level were stone axe- and arrow-heads, fossils and stones with holes in them, all of which were used as protective amulets in a variety of situations.

Bent or perforated coins were also common. Friederich Behaim wrote to his mother from school in Altdorf in 1579: 'I am also sending you a *groschen* I received because I have been promoted. I want you to have it made into a charm and returned to me', that is to have a hole drilled in it so that he could wear it round his neck. More unusual were the amulets made from the Maundy money distributed by English sovereigns, and 'cramp rings' also made from coins offered by the monarchs. Lady Lisle in the early sixteenth century gave these to her relatives and friends. Medals and medallions of all kinds were very popular. They were produced for example in Scandinavia from the fifth century with a variety of devices: animals, gods and goddesses, 'symbols of power' and of fertility. Later medallions were Christianized. In the Abruzzi, medals of St Benedict, made and sold by local jewellers in modern times, gave protection against hail, lightning and thieves; while medals of St Anthony lent protection to cattle and horses. Among other metal objects were keys. In the Abruzzi again, 'small iron keys were hung round a baby's neck to prevent epilepsy, and brass or silver keys to prevent convulsions'.[16] Keys were associated with the cult of St Peter, who has custody of the keys to Paradise, and keys from the shrine of the saint in the Vatican were distributed in the early medieval period as relics.

We have already discussed the use of animals parts in healing and in magic generally. They figure again as amulets. Feet were commonly worn. In modern Provence, a mole's paw gave special protection to babies during teething. Badgers' and hares' feet gave general protection in many places. Samuel Pepys carried a hare's foot, and this was mentioned as commonplace in Swift's satirical guide to 'polite conversation' in 1738. King Ferdinand I of Naples was reported always to wear a heron's foot in his button-hole when he went out hunting, 'as the most effective charm against the *Monacello* [the Neapolitan hobgoblin], or against the ill-luck of meeting an old woman or a priest as he crosses the threshold – both ill omens for the day'.[17]

Written charms could also serve as amulets, some authors reserving the term 'talisman' for this type. In the fourteenth century Gerson criticized the practice of hanging round the neck 'certain words' written on parchment or unknown characters in a triangle, but another canon lawyer, Henry of Gorkum, allowed that writing the name of the Three Magi on paper and hanging it around one's neck was licit.[18]

As this and the case of medallions show, many amulets were Christianized in some way. In the Abruzzi, all charms were generally blessed by the priest, while the special amulet known as a *greve* was 'slipped under the altar cloth' so that it would be sanctified during mass. Everywhere amulets linked to saints and shrines were common, and they were manufactured and sold on a commercial basis from the central medieval period onwards. Very often amulets were eclectic and composite, including non-Christian and Christian elements. The Basque *kutun* usually contained 'an assortment of substances such as jet, charcoal, ashes, laurel and other herbs, holy bread and chicken dung'; while the *greve* made by folk healers from the Abruzzi comprised a specific number of hairs of the patient, 'a bit of the consecrated host, a palm leaf, a grain ... a paper bearing the image of a saint, a prayer written on a piece of cloth (often a vestment stolen from a priest)' and a horn of coral.[19]

Images were used in magic from earliest times. The Great Magical Papyrus in Paris, written in the early fourth century, instructed devotees how to make wax or clay human figures, male and female, on which the names of those whom one wished to attract were written together with other magical words. The head and body were then pricked with thirteen needles to 'make sure that he or she thinks of no one but me'. An eighth-century list of 'superstitions' referred to 'idols' made of dough or rags; and an Anglo-Saxon charter of 963 to an effigy of one Aelsi, father of Wulfstan, having nails driven into it. In the *Inferno*, Dante mentions women 'doing evil with herbs and with images'. Late medieval and Renaissance high magic employed images, while the use in England of the term 'poppet' to designate doll-like figures made for magic purposes, which became common from the same period, suggests that the practice was also common.[20]

Images were often and still are associated with harmful magic. The use of image magic was alleged at both the French and the English courts in the late medieval period. The bishop of Troyes was accused in 1308 of having 'caused the death of the former Queen Jeanne by having baptized and impaled a wax image which represented her'; and similar charges were made against the wife of Marigny, minister of Philip the Fair, in 1314. We have seen that Eleanor Cobham, wife of the duke of Gloucester, who supposedly used an image in a ritual 'to enable her to bear a child', was accused in 1441 of trying 'to kill the king by witchcraft'. Bewitching via wax and other images also figures in the 'classic' witch trials of the sixteenth and seventeenth centuries. A clay mannekin was reported to have been used by a group of women at Auldearne in 1662, for example, to cause the death of the male children of the laird of Park. Here the carefully made likeness of a little boy was burned in the fire, 'until the child it represented was dead'. Abbé Thiers noted that in the Chartres region around 1700 certain people 'make figures of wax or some other material and stick pins in them, or put them near the fire or pull them apart, so that the living originals (for whom they stand) may feel the same affronts and the same pains on their bodies and in their persons'. In a Danish text from the 1930s, a servant girl 'felt as if someone was sticking pins into her, first on one side and then on the other' and 'became very ill'. Later a doll was found in the closet of her employer with pins stuck in it that corresponded exactly with the pains of the girl.[21] There could not be a clearer instance of sympathetic magic.

But images were used in other kinds of magic. As in the Great Magical Papyrus, images were used in love magic. Wax statues were bought or made and stuck with pins or held by the fire to arouse love in sixteenth-century Venice and the Veneto. Statues of Christ were sometimes employed here to represent the victim, the ritual of heating them by the fire being called *fritto Cristo* or 'frying Christ'. The Christ-figure presumably gave extra power to the rite. In a case in 1588, a middle-class girl from Feltre, who had been seduced by a local noble, acquired 'a detailed wax figure of a nude man', complete with genitals, and stuck 'needles all over it, especially in the eyes temple, heart and phallus'. She then placed it near the altar in a church – all in order to force the man to marry her. At Entrevaux in Provence in modern times, 'girls or widows looking for a husband simply fashioned a little man out of clay, resembling the person they want and having obvious sexual characteristics'. Images were also used in healing. The doctor of physic in Chaucer's *Canterbury Tales* had 'images for his patients'. These were hung on the sufferer's body 'at hours when his horoscope indicated that the planets were favourably placed for him'. Virtue was supposed to descend to the image and hence to the person. A Norfolk monk, William Stapleton, told Cardinal Wolsey in 1528 that he had made 'an image of wax' to the duke of Norfolk's 'similitude' in an attempt to heal him of his sickness.[22]

'Every word, every formula uttered aloud acts like a force and more than ever when the words are of a sacred or magical character.' We have come across much testimony to the truth of Lévy-Bruhl's observation in both respects. As far as particular words of power are concerned, magic borrows from religion and vice-versa. Religious names and formulae figure in charms, and gods, clergy and saints use magic words. The Scandinavian god Odin was 'the great word-master' and maker of runes. St Martin of Tours banished some voracious waterfowl 'with words of power'. Less often, but significantly, some victims of magic were struck dumb. With their voices, they lost power and standing in the community. The importance of the verbal element in magic varied from milieu to milieu, and a distinction should always be made between spoken and written words. 'Spoken or chanted spells' were 'the most important instrument of supernatural power' in medieval and early modern Iceland; while 'scraps of paper with different types of writing were commonplace' in sixteenth-century Venice. This is partly the reflection of a contrast between a less developed country with an oral culture and one of the prime commercial centres of Europe where literacy was widespread, but not entirely. As we have noted, the written word had special cachet in non- or semi-literate circles, and 'words of power' accrued further power from being esoteric. A student of early modern Portugal 'found several cases of illiterate sorceresses who included written formulae ... in their procedures, or began their divination by asking someone to read magic words'.[23]

The folklorist Edward Clodd proposed a typology of words of power in 1898. These were: 1. Creative words, such as the 'Let there be light' of the Creation story in Genesis; 2. Mantras, which would include repetitive prayers, the names of God and perhaps mysterious words used in magic, such as *abracadabra*; 3. Passwords like 'Open Sesame'; 4. Spells and incantations for conjuring up spirits; and 5. Cure charms. The categories are overlapping, and they are not exhaustive. Into what category does the consecration formula of the mass fall, which was so often evoked in magic? Or the 'divine locutions' received by mystics like St Teresa of Ávila?[24]

Esoteric words do figure in popular magic. They are found, for example, in Carolingian and Anglo-Saxon charms and spells, and they occur in later material. But they are more a feature of learned magic, as one might expect, and popular examples tends to be confined to just a few words, often taken from the Latin liturgy. Mention should also be made of word diagrams, occasionally used as amulets and for other purposes. An instance is the SATOR square, based on the letters of the Paternoster. 'Its earliest appearance is in a Christian church at Pompeii, destroyed in 70 AD', and it was used in Anglo-Saxon and later magic:

SATOR
AREPO
TENET
OPERA
ROTAS

Invoking, commanding and exorcizing spirits by pronouncing their names was another component of high magic, but one that had its echoes or equivalents at the popular level. In the 'Rumpelstilstkin' or 'Tom Tit Tot' folk-tale motif, the girl escapes from the power of her supernatural helper by discovering and revealing his name.[25]

In everyday verbal rites, the main types were blessings and curses; and oral and written spells. In some cases, anyone could utter, write or show the words, but usually the role of the person was significant. Only a priest could effectively utter the consecration and other formulae. Magicians knew 'secret' words. Blessings and curses, as we shall see, were of particular power if pronounced by parents. In many traditional societies, women had a special relationship to words. They commented on or incited to action performed by men. They lamented the dead and called for murders to be avenged. When Prince Edward is killed in Shakespeare's *King Henry VI Part III*, Richard of Gloucester offers to kill Queen Margaret too: 'Why should she live to fill the world with words?'[26]

Both blessing and cursing, indeed all spoken magic, depended on the power also believed to reside in the tongue. The tongue could be a force for good, notably as the instrument for preaching God's word. The *Fioretti* declared of the early Franciscan Brother Lucido the Elder that 'his glorious tongue, informed by the Holy Spirit, brought forth marvellous fruit in preaching'. Saints' tongues were sometimes preserved as relics. For example, at the convent of the Visitation of Avignon, there was kept 'the most precious of the relics [of St François de Sales] after his heart: his tongue, which declared so many admirable things'. It was exposed for veneration and kissing every year for a week at Corpus Christi. But much more often the tongue was regarded in a negative way, as a source of evil and conflict. A passage from the Epistle of James was frequently cited by the clergy. According to this, the tongue was a small member, but it could do huge damage: 'No man can subdue the tongue. It is an intractable evil, charged with deadly venom'. It was used to praise God but also to curse our fellow men. It represented among our members the world with all its wickedness; it defiled our whole being. All this explains the importance of silence in the religious life, insisted on in varying degrees by all monastic Rules. But this was by no means an exclusively clerical view. Chaucer wrote that 'a wicked tongue is worse than a fiend'.[27] He also likened it to a cutting instrument, severing friendships. The same metaphor is found in other popular writers and in proverbs: the tongue wounds like a sword or a lance.

Making the tongue responsible for the word it uttered was reflected in penal practice, both informal and formal. According to Brother Leo, another early Franciscan insulted a brother with harsh words. When he saw that the other brother was distressed, he was angry with himself 'and, taking up the droppings of an ass, he put them into his mouth and chewed them with his teeth, saying: "The tongue that has spewed out the venom of malice against my brother shall taste dung" '. Later another Franciscan, St Charles of Sezze, recalled being punished for 'faults in speech' by having 'to drag my tongue many times along the entire length of the [convent] kitchen'.[28] Courts also imposed this type of punishment. In an early modern Scottish example, a man who had falsely accused his wife of adultery had to do penance holding his tongue. More serious offences relating to the tongue might be penalized by mutilation of that organ. Church courts on the Continent prescribed cutting out or slitting the tongue as penalties for heresy or blasphemy.

The blessing was a universal feature of social intercourse in traditional Europe. We have encountered it in the context of calendar customs, where those engaged in ritual begging extended a blessing to those who accommodated them. A typical Hogmanay blessing from the Hebrides ran:

> If it be well tonight,
> May it be sevenfold better a year from tonight;
> May God bless the house and all in it,
> Between man and wife and children,
> Much food and plenty of clothing,
> And the wealth of men be in it.

In another example from the Limousin, children begging eggs on Easter Saturday expressed these wishes, if their requests were granted:

> If there are girls to be married,
> May they find good parties ...
> If there are youths,
> May they get good numbers in the draft lottery.

Blessing also occurred within communities among neighbours. O'Sullivan recounts for example, that on the Blasket Islands and at Dingle in the West of Ireland, 'God save all here', 'God and Mary save you' and 'God bless you' were normal greetings on entering a house.[29]

Blessings were also sought from those with a specific status or in a specific relationship. We have seen that the priest's blessing of both objects and persons was believed to be particularly efficacious. The poor and real beggars also blessed their benefactors. In the Cotswolds in the late nineteenth century, tramps who were given food returned: 'God bless ye'. An old beggar woman in Almeria (Granada) always 'poured out a stream of blessings' on those who gave to her: 'May the Blessed Virgin give you everything you wish for! May she give you and your father and your mother long lives! ... May St Gabriel and St Michael and the holy choir of angels come down through the air and carry you up to Heaven!'.[30]

Blessings also reflected and reinforced hierarchical relationships, passing from superior to inferior, from master to servants, from elder to younger, and especially from parents to child. The parental blessing was regular and often formal in all countries and all classes. George Basset wrote typically in

1539 to his stepfather and mother, Lord and Lady Lisle: 'I recommend me unto you; beseeching to have your daily blessing', and the other Lisle children sought the parental blessing in the same way either directly or indirectly through the letters of others. One of the Lives of Sir Thomas More relates a more formal but striking instance, dating from the time when More was Lord Chancellor.

> Whensoever he passed through Westminster Hall to his place in the Chancery, by the Court of the King's Bench, if his father, who sat there as a judge, had been set down ere he came, he would go to him, and reverently kneeling down in the sight of all, ask his blessing. This virtuous custom he always solemnly observed though then men after their marriages thought themselves not bound to these duties of younger folks.

'The habit of kneeling, both morning and evening, before parents' to ask for their blessing persisted in England down to the eighteenth century, and blessing on special occasions for even longer. The last blessing of children by parents on their death-beds was of particular importance in England and on the Continent. 'If any of my sons were to go to law, and to dispute my will', Lapo Niccolini ordered in 1430, 'I leave him without my paternal benediction, as one should do to such a wicked son.' St Charles of Sezze, who was unable to be present at his father's death, took comfort from reports that, 'though I was not there, as he wished, he also gave me his blessing, wherever I might be, mentioning my name many times'.[31]

'A curse is a wish, expressed in words, that evil ... may befall a certain person.' 'My curses on her!', King Lear declared of Regan.

> All the stor'd vengeances of heaven fall
> On her ingrateful top! Strike her young bones,
> You taking airs, with lameness! ...

Among curses reported to the Chancery court in York in the 1590s were: 'An evil plague ... light upon thee'; and 'Fie upon thee, I ask a vengeance of thee, and that an evil end may come upon thee as ever did to man'. The curse was the malevolent equivalent of the blessing, and it could be directed against places, seasons, stars, plants, ships, animals and activities like fishing as well as against persons, though persons remained its main target. Cursing was a feature of all traditional societies from the earliest times. Oedipus, for example, utters a series of curses through the Theban Plays of Sophocles. In the *Aeneid*, Dido curses Aeneas when he abandons her, invoking the Avenging Furies, which were also known as the 'Curses'. Tombs in the Ancient world were frequently protected by inscriptions promising vengeance on their violators. One from Halicarnassus read: 'May the land not be fruitful for him [the violator], nor the sea navigable. May he have no profit from his children, nor a hold on life, but may he encounter destruction'.[32]

A distinction should be drawn between public and private curses. In Shakespeare's *King John*, for example, Cardinal Pandulph tells the king that he will 'stand curs'd and excommunicate', that is he officially excommunicates him. Constance then adds her unofficial curses, inviting the cardinal to second them; but he objects that his curses, unlike hers, have 'law and warrant'. As Crawley notes, 'throughout their history, private cursing and blessing preponderate over public and unofficial over official'. However, it is important to realize that public and official cursing was a well-established practice in Europe, particularly in the medieval period. There are many manifestations of this, and curses or the threat of curses were used in various important circumstances. First, curses were used to strengthen and sanction gifts or exchanges of property. An assembly in 657 confirmed and extended the privileges and lands of the monastery of Peterborough: 'Then they laid the curse of God and the curse of all his saints and of all Christian people upon anyone who should abrogate anything that was done there'. Across Europe through the early and central Middle Ages such curses were written into charters. The foundation charter of the abbey of Cluny in 909 or 910, for example, 'ends with a terrible curse on any man who should try to upset it or to violate its provisions'.[33] Provisional curses were also written into laws and wills.

Official curses were a special weapon of the clergy. The Church generally used malediction as a sanction in its processes of excommunication and anathema, which were used against major and minor offences, such as the failure to pay tithes. Monasteries employed liturgies of malediction, the 'clamour', from the ninth to the twelfth centuries. And individual clerics, at all levels, issued or threatened curses. In a letter of 722, commending Bishop Boniface to the Germans, Pope Gregory II declared that if anyone hindered his work, 'let him be cursed by the judgment of God and condemned to eternal damnation'. In a twelfth-century Life, Thomas Becket, shortly before his death,

> cursed all those who had been the means of his falling-out with the king ... 'Christ Jesus curse them all!', he said, and threw the candle down upon the paved floor as a sign that their memory should be erased from the book and they themselves expelled from the realm to which the good are called.

Pope Pius II laid a curse in 1462 on anyone who should change the appearance and lay-out of his church at Pienza. Later clergy, including Protestants, also deployed curses against religious opponents, sinners and others who displeased them. The curses of the clergy were particularly powerful since they were able to invoke God's aid and to cite Scriptural texts and precedents. Monastic clamours used the Psalms and Chapters 27 and 28 from Deuteronomy. In an English anathema against tithe-dodgers, 'the sinner was to be accursed by Father, Son and Holy Spirit and all the host of heaven ... [he] was condemned to share the pains of Hell "with Judas that betrayed our Lord Jesus Christ" and [he was] ... "to be put out of the Book of Life" '.[34] Official cursing was also more generally present in the ecclesiastical context via the services of Commination performed on Ash Wednesday and other occasions.

We turn now to private and unofficial curses. The power of the curse depended in part on the position of the curser, as we have seen with the clergy, and on his or her relationship to the cursed, and certain kinds of curse were therefore more dreadful and dreaded than others. Parents ought to bless their children. The parental curse was thus particularly serious. One of the categories of Greek vampire was a person who had died under it.

We have cited King Lear's paternal curses of his ungrateful daughters and many other examples may be found in literature from Cervantes to Balzac. This reflected reality. According to Giovanni di Ceprano, St Francis' father cursed him, when he decided to adopt the religious life – a not uncommon occasion for this. In 1380, the Florentine Simone di Rinieri de' Peruzzi added a codicil to his will, in which he stated: 'I curse my son Benedetto; may he be accursed to the extent of my power ... May he be accursed by God, amen!' In a much more recent and non-Christian example, when Elias Canetti's father decided to leave Bulgaria in 1911 to go to England against the wishes of his father, the latter 'cursed his son solemnly in the courtyard, in front of the relatives who were present and who listened in horror ... Nothing, they said, was more dreadful than a [Jewish] father's cursing his son'. When Canetti's father subsequently died prematurely in Manchester, the grandfather 'was convinced that his curse had killed my father'.[35]

A mother's curse was equally if not more dangerous. After fratricidal killing within the ruling Baglioni family at Perugia around 1500, Atalanta, mother of Grifone, cursed her son, so 'that it seemed that the earth must open and swallow up the unhappy youth'. A renegade friar, running a shop in Geneva in the 1550s, 'had received his mother's curse for breaking his vows and leaving the church' to become a Protestant. In a witchcraft trial at Basel in 1615, the widow of Jehanperrin Bourgeois was said to have quarrelled with her own daughter and cursed her. Within three or four days the daughter died, a witness saying she 'did not know whether from such maledictions or not'. A particular twist could be lent the maternal curse by reference to the breast-feeding tie. One of the worst curses in the modern Balkans was the restrospective: 'May my milk poison you!', uttered to an adult child.[36]

Children also cursed parents, and their curses too were heavily loaded. The German confessional manual of around 1470, *The Mirror of the Sinner*, asked children: 'Have you insulted or cursed your parents ... ?' After she became a nun in 1610, the widowed Madame de Chantal, aged thirty-eight, effectively abandoned her children, and she dreamed that her relatives, including her children, cursed her for this course of action. Much later, in Balzac's novel of 1838 Victor Grandet wrote to his brother about his bankruptcy and referring to his son: 'Will he not live to curse me? Oh! my brother ... our children's curse is a terrible thing! They may appeal against your curse, but there is no appeal against theirs'.[37]

The curse was 'particularly the weapon of the wronged and oppressed against their more powerful enemies'. In cursing Creon, Oedipus declares: 'I, who am so ill-used, have no defence but cursing'. Curses were therefore likely to emanate from the poor and those seeking alms and to be directed against the rich, and they had religious and social sanction. 'Do not avert your eye from the needy', advised Ecclesiasticus, 'nor give a man occasion to curse you: For if in bitterness of soul he calls down a curse upon you, his Creator will hear his prayer.' According to Matthew Paris writing in 1247, King Henry III of England gave so much away to his relatives that he had little left for almsgiving, 'and those who sincerely and truly loved him feared not a little ... the curses of the poor people heaped on his head'. Cursing was also the response to the breach of community norms represented by not entertaining ritual beggars. Instead of the ritual blessing the guisers would then issue a ritual curse.

> The Malison of God and of Hogmanay be on you,
> And the scath of the plaintive buzzard ...
> And the scath of the sneaking fox

and so on, they said on Barra.[38] All of this explains the classic pattern of the witchcraft accusation against a beggar refused, who utters a curse, which is followed by some disaster.

Indeed curses were believed to be one of the most effective weapons of witches generally, and examples may be cited from trial evidence from Portugal to Russia. These ranged from name-calling to the deployment of elaborate formulae. The witches of Llanddona on Anglesey uttered this curse against a man who had offended them:

> May he wander for ages many;
> And at every step, a stile;
> At every stile, a fall;
> At every fall, a broken bone;
> Not the largest, nor the least bone,
> But the chief neck bone, every time.[39]

Curses were sometimes accompanied by ritual gestures, like Becket's dropping the candle to the ground. The Llanddona witches uttered their curse at a particular well, and cursing wells or springs were not uncommon in North Wales. A woman served at St Aelian's well in Denbighshire down to modern times. 'Pilgrims' with grudges came and paid her money. She wrote the name of the victim in a book and dropped a pin in the water. Elsewhere pieces of slate with victims' names scratched on them were thrown into the well or frogs pierced with pins. In Ireland, stones with cups in them made by other stones (probably communal mortars originally) were used into recent times as cursing stones. The curse was apparently uttered while turning a pebble in the cup. Most curses were oral, but, as the Welsh examples show, they might have a written element and in some curses this element might be predominant. Public curses were placed on inscriptions in the Ancient world, and private curse tablets, often made of lead, and sometimes transfixed with nails, were fixed to posts, dropped in wells, and placed in graves and other situations. Later examples of written curses are reported, though they seem to have been rare. Two leaden plates were found, for example, under a heap of stones on Gatherley Moor in Yorkshire in the late nineteenth century. On one was inscribed: 'I do make this that James Philipp, John Philipp his son, Christopher and T[h]omas his sons shall flee Richmondshire and nothing prosper with any of them in Richmondshire'. This seems to have related to a property dispute, in which the family had been engaged.[40]

Curses tended to have an automatic effect. Once uttered, they could not easily be cancelled. Among the Sarakatsani, 'there was no defence against a mother's curse'. The curse was in effect also a kind of prophecy. It was referred to in ancient Welsh literature, like the *Mabinogion*, as a 'destiny'. Often the best that could be done was to mitigate or to divert the curse on to some other object. Gregory of Tours related that 'in order to avoid the curse pronounced in the pact between his brothers and himself on whichever of them should enter Paris without the agreement of the others, King Chilperic sent the relics of saints on ahead, and then marched into the city himself '. Here the saints countered the effects of the curse or even took it upon themselves. In order to escape his father's curse, St Francis deployed the countervailing power of a beggar's blessing. He adopted

> a despised beggar ... in his father's stead. He said to him: 'Come with me, and I will share the alms I receive with you, and when you see my father cursing me, I will say to you: Bless me, my father. Then you must make the sign of the cross over me and bless me'.

In modern Greece,

it is a common custom for a dying man to put a handful of salt into a vessel of water, and when it is dissolved to sprinkle with the liquid all those who are present, saying ... 'As the salt dissolves, so may my curses dissolve'. By this ceremony all persons whom he has cursed are released from the bonds of an imprecation, which after death he would no longer be able to revoke or annul.[41]

The power of curses depended, we have seen, on the status and relationship of those involved, but a moral dimension could be present. Here curses might return to harm those who had originally uttered them. Matthew Paris related that the prior of Peterborough frequently cursed the abbot of St Albans, after the latter had refused to let his nephew become a monk because he was too young. 'But all these curses ultimately rebounded to his own head'; and the prior died while sitting on a latrine and was supposedly carried off by the Devil. It was said of the cursing stones at Killinagh in County Cavan that 'you would think twice before turning the stones, because the curse would come back on you unless the cause was just'.[42]

Magic spells or charms came in a great variety of forms, oral and written. These include tales, epics and narratives; vows; conjurations; children's rhymes; brief formulae often comprising unintelligible combinations of words, letters and signs or puzzles. As we have seen, they were used in a whole spectrum of situations. So there were protective spells, healing spells, love spells, spells to cause harm, spells to undo other spells. Special magical words were sometimes arranged in a particular format, like the SATOR square, which could be read, horizontally and vertically, backwards and forwards. Addison in *The Spectator* at the start of the eighteenth century referred to 'a little acrostic called the Witches' prayer, that fell into verse when it was read either backward or forward, excepting only that it cursed one way and blessed the other'. Saying prayers or charms backwards was a general ploy. Special words or other formulae could also be repeated, each time dropping a letter or a word, thus providing a reducing or disappearing spell. Special or secret words were often taken from the Ancient languages, Hebrew, Greek and Latin. Hebrew was almost exclusively confined to learned magic. During the Carolingian period, Greek was a virtually unknown language in the West. This 'led men to look on Greek rather as a branch of magic than a language, so that the very letters of the alphabet were individually endowed with mystical meanings'. *Beta*, for example, meant *vetus* or 'old' or *beatitudo* or 'happiness'. The use of Latin words was much more common, particularly in later centuries.

> They'd make men think the Devil were fast and loose,
> With speaking fustian Latin,

says the conjuror in Webster's *The White Devil*. A man prosecuted at St Albans early in the sixteenth century, for example, used incantations to cure horses. These were apparently Latin formulae, which were written on a piece of paper that was then tied to the mane or tail of the animal. Again, a sorcerer from the Yonne in the nineteenth century used this formula to give a person lice: '*Niger, nigrum. Conculabis basiliscum et aspidem*'.[43] Very often Latin words and formulae were taken from the liturgy, only one example, as we have seen, of extensive borrowing from religious sources.

Magical procedures involved a range of ritual gestures. In Sardinia in the 1920s, St Anthony was made to grant a wish by lighting lamps in front of his image, 'placing one's head downwards and tearing one's breast, while shouting at the top of one's voice and insistently: I wish it; you owe it'.[44] In the Abruzzi and elsewhere, men guarded against the effects of the evil eye by grasping their genitals. Among such bodily gestures, we have already discussed the healing touch, spitting and the harmful look. Two others were movements with the hand and use of the breath.

Raising the hand with certain fingers extended was a common religious and magical gesture from Roman times. The thumb might be joined to particular fingers to form a circle; or the first two fingers used to make a V-sign; or all fingers could be extended and sometimes placed against the palm. The gestures could be precautionary, beneficent or aggressive. Placing the thumb inside the clasped fist of the opposite hand was used against the evil eye in southern Italy. In modern Greece, pointing the five fingers could be prophylactic, but it could also 'intend a curse upon the person to whom it is directed'. The hand could also be holding or in contact with some object of significance. In an early modern love charm, the hands were placed by the chimney wall or on the ground, with the words: 'I place ten fingers on the ground; I conjure heaven and earth'. In the Outer Hebrides, the special piece of wool used to counter spells on livestock had to be carried 'in silence, and in the palm of the hand – not between the finger and the thumb, because with them Eve plucked the apple and they are not blessed'.[45] As we shall see, much significance could be attached to whether the left or the right hand was used.

A person's 'soul' was very often thought of as existing in his or her breath. Hence the Creation myth in Genesis, in which God 'breathed into his nostrils the breath of life; and man became a living soul'. The vitality of the pagan gods was also associated with their breath. The last breath signified dying in many cultures. In Corsica, 'when a person dies, they said, it is the breath that goes'. All of this lent great power and meaning to human breath. We have seen that insufflation on the forehead, ears and nose was an integral part of the traditional baptismal rite, and its significance was clear. As St Augustine wrote, infants were thereby 'exorcized, so that the power of the Devil may be expelled from them'. Breathing or blowing was also used in regular exorcisms. A medieval practice involved the *Christus vincit* formula combined with 'a puff in the eyes'. Though averse to many of these Catholic rituals, Protestants still employed blowing in their own way. The seventeenth-century 'prophet' Du Serre breathed into the mouths of his followers 'to convey the gift of the Pentecost', while the Camisards in their struggles against persecution also breathed 'into each other's mouths to give an inspiration of supernatural courage'.[46]

Blowing was used in magic to give protection against supernatural forces and especially the Devil, echoing liturgical exorcisms. 'The Devil it is that's thy master', Lafew tells Parolles in Shakespeare's *All's Well That Ends Well*, '... I think thou wast created for men to breathe themselves upon thee.' Human breath was also thought to possess healing power, which could be exercised on humans and animals. Bede related that Bishop John of Hexham 'blew in the face' of a priest badly injured on the head by a fall from a horse. In another early English example, a person performing 'The Nine Herbs Charm' was instructed to 'sing the same charm into the mouth of the man [to be cured] and into both of his ears and on the wound before you apply the salve'. In eighteenth- and nineteenth-century France, healers who cured by this means were common enough to be known as *souffleurs* or breathers. Breathing could also resuscitate babies, dispel pests and cause harm. In a case in Galloway in 1810, a child was supposedly made ill by the breath of an ill-wisher. In modern Greece, the breath of witches could cause insanity or death. Blowing through the keyholes of churches was said to be part of the initiation of witches in early modern Denmark. More mundanely and returning to the identity of life and breath, the daily rekindling of the household fire by blowing on it might be thought of as a quasi-magical rite. In modern Tuscany, for example, this was done by the mother of the house, 'who stooped in front of the andirons to blow on the fire to communicate [to it] ... the vital breath that popular belief considered to be exactly like fire'.[47]

We turn now to more general gestures, starting with measuring and weighing. We have seen that measuring a person and burning a candle the same length was a procedure used in the diagnosis and cure of illnesses. Measuring a baby's swaddling was a way of evaluating its illness in sixteenth-century Venice. Pilgrims to Jerusalem in the late medieval period and probably at other times measured the dimensions of the holy places with threads and girdles which were kept as relics. In the County of Foix in the fourteenth century, 'before undertaking a dangerous trip, the Cathar leader Bélibaste ... took a shoe to measure the distance from the hearth to the door [in a neighbour's house]. At the door, the shoe overlapped the threshold by half its length', which was taken to be 'a sign that he would not return'. In Venice again, 'measuring the hearth, a wall, or a cord with their hand or forearm' was admitted to by women interviewed by the Inquisition, a procedure which 'often seems to have been concerned with evaluating the relationship between people'. Women also measured the erect penises of their lovers for love magic – to bind the men to them. In one of the miracles attributed to St Martin of Tours, the King of Galicia, seeking a cure for his son, sent gifts to the saint's shrine, and 'gold and silver were weighed there to the weight of ' the sufferer. Silk cloths placed on St Martin's tomb in other circumstances became 'heavy' with grace; and the same phenomenon was observed at St Peter's shrine in Rome.[48]

We have come across many examples of circumambulation of sacred and other sites, especially in calendar customs, and of going and turning round in other magical rites. Circumambulation was an ancient religious procedure. A sucking pig was carried round the area in Ancient Athens in which the assembly was held to purify it and make it a consecrated enclosure. In Ancient Rome there were festivals to trace the city enclosure and the limits of its territory. 'On those days, the citizens formed a grand procession, clad in white, and crowned with leaves; they made the circuit of the city or territory, chanting prayers; at the head walked priests, leading victims, which they sacrificed at the close of the ceremony.'[49] This was the model for the later Rogations. Circumambulations were also performed at the rites of passage.

In the Christian era, all kinds of objects and buildings were processed around in rituals of different kinds. In calendar rituals all over Europe, especially those at the solstices, people and animals went round fires. Stones, trees and houses were also circuited. The tenants of Knightlow Hundred walked three time round a great stone before paying 'Wroth Silver' to their lord, the duke of Buccleuch. In *Grettir's Saga*, hostile magic practised by an old woman involved carving runes in the trunk of a tree, smearing them with her blood, and walking counterclockwise around it. In parts of the Highlands, the Hogmanay lads walked round the house sunwise; while the Căluş dancers in Rumania danced 'three times counterclockwise around the house, so that the evil spirits would not approach it'.[50] According to a sixteenth-century French source, it was good for a cow to go three times round a bull before coupling.

Very common also was the circuit of the church. Churches were generally circumambulated when they were consecrated. Capitularies in the ninth century ordered the clergy to process round churches every Sunday, carrying holy water, and similar provisions were made in times of crisis in later centuries. Following the Stations of the Cross was a regular internal circuit from the eighteenth century, if not before. Going round the church, chapel or holy well was a feature of many pilgrimages. For example, an old woman who

went often as a proxy pilgrim to the Breton shrine of Our Lady of Rumengol
would walk three times bare-footed round the chapel, reciting a ballad of the
Virgin, before she entered it. Pilgrims to the chapel of Le-Bois-du-Rat in the
Limousin carried out a particularly elaborate set of rituals on 6 May. First, the
women went three times round the cross facing the chapel, then three times
round the tower. Then the pilgrims went inside and processed around the
interior, touching various sacred spots. Other shrines saw circuits by the sick,
by those wishing to marry, and by animals. We should also mention the
related custom of forming a circle around a church. At Painswick, for
example, at its feast on the Sunday nearest the Nativity of the Virgin, the
ritual of 'clipping the church' took place. This consisted, in modern times, of
children forming a complete circle round the building.[51] Elsewhere in
different parts of Europe ribbons, scarves, threads, or wax cords were placed
around churches. On the day of the *pardon*, for example, the chapel of St
Anne at Prat had immense wax cords wrapped round it; while many churches
dedicated to St Leonard in the Limousin had iron chains round them.
Saintyves suggests that both circumambulation and surrounding with cords
and so on were means of taking possession and also of creating a protective
barrier around the church or other place or object to keep off evil spirits ad
witches.

   As some of our examples have indicated, the direction of the circumambulation was important. In rituals to do with fertility, the circuit was nearly always
sunwise or clockwise. In Scotland circuits of fires at Beltane and St John's went
sunwise, as did Michaelmas cavalcades of horses round the burial grounds.
Beating the bounds in Scotland and England went the same way. In Ireland,
'when starting on fishing expeditions the crews were very careful that their
craft should leave the shore in a direction sunways', while the same concern
governed the subsequent course of the boat, casting the nets and other actions.
The same prescription attached to other circumstances. In Ireland again,
funeral processions used to make 'a sunwise circle around some place or
object on the way to the burial place'; while in well cults also 'a sunwise circuit
of the well was made'. In the Outer Hebrides, 'everything should be done
dessil, i.e. sunwards. When a child is choking, they say, *Dessil*, possibly part of
some old invocation'. Moreover, 'it is not right to come to a house ... north-
ward' or the reverse of *dessil*. Some healing rituals also include sunwise turns
or circuits, for example, when a sick child was passed through a tree in modern
Somerset.[52]

   By contrast, 'withershins or widdershins, i.e. against the sun, or counter-
clockwise has a special potency as reverse [or hostile] magic'. As such, it too
could be used in cures. At Men-an-tol in Cornwall, for example, scrofulous
children were 'passed naked three times' through the holed stone there 'and

then drawn three times on the grass, against the course of the sun'. The old nurse in Spenser's *The Fairy Queen*, trying to reverse her daughter's conception, muttered prayers, and

> That said, her round about she from her turn'd,
> She turned her contrary to the sun,
> Thrice she her turn'd contrary and return'd,
> All contrary, for she the right did shun.

Witches of course were believed to move withershins in the accomplishment of their evil. Janet Macmurdoch from Dumfries, according to trial evidence from 1671, 'went thrice widdershins round all the yards [of her neighbours], barefooted', which caused illness in the animals. The same contrary movement could be used to control spirits. In the tale of Childe Roland, the hero encircled the fairy knowe 'three times widdershins, crying, Open door! Open door!' to gain access to Elfland. Occasionally movement both ways is found in the same ritual. In the ceremony of the Ceri at Gubbio, the procession took a sunwise path through the city to arrive at the main square, where it went round against the sun; but the gyration of the giant candle with the statue of St Ubaldo on top of it was always 'withershins'.[53]

Related to all this, circles were traced in the course of magical rites. In Anglo-Saxon cures, they were made around the patient or the wound or swelling. More generally, circles were drawn around plants before they were picked for magical purposes; while magic circles were 'traced on the ground with a sword or a knife or else inscribed on a piece of parchment or cloth' in late medieval and Renaissance high magic. For the Rumanian Câluş dance, the mute drew a circle on the ground with a sword to make the space for the dance to take place. As Delatte explains, encirclement of plants had three functions. It signified 'a taking of possession'; whatever was encircled came into the power of the magician; in the case of a plant, its occult virtue was held in and could not escape. The magic circle also 'purified the plant of any element that could harm or weaken its properties'. Finally, the circle, which might also be drawn around plant *and* gatherer, was protective; it kept both 'safe from any harmful external influence'. Much of this would apply more generally. The direction in which the circle was drawn was also significant, as with circumambulations. The Căluş circle was drawn anti-clockwise. This consideration is also found with the swastika symbol, which was quite widespread in Europe: it was regarded 'as a talisman; for good if the lines bend clockwise, for evil if they go widdershins'.[54]

Another range of magical gestures involved tying and untying. As Mauss noted, tying and binding were terms often used to mean magical control generally, an indication of their prominence. The Ancient Fates determined the destiny of humans with threads, which they spun and cut. The Ancient Gods bound and freed each other and mortals. Odin, for example, was 'famed for his power to free men from bonds, either material or psychological, and to bind his enemies' with special words and in other ways.[55]

On the human level, binding was sometimes done in the course of normal 'tying' work. 'Have you been present at, or consented to the vanities which women practise in their woollen work, in their weaving', asked Burchard of Worms, 'who, when they begin their weaving, hope to be able to bring it about that with incantations and with their actions the threads of the warp and the woof become so intertwined that unless [someone] makes use of ... other diabolical counter-incantations, he will perish totally?' At *veillées* or bees in Transylvania, 'girls used to collectively perform ritual love charms to attract the young men'. As they spun, they chanted verses to induce all the bachelors to leave what they were doing and come to their bee. 'What are you spinning?', one asked and received the reply:

> I'm not spinning but unspinning:
> Bachelors from all work bees ...
> From all the houses ...
> All of them to come here.[56]

Perhaps more frequently, special knots were tied and untied in ropes, strings, ribbons, handkerchiefs and other articles of clothing. Here it is important to know that clothing in the past in Europe had many more laces, ties and 'points' than modern dress. Buttons were little used before the later Middle Ages and were then restricted to the well-to-do. In the Limousin, safety-pins only began to replace strings on babies' swaddling in the 1890s.

Tying was especially associated with relations between the sexes. In England and Wales from the seventeenth to the nineteenth century, young men made lovers' knots, which they presented to their sweethearts, often on St Valentine's Day. Ribbons, girdles and garters were given at betrothals and were probably 'construed [in early modern England and elsewhere] to bind or coerce the party to whom they were given'. 'We shall have points and bride-laces', declares Penthea in Ford's *The Broken Heart*, at the prospect of a wedding. A veil was used in the marriage ritual and in some places had knots tied in it, while knotted ribbons were distributed as 'bride favours'. In common parlance in England, marriage was referred to as 'tying the knot', the knot 'pointing out the indissoluble tie of affection and duty', in the words of a popular book on manners and customs in 1827.[57]

Tying and binding were thus unsurprisingly a common feature in love magic. A procedure was reported in England in the early nineteenth century, in which young men or women knitted 'the left garter about the right-legged stocking' on St Agnes Eve, saying at every stitch:

> This knot I knit,
> To know the thing I know not yet,
> That I may see,
> The man [or woman] that shall my husband [or wife] be.

The future spouse would then appear in a subsequent dream. In a poem by
Marie de France from the twelfth century, two lovers were bound by special
knots: 'The knot that the hero Guigemar's beloved makes in his tunic is made
in such a way that no one else can undo it; Guigemar, for his part, wraps a belt
around his naked lover's waist which no one else can break or cut'. In early
modern Venice, victims of love magic were said to be 'bound' or 'tied', and
garters, ties from clothing, and rope were used in spells. Within this sphere,
too, we have seen that knots were tied maliciously, or so it was believed, to
cause infertility or impotence. Lovers could also be separated by reversing
procedures of these kinds. A magician from Bayonne in 1750 claimed to be
able 'to untie two married people'.[58]

Tying and untying were also employed in other kinds of magic. In
Scandinavia and elsewhere, knots were tied in ropes and handkerchiefs and
then untied to cause winds to blow at sea. Belts we have seen were tied round
women in childbirth, and knots untied in the birth-room. Similar procedures
were used in healing and to ease dying. In some parts of Europe, it was
believed that ghosts or *revenants* could be diverted by giving them knots to
untie, so nets or stockings were buried with corpses in north Germany. But
elsewhere, for example in Greece, the presence of knots in the grave
prevented the corpse from being 'loosed', that is from decomposing. Tying
was also a device to protect or control animals. Burchard of Worms referred
to the use of ligatures to protect one's own animals from disease or to destroy
those of others. Sir Walter Scott noted that 'among the almost innumerable
droves of bullocks which come down every year from the Highlands for the
south, there is scarce one but has a curious knot upon his tail, which is ... a
precaution lest an evil eye or an evil spell may do the animal harm'. In order
to protect poultry from predators in Sicily, a magician was called in

> who had the power to bind these chicken-killing animals. He would take a leather
> shoelace from his big boots, make three knots and, holding the lace straight
> between thumb and index finger of both hands, recite this formula:

> > Bring laces, irons and chains
> > To tie up foxes and martens:
> > Spare me the brood hen and her pullets,
> > In the name of the Father, the Son and the Holy Spirit!

In the Apennines, a similar kind of spell prevented a dog from biting. Knots were tied in a strip of the skin of a dead dog and a formula uttered. 'All this should be done three times, and the [living] dog will remain paralysed until the knots are undone, and the words each time repeated backwards.' Untying was a way of curing animals, too. In modern Ireland, calves believed to be suffering from intestinal knots were healed 'by drawing apart over the animals' backs the loose ends of a string tied in a complicated witch-knot of the type which comes undone when pulled'.[59]

As this indicates, tying or binding was one of the ways of bewitching an animal or a person. The early medieval Pseudo-Apuleius, for example, includes a counter-spell for 'unbinding ... one bewitched with a knot'. 'A white cloth ... with strings, whereon was many knots' was discovered under the clothing of a woman burned as a witch at St Andrews in 1572, and was taken to be strong evidence against her. More recently in southern Italy in the 1950s, De Martino came across several cases of persons being 'tied' by witches, where the remedy consisted of finding and untying the knots. In one instance, a baby had its penis tied with a cotton thread, which was removed and burnt. People were also 'tied' by spirits and fairies. Pennant encountered a man in the Highlands of Scotland in the 1760s who was attacked by spirits of the dead flying through the air: 'He then found that his hair was all tied in double knots'. In England elves were supposed to tangle the hair of children and adults during sleep: hence Edgar's 'Elf all my hairs in knots' in *King Lear*. In Sicily, knots in children's hair were caused by the 'house-women' or Fates. If they were cut, this might cause the child serious injury.[60]

Repetition was a very important element in many magical rites, as we have repeatedly seen. This relates in turn to the number symbolism that was a prominent feature of both religion and magic. Numbers were very significant, for example, in The Revelation of St John, where we have the four horsemen of the Apocalypse, the seven seals, the seven angels with seven plagues, and the beast with seven heads and ten horns ridden by the whore of Babylon. A fascination with numbers was characteristic of the medieval Church and its devotions. Prayers recommended in the thirteenth-century *Nun's Rule* mentioned 'the four Gospels', 'the five wounds of Christ', 'the seven gifts of the Holy Ghost' and 'the ten commandments'. To these might be added the seven words on the Cross, the fifteen O's of St Bridget and of course the Trinity. The fourteenth-century ascetic Henry Suso, it is reported 'swallowed five times [when he drank] for the wounds of Jesus ... and cut any large fruit into four parts, three for the Trinity and the fourth part for Mary'. But such concerns were not confined to this period. Healing rites in modern Portugal were performed a set number of uneven times, and specific reference was made to their religious significance: 'Five (for the wounds of

Christ), seven (for the sacraments), and nine (for the number of months Our Lady carried Jesus in her womb)'.[61]

But the numbers had a wider and deeper meaning than this, and some numbers were of particular importance. We have seen that doing or saying things three times figures again and again in magical rites. In Anglo-Saxon magic, for example, 'no magic device was so frequent as the number three'. Various rites included stepping three times over a grave; letting holy water drip three times over sods, then turning three times and saying three Paternosters; letting three drops of wax fall into animal prints; having three masses said over charms; and tracing three crosses with the oil of extreme unction. In the seventeenth-century charm for ague from Lincolnshire, the patient had to 'three days shiver three days shake'. For the Christmas Eve supper in Provence, 'the table was ritually covered with three cloths and set out for the three feasts: Christmas, Circumcision and Epiphany, and lit with three candles'. Mainly a propitious number, three could also be unlucky. In the Mourne region of Ireland, 'it was unlucky to be the third boat out on leaving harbour';[62] while in Provence and elsewhere, people died in threes. The number three was associated with the Trinity, as we have noted; and tripartite divisions were a fundamental feature of Indo-European social and cultural ordering being manifested in the notion of the Three Orders or Estates.

Seven was another special number. In one of their conversations in Sterne's *Tristram Shandy* (1759), Dr Slop and Uncle Toby mention the seven sacraments, the seven deadly sins, the seven days of the week, the seven wonders of the world, the seven planets and the seven plagues, and we have seen that seven had a particular significance in Revelation. In magic, we have seen that seventh children had extraordinary powers. A West Sussex cure required: 'Eat seven sage leaves for seven mornings'. In a spell to harm their neighbours in Spanish Galicia, people 'take oil from the lamps burning before the altar containing the Blessed Sacrament in seven churches'.[63]

Nine, a multiple of three, was also very common in magical procedures. In a remedy prescribed by a Scottish folk-healer in the early seventeenth century, the patient was directed to kneel by his bedside 'three several nights, and every night, thrice nine times, to ask his health ... in the name of Jesus'; and again, he was 'to take nine pickles of wheat and nine pickles of rowan tree, and to wear them continually upon [himself] for his health'. In early modern Venice, objects used in magic were given power by making 'nine crossings' of a canal. Among the Huculs and the Rumanians of the East Carpathians, 'drinking nine lice in a glass of brandy' was a cure for fever; 'dung inserted under a horse-shoe for nine days' for tuberculosis; while 'water from nine wells drawn nine times from each' was sure to extinguish fires. In a cure for impetigo at Avignon, 'the child had a red string tied round its chest for nine days; its mother had to beg alms from nine widows; and with the amount thus raised have a mass said at the Carmelite church and prepare a special soup, which the child was to drink for nine days running'.[64]

Thirteen is now regarded as an unlucky number. People avoid sitting down thirteen to dinner, and the number is avoided for hotel rooms. The aversion seems to be pre-Christian, though it was reinforced by the fact that Christ and the twelve Apostles made up the number, notably at the Last Supper. It was not of much significance in magical rites, though some examples may be found. The modern Sardinian procedure to make St Anthony grant a wish involved lighting thirteen oil lamps in front of his image. As this shows, though powerful, thirteen was not necessarily harmful. In early modern England, testators might provide for thirteen paupers to follow their funerals.

Forty was also a significant number, mainly though not exclusively in the Orthodox world. Women were unclean after childbirth for forty days. In northern Greece, the *liokra*, an amulet made with the skin of a horned snake was washed by forty waves in the sea and then blessed by forty liturgies in church. A charm to prevent miscarriages was 'made with forty coins, begged from forty homes, and blessed again with forty liturgies. A net with forty knots, worn during intercourse by her parents, served to protect a bride against a binding curse'.[65]

Numbers could also be used in more complicated ways. Magic squares in which rows or columns of numbers added up to the same figure or to some significant figure were a feature of learned magic from the early medieval period onwards. Circles of Pythagoras or tetragons were used in the Carolingian period and later to diagnose illnesses. A square was divided into two sections, an upper and a lower, each with three columns.

> The patient had to say what day of the lunar cycle he fell ill and give the numerical value of his name, each letter corresponding to a figure. These numbers were combined and divided by thirty, from which a final number was obtained which matched one of those in the tetragon. If it was a number in the upper part, the patient would be cured ... If in the lower half, the patient would soon die.

A similar device from Lancashire in the eighteenth century included the cabbalistic names of God and algebraic symbols. It was not read, however, but simply placed in a barn, it seems to protect the livestock and grain. We have come across examples of counting down or reducing spells, where a complaint is meant to diminish as the numbers in it decrease. As an Anglo-Saxon charm against a furuncle went:

> Nine were Noththe's sisters,
> Then the nine became eight
> And the eight became seven
> And the seven became six

and so on until 'the one became none'.[66] One also finds the phenomenon of personal lucky or significant numbers, a feature of modern children's lore. Richard Gough noted, for example, that his Uncle William was born in 1588, married when he was sixty-eight, in the eighth year of the reign of Charles II, and died in 1668 aged eighty.

Mauss referred to 'the idea of secrecy and mystery with which magic is imbued and which provides its distinctive features', and there is much in European magic to support this idea. High magic from Classical times onwards was surrounded by secrecy, and occult elements were present in the more general popular magic with which we are mainly concerned. Healers, for example, often had their 'secrets', whose divulgence would make them ineffective. A modern Norwegian practitioner required everyone to leave the room before working her cures; while of another it was said that 'nobody was allowed to listen or watch her when she worked'. A witness told the Inquisition in Venice in 1624: 'I know that women who throw the rope [a divining procedure used in love magic] recite words, but they say them quietly so that others won't learn them'. In Portugal people visited *bruxa* or magicians at night and tried to keep the fact from their neighbours, and so great was peasants' fear of witchcraft that they were 'unwilling to mention it'. In the Balkans, the special powers associated with being born with the caul depended on this being concealed, and the powers could be repudiated by announcing the circumstance. We should also mention the use of euphemisms to refer to the Devil, to fairies and to other beings and creatures. While cooking sausages after the pig-killing in Scandinavia, the pig was never referred to as such; while in south-western France talking while cooking the sausages would cause them to burst. As this indicates, secrecy often implied silence. 'Scarify the neck after sunset', an Anglo-Saxon curing procedure ordered; 'silently pour the blood into running water ... Go back to the house ... in silence.'[67]

Secrecy was encouraged by extraneous factors: fear of official disapproval and, in the early modern period particularly, of prosecution; and in later centuries fear of ridicule; but there is no doubt that it was often regarded as an essential part of some magical rites. But it was not a feature of all magic. Collective rites, like calendar customs and pilgrimages, were necessarily public. Distinctions were sometimes made here between different kinds of ritual. In the modern Limousin, for example, rituals at dolmens were secret, but those at fountains were not. Hostile magic was always likely to be carried out clandestinely. Nor did magic have a monopoly on secrecy. Early Christianity was a mystery religion, whose rites and doctrines were only known by initiates, and the cultural gap between clergy and laity, together with the Latin liturgy, tended to preserve this quality. Priests whispered the words of the mass, 'lest they be caught by the profane'. Secrecy was also present generally in popular culture. Skills, such as those of the blacksmith, the pig-curer or the cook, were jealously guarded and handed on like magical secrets when their possessors were on the point of dying.[68] Families had their secrets, too, which they tried to keep away from the ears of communal gossip.

We have seen too that noise was an important component of many festive rituals, including weddings, calendar customs and the charivaris mounted against those who breached community norms, particularly in the area of marriage. Charivaris involved the banging of pots and pans and sounding of horns. In modern times, fireworks and gunshots were added to the traditional noises. Noise provided publicity, but Frazer and others were in no doubt that it was also intended to drive off evil forces.

> Thus at Brunnen on the Lake of Lucerne, boys go about in procession on Twelfth Night carrying torches and making a great noise with horns, bells, whips and so forth to frighten away two female spirits of the wood ... The people think that if they do not make enough noise, there will be little fruit that year.[69]

Noise also accompanied childbirth and baptisms, and was deployed to drive off storms.

Certain times and places were especially propitious for magical activity or even required. 'Some ceremonies may take place only at night, or at special hours of the night ... Others occur at special times in the day, at sunset or sunrise – two periods which are specially magical', presumably because of their liminal position between day and night. We saw the significance of dusk and dawn in gathering plants. Noon was also a magical time, particularly it seems in the Mediterranean region. According to Leopardi,

> the weariness, rest, and silence that prevail during the midday hour, rendered the time mysterious and sacred to the Ancients, like the hours of night – so that it was believed that it was especially at midday that the Gods, nymphs and fauns, and the souls of the dead, might be seen and heard by men.

In modern Calabria, noon was known as 'Controra ... the ominous hour. Man and beast are fettered in sleep, while spirits walk abroad, as at midnight'. In

Greece, it was the 'heavy', the 'bad' or the 'dangerous' hour, sometimes personified as an evil spirit which caused illness especially in children. Psalm 90 or 91 referred to the *daemonium meridianum*, 'the destruction that wasteth at noonday'.[70]

In traditional Europe, without artificial lighting beyond rushes, tallow and expensive wax candles, night was clearly contrasted with day. It was 'a time of danger and fear' – 'black, fearful, comfortless and horrible'. People slept and kept indoors, afraid to go out. This simple fear of the dark was compounded by or projected into the belief that all kinds of evil forces were abroad at night: ghosts, fairies, spirits and demons, witches. Burchard of Worms referred to those who 'when they have occasion to go out somewhere before daylight, they dare not go, saying that ... it is not permitted to go out before cock-crow and that it is dangerous because the unclean spirits have more power to harm before cock-crow than after'. Both the general and the particular belief remained lively down to modern times.

> The cocks do not crow; I hear no sound ...
> All kinds of phantoms, bodies without bodies,
> Freely visit the domain of the dead,

wrote the French poet Racan. Night was thus the most propitious time for many kinds of magical activity from picking herbs to raising spirits. Bolingbroke tells the Duchess of Gloucester in *King Henry VI, Part II*:

> ... wizards know their times:
> Deep night, dark night, the silent of the night ...
> The time when screech-owls cry, and ban-dogs howl,
> And spirits walk, and ghosts break up their graves;
> That time best fits the work we have in hand.[71]

Night of course was the time when the moon shone, and we have seen how important the phases of the moon were in relation to agriculture, breeding livestock, human conception, childbirth and child-rearing and health. In Ancient and medieval times, eclipses of the moon were attributed to evil spirits or witches. In order to counter their activities and restore the moon to its normal functions, peasants blew horns, rang bells, broke pots and made other noises and shot arrows or threw torches into the sky. The moon was changing and ambiguous, and its power could be dangerous. Sleeping in the light of the moon could turn one mad. One finds rituals therefore to placate the moon. In Calabria in modern times, children sang to the moon to bring them luck. In Rumania, the new moon was hailed with the words:

> Moon, new moon,
> Cut the bread in two
> And give us,
> Half to thee,
> And health to me!

In Macedonia, a more elaborate ritual is reported by a participant. A loaf or specially prepared cake was placed on the head of a child and a silver coin put in its pocket, both echoing the moon. The child was turned round three times, and an adult female recited a prayer to the moon: 'Moon, new moon, let goodness be like the dew; as much sand in the river, so the purse of the father; as the cinders in the house, so many guests at our table; thou like me, and I like thee!'[72]

Particular days had special significance. They were suited or unsuited to specific activities; they were lucky or unlucky. Both the Ancient Greeks and the Ancient Romans had a belief in propitious and unpropitious days. On unpropitious days in Athens 'no marriage took place, no enterprise was begun, no assembly held, and justice was not administered. The eighteenth and nineteenth day of every month was employed in purifications. The day of the Plynteria – a day unlucky above all – they veiled the statue of the great Athene Polias'. Similar restrictions attended the *dies nefasti* at Rome, when the courts were closed and public life suspended. In addition to such official behaviour, there were private and personal practices. Suetonius relates that Augustus 'had a superstition against starting a journey on the day after a market day, or undertaking any important task on the Nones of the month'.[73]

Some early Christians were unhappy with the observation of special days and months; but in practice, as we have seen, the medieval Church established an elaborate calendar of festivals and saints' days. Radical Protestants wished to do away with this calendar and with the cults associated with it, but, as in England, much of the old calendar with its significant days survived the Reformation. Only a minority of 'Puritans' would have agreed with the sentiments expressed by William Thompson of North Shields in a letter written on 5 January 1840:

> 'The compliments of the season', I seldom use, they are too often unmeaning compliments, the offspring of superstition and folly. I consider it my duty as a Christian to wish every person as well and as happy on any and every day as on the first day of a new year or any other particular day.[74]

For most, days and seasons did have meaning.

From the time of Hesiod, the timing of agricultural tasks had been laid down according to the calendar. This norm existed, as we have seen in

Christian Europe and is illustrated in Books of Hours, the sculpture on cathed-ral portals and almanacs. There was also a more finely-tuned prescription of what tasks should be performed and what avoided at particular times. The priest of Senneley in the late seventeenth century noted, for example, that

> the people of the Sologne believe that they would offend God if they winnowed their flour on the day of St Thomas, because there is a false tradition among them that this holy Apostle was martyred with a winnowing sieve, and they have a saying to this effect.[75]

The association of tasks with particular dates has a real basis in the object-ive round of the seasons and their conditions, but other more mystical notions also became attached to calendar dates. In different parts of Europe, as we have seen, New Year's Day was a microcosm foretelling events and fortune in the year to come. So, in Sicily, there were sayings: 'Whoever is sick on New Year's Day will be sick all the year'; or 'Whoever eats macaroni on New Year's Day will have a hard time the whole year'. In Scotland, the ashes on the hearth might be investigated to see who in the family was going to die during the year. Unhappy events such as breaking glass on that day might also indicate deaths to come, and special significance was attached to the first person or animal seen or encountered. Other dates had special meaning for other reasons. In some parts of Europe, such as the Veneto, Christmas was a dangerous time when 'witchcraft is done and undone'. But elsewhere, as in the Limousin and parts of England, Christmas Eve in particular was a time when evil forces were powerless:

> And then, they say, no spirit dare stir abroad,
> The nights are wholesome, then no planets strike,
> No fairy takes, nor witch hath power to charm,
> So hallow'd and so gracious is the time.

In Calabria, the Fortune's Grass 'oracle' was 'chiefly consulted on Ascension Day, when it is asked to tell the secrets confided to it by Christ when He walked upon the earth'. Again, in Sicily, the dew falling on the eve of Ascension Day had curative properties. 'At dawn both men and women eagerly washed their faces in it in order to prevent or remove common skin disorders', while bathing the buttocks paradoxically cured or stopped headaches.[76]

This is only one example of the linkage between healing and special days or seasons. We have seen that it was important to pick medicinal plants at partic-ular times, and folk-healers might acquire their powers from being born or carrying out rituals on specific days. Hucul healers were 'supposed to practise self-incantations to ensure their powers and personal security during the forth-coming year' on 4 December or 1 January. There were also propitious days for cures. 'The first Wednesday in May for example was the day in Cornwall for bathing rickety children, and on the first three Wednesdays of May children suffering from mesenteric disease are dipped' in the well at Chapell Uny. Again, in Pseudo-Apuleius, 'vervain is recommended for sore of the liver ... if taken on Midsummer Day, and lithewort ... for another complaint, if taken before the rising of the sun' in July.[77] The fifteenth-century leechbook that we have cited lays down in great detail what foods should be eaten and which avoided every month, and what time are suitable for bleeding.

More generally, there were lucky and unlucky days. There was a debate in Florence among the priors in 1454 as to when the Peace of Lodi should be proclaimed. Marco Parenti relates that he argued for Palm Sunday, the date ultimately chosen, since it 'seemed to me a day most suited to peace and augurs well'. In Scotland in the eighteenth and nineteenth centuries, it was popularly believed that 'the first day of every quarter, Midsummer and New Year's Day, are the most fortunate times for accomplishing any design'. In the medieval period, clerical authors designated certain days: 'the Egyptian Days' or 'the unfortunate days'. The basis on which this classification was made is not clear but it may bear some relationship to the Ancient Egyptian calendar. There were thirty-two such days and they fell on two or three apparently random dates during the month. We have seen that it was unlucky to be born on such a day. In the words of the fifteenth-century leechbook,

> whoso weddeth a wife on any of those days, he shall not long have joy of her. And who that taketh any great journey, shall never come back again, or some misfort-une shall befall him. And he that beginneth any great work shall never make end thereof. And he that letteth blood shall soon die.

The belief in unlucky days survived in post-Reformation Britain, and some of these days were related to the old Egyptian Days. Pennant reported, for example, in the 1760s that 'a Highlander never begins anything of conse-quence on the day of the week on which the third of May falls, which he styles ... the dismal day'. This day was still considered unlucky in the twentieth century. It was avoided 'especially for digging peat or taking an account of the sheep or cattle on a farm'. The situation was the same on the Continent. In Provence in the modern period the last three days of February and the first three days of March were unlucky, being known as 'the days of the Old Woman'. Other unlucky days nearly everywhere were Holy Innocents and Good Friday. In early modern and modern England, blacksmiths would not shoe horses on Good Friday, miners would not go down mines, and house-wives would not sweep their houses; it was also very unlucky to wash clothes or linen.[78] Elsewhere, we have seen, Good Friday was avoided when planting certain crops or weaning infants. On the other hand, bread or buns baked on Good Friday might have special preservative and curative powers.

The particular days of the week were also considered lucky or unlucky for all or some activities: ploughing, sowing, baptism, healing, for example. In fifteenth-century Florence, Mondays, Tuesdays, Fridays and Saturdays were believed to be unlucky, while Wednesdays and Sundays were days of good fortune. An English clerical text of 1502 condemned 'they which vow never to comb themselves on the Friday or not to spin on the Saturday'. Special significance, we have seen, attached to particular birthdays, and the days on which weddings were held could foretell their outcome. According to an English rhyme:

> Monday [was] for wealth,
> Tuesday for health,
> Wednesday the best day of all;
> Thursday for crosses,
> Friday for losses,
> Saturday no luck at all.[79]

All the days of the week had different associations in different places. Among the shepherds of the Coscione in Corsica, for example, 'Monday was unlucky, and no sales were ever effected on that day', and Monday was an inauspicious day for shaving in modern Ireland. But in Languedoc Monday was the best day for working in the fields. Tuesday (together with Friday) was especially unlucky in Rome and elsewhere in Italy in the nineteenth century; 'on these days no one would marry or undertake a journey, or commence work'. However, in Alsace, Tuesday was the 'lucky day' for Jewish weddings. At Sennely-en-Sologne, 'they say that husbands will have unfaithful wives if they marry on Wednesdays' and in practice weddings were only celebrated on Sundays and Tuesdays. In modern Greece people were advised not to cut their nails on a Wednesday or a Friday. In Venice, Thursdays were associated with magical activity, and especially the first Thursday of a new lunar month, and weddings were therefore not held on this day. Its association with the Crucifixion made Friday a generally inauspicious day. It was also a fast day. In an account from northern Greece, a girl 'brought eggs to her father on Friday. She felt a power pushing her from behind and the basket turned upside down so that the eggs were broken. She said it was a saint's miracle, since she had intended to eat those eggs on a Friday'. But Friday could be a propitious day for healing. In Ireland, Friday was the best day to visit 'a seventh son', and often elsewhere to collect or to administer medicines. We have seen that Saturdays were often regarded as unlucky. Normal work was not allowed on

Sundays, but there were other proscriptions. In parts of Greece, people did not bathe on Sundays, for example. The conjunction of calendar festivals and days of the week could also be of great moment. In late medieval England, 'prognostications based on the day on which festivals like Christmas or the feast of St Paul fell, were extremely common';[80] while in modern Scotland it was extremely inauspicious if Beltane fell on a Thursday.

'Cemeteries, crossroads, woods, marshes, rubbish heaps – were all places where ghosts and demons might be found and were highly favoured for the performance of magic.' These are places at the boundaries, on the edge, in the wild, and we have already encountered them and noted their role. Something more may be said about crossroads. One writer suggests that 'the crossroads was the opposite pole to the church, a place where evil spirits consorted and led people astray'. Like the other places mentioned, they were on the margins. In Rumania, gypsies, regarded as beyond the proper human pale, often camped there or by rivers or on the edge of the forest. 'Society's marginals reinforced their stigma by choosing to live in marginal, feared places'. In the Ancient world, crossroads were associated with the dark deities. Hecate was invoked at a crossroads in the *Aeneid*. On the other hand, they were guarded by the public *lares*, a custom continued perhaps in the statues of saints or crosses placed there later. There is some evidence, too, of a continuation of old precautionary rituals. In the sixth century, 'Martin of Braga mentions with dismay a habit travellers had of piling up stones into a cairn, for a sacrifice in honour of Mercury, whenever they passed a crossroads', a custom also referred to by Burchard of Worms. Criminals were executed at crossroads, and they might be buried there. Placing stones was probably related to this custom also. Plato recommends in *The Laws* that 'certain criminals should be buried at a crossroads with a stone over their heads'. In nineteenth-century Corsica, stones were accumulated where persons had been killed in the wild. Suicides were also buried at crossroads. At Myddle in the seventeenth century, when Richard Wolph poisoned himself, the coroner's inquest declared him a suicide, 'and he was buried on Myddle Hill, at that crossway'. Given all this, it is not surprising that ritual and magic should take place at crossroads. St John's Eve bonfires were lit there in Spain and Sweden. Curing procedures involved leaving objects and burying animal carcases there. In the Tenby district in the nineteenth century, women sowed hemp seed at crossroads for use in marriage divination; while in modern Greece babies were taken there to undo spells laid on them. Meetings of witches and communication with the Devil were also supposed to take place at crossroads in many parts of Europe.[81]

Direction was another factor in magic. Turning to the east, that is towards the rising sun, figures in a number of Anglo-Saxon rites. In the modern

Limousin, too, the direction of the rising sun was *jauvent* or lucky. Some folk-healers there turned east to say their prayers or charms, as did girls wanting husbands; and the heads of corpses were pointed in the same direction in their graves.[82]

The opposition between left and right was a fundamental principle in most cultures and religions. This reflects a clear distinction in the use of the two hands, the left being retained very often for dirty tasks, while the right is used for eating, greeting and sacred gestures. In the Christian scheme of things, Christ will sit at Judgment Day at the right hand of God, while the everyday clerical blessing is given with the right hand. Left and right, in Europe as else-where, were also linked to gender, the left with the female and the right with the male. The Sarum Manual, for example, directed that, when a child was brought to the church door for baptism, 'a male be set on the right of the priest: but a female on the left'. On Skara Brae in Ireland, 'the women occup-ied the left side of the fire and the men the right'. Left and right were linked, too, to moral or practical evil and good. Joan of Arc's 'voices came from her right, so she knew they were good rather than evil'. In the Pyrenees, the fairies who visited houses on New Year's Eve 'brought good fortune with their right hand and bad fortune with their left'.[83]

Magical ritual used and referred to these various meanings of the left/right polarity, with a general tendency to favour the left. An Anglo-Saxon cure for dysentery required a person to 'cut nine chips from a bramble root on to your left hand'; while to discover a thief one had to write that one had been robbed and put the message 'in your left shoe'. The remedy to make a baby's cranial suture close up in southern Italy required a ribbon to be tied round its head with the left hand. Le Père Dodu in the Valois in the nineteenth century, according to Nerval, cured cows 'by making the sign of the cross with his left foot'. At Tonnerre in the Yonne, reliquaries containing the remains of several saints were processed on the fourth Sunday after Easter. 'During this procession, the women who want to have good calves, fat pigs and cocks that crow well, hit the windows of the *châsses* and pass under them', but these procedures would only be effective, it was believed, if the left-hand sides of the reliquaries were hit and not the right-hand, and if the women approached them to go under from the left also. Left and right might also be important in harmful magic. In a case at Noville in 1607, for example, a child confessed that he had, at his mother's behest, touched a victim on the left arm.[84]

17

Magic and Religion

We have already discussed in the Introduction and elsewhere some of the problems involved in defining the spheres of religion and magic, and of distinguishing in practice between them. Always in the millennium or more that we have covered, there existed an official religious body or bodies, a Church or Churches, with clergy providing official rituals and some teaching on doctrine and morals and a view of how the universe worked and for what purpose. Alongside this were the host of rituals that we have described, performed sometimes by 'lay' people privately or collectively, sometimes by experts. These had no equivalent organized body to sustain them, and no formally worked out body of belief, no 'theology', although they were embedded in the common traditional culture and they did have their own coherence. Some people have always stressed the difference, the opposition between these two fields. The 'radical conflict of principle between magic and religion', Frazer wrote, 'sufficiently explains the relentless hostility with which the priest has often pursued the magician'. Putting the same point another way, magical rituals 'were particularly objectionable to theological opinion', a more recent student agrees, 'because they were aimed at 'coercion ... through the subversion of free will'.[1] The clergy were also jealous of their ritual role and suspicious of practices that predated Christianity and seemed to be closely allied with paganism.

There are several examples in the New Testament of the discomfiture of magicians at the hands of the Apostles: Simon Magus by St Peter, Simon in Samaria by St Philip; Elymas in Cyprus and the magicians of Ephesus by St Paul. Early medieval rulers and clergy condemned magic and laid down severe penalties for those found practising it. The Counter-Reformation Church stepped up the campaign against 'superstitious' magical practices, including the relatively new offence of demonologically inspired witchcraft, and used the Inquisitions to try to root them out. The catechism issued by the bishop of Aleria in Corsica in 1565 called typically for the laity to promise:

> We will take care not to recite the prayers sold by charlatans or taught by witches, sorcerers and other ignorant and superstitious persons. We will only say the prayers approved and confirmed by the usage of the Church.

The new Protestant clergy were even more hostile to magic (a term which they used to include many Catholic practices). 'The various kinds of superstition which prevailed here', Dr Johnson wrote of the Hebrides in 1775 – another paradigmatic case – '... are by the diligence of the Ministers almost extirpated.'[2]

In fact, however, the campaign of the Church or Churches against magic was both more fitful and more ambiguous, particularly as far as the Catholic Church was concerned. Miracles performed by the Apostles, but above all by Christ Himself, are a prominent feature of the New Testament. These were seen as magic by pagan contemporaries and were only distinguished then and later from demonic and other 'wonders' by elaborate and interested arguments. Moreover, the more hostile stance of the late antique period, represented by St Augustine, gave way to one of selectivity or the provision of approved ecclesiastical magic. There was a 'Christian remodelling of non-Christian methods of magical control'. 'We advise that none should seek anything from the soothsayers', Gregory of Tours wrote in the sixth century in connection with the miracles of St Martin, 'because they never profit the sick. For a little of the dust of the basilica [at Tours] has more power than these men with their witless remedies.' Similarly Aelfric around 1000 condemned 'magic', 'sorcery' and 'enchantments' but allowed such practices as performing certain agricultural tasks at full moon and especially charms to heal using Christian words and gestures. Many such practices encouraged by the clergy at this time were later condemned. There was also a refocusing of the Church's hostility on to magic used for selfish ends or that appeared to override free will, and a consequent acceptance of much of the magic for fertility and welfare that we have described. Stress came to be laid also on the power of the Church, clergy and saints to provide protection against or to overcome 'malevolent magic'. Such was the relative position of religion and magic with ups and downs for much of the period in question, particularly at the parish level. Peasants adopted and adapted what the clergy had to offer, and they were more attached to some kinds of their own magic than to others. As late as the 1930s, the Uniate clergy in the Carpathians had been relatively successful in 'its struggle against sorcery', but folk-healing was untouched.[3]

Again and again, we have seen that elements drawn from religion were used in popular and everyday magic all over Europe.

Just like the clerical exorcist, the sorcerer or undoer of spells used holy water and salt, multiplied signs of the cross, invoked the mysteries of the Trinity, the Incarnation and Redemption; while folk-healers muttered incantations in Latin, accompanied by quasi-sacramental gestures, and recommended religious amulets.[4]

Most obvious in Catholic areas, these practices or their equivalent are found too in the Orthodox world and survived under Protestantism.

Magical powers were ascribed at all times and places to the clergy. They were learned. They administered the sacraments and were the mediators of the religious power of the Church. From the central medieval period in the West, they were celibate. All of this lent them a charisma *ex officio*, which could extend beyond their official role. Bede recounts that when St Augustine of Canterbury and his companions first preached on the Isle of Thanet in 597, King Ethelbert made them do so 'in the open air ... for he had taken the precaution that they should not come to him in any house, lest, according to the custom of augurers, they might practise magical arts and so get the better of him'. Much later in southern Italy and elsewhere, clerics were believed to be able to control storms and repel pests, while thread from a priest's stole was used as a protective amulet and in healing. In modern Greece, priests 'can direct powers to the good ... or they can direct the powers to work evil'; in particular, they could cure those 'affected by the nereids or exotica', that is spirits of the wild. In Scandinavia, Protestant ministers were often believed to have similar or more extensive powers. Some obtained these from magical books; some could 'exorcize the Devil but [they could also] employ the Devil's services for [their] ... own purposes'.[5]

The official rituals performed by the clergy provided their own magic. The magical potential of the mass was increased by the elaboration of the doctrine of transubstantiation in the central medieval period, and the clergy connived at or encouraged magical attitudes towards the rite. There was a common belief from the late Middle Ages that seeing the sacrament was 'equivalent to tasting it'. Members of boys' confraternities in fifteenth-century Florence, for example, were made to 'attend mass every morning or at least to try to see the body of Christ'. In England and elsewhere at the same time and later 'mothers in labour could secure safe delivery, travellers safe arrival, eaters and drinkers good digestion, by gazing on the host at mass'. Beyond this there was further magical manipulation of the Catholic rite. We have seen that herbs, images and amulets were placed on, under or near altars to be imbued with power via the performance of the mass in their vicinity. The magic spear that alone could kill Lleu Llaw Gyffes in the *Mabinogion* had to be made over a year during the time 'when folk were at mass on Sunday'. A powder made of blood and hairs and used in love magic in Lucania was activated in church during the elevation at mass, when the woman using it murmured over it the formula: 'Blood of Christ, Devil, attach to me who must be so bound and let him not be split away'.[6]

Sometimes the liturgy was that associated with a particular calendar festival or rite of passage or saint. Bénigne Morant, a valet from a village in

Burgundy, 'wrote or marked certain letters or characters with the point of a pin on a laurel leaf during the divine service of the Passion [on Good Friday 1634]', claiming afterwards that it was a charm that would prevent 'a hen that ate the leaf from being killed with a shot from an arquebus'. In the Limousin in modern times, there were legends about rocks opening up to reveal treasures during the elevation at the Christmas Eve mass. Impotence could be caused, we have seen, by tying knots at the moment 'of the elevation in a nuptial mass', while in the Périgord, the 'dry mass' used in hostile magic to 'dry up' an enemy took place after churching or *relevailles*. In late medieval England, it was believed that saying or hearing masses or series of masses linked to particular saints would bring special benefits. The official rubric in the York missal, for example, promised immunity for a year from a long list of diseases and general protection against misfortune to anyone attending the mass of St Anthony.[7]

Devotion at the mass centred on the Eucharistic elements and especially the host or bread available to the laity. As the Rising Christ declares in the Chester Mystery Plays:

> I am very bread of life ...
> Who eateth that bread, man or wife,
> Shall live with me without end.
> And that bread that I you give
> Your wicked life for to amend,
> Becomes my flesh through your belief
> And doth release your sinful bond.[8]

The host was treated with the utmost care. A ninth-century penitential laid down that any portion of the consecrated host falling to the ground should be burned and the ashes concealed beneath the altar. Devotion to the host escalated in the twelfth and thirteenth centuries, and the feast of Corpus Christi was instituted in 1264. At the same time bleeding host legends proliferated, as we have seen. By the sixteenth century the host had become the supreme focus of the old religion and thus the special target of Protestant attack and iconoclasm.

The host had always been deployed for profane purposes. According to Adhemar of Chabannes in the eleventh century, Christian forces were victorious against the Saracens in a battle near Narbonne against all the odds, because they had been provided with the Eucharist. Corpus Christi processions went through the fields 'to ensure the fertility of the crops'; and consecrated hosts were used as amulets against illness and storms. Oaths were taken on the sacrament for good or nefarious purposes. The Duke of York reports in Shakespeare's *King Richard II* that

A dozen of them here have ta'en the sacrament,
And interchangeably set down their hands
To kill the king at Oxford.

In early modern Corsica 'synods forbade and threatened with the severest sanctions those who swore on the Eucharist or on the altar [by the reserved sacrament]'.[9] The sacrament was also taken through the medieval and early modern periods as a kind of ordeal to clear oneself of serious crimes, including witchcraft.

These were public or semi-public actions, but the host was also used in secret procedures. In a miracle story told by Peter Damian, a woman used a portion of the host to discover whether her husband was being unfaithful to her. Again, in a case before the Inquisition in Venice in the sixteenth century, a woman was accused of using a consecrated host, given her by a priest, in love magic. Here communicants were suspected of or confessed to retaining the host in their mouths and then keeping it to work magic. A Danish author related that down to the nineteenth century, 'the Laplanders ... took a cloth always into church with them into which they spit out the sacramental bread, which they then wrapped carefully up and divided at home into numerous small crumbs', which they fed to their livestock to secure them 'from all injury'.[10] Suspected witches were often induced in the early modern period to admit that they had retained the host in a similar way, sometimes consequently desecrating it or using it in harmful magic. In a series of paintings by Uccello, a woman again fails to swallow the host at communion and sells it to the Jews, who were supposed to use it in their rituals.

The wine of the mass, reserved to the clergy before the Reformation, did not accumulate the same popular magical aura about it. It was treated, however, with awe by the clergy. A ninth-century penitential laid down penalties for those who allowed the chalice to drip on the altar or, much worse, on the ground. In the latter case, the drops should 'be licked up with the tongue', and the floorboards scraped and the scrapings burned. John of Salisbury relates that whilst the pope was celebrating mass in the cathedral of Reims after the council there in 1148, one of his assistants

> was careless enough to spill the consecrated wine on the carpet before the altar. This gave rise to general consternation. The pope at once sent his chancellor ... to cut out the piece of carpet on which the blood of Our Lord had fallen, and place it among the relics.

A Norwegian narrative from the nineteenth century provides a rare example of popular-cum-clerical beliefs relating to the chalice in Protestant setting. A minister administering Holy Communion pushed away a woman, preventing her from taking the wine. He explained later that he had known she was a witch, because, 'when he came to the woman with the chalice, the wine rotated counter-clockwise'.[11] This also illustrates the more general point that receiving communion (in one or both kinds) represented a communion literally with one's neighbours. The witch's anti-social nature was recognized by refusing her communion from the common cup. In the same way, to voluntarily reject or pervert the host was to place oneself beyond the normal bounds and to prepare oneself as often as not to harm one's fellows.

> Holy water and similar consecrations are not called sacraments, because they do not have as a necessary consequence the conferring of grace; but they are means or dispositions for the reception of the sacraments. These dispositions consist either of warding off obstacles to their reception – thus holy water is directed against the attacks of the Devil and against venial sins – or to facilitate their accomplishment and administration – thus the altar and its paraphernalia are consecrated from respect for the Eucharist.

Thus St Thomas Aquinas distinguished between the sacraments and the elements used in them, and sacramentals, other substances and objects blessed by the clergy, such as holy water, palms and candles. As we have seen again and again, the latter were believed to possess great power and were used in a huge variety of circumstances – with clerical approval. In the words of a Württemberg preacher in 1592, 'one should seek medicine against sorcery, diabolical spirits and witchcraft ... and one should use thereby blessed salt, water, herbs, palms and candles. These things were ordained by the Christian Church for the expulsion of demons and witchcraft'. Holy water was used, for example, to repel demons, as these texts suggest, to provide general protection for houses and their occupants, byres and theirs, to cure the sick, and in love magic. Holy oil was strictly an element associated with the sacraments proper: baptism, extreme unction and ordination; but it was used like other sacramentals – this time against clerical advice. It was a feature, for example, of Venetian love magic; and it was used in the early medieval period in attempts to frustrate 'the divine judgment' supposedly expressed in officially sponsored ordeals.[12]

Church bells were a special kind of sacramental. They had a practical function 'telling the hours, announcing fire or an approaching enemy, calling the people to arms or to peaceful assemblies, telling them when to go to bed and when to get out of it, when to work [and] when to pray'. But, as the last phrase reminds us, bells also had a ritual function. A Latin verse on an English bell proclaimed: 'I praise the true God, call the people, assemble the clergy, toll for funerals, subdue the lightning, signal the Sabbath, mourn the dead, drive away the plague, and beautify festivals'; and we have come across examples of all these. Protestants sought to ban or seriously reduce the amount of bell-ringing, but this met with popular resistance. Bells were also involved in unorthodox and magical rituals other than simple ringing. We have seen that they might be 'baptized', and they might be the sources of magical material or quasi-relics, like other parts of the church and churchyard. According to a Norwegian narrative relating to around 1700, 'people say that every Easter night witches came to the church [at Brunkeberg] to scrape rust and copper off the church bell'.[13]

As Duffy has shown for late-medieval England – but the observation applies much more widely – intrinsic power was popularly attributed to certain passages of Scripture, for example the opening passage of St John's Gospel, to certain religious formulae and to certain prayers or combinations of prayers. 'Apotropaic forces were said to dwell' through the medieval period in the formula: *Christus vincit, Christus regnat, Christus imperat* from the liturgy for Lauds. The words 'were used as a spell, and rings inscribed with them were believed to protect the bearer from evil. The three clauses were sung as a charm to keep droughts and tempests away', and they were also used to cure disease. Aves, Paternosters and Creeds were regularly used in healing and other charms down the centuries. They were often said three or nine times. Multiple recitations occurred in unusual circumstances. A love charm in sixteenth-century Venice involved 'saying thirty-three Paternosters for the meanest soul that had been executed ... with my hands behind my back walking through the house with all the doors open'.[14] An old couple in the Périgord in modern times, who believed they were bewitched, were told to say 6000 Paternosters and 60,000 Aves to counter the spell.

Many of these formulae or prayers were used in a pious spirit, but deliberately unorthodox use of prayers was also reported, though far less often. The so-called White Paternoster was used in early modern England and elsewhere; this was a variable prayer-charm loosely based on the Lord's Prayer. In the Périgord, conjurors omitted the name of the Holy Ghost from invocations of the Trinity, substituting that of saints, for example: 'In the name of the Father, the Son and of St Peter and St Paul'. Prayers were also said backwards, especially the Paternoster. The rosary of course was used to say multiple prayers for orthodox purposes, but unorthodox use was also made of it and irregular rosaries are also occasionally reported. Searches at Amiens in the early eighteenth century, for example, discovered 'certain little rosaries made with hemp or silk, of horsehair and feathers', which were believed to be employed in witchcraft. In Venice, Paternosters were said with a crossless rosary in a love magic rite, but leaving out the clause: 'Lead us not into temptation'. The rosary was then thrown over the shoulders and Judas invoked. In a Greek folk-song from Calabria, a girl, bettered by another in love, says 'that she will put up a vow in a chapel, so as to be enabled' to damage her rival. The ex-voto is here being used like a curse tablet.[15]

Finally, we may point to instances in which religious ritual was used by those accused of witchcraft, often demonic. So the 'witch' of Jasmin in nineteenth-century Languedoc takes refuge at the shrine of Roquefort dedicated to St Peter, and she also went on the Marian pilgrimage of the Bon-Encontre. In a trial at Vesoul in the 1620s, Claudine Oudet said that she had been told that a talisman with the *Agnus Dei* in it could save a witch from being arrested by the court authorities. She had also been induced to believe that re-confirmation by the bishop could reverse her dedication to witchcraft, 'but it was necessary to know where the Devil had touched her, so as to put the holy chrism in the same spot'.[16]

The aim of Ancient Roman religion was to maintain good relations with the powers that controlled the universe, 'the mysterious impersonal life-giving and death-dealing powers ... The former they sought to keep kindly; the latter they sought to drive away. Their rites were what are called magical'.[17] The advent of Christianity brought little change to the function of religion as far as most people were concerned. The clergy provided general rituals which maintained a right relationship with the mysterious powers, as well as rites of passage and other more specific rituals to ensure the fertility of the fields, the health of humans and livestock and so on. These were selected from, appropriated and adapted to suit the needs and purposes of peasants. They had a symbiotic relationship with other, older more purely magical rites, whose primary functions they shared. The personal element in popular Christianity very often consisted of a relationship with a saint or saints, conceived of as helpful or dangerous 'godlings' to be cajoled, coerced or placated. Of course, a minority, clerical and lay, had a different view of Christianity and exemplified a more 'spiritual' religiosity, and this minority sought to impose its view and spread its spirituality through the centuries, bearing down on what it regarded as 'superstitions'. But its success was limited and slow, and only came to fruition with the virtual demise of Christianity itself in Europe in the twentieth century.

Many basic features of Catholic Christianity in particular enabled or encouraged the symbiosis with magic. Medieval and later Catholicism perceived 'grace' as a substance placed within the elements of the sacraments rather like 'mana'. Again, the effect of the words and gestures of the sacramental liturgies, the mass, baptism and so on, was automatic.[18] These were magical traits. Moreover, the Church promoted the idea of miracles, supernatural events brought about by God directly or through the saints, and not easy for the simple mind to distinguish from the accomplishments or claimed accomplishments of magicians. Christianity also shared with magic the mentality which excluded accidents from the explanation of day-to-day events. Divine Providence filled the same role as magical intervention.

On a more superficial level, members of the clergy themselves believed in magic and some of them practised it or consulted those who did. Guido Ruggiero has told the story of Fra Aurelio, a renegade cleric in sixteenth-century Venice, who made a living from doing predictions, love magic and healing. He was patronized, it seems, by rich and poor. He was by no means alone either in Venice at that time or in Europe much more generally. Fra Basileo da Parma was examined by the Inquisition at Bologna in 1584. His former superior acknowledged 'that he is famous for expelling spirits', but since he was 'ignorant and led rather a low life', the superior suspected, along with others, that he might have 'some Key of Solomon or pact with the demon or some other special secret for discovering spirits'. This is as valuable as an indicator of the superior's views as it is of Fra Basileo's behaviour. Clerical involvement in magic was not confined either to Catholics, rene-gades or the ignorant. In sixteenth-century Brandenburg-Ansbach, the Protestant clergy and their wives freely consulted cunning folk. In 1732, the wife of the vicar of Sustead in Norfolk went 'to the cunning man, about her being a widow, and what sort of husband she should have', thus anticipating her husband's death. We have seen that divination with the Bible and by other means was practised by the upper clergy in the medieval period and later. A group of Jesuits on their way to the Far East 'tossed tiny talismans made from the wax from the paschal candles of Rome into the stormy seas as they rounded the Cape of Good Hope in 1578', trusting that they would have an assuaging effect. Such attitudes survived into stricter modern times. Douglas recounts that the bishop of Pozzuoli in Calabria in the 1890s, 'among hundreds of other clients, was wont to drive up' to the door of a *santa* in Naples, 'once a week for a consultation'.[19]

Magical rites accompanied all the activities of everyday life from cooking and child-rearing to the major agricultural tasks. All the events of the life cycle, weddings, births and deaths, were marked and surrounded by a complex of protective gestures and words. Illness of all kinds was similarly diagnosed and treated via magical means. Always the aim was to guard over, to ensure fertility and well-being, and to keep at bay the forces that threatened disaster or death. The universe was hostile, but it was not inanimate or indifferent. It was informed by forces of various kinds, impersonal and personal, that could be influenced or manipulated. Magical ritual here operated on the general principle of sympathy, but it was eclectic, taking in features from religion, as we have seen, or even invading or colonizing religion itself. More fundament-ally, magic used substances and objects from everyday life: bodily fluids or excreta, animal parts, salt and iron, tools, fire and water, transforming them into its own 'sacramental' elements. It also transformed words and gestures, lending them special significance and power.

Magic in all this was not a marginal activity or an esoteric mind-set, though it had its occult aspects. Magical ritual was central to the concerns of most people and magical thought was in the mainstream of both elite and popular mentalities. There were learned and unlearned kinds of magic, and we have focused on the latter, but they operated on the same principles and they over-lapped. Only in the modern period did any serious or widespread scepticism about magic arise, abandoning it to the mainly rural working population. Over the centuries till our time, magic was perennial, relatively unchanging, relating to a world that was relatively unchanging as far as agriculture, the life-cycle and illness in particular were concerned. Only with the advent of new technological and 'scientific' controls over these spheres of life, did the magical universe lose its meaning and disappear.

Notes

INTRODUCTION

1. Orwell, *Collected Essays*, p. 181.
2. Lévy-Bruhl, pp. 58–9.
3. Frazer, p. 11; Mauss (1972), pp. 64, 73, 51–2 and 102; Blum, pp. 249–50.
4. Pina-Cabral, p. 197.
5. Mauss (1972), pp. 12 and 88–9; Frazer, p. 50; Bendix, p. 88; Durkheim, p. 44.
6. Mauss (1972), pp. 40, 124 and 54; Blum, p. 244.
7. Mauss (1972), pp. 51, 70, and 44; Raglan, p. vii.
8. Febvre (1957), pp. 293–300; Valéry, p. 28.
9. Laget (1982), p. 13.
10. 'They have banished the demons and the fairies:/The graces are stifled under reason's sway,/And hand our hearts over to insipidness;/Sadly reasoning gains credit day by day;/Everyone, alas, runs after the truth:/Ah! believe me, error has its merits.' Voltaire, 'Ce qui plaît aux dames' (1764), *Oeuvres complètes*, X, p. 19.

CHAPTER 1

1. Varagnac, p. 189.
2. Kligman (1988), p. 31.
3. E. Estyn Evans, pp. 30 and 41.
4. Merrifield, pp. 187–8; Frazer, p. 151; E. Estyn Evans, p. 213; Howard.
5. Maxwell, p. 10; Poueigh, p. 146.
6. Scribner, p. 43; E. Estyn Evans, p. 99.
7. Elliott, p. 259; Benoît, p. 77; Goursaud, 3, p. 725.
8. Gallop (1930), p. 176; E. Estyn Evans, pp. 68 and 71; Trefor M. Owen (1991), p. 24; Pina-Cabral, p. 39.
9. Benoît, pp. 109–10.
10. Salomone-Marino, p. 63; Pina-Cabral, p. 41; Benoît, pp. 83 and 87; Banks, II, p. 55.
11. Fabre-Vassas, pp. 426ff.
12. Casta (1965a), p. 115; Dickens, *Pickwick Papers*, p. 366; Poueigh, pp. 34–5; W.J. Rose (ed.), p. 47.
13. K.M. Briggs (1959), pp. 14 and 19–20.
14. Goodrich-Freer, pp. 260–1; Poueigh, p. 81; Riché (1981), p. 132; Thuillier, p. 215.
15. Douglas (1923), p. 143; Jolas, p. 12.
16. Cit. Flint, p. 205; Stahl, pp. 152–3; Gélis (1984), p. 93; Goursaud, III, pp. 643 and 641; K.M. Briggs (1953), p. 456.
17. Hole (1975), p. 37; Benoît, p. 273; Storms, pp. 74–5.
18. H.E. Davidson (1993), p. 39; Storms, pp. 172–7; E. Estyn Evans, pp. 100–1.
19. Guillaumin, *Life of a Simple Man*, p. 156.
20. Storms, p. 177; Lebrun, p. 463; E. Estyn Evans, p. 142.
21. Thiriat, pp. 457–8; E. Estyn Evans, pp. 142 and 270; Rocal, p. 124.
22. James Boswell, *Journal of a Tour to the Hebrides*, p. 214; S. Johnson. *Journey to the Western*

Islands, p. 742; G. Rose, pp. 87ff.

23. Trefor M. Owen (1991), pp. 12ff; Banks, II, pp. 12–13 and 10; C. Leroy, p. 239; Joutard, p. 154.

24. F.M. McNeill, II, pp. 161ff; E. Estyn Evans, p. 142; Poueigh, p. 96.

25. Virgil, *Georgics*, Book I, vv. 347–50, I, pp. 104–5; Claude Gauchet, cit. Sébillot (1968), III, p. 465; Salomone-Marino, pp. 75–8; Carmichael, cit. E. Estyn Evans, p. 160.

26. E. Estyn Evans, pp. 188–9; T. Davidson (1957–8), p. 246.

27. Cit. Williams, Introduction, Thomas Platter (junior), *Travels in England*, p. 108; Bushaway (1982), p. 126; Trefor M. Owen (1991), pp. 12ff.

28. Varagnac, p. 25; Sydow, p. 98.

29. Cit. Hutton (1996), p. 343; Mistral, *Mémoires et récits*, p. 18; Kvideland and Sehmsdorf (eds), p. 234; Devos, p. 138.

30. Beauquier, p. 358; Trefor M. Owen (1991), p. 15; William Cole, *Blecheley Diary*, p. 75.

31. Propertius, Book IV, ii, Trans. A.E. Watts, p. 144; Joan Evans, pp. 84–5; Frazer, p. 481; E. Estyn Evans, p. 160; Salomone-Marino, pp. 59–61; Mistral, *Mirèio*, pp. 122–3.

32. Grenadou and Prévost, p. 157.

33. Frazer, pp. 530–1; Moiset, pp. 26–7; Sébillot (1968), III, pp. 38–9; Shakespeare, *As You Like It*, Act III, Sc. II, p. 69; Camporesi (1988), p. 97.

34. Sébillot (1968), III, pp. 310–12; Cocchiara, p. 161.

35. Montaigne, *Journal de voyage en Italie*, p. 138; Blum, p. 94.

36. Webb and Walker (eds), p. 71; De Rosa, pp. 252–3.

37. Christian (1981b), pp. 60–1; T. Johnson, p. 197.

38. Rocal, pp. 139–41; Camporesi (1988), p. 80; Durbec, pp. 265–8.

39. Cohen, p. 13.

40. Cit. Luck, p. 197; Kieckhefer, p. 177; cit. E. Peters (1978), p. 170; Finot, pp. 47–8.

41. Reymond, pp. 84–5; Ginzburg (1983), p. 29; Sébillot (1968), III, p. 461; Barbey d'Aurevilly, *L'Ensorcelée*, p. 240.

42. Tibullus, I, viii, pp. 234–5; Lévi-Strauss, p. 111; W. Scott, *Demonology and Witchcraft*, pp. 231–2.

43. Foster (1965), p. 296.

44. Jolas and Zonabend, p. 141.

CHAPTER 2

1. Frazer, p. 322.

2. Ovid, *Fasti*, pp. 42–3; H.E. Davidson (1993), p. 93.

3. Varagnac, p. 140.

4. Benoît, p. 218; Mistral, *Mirèio*, pp. 488–9; Thomas Platter (junior), *Journal of a Younger Brother*, pp. 146–7 and 268.

5. Camporesi (1988), p. 263.

6. Bushaway (1982), pp. 157–8.

7. Beauquier, pp. 669–70; Hole (1975), p. 16.

8. Pina-Cabral, pp. 122–3; Poueigh, pp. 242–3; Flint, p. 192.

9. Banks, II, pp. 60–1 and 52–3.

10. Hutton (1994), pp. 16–17; Hole (1975), p. 23.

11. Duffy, pp. 15–18; Vloberg (1936), pp. 23–7.

12. Trefor M. Owen (1973).

13. Hole (1975), p. 41; F.M. McNeill, II, p. 45.

14. Goursaud, II, pp. 413–14; Varagnac, p. 109.

15. Frazer, p. 610; Beauquier, p. 109; J. Larner (1965), p. 121.

16. Rocal, p. 149; Duffy, p. 26.

17. Brenan, pp. 59–60; Casta (1965b); Trefor M. Owen (1987), p. 84; Rocal, p. 125.

18. Poueigh, p. 215; cit. Tyack, p. 31.
19. Chouraqui (1979), pp. 154–5; Dimnet, *My Old World*, p. 91.
20. Traimond, p. 163; Hole (1975), pp. 41–2; Bushaway (1995), pp. 205–6.
21. Beauquier, pp. 304–5; Montaigne, *Journal de voyage en Italie*, pp. 270 and 272.
22. Hole (1975), p. 64.
23. Cit. Le Roux, p. 181; F.M. McNeill, II, p. 68; Thomas Pennant (1769), cit. Youngson (ed.), pp. 135–6; Banks, II, pp. 225–6.
24. Cit. Trefor M. Owen (1987), pp. 97–8.
25. Shakespeare, *Measure for Measure*, Act III, Sc. II, p. 91; Gueusquin-Barbichon, pp. 33–4; Beauquier, pp. 307–8.
26. Klauser, p. 89; Gallop (1961), p. 162; cit. Page, p. 184.
27. Beauquier, pp. 308–9; Salomone-Marino, p. 142.
28. Hutton (1994), p. 105; Articles of Visitation for the Diocese of London, 1601, Kennedy, III, p. 337; Nelson, *Festivals and Fasts of the Church of England*, p. 425.
29. McClatchey, p. 30; William Cole, *Blecheley Diary*, p. 46; Woodforde, *Diary*, pp. 161–2.
30. Kligman (1981), pp. 2 and passim.
31. Burke, p. 181; Brenan, p. 104.
32. Belmont (1971), pp. 99–100; Goursaud, II, pp. 454–6; F.M. McNeill, II, p. 91. E. Estyn Evans, p. 275.
33. Frazer, p. 630; Poueigh, p. 226.
34. Stow, *Survey of London*, p. 126; Beard, p. 25.
35. N. Sykes, cit. McClatchey, p. 86; Vloberg (1936), pp. 178–9.
36. E. Estyn Evans, p. 73.
37. *Manners and Customs* (1827), p. 253; Hole (1975), p. 98; Swift, *Journal to Stella*, II, pp. 404–5; Cowper, *Letters*, p. 216.
38. Hutton (1996), p. 362.
39. *Lives of the Desert Fathers*, p. 86; Vauchez (1981), p. 543; Le Braz (1937), p. 57.
40. Christian (1981b), pp. 115–17; Banks, II, pp. 150ff; Beauquier, p. 508.
41. Barbin and Duteil, p. 249; Raison-du-Cleuziou; Le Braz (1900), pp. xi–xiv; Stendhal, *Mémoires d'un touriste*, II, p. 20.
42. Le Roy Ladurie (1981), pp. 102–3 and 295–6; Salomone-Marino, pp. 73–4.
43. Spranger, p. 307; Moss and Cappannari (1953), pp. 320–2.
44. Rocal, pp. 187–8; F.M. McNeill, II, p. 105ff.
45. Mellot, pp. 291–2; Poueigh, p. 204; Origo (1970), p. 209.
46. Schama, pp. 177 and 607; Pepys, *Diary* (1662), p. 10; G. Huxley, p. 89.
47. Storms, pp. 176–7; cit. Runeberg, p. 201; J. Larner (1965), pp. 120–1; Trigg, p. 199.
48. Saintyves (1935), p. 31.
49. Chaucer, Prologue, *The Pardoner's Tale*, *Complete Works*, p. 149; and *The Canterbury Tales*, Penguin, p. 260; cit. Godin, p. 361; Ozment (1975), p. 33.
50. St. Bernard, *On the Christian Year*, p. 20; St Bernard, 'In Praise of the New Chivalry', in Herlihy (ed.) (1970), p. 298; cit. Karrer (ed.), p. 3; Casta (1965a), p. 130.

CHAPTER 3

1. Giovanni Levi, pp. 125–6; Guillaumin, *Life of a Simple Man*, p. 116; Bloch (1961–4), p. 216.
2. Clare, *The Shepherd's Calendar*, p. 2; Hermann, p. 58; Poueigh, p. 56.
3. Goursaud, II, pp. 439–40 and 486–7; and III, pp. 583–6; Banks, II, p. 26.
4. Hermann, p. 124; Canziani (1928b), p. 94.
5. Canziani (1928b), p. 89; Banks, II, p. 143; Beauquier, p. 100.
6. Bollême, p. 56; Mellot, pp. 291–2; Banks, II, pp. 140–1.
7. Canziani (1928b), p. 92; Simon, p. 137.
8. Gallop (1961), p. 54; Boussel, pp. 107–8; cit. Gélis (1984), p. 528; Shakespeare, *Pericles*, Act

III, Sc. I, p. 82.

9. Shakespeare, *Macbeth*, Act II, Sc. IV, p. 69; St Bonaventura, *Life of St Francis*, Karrer (ed.), p. 163; Saintyves (1935), pp. 15–16; Sabean, p. 65.
10. Rocal, p. 101; Carmichael, p. 42; Joseph Greene, *Correspondence*, pp. 124 and 136.
11. Mauriac, *Second Thoughts*, pp. 170–1.
12. Shakespeare, *King Lear*, Act III, Sc. IV, pp. 87–8; Benoît, pp. 256–7; Lawson, p. 52; Canziani (1928b), pp. 70–1 and 308–9.
13. Hesiod, *Theogony*, p. 15; H.E. Davidson (1993), p. 80; Lawson, pp. 51–2; *The Book of Job*, Chapter 37.
14. Margery Kempe, p. 239; Tusser, *Five Hundred Points of Good Husbandry*, p. 192; Cohn, p. 307; cit. Brayshaw, pp. 46 and 51; Kilvert, *Diary*, pp. 204–5.
15. Cit. Manning, p. 89; Montaigne, *Essays*, I, p. 164; Ozment (1975), pp. 94–5; Macfarlane, p. 189; Schama, p. 27; Villari, pp. 155, 413 and 640.
16. Cit. E. Peters (1978), p. 96; Flynn, p. 40.
17. John Capgrave, *The Life of St Norbert*, p. 52; Joisten, pp. 278–9; F.M. McNeill, II, pp. 20–1; Gallop (1930), p. 168; K.M. Briggs (1959), p. 45; Orme, p. 82.
18. Bede, *Ecclesiastical History*, p. 25; Le Roy Ladurie (1980), pp. 293 and 322; Saintyves (1935), p. 61; cit. Manning, pp. 90–1; Ronsard, *Oeuvres complètes*, II, pp. 167–70; Canziani (1928b), pp. 70–2 and 308–9.
19. Canziani (1928b), pp. 71–2.
20. Lucan, *The Civil War*, Book VI, lines 461ff, pp. 338–41; Flint, pp. 110–11; *Malleus Maleficarum*, Part II, Question 1, Chapter XV; Shakespeare, *Macbeth*, Act I, Sc. I and Sc. III; and Act IV, Sc. I, pp. 3, 11–14 and 109–10.
21. Bavoux (1956), p. 176; Ginzburg (1983), p. 121; Levack, p. 198; Klaniczay (1990b), p. 161.
22. Elias Owen, p. 219; Muchembled (1979), p. 240; C. Larner (1984), pp. 16–17.
23. W.L. Strauss (ed.), Figure 29 (1500), pp. 92–3; Marrow and Shestack (eds), Figures 18A (1510) and 18B (1523), pp. 116–17 and 119; Cyrano de Bergerac, *Les Etats et Empires de la Lune* (1657), cit, Sébillot (1968), I, p. 99; Shakespeare, *The Tempest*, Act I, Sc. II, pp. 22–3.
24. Christian (1981b), p. 30; Sébillot (1968), I, p. 110; Synge, *The Aran Islands*, p. 53.
25. Lawson, p. 56; Dodds (1973), p. 145; Blum, p. 369; Poueigh, p. 204; Dawes and Baynes (eds), pp. 21–3; McCulloh, p. 149.
26. Hole (1975), pp. 88–9; Sébillot (1968), I, p. 103; Christian (1981b), pp. 33–5; Margery Kempe, pp. 123–4.
27. Benoît, p. 229.
28. Steer, plate 152, pp. 182–6.
29. Bloch (1989), p. 42; Le Roy Ladurie (1983), p. 63; Joisten, p. 334.
30. Pseudo-Apuleius, cit. Delatte, p. 133.
31. *The Saga of Gisli*, p. 27; Sébillot (1968), I, p. 102; Frazer, p. 81; Fielding, *The Journal of a Voyage to Lisbon*, pp. 225 and 272.
32. *The Mabinogion*, pp. 159–61; J.T. McNeill (1933), p. 459; Sébillot (1968), II, pp. 229–30; Regné, pp. 487 and 497; Addison, *Selections from The Spectator*, note by editor, p. 478; Reymond, pp. 84–5.
33. Thomas Platter (junior), *Travels in England*, p. 189; Sébillot (1968), II, p. 224; J.T. McNeill and Gamer (eds), p. 341; Beza, pp. 27–8.
34. Zguta (1977a), pp. 225ff.
35. Aubrey, *Three Prose Works*, pp. 255–8; Opie, No. 435, pp. 360–1; Gaboriau, p. 3; Canziani (1928b), p. 71; De Martino, pp. 48ff; Deonna, pp. 27–8.
36. Benoît, pp. 272–3.
37. Webster and Ford, *Plays*, p. 83; Kieckhefer, p. 45; Canziani (1928b), p. 310.
38. Wickersheimer, p. 374; Bouchard, p. 318.
39. Peacock, p. 37; Moiset, pp. 119–21; Goursaud, III, p. 577.
40. Flint, p. 190; Zonabend (1980), p. 102; Lebrun, pp. 456 and 458; cit. Elias Owen, p. 173; Hoffmann, p. 25.

41. McManners, pp. 14–15; Zika, pp. 33–5.
42. Rocal, pp. 126–8; Hufton, p. 366.
43. More, *Utopia* and *A Dialogue of Comfort*, p. 193; Chanaud, p. 74; Mme de Sévigné, *Letters*, 19 June and 7 August 1675, pp. 123–4 and 132.
44. Rocal, pp. 103–2; Mauriac, *Second Thoughts*, p. 172.
45. Abray, p. 28.
46. Lebrun, p. 463; Chanaud, p. 101.
47. Rocal, pp. 134–5; Brenan, pp. 107–8; Henri Estienne, cit. Delumeau, p. 102; Bourgeaux, pp. 356–7.
48. Cit. Devos, pp. 139–40; Southwell Colucci, p. 154; Rocal, pp. 136–7.
49. Froeschlé-Chopard (1974), p. 95.
50. Bordes, pp. 386–7; cit. Saintyves (1935), p. 22; Fribourg, p. 359.
51. Lady Tennyson, *Journal*, May 1869, p. 292; Keynes, *The Gates of Memory*, p. 8.
52. Eire, p. 9; cit. Duffy, pp. 437–8; Martinengo-Cesaresco, pp. 169–70.
53. Rocal, pp. 149–50; Varagnac, pp. 226–7; Mérimée, *Notes d'un voyage en Corse*, pp. 715–16; Belmont (1973), pp. 99–100; Canziani (1928a), p. 211; Froeschlé-Chopard (1974), p. 90; Christian (1981b), pp. 190–1.
54. Pinard, p. 240; Moiset, p. 121; Goursaud, III, p. 576.
55. Origo (1963), p. 167; Brenan, p. 107.
56. Delehaye, p. 312; Manning, p. 129; Pourrat, p. 153; Dancu, p. 34; Saintyves (1935), p. 5.
57. Cocchiara, p. 154; *Ex-voto du terroir marseillais*, No. 97, p. 97; Bower, p. 37.
58. Cit. Christian (1981b), p. 128; cit. Lacroix, p. 223; Origo (1963), pp. 5 and 178.
59. Goursaud, III, pp. 578 and 722.
60. Bede, *Ecclesiastical History*, pp. 184–5; Vicaire, p. 255.
61. Guesquin-Barbichon, p. 42; Ashby, p. 97.
62. Christian (1981b), p. 49; cit. Saintyves (1935), p. 19; Cervantes, *Don Quixote*, I, p. 418.
63. Villari, pp. 306–1, 464 and 467; Trexler (1972).
64. Clay (ed.) (1965), p. 106; Brandon-Albini, p. 50; Moss and Cappannari (1960). p. 100.
65. Benoît, p. 245; Sébillot (1968), II, pp. 376–8; Saintyves (1935), p. 4.
66. Loubet, plate 3, p. 218; Saintyves (1935), p. 23.
67. Martinengo-Cesaresco, p. 150; 1834 account, cit. Raison-du-Cleuziou, p. 293.

CHAPTER 4

1. E. Estyn Evans, p. 42; Benoît, p. 48; Ford, *Gatherings from Spain*, pp. 140–1; Gallop (1930), p. 253; Poueigh, p. 37; K. Thomas (1984), pp. 70–1; Salomone-Marino, pp. 226–7.
2. F. Thompson, *Lark Rise to Candleford*, p. 26; Cervantes, *Don Quixote*, I, p. 161; St Charles of Sezze, *Autobiography*, p. 23; Hélias, *The Horse of Pride*, p. 59; Poueigh, p. 143.
3. Beauquier, pp. 663 and 2–3; E. Estyn Evans, p. 117.
4. Banks, II, pp. 197–8; Poueigh, p. 205; Fabre-Vassas.
5. W.J. Rose (ed.), p. 138.
6. Salomone-Marino, pp. 142–4; Alford (1932), p. 50.
7. Pourrat, p. 58; Gallop (1930), p. 225.
8. Cit. Goursaud, II, p. 523.
9. F.M. McNeill, II, p. 84; Poueigh, p. 231.
10. Hole (1975), pp. 13–14; Francis Jones, pp. 106–7; Trefor M. Owen (1991), p. 77; Sébillot (1968), II, pp. 289–91, citing an eighteenth-century text; Pasternak, *An Essay in Autobiography*, p. 39.
11. Boccaccio, *Decameron*, III, p. 35; Origo (1970), p. 209; Beauquier, p. 13; Cornelisen, pp. 260–1; Story, *Roba di Roma*, II, p. 232; Lisón-Tolosana (1966), p. 304.
12. Bouchard, pp. 299–300; Gallop (1961), pp. 132–3; Ford, *Gatherings from Spain*, p. 141.
13. Pourrat, p. 58; Guesquin-Barbichon, p. 42; Benoît, pp. 243–4.
14. Sedgewick, pp. 180–2; Le Braz (1937), pp. 156–7; C. Leroy, pp. 230–5.

15. Brenan, pp. 60–1; Mistral, *Mémoires et récits*, p. 290; Bertrand-Rousseau, p. 107.
16. Sébillot (1968), III, pp. 107–9; Gallop (1961), pp. 137–8; E. Estyn Evans, pp. 268–9.
17. Casta (1974), p. 69; Story, *Roba di Roma*, II, p. 231; Dancu, p. 35.
18. F.M. McNeill, II, pp. 61–4 and 97; Banks, II, pp. 9 and 15; Bertrand-Rousseau, p. 107.
19. Fermor, pp. 180–1; Canziani (1928b), p. 2; Gallop (1961), p. 60; Clare, *The Shepherd's Calendar*, p. 35; Ford, *Gatherings from Spain*, pp. 86–7; Poueigh, p. 94.
20. E. Estyn Evans, p. 98; Benoît, p. 78.
21. Moiset, pp. 125–6; Sébillot (1968), III, p. 31; Banks, II, p. 22.
22. Cit. Rivals, p. 163; Cocchiara, pp. 159–60; Poueigh, p. 134.
23. Cit. Sébillot (1968), III, p. 36.
24. F.M. McNeill, II, p. 106; cit. Bushaway (1995), p. 211.
25. Rocal, p. 120; cit. Sébillot (1968), III, p. 135; Traimond, p. 77; Elias Owen, p. 245.
26. E. Estyn Evans, p. 304; Bouchard, p. 364; Moulis, p. 125; Le Braz (1937), p, 156.
27. Vuillier, p. 183; Chaucer, Prologue, *The Pardoner's Tale, Complete Works*, pp. 148–9.
28. *The Dialogues of Sulpicius Severus*, Hoare (ed.), pp. 114–15.
29. Coulton (1944), p. 181; Riché (1978), p. 144; J.T. McNeill and Gamer (eds), p. 331; Gurdon; D. Edmondes Owen, pp. 111–12; cit. Gallop (1930), p. 223.
30. Hair (ed.), p. 209; Bushaway (1995), p. 198.
31. Clark and Morgan, pp. 35–6; cit. Newman, p. 27; Fincham, p. 121; W.G. Black, p. 74.
32. C. Larner (1983), p. 180; E.P. Evans, pp. 138–9; Sabean, Ch. 6.
33. Simpson, p. 67; *The Dialogues of Sulpicius Severus*, Hoare (ed.), pp. 104–6; Cagnat, pp. 165–8; Poly and Bournazel, p. 315; Scribner, p. 11.
34. Christian (1972), p. 193; Fels et al., p. 16; G.E. Evans (1967), pp. 240ff; G.E. Evans (1971), pp. 204ff; E. Porter, pp. 55–9; Kvideland and Sehmsdorf (eds), p. 188.
35. G.E. Evans (1967), pp. 263–4; G.E. Evans (1971), pp. 214–16; Albert-Llorca, p. 24; Poueigh, p. 46.
36. W. Scott, *Demonology and Witchcraft*, p. 273; *Malleus Maleficarum*, pp. 144–7; C. Larner (1983), pp. 121–2.
37. Ronsard, Ode 14, Book II, *Oeuvres complètes*, pp. 451–2.
38. Muchembled (1979), p. 244; *Malleus Maleficarum*, pp. 189–90; Guazzo, *Compendium Maleficarum*, p. 23; J.T. McNeill and Gamer (eds), p. 349; Goodrich-Freer, p. 275; W.J. Rose (ed.), p. 137; Sebald, p. 186; Favret-Saada, p. 135; Blum, pp. 76 and 97.
39. G.F. Black (1938), p. 81; T. Davidson (1958), p. 23; Henri Pourrat, *Gaspard des Montagnes* (1922), cit. Evemy, p. 31.
40. Leproux (1954), p. 247; Goursaud, II, p. 443; Banks, II, pp. 42 and 98.
41. F.M. McNeill, II, pp. 63–4; Kvideland and Sehmsdorf (eds), pp. 52–3.
42. James Boswell, *Journal of a Tour to the Hebrides*, p. 87; Opie (1989), no. 116, p. 137; T. Davidson (1958), p. 28; Frazer, p. 119; E. Estyn Evans, pp. 303–4.
43. E. Estyn Evans, pp. 304–5.
44. Anne Wilson, p. 142; Goubert (1968), p. 143; W.J. Rose (ed.), p. 141.
45. Lisón-Tolosana (1973), p. 832; Favret-Saada, pp. 146–7.

CHAPTER 5

1. Tusser, *Five Hundred Points of Good Husbandry*, p. 25; cit. Gélis (1984), p. 25; Laget (1982), p. 97.
2. Saintyves (1935), p. 31; *La Gazette des Tribunaux*, 8 August 1834; Cobb, p. 205.
3. Fermor, pp. 42–3.
4. Varagnac, p. 75; Frazer, p. 299; Gallop (1961); Roubin, p. 168; E. Estyn Evans, p. 273.
5. Frazer, p. 406.
6. F.M. McNeill, II, pp. 104–5.
7. Salomone-Marino, pp. 91–3 and 126–9.

8. Kligman (1981), p. 137; E. Estyn Evans, p. 10; Schnucker, p. 638; St Augustine, *The City of God*, book VI, ch. 9, pp. 244–5.
9. Lea (1939), III, p. 1107.
10. Thiriat, p. 453.
11. Synge, *The Aran Islands*, p. 122; Kostic, pp. 152–3; cit. Flandrin, p. 174; cit. Abray, p. 218; Psalms, 127, v. 5; and 218, v. 3; Schnucker, p. 642; Wyatt-Brown, p. 205.
12. Douglas (1948), p. 80; Zmigrodzki, p. 389; Pina-Cabral, p. 124.
13. Ravis-Giordani, p. 12; cit. Martynova, pp. 171–2; E. Estyn Evans, p. 10; Leproux (1959), p. 3; Goursaud, IV, p. 290; Shakespeare, *King Lear*, Act I, Sc. IV, pp. 48–9.
14. F. Thompson, *Lark Rise to Candleford*, p. 429.
15. Shahar, p. 12; Dilys Powell, pp. 133–4; Maraspini, p. 248.
16. Djilas, p. 104; Grenadou and Prévost, p. 155; Kligman (1988), p. 44; Klapisch-Zuber (1985b), p. 102.
17. Douglas (1948), p. 215; St Charles of Sezze, *Autobiography*, p. 205; Gaspar, p. 23; B. Rowland (ed.), p. 35; Laget (1982), p. 87; Klapisch-Zuber (1985b), pp. 101–2.
17. Cit. Bollême, p. 34; Hunt, p. 233.
19. *Malleus Maleficarum*, p. 143; Pentikäinen, p. 57.
20. McClaren, pp. 107–8.
21. Farge, p. 19; Zmigrodzki, p. 389.
22. Graef, I, pp. 60–1; Blum, p. 260; cit. Gélis, Laget and Morel, p. 28.
23. Gallop (1961), p. 98; Martinengo-Cesaresco, pp. 191–2.
24. Goursaud, II, p. 437; Kligman (1988), p. 331; Hole (1975), p. 58.
25. Benoît, p. 273; Sébillot (1968), IV, p. 56; cit. E. Estyn Evans, p. 286.
26. Bollême, pp. 160–1; Eliade (1975), p. 163; Sébillot (1968), IV, p. 138; Benoît, p. 247.
27. K.M. Briggs (1953), p. 461; Ford, *Gatherings from Spain*, p. 271.
28. Cit. Dorson, p. 20; Beauquier, p. 625; Goursaud, II, pp. 334–6.
29. Cit. Howlett, p. 112; J.T. McNeill and Gamer (eds), p. 331; Le Roy Ladurie (1980), p. 289.
30. Stevenson, pp. 43 and 173.
31. Cressy (1997), p. 338.
32. Cit. F. Wilson (ed.), p. 70; cit. Hole (1953), pp. 17–18; Cressy (1997), p. 352; Howlett, pp. 118–19.
33. Kligman (1988), pp. 99 and 107ff; Goursaud, II, p. 359; N.Z. Davis (1985), p. 18; Gallop (1961), p. 93; Brandon-Albini, pp. 58–9.
34. Cressy (1997), p. 357; E. Estyn Evans, p. 288; Gaspar, p. 19; Howlett, pp. 118–19.
35. Sébillot (1968), II, p. 232; Goursaud, II, p. 491.
36. Blum, p. 18; Gallop (1961), p. 86; E. Porter, p. 7.
37. Varagnac, p. 80; Trigg, p. 203; Faulkner, *The Hamlet*, pp. 215–16.
38. Origo (1963), p. 165; Prescott (ed.), p. 214; Gaspar, p. 22; Cockayne (ed.), II, p. 329.
39. Crawley, p. 97; H. Leyser, p. 122; Laget (1982), p. 39; cit. Goubert (1973), p. 281; Gaspar, p. 24; cit. Hunt, p. 39.
40. Hole (1954), p. 11; Le Braz (1900), p. 305; Goursaud, II, p. 291; Chanaud, p. 54; Pourrat, p. 156; Douglas (1923), pp. 39–40.
41. Kittredge, pp. 81–2; Opie (1974), p. 33, citing 1621 edn. of *The History of Tom Thumb*.
42. *Aucassin and Nicolette*, p. 107; Rocal, p. 29; Archives Nationales, Paris, BB[18] 1586.
43. Dawes and Baynes (eds), pp. 178–9; Poly and Bournazel, p. 341; Elkins, p. 206; Blanc, pp. 10–121.
44. Martinez de Toledo, p. 137; Laget (1982), pp. 40–1; B. Cole, p. 79.
45. Sautman, p. 85; Osbern Bokenham, cit. G.M. Gibson, p. 107; Aubrey, *Three Prose Works*, p. 164; Gélis (1984), pp. 54–5.
46. Hole (1954), p. 112.
47. Boussel, p. 216.
48. Cit. McClaren, p. 48.
49. Francis Jones, p. 65; Gaspar, pp. 18–19; Le Braz (1937), pp. 130–2.

50. Cit. Opie (1974), p. 22; Gélis (1984), p. 65.
51. Gaspar, p. 27.
52. Djilas, p. 104; B. Rowland (ed.), p. 169.
53. Cit. E. Peters (1978), p. 171; Canziani (1928a), p. 213; Mistral, *Mirèio*, pp. 124–5; Loux (1978), p. 38; Gaspar, p. 28.
54. Régné, p. 500; Klapisch-Zuber (1985b), pp. 190–1.
55. Thomas Platter (junior), *Journal of a Younger Brother*, pp. 171–2; Lea, II, pp. 935–6 and 557; *Quinze Joyes de mariage*, p. 11; Frazer, pp. 240–1.
56. Cit. Lea (1939), II, p. 751; Hair (ed.), p. 182; B. Rowland (ed.), pp. 157–9; E. Muir, p. 40.
57. Cit. J.T. McNeill and Gamer (eds), p. 340; Robert Cotgrave, cit. McClaren, p. 165.
58. Delumeau, cit. Gélis (1984), p. 553; N.Z. Davis (1985), pp. 19–21; Wickersheimer, p. 385.
59. Cit. Lea (1939), II, p. 1009; Ruggiero, pp. 168–9; Sébillot (1968), IV, p. 140.
60. K.M. Briggs (1977), p. 20.
61. Cit. H. Leyscr, p. 266; cit. Flint, p. 232; Delatte, p. 116.
62. Ruggiero, p. 31; R. Martin, pp. 127–8.
63. R. Martin, pp. 130–1.
64. Ruggiero, pp. 43 and 88ff; Origo (1963), p. 165; Kieckhefer, pp. 59–60.
65. Rackham, plate B and p. 14.
66. Cervantes, *Don Quixote*, I, p. 152; St Teresa of Ávila, *Life*, pp. 28–9.
67. Bollême, pp. 38–9.
68. Shakespeare, *The Merry Wives of Windsor*, Act II, Sc. II, p. 54; Clark and Morgan, p. 43; Emmison (1973), pp. 299–300; Dorson, p. 9–10; K.M. Briggs (1953), p. 456.
69. Pina-Cabral, p. 178.
70. Benoît, p. 274; Bouteiller (1958), p. 103; Leproux (1954), p. 251.
71. De Martino, p. 17.
72. Le Goff (1984), p. 306; Zguta (1977b), p. 1194.
73. Hole (1973), pp. 87–8; Shakespeare, *Othello*, Act I, Sc. II, pp. 24–5.

CHAPTER 6

1. Cit. Laget (1982), p. 34; Plutarch, *Essays*, p. 280.
2. Shakespeare, *King Henry IV, Part II*, Act IV, Sc. III, pp. 136–7; Gerald of Wales, *The Journey through Wales*, pp. 190–2; Sterne, *Tristram Shandy*, esp. pp. 5–10; Myer, pp. 99–100.
3. R. and D. Porter, p. 66; cit. Gélis (1984), p. 118.
4. Vicaire, p. 21; Garnier, *Becket*, p. 6.
5. Pina-Cabral, p. 122; cit. Rawcliffe, p. 41.
6. Chojnacki, p. 579, re Renaissance Venice; cit. Laget (1982). p. 48.
7. Cit. B. Rowland (ed.), p. 34; *Malleus Maleficarum*, p. 118; De Martino, pp. 30–1.
8. Laget (1982), p. 55; *Oxford Book of Ballads*, pp. 36–9.
9. Gélis (1984), p. 110.
10. E. Estyn Evans, p. 199; Bloch (1967), p. 145.
11. Goursaud, II, p. 294; Bede, *Ecclesiastical History*, pp. 42–3; Klapisch-Zuber (1985b), pp. 145 and 159–61.
12. Abray, p. 218; cit. Gélis (1984), p. 136; cit. Grattan and Singer, pp. 188–91; Margery Kempe, pp. 62–3; Macfarlane, p. 84.
13. Gélis (1984), p. 140; Da Rocha Brito; Thuillier, p. 85.
14. De Martino, p. 32.
15. Gallop (1961), p. 85; Pina-Cabral, p. 109; E. Estyn Evans, p. 13.
16. McManners, p. 13; Boussel, pp. 184–5.
17. Zmigrodzki, p. 389; Leproux (1959), p. 10.
18. Pina-Cabral, p. 108.

19. Kvideland and Sehmsdorf (eds), p. 133; Zmigrodzki, p. 390; Moiset, p. 123; Pina-Cabral, pp. 105–6.
20. Marbodus, cit. Bromehead, p. 19; Cunnington and Lucas, pp. 13–14.
21. Gaspar, p. 38; Kvideland and Sehmsdorf (eds), p. 75; Grattan and Singer, pp. 188–91; McClaren, p. 47.
22. Montaigne, *Essays*, I, p. 102; Shakespeare, *The Winter's Tale*, Act IV, Sc. IV, p. 106.
23. Simpson, p. 112; Gélis (1984), pp. 119–20; Lady Mary Wortley Montagu, *Letters*, p. 528.
24. Kilvert, *Diary*, p. 137; Grimm, *Tales*, pp. 375–9.
25. Glyde, p. 177; Simpson, p. 111; De Martino, pp. 30–1.
26. Rolleston, p. 287; cit. Beier, p. 233.
27. Lebrun, p. 447; Gallop (1961), pp. 84–5; Lawson, p. 56; cit. Slater, p. 125.
28. Culpeper, *Complete Herbal*, p. 231; Fielding, *Joseph Andrews*, p. 174; Pina-Cabral, pp. 105–6; Sterne, *Tristram Shandy*,p. 269.
29. Pius II, *Commentaries*, p. 35; Marcotti, cit. Klapisch-Zuber (1985b), p. 317; Addison, *Selections from The Spectator*, p. 1; Webb and Walker (eds), p. 14.
30. Laget (1982), pp. 87 and 90–1; McClaren, p. 46; Moss and Cappannari (1960), pp. 96–7.
31. Cit. Laget (1982), pp. 84–5 and 88–9.
32. Storms, p. 203; Ozment (1983), p. 113.
33. E. Porter, p. 12.
34. Cit. Lebrun, p. 447.

CHAPTER 7

1. Goubert (1986), p. 47.
2. Laget (1982), p. 127; Schama, p. 532.
3. Cit. Ozment (1975), p. 28; e.g. *The First Prayer Book of Edward VI*, pp. 278–9; cit. Laget (1982), p. 160; Shakespeare, *All's Well That Ends Well*, Act I, Sc. III, p. 28; Shakespeare, *King Henry VIII*, Act V, Sc. I, p. 148; cit. Beier, pp. 234–5.
4. Montaigne, *Essays*, I, p. 279; Cressy (1997), pp. 24–5; Bouteiller (1963), p. 88; Gallop (1961), p. 85.
5. K.M. Briggs (1959), p. 240; cit. B. Rowland (ed.), p. 34; Fisher (1970), p. 135; Villette (1961), pp. 148–9; Lea (1939), III, p. 1105; Kahk, p. 274; Bouteiller (1963), p. 88.
6. Abbott, cit. Foster (1972), p. 175; Frieden, p. 249, referring to a manual of 1903; F. Thompson, *From Lark Rise to Candleford*, pp. 133–5.
7. Gaspar, p. 53; cit. Lea (1939), I, p. 264; E. Porter, p. 15.
8. Thomas Platter (senior), *Autobiographie*, p. 83; Jacobsen, p. 108; cit. Ozment (1983), p. 115; Laget (1982), p. 136.
9. Sterne, *Tristram Shandy*, p. 12.
10. Cutileiro, pp. 277–8.
11. Cit. Fisher (1970), p. 135; McManners, p. 144; oath, Canterbury diocese, 1567, cit. Graham, p. 104; Kligman (1988), pp. 343–4.
12. Schama, p. 454; Thomas Heywood, *The Wise-Woman of Hogsden* (1638), cit. Beier, p. 29.
13. *Malleus Maleficarum*, pp. 115 and 269; *Fugger News-Letters*, pp. 118–25; Kligman (1988), pp. 65–6.
14. Adrian Wilson, p. 135; cit. Graham, pp. 195–6; Zmigrodzki, p. 391.
15. Zmigrodzki, p. 390; Frazer, p. 226.
16. Cit. Gélis (1984), pp. 198–9 and 233; Gélis, Laget and Morel, p. 84.
17. Gaspar, p. 50; Bertrand-Rousseau, pp. 55–6.
18. Kennedy, III, p. 166; G.F. Black (1938), p. 50.
19. Cit. Payne, pp. 131–2; and H. Leyser, pp. 123–4; Origo (1963), p. 164; Forbes (1971), pp. 302–3; Kieckhefer, p. 78.
20. Ozment (1983), p. 114; Beier, p. 125; Bloch (1989), pp. 92–107; cit. B. Rowland (ed.), pp.

33-4; cit. Graham, p. 129.

21. Bouteiller (1963), p. 88; E. Porter, p. 389.
22. B. Rowland (ed.), p. 139; Leproux (1959), p. 16; Schneid, pp. 38-9.
23. Hugues Dedieu, p. 234; cit. Forbes (1966), p. 125.
24. Hughes, pp. 100-1; cit. Graham, p. 237.
25. Cit. Lebrun, pp. 447-8; Gallop (1961), p. 85.
26. Laget (1982), p. 136; Gaspar, pp. 51-2; Chapman, pp. 38-9; cit. Hugh Brody, p. 111; Sharpe, p. 45; St Charles of Sezze, *Autobiography*, p. 124.
27. Sharpe, pp. 166-7.
28. Bouteiller (1963), p. 88; E. Estyn Evans, p. 289.
29. Gorceix, p. 9; Rolleston, p. 295.
30. Cit. Linnell, pp. 11-12; Thomas Platter (senior), *Autobiographie*, p. 83; Albarel, p. 231.
31. Bouteiller (1963), p. 88; Cousin (1979), p. 109; Bertrand-Rousseau, p. 53.
32. Dante, *Paradiso*, Canto XV, line 133, pp. 188-90; Thomas Platter (junior), *Journal of a Younger Brother*, p. 221.
33. Alcini Tartaglini, p. 194; Gaspar, p. 43; cit. Folet, pp. 204-5.
34. De Rosa, p. 257; Bertrand, pp. 202-3.
35. T. Johnson, p. 197; Ghéon, p. 126; Prescott (ed.), p. 214; Kvideland and Sehmsdorf (eds), p. 147.
36. Boussel, pp. 106-7; Duffy, p. 490.
37. Cressy (1997), p. 64; *Quinze Joyes de mariage*, pp. 35 and 116-22; Cassar, pp. 23 and 27.
38. Duby and Duby, p. 63; cit. Forbes (1966), p. 145.
39. Cit. B. Rowland (ed.) pp. 31ff.
40. Gaspar, pp. 48-9; Scribner, pp. 6 and 32.
41. Smollett, *Humphry Clinker*, p. 249; *Customs of the World*, p. 1157.
42. Ozment (1983), p. 111.
43. Pina-Cabral, p. 112; Woman's testimony, 1954, cit. Dolci (1960), pp. 225-6.
44. Pentikäinen, pp. 205-7.
45. Laget (1982), p. 183.
46. Pina-Cabral, p. 112.
47. Arrighi, pp. 221-2; Gallop (1961), pp. 86-7.
48. Ovid, *Fasti*, pp. 215ff; Abray, p. 218; cit. J. Dover Wilson, p. 37.
49. Blum, p. 11; Martynova, p. 179.
50. Laget (1982), pp. 173 and 183; Gélis (1976), p. 330; Blumenfeld-Kosinski, p. 16, citing Soranus of Ephesus; Durham, p. 191.
51. Gaspar, p. 58; Ozment (1983), p. 116; Moiset, p. 121.
52. Cit. Shahar, p. 40; Gaspar, p. 83; T.W. Thompson, pp. 166-7; Canziani (1928a), p. 213; *Customs of the World*, p. 1157; W.G. Black, p. 179.
53. Pina-Cabral, p. 115; Kligman (1988), p. 48.
54. *Customs of the World*, p. 1157; Fermor, p. 41; H.E. Davidson (1993), p. 101; Ghéon, p. 93.
55. Belmont (1976), p. 2; *Customs of the World*, p. 1109; De Martino, p. 34; cit. Cressy (1997), p. 81.
56. Glyde, p. 177; Simpson, p. 114; Forsyth, fig. 1 and p. 32; *Malleus Maleficarum*, pp. 66 and 141; Forbes (1966), p. 128.
57. Kaganoff, pp. 95-6; G. Strauss, p. 62.
58. Belmont (1976); Pentikäinen, pp. 73-4; Lynch, p. 126; Durantini, pp. 303-6.
59. Jacopone da Todi, *Lauds*, p. 109; Lisón-Tolosana (1973), p. 831; Durham, p. 191.
60. De Martino, p. 35; Laget (1982), p. 89.
61. Webb and Walker (eds), pp. 14-15.
62. Lebrun, p. 228; Fermor, p. 41.
63. Gaspar, p. 89; Elias Owen, p. 52; G.E. Evans (1971), p. 57; Gallop (1961), p. 87.
64. Trexler (1973-4), p. 269; Filippi, p. 465; Cutileiro, p. 274; Gallop (1961), pp. 60-1.
65. Cutileiro, pp. 274-5; Lebrun; B. Cole, plate 44 and colour plate 5.

66. Cunnington and Lucas, p. 26; *Customs of the World*, p. 1057.
67. Laget (1982), p. 188; Gallop (1961), p. 87.
68. W.G. Black, p. 179; Loux and Morel, p. 311; cit. H. Leyser, p. 134.
69. Fels et al., Plate 45; Simpson, p. 14; Durham, p. 191; Mistral, *Mémoires et récits*, p. 8; Gélis (1984), p. 264; Belmont (1973), p. 51; Ahl.
70. Durantini, p. 303; Jacobsen, pp. 93 and 103ff; Shahar, p. 43.

CHAPTER 8

1. Persius, *Satires*, II, pp. 336–9; Story, *Roba di Roma*, II p. 120; H.E. Davidson (1993), p. 101.
2. Martinengo-Cesaresco, pp. 261–2; Blum, p. 100; *Customs of the World*, p. 1157; Lawson, p. 201; Fermor, p. 41.
3. Canziani (1928b), pp. 37–8; Grimm, *Household Stories*, pp. 204–5.
4. Shakespeare, *King Henry VI Part III*, Act V, Sc. VI, pp. 137–8; Nesta Evans, p. 108.
5. *Customs of the World*, p. 1057; Gurdon, p. 11.
6. Opie (1989), no. 353, pp. 309–10; Crawley, pp. 142–4; Dickens, *David Copperfield*, p. 1; Ford, *Gatherings from Spain*, p. 116.
7. Gaspar, pp. 71–3; cit. Origo (1963), p. 165; Shakespeare, *King John*, Act III, Sc. I, p. 60.
8. Gélis (1984), pp. 274–5; E. Estyn Evans, p. 24.
9. Juvenal, *Satires*, Penguin, p. 170, and Loeb, pp. 152–3; Shakespeare, *King Henry IV, Part II*, Act IV, Sc. I, p. 102; Vasari, *Lives of the Artists*, I, p. 326; S. Johnson, *Lives of the Poets*, II, p. 4.
10. Hardy, *The Return of the Native*, pp. 29–30; Trefor M. Owen (1987), p. 144.
11. Radford (1978b), p. 27; Shakespeare, *King Henry IV, Part I*, Act II, Sc. I, p. 88. Martinengo-Cesaresco, p. 217; Ozment (1983), pp. 114–15.
12. *Le Grand Calendrier des bergiers*, pp. cvii–viii.
13. Ginzburg (1983), p. 73; Belmont (1971).
14. Gélis (1984), pp. 279–80.
15. Radford (1978a), p. 117; Simpson, p. 113; Shakespeare, *King Henry VI, Part III*, Act V, Sc. VI, pp. 138–9; Klaniczay (1990a), p. 245.
16. Cit. Belmont (1971), pp. 29–30; Jonson, *The Alchemist*, Act I, Sc. II, p. 24; Mistral, *Mirèio*, p. 122; Radford (1978b), p. 32; Hardy, *The Return of the Native*, p. 274.
17. Klapisch-Zuber (1985b), p. 292; Belmont (1971), p. 44.
18. Forbes (1953), p. 497.
19. Forbes (1953), pp. 499 and 500; and Graham, p. 126, citing 1659 edn. of Bourgeois; cit. Belmont (1971), p. 22.
20. Forbes (1953), p. 499.
21. Forbes (1953), p. 499; Ginzburg (1983), pp. 60–1; Radford (1978b), pp. 33–4.
22. Belmont (1971), pp. 21 and 202.
23. A. Lynn Martin, p. 135; D.J. Ward, p. 201; cit. Hair (ed.), p. 94.
24. Stith Thompson, p. 96; Frazer, p. 66; Gaspar, p. 55.
25. See especially Park and Daston; and Said, p. 144.
26. Cit. Shakespeare, *Macbeth*, appendix, p. 166; cit. Park and Daston, p. 34.
27. Hand (1980–1), pp. 60–1; Lilly (ed.), pp. 194–6; cit. Stannard, pp. 89–90; K. Thomas (1984), pp. 47–8.
28. *Fugger News-Letters*, p. 187; cit. Gélis, Laget and Morel, p. 26; B. Rowland (ed.), p. 63.
29. Theis, p. 15; Blum, p. 46.
30. Shakespeare, *King Richard III*, Act I, Sc. II, p. 137; Finot, p. 15; Beckman, pp. 449–50; Shakespeare, *A Midsummer Night'S Dream*, Act V, Sc. I, p. 126.
31. Guazzo, *Compendium Maleficarum*, pp. 32–3.
32. *Malleus Maleficarum*, p. 105; Stith Thompson, p. 248.
33. Banks, II, p. 154; John Boswell, pp. 291–2.

34. Cit. Ranum, p. 82; Cressy (1997), p. 66; Fermor, p. 41.
35. Shahar, p. 51; cit. Gittings, pp. 112 and 118; Howlett, p. 142.
36. Cit. Casta (1974), p. 42.
37. Hampe, p. 106; Burgess, p. 222; Esdaile, Illus. 65.
38. Humphreys, Shakespeare, *King Henry IV, Part II*, p. 177.
39. Shahar, pp. 34–5; *La Gazette des Tribunaux*, 2nd February 1837, no. 3556; Kselman, p. 192.
40. J.T. McNeill and Gamer (eds), pp. 339–40; Laget (1982), p. 274; Trefor M. Owen (1991), p. 82.

CHAPTER 9

1. *Malleus Maleficarum*, pp. 99–100; Kieckhefer, p. 59; Dorson, p. 153; 'Les enfants morts sans baptême', p. 15.
2. Kennedy, II, p. 73; Leproux (1959), p. 269; Gallop (1930), p. 211.
3. J.T. McNeill and Gamer (eds), p. 339; Blum, p. 96; Kligman (1988), pp. 165–6.
4. S. Mercier, *The Picture of Paris*, p. 78; Gittings, p. 84; Pina-Cabral, p. 117.
5. Cit. Moorman, p. 83; cit. Ozment (1983), p. 102; St Vincent Ferrer, pp. 82–3; cit. Coulton (1922), p. 5.
6. J. Larner (1980), p. 229; Baxter, *Autobiography*, pp. 28 and 281; cit. Youngson (ed.), pp. 61–2; Lamb, *Essays of Elia*, p. 81.
7. Fisher (1970), pp. 73–4; Kennedy, II, p. 73.
8. J.G. Davies, p. 54; Warren, p. 164; John Boswell, p. 279; Gélis (1984), p. 521.
9. Fisher (1970), p. 27; *The First Prayer Book of Edward VI*, p. 242; Cornford (ed.), p. 174; Emmison (1973), p. 139.
10. Brucker (ed.) (1967), pp. 115ff.; Pegeot, p. 55; Gélis (1984), p. 522; Laget (1975), p. 13; Gennep (1972), I, p. 127.
11. Cressy (1997), p. 101; cit. Gérin, p. 11; Laget (1975), p. 13.
12. Robert of Brunne, *Handlyng Synne*, p. 300.
13. Fisher (1970), p. 137; Monter, pp. 51–2.
14. William Cole, *Blecheley Diary*, pp. 44–5; Dickens, *Bleak House*, p. 140.
15. Robert of Brunne, *Handlyng Synne*, pp. 300–1.
16. St Vincent Ferrer, p. 80; Woodforde, *Diary*, p. 137; cit. Fisher (1970), p. 86.
17. *Aucassin et Nicolette*, p. 86; Hardy, *The Return of the Native*, p. 29.
18. St Augustine, cit. Benko, pp. 76–7; Le Roy Ladurie (1980), pp. 296 and 310–11; Gurdon, p. 25; Simpson, pp. 104 and 115; Lehndorff, p. 216; Huxley, *Beyond the Mexique Bay*, p. 112.
19. De Martino, p. 35; Trigg, pp. 78ff and 202; Martinengo-Cesaresco, p. 258.
20. Albarel, pp. 231–3; Boussel, p. 152; Blum, pp. 59–60 and 83–4.
21. Collinson, p. 275; Laget (1982), p. 106.
22. Perdrizet, p. 157; Shahar, p. 48; Trexler (1973–4), p. 282; Laget (1982), p. 114; Larquié, p. 132.
23. Brissaud, p. 241; Case, Assize Court, Bastia. Archives Nationales, Paris. BB^{20} 273.
24. Hawkins, pp. 496–9; Gélis (1976), pp. 335–7 and 340.
25. Benoît, p. 133.
26. Forsyth, Fig. 6 and pp. 38–9; Salet, no. 20, plate 45; Webb (ed.), pp. 150–1.
27. Gélis (1981); and (1984), p. 485; Saintyves (1911), pp. 70 and 74; Rebouillat, p. 180.
28. Cit. Vloberg (1960), p. 18.
29. Rebouillat, p. 180.
30. Cit. Saintyves (1991), pp. 70–1; and Didier (1968), pp. 9ff.
31. Eire, p. 140.
32. Rubellin, pp. 41–2.
33. Fisher (1965), pp. 158–79; cit. Russell, p. 126.
34. J.G. Davies, p. 109.
35. Tebbenhoff, p. 575; J.T. McNeill (1954), p. 88; E. Peters, Introduction, Zwingli, *Selected*

Works, p. xxiii.

36. Cit. J.G. Davies, p. 94; Fisher (1970), pp. 23–5, 93ff and 119.
37. Canziani (1928a), p. 213; *L'Homme et son corps*, Items 245 and 246; Zonabend (1978), p. 658; Hélias, *The Horse of Pride*, p. 33.
38. *Customs of the World*, p. 1060; Gaspar, pp. 75–9; W.G. Black, p. 181.
39. Origo (1963), pp. 119–20; Hole (1953), p. 139; Cunnington and Lucas, p. 45; Casta (1965a), p. 124; Benoît, p. 133; E. Estyn Evans, p. 289.
40. Gélis (1984), pp. 532–3; Pannet, pp. 119–20.
41. Maertens, p. 264; Story, *Roba di Roma*, II, p. 122; Pina-Cabral, p. 117.
42. Fisher (1965), p. 175.
43. *The First Prayer Book of Edward VI*, pp. 240–1; Jansson, pp. 92–4; Shakespeare, *King Henry V*, Act II, Sc. III, p. 46; Hole (1953), p. 139; Howlett, p. 143. Laslett, p. 123, believes that 'chrissoms' were those who died without baptism.
44. Myrc, *Instructions for Parish Priests*. p. 86, note by editor; Gennep (1972), p. 132, referring especially to the Ille-et-Vilaine and the Hautes-Vosges; Lebrun, pp. 448–9; G. Anderson, p. 43.
45. Kennedy, III, p. 248.
46. *Customs of the World*, p. 1060; Benoît, p. 134; G. Anderson, p. 48.
47. Cit. Bouchard, p. 317.
48. *Customs of the World*, p. 1060; Fine (1987b), p. 868.
49. Talbot (ed.), pp. 94 and 119–20; Puniet, Cabrol and Leclercq (eds), 2, part 1, col. 343; Myrc, *Instructions for Parish Priests*, pp. 18–19.
50. Ryan, p. 365.
51. Thorpe (ed.) (1969), pp. 168–9; Fine (1987b), p. 870; Simpson, p. 104.
52. Cit. Busk, pp. 70–1; Rémy, *Demonolatry*, p. 166.
53. Benham, p. 97; Francis Jones, p. 150; cit. Kieckhefer, p. 181; Cocchiara, p. 138; Potts, *Discovery of Witches*, p. K1; Fisher (1965), p. 178; cit. J.G. Davies, p. 70.
54. Sedgewick, pp. 181–2.
55. De Martino, p. 36; Vloberg (1936), p. 166; Goubert (1973), p. 281, citing Poitrineau.
56. Sébillot (1899c), pp. 390–1.
57. Zonabend (1980), p. 102; cit. Ozment (1975), p. 81.
58. G. Anderson, p. 51; Campbell, p. 221.
59. Patlagean, p. 627; Lynch, ch. 8; Lebrun, p. 448.
60. Dillenberger (ed.), p. 333; Prümmer, p. 449.
61. Robert of Brunne, *Handlying Synne*, pp. 304–5; cit. Gélis (1984), p. 528; Weibust, p. 106; J. Davis, p. 231.
62. J. Davis, p. 230; G. Anderson, pp. 48–9.
63. Mintz and Wolf, p. 354; Gennep (1972), I, p. 130.
64. *Customs of the World*, p. 1096; Campbell, pp. 220–1; Poueigh, p. 213.
65. F. Wilson, p. 39; Pitt-Rivers (1976), p. 319; G. Anderson, pp. 39–40.
66. Zonabend (1978), p. 664.
67. Kligman (1988), p. 96; G. Anderson, p. 40.
68. Gaspar, pp. 81–2; Fine (1987a), p. 127; Thrupp, p. 178; Kligman (1988), p. 37.
69. Fine (1987a), esp. pp. 133ff; Canziani (1928b), p. 39.
70. Fine (1987a), pp. 129 and 133; Campbell, p. 220.
71. Fine (1987a), pp. 123 and 140; Gudeman, p. 61.
72. Shahar, pp. 117–18; Klapisch-Zuber (1985a); G. Anderson, p. 48.
73. Weibust, pp. 103 and 105; Maurois, p. 34; Gallop (1961), p. 82.
74. Fine (1984), p. 109; W.G. Black, p. 181; Leproux (1959), p. 48.
75. S. Wilson (1998), p. 87; Martinengo-Cesaresco, p. 88; Clodd (1920), pp. 99 and 104; Dégh, p. 124.
76. Febvre (1968), p. 309.
77. Birket-Smith, pp. 153–4; Gluckman, p. 43.

78. S. Wilson (1998), p. 224. citing F.W. Kent; Danforth, p. 134.
79. Saravelli-Retali, p. 164.

CHAPTER 10

1. *Lisle Letters*, p. 270, editor's note; Cressy (1997), p. 203; Blum, pp. 11 and 19; Kligman (1988), p. 65; Gaspar, p. 60.
2. W.J. Rose (ed.), p. 136; Duby (1985), pp. 234–5; Edward Lhwyd, cit. Kittredge, p. 145; cit. Cressy (1997), p. 207; Bavoux (1956), pp. 135–44; Thuillier, p. 86; Blum, pp. 20 and 49.
3. Devos, p. 143.
4. Awty, pp. 27 and 8.
5. Cit. Fisher (1970), p. 136; *The First and Second Prayer Books of Edward VI*, pp. 278–9 and 428–9; Cressy (1997), pp. 205 and 208.
6. Dupin, pp. 306–7; Casta (1978), p. 176; Casta (1965a), p. 126; Arx, pp. 66–8; Rushton (1983), p. 122; Herrick, 'Julia's Churching, or Purification', *Hesperides and Noble Numbers*, p. 326; Cunnington and Lucas, pp. 18–19; Addleshaw and Etchells, pp. 84–6 and 94.
7. Kennedy, III, p. 202; Nesta Evans, p. 19.
8. Crabbe, 'The Parish Register', *Poetical Works*, p. 49; Cressy (1997), pp. 210. and 216; Awty, p. 24; Young and Willmott, p. 57.
9. Cit. Rushton (1983), p. 124; cit. Kittredge, p. 145.
10. Webster and Ford, *Plays*, p. 44; Schnucker, p. 645; cit. Kvideland and Sehmsdorf (eds), p. 106; Busk, p. 56.
11. Luke, ch. 11, v. 27; Platelle, p. 187; Carlo Levi, *Christ Stopped at Eboli*, p. 88.
12. Aeschylus, *The Oresteia*, p. 216; St Jerome, *Letters*, pp. 30–33; Salis, *De l'Éducation chrétienne*, p. 50; Odenkirchen, p. 153; *The Chester Mystery Cycle*, p. 287.
13. Sébillot (1968), III, p. 60.
14. Cit. Sussman, p. 6; Wrightson, p. 17; Fanshawe, *Memoirs*, p. 18; Thomas Wilson, *Diaries*, p. 122; cit. J.-P. Peter, p. 30; Hansen, p. 345.
15. Origo (1957), p. 129; Gaspar, pp. 68–9.
16. Shahar, p. 59; Shakespeare, *Macbeth*, pp. 180–1, appendix.
17. Sand, *La Petite Fadette*, pp. 10–11; Traimond, p. 39; Shahar, p. 61; Jean Itard, in Malson, p. 168; cit. Sussman, p. 4.
18. Le Fort, p. 373; Thrupp, pp. 226–7; Klapisch-Zuber (1985), pp. 132ff; Tilly and Scott, p. 46; Sussman, p. 12.
19. Webb and Walker (eds), p. 14; cit. Ozment (1983), p. 119; Marshall, p. 45.
20. Cit. Schnucking, p. 645; Duby (1985), p. 137; Régnier-Bohler, p. 336; *Oxford Dictionary of Proverbs*, p. 784; cit. Durantini, p. 19; Lindemann, p. 383; Minois, p. 129; cit. Ross, p. 185; Vasari, *Lives of the Artists*, I, p. 326; Eliade (1978), p. 108.
21. Sherwood, p. 168; Martinengo-Cesaresco, p. 243; Cressy (1997), p. 90.
22. J. Davis, pp. 237–8; Solnon, p. 356; Herlihy (1985), p. 120.
23. Belmont (1982), p. 3.
24. Cit. Morel, p. 52.
25. V. Phillips (1978b), p. 163; Pina-Cabral, p. 116; De Martino, pp. 42–3; Goursaud, II, p. 297.
26. Finley, p. 13; Rocal, p. 46; Gaspar, p. 63.
27. De Martino, p. 42; Moss and Cappannari (1960), p. 97.
28. Hunt, p. 200; Culpeper, *Complete Herbal*, p. 57; Moulis, p. 122.
29. Grattan and Singer, pp. 190–1; Dawson (ed.), p. 197; Camporesi (1988), p. 264.
30. Rocal, p. 38; De Martino, p. 43.
31. Thiriat, pp. 457–8; Dolci (1966), p. 210.
32. Sébillot (1968), II, p. 236; Vloberg (1936), p. 189; Francis Jones, p. 180.
33. Sébillot (1968), I, p. 478; Origo (1970), pp. 210–11.
34. Le Braz (1937), pp. 4–5.

35. MacCulloch, p. 141; Douglas (1923), p. 250; *Le Saint Voyage de Jhérusalem du Seigneur d'Anglure*, cit. Jusserand, p. 401; Bétérous, p. 405.
36. Vacandard, p. 203; cit. Erikson, p. 68; Froeschlé-Chopard (1976), p. 504.
37. Martinengo-Cesaresco, p. 236; *Oxford Book of Ballads*, p. 443.
38. Bynum, p. 170; Delooz, p. 209; Gennep (1924), p. 31; Thuillier, p. 73.
39. Laget (1982), p. 194; Rocal, pp. 45–7.
40. Bertrand-Rousseau, p. 57; Cornelisen, p. 244; E. Porter, p. 17.
41. A.E. Green (ed.), p. 17; C. Larner (1977), pp. 240–1; G.F. Black (1938), p. 49; Rémy, *Demonolatry*, pp. 119 and 160; Bavoux (1954), p. 125.
42. Culpeper, *Complete Herbal*, pp. 99 and 258; A. Mercier, p. 91; Laget (1982), p. 195.
43. Cit. Forbes (1971), p. 301; Brenan, p. 99; cit. Graham, p. 238.
44. Francis Jones, p. 161; Gennep (1972), I, p. 118; M.D. Anderson, pp. 186 and 189–90.
45. Cit. C.T. Wood, p. 719; cit. Crawford (1986), p. 30; Fedotov, II, p. 97; Hildburgh, pp. 434–5 and 442; Corbin, p. 36.
46. Dawson (ed.), pp. 22–3; Beier, p. 125; Zuccarelli, p. 47.
47. Dupin, p. 307; cit. Schnucking, p. 650.
48. Laget (1982), p. 192.
49. Dorson, p. 407; Bakhtin, p. 331.
50. Gennep (1972), I, p. 147.
51. Klapisch-Zuber (1985b), pp. 149–50; Herrick, *Hesperides and Noble Numbers*, p. 323.
52. Aubrey, *Three Prose Works*, pp. 109–10; R. Scot, *The Discovery of Witchcraft*, p. 239.
53. Cit. Clark and Morgan, p. 39; Klapisch-Zuber (1985b), p. 105; Camporesi (1988), pp. 132–3.
54. Segalen (1983), p. 121; Goursaud, II, p. 313; Fermor, p. 40; Vloberg (1936), p. 153; Guesquin-Barbichon, p. 41.
55. Cit. Lea, I, pp. 262 and 266–7; Potts, *Discovery of Witches*, p. B3; Gallop (1930), p. 170.
56. *Malleus Maleficarum*, p. 91; *Fugger News-Letters*, p. 123; Ford, *Gatherings from Spain*, p. 258.
57. Lawson, p. 56; cit. Caraman, p. 73; Awty, p. 9; G. Anderson, p. 43.
58. Martinengo-Cesaresco, p. 260; Tomasi, pp. 21–36.
59. Martynova, pp. 180–2; Martinengo-Cesaresco, p. 239.
60. Moiset, p. 121; Pina-Cabral, pp. 115–16; Leproux (1959), p. 61; Benoît, p. 135.
61. Martinengo-Cesaresco, p. 261; Gallop (1961), pp. 87–8.
62. Laget (1982), p. 187; Loux and Morel, pp. 314 and 323; Gaspar, p. 83; *Customs of the World*, p. 1058; Leproux (1959), p. 61.
63. Graham, p. 157; *Apocrypha*, p. 109.
64. Mead (ed.), pp. 453–4; cit. Loux and Morel, p. 313; cit. Cunnington and Lucas, p. 31; Mistral, *Mémoires et récits*, p. 8; Hélias, *The Horse of Pride*, p. 32.
65. Hélias, *The Horse of Pride*, p. 32; e.g. Rösslin, cit. Ozment (1983), p. 116; Margery Kempe, pp. 24–5; Cornelisen, pp. 245–6.
66. Loux and Morel, p. 318; Goursaud, II, p. 312; *L'Homme et son corps*, p. 134; Leproux (1959), pp. 34–5; cit. Pinchbeck and Hewitt, p. 6.
67. Gallop (1961). p. 88; cit. Radford (1978b), pp. 106–7.
68. Hieronymus Bosch, 'Christ Child with a Walking-Frame' on reverse of 'Christ Carrying the Cross', Kunsthistorisches Museum, Vienna, W.S. Gibson, plate 15; Thiriat, p. 477.
69. Mistral, *Mémoires et récits*, p. 8; Vloberg (1936), p. 86; Benoît, p. 135.
70. Benoît, p. 136; cit. Gélis (1984), p. 468; Gougaud (1914), pp. 239–40.
71. Gaspar, p. 83; Canziani (1928a), p. 213; Gallop (1961), p. 87.
72. Senior, p. 371; Sussman, p. 90; Ozment (1983), p. 127; Leproux (1959), pp. 10–11.
73. Origo (1963), p. 24; Shakespeare, *Romeo and Juliet*, Act I, Sc. III, p. 101.
74. Benoît, p. 132; Crawford (1986), p. 35.
75. Cit. Fildes, p. 51; Gallop (1961), p. 88; cit. Ozment (1983), p. 136; Durantini, pp. 14 and 120.
76. Jacopone da Todi, *Lauds*, p. 83; cit. Youngson (ed.), p. 181; Gélis (1984), pp. 435ff.
77. Loux and Morel, p. 320.

78. Dégh, pp. 125–8.
79. Gaspar, pp. 84–5; Kvideland and Sehmsdorf (eds), pp. 49–50.
80. Leproux (1957), p. 159 and passim.
81. Lecotté, pp. 113 and 100; Bouteiller, Loux and Segalen, p. 37.

CHAPTER 11

1. Durkheim and Mauss, p. 15.
2. Gough, *The History of Myddle*, p. 87; Blum, p. 124; Shakespeare, *Macbeth*, Act II, Sc. II, p. 51; Simpson, p. 120.
3. Kselman, p. 42; Stevens, pp. 31–2; Kvideland and Sehmsdorf (eds), pp. 61 and 63; S. Wilson (1988), p. 410; *The Miracles of St Martin*, E. Peters (ed.) (1975), p. 153.
4. Banks, II, p. 198; A. Wood, p. 196; Trefor M. Owen (1991), p. 38; Kselman, p. 42.
5. Radford (1978a), pp. 41–2; Brékilien, pp. 214–15, summarized in S. Wilson (1988), p. 413.
6. S. Wilson (1988), pp. 410–12, based mainly on Vuillier, pp. 148 and 158–61; and Carrington and Lamotte (1957).
7. Bouchard, p. 317.
8. Kieckhefer, p. 181; Kselman, p. 50; *Customs of the World*, p. 1126; Forbes, (1953), p. 501.
9. Cit. Rocal, pp. 194–5.
10. Kligman (1988), p. 161; Shakespeare, *King Henry V*, Act II, Sc. III, p. 46; Dickens, *David Copperfield*, p. 445; Lady Tennyson, *Journal*, p. 266.
11. Kligman (1988), p. 170.
12. Cressy (1997), p. 422; Trefor M. Owen (1987), pp. 176–7.
13. Pennant, cit. Youngson (ed.), p. 136; Gittings, p. 111.
14. Kligman (1988), p. 171.
15. Cit. Simpson, p. 123; Gaspar, pp. 88–9.
16. Cit. Youngson (ed.), p. 136; Ford, *Gatherings from Spain*, p. 232; Shakespeare, *King Henry V*, Act II, Sc. I, p. 34; Barber, p. 194.
17. Kvideland and Sehmsdorf (eds), p. 80; Howlett, p. 131; Trefor M. Owen (1987), p. 174.
18. Trefor M. Owen (1987), p. 177; Simpson, p. 126; Kligman (1988), p. 196.
19. Gittings, p. 111; Kligman (1988), pp. 171–2.
20. Cressy (1997), p. 466.
21. Varagnac, p. 220; Kvideland and Sehmsdorf (eds), pp. 10–11; Kselman, pp. 58–9; Ribeyrol and Schnapper, pp. 223 and 228.
22. Flint, p. 213.
23. Kligman (1988), pp. 172–3; S. Wilson (1988), p. 397.
24. Kennedy, II, p. 72; Trefor M. Owen (1987), pp. 185–6; Simpson, p. 130.
25. Ribeyrol and Schnapper, pp. 226 and 228; Kligman (1988), pp. 157–8; Beza, p. 42; Lewin, pp. 159–60.
26. Cit. Gittings, p. 45; Poueigh, pp. 233ff; Riché (1981), p. 132; Desaivre, p. 572.
27. Longman and Loch, p. 49; Zonabend (1973), p. 21.
28. E. Muir, p. 51.
29. Le Goff (1984), p. 269; Shakespeare, *Hamlet*, Act I, Sc. V, p. 216; Shakespeare, *Julius Caesar*, Act IV, Sc. III, pp. 111–12; K. Thomas (1973), pp. 711–19.
30. Klaniczay (1990b), p. 178; Blum, pp. 70–1; Zonabend (1973), p. 20.
31. Runeberg, p. 112; Almqvist, p. 107; Ginzburg (1990), p. 125; K.M. Briggs (1959), pp. 30 and 117ff.
32. Jansson, p. 8; cit. Dorson, p. 114; Blum, p. 74; Klaniczay (1990b), p. 178.
33. Flint, p. 215; R. Martin, p. 86; M.R. O'Neil (1984), p. 62; Hastrup, pp. 391–2.
34. Sophocles, *The Theban Plays*, p. 158; Kligman (1988), pp. 216, 220–1 and 245; cit. Gittings, p. 193.
35. Gélis (1984), pp. 104–5.

36. Dodds (1973), p. 147; Benoît, p. 212; Varagnac, p. 84; E. Estyn Evans, p. 276.
37. Ginzburg (1983), pp. 56–7; O'Sullivan, p. 81.
38. Barber, pp. 135–6; Ford, *Gatherings from Spain*, pp. 273–4.
39. Blum, pp. 17 and 32; Ruggiero, pp. 168–9; *Revue des Traditions Populaires* 14(1899), p. 718; Le Roy Ladurie (1983), p. 63; E.P. Evans, p. 188; E. Estyn Evans, p. 294; Dorson, p. 184.

CHAPTER 12

1. Beier, p. 258; Garnier, *Becket*, p. 41; cit. M. Phillips, p. 110.
2. J.-P. Peter, p. 24; Gentilcore, p. 125; Rawcliffe, p. 42; R. and D. Porter, p. 156.
3. Rawcliffe, pp. 84 and 87; Blum, p. 13; Cocchiara, p. 176; Pullan, p. 115; cit. R. and D. Porter, p. 157.
4. J. Larner (1980), p. 258; Seznec, p. 58; R. Porter, p. 25.
5. De Rosa, cit, Prandi, p. 122.
6. Delaruelle, pp. 229–30; cit. Ozment (1975), p. 29; Milton, *Poetical Works*, pp. 434–6; cit. P. Brown, p. 100; Hand (1980), p. 63.
7. A. Lynn Martin, p. 134; Hoffmann, p. 46.
8. Beier, p. 156; R. Porter, p. 27; *The Nun's Rule*, pp. 136–7; Ro. Ba., *The Life of Syr Thomas More*, p. 128; Casta (1965a), pp. 146–7; Baxter, *Autobiography*, pp. 8 and 249.
9. Russell, pp. 127–8.
10. Schama, p. 171; Benoît, p. 189; Thun, p. 381.
11. Giovanni Levi, p. 22; Thiriat, p. 479; Pina-Cabral, p. 188; Zguta (1978), p. 439.
12. Salomone-Marino, p. 202; C. Larner (1983), pp. 120 and 122; Shakespeare, *The Tempest*, Act III, Sc. III, p. 90; Cannaert, pp. 66–7.
13. Neuman, p. 192; M.R. O'Neil (1984), p. 61; Zguta (1978), p. 440; Sébillot (1899b), pp. 602–3.
14. Beier, pp. 198ff; Mozart, Letter to his father, 3 July 1778, *Letters*, p. 106; Pina-Cabral, p. 187.
15. Addison, *Selections from The Spectator*, p. 237; Ramsey, p. 136.
16. R. Porter (1987), pp. 18–20; Braudel, p. 548; Ramsey, pp. 58ff and 62; cit. K. Thomas (1973), p. 209; Gross, p. 211.
17. Cit. Burstein, p. 19; Jonson, *The Alchemist*, p. 35.
18. Riddle, p. 174; Goursaud, III p. 688; Beier, pp. 107–8; R. Porter (1995), p. 129.
19. Payne, pp. 14–16; Michaelis-Jena, p. 39.
20. Ramsey, p. 68; Brandon-Albini, p. 62.
21. Cit. Jolly, p. 285; cit. Jacob, p. 45; cit. Beier, p. 170; Camporesi (1988), p. 73.
22. Muchembled (1982), p. 216; Flint, p. 89; *The Letters of Abelard and Heloise*, p. 215.
23. Vogler, p. 148; Beier, pp. 204–5; Baxter, *Autobiography*, p. 76.
24. Shaw (ed.), p. 119; Beier, pp. 220–1; Wear, p. 70; Baxter, *Autobiography*, p. xviii, J.M. Lloyd Thomas, Introd.
25. Cit. Rawcliffe, p. 95; Ford, *Gatherings from Spain*, p. 285.
26. Casta (1965a), p. 16; Minois, pp. 296–7.
27. Rocal, pp. 52–4; Sébillot (1968), II, p. 270; M.R. O'Neil (1984), pp. 57–8.
28. Le Braz (1900), pp. 95–7; Maraspini, pp. 226–7; *L'Homme et son corps*, items 401 and 402.
29. W.G. Black, p. 93.
30. Storms, p. 56; cit. Prandi, p. 130.
31. Rocal, pp. 55–60.
32. Saintyves (1935), p. 28; Rocal, p. 63; *The Life of St Leoba*, Talbot (ed.), pp. 225–6; Trefor M. Owen (1991), pp. 77–8.
33. Banks, II, pp. 131–4.
34. Gaidoz; Chaumartin, esp. pp. 32–5.
35. Eugène Le Roy, *Jacquou le croquant*, pp. 163–4; E. Peters (ed.) (1975), pp. 162, 169–70 and

176; Benoît, p. 265.

36. Montaigne, *Journal de voyage en Italie*, pp. 318–21.
37. Vicaire, p. 248; Canziani (1928b), pp. 49–50.
38. Dimnet, *My Old World*, pp. 94–5.
39. Coutil, pp. 240 and 217.
40. Goursaud, II, pp. 463 and 503; B. Ward, p. 85.
41. Trigg, pp. 184–9.
42. Goursaud, II, p. 503; Sigal, p. 1528; Gonthier and Le Bas, p. 16; cit. Huizinga, p. 175; Folet, pp. 203–4; Barnaby Googe, cit. I.B. Jones, p. 442; Rocal, pp. 49–51 and 60–1.
43. Cit. Folet, p. 207; Rocal, pp. 49 and 117; Leproux (1957) pp. 996.

CHAPTER 13

1. Cutileiro, p. 273.
2. Cit. Burstein, p. 19; Thuillier, p. 102; Sand, *La Petite Fadette*, pp. 67–8; Beer, *Mrs Beer's House*, p. 81.
3. Hand (1971), p. 264; Joutard, pp. 155–6.
4. Hand (1971), pp. 266 and 268; Brenan, p. 99; Gallop (1961), p. 74.
5. Hole (1953), p. 80; Pina-Cabral, p. 187; Ginzburg (1983), pp. 52–3.
6. Elias Owen, p. 254; Stevens, p. 32; Fraysse, p. 104.
7. Sébillot (1968), III, pp. 276–7.
8. Vuillier, pp. 195–7; Trigg, p. 36; Brandon-Albini, p. 62; Rushton (1982), pp. 14–15; Finot, p. 35; Traimond, pp. 74 and 148–9.
9. Cit. Chandos, p. 132.
10. Salomone-Marino, pp. 204–4; Cocchiara, pp. 142–6.
11. Rocal, pp. 104–5; Jonson, *The Alchemist*, p. 81.
12. Story, *Roba di Roma*, II, p. 333; Dawson (ed.), p. 89; Rawcliffe, p. 54.
13. Goursaud, III, p. 687; Storms, p. 79; Hole (1953), pp. 82–3; Moulis, pp. 117–19.
14. Dawson (ed.), p. 269; Sébillot (1968), III, p. 475.
15. Origo (1957), p. 302; Delatte, pp. 49 and 54; Shakespeare, *The Merchant of Venice*, Act V, Sc. I, pp. 124–5; Banks, II, p. 178; Reynolds and Sawyer, p. 515; Shakespeare, *Macbeth*, Act IV, Sc. I, p. 107; Shakespeare, *Hamlet*, Act III, Sc. II, pp. 303–4.
16. Luck, pp. 86–7; Benoît, pp. 185 and 258; Blum, p. 46; Storms, p. 79; Larkin, *The Less-Deceived*, p. 28.
17. Delatte, pp. 76–7.
18. Delatte, p. 95.
19. Delatte, p. 180; cit. Payne, pp. 72–4; Frazer, p. 661.
20. Delatte, pp. 151, 156–7 and 163.
21. J.T. McNeill and Gamer (eds.), pp. 330–1; Storms, pp. 186–7; Delatte, p. 128.
22. I.B. Jones, p. 437; Origo (1957), p. 302; Delatte, p. 147; K.M. Briggs (1953), pp. 454–5; W.G. Black, pp. 193–4.
23. Delatte, p. 195; Kligman (1981), pp. 6–7.
24. Nalle, pp. 83–4; Frazer, p. 661.
25. Cit. Ruggiero, p. 164; K. Thomas (1973), p. 219; Frijhoff, p. 211; Rushton (1982), p. 120.
26. Rocal, pp. 95–7; Goursaud, III, pp. 714–16 and 677–8; Eugène Le Roy, *Le Moulin du Frau*, pp. 389–91.
27. Camporesi (1988), pp. 12–13; Cockayne (ed.), II, p. 63; B. Rowland (ed.), p. 161; Trigg, p. 39.
28. Shakespeare, *Twelfth Night*, Act III, Sc. IV, p. 98; G.E. Evans (1971), p. 84; cit. Sébillot (1968), III, p. 497; G.F. Black (1941), p. 416.
29. W.G. Black, p. 146; De Martino, p. 30.
30. I.B. Jones, p. 437; Webster and Ford, *Plays*, p. 110.
31. Hand (1980), pp. 108–9.

32. Jacob, pp. 45–6; Origo (1970), p. 210.
33. Hand (1980), p. 9.
34. Gallop (1961), p. 70; Goursaud, III, p. 713; cit. Klagstad, p. 136; K. Thomas (1973), pp. 211–12.
35. Payne, p. 137; Kvideland and Sehmsdorf (eds.), pp. 138–9; cit. Kieckhefer, p. 71; Gennep (1927), p. 59.
36. Cit. Frazer, p. 17; cit. Vloberg (1936), p. 167; Hélias, *The Horse of Pride*, pp. 83–4; Aubrey, *Three Prose Works*, p. 87; Glyde, p. 171; W.G. Black, p. 58.
37. Neuman, pp. 196–7; Cocchiara, p. 161.
38. Hand (1980), p. 123; cit. Payne, p. 135; Mailand, p. 582; R. Martin, p. 142; Ruggiero, p. 150.
39. Hand (1980), p. 18; K. Thomas (1973), p. 221; Montaigne, *Essays*, I, p. 92.
40. C. Larner (1983), p. 179; W.G. Black, p. 44.
41. Kvideland and Sehmsdorf (eds.), p. 138; Febvre (1957), p. 297; cit. Forbes (1971), p. 312; W.G. Black, p. 43; Hand (1980), p. 13.
42. Trigg, p. 40.
43. Febvre (1957), p. 296; Francis Jones, p. 104; Trigg, p. 40.
44. Sébillot (1968), III, pp. 412–15; Moulis, p. 121; Forbes (1971), p. 295; cit. W.G. Black, p. 38; Salomone-Marino, p. 145.
45. Hand (1980), pp. 32–3 and 82–9.
46. Sébillot (1968), II, pp. 284 and 293; cit. Payne, pp. 134–5.
47. Hand (1980), p. 3; De Martino, pp. 28–9; Bloch (1989), p. 216.
48. White, *The Natural History of Selborne*, p. 194; Sébillot (1899a), p. 453; M.R. O'Neil (1987), p. 93; Tax Freeman, p. 108.
49. Simpson, p. 108; Hand (1980), pp. 139 and 145.
50. Leproux (1959), p. 61; Moss and Cappannari (1960), p. 97; Hand (1980), pp. 270–1.
51. W.G. Black, p. 89.
52. Simpson, p. 102; Woodforde, *Diary*, p. 396; Pepys, *Diary*, II, p. 431; Douglas (1923), p. 57.
53. Trigg, pp. 39–40; Dawson (ed.), p. 155; Benoît, p. 271; Douglas (1923), p. 57.
54. Cit. W.G. Black, p. 51.
55. Hughes, p. 122; Dawson (ed.), pp. 89, 99 and 129; Storms, p. 57; cit. W.G. Black, pp. 154–5.
56. Douglas (1923), p. 57; Gallop (1961), pp. 71–2; cit. Cockayne, I, pp. 326–9.
57. Dawson (ed.), p. 273; cit. J. Dover Wilson, p. 136.
58. Loux and Morel, pp. 320–1.
59. G.E. Evans (1971), p. 84; W.G. Black, pp. 108–12 and 55; K. Thomas (1973), p. 225.
60. De Martino, p. 21.
61. Bouchard, pp. 320–1; W.G. Black, p. 187.
62. Elias Owen, p. 264; Cutileiro, p. 273.
63. K. Thomas (1973), p. 215.
64. Joseph Greene, *Correspondence*, p. 82; W.G. Black, p. 33; Carmichael, pp. 41–2; Hertz (1970), p. 174; Giovanni Levi, p. 15.
65. Ramsey, p. 241; R. Porter (1981), p. 15; Garnier, *Becket*, p. 197; Burstein, p. 21.
66. Payne, p. 125; Giovanni Levi, pp. 12–13.
67. Cit. Forbes (1971), pp. 305–6.
68. Must, p. 197; Riché (1981), p. 232; Forbes (1971), p. 296; H.E. Davidson (1970), p. 181; K.M. Briggs (1959), p. 190; Rawcliffe, p. 99.
69. T.W. Thompson, p. 167.
70. Traimond, p. 76; Tommaséo, *Canti popolari corsi*, pp. 51–4; M.R. O'Neil (1984), pp. 65 and 68.
71. Ramsey, pp. 37–8.
72. Ramsey, pp. 169–70; Hand (1980), p. 3.
73. Ramsey, p. 199; Mauriac, *The Unknown Sea*, p. 165.
74. Bonser. p. 13; Scribner, p. 31; Bede, *Ecclesiastical History*, p. 105; Bloch (1989), pp. 52 and 307–8; Ruggiero, pp. 144–5.

75. W.G. Black, p. 89; Walter Daniel, *Life of Ailred*, p. 32; Cockayne, II, p. 137.
76. Payne, p. 121; W.G. Black, p. 89.
77. K. Thomas (1973), p. 211; Cervantes, *Don Quixote*, I, pp. 105–6; De Martino, pp. 39–40; Forbes (1971), pp. 295–6; M.R. O'Neil (1984), p. 57; W.G. Black, p. 91.
78. Kieckhefer, p. 3; Forbes (1971), pp. 294–5; Moulis, p. 120.
79. Kieckhefer, p. 186; Zguta (1978), p. 445.
80. Singer, introduction, Cockayne, I, p. xxx; I.B. Jones, p. 438; cit. W.G. Black, p. 169.
81. Elias Owen, p. 267.
82. Cocchiara, p. 147; Haggard and Williamson, p. 192; Glyde, p. 173; cit. W.G. Black, pp. 79–80; Forbes (1971), p. 311; Hughes, p. 32.
83. Goursaud, III, pp. 711–12.
84. C. Larner (1983), p. 140; Fraysse, p. 102; W.G. Black, p. 82.
85. K.M. Briggs (1953), pp. 452–4.

CHAPTER 14

1. Lévy-Bruhl, pp. 70–1.
2. Fagles and Stanford, Introduction, Aeschylus, *The Oresteia*, pp. 25 and 107.
3. Livy, Book III, Loeb Vol. II, pp. 34–7; Tacitus, *Annals*, pp. 271 and 355; Tibullus, II, pp. 276–7.
4. Acts, II, vv. 19–20, *New Testament*, p. 199.
5. Gregory of Tours, *History of the Franks*, pp. 395 and 449; *Anglo-Saxon Chronicle*, pp. 44–5, 54–6 and 261–3.
6. *Song of Roland*, laisse 111, pp. 74–5; cit. Duby (1981), p. 54.
7. Cit. Niccoli, p. xiii; Matarazzo, *Chronicles*, pp. 102, 107 and 223–4; St Teresa of Ávila, *Life*, p. 178.
8. A. Lynn Martin, p. 134; T. Johnson, p. 198; Abray, p. 82; Baxter, *Autobiography*, pp. 5, 161 and 191; cit. Rasmussen, pp. 107–8.
9. Shakespeare, *King Lear*, Act I, Sc. II, pp. 28–9; *King Richard II*, Act II, Sc. IV, pp. 88–9; *King John*, Act III, Sc. III, p. 86; and Act IV, Sc. II, pp. 105–6.
10. Cit. J. Dover Wilson, pp. 46–7; Macfarlane, pp. 189–91; White, *The Natural History of Selborne*, pp. 284–5.
11. Knox, p. 363; Turgenev, *A Sportsman's Notebook*, pp. 108–10; Goursaud, III, p. 570.
12. Henry Vaughan, 'The Rain-Bow', *Sacred Poems*, p. 195; Shakespeare, *Julius Caesar*, Act II, Sc. II, p. 52; Price, p. 76; Bede, *Ecclesiastical History*, pp. 278–9.
13. Kieckhefer, p. 124; cit. Bollème, pp. 66–7; Canetti, *The Tongue Set Free*, pp. 20–1.
14. Ozment (1990), p. 52.
15. Milton, 'Of Reformation in England', *Areopagitica and Other Prose Works*, p. 85; Garin, p. 16; Seznec, p. 52; Flint, pp. 20 and 128; Ruggiero, p. 202.
16. Webster and Ford, *Plays*, p. 120; Story, *Roba di Roma*, II, p. 346.
17. Haller, p. 229; Woodforde, *Diary*, pp. 57, 70 and 532–3.
18. J.T. McNeill and Gamer (eds.), p. 337; Godin, p. 353; Trevelyan, p. 48; Clare, *The Shepherd's Calendar*, p. 117; Gough, *The History of Myddle*, p. 18; Goursaud, III, p. 727; Gomme, p. 329.
19. Gough, *The History of Myddle*, p. 122; Verga, *I Malavoglia*, p. 72.
20. Schama, pp. 133 and 136–40; Shakespeare, *Pericles*, Act II, Sc. I, p. 43.
21. Cit. Sébillot (1968), III, pp. 23–4; Warren, p. 38.
22. Hunt and Edgar (eds.), I, pp. 436–9; Juvenal, *Satires*, Penguin, p. 148.
23. Godin, p. 353; Woodforde, *Diary*, pp. 240–3; Blum, pp. 60–1.
24. J.T. McNeill and Gamer (eds), pp. 275–6 and 335; Flint, p. 117; La Bruyère, *Characters*, p. 280; Martinengo-Cesaresco, p. 220; Banks, II, pp. 42 and 26.
25. *The Life of St Willibrord*, Talbot (ed.), pp. 10–11; J.T. McNeill and Gamer (eds.), p. 330; R.

Martin, p. 121; cit. Youngson (ed.), pp. 180–1.

26. J.T. McNeill and Gamer (eds.), pp. 228–9; Flint, p. 222; cit. Karrer (ed.), p. 16; cit. Knox, p. 489.
27. Brodrick, p. 98.
28. Niccoli, pp. 195 and passim.
29. La Bruyère, *Characters*, p. 280; J.T. McNeill and Gamer (eds.), p. 335; Chaucer, *Complete Works*, p. 48; Clay (ed.) (1979), p. 131.
30. Orme, p. 83; Kieckhefer, pp. 89–90.
31. M.R. O'Neil ((1984), p. 67; M.R. O'Neil (1987), p. 90; Ruggiero, p. 119; Lea (1973), p. 111.

CHAPTER 15

1. Webster and Ford, *Plays*, p. 30.
2. Cit. *The Penguin Book of Comic and Curious Verse*, pp. 15–16; Turgenev, *A Sportsman's Notebook*, p. 12; Douglas (1923), p. 58; Pina-Cabral, pp. 189–90.
3. Mauss (1974), p. 327.
4. Luck, p. 6; T.W. Thompson, p. 159; Blum, p. 36; Slack, p. 53; Braudel (1990), pp. 307–8, citing Nelli; Mauss (1972), p. 29.
5. Blum, p. 161; Ruggiero, p. 170.
6. Pressey, p. 18; Loux (1977), pp. 54–5.
7. Scudder, introduction, Bede, *Ecclesiastical History*, p. xi; cit. Youngson (ed.), pp. 180–1.
8. Milton, *Poetical Works*, p. 124; cit. Chaunu, p. 346.
9. Apuleius, *Apologia*, pp. 77ff; Dodds (1973), pp. 189–90; cit. K.M. Briggs (1959), p. 174; cit. E. Peters (1978), p. 47; R. Martin, p. 93; Storms, p. 93; Dawson (ed.), pp. 85 and 99; Cocchiara, pp. 153–4; *Customs of the World*, p. 1097; Delumeau, p. 111; Joutard, pp. 153–4.
10. Culpeper, *Complete Herbal*, pp. 15, 21, 82 and *passim*.
11. Whitaker, pp. 4 and 77; H. Leyser, pp. 38–9 and 266.
12. Frazer, p. 606; Pliny, *Natural History*, Book VII, xv, 64, Vol. 2, pp. 548–9. Flint, p. 28; Gélis (1984), p. 35; Sébillot (1968), II, p. 87; Victor Hugo, *Choses vues 1830–46*, p. 441; Kligman (1988), p. 68.
13. Crawford (1981), p. 61; S.N. Brody, pp. 55 and 119; Shahar, p. 275; Pullan, p. 81.
14. Ginzburg (1983), p. 100; Blum, p. 17; Durbec, p. 266; Camporesi (1988), p. 173.
15. Le Roy Ladurie (1980), pp. 32 and 189; Brucker (ed.) (1971), pp. 270–1.
16. Dante, *Inferno*, Canto XX, pp. 222–3; *Malleus Maleficarum*, pp. 41–8; Levack, p. 124; Ankarloo and Henningsen (eds.), pp. 310ff and 350; R. Martin, pp. 226–7; Henningsen (1982), p. 135; Traimond, p. 31.
17. Cit. Robbins, p. 12; Levack, pp. 128–9.
18. Cit. Bethencourt, pp. 414–15; Bigot, p. 447; Blum, p. 147; Hand (1980), pp. 239–40.
19. Zuccarelli, p. 49; Blum, p. 43; Potts, *Discovery of Witches*, p. G; Notestein, p. 217; Lea (1939), II, p. 867; Favret-Saada, p. 137; Campbell, p. 240.
20. Cit. Lea (1939), III, p. 1342; Rushton (1982), p. 128; Burr (ed.), pp. 223–5 and 227, citing C. Mather; Bouteiller (1958), pp. 90–1; Campbell, p. 340.
21. Shakespeare, *King Richard III*, Act IV, Sc. I, p. 261.
22. Cit. Robert, pp. 7–8; E. Muir, p. 76; Mead (ed.), p. 452; *Le Grand Calendrier des bergiers*, p. F xlii; cit. Baxandall, p. 58; Hazlitt, *Table Talk* (1821–2), p. 39; John Boswell, p. 274; Wyatt-Brown, p. 49.
23. K. Leyser, p. 83; Eire, pp. 190–1; *Two Lives of Charlemagne*, p. 152.
24. *The Nun's Rule*, p. 48; Jacopone da Todi, *Lauds*, pp. 79 and 81; Duby (1981), p. 235; Castiglione, *The Book of the Courtier*, p. 271; Brookes, introduction, Shakespeare, *A Midsummer Night's Dream*, p. cxxxiv; e.g. Falassi, p. 344; Mistral, *Mirèio*, pp. 112–13.
25. *Customs of the World*, p. 1073; Bigot, p. 497; Joutard, p. 151; Blum, p. 147.
26. *Malleus Maleficarum*, pp. 12–13, 17–18 and 38; Scot, *The Discovery of Witchcraft*, ch. 9, pp.

408–9; Clay (ed.) (1965), pp. 64–5.
27. Villette (1961), p. 151; Bartoli, I, p. 250; Dilys Powell, *An Affair of the Heart*, pp. 107 and 132; Dégh, p. 125.
28. Aubrey, *Three Prose Works*, pp. 109–10; Campbell, p. 338; cit. Pomponi, p. 13; Pina-Cabral, p. 180; Blum, p. 221; Lisón-Tolosana (1973), pp. 831–3.
29. Mistral, *Mirèio*, pp. 122–3.
30. Martinengo-Cesaresco, p. 218; S. Johnson, *A Journey to the Western Islands*, pp. 741–2; Milton, *Poetical Works*, p. 91; *Histoire ... d'un petit ramoneur savoyard*, p. 43; J.T. McNeill and Gamer (eds), p. 335; Ruggiero, p. 170.
31. W. Scott, *Rob Roy*, II, p. 160; Shakespeare, *A Midsummer Night's Dream*, Act II, Sc. I, p. 28; Jonson, 'The Entertainment at Althorp', *Poems*, pp. 357–8; Clare, *The Shepherd's Calendar*, pp. 13–14; Blum, pp. 119–22.
32. Elias Owen, p. 68.
33. Stuart, p. 313; Kligman (1981), p. 53.
34. Stenton, pp. 97–8; Bede, *Ecclesiastical History*, p. 53.
35. Benoît, pp. 218–20.
36. Banks, II, pp. 218 and 188; Frazer, pp. 457–8.
37. Burkert, pp. 8–9.
38. Trefor M. Owen (1987), p. 73; Thun, pp. 393–4; Cannaert, p. 56.
39. K.M. Briggs (1959), pp. 76–7; S. Johnson, *A Journey to the Western Islands*, p. 763; E. Estyn Evans, p. 279; H.E. Davidson (1993), p. 99.
40. Beza, p. 37; Benoît, pp. 308–13; Runeberg, p. 12; H.E. Davidson (1993), pp. 91–3.
41. Robert Rowland, p. 166.
42. Cit. Osborne, p. 180; Burkert, pp. 16 and 140; H.E. Davidson (1993), p. 81; Piggott, pp. 110ff.
43. Douglas (1923), p. 261.
44. Gregory of Tours, *History of the Franks*, pp. 484–5.
45. Douglas (1923), pp. 56–7; Kieckhefer, p. 22.
46. Gomme, p. 240; E. Estyn Evans, pp. 277–8; Kvideland and Sehmsdorf (eds), p. 320; Forbes (1953), pp. 503–5; R. Martin, p. 128.
47. Shakespeare, *Macbeth*, Act IV, Sc. I, p. 106; Propertius, *Poems*, p. 152; and Loeb, pp. 294–5; Mallett, p. 227.
48. Clodd (1920), pp. 89ff.
49. E. Estyn Evans, p. 271; Hole (1975), pp. 46–7; K.M. Briggs (1977), pp. 295–6; Régné, pp. 486 and 492; Reymond, p. 91.
50. Beckman, p. 451; E. Porter, p. 50; Hole (1954). p. 119; cit. L.R. Muir, p. 177; cit. J. Larner (1965), p. 29.
51. Rothkrug, p. 51.
52. Shakespeare, *Macbeth*, p. 106 note; Leproux (1954), p. 203.
53. Goursaud, III, p. 623; Kilvert, *Diary*, p. 108.
54. G.E. Evans (1971), pp. 217–19; and (1967), pp. 260–2.
55. Randell, *Sixty Years a Fenman*, pp. 95–6.
56. Maclaren, p. 47.

CHAPTER 16

1. Mauss (1972), p. 48; Goodrich-Freer, p. 270.
2. Blum, p. 138; Fustel de Coulanges, p. 180; Bloch (1989), p. 158; Dickens, *Great Expectations*, p. 105.
3. Poueigh, p. 55; third-century liturgy, cit. Russell, p. 125; *Stowe Missal*, cit. Whitaker, pp. 205–6; *pace* R. Martin, pp. 97–8; and Ruggiero, pp. 110–11, who follow the Inquisition's view that this was a payment to or even a means of invoking the Devil.
4. Shakespeare, *The Comedy of Errors*, Act IV, Sc. III, p. 77; Blum, pp. 30 and 32; J. Dover

Wilson, p. 36; Le Roy Ladurie (1980), pp. 31–2.

5. Lady Tennyson, *Journal*, p. 89.
6. Lebrun, p. 461.
7. Nicolson, p. 35; Lebrun, p. 461; E. Estyn Evans, p. 303; Clodd (1898), citing Brand.
8. Cit. Forbes (1971), p. 306; Gallop (1961), p. 68.
9. Pius II, *Commentaries*, p. 366; Forey, p. 232; Eire, p. 138.
10. Francis Jones, pp. 37–8; Cassin, p. 183; Dewez and Iterson, pp. 165ff; Bétérous, p. 405; Blum, p. 132.
11. Seneca, *Medea*, cit. Luck, p. 88.
12. *The Chester Mystery Cycle*, p. 354; St Teresa of Ávila, *Life*, p. 455; Cohn, pp. 143–4.
13. Vespasiano, *Memoirs*, p. 124.
15. Cit. *Manners and Customs*, pp. 681–2; Canziani (1928b), p. 8.
16. Ozment (1990), p. 125; H.E. Davidson (1993), pp. 37–41; Canziani (1928b), p. 8.
17. Harold Acton, Introduction, Clay (ed.) (1979), p. 5.
18. Bonney, p. 96.
19. Canziani (1928b), p. 8; Moss and Cappanari (1960), p. 101; Gallop (1930), p. 254.
20. Luck, p. 92; J.T. McNeill and Gamer (eds.), pp. 420–1; Hole (1973), p. 83; Dante, *Inferno*, Canto XX, 121–2, pp. 222–3; Orme, p. 57.
21. Partner, pp. 54–6; Hole (1973), pp. 82–3 and 85–7; Kvideland and Sehmsdorf (eds.), pp. 161–2.
22. R. Martin, pp. 126–7; Ruggiero, pp. 57ff; Chaucer, General Prologue, *Complete Works*, p. 21; and *Canterbury Tales*, p. 510, note by Coghill; K.M. Briggs (1959), p. 260.
23. Lévy-Bruhl, p. 184; Jansson, pp. 15–17; Sulpicius Severus, *Three Letters*, Hoare (ed.), p. 57; Blum, p. 229; Kieckhefer, p. 51; Hastrup, p. 387; R. Martin, p. 98; Bethencourt, p. 413.
24. Clodd (1898), pp. 198ff; Ruggiero, pp. 102–3; St Teresa of Ávila, *Life*, pp. 215–16 and 407–8.
25. Storms, p. 281; Kieckhefer, pp. 39–40; Stith Thompson, p. 48.
26. Mauss (1972), p. 54; Shakespeare, *King Henry VI, Part III*, Act V, Sc. V, p. 133.
27. Karrer (ed.), p. 233; Boussel, p. 81; Epistle of James, 3, vv. 5–10; Chaucer, *The Manciple's Tale, Complete Works*, p. 227.
28. Cit. Karrer (ed.), p. 78; St Charles of Sezze, *Autobiography*, p. 40.
29. Banks, II, p. 64; Goursaud, II, p. 437; O'Sullivan, pp. 12 and 19.
30. F. Thompson, *From Lark Rise to Candleford*, p. 124; Brenan, p. 217.
31. *Lisle Letters*, pp. 143–4; Ro. Ba., *The Life of Syr Thomas More*, pp. 59–60; Schucking, p. 73; Cressy (1997), p. 392; Niccolini di Camugliano, p. 121; St Charles of Sezze, *Autobiography*, p. 71.
32. Crawley, p. 3; Shakespeare, *King Lear*, Act III, Sc. IV, pp. 86–8; Marchant, p. 73; Walker, p. 58.
33. Shakespeare, *King John*, Act III, Sc. I, pp. 64–5; Crawley, p. 27; *Anglo-Saxon Chronicle*, pp. 32–3; Joan Evans, p. 6.
34. Geary, pp. 123ff; Talbot (ed.), p. 72; Garnier, *Becket*, p. 132; Moorman, p. 125.
35. Cit. Brucker (ed.) (1971), p. 63; Canetti, *The Tongue Set Free*, pp. 33 and 62.
36. Matarazzo, *Chronicles*, pp. 127–8; A. Lynn Martin, p. 88; Diricq, p. 118; Durham, p. 279.
37. Ozment (1975), p. 4; Balzac, *Eugénie Grandet*, p. 80.
38. Crawley, p. 23; Sophocles, *The Theban Plays*, p. 98; Sirach, 4, vv. 5–6, *Apocrypha*, p. 133; Matthew Paris, *Chronicles*, p. 125; Banks, II, p. 52.
39. Elias Owen, p. 223.
40. Hole (1954), p. 12; E. Estyn Evans, pp. 299–300; Clodd (1920), p. 177.
41. Campbell, p. 167; *The Mabinogion*, pp. 64–8; Gregory of Tours, *History of the Franks*, p. 355; Giovanni di Ceprano, cit. Karrer (ed.), p. 14; Lawson, pp. 388–9.
42. Matthew Paris, *Chronicles*, p. 18; E. Estyn Evans, p. 300.
43. Kvideland and Sehmsdorf (eds.), p. 21; Addison, *Selections from the Spectator*, p. 333; Bolgar, pp. 123 and 409; Webster and Ford, *Plays*, p. 30; Fincham, p. 120; Moiset, p. 73.
44. Cocchiara, p. 129.

45. Blum, p. 30; R. Martin, pp. 103–4; Goodrich-Freer, p. 279.
46. Genesis, 2, v. 7; Casta (1978), p. 174; St Augustine, cit. Whitaker, p. 91; Kantorowicz, p. 21; Knox, pp. 358 and 362.
47. Shakespeare, *All's Well That Ends Well*, Act II, Sc. III, pp. 63–4; Kvideland and Sehmsdorf (eds), p. 45; Bede, *Ecclesiastical History*, p. 232; Storms, p. 62; Ramsey, p. 242; Falassi, p. 8.
48. Llobet, p. 114; Ruggiero, p. 111; Gregory of Tours, *Miracles of St Martin*, E. Peters (ed.) (1975), pp. 159–60.
49. Aristophanes, *The Acharnians*, pp. 50 and 239; Fustel de Coulanges, p. 159.
50. Hole (1975), p. 122; Kieckhefer, p. 49; Kligman (1981), pp. 28–9.
51. Hole (1975), p. 94.
52. E. Estyn Evans, pp. 293, 298 and 303; Goodrich-Freer, p. 268; Hand (1980), p. 4.
53. Hand (1980), pp. 4–5; W.G. Black, p. 66; Spenser, *The Fairy Queen*, Book III, Canto II, 51, *Poetical Works*, p. 153; cit. McClaren, p. 100; C. Larner (1983), p. 123; cit. K.M. Briggs (1959), p. 200; Bower, p. 10.
54. Kieckhefer, p. 159; Delatte, pp. 98 and 100; Gallop (1930), p. 222.
55. H.E. Davidson (1993), p. 77.
56. Cit. Flint, p. 227; Kligman (1988), p. 59.
57. Cressy (1997), p. 266; Webster and Ford, *Plays*, p. 244; Stevenson, p. 61; *Manners and Customs*, pp. 286–7.
58. *Manners and Customs*, p. 682; Régnier-Bohler, p. 333; Ruggiero, pp. 102, 124 and 167; Traimond, p. 107.
59. Barber, p. 49; W. Scott. *Demonology and Witchcraft*, p. 273; Salomone-Martino, pp. 223–4; Canziani (1928b), p. 25; E. Estyn Evans, p. 304.
60. Cockayne, I, p. xxviii; W.G. Black, p. 186; De Martino, pp. 60ff; cit. Dorson, p. 33; Shakespeare, *King Lear*, Act II, Sc. III, p. 76; Martinengo-Cesaresco, pp. 261–2.
61. *The Nun's Rule*, pp. 22–4; Duffy, pp. 246ff; Bynum, p. 105; Cutileiro, p. 274.
62. Storms, p. 98; Forbes (1971), p. 294; Benoît, p. 217; E. Estyn Evans, p. 303.
63. W.G. Black, p. 122; Lisón-Tolosana (1973), p. 829.
64. W.G. Black, pp. 118–19; R. Martin, p. 137; Neuman, pp. 195–6; Benoît, p. 265.
65. Blum, pp. 47, 128 and 167–9.
66. Riché (1981), p. 136; Storms, pp. 150–1.
67. Mauss (1972), p. 128; Blum, p. 162; Kvideland and Sehmsdorf (eds.), pp. 131 and 143; R. Martin, p. 123; Gallop (1961), p. 55; Storms, p. 94.
68. Camporesi (1995), p. 59; Zonabend (1980), p. 140.
69. Frazer, p. 561.
70. Mauss (1972), p. 45; cit. Origo (1953), p. 110; Douglas (1923), p. 321; Blum, pp. 101ff; Psalm 91 (*Vulgate* 90), v. 6.
71. Gourevitch, pp. 109–10; Shakespeare, *King John*, Act V, Sc. VI, p. 140; J.T. McNeill and Gamer (eds.), pp. 337–8; cit. Mandrou, p. 83; Shakespeare, *King Henry VI, Part II*, Act I, Sc. IV, p. 32.
72. Beza, pp. 21–2.
73. Fustel de Coulanges, pp. 217 and 163; Suetonius, p. 100.
74. Letter, St Boniface to Pope Zacharias (742), Talbot (ed.), p. 101; *Ames Correspondence*, p. 57.
75. Bouchard, pp. 316–17.
76. Salomone-Marino, pp. 148–9 and 145; R. Martin, p. 187; Shakespeare, *Hamlet*, Act I, Sc. I, p. 177; Martinengo-Cesaresco, p. 220.
77. Neuman, p. 194; W.G. Black, pp. 134–5.
78. M. Phillips, p. 66; Banks, II, pp. 20 and 247; Dawson (ed.), p. 329; Youngson (ed.), p. 135; Benoît, p. 228; Hole (1975), p. 42.
79. E. Muir, pp. 74–5; cit. Duffy, p. 49; Opie (1989), No. 353, p. 309; Menefee, p. 49.
80. Vuillier, p. 183; Story, *Roba di Roma*, II, p. 265; Burns, p. 6; Bouchard, p. 317; Blum, p. 88; W.G. Black, p. 133; Duffy, p. 49.

81. Mauss (1972), pp. 46–7; Baston, p. 322; Kligman (1981), p. 181; Flint, p. 206; Barber, p. 79; Gough, *The History of Myddle*, p. 173; Bethencourt, p. 419.
82. Goursaud, III, p. 564.
83. Lévi-Strauss, p. 144; Fisher (1965), p. 158; E. Estyn Evans, p. 65; Duby (1991), p. 289; Saintyves (1935), p. 31.
84. Storms, p. 91; Gérard de Nerval, *Sylvie, Oeuvres*, I, p. 619; Moiset, p. 124; Beckman, p. 449.

CHAPTER 17

1. Frazer, p. 52; M.R. O'Neil (1987), p. 98.
2. Casta (1965a), p. 115; S. Johnson, *Journey to the Western Islands*, pp. 741–3.
3. Flint. pp. 186 and 183; Gregory of Tours, *Miracles of St Martin*, E. Peters (ed.), (1975), p. 169; Jolly, p. 284; Neuman, p. 194.
4. Léonard, p. 503.
5. Bede, *Ecclesiastical History*, p. 35; Blum, pp. 24 and 50; Kvideland and Sehmsdorf (eds), p. 7.
6. Sinanoglou, p. 499; Trexler (1974), pp. 211–12; Duffy, p. 100; *The Mabinogion*, p. 70; De Martino, pp. 17–18.
7. Finot, p. 64; Muchembled (1990), p. 152; Rocal, pp. 43–6; Duffy, p. 294.
8. *The Chester Mystery Cycle*, p. 323.
9. Martindale, p. 174; Kieckhefer, p. 79; Shakespeare, *King Richard II*, Act V, Sc. II, p. 158; Casta (1965a), p. 129.
10. Cit. Newton, *Diary*, 1818, p. 153.
11. J.T. McNeill and Gamer (eds.), p. 310; John of Salisbury, *Historia Pontificalis*, pp. 10–11; Kvideland and Sehmsdorf (eds.), pp. 198–9.
12. Cit. Vandenbroucke, p. 257; Scribner, p. 268; J.T. McNeill and Gamer (eds), p. 339.
13. Cipolla, p. 38; Cressy (1989), p. 71; Kvideland and Sehmsdorf (eds), p. 180.
14. Kantorowicz, p. 1; Ruggiero, p. 122.
15. Rocal, p. 100; Deyon, p. 456; Martinengo-Cesaresco, p. 135.
16. Finot, pp. 33–4.
17. Yerkes, p. 56.
18. Whale, pp. 48–9.
19. M.R. O'Neil (1984), p. 72; Ketton-Cremer, pp. 88–90; Spence, p. 19; Douglas (1923), p. 58.

Bibliography

Abray, Lorna Jane (1985). *The People's Reformation: Magistrates, Clergy, and Commons in Strasbourg, 1500–1598* (Oxford, Blackwell).

Addison, Joseph (1890). *Selections from The Spectator*, ed. Thomas Arnold (Oxford, Clarendon Press).

Addleshaw, G.W.O. and Etchells, Frederick (1948). *The Architectural Setting of Anglican Worship.* (London, Faber).

Aeschylus (1979). *The Oresteia*, ed. Robert Fagles and W.B. Stanford (Harmondsworth, Penguin).

Ahl, Diane Cole (1981–2). 'Renaissance Birth Salvers and the Richmond *Judgment of Solomon*', *Studies in Iconography*, 7–8, pp. 157–74.

Albarel, Dr P. (1924). 'L'oraison de sainte Marguerite pour les femmes en couches', *La Chronique Médicale*, 31, pp. 231–3.

Albert-Llorca, Marlene (1988). 'Les "servantes du Seigneur": l'abeille et ses oeuvres', *Terrain*, 10, pp. 23–26.

Alciani Tartaglini, Clara (1963). 'La feste dei santi patroni nel territorio di Civitella de' Pazzi', *Lares*, 29, pp. 191–200.

Alford, Violet (1932). 'Some Pyrenean Folk Customs', *Folk-Lore*, 43, pp. 49–54.

Alford, Violet (1948). 'Ceremonial Animals of Languedoc and the Sinibelet', *Folk-Lore*, 59, pp. 184–7.

Almqvist, Bo (1971). 'Nitha(n)grísur: The Faroese Dead-Child Being', *Arv*, 27, pp. 97–120.

Altorki, Soraya (1980). 'Milk-Kinship in Arab Society: An Unexplored Problem in the Ethnography of Marriage', *Ethnology*, 19, pp. 233–44.

Ames Correspondence, The (1962). Ed. J.A. Robinson, *Norfolk Record Society*, 81.

Anderson, Gallatin (1957). 'Il Comparaggio: The Italian Godparenthood Complex', *Southwestern Journal of Anthropology*, 13, pp. 32–53.

Anderson, M.D. (1964). *A Saint at Stake: The Strange Death of William of Norwich, 1144* (London, Faber).

Andree, Richard (1904). *Votive und Weihegaben des katholischen Volks in Süddeutschland: ein Beitrag zur Volkskunde* (Braunschweig).

Anglo-Saxon Chronicle, The (1972). Ed. G.N. Garmonsway (London, Dent).

Ankarloo, Bengt and Henningsen, Gustav (eds) (1990). *Early Modern Witchcraft: Centres and Peripheries* (Oxford, Clarendon Press).

Apocrypha, The (1965). Ed. Bruce M. Metzger (New York, OUP).

Apuleius (1909). *The Apologia* and *Florida*, trans. H.E. Butler (Oxford, Clarendon Press).

Aristophanes (1973). *The Acharnians, The Clouds, Lysistrata*, ed. Alan H. Sommerstein (Harmondsworth, Penguin).

Arrighi, Paul (1970). *La Vie quotidienne en Corse au XVIIIe siècle* (Paris, Hachette).

Arx, Walter von (1979). 'The Churching of Women after Childbirth: History and Significance', in David Power and Luis Maldonado (eds), *Liturgy and Human Passage.* (New York: Seabury Press), pp. 63–72.

Ashby, Thomas (1929). *Some Italian Scenes and Festivals* (London, Methuen).

Aubrey, John (1972). *Three Prose Works*, ed. John Buchanan-Brown (Fontwell).

Aucassin and Nicolette and Other Mediaeval Romances and Legends (1949). Ed. Eugene Mason (London, Everyman).

Augustine, St (1972). *City of God*, ed. David Knowles (Harmondsworth, Penguin).

Awty, Julia (1997). 'The Churching of Women after Childbirth: A Study of its History and its Functions' (University of East Anglia, Unpublished Third Year Dissertation in History).

Bakhtin, Mikhail (1968). *Rabelais and his World* (Cambridge, Mass, MIT Press).

Balzac, Honoré de (1955), *Eugénie Grandet* (Harmondsworth, Penguin; original edn, 1838).

Banks, M. Macleod (1939). *British Calendar Customs, Scotland, II* (London), Publications of the Folk-Lore Society, 104.

Barb, A.A. (1950). 'Birds and Medical Magic, 1. The Eagle-Stone', *Journal of the Warburg and Courtauld Institutes*, 13, pp. 316–22.

Barber, Paul (1988). *Vampires, Burial and Death: Folklore and Reality* (New Haven and London, Yale).

Barbey d'Aurevilly (no date). *L'Ensorcelée* (Paris, Alphonse Lemerre; original edn, 1854).

Barbin, Hervé and Duteil, Jean-Pierre (1975). 'Miracle et pèlerinage au XVIIe siècle', *Revue d'Histoire de l'Eglise de France*, 61, pp. 246–56.

Bartoli, Abbé (1898). *Histoire de la Corse*, I (Paris).

Ba. (sset), Ro. (bert) (1950). *The Life of Syr Thomas More*, ed. E.V. Hitchcock and Mgr P.E. Hallett (London), Early English Text Society, Original Series, 222.

Bastow, A. (1936). 'Peasant Customs and Superstitions in Thirteenth-Century Germany', *Folk-Lore*, 47, pp. 313–28.

Baudouin de Gaiffier (1967). 'Le Diable voleur d'enfants', in *Etudes critiques d'hagiographie et d'iconologie* (Brussels, Société des Bollandistes), pp. 169–94.

Bavoux, Francis (1954). *La Sorcellerie en Franche-Comté (Pays de Quingey)* (Monaco).

Bavoux, Francis (1956). *Hantises et diableries dans la terre abbatiale de Luxeuil: d'un procès de l'Inquisition (1529) à l'épidémie démoniaque de 1628–1630* (Monaco).

Baxandall, Michael (1988). *Painting and Experience in Fifteenth-Century Italy* (Oxford, OUP).

Baxter, Richard (1931). *Autobiography* (London, Everyman).

Beard, Mary (1980). 'The Sexual Status of Vestal Virgins', *Journal of Roman Studies*, 70, pp. 12–27.

Beauquier, C. (1899). 'Les mois en Franche-Comté', *Revue des Traditions Populaires*, 14, passim.

Beaver, M.W. (1973). 'Population, Infant Mortality and Milk', *Population Studies*, pp. 243–54.

Beckman, Jacques (1968). 'Une épidémie de sorcellerie à Noville-les-Bois au début du XVIIe siècle', *Annales de la Société Archéologique de Namur*, pp. 425–63.

Bede (1927). *The Ecclesiastical History of the English Nation* (London, Everyman).

Beer, Patricia (1978). *Mrs Beer's House* (London, Anthony Mott).

Beier, Linda McCray (1987). *Sufferers and Healers: The Experience of Illness in Seventeenth-Century England* (London).

Belmont, Nicole (1971). *Les Signes de la naissance: études des représentations symboliques associées aux naissances singulières* (Brionne).

Belmont, Nicole (1973). *Mythes et croyances dans l'ancienne France* (Paris).

Belmont, Nicole (1976). 'Levana; or How to Raise Up Children', in Robert Forster and Orest Ranum (eds), *Family and Society: Selections from the Annales* (Baltimore and London, Johns Hopkins), pp. 1–15.

Belmont, Nicole (1982). 'The Symbolic Function of the Wedding Procession in the Popular Rituals of Marriage', in Robert Forster and Orest Ranum (eds), *Ritual, Religion, and the Sacred: Selections from the Annales* (Baltimore and London, Johns Hopkins), pp. 1–17.

Bendix, Reinhard (1962). *Max Weber: An Intellectual Portrait* (New York, Doubleday Anchor).

Benedictow, Ole Jørgen (1985). 'The Milky Way in History: Breast Feeding, Antagonism between the Sexes, and Infant Mortality in Medieval Norway', *Scandinavian Journal of History*, 10, pp. 19–53.

Benedikz, B.S. (1964). 'The Master Magician in Icelandic Folk-Legend', *Durham University Journal*, pp. 22–34.

Benham, Rev. Canon (1895). 'Customs and Superstitions of Baptism', in William Andrews (ed.), *Curious Church Customs* (Hull, William Andrews), pp. 78–98.

Benko, Stephen (1964). *The Meaning of Sanctorum Communio* (Naperville, Ill.), Studies in Historical Theology, 3.

Benoît, Fernand (1975). *La Provence et le Comtat Venaissin: arts et traditions populaires* (Avignon, Aubanel).

Bernard, St (1954). *On The Christian Year: Selections from his Sermons* (London, Mowbray).

Bernos, Marcel (1970). 'Refléxions sur un miracle à l'Annonciade d'Aix-en-Provence: contribution à l'étude des sanctuaires "à répit" ', *Annales du Midi*, 82, pp. 5–20.

Bernos, Marcel (1980). 'Une "suscitation" au Buis-les-Baronnes en 1669: nouvelle contribution à l'étude des sanctuaires "à répit" ', *Annales du Midi*, 92, pp. 87–93.

Bertrand, Raymond de (1853–4). 'Dévotions populaires chez les Flamands de France de l'arrondissement de Dunkerque', *Annales du Comité Flamand de France*, pp. 191–235.

Bertrand-Rousseau, Pierrette (1978). *Ile de Corse et magie blanche: étude des comportements magico-thérapeutiques* (Paris, Publications de la Sorbonne).

Bétérous, Paule-V. (1975). 'A propos d'une des légendes mariales les plus répandues: le "lait de la Vierge" ', *Bulletin de l'Association Guillaume Budé*, 4, pp. 403–11.

Beza, Marcu (1928). *Paganism in Roumanian Folklore* (London).

Bigot, Maximilien (1890). *Paysans corses en communauté: porchers-bergers des montagnes de Bastelica, propriétaires ouvriers, dans le système du travail sans engagements d'après les renseignements recueillis sur les lieux en 1869*, Les Ouvriers des Deux Mondes, 2nd series, II, No. 64, pp. 433–524.

Biller, P.P.A. (1982). 'Birth-Control in the West in the Thirteenth and Early Fourteenth Centuries', *Past and Present*, 94, pp. 3–26.

Binns, Alison (1989). *Dedications of Monastic Houses in England and Wales, 1066–1216* (Woodbridge, Boydell Press).

Birket-Smith, Kaj (1959). *The Eskimos* (London).

Black, George F. (1938). *A Calendar of Cases of Witchcraft in Scotland, 1510–1727* (New York).

Black, George F. (1941). 'Some Unpublished Scottish Witch Trials', *Bulletin of the New York Public Library*, 45, no. 4, pp. 335–42 and 413–22; and no. 8, pp. 671–84 and 763–80.

Black, William George (1883). *Folk-Medicine: A Chapter in the History of Culture* (London).

Blanc, J. (1982). *L'Abbaye de Saint-Papoul* (Carcassonne, CAMI).

Bloch, Marc (1961–4). *Les Caractères originaux de l'histoire rurale française* (Paris, Armand Colin, 2 vols; original edn, 1931).

Bloch, Marc (1967). *Land and Work in Mediaeval Europe: Selected Papers* (London, Routledge).

Bloch, Marc (1989). *The Royal Touch: Monarchy and Miracles in France and England* (New York: Dorset Press; original edn, 1923).

Blum, Richard and Eva (1970). *The Dangerous Hour: The Lore of Crisis and Mystery in Rural Greece* (London, Chatto and Windus).

Blumenfeld-Kosinski, Renate (1990). *Not of Woman Born: Representations of Caesarean Birth in Medieval and Renaissance Culture* (Ithaca and London, Cornell).

Boccaccio, Giovanni (1822). *Il Decameron* (Florence, Leonardo Ciardetti), 4 vols.

Bolgar, R.R. (1973). *The Classical Heritage and its Beneficiaries* (Cambridge, CUP).

Bollême, Geneviève (1971). *La Bibliothèque bleue: la littérature populaire en France du XVIe au XIXe siècle* (Paris, Julliard, Collection Archives).

Bolton, H.C. (1888). *The Counting-Out Rhymes of Children, Their Antiquity, Origin and Wide Distribution: A Study in Folk-Lore* (London).

Bonney, Françoise (1971). 'Autour de Jean Gerson: opinions de théologiens sur les superstitions et la sorcellerie au début du XVe siècle', *Moyen Age*, pp. 85–98.

Bonser, W. (1956). 'Medical Folklore of Venice and Rome', *Folk-Lore*, 67, pp. 1–15.

Bordes, Maurice (1978). 'Contribution à l'étude des confréries de pénitents à Nice aux XVIIe–XVIIIe siècles', *Annales du Midi*, 90, pp. 377–88.

Boswell, James (1955). *The Journal of a Tour to the Hebrides with Samuel Johnson* (London and Glasgow, Collins; original edn, 1785).

Boswell, John (1988). *The Kindness of Strangers: The Abandonment of Children in Western Europe from Late Antiquity to the Renaissance* (New York, Pantheon Books).

Bouchard, Gerard (1972). *Le Village immobile: Sennely-en-Sologne au XVIIIe siècle* (Paris, Plon).

Bourgeaux, Arsène (1977). 'Interférences religieuses dans les mentalités populaires à Brison et au Mont-Saxonnex en Faucigny', *Religion Populaire: Le Monde Alpin et Rhodanien*, 5, pp. 339–57.

Boussel, Patrice (1971). *Des Reliques et de leur bon usage* (Paris, Balland).

Bouteiller, Marcelle (1958). *Sorciers et jeteurs de sort* (Paris).

Bouteiller, Marcelle (1963). 'Rites et croyances de la naissance et de l'accouchement dans les provinces traditionnelles françaises', *La Vie Médicale*, December, pp. 87–92.

Bouteiller, Marcelle (1970). 'Tradition folklorique et "parentés parallèles": le couple parrain-marraine et ses implications dans les lignées familiales', in J. Pouillon and P. Maranda (eds.), *Echanges et communications: mélanges offertes à Claude Lévi-Strauss à l'occasion de son 60e anniversaire* (The Hague and Paris), I, pp. 153–61.

Bouteiller, Marcelle, Loux, Françoise and Segalen, Martine (1973). *Croyances et coutumes.* (Paris, Editions des Musées Nationaux), Guides ethnologiques, 12.

Bower, Herbert M. (1897). *The Elevation and Procession of the Ceri at Gubbio: An Account of the Ceremonies* (London) Folk-Lore Society, 39.

Brandon-Albini, Maria (1963). *Midi vivant: peuple et culture en Italie du Sud* (Paris, PUF).

Braudel, Fernand (1981). *The Structures of Everyday Life* (London, Collins).

Braudel, Fernand (1990). *The Identity of France*, II (London, Harper Collins).

Brayshaw, A. Neave (1933). *The Personality of George Fox* (London, Allenson).

Brékilien, Yves (1966). *La Vie quotidienne des paysans en Bretagne au XIXe siècle* (Paris, Hachette).

Brenan, Gerald (1958). *South from Granada* (London, Hamish Hamilton).

Briggs, K.M. (1953). 'Some Seventeenth-Century Books of Magic'. *Folk-Lore*, 64, pp. 445–62.

Briggs, K.M. (1959). *The Anatomy of Puck: An Examination of Fairy Beliefs among Shakespeare's Contemporaries and Successors* (London, Routledge).

Briggs, K.M. (1977). *British Folk Tales and Legends: A Sampler* (London, Paladin).

Briggs, Robin (1996). *Witches and Neighbours: The Social and Cultural Context of European Witchcraft* (London, Harper Collins).

Brissaud, Y.-B. (1972). 'L'infanticide à la fin du moyen âge, ses motivations psychologiques et sa répression', *Revue Historique de Droit Français et Étranger*, 50, pp. 229–56.

Brodrick, James, S.J. (1961). *Robert Bellarmine, Saint and Scholar* (London, Catholic Book Club).

Brody, Hugh (1973). *Inishkillane: Change and Decline in the West of Ireland* (London, Allen Lane).

Brody, S.N. (1974). *The Disease of the Soul: Leprosy in Medieval Literature* (Ithaca, Cornell).

Bromehead, C.N. (1947). 'Aetites or the Eagle-Stone'. *Antiquity*, 21, pp. 16–22.

Brown, Peter (1981). *The Cult of the Saints: Its Rise and Function in Latin Christianity* (Chicago).

Brown, Theo (1979). *The Fate of the Dead: A Study in Folk-Eschatology in the West Country after the Reformation* (London, Folklore Society).

Brucker, Gene (ed.) (1967). *Two Memoirs of Renaissance Florence: The Diaries of Buonaccorso Pitti and Gregorio Dati* (New York, Harper Torchbooks).

Brucker, Gene (ed.) (1971). *The Society of Renaissance Florence: A Documentary Study* (New York, Harper Torchbooks).

Brunne, Robert of (1901). *Handlyng Synne*, ed. F.J. Furnivall (London), Early English Text Society, 119.

Bühler, Curt F. (1964). 'Prayers and Charms in Certain Middle English Scrolls', *Speculum*, 39, pp. 270–8.

Burgess, Frederick (1963). *English Churchyard Monuments* (London, Lutterworth Press).

Burke, Peter (1978). *Popular Culture in Early Modern Europe* (London, Temple Smith).

Burkert, Walter (1983). *Homo Necans: The Anthropology of Ancient Greek Sacrificial Ritual and Myth* (Berkeley, University of California).

Burns, Michael (1991). *Dreyfus: A Family Affair, 1789–1945* (New York, Harper Collins).

Burr, George Lincoln (ed.) (1968). *Narratives of the Witchcraft Cases, 1648–1706* (New York; original edn, 1914).

Burstein, Sonia Rosa (1956). 'Demonology and Medicine in the Sixteenth and Seventeenth Centuries', *Folk-Lore*, 67, pp. 16–33.

Bushaway, Bob (1982). *By Rite: Custom, Ceremony and Community in England, 1700–1880* (London, Junction Books).

Bushaway, Bob (1995). ' "Tacit, Unsuspected, but Still Implicit Faith": Alternative Belief in Nineteenth-Century Rural England', in T. Harris (ed.), *Popular Culture in England, c. 1500–1850* (London, Macmillan), ch. 9.

Busk, R.H. (1887). *The Folk-Songs of Italy* (London).

Bynum, Caroline Walker (1987). *Holy Feast and Holy Fast: The Religious Significance of*

Food to Medieval Women (Berkeley, University of California).

Cabrol, Dom Fernand and Leclercq, Dom Henri (eds) (1924–53). *Dictionnnaire d'archéologie chrétienne et de liturgie* (Paris, Letouzey), 15 vols.

Cagnat, M.R. (1903–4). 'La sorcellerie et les sorciers chez les Romains', *Annales du Musée Guimet*, 15, pp. 134–75.

Cameron, M.L. (1983). 'Bald's *Leechbook*: Its Sources and their Use in its Compilation', *Anglo-Saxon England*, 12, pp. 153–78.

Cameron, M.L. (1988). 'Anglo-Saxon Medicine and Magic', *Anglo-Saxon England*, 17, pp. 191–215.

Campbell, J.K. (1964). *Honour, Family and Patronage: A Study of Institutions and Moral Values in a Greek Mountain Community* (Oxford, Clarendon Press).

Camporesi, Piero (1988). *The Incorruptible Flesh: Bodily Mutation and Mortification in Religion and Folklore* (Cambridge, CUP).

Camporesi, Piero (1995), *Juice of Life: The Symbolic and Magic Significance of Blood* (New York, Continuum).

Canetti, Elias (1989). *The Tongue Set Free: Remembrance of a European Childhood* (London, Picador).

Cannaert, J.-B. (1847). *Olim: procès des sorcières en Belgique sous Philippe II et le gouvernement des Archiducs* (Ghent).

Canziani, Estella (1928a). 'Abruzzese Folklore', *Folk-Lore*, 39, pp. 208–19.

Canziani, Estella (1928b). *Through the Apennines and the Lands of the Abruzzi: Landscape and Peasant Life* (Cambridge, Heffer).

Capgrave, John (1977). *The Life of St Norbert*, ed. C.L. Smetana (Toronto, Pontifical Institute of Mediaeval Studies).

Caraman, Philip (1957). *Henry Morse: Priest of the Plague* (London, Longmans).

Carmichael, Ann G. (1986). *Plague and the Poor in Renaissance Florence* (Cambridge, CUP).

Carrington, Dorothy and Lamotte, Pierre (1957). 'Les "Mazzeri" ', *Etudes Corses*, 15/16, pp. 81–91.

Carsch, Henry (1969). 'Witchcraft and Spirit Possession in Grimm's Fairy Tales', *Journal of Popular Culture*, 2, pp. 627–48.

Cassar, Paul (1964). 'Medical Votive Offerings in the Maltese Islands', *Journal of the Royal Anthropological Institute*, 94, pp. 23–9.

Cassin, Elena (1958). *San Nicandro: The Story of a Religious Phenomenon* (London, Cohen and West).

Casta, François J. (1965a). *Evêques et curés corses dans la tradition pastorale du Concile de Trente (1570–1620)*, *Corse Historique*, 5, nos 17–18.

Casta, François J. (1965b). 'La Granitula: refléxions autour d'une antique tradition corse du Vendredi Saint', *Corse Historique*, 5, no. 20, pp. 5–10.

Casta, François J. (1974). *Le Diocèse d'Ajaccio* (Paris, Editions Beauchesne).

Casta, François J. (1978). 'La religion populaire: à la recherche de ses formes d'expression', in M. Caisson et al. (eds), *Pieve e Paesi: communautés rurales corses* (Paris, CNRS), ch. 7.

Castellan, Yvonne (1967). *La Culture serbe au seuil de l'indépendance (1800–1840): essai d'analyse psychologique d'une culture à distance temporelle*. Paris: PUF.

Castiglione, Baldassar (1959). *The Book of the Courtier*, trans. Charles S. Singleton (New York, Doubleday Anchor).

Catedra, Maria (1987). 'Entre bêtes et saints: esprits des vivants et esprits des morts chez les *vaqueiros de alzada*', *Etudes Rurales*, 105–6, pp. 65–78.

Cawte, E.C. (1978). *Ritual Animal Disguise: A Historical and Geographical Study of Animal Disguise in the British Isles* (Cambridge, CUP).

Ceramiche Tusci da speziera e d'amore nel Rinascimento Italiano (1993). (Monte San Savino).

Cerulli, Enrico (1943). *Il Libro Etiopico dei miracoli di Maria e le sue fonti nelle letterature del medio evo latino* (Rome).

Cervantes Saavedra, Miguel de (1947). *Don Quixote* (London, Everyman), 2 vols.

Chanaud, Robert (1977). 'Folklore et religion dans le diocèse de Grenoble à la fin du XVIIe siècle: les visites pastorales de Mgr Le Camus', *Religion Populaire: Le Monde Alpin et Rhodanien*, 5, pp. 33–103.

Chandos, John (ed.) (1971). *In God's Name: Examples of Preaching in England from the Act of Supremacy to the Act of Uniformity, 1534–1662* (London, Hutchinson).

Chapman, John Mitchel (1908). *Corsica: An Island of Rest* (London).

Charles of Sezze, St (1963). *Autobiography*, trans. and ed. Leonard Perotti, O.F.M. (London, Catholic Book Club).

Chaucer, Geoffrey (1974). *Complete Works*, ed. F.N. Robinson (Oxford, OUP).

Chaucer, Geoffrey (1975). *The Canterbury Tales*, trans. Nevill Coghill. (Harmondsworth, Penguin).

Chaumartin, Henry (1946). *Le Mal des ardents et le feu Saint-Antoine: étude historique, médicale, hagiographique et légendaire.*

Chaunu, Pierre (1978). *La Mort à Paris, XVIe, XVIIe et XVIIIe siècles* (Paris: Fayard).

Chauvin, Yves (1975). 'Le livre des miracles de Saint-Catherine-de-Fierbois', *Bulletin de la Société des Antiquaires de l'Ouest et des Musées de Poitiers*, 4th series, 13, pp. 281–311.

Chester Mystery Cycle, The (1992). Ed. David Mills (East Lansing, Colleagues Press).

Chojnacki, S. (1975). 'Dowries and Kinsmen in Early Renaissance Venice', *Journal of Interdisciplinary History*, 5, pp. 571–600.

Chouraqui, Jean-Marc (1979). 'Le cycle de Carême en Provence: rites et coutumes (XVIe–XIXe siècle), *Annales du Midi*, 91, pp. 153–64.

Chouraqui, Jean-Marc (1985). 'Le "combat de Carnaval et de Carême" en Provence du XVIe au XIXe siècle', *Revue d'Histoire Moderne et Contemporaine*, 32, pp. 114–24.

Christian, William A. (1972). *Person and God in a Spanish Valley* (New York and London, Seminar Press).

Christian, William A. (1981a). *Apparitions in Late Medieval and Renaissance Spain* (Princeton).

Christian, William A. (1981b). *Local Religion in Sixteenth-Century Spain* (Princeton).

Cipolla, Carlo M. (1967). *Clocks and Culture, 1300–1700* (London, Collins).

Clare, John (1964). *The Shepherd's Calendar*, ed. Eric Robinson and Geoffrey Summerfield (London, OUP; original edn, 1827).

Clark, Stuart and Morgan, P.T.J. (1976). 'Religion and Magic in Elizabethan Wales: Robert Holland's *Dialogue on Witchcraft*', *Journal of Ecclesiastical History*, 27, pp. 31–46.

Clay, Edith (ed.) (1965). *Ramage in South Italy* (London, Longmans).

Clay, Edith (ed.) (1979). *Lady Blessington at Naples* (London, Hamish Hamilton).

Clodd, Edward (1898). *Tom Tit Tot: An Essay on Savage Philosophy in Folk-Tale* (London).

Clodd, Edward (1920). *Magic in Names* (London, Chapman and Hall).

Cobb, Richard (1972). *The Police and the People: French Popular Protest, 1789–1820* (Oxford, OUP).

Cocchiara, Giuseppe (1951). *Il linguaggio della poesia popolare* (Palermo, Palumbo).

Cockayne, T.O. (ed.) (1961). *Leechdoms, Wortcunning and Starcraft of Early England.* (London, Holland Press), 2 vols; original edn. 1864–6.

Cohen, Esther (1986). 'Law, Folklore and Animal Lore', *Past and Present*, 110, pp. 6–37.

Cohn, Norman (1970). *The Pursuit of the Millennium: Revolutionary Millenarians and Mystical Anarchists of the Middle Ages* (London, Paladin).

Cole, Bruce (1991). *Piero della Francesca: Tradition and Innovation in Renaissance Art* (London, Harper Collins).

Cole, William (1931). *The Blecheley Diary, 1765–67*, ed. F.G. Stokes (London, Constable).

Collinson, Patrick (1984). *The Religion of Protestants: The Church in English Society, 1559–1625* (Oxford, Clarendon Press).

Corbin, Alain (1986). *The Foul and the Fragrant: Odour and the French Social Imagination* (Leamington Spa, Berg).

Cornelisen, Ann (1969). *Torregreca: A World in Southern Italy* (London, Macmillan).

Cornford, James (ed.) (no date). *The Book of Common Prayer with Historical Notes.* (London, SPCK).

Coulton, G.G. (1922). *Infant Perdition in the Middle Ages* (London) Mediaeval Studies, 16.

Coulton, G.G. (1944). *Fourscore Years: An Autobiography* (New York, Macmillan).

Cousin, Bernard (1976). 'Deux cent miracles en Provence sous Louis XIV', *Revue d'Histoire de la Spiritualité*, 207–8, pp. 225–44.

Cousin, Bernard (1977). 'Dévotion et société en Provence: les ex-voto de Notre-Dame-de-Lumières', *Ethnologie Française*, 7, pp. 121–42.

Cousin, Bernard (1979). 'L'ex-voto: document d'histoire, expression d'une société', *Archives de Sciences Sociales des Religions*, 48, pp. 107–24.

Coutil, Leon (1917). 'La chapelle Saint-Eloi de Nassandres: étude sur le culte des pierres, des sources et des arbres dans les départements de l'Eure, la Seine-Inférieure et la Normandie', *Recueil des Travaux de la Société Libre d'Agriculture, Sciences, Arts et Belles-Lettres de l'Eure*, 7th series, 5, pp. 159–276.

Cowper, William (1926). *Selected Letters* (London, Everyman).

Crabbe, George (1854). *The Poetical Works* (Edinburgh, Gall and Inglis).

Crawford, Patricia (1978). 'Attitudes to Pregnancy from a Woman's Spiritual Diary, 1687–8', *Local Population Studies*, 21, pp. 43–5.

Crawford, Patricia (1981). 'Attitudes to Menstruation in Seventeenth-Century England', *Past and Present*, 91, pp. 47–73.

Crawford, Patricia (1986). ' "The Sucking Child": Adult Attitudes to Child Care in the First Year of Life in Seventeenth-Century England', *Continuity and Change*, 1, pp. 23–52.

Crawley, Ernest (1934). *Oath, Curse and Blessing* (London, Watts).

Cressy, David (1989). *Bonfires and Bells: National Memory and the Protestant Calendar in Elizabethan and Stuart England* (London, Weidenfeld and Nicolson).

Cressy, David (1997). *Birth, Marriage, and Death: Ritual, Religion and the Life-Cycle in Tudor and Stuart England* (Oxford, OUP).

Culpeper, Nicholas (no date). *Complete Herbal* (London, Foulsham).

Cunnington, Phillis and Lucas, Catherine (1972). *Costume for Births, Marriages and Deaths* (London, Black).

Customs of the World (no date). Ed. Walter Hutchinson (London, Hutchinson), 2 vols.

Cutileiro, Jose (1971). *A Portuguese Rural Society* (Oxford, OUP).

Dancu, Juliana and Dumitru (1982). *Folk Glass-Painting in Romania* (Bucharest,

Meridiane).

Danforth, Loring M. (1982). *The Death Rituals of Rural Greece* (Princeton).

Daniel, Walter (1950). *Life of Ailred, Abbot of Rievaulx*, ed. F.M. Powicke (London, Nelson).

Danigo, J. (1973). 'Les anciens ex-voto de Saint-Anne d'Auray', *Bulletin de la Société Polymathique du Morbihan*, pp. 63–89.

Dante Alighieri (1929), *The Inferno* (London, Dent).

Dante Alighieri (1900). *The Paradiso* (London, Dent).

D'Arbois de Jubainville (1854). 'Les excommunications d'animaux', *Revue des Questions Historiques*, pp. 275–80.

Da Rocha Brito, A. (1935). 'Statues de la Vierge enceinte en Portugal', *Aesculape*, pp. 257–9.

Davidson, Hilda Ellis (1970). 'Scandinavian Folklore in Britain', *Journal of the Folklore Institute*, 7, pp. 177–86.

Davidson, Hilda Ellis (1993). *The Lost Beliefs of Northern Europe* (London, Routledge).

Davidson, Thomas (1957–8). 'Animal Charm Cures and Amulets', *Amateur Historian*, 3, pp. 237–48.

Davidson, Thomas (1958). 'Cattle-Milking Charms and Amulets', *Gwerin*, 2, pp. 22–37.

Davies, J.G. (1962). *The Architectural Setting of Baptism* (London).

Davis, J. (1977). *People of the Mediterranean: An Essay in Comparative Social Anthropology* (London, Routledge).

Davis, Natalie Zemon (1985). *The Return of Martin Guerre* (Harmondsworth, Penguin).

Dawes, Elizabeth and Baynes, Norman H. (eds) (1977). *Three Byzantine Saints: Contemporary Biographies of St Daniel the Stylite, St Theodore of Sykeon and St John the Almsgiver* (London, Mowbrays).

Dawson, Warren R. (ed.) (1934). *A Leechbook or Collection of Medical Recipes of the Fifteenth Century* (London).

Dedieu, Hugues (1966). 'Quelques traces de religion populaire autour des frères mineurs de la province d'Aquitaine', *Cahiers de Fanjeaux*, 11, pp. 227–49.

DeDieu, Jean-Pierre (1986). 'The Archives of the Holy Office of Toledo as a Source for Historical Anthropology', in Gustav Henningsen and John Tedeschi (eds), *The Inquisition in Early Modern Europe: Studies on Sources and Methods* (Dekalb, Northern Illinois University Press), pp. 158–75.

DeDieu, Jean-Pierre (1987). 'The Inquisition and Popular Culture in New Castile', in Stephen Haliczer (ed.), *Inquisition and Society in Early Modern Europe* (London, Croom Helm).

Dégh, Linda (1969). *Folktales and Society: Story-Telling in a Hungarian Peasant Community* (Bloomington, Indiana University Press).

Delaruelle, Etienne (1975). *La Piété populaire au moyen âge* (Turin).

Delatte, Armand (1961). *Herbarius: recherches sur le cérémonial usité chez les anciens pour la cueillette des simples et des plantes magiques* (Brussels): Académie Royale de Belgique, Classes des lettres et des sciences morales et politiques, Mémoires, 54, Part 4; original edn. 1936.

Delcambre, Etienne (1954). 'La psychologie des inculpés lorrains de sorcellerie', *Revue Historique du Droit Français et Étranger*, 32, pp. 508–25.

Delehaye, H. (1925). 'Les recueils antiques de miracles de saints', *Analecta Bollandiana*, 43, pp. 5–85 and 305–25.

Delooz, Pierre (1983). 'Towards a Sociological Study of Canonized Sainthood in the

Catholic Church', in Stephen Wilson (ed.), *Saints and their Cults: Studies in Religious Sociology, Folklore and History* (Cambridge, CUP), ch. 6; original edn. 1962.

Delumeau, Jean (ed.) (1976). *La Mort des pays de Cocagne: comportements collectifs de la Renaissance á l'âge classique* (Paris, Publications de la Sorbonne), Série 'Etudes', 12.

De Martino, Ernesto (1966). *Sud e magia* (Milan, Feltrinelli).

Deonna, W. (1928). 'Talismans chrétiens', *Revue de l'Histoire des Religions*, 95, pp. 19–42.

De Rosa, Gabriele (1976). 'Sainteté, clergé et peuple dans le Mezzogiorno italien au milieu du XVIIIe siècle', *Revue d'Historie de la Spiritualité*, 52, pp. 245–64.

Desaivre, Leo (1899). 'Creuse', *Revue des Traditions Populaires*, 14, p. 572.

Desnoyers, J. (1985). 'Excommunication des insectes et d'autres animaux nuisibles à l'agriculture', *Bulletin du Comité Historique des Monuments Écrits de l'Histoire de France*, 4, pp. 36–54.

Devos, Roger (1977). 'Pratiques et mentalités religieuses dans la Savoie du XVIIIe siècle: la paroisse de Combloux', *Religion Populaire: Le Monde Alpin et Rhodanien*, 5, pp. 105–43.

Dewez, Leon and Iterson, Albert van (1956). 'La lactation de Saint Bernard: légende et iconographie'. *Cîteaux in de Nederlanden*, 7, pp. 165–89.

Deyon, Pierre (1962). 'Mentalités populaires: un sondage à Amiens au XVIIe siècle', *Annales*, 17, pp. 448–58.

Dickens, Charles (1932). *Bleak House* (London, Everyman; original edn, 1852-3).

Dickens, Charles (no date). *Great Expectations* (Oxford, OUP; original edn, 1861).

Dickens, Charles (1949). *The Personal History of David Copperfield* (Oxford, OUP; original edn, 1849–50).

Dickens, Charles (1991). *The Posthumous Papers of the Pickwick Club* (Oxford, OUP; original edn, 1836-7).

Didier, J.C. (1953). 'La question du baptême des enfants chez S. Bernard et ses contemporains', *Analecta Sacri Ordinis Cisterciensis*, 3–4, pp. 191–201.

Didier, J.C. (1956). 'Saint Augustin et le baptême des enfants', *Revue des Etudes Augustiniennes* (*Mémorial Bardy*), pp. 109–29.

Didier, J.C. (1959). *Le Baptême des enfants dans la tradition de l'église* (Tournai).

Didier, J.C. (1968). 'Un sanctuaire à "répit" du diocèse de Langres: l'église de Fayl-Billot, Haute-Marne, d'après des actes notariés du XVIIe siècle', *Mélanges de Science Religieuse*, pp. 3–21.

Diethelm, Oskar (1970). 'The Medical Teaching of Demonology in the 17th and 18th Centuries', *Journal of the History of Behavioural Sciences*, 6, pp. 3–15.

Dillenberger, John (ed.) (1961). *Martin Luther: Selections from his Writings* (New York, Doubleday Anchor).

Dimnet, Ernest (1939). *My Old World* (London, Cape).

Diricq, Edouard (1910). *Maléfices et sortilèges: procès criminels de l'ancien évêché de Bâle pour faits de sorcellerie* (1549–1670) (Lausanne).

Djilas, Milovan (1958). *Land without Justice* (New York).

Dodds, E.R. (1951). *The Greeks and the Irrational* (Berkeley, University of California).

Dodds, E.R. (1973). *The Ancient Concept of Progress and Other Essays on Greek Literature and Belief* (Oxford, Clarendon Press).

Dolan, John P. (1972). 'Religious Festivities during the Reformation and Counter-Reformation: Challenge and Response', *Societas*, 2, pp. 95–120.

Dolci, Danilo (1960). *The Outlaws of Partinico* (London, Macgibbon and Kee).

Dolci, Danilo (1966). *Poverty in Sicily* (Harmondsworth, Penguin).

Dorson, Richard M. (1968). *The British Folklorists: A History* (London, Routledge).

Douglas, Norman (1923). *Old Calabria* (London, Secker; original edn, 1915).

Douglas, Norman (1948). *Siren Land* (Harmondsworth, Penguin; original edn, 1911).

Duby, Georges (1981). *The Age of the Cathedrals: Art and Society, 980–1420* (London, Croom Helm).

Duby, Georges (1985). *The Knight, the Lady and the Priest: The Making of Modern Marriage in Medieval France* (Harmondsworth, Penguin).

Duby, Georges (1991). *France in the Middle Ages, 987–1460* (Oxford, Blackwell).

Duby, Georges and Andrée (1973). *Les Procès de Jeanne d'Arc* (Paris, Gallimard/Julliard), Collection Archives.

Dupin, L.E. (1970). *Nouvelle bibliothèque des auteurs ecclesiastiques*, iv, *Des auteurs du sixième siècle* (Westmead, Gregg; original edn, 1703).

Duffy, Eamon (1992). *The Stripping of the Altars: Traditional Religion in England, 1400–1580* (New Haven and London, Yale).

Durantini, Mary Frances (1983). *The Child in Seventeenth-Century Dutch Painting* (Ann Arbor), Studies in the Fine Arts: Iconography, 7.

Durbec, J.-A. (1952). 'Notes historiques sur quelques pèlerinages, processions, fêtes et jeux de Provence', *Actes du soixante-dix-septième congrès des sociétés savantes, Grenoble, 1952*, Section d'histoire moderne et contemporaine, pp. 247–86 (Paris).

Durham, M.E. (1928). *Some Tribal Origins, Laws and Customs of the Balkans* (London).

Durkheim, Emile (1976). *The Elementary Forms of Religious Life* (London, Allen and Unwin; original edn, 1912).

Durkheim, Emile and Mauss, Marcel (1963), *Primitive Classification* (London, Cohen and West; original edn, 1903).

Eire, Carlos M.N. (1989). *War against the Idols: The Reformation of Worship from Erasmus to Calvin* (Cambridge, CUP).

Eliade, Mircea (1975). 'Some Observations on European Witchcraft', *History of Religions*, 14, pp. 149–72.

Eliade, Mircea (1978). *No Souvenirs: Journal, 1957–1969* (London, Routledge).

Elkins, Sharon K. (1988). *Holy Women of Twelfth-Century England* (Chapel Hill, University of North Carolina).

Elliott, Ralph W.V. (1957). 'Runes, Yews and Magic', *Speculum*, 32, pp. 250–61.

Emmison, F.G. (1973). *Elizabethan Life: Morals and the Church Courts* (Chelmsford), Essex Record Office Publications, 63.

Emmison, F.G. (1976). 'Tithes, Perambulations and Sabbath-Breach in Elizabethan Essex', in F.G. Emmison and Roy Stephens (eds.), *Tribute to an Antiquary: Essays Presented to Marc Fitch* (Leopard's Head Press), pp. 177–209.

'Enfants morts sans baptême, Les' (1899). *Revue des Traditions Populaires*, 14, pp. 15, 205 and 579–80.

Erikson, Erik H. (1972). *Young Man Luther: A Study in Psychoanalysis and History* (London, Faber).

Esdaile, Katharine A. (1927). *English Monumental Sculpture since the Renaissance* (London, SPCK).

Evans, E, Estyn (1988). *Irish Folk Ways* (London, Routledge; original edn, 1957).

Evans, E.P. (1987). *The Criminal Prosecution and Capital Punishment of Animals* (London, Faber; original edn, 1906).

Evans, George Ewart (1967). *The Horse in the Furrow* (London, Faber).

Evans, George Ewart (1971). *The Pattern under the Plough: Aspects of the Folk-Life of East Anglia* (London, Faber).

Evans, Joan (1968). *Monastic Life at Cluny, 910–1157* (Hamden, Conn., Archon Books; original edn, 1931).

Evans, G. Nesta (1953). *Religion and Politics in Mid-Eighteenth-Century Anglesey* (Cardiff, University of Wales).

Evemy, F.S. (1979). 'La Vie rurale en France au XIXe siècle à travers la littérature' (University of East Anglia, Unpublished Third Year Dissertation, European Studies).

Ewen, C. L'Estrange (1936). 'A Noted Case of Witchcraft at North Moreton in the Early Seventeenth Century', *Berkshire Archaeological Journal*, 40, pp. 207–13.

Ex-voto du terroir marseillais (1978). (Marseille, Archives Communales).

Fabre-Vassas, Claudine (1991). 'La cuisine des sorcières', *Ethnologie Française*, 21, pp. 423–37.

Falassi, Alessandro (1980). *Folklore by the Fireside: Text and Context of the Tuscan Veglia* (London, Scolar Press).

Fanshawe, Ann, Lady (1907). *The Memoirs* (London, John Lane).

Farge, Arlette (1976). 'Accouchement et naissance au XVIIIe siècle', *Revue de Médecine Psychosomatique*, 18, pp. 19–26.

Faulkner, William (1956). *The Hamlet* (New York, Vintage Books).

Favret-Saada, Jeanne (1977). *Les Mots, la mort, les sorts: la sorcellerie dans le Bocage* (Paris, Gallimard).

Febvre, Lucien (1957). *Au coeur religieux du XVIe siècle* (Paris, SEVPEN).

Febvre, Lucien (1968). *Le Problème de l'incroyance au XVIe siècle: la religion de Rabelais* (Paris, Albin Michel; original edn, 1942).

Fedotov, G.P. (1966). *The Russian Religious Mind* (Cambridge, Mass., Harvard), 2 vols.

Fél, Edit, Hofer, Tamás and Csilléry, Klára K. (1958). *Hungarian Peasant Art* (Budapest, Corvina).

Fermor, Patrick Leigh (1966). *Roumeli: Travels in Northern Greece* (London, John Murray).

Fielding, Henry (1932). *Jonathan Wild* and *The Journal of a Voyage to Lisbon* (London, Everyman; original edn of latter 1755.

Fielding, Henry (1960). *Joseph Andrews* (London, Everyman; original edn, 1742).

Fildes, Valerie (1988). *Wet Nursing: A History from Antiquity to the Present* (Oxford, Blackwell).

Filippi, J.-M. (1906). *Recueil de sentences et dictons usités en Corse avec traduction et lexique* (Paris).

Fincham, Francis W.X. (1921). 'Notes from the Ecclesiastical Court Records at Somerset House', *Transactions of the Royal Historical Society*, 4th Series, 4, pp. 103–39.

Fine, Agnès (1984). 'Transmission des prénoms et parenté en pays de Sault, 1740–1940', in Jacques Dupâquier et al. (eds.), *Le Prénom: mode et histoire* (Paris, Editions de l'Ecole des Hautes Etudes en Sciences Sociales), pp. 109–25.

Fine, Agnès (1987a). 'Le parrain, son filleul et l'au-delà', *Etudes Rurales*, 105–6, pp. 123–46.

Fine, Agnès (1987b). 'L'héritage du nom de baptême', *Annales*, pp. 853–77.

Finley, M.I. (1968). *Aspects of Antiquity: Discoveries and Controversies* (London, Chatto and Windus).

Finot, Jules (1875). 'Procès de sorcellerie au bailliage de Vesoul de 1606 à 1636', *Bulletin de la Société d'Agriculture, Sciences et Arts du Département de la Haute-Saône*, pp. 1–71.

First and Second Prayer Books of King Edward the Sixth, The (1927). (London, Everyman).

Fisher, J.D.C. (1965). *Christian Initiation: Baptism in the Medieval West, A Study in the Disintegration of the Primitive Rite of Initiation* (London, SPCK), Alcuin Club

Collections, 47.

Fisher, J.D.C. (1970). *Christian Initiation: The Reformation Period, Some Early Reformed Rites of Baptism and Confirmation and Other Contemporary Documents* (London, SPCK), Alcuin Club Collections, 51.

Flandrin, Jean-Louis (1976). *Familles: parenté, maison, sexualité dans l'ancienne société* (Paris, Hachette).

Flint, Valerie I.J. (1991). *The Rise of Magic in Early Medieval Europe* (Oxford, Clarendon, Press).

Flynn, Maureen (1995). 'Blasphemy and the Play of Anger in Sixteenth-Century Spain', *Past and Present*, 149, pp. 29–56.

Folet, H. (1906). 'Rabelais et les saints préposés aux maladies', *Revue des Etudes Rabelaisiennes*, 4, pp. 199–216.

Follonier, Jean (1954). 'Maléfices: "Le mal donné" (La mâ baïa)', *Folklore Suisse*, 44, pp. 40–4.

Forbes, Thomas R. (1953). 'The Social History of the Caul', *Yale Journal of Biology and Medicine*, 25, pp. 495–508.

Forbes, Thomas R. (1966). *The Midwife and the Witch* (New Haven, Yale).

Forbes, Thomas R. (1971). 'Verbal Charms in British Folk Medicine', *Proceedings of the American Philosophical Society*, 115, part 4, pp. 293–316.

Ford, Richard (1913). *Gatherings from Spain* (London, Everyman; original edn, 1846).

Forey, Alan (1992). *The Military Orders from the Twelfth to the Early Fourteenth Centuries* (London, Macmillan).

Forsyth, Ilene H. (1976–7). 'Children in Early Medieval Art: Ninth through Twelfth Centuries', *Journal of Psychohistory*, 4, pp. 31–70.

Foster, George M. (1965). 'Peasant Society and the Image of Limited Good', *American Anthropologist*, 67, pp. 293–315.

Foster, George M. (1972). 'The Anatomy of Envy: A Study in Symbolic Behavior', *Current Anthropology*, 13, pp. 165–202.

Fouju, G. (1889). 'Amulettes pour les convulsions et la dentition des enfants', *Revue des Traditions Populaires*, 4, p. 576.

Fraysse, Camille J.B. (1961). 'Au pays de Baugé (Maine-et-Loire): la thérapeutique populaire et les sorciers guérisseurs', *Arts et Traditions Populaires*, 9, pp. 100–8.

Frazer, James George (1932). *The Golden Bough: A Study in Magic and Religion* (London, Macmillan).

Fribourg, Jeanine (1979). 'Rapports entre morts et vivants en Espagne (dans des villages du N.E.: Aragón, Navarre, Catalogne)', *Etudes Corses*, 7, nos 12–13, pp. 343–59.

Frieden, Nancy M. (1978). 'Child Care: Medical Reform in a Traditionalist Culture', in David L. Ransel (ed.), *The Family in Imperial Russia: New Lines of Historical Research* (Urbana, University of Illinois), pp. 236–59.

Frijhoff, Willem (1993), 'The Kiss Sacred and Profane: Reflections on a Cross-Cultural Confrontation', in Jan Bremmer and Herman Roodenburg (eds), *A Cultural History of Gesture, From Antiquity to the Present Day* (Cambridge, Polity Press), ch. 9.

Froeschlé-Chopard, M.H. (1974). 'Les dévotions populaires d'après les visites pastorales: un exemple, le diocèse de Vence au début du XVIIIe siècle', *Revue d'Histoire de l'Eglise de France*, 60, pp. 85–97.

Froeschlé-Chopard, M.H. (1976). 'Univers sacré et iconographie au XVIIIe siècle: églises et chapelles des diocèses de Vence et de Grasse', *Annales*, 31, pp. 489–519; and in Robert Forster and Orest Ranum (eds), *Ritual, Religion, and the Sacred: Selections from the*

Annales (Baltimore, Johns Hopkins, 1982), ch. 8.

Fugger News-Letters, The (1928). Ed. Victor von Klarwill, First Series (London, John Lane).

Fustel de Coulanges, Numa Denis (no date). *The Ancient City* (New York, Doubleday Anchor; original edn, 1864).

Gaboriau, Patrick (1987). 'Les livres de sorcellerie: rejet et fascination de la culture lettrée', *Anthropologie sociale et ethnologie de la France*, Colloque du Centre d'ethnologie française et du Musée national des arts et traditions populaires, Paris, November 1987, Communications, II, Atélier 5.

Gaidoz, Henri (1887). *La Rage et St Hubert* (Paris, Alphonse Picard).

Gallop, Rodney (1930). *A Book of the Basques* (London, Macmillan).

Gallop, Rodney (1936). '*Couvade* and the Basques', *Folk-Lore*, 47, pp. 310–13.

Gallop, Portugal (1961). *Portugal: A Book of Folk-Ways* (Cambridge, CUP; original edn, 1936).

Ganiage, Jean (1973). 'Nourrissons parisiens en Beauvaisis', in *Hommage à Marcel Reinhard: sur la population française au XVIIIe et au XIXe siècle* (Paris), pp. 271–89.

Garin, Eugenio (1983). *Astrology in the Renaissance: The Zodiac of Life* (London, Routledge).

Garnier (1975). *Becket (Vie Saint Thomas le Martyr de Cantorbire)*, ed. Janet Shirley (Chichester, Phillimore).

Gaspar, Enrique Casas (1947). *Costumbres españoles de naciamiento, noviazgo, casamiento y muerte* (Madrid).

Gasparini, Evel (1962). 'Studies in Old Slavic Religion: *Ubrus*', *History of Religions*, 2, pp. 112–39.

Geary, Patrick (1983). 'Humiliation of Saints', in Stephen Wilson (ed.), *Saints and their Cults: Studies in Religious Sociology, Folklore and History* (Cambridge: CUP), ch. 3.

Gélis, Jacques (1976). 'L'accouchement au XVIIIe siècle: pratiques traditionnelles et contrôle médical', *Ethnologie Française*, 6, pp. 325–40.

Gélis, Jacques (1981). 'De la mort à la vie: les "sanctuaires à répit" ', *Ethnologie Française*, 11, pp. 211–24.

Gélis, Jacques (1984). *L'Arbre et le fruit: la naissance dans l'Occident moderne (XVIe–XIXe siècle)* (Paris, Fayard).

Gèlis, Jacques, Laget, Mireille and Morel, Marie-France (eds) (1978). *Entrer dans la vie: naissances et enfances dans la France traditionnelle* (Paris, Gallimard/Julliard), Collection Archives.

Gennep, Arnold van (1924). 'Le culte populaire de sainte Agathe en Savoie', *Revue d'Ethnographie*, 17, pp. 28–36.

Gennep, Arnold van (1927). 'La Saint-Jean dans les croyances et coutumes populaires de la Savoie', *Journal de Psychologie Normale et Pathologique*, pp. 26–77.

Gennep, Arnold van (1972). *Manuel de folklore français contemporain* (Paris, Auguste Picard; original edn, 1937–58), 7 vols.

Gentilcore, David (1995). 'Contesting Illness in Early Modern Naples: *Miracolati*, Physicians and the Congregation of Rites', *Past and Present*, 148, pp. 117–48.

Gerald of Wales (1978). *The Journey through Wales* and *The Description of Wales*. Ed. Lewis Thorpe (Harmondsworth, Penguin).

Gérin, Winifred (1970). *Horatia Nelson* (Oxford).

Ghéon, Henri (1939). *St Vincent Ferrer* (London, Sheed and Ward).

Gibson, Gail McMurray (1990). 'Saint Anne and the Religion of Childbed: Some East

Anglian Texts and Talismans', in Kathleen Ashley and Pamela Sheingorn (eds.), *Interpreting Cultural Symbols: Saint Anne in Late Medieval Society* (Athens: University of Georgia), pp. 95–110.

Gibson, Walter S. (1973). *Hieronymus Bosch* (London, Thames and Hudson).

Ginzburg, Carlo (1983). *The Night Battles: Witchcraft and Agrarian Cults in the Sixteenth and Seventeenth Centuries* (London, Routledge; original edn, 1966).

Ginzburg, Carlo (1990). 'Deciphering the Sabbath', in Bengt Ankarloo and Gustav Henningsen (eds), *Early Modern Witchcraft: Centres and Peripheries* (Oxford, Clarendon Press), ch. 4.

Gittings, Clare (1988). *Death, Burial and the Individual in Early Modern England* (London, Routledge).

Gluckman, Max (1973). *The Judicial Process among the Barotse of Northern Rhodesia (Zambia)* (Manchester, MUP).

Glyde, John (1976). *Folklore and Customs of Suffolk (The New Suffolk Garland)* (Wakefield, EP Publishing; original edn, 1866).

Godin, André (1964). 'La société au XVI siècle vue par J. Glapion (1460?–1522), frère mineur, confesseur de Charles-Quint', *Revue du Nord*, 46, pp. 341–70.

Gomme, G.L. (1889). 'Totemism in Britain', *Archaeological Review*, 3, pp. 217–42.

Gonthier, Dominique and Le Bas, Claire (1974). 'Analyse socio-économique de quelques recueils de miracles dans la Normandie du XIe au XIIIe siècle', *Annales de Normandie*, 24, pp. 3–36.

Goodrich-Freer, A. (1899). 'The Powers of Evil in the Outer Hebrides', *Folk-Lore*, 10, pp. 259–82.

Goody, Jack (1983). *The Development of the Family and Marriage in Europe* (Cambridge, CUP).

Gorceix, Septime (1913). 'Saint Léonard accoucheur: les vertus de ses reliques et leur rôle dans la naissance de Louis XIV', *Aesculape*, 3, pp. 7–11.

Goubert, Pierre (1968). *Cent mille provinciaux au XVIIe siècle: Beauvais et le Beauvaisis de 1600 à 1730* (Paris, Flammarion).

Goubert, Pierre (1973). *The Ancien Régime: French Society, 1600–1750* (London, Weidenfeld and Nicolson).

Goubert, Pierre (1986). *The French Peasantry in the Seventeenth Century* (Cambridge, CUP).

Gougaud, L., O.S.B. (1914). 'La danse dans les églises', *Revue d'Histoire Ecclésiastique*, 15, pp. 5–22 and 229–45.

Gougaud, L., O.S.B. (1924). 'La pratique de la phlébotomie dans les cloîtres', *Revue Mabillon*, 14, pp. 1–13.

Gough, Richard (1981). *The History of Myddle*, ed. David Hey (Harmondsworth, Penguin).

Gourevitch, Aaron J. (1983). *Les Catégories de la culture médiévale* (Paris, Gallimard).

Goursaud, A. (1977–8), *La Société Rurale traditionelle en Limousin: ethnographie et folklore du Haut-Limousin et de la Basse-Marche* (Paris: G.-P. Maisonneuve et Larose), vols 2 and 3.

Graef, Hilda (1963–5). *Mary: A History of Doctrine and Devotion* (London, Sheed and Ward), 2 vols.

Graham, Harvey (1960). *Eternal Eve: The Mysteries of Birth and the Customs that Surround It* (London, Hutchinson).

Grand Calendrier et compost des bergiers avec leur astrologie (1976) (Paris, Editions Siloe).

Grattan, J, H.G. and Singer, Charles (1952). *Anglo-Saxon Magic and Medicine: Illustrated Specially from the Semi-Pagan Text 'Lacnunga'* (Oxford, OUP).

Green, A.E. (ed.) (1971). *Witches and Witch-Hunters* (Wakefield).

Green, Roger Lancelyn (1962). 'Shakespeare and the Fairies', *Folk-Lore*, 73, pp. 89–103.

Greene, Rev. Joseph (1965). *Correspondence*, ed. Levi Fox (London, Historical Manuscripts Commission), JP 8.

Grégoire, Henri (1949). 'Asklépios, le dieu-taupe', *Flambeau*, 32, pp. 22–54.

Gregory of Tours (1974). *The History of the Franks*, ed. Lewis Thorpe (Harmondsworth, Penguin).

Grenadou, Ephraïm and Prévost, Alain (1966). *Grenadou paysan français* (Paris, Editions du Seuil).

Grimm, Jakob and Wilhelm (1963). *Household Stories* (New York, Dover).

Grimm, Jakob and Wilhelm (1978). *Tales for Young and Old: The Complete Stories* (London).

Gross, Hanns (1990). *Rome in the Age of Enlightenment: The Post-Tridentine Syndrome and the Ancien Régime* (Cambridge, CUP).

Guazzo, Francesco Maria (1970). *Compendium Maleficarum*, trans E.A. Ashwin (London, original edn, 1608 and 1626).

Gudeman, Stephen (1972). 'The *Compadrazgo* as a Reflection of the Natural and Spiritual Person', *Proceedings of the Royal Anthropological Institutes of Great Britain and Ireland for 1971*, pp. 45–71.

Guesquin-Barbichon, Marie-France (1977). 'Organisation sociale de trois trajets rituels (les Rogations, la Fête-Dieu et la Saint-Roch) à Bazoches, Morvan', *Ethnologie Française*, 7, pp. 29–44.

Guillaumin, Emile (1983). *The Life of a Simple Man* (London, Sinclair Browne, original edn, 1904).

Gurdon, Lady Eveline Camilla (ed.) (1893). *Country Folk-Lore: Printed Extracts, No. 2, Suffolk* (London and Woodbridge).

Haffter, Carl (1968). 'The Changeling: History and Psychodynamics of Attitudes to Handicapped Children in European Folklore', *Journal of the History of the Behavioural Sciences*, 4, pp. 55–61.

Haggard, Lilias Rider and Williamson, Henry (1943). *Norfolk Life* (London, Faber).

Hair, Paul (ed.) (1972). *Before the Bawdy Court: Selections from Church Court and Other Records Relating to the Correction of Moral Offences in England, Scotland and New England, 1300–1800* (London, Elek).

Haller, William (1938). *The Rise of Puritanism, 1570–1643* (New York, Columbia).

Hampe, Theodor (1929). *Crime and Punishment in Germany: As Illustrated by the Nuremberg Malefactors' Books* (London, Routledge).

Hanawalt, Barbara A. (1977). 'Childrearing among the Lower Classes of Late Medieval England', *Journal of Interdisciplinary History*, 8, pp. 1–22.

Hand, Wayland D. (1971). 'The Folk Healer: Calling and Endowment', *Journal of the History of Medicine*, 26, pp. 263–75.

Hand, Wayland, D. (1980). *Magical Medicine: The Folkloric Component of Medicine in the Folk Belief, Custom and Ritual of the Peoples of Europe and America* (Berkeley).

Hansen, Elizabeth de G.R. (1979). ' "Overlaying" in Nineteenth-Century England: Infant Mortality or Infanticide?', *Human Ecology*, 7, pp. 333–52.

Hart, Rev. Richard (1864). 'The Shrines and Pilgrimages of the County of Norfolk', *Norfolk Archaeology*, 6, pp. 277–94.

Haskell, Arnold and Lewis, Min (1971). *Infantalia: The Archaeology of the Nursery* (London).

Hasluck, Margaret (1939). 'Couvade in Albania', *Man*, 39, nos 17–18, pp. 18–20.

Hastrup, Kirsten (1990). 'Iceland: Sorcerers and Paganism', in Ankarloo and Henningsen (eds), ch. 15.

Hawkins, L.H. (1970). 'The History of Resuscitation', *British Journal of Hospital Medicine*, October, pp. 495–500.

Hazlitt, William (1942). *Table Talk: or Original Essays on Men and Manners* (London, Everyman; original edn, 1824.)

Hélias, Pierre-Jakez (1978). *The Horse of Pride: Life in a Breton Village* (New Haven, Yale).

Henningsen, Gustav (1982). 'Witchcraft in Denmark', *Folklore*, 93, pp. 131–7.

Herlihy, David (ed.) (1979). *The History of Feudalism* (New Jersey, Humanities Press).

Herlihy, David (1985). *Medieval Households* (Cambridge, Mass., Harvard).

Herman, Marie-Thérèse (1987). *La Savoie traditionnelle* (Apremont, Curandera).

Herrick, Robert (1908). *Hesperides and Noble Numbers* (London, Everyman; original edn, 1648).

Hertz, Robert (1970a). 'Contes et dictons recueillis sur le front parmi les poilus de la Mayenne et d'ailleurs', in Hertz, *Sociologie religieuse et folklore* (Paris, PUF), pp. 161–88; original edn, 1917.

Hertz, Robert (1970b). 'La prééminence de la main droite: étude sur la polarité religieuse', in ibid., pp. 84–109; original edn, 1909.

Hesiod (1983). *Theogony, Works and Days, Shield*, ed. A.N. Athanassakis (Baltimore, Johns Hopkins).

Hildburgh, W.L. (1951). 'Some Spanish Amulets connected with Lactation', *Folk-Lore*, 62, pp. 430–48.

Hill, Thomas D. (1977). 'The *Aecerbot* Charm and its Christian User', *Anglo-Saxon England*, 6, pp. 213–21.

Histoire passionnante de la vie d'un petit ramoneur savoyard (1981) (Paris, Le Sycomore).

Hoare, F.R. (ed.) (1954). *The Western Fathers: Being the Lives of SS. Martin of Tours, Ambrose, Augustine of Hippo, Honoratus of Arles and Germanus of Auxerre* (London, Sheed and Ward).

Hoffmann, Léon-François (1964). *La Peste à Barcelone* (Princeton, and Paris, PUF).

Hole, Christina (1953). *The English Housewife in the Seventeenth Century* (London, Chatto and Windus).

Hole, Christina (1954). *English Shrines and Sanctuaries* (London, Batsford).

Hole, Christina (1975). *English Traditional Customs* (Totowa, N.J., Rowman and Littlefield).

Hole, Christina (1973). 'Some Instances of Image-Magic in Great Britain', in Venetia Newall (ed.), *The Witch Figure* (London, Routledge), ch. 5.

Homme et son corps dans la société traditionnelle, L' (1978). (Paris, Editions de la Réunion des Musées Nationaux).

Howard, Margaret M. (1951). 'Dried Cats', *Man*, November, pp. 148–51.

Howlett, England (1895). 'Marriage Customs', and 'Burial Customs', in William Andrews (ed.), *Curious Church Customs* (Hull, William Andrews), pp. 99–146.

Hufton, Olwen (1974). *The Poor of Eighteenth-Century France, 1750–1789* (Oxford, Clarendon Press).

Hughes, Muriel Joy (1987). *Women Healers in Medieval Life and Literature* (Salem, N.H.; original edn, 1943).

Hugo, Victor (1972). *Choses vues: souvenirs, journaux, cahiers, 1830–1846* (Paris, Gallimard).

Huizinga, J. (1955). *The Waning of the Middle Ages: A Study of the Forms of Life, Thought and Art in the Fourteenth and Fifteenth Centuries in France and the Netherlands* (Harmondsworth, Penguin; original edn, 1924).

Hulst, P. Cesario van (1944). 'La storia della divozione a Gesù Bambino nelle immagini plastiche isolate', *Antonianum*, 19, pp. 35–54.

Hunt, Tony (1990). *Popular Medicine in Thirteenth-Century England: Introduction and Texts* (Cambridge, Brewer).

Hunt, A.S. and Edgar, C.C. (1970). *Select Papyri*, I, *Non-Literary Papyri, Private Affairs* (Cambridge, Mass., Harvard, and London; Heinemann) Loeb.

Hutton, Ronald (1994). *The Rise and Fall of Merry England: The Ritual Year, 1400–1700* (Oxford, OUP).

Hutton, Ronald (1995). 'The English Reformation and the Evidence of Folklore'. *Past and Present*, 148, pp. 89–116.

Hutton, Ronald (1996). *The Stations of the Sun: A History of the Ritual Year in Britain* (Oxford, OUP).

Huxley, Aldous (1955). *Beyond the Mexique Bay: A Traveller's Journal* (Harmondsworth, Penguin; original edn, 1934).

Huxley, Gervas (1967). *Victorian Duke: The Life of Hugh Lupus Grosvenor, First Duke of Westminster* (London, OUP).

Inman, W.S. (1941). 'The Couvade in Modern England', *British Journal of Medical Psychology*, 19, pp. 37–55.

Jacob, E.F. (1968). *Essays in Later Medieval History* (Manchester).

Jacobsen, Grethe (1984). 'Pregnancy and Childbirth in the Medieval North: A Typology of Sources and a Preliminary Study', *Scandinavian Journal of History*, 9, pp. 91–111.

Jacopone da Todi (1982). *The Lauds* (London, SPCK), Classics of Western Spirituality.

Jansson, Sven B.F. (1962). *The Runes of Sweden* (Stockholm, Norstedt and Söner).

Jeanton, Jean (1937). 'Le folklore des eaux en Mâconnais', *Ethnographie*, 33/34, pp. 65–92.

Jerome, St (1954). *Select Letters* (London, Heinemann, and Cambridge, Mass., Harvard), Loeb.

John of Salisbury (1956). *Historia Pontificalis*, ed. Marjorie Chibnall (London, Nelson), Medieval Texts.

Johnson, Samuel (1963). *A Journey to the Western Islands of Scotland*, in *Prose Prose and Poetry*, ed. Mona Wilson (London, Hart-Davis, pp. 655–789; original edn, 1775).

Johnson, Samuel (No date). *Lives of the English Poets* (London, Everyman; original edn, 1777–80), 2 vols.

Johnson, Trevor (1996). 'Blood, Tears and Xavier-Water: Jesuit Missionaries and Popular Religion in the Eighteenth-Century Upper Palatinate', in Bob Scribner and Trevor Johnson (eds), *Popular Religion in Germany and Central Europe, 1400–1800* (London, Macmillan), Ch. 9.

Joisten, Charles (1977). 'La mort, Dieu et le diable dans un ethnotexte du Haut-Embrunais', *Religion Populaire: Le Monde Alpin et Rhodanien*, 5, pp. 271–338.

Jolas, Tina (1977). 'Parcours cérémoniel d'un terroir villageois', *Ethnologie Française*, 7, pp. 8–28.

Jolas, Tina, Verdier, Yvonne and Zonabend, Françoise (1970). ' "Parler famille" '. *L'Homme*, 10, part 3, pp. 5–26.

Jolas, Tina and Zonabend, Françoise (1977). 'Tillers of the Fields and Woodspeople', in

Robert Forster and Orest Ranum (eds.), *Rural Society in France: Selections from the Annales* (Baltimore, Johns Hopkins), ch. 7.

Jolly, Karen Louise (1985). 'Anglo-Saxon Charms in the Context of a Christian World View', *Journal of Medieval History*, 11, pp. 279–93.

Jones, Francis (1954). *The Holy Wells of Wales* (Cardiff, University of Wales).

Jones, I.B. (1937). 'Popular Medical Knowledge in Fourteenth-Century English Literature', *Bulletin of the Institute of the History of Medicine*, 5, pp. 405–51 and 538–88.

Jones, William R. (1971–2). 'Political Uses of Sorcery in Medieval Europe', *The Historian*, 34, pp. 670–87.

Jonson, Ben (1966). *The Alchemist*, ed. Douglas Brown (London, Benn; original edn, 1610).

Jonson, Ben (1975). *Poems*, ed. Ian Donaldson (London, OUP).

Joutard, Philippe (1977). 'Protestantisme populaire et univers magique: le cas cévenol', *Religion Populaire: Le Monde Alpin et Rhodanien*, 5, pp. 145–71.

Jussen, Bernhard (1992). 'Le parrainage à la fin du moyen age: savoir public, attentes théologiques et usages sociaux', *Annales*, 47, pp. 467–502.

Jusserand, J.J. (1891). *English Wayfaring Life in the Middle Ages* (London, Unwin).

Juvenal (1974). *The Sixteen Satires*, ed. Peter Green (Harmondsworth, Penguin).

Juvenal and Persius (1918 and 1961). Ed. G.G. Ramsay (London, Heinemann, and Cambridge, Mass., Harvard) Loeb.

Kaganoff, Benzion C. (1978). *A Dictionary of Jewish Names and Their History* (London, Routledge).

Kahk, Juhan (1990). 'Estonia II: The Crusade against Idolatry', in Ankarloo and Henningsen (eds), ch. 10.

Kantorowicz, Ernst H. (1958). *Laudes Regiae: A Study in Liturgical Acclamations and Medieval Ruler Worship* (Berkeley, University of California).

Karrer, Otto (ed.) (1947). *St Francis of Assisi: The Legends and Lauds* (London, Sheed and Ward).

Kempe, Margery (1954). *The Book of*, ed. W. Butler-Bowdon (London, OUP), World's Classics.

Kennedy, W.P.M. (ed.) (1924). *Elizabethan Episcopal Administration* (London, Mowbray), Alcuin Club Collections, 25–7, 3 vols.

Kent, Francis William (1977). *Household and Lineage in Renaissance Florence: The Family Life of the Capponi, Ginori and Rucellai* (Princeton).

Kerlouegan, François (1968–9). 'Essai sur la mise en nourriture et l'éducation dans les pays celtiques d'après le témoignage des textes hagiographiques latins', *Etudes Celtiques*, 12, pp. 101–46.

Ketton-Cremer, R.W. (1951). *Country Neighbourhood* (London, Faber).

Keynes, Geoffrey (1983). *The Gates of Memory* (Oxford, OUP).

Kieckhefer, Richard (1989). *Magic in the Middle Ages* (Cambridge, CUP).

Kilvert, Francis (1977). *Diary, 1870–1879: Selections*, ed. William Plomer (London, Cape).

Kingsford, H.S. (1921). *Illustrations of the Occasional Offices of the Church in the Middle Ages from Contemporary Sources* (Oxford), Alcuin Club Collections, 24.

Kittredge, George Lyman (1929). *Witchcraft in Old and New England* (Cambridge, Mass.).

Klagstad, Harold L. (1958). 'Great Russian Charm Structure', *Indiana Slavic Studies*, 2, pp. 135–44.

Klaniczay, Gábor (1990a). 'Hungary: The Accusations and the Universe of Popular Magic', in Ankarloo and Henningsen (eds), ch. 8.

Klaniczay, Gábor (1990b). *The Uses of Supernatural Power: The Transformation of Popular Religion in Medieval and Early Modern Europe* (Cambridge, Polity Press).

Klapisch-Zuber, Christiane (1985a). 'Compérage et clientèlisme à Florence (1360–1520)', *Richerche Storiche*, 15, pp. 61–76.

Klapisch-Zuber, Christiane (1985b). *Women, Family and Ritual in Renaissance Italy* (Chicago).

Klapisch-Zuber, Christiane (1986). 'Parrains et filleuls: une approche comparée de la France, l'Angleterre et l'Italie médiévales', *Medieval Prosopography*, 6, pp. 51–77.

Klauser, Theodor (1969). *A Short History of the Western Liturgy: An Account and Some Reflections* (London, OUP).

Kligman, Gail (1981). *Căluş: Symbolic Transformation in Romanian Ritual* (Chicago).

Kligman, Gail (1988). *The Wedding of the Dead: Ritual, Poetics, and Popular Culture in Transylvania* (Berkeley, University of California).

Knox, R.A. (1950). *Enthusiasm: A Chapter in the History of Religion with Special Reference to the XVII and XVIII Centuries* (Oxford, Clarendon Press).

Kostić, Cvetko (1957). 'Changement de structure du village en Yougoslavie', *Cahiers Internationaux de Sociologie*, 23, pp. 142–56.

Kselman, Thomas A. (1993). *Death and the Afterlife in Modern France* (Princeton).

Kvideland, Reimund and Sehmsdorf, Henning K. (eds.) (1991). *Scandinavian Folk Belief and Legend* (Oslo, Norwegian University Press).

Labriolle, Pierre de (1934). 'Le "Démon du Midi" ', *Bulletin Du Cange*, 9, pp. 46–54.

La Bruyère, Jean de (1970). *Characters*, ed. Jean Stewart (Harmondsworth, Penguin; original edn, 1668–94).

Lacroix, Pierre (1975). 'Un centre jurassien de piété populaire: Notre-Dame de Mièges', *Actes du 99e congrès national des sociétés savantes, Besançon, 1974*, Section d'histoire moderne, 2, pp. 215–35.

Laget, Mireille (1975). 'Recherches sur les ondoyements et baptêmes à Lodève et dans son diocèse aux XVII et XVIIIe siècles', *Etudes sur Pézenas et sa région*, 3, pp. 5–18.

Laget, Mireille (1980). 'Childbirth in Seventeenth- and Eighteenth-Century France: Obstetrical Practices and Collective Attitudes', in Robert Forster and Orest Ranum (eds.), *Medicine and Society in France: Selections from the Annales* (Baltimore, Johns Hopkins), ch. 7.

Laget, Mireille (1982). *Naissances: l'accouchement avant l'âge de la clinique* (Paris, Editions du Seuil).

Lamb, Charles (1951). *The Essays of Elia* and *The Last Essays of Elia* (London, OUP, World's Classics; original edn, 1820–33).

Larkin, Philip (1955). *The Less Deceived: Poems* (Hessle, Marvell Press).

Larner, Christina (1977). 'Two Late Scottish Witchcraft Tracts: *Witch-Craft Proven* and *The Tryal of Witchcraft*', in Sydney Anglo (ed.), *The Damned Art: Essays in the Literature of Witchcraft* (London), ch. 10.

Larner, Christina (1983). *Enemies of God: The Witch-Hunt in Scotland* (Oxford, Blackwell).

Larner, Christina (1984). *Witchcraft and Religion: The Politics of Popular Belief* (Oxford, Blackwell).

Larner, John (1965). *The Lords of Romagna: Romagnol Society and the Origins of the Signorie* (London, Macmillan).

Larner, John (1980). *Italy in the Age of Dante and Petrarch, 1216–1380* (London, Longman).

Larquié, Claude (1985). 'La mise en nourrice des enfants madrilènes au XVIIe siècle',

Revue d'Histoire Moderne et Contemporaine, 32, pp. 125–44.

Laslett, Peter (1965). *The World We Have Lost* (London, Methuen).

La Sorsa, Saverio (1962). 'Religiositá popolare pugliese', *Lares*, pp. 134–42.

Lawson, John Cuthbert (1910). *Modern Greek Folklore and Ancient Greek Religion: A Study in Survivals* (Cambridge, CUP).

Lea, Henry Charles (1939). *Materials toward a History of Witchcraft*, ed. Arthur C. Howland (Philadelphia), 3 vols.

Lea, Henry Charles (1973). *The Ordeal*, ed. Edward Peters (Philadelphia, University of Pennsylvania; original edn, 1866).

Le Braz, Anatole (1900). *Au Pays des pardons* (Paris, Calmann-Lévy).

Le Braz, Anatole (1937). *Les Saints Bretons d'après la tradition populaire en Cornouaille* (Paris).

Lebrun, François (1976). 'Le "Traité des superstitions" de Jean-Baptiste Thiers: contribution à l'ethnographie de la France du XVIIe siècle', *Annales de Bretagne et des Pays de l'Ouest*, pp. 443–65.

Lecotté, Roger (1953). *Recherches sur les cultes populaires dans l'actuel diocèse de Meaux (Département de Seine-et-Marne)*, Mémoires de la Fédération Folklorique d'Ile-de-France, 4 (Paris).

Le Fort, Léon (1870). 'La mortalité des nouveau-nés et l'industrie des nourrices en France', *Revue des Deux Mondes*, 86, 15 March, pp. 363–91.

Le Goff, Jacques (1980). 'Ecclesiastical Culture and Folklore in the Middle Ages: Saint Marcellus of Paris and the Dragon', in Le Goff, *Time, Work and Culture in the Middle Ages* (Chicago), pp. 159–88.

Le Goff, Jacques (1984). *The Birth of Purgatory* (London, Scolar Press).

Lehndorff, Hans Graf von (1964). *Token of a Covenant: Diary of an East Prussian Surgeon, 1945–47* (Chicago, Henry Regnery).

Léonard, Jacques (1980). 'Les guérisseurs en France au XIXe siècle', *Revue d'Histoire Moderne et Contemporaine*, 27, pp. 501–16.

Leproux, Marc (1954). *Contributions au folklore charentais: médecine, magie et sorcellerie* (Paris, PUF).

Leproux, Marc (1957). *Contributions au folklore charentais: dévotions et saints guérisseurs* (Paris, PUF).

Leproux, Marc (1959). *Contributions au folklore charentais: du berceau à la tombe* (Paris, PUF).

Lerou, Paule et Roger (1977). 'Les itinéraires cérémoniels des fêtes de saint Fiacre', *Ethnologie Française*, 7, pp. 83–94.

Le Roux, Françoise (1962). 'Etudes sur le festiaire celtique', *Ogam*, 14, pp. 174–84.

Le Roy, C. (1934). 'Le culte de Saint Eloi en Artois et dans le Nord de la France', *Revue de Folklore Français et Colonial*, 5, pp. 217–52.

Le Roy, Eugène (1937). *Le Moulin du Frau* (Paris, Nelson; original edn, 1895).

Le Roy, Eugène (1978). *Jacquou le croquant* (Paris, Presses Pocket; original edn, 1899).

Le Roy Ladurie, Emmanuel (1974). 'L'aiguillette', *Europe*, 539, pp. 134–46.

Le Roy Ladurie, Emmanuel (1980). *Montaillou: Cathars and Catholics in a French Village, 1294–1324* (Harmondsworth, Penguin).

Le Roy Ladurie, Emmanuel (1981). *Carnival in Romans: A People's Uprising at Romans, 1579–1580* (Harmondsworth, Penguin).

Le Roy Ladurie, Emmanuel (1983). *La Sorcière de Jasmin* (Paris, Editions du Seuil).

Letters of Abelard and Heloise, The (1974). Ed. Betty Radice (Harmondsworth, Penguin).

Levack, Brian P. (1987). *The Witch-Hunt in Early Modern Europe* (London, Longman).

Levi, Carlo (1948). *Christ Stopped at Eboli* (London, Cassell).

Levi, Giovanni (1988). *Inheriting Power: The Story of an Exorcist* (Chicago).

Lévi-Strauss (1972). *The Savage Mind* (*La Pensée Sauvage*) (London, Weidenfeld and Nicolson).

Lévy-Bruhl (1936). *Morceaux choisis* (Paris, Gallimard).

Lewin, Moshe (1990). 'Popular Religion in Twentieth-Century Russia', in Ben Eklof and Stephen Frank (eds.), *The World of the Russian Peasant: Post-Emancipation Culture and Society* (Boston, Unwin Hyman), ch. 8.

Leyser, Henrietta (1995). *Medieval Women: A Social History of Women in England, 450–1500* (London, Weidenfeld and Nicolson).

Leyser, K.J. (1979). *Rule and Conflict in an Early Medieval Society: Ottonian Saxony* (London, Edward Arnold).

Lilly, Joseph (ed.) (1870). *A Collection of Seventy-Nine Black-Letter Ballads and Broadsides Printed in the Reign of Queen Elizabeth* (London).

Lincoln, Bruce (1976–7). 'Treatment of Hair and Fingernails among the Indo-Europeans', *History of Religions*, 16, pp. 315–62.

Lindemann, Mary (1981). 'Love for Hire: The Regulation of the Wet-Nursing Business in Eighteenth-Century Hamburg', *Journal of Family History*, 6, pp. 379–95.

Linnell, Rev. C.L.S. (1962). *Norfolk Church Dedications* (York), St Anthony's Hall Publications, 21.

Lisle Letters, The (1985). Ed. Muriel St Clare Byrne and Bridget Boland (Harmondsworth, Penguin).

Lisón-Tolosana, Carmelo (1966). *Belmonte de Los Caballeros: A Sociological Study of a Spanish Town* (Oxford, OUP).

Lisón-Tolosana, Carmelo (1973). 'Some Aspects of Moral Structure in Galician Hamlets', *American Anthropologist*, 75, pp. 823–34.

Little, Lester K. (1979). 'La morphologie des malédictions monastiques', *Annales*, 34, pp. 43–60.

Lives of the Desert Fathers, The (1981). Eds. Norman Russell and Benedicta Ward (London, Mowbray).

Livy (1919–59). *Histories*, Ed. B.O. Foster et al. (London, Heinemann, and Cambridge, Mass., Harvard), Loeb, 14 vols.

Llobet, Gabriel de (1966). 'Variété des croyances populaires au comté de Foix au début du XIVe siècle d'après les enquêtes de Jacques Fournier', *Cahiers de Fanjeaux*, 11, pp. 109–26.

Longman, E.D. and Loch, S. (1911). *Pins and Pincushions* (London, Longmans).

Lorand, Sandor (1947). 'The Anathema of the Dead Mother', *Psychoanalysis and the Social Sciences*, 1, pp. 235–44.

Lottin, Alain (1970). 'Naissances illégitimes et filles-mères à Lille au XVIIe siècle', *Revue d'Histoire Moderne et Contemporaine*, 17, pp. 278–322.

Loubet, Christian (1977). 'Ex-voto de Notre-Dame d'Oropa en Piémont (XVIe-XXe siècles): images d'une dévotion populaire', *Religion Populaire: Le Monde Alpin et Rhodanien*, 5, pp. 213–45.

Loux, Françoise (1977). 'Pratiques médicales préventives et recours religieux: les soins aux enfants en Haute-Normandie', *Archives de Sciences Sociales des Religions*, 44, pp. 45–58.

Loux, Françoise (1978). *Le Jeune Enfant et son corps dans la médecine traditionnelle* (Paris,

Flammarion).

Loux, Françoise and Morel, Marie-France (1976). 'L'enfance et les savoirs sur le corps: pratiques médicales et pratiques populaires dans la France traditionnelle', *Ethnologie Française*, 6, pp. 309–24.

Lucan (1957). *The Civil War*, Trans, J.D. Duff (London: Heinemann, and Cambridge, Mass., Harvard) Loeb.

Luck, Georg (1987). *Arcana Mundi: Magic and the Occult in the Greek and Roman Worlds* (London, Crucible).

Lynch, Joseph H. (1986). *Godparents and Kinship in Early Medieval Europe* (Princeton).

Mabinogion, The (1977). Ed. Gwyn and Thomas Jones (London, Everyman).

MacCulloch, J.A, (1932). *Medieval Faith and Fable* (London, Harrap).

Macfarlane, Alan (1970). *The Family Life of Ralph Josselin, a Seventeenth-Century Clergyman: An Essay in Historical Anthropology* (Cambridge, CUP).

Mackinney, Loren C. (1943). 'An Unpublished Treatise on Medicine and Magic from the Age of Charlemagne', *Speculum*, 18, pp. 494–6.

Mackinney, Loren C. (1960). 'Childbirth in the Middle Ages as Seen in Manuscript Illustrations', *Ciba Symposium*, 8, pp. 230–6.

Macrides, Ruth (1987). 'The Byzantine Godfather', *Byzantine and Modern Greek Studies*, 11, pp. 139–62.

Maertens, T. (1962). *Histoire et pastorale du rituel du catéchuménat et du baptême* (Bruges), Collection de Pastorale liturgique, 56.

Mailand, Oscar (1899). 'Folk-lore des Roumains de la Hongrie: enchantements ou incantations', *Revue des Traditions Populaires*, 14, pp. 581–5.

Maître, J. (1967–8). 'Problèmes épistémologiques posés par une sociologie du baptême', *Epistémologie Sociologique*, 5, pp. 397–429.

Mallett, Michael (1969). *The Borgias: The Rise and Fall of a Renaissance Dynasty* (London, Bodley Head).

Malleus Maleficarum (1969). Ed. Rev. Montague Summers (London, Hogarth Press).

Maloney, Clarence (ed.) (1976). *The Evil Eye* (New York, Columbia).

Malson, Lucien (1972). *Wolf Children*, with Jean Itard, *The Wild Boy of Aveyron* (1801–7) (London, NLB).

Mandrou, Robert (1974). *Introduction à la France moderne (1500–1640): essai de psychologie historique* (Paris, Albin Michel).

Manners and Customs of All Nations (1827). Ed. Rev. John Platts (London, Henry Fisher).

Manning, Bernard, Lord (1919). *The People's Faith in the Time of Wyclif* (Cambridge, CUP).

Maraspini, A.L. (1968). *The Study of an Italian Village* (The Hague, Mouton).

Marchant, Ronald A. (1969). *The Church under the Law: Justice, Administration and Discipline in the Diocese of York, 1560–1640* (Cambridge, CUP).

Marrow, James H. and Shestack, Alan (eds.) (1981). *Hans Baldung Grien: Prints and Drawings* (Chicago).

Marshall, Rosalind K. (1984). 'Wet-Nursing in Scotland, 1500–1800', *Review of Scottish Culture*, 1, pp. 43–51.

Martin, A. Lynn (1988). *The Jesuit Mind: The Mentality of an Elite in Early Modern France* (Ithaca, Cornell).

Martin, Ruth (1989). *Witchcraft and the Inquisition in Venice, 1550–1650* (Oxford, Blackwell).

Martindale, Jane (1992). 'Peace and War in Early Eleventh-Century Aquitaine', in

Christopher Harper-Bill and Ruth Harvey (eds.), *Medieval Knighthood*, 4 (Woodbridge, Boydell Press), pp. 147–76.

Martinengo-Cesaresco, Countess (no date). *Essays in the Study of Folk-Songs* (London, Everyman; original edn, 1886).

Martinez de Toledo, Alfonso (1959). *Little Sermons on Sin: The Archpriest of Talavera* (Berkeley, University of California).

Martynova, Antonina (1978). 'Life of the Pre-Revolutionary Village as Reflected in Popular Lullabies', in David. L. Ransel (ed.), *The Family in Imperial Russia: New Lines of Historical Research* (Urbana, University of Illinois), pp. 171–85.

Massing, Jean-Michel (1977). 'A Sixteenth-Century Illustrated Treatise on Comets', *Journal of the Warburg and Courtauld Institutes*, 40, pp. 318–22.

Matarazzo, Francesco (1905). *Chronicles of the City of Perugia, 1492–1503*, ed. E.S. Morgan (London, Dent).

Mauriac, François (1948). *The Unknown Sea* (London, Eyre and Spottiswoode).

Mauriac, François (1961). *Second Thoughts: Reflections on Literature and Life* (London, Darwen Finlayson).

Maurois, André (1957). *Three Musketeers: A Study of the Dumas Family* (London, Cape).

Mauss, Marcel (1972). *A General Theory of Magic* (London, Routledge; original edn, 1904).

Mauss, Marcel (1974). *Oeuvres, 2. Représentations collectives et diversité des civilisations* (Paris, Editions de Minuit).

Maxwell, Gavin (1957). *God Protect me from my Friends* (London, Longman).

McClatchey, Diana (1960). *Oxfordshire Clergy, 1777–1869: A Study of the Established Church and of the Role of its Clergy in Local Society* (Oxford, Clarendon Press).

McCulloh, John M. (1976). 'The Cult of Relics in the Letters and "Dialogues" of Pope Gregory the Great: A Lexicographical Study', *Traditio*, 32, pp. 145–84.

McLaren, Angus (1984). *Reproductive Rituals: The Perception of Fertility in England from the Sixteenth Century to the Nineteenth Century* (London, Methuen).

McManners, John (1960). *French Ecclesiastical Society under the Ancien Régime: A Study of Angers in the Eighteenth Century* (Manchester, MUP).

McNeill, F. Marian (1959). *The Silver Bough*, II, *A Calendar of Scottish National Festivals, Candlemas to Harvest Home* (Glasgow, William Maclellan).

McNeill, John T. (1933). 'Folk-Paganism in the Penitentials', *Journal of Religion*, 13, pp. 450–66.

McNeill, John T. (1954). *The History and Character of Calvinism* (New York, OUP).

McNeill, John T. and Gamer, Helena M. (eds.) (1938). *Medieval Handbooks of Penance: A Translation of the Principal Libri Poenitentiales and Selections from Related Documents* (New York, Columbia), Records of Civilization, Sources and Studies, 29.

Mead, Margaret (ed.) (1959). *An Anthropologist at Work: Writings of Ruth Benedict* (Boston, Houghton Mifflin).

Mellot, Jean (1971). 'Le culte de Saint Vincent en Berry depuis la fin de la période révolutionnaire', *Actes du 94e congrès national des sociétés savantes*, Pau, 1969, Section d'histoire moderne et contemporaine, 2 (Paris, Bibliothèque Nationale), pp. 289–300.

Menefee, Samuel Pyeatt (1981). *Wives for Sale: An Ethnographic Study of British Popular Divorce* (Oxford, Blackwell).

Mercier, André (1925). 'Les plantes dans la médecine populaire au XVIIe siècle', *Ethnographie*, 31/32, pp. 81–103.

Mercier, Louis Sébastien (1929). *The Picture of Paris*, ed. W. and E. Jackson (London, Routledge).

Mérimée, Prosper (1971). *Notes d'un voyage en Corse, 1840* in *Notes de voyages* (Paris), pp. 645–745.

Merrifield, Ralph (1987). *The Archaeology of Ritual and Magic* (London, Batsford).

Michaelis-Jena (1970). *The Brothers Grimm* (London, Routledge).

Miller, B.D.H. (1962). ' "She Who Hath Drunk Any Potion" ... ', *Medium Aevum*, 31. pp. 188–93.

Milton, John (1950). *Areopagitica and Other Prose Works* (London, Everyman).

Milton, John (1966). *Poetical Works*, ed. Douglas Bush (London, OUP).

Minois, Georges (1989). *Les Religieux en Bretagne sous l'Ancien Régime* (Luçon, Editions Ouest-France).

Mintz, Sidney W. and Wolf, Eric R. (1950). 'An Analysis of Ritual Co-Parenthood (Compadrazgo)', *Southwestern Journal of Anthropology*, 6, pp. 341–68.

Mistral, Frédéric (1978). *Mireille* (*Mirèio*) (Paris, Garnier-Flammarion; original edn, 1859).

Mistral, Frédéric (1980). *Mémoires et récits* (Raphèle-lès-Arles, Marcel Petit; original edn, 1906).

Moiset, M.C. (1888). 'Les usages, croyances, traditions, superstitions, etc., ayant existé autrefois ou existant encore dans les divers pays du département de l'Yonne', *Bulletin de la Société des Sciences Historiques et Naturelles de l'Yonne*, 42, Ier sémestre, pp. 5–157.

Montagu, Lady Mary Wortley (1914). *Letters 1709 to 1762* (London, Everyman).

Montaigne, Michel de (1940). *Essays* (London, Everyman), 3 vols.

Montaigne, Michel de (1946). *Journal de voyage en Italie en 1580 et 1581*, ed. Charles Dédéyan (Paris, Société Les Belles Lettres).

Monter, William (1983). *Ritual, Myth and Magic in Early Modern Europe* (Brighton, Harvester Press).

Moorman, J.R.H. (1946). *Church Life in England in the Thirteenth Century* (Cambridge, CUP).

More, Thomas (1951). *Utopia* and *A Dialogue of Comfort*, ed. John Warrington. (London, Everyman).

Morel, Marie-France (1980). 'City and Country in Eighteenth-Century Discussions about Early Childhood', in Robert Forster and Orest Ranum (eds.), *Medicine and Society in France: Selections from the Annales* (Baltimore, Johns Hopkins), ch. 3.

Morin, Louis (1892). 'Empiriques et guérisseurs de l'Aube', *Revue des Traditions Populaires*, 7, pp. 88–90.

Moss, Leonard W. and Cappannari, Stephen C. (1953). 'The Black Madonna: An Example of Cultural Borrowing', *Scientific Monthly*, 76 (June), pp. 319–24.

Moss, Leonard W. and Cappannari, Stephen, C. (1960). 'Folklore and Medicine in an Italian Village', *Journal of American Folklore*, 73, pp. 95–102.

Moulis, Adelin (1961). 'Médecine populaire en Ariège: devins et guérisseurs', *Arts et Traditions Populaires*, 9, pp. 115–25.

Mozart, W.A. (1956). *Letters*, ed. Eric Blom (Harmondsworth, Penguin).

Muchembled, Robert (1973). 'Sorcellerie, culture populaire et christianisme au XVIe siècle principalement en Flandre et en Artois', *Annales*, 28, pp. 264–84; and in Robert Forster and Orest Ranum (eds.), *Ritual, Religion, and the Sacred: Selections from the Annales* (Baltimore, Johns Hopkins), ch. 10.

Muchembled, Robert (1979). 'The Witches of the Cambrésis: The Acculturation of the Rural World in the Sixteenth and Seventeenth Centuries', in James Obelkevich (ed.), *Religion and the People, 800–1700* (Chapel Hill, University of North Carolina), ch. 6.

Muchembled, Robert (1990) 'Satanic Myths and Cultural Reality', in Ankarloo and Henningsen (eds.), ch. 5.

Muir, Edward (1997). *Ritual in Early Modern Europe* (Cambridge, CUP).

Muir, Lynette R. (1985). *Literature and Society in Medieval France: The Mirror and the Image, 1100–1500* (London, Macmillan).

Must, Gustav (1960). 'A Gaulish Incantation in Marcellus of Bordeaux', *Language*, 36, pp. 193–7.

Myer, Valerie Grosvenor (1984). 'Tristram and the Animal Spirits', in Myer (ed.), *Laurence Sterne: Riddles and Mysteries* (London and Totowa), ch. 7.

Myrc, John (1868). *Instructions for Parish Priests*, ed. Edward Peacock (London), Early English Text Society, 31.

Nalle, Sara (1987). 'Popular Religion in Cuenca on the Eve of the Catholic Reformation', in Stephen Haliczer (ed.), *Inquisition and Society in Early Modern Europe* (London, Croom Helm), Ch. 4.

Naroll, Frada (1960). 'Child Training among Tyrolean Peasants', *Anthropological Quarterly*, 33, pp. 106–14.

Nelson, Robert (1722). *Companion for the Festivals and Fasts of the Church of England* (London, R. Bonwicke et al.; 12th edn).

Nerval, Gérard de (1958). *Oeuvres*, I (Paris, Garnier).

Neuman, Dov (1956). 'Five Hucul Healing Incantations', *Indiana Slavic Studies*, 1, pp. 191–207.

Newman, L.F. (1946). 'Some Notes on the History and Practice of Witchcraft in the Eastern Counties', *Folklore*, 57, pp. 12–33.

New Testament, The New English Bible (1961) (OUP/CUP).

Newton, Benjamin (1933). *Diary, 1816–1818*, ed. C.P. Fendall and E.A. Crutchley (Cambridge, CUP).

Niccoli, Ottavia (1990). *Prophecy and People in Renaissance Italy* (Princeton).

Niccolini di Camugliano, Ginevra (1933). *The Chronicles of a Florentine Family, 1200–1470* (London, Cape).

Nicolson, Frank W. (1897). 'The Saliva Superstition in Classical Literature', *Harvard Studies in Classical Philology*, 8, pp. 23–40.

Nun's Rule, The (1926). Ed. James Morton (London, Chatto and Windus).

Odenkirchen, Carl J. (ed.) (1978). *The Life of St Alexius in the Old French Version of the Hildesheim Manuscript* (Brookline, Mass., and Leyden), Classical Folia Editions.

O'Neil, Mary R. (1984). '*Sacerdote ovvero strione*: Ecclesiastical and Superstitious Remedies in Sixteenth-Century Italy', in Steven L. Kaplan (ed.), *Understanding Popular Culture: Europe from the Middle Ages to the Nineteenth Century* (Berlin, Mouton), pp. 53–83.

O'Neil, Mary R. (1987). 'Magical Healing, Love Magic and the Inquisition in Late Sixteenth-Century Modena', in Stephen Haliczer (ed.), *Inquisition and Society in Early Modern Europe* (London, Croom Helm), ch. 5.

Opie, Iona and Peter (eds.) (1974). *The Classic Fairy Tales* (Oxford, OUP).

Opie, Iona and Peter (eds.) (1989). *The Oxford Dictionary of Nursery Rhymes* (Oxford, OUP).

Origo, Iris (1953). *Leopardi: A Study in Solitude* (London, Hamish Hamilton).

Origo, Iris (1957). *The Merchant of Prato: Francesco di Marco Datini* (London, Cape).

Origo, Iris (1963). *The World of San Bernardino* (London, Cape).

Origo, Iris (1970). *Images and Shadows: Part of a Life* (London, John Murray).

Orme, Nicholas (1995). 'The Culture of Children in Medieval England', *Past and Present*, 148, pp. 48–88.

Orwell, George (1961). *Collected Essays* (London, Secker and Warburg).

Osborne, Robin (1987). *Classical Landscape with Figures: The Ancient Greek City and its Countryside* (London, George Philip).

O'Sullivan, Maurice (1975). *Twenty Years A-Growing* (London, OUP), World's Classics; original edn, 1933.

Otis, Leah L. (1986). 'Municipal Wet Nurses in Fifteenth-Century Montpellier', in Barbara A. Hanawalt (ed.), *Women and Work in Preindustrial Europe* (Bloomington, Indiana University), ch. 5.

Ovid (1872). *The Fasti, Tristia, Pontic Epistles*, ed. Henry T. Riley (London, Bell and Daldy), Bohn.

Owen, Rev. D. Edmondes (1910–11). 'Pre-Reformation Survivals in Radnorshire', *Transactions of the Honourable Society of Cymmrodorion*, pp. 92–114.

Owen, Rev Elias (1976). *Welsh Folk-Lore: A Collection of the Folk-Tales and Legends of North Wales* (Wakefield, EP Publishing; original edn, 1896).

Owen, Trefor M. (1961). 'A Breconshire Marriage Custom', *Folklore*, 72, pp. 372–84.

Owen, Trefor M. (1973). 'The Celebration of Candlemas in Wales', *Folklore*, 84, pp. 238–51.

Owen, Trefor M. (1987). *Welsh Folk Customs* (Llandysul, Gomer).

Owen, Trefor M. (1991). *The Customs and Traditions of Wales: A Pocket Guide.* (Cardiff, University of Wales).

Oxford Book of Ballads, The (1910). Ed. Arthur Quiller-Couch (Oxford, Clarendon Press).

Oxford Dictionary of English Proverbs, The (1970). Ed. William George Smith and F.P. Wilson (Oxford, Clarendon Press, 3rd edn).

Ozment, Steven E. (1975). *The Reformation in the Cities: The Appeal of Protestantism to Sixteenth-Century Germany and Switzerland* (New Haven, Yale).

Ozment, Steven E. (1983). *When Fathers Ruled: Family Life in Reformation Europe* (Cambridge, Mass., Harvard).

Ozment, Steven E. (ed.) (1990). *Three Behaim Boys: Growing up in Early Modern Germany* (New Haven, Yale).

Page, John T. (1895). 'Beating the Bounds', in William Andrews (ed.), *Curious Church Customs* (Hull, William Andrews), pp. 182–90.

Pancino, Claudia (1981). 'La comare levatrice: crisi di un mestiere nel XVIII secolo', *Società e Storia*, 13, pp. 593–638.

Pannet, Robert (1974). *Le Catholicisme populaire: trente ans après 'La France, pays de mission?'* (Paris: Editions du Centurion).

Paris, Matthew (1984). *Chronicles: Monastic Life in the Thirteenth Century*, ed. Richard Vaughan (Gloucester, Alan Sutton).

Park, Katharine and Daston, Lorraine J. (1981). 'Unnatural Conceptions: The Study of Monsters in Sixteenth- and Seventeenth-Century France and England', *Past and Present*, 92, pp. 20–54.

Partner, Peter (1987). *The Murdered Magicians: The Templars and their Myth* (London, Crucible).

Pasternak, Boris (1959). *An Essay in Autobiography* (London, Collins and Harvill Press).

Patlagean, E. (1981). 'Christianisation et parentés rituelles: le domaine de Byzance', in Patlagean, *Structure sociale, famille, chrétienté à Byzance, IVe–XIe siècles* (London, Variorum Reprints), pp. 625–36.

Payne, Joseph Frank (1904). *English Medicine in the Anglo-Saxon Times* (Oxford).

Peacock, Florence (1895). 'Church Bells: When and Why they were Rung', in William Andrews (ed.), *Curious Church Customs* (Hull, William Andrews), pp. 33–63.

Peele, George (1908). *The Old Wives Tale (1595).* (Oxford), Malone Society Reprint.

Pegeot, Pierre (1982). 'Un exemple de parenté baptismale à la fin du moyen age: Porrentruy, 1482–1500', in *Les Entrées dans la vie: initiations et apprentissages* (Nancy, Presses Universitaires).

Penguin Book of Comic and Cuious Verse, The (1952). Ed. J.M. Cohen (Harmondsworth).

Pentikäinen, Juha (1968). *The Nordic Dead-Child Tradition: A Study in Comparative Religion* (Helsinki, Academia Scientiarum Fennica).

Pepys, Samuel (1970). *Diary*, III, *1662*, ed. Robert Latham and William Matthews. (London, Bell).

Perdrizet, Paul (1933). *Le Calendrier parisien à la fin du moyen âge d'après le bréviaire et les livres d'heures* (Gap, Editions Ophrys), Publications de la Faculté des Lettres de l'Université de Strasbourg, 63.

Perry, Mary Elizabeth (1987). 'Beata and the Inquisition in Early Modern Seville' in Stephen Haliczer (ed.), *Inquisition and Society in Early Modern Europe* (London, Croom Helm), Ch. 8.

Persius (1918 and 1961). In Juvenal and Persius. Ed G.G. Ramsay.

Peter, Jean-Pierre (1971). 'Les mots et les objects de la maladie: remarques sur les épidémies et la médecine dans la société française de la fin du XVIIIe siècle', *Revue Historique*, 246, pp. 13–38.

Peters, Edward (ed.) (1975). *Monks, Bishops and Pagans: Christian Culture in Gaul and Italy, 500–700* (Philadelphia, University of Pennsylvania).

Peters, Edward (1978). *The Magician, the Witch and the Law* (Hassocks, Harvester Press).

Philipps, Mark (1989). *The Memoir of Marco Parenti: A Life in Medici Florence.* (London, Heinemann).

Philipps, Virginia (1978a). ' "Brought up by Hand": Dickens's Pip, Little Paul Dombey, and Oliver Twist', *The Dickensian*, 74, pp. 144–7.

Philipps, Virginia (1978b). 'Children in Early Victorian England: Infant Feeding in Literature and Society, 1837–1857', *Journal of Tropical Pediatrics*, 24, pp. 158–66.

Piggott, Stuart (1962). 'Heads and Hoofs', *Antiquity*, 36, pp. 110–18.

Pina-Cabral, João de (1986). *Sons of Adam, Daughters of Eve: The Peasant Worldview of the Alto Minho* (Oxford, Clarendon Press).

Pinard, Joseph (1976). 'La piété populaire en Franche-Comté à travers les mémoires de Claude et Jean-François Pinard', *Actes du 99e congrès national des sociétés savantes, Besançon, 1974*, Section d'histoire moderne et contemporaine, 2, pp. 237–47.

Pinchbeck, Ivy and Hewitt, Margaret (1969). *Children in English Society*, I, *From Tudor Times to the Eighteenth Century* (London).

Pitt-Rivers, Julian A. (1971). *The People of the Sierra* (Chicago, 2nd edn).

Pitt-Rivers, Julian A. (1976). 'Ritual Kinship in the Mediterranean: Spain and the Balkans', in J.G. Peristiany (ed.), *Mediterranean Family Structures* (Cambridge, CUP), ch. 16.

Pius II, Pope (Aeneas Sylvius Piccolomini) (1960). *Memoirs of a Renaissance Pope: The Commentaries*, ed. Leona C. Gabel (London, Allen and Unwin).

Platelle, Henri (ed.) (1968). *Les Chrétiens face au miracle: Lille au XVIIe siècle* (Paris, Editions du Cerf).

Platelle, Henri (1980). 'Crime et châtiment à Marchiennes: étude sur la conception et le fonctionnement de la justice d'après les Miracles de Sainte Rictrude (XIIe siècle)',

Sacris Erudiri, 24, pp. 155–202.

Platter, Thomas (junior) (1937). *Travels in England 1599*, ed. Clare Williams (London, Cape).

Platter, Thomas (junior) (1963). *Journal of a Younger Brother: The Life of Thomas Platter as a Medical Student in Montpellier at the Close of the Sixteenth Century*, ed. Sean Jennett (London, Frederick Muller).

Platter, Thomas (senior) (1964). *Autobiographie*, ed. Marie Helmer (Paris, Armand Colin), Cahiers des Annales, 22.

Pliny the Elder (1938–63). *Natural History*, ed. H. Rackham et al. (London, Heinemann, and Cambridge, Mass., Harvard), Loeb, 10 vols.

Plutarch (1992). *Essays*, ed. Ian Kidd and Robin Waterfield (Harmondsworth, Penguin).

Poly, Jean-Pierre and Bournazel, Eric (1991). *The Feudal Transformation, 900–1200* (New York, Holmes and Meier).

Pomponi, Francis (1978). 'A la recherche d'un "invariant" historique: la structure clanique dans la société corse', in M. Caisson et al. (eds.), *Pieve e Paesi: communautés rurales corses* (Paris, CNRS), ch. 1.

Porter, Enid (1969). *Cambridgeshire Customs and Folklore* (London, Routledge).

Porter, Roy (ed.) (1985). *Patients and Practitioners: Lay Perceptions of Medicine in Pre-Industrial Society* (Cambridge, CUP).

Porter, Roy (1987). *Disease, Medicine and Society in England, 1550–1860* (London, Macmillan).

Porter, Roy (1995). 'The People's Health in Georgian England', in Tim Harris (ed.), *Popular Culture in England, c. 1500–1850* (London, Macmillan), ch. 6.

Porter, Roy and Dorothy (1988). *In Sickness and in Health: The British Experience, 1650–1850* (London).

Potts, Thomas (1845). *Discovery of Witches in the County of Lancaster: Reprinted from the Original Edition of 1613*, ed. James Crossley. Chetham Society, 6.

Poueigh, Jean (1976). *Le Folklore des Pays d'Oc: la tradition occitane* (Paris, Payot).

Pourrat, Annette (1976). *Traditions d'Auvergne* (Verviers, Marabout).

Powell, Dilys (1957). *An Affair of the Heart* (London, Hodder and Stoughton).

Prandi, Carlo (1977). 'Religion et classes subalternes en Italie: trente années de recherches italiennes', *Archives de Sciences Sociales des Religions*, 43, pp. 93–139.

Prescott, H.F.M. (1954). *Jerusalem Journey: Pilgrimage to the Holy Land in the Fifteenth Century* (London).

Pressey, Rev. W.J. (1930). 'The Records of the Archdeaconries of Essex and Colchester', *Transactions of the Essex Archaeological Society*, NS 19, pp. 1–21.

Price, Simon (1987). 'From Noble Funerals to Divine Cult: The Consecration of Roman Emperors', in David Cannadine and Simon Price (eds.), *Rituals of Royalty, Power and Ceremonial in Traditional Societies* (Cambridge, CUP), ch. 2.

Propertius (1912). Trans. H.E. Butler (London and Cambridge, Mass.), Loeb.

Propertius (1961). *Poems.* trans. A.E. Watts. (London, Centaur Press).

Prümmer, Dominic M. (1956). *Handbook of Moral Theology* (Cork).

Pullan, Brian (1983). *The Jews of Europe and the Inquisition of Venice, 1550–1670* (Oxford, Blackwell).

Quinze Joyes de mariage, Les (1918). Ed. François Tulou (Paris, Garnier).

Rackham, Bernard (1952). *Italian Maiolica* (London, Faber).

Radford, E. and M. (1978a). *Superstitions of Death and the Supernatural*, ed. Christina Hole (London, Arrow Books).

Radford, E. and M. (1978b). *Superstitions of Love and Marriage*, ed. Christina Hole (London, Arrow Books).

Raglan, Lord (1940). *Jocasta's Crime: An Anthropological Study* (London, Watts).

Raison-du-Cleuziou, Abbé J. (1952). 'Contribution à l'histoire du pardon de Saint-Servais', *Actes du 77e congrès national des sociétés savantes, Grenoble 1952*. pp. 287–95.

Ramsey, Matthew (1988). *Professional and Popular Medicine in France, 1770–1830: The Social World of Medical Practice* (Cambridge, CUP).

Randell, Arthur (1966). *Sixty Years a Fenman*, ed. Enid Porter (London, Routledge).

Ranum, Orest (1979). *Paris in the Age of Absolutism* (Bloomington, Indiana University Press).

Rasmussen, Steen Eiler (1960). *London: The Unique City* (Harmondsworth, Penguin).

Ravis-Giordani, Georges (1976). 'La femme corse dans la société villageoise traditionnelle: statuts et rôles' *Etudes Corses*, 4, pp. 6–19.

Rawcliffe, Carole (1995). *Medicine and Society in Later Medieval England* (Stroud, Alan Sutton).

Rebouillat, Marguerite (1976). 'Les sanctuaires de Bourgogne dits "à répit"', *Actes du 99e congrès national des sociétés savantes, Besançon, 1974*, Section d'histoire moderne et contemporaine, 1, pp. 173–92.

Régné, Jean (1913). 'La sorcellerie en Vivarais et la répression inquisitoriale et séculière du XVe au XVIIe siècle', in *Mélanges d'histoire offerts à M. Charles Bémont* (Paris, Alcan), pp. 481–508.

Régnier-Bohler, Danielle (1988). 'Imagining the Self, Exploring Literature', in Georges Duby (ed.), *A History of Private Life*, II, *Revelations of the Medieval World* (Cambridge, Mass., Harvard, Belknap Press), ch. 3.

Rémy, Nicolas (1930 and 1970). *Demonolatry in Three Books*, trans. E.A. Ashwin (London).

Reymond, Maxime (1909). 'Cas de sorcellerie en pays fribourgeois au quinzième siècle', *Schweizerisches Archiv für Volkskunde*, 12, pp. 81–94.

Reynolds, Lou Agnes and Sawyer, Paul (1959). 'Folk Medicine and the Four Fairies of *A Midsummer Night's Dream*', *Shakespeare Quarterly*, pp. 513–21.

Ribeyrol, Monique and Schnapper, Dominique (1976). 'Cérémonies funéraires dans la Yougoslavie orthodoxe', *Archives Européennes de Sociologie*, 17, pp. 220–46.

Riché, Pierre (1978). *Daily Life in the World of Charlemagne* (Liverpool).

Riché, Pierre (1981). 'La magie à l'époque carolingienne', in Riché, *Instruction et vie religieuse dans le haut moyen âge* (London, Variorum Reprints), ch. 22.

Riddle, John M. (1974). 'Theory and Practice in Medieval Medicine', *Viator*, 5, pp. 157–84.

Riet, Didier (1986). 'Infanticide et société au XVIIIe siècle: bruits publics et rumeurs dans la communauté', *Ethnologie Française*, 16, pp. 401–6.

Rivals, Claude (1987). 'Renard trop humain? D'après les recherches d'Eugène Rolland sur la *Faune populaire*', in Jacques Hainard and Roland Kaehr (eds.), *Des Animaux et des hommes* (Neuchâtel, Musée d'Ethnographie).

Robbins, Rossell Hope (1978). *Witchcraft: An Introduction to the Literature* (New York, KTO Press).

Robert, C.-M. (1905). *Phraséologie française: répertoire systématique de proverbes, dictons et locutions idiomatiques* (Groningen, Wolters).

Roberts, J.A. Fraser (1959). 'The Unborn Child', *Journal of the Royal Anthropological Institute*, 89, pp. 117–27.

Rocal, Georges (1922). *Les Vieilles Coutumes dévotieuses et magiques de Périgord.*

(Toulouse, Librairie Marqueste).

Rolleston, J.D. (1943). 'The Folklore of Children's Diseases', *Folk-Lore*, 54, pp. 287–307.

Ronsard, Pierre de (1965–6). *Oeuvres complètes* (Gallimard, Bibliothèque de la Pléiade), 2 vols.

Roodenburg, Herman W. (1984–5). 'The Autobiography of Isabella de Moerloose: Sex, Childrearing and Popular Belief in Seventeenth-Century Holland', *Journal of Social History*, 18, pp. 517–39.

Rose, Georges (1981). *Ecologie et tradition: influences cosmiques dans l'agriculture biologique et les traditions populaires. Le calendrier annuel, le cycle des douze jours, la lune* (Paris, Maisonneuve et Larose).

Rose, William John (ed.) (1941). *From Serfdom to Self-Government: Memoirs of a Polish Village Mayor, 1842–1927* (London, Minerva).

Ross, James Bruce (1976). 'The Middle-Class Child in Urban Italy, Fourteenth to Early Sixteenth Century', in Lloyd de Mause (ed.), *The History of Childhood* (London, Souvenir Press), ch. 4.

Rothkrug, Lionel (1979). 'Popular Religion and Holy Shrines: Their Influence on the Origins of the German Reformation and their Role in German Cultural Development', in James Obelkevich (ed.), *Religion and the People, 800–1700* (Chapel Hill, University of North Carolina), ch. 2.

Roubin, Lucienne (1977). 'Male Space and Female Space within the Provençal Community, in Robert Forster and Orest Ranum (eds.), *Rural Society in France, Selections from the Annales* (Baltimore, Johns Hopkins), ch. 8.

Rougé, J. (1968). 'Topos et realia: la tempête apaisée de la Vie de Saint Germain d'Auxerre', *Latomus*, 27, pp. 197–202.

Rousselle, Aline (1983). 'La sage-femme et le thaumaturge dans la Gaule tardive: les sages-femmes ne font pas de miracles', *Revue Archéologique du Centre de la France*, 22, pp. 261–71.

Beryl Rowland (ed.) (1981). *Medieval Woman's Guide to Health: The First English Gynecological Handbook* (Kent, Ohio).

Rowland, Robert (1990). '"Fantasticall and Devilishe Persons": European Witch-Beliefs in Comparative Perspective', in Ankarloo and Henningsen (eds.), ch. 6.

Rubellin, Michel (1982). 'Entrée dans la vie, entrée dans la chrétienté, entrée dans la société: autour du baptême à l'époque carolingienne', in *Les Entrées dans la vie: initiations et apprentissages* (Nancy, Presses Universitaires), pp. 31–51.

Ruggiero, Guido (1993). *Binding Passions: Tales of Magic, Marriage and Power at the End of the Renaissance* (New York and Oxford, OUP).

Runeberg, Arne (1947). *Witches, Demons and Fertility Magic: Analysis of their Significance and Mutual Relations in West-European Folk Religion* (Helsinki), Societas Scientiarum Fennica Commentationes Humanarum Litterarum, 14: 4.

Rushton, Peter (1982). 'Women, Witchcraft and Slander in Early Modern England: Cases from the Church Courts of Durham, 1560–1675', *Northern History*, 18, pp. 116–32.

Rushton, Peter (1983). 'Purification or Social Control? Ideologies of Reproduction and the Churching of Women after Childbirth', in Eva Gamarnikow et al. (eds.), *The Public and the Private* (London, Heinemann), ch. 10.

Russell, Jeffrey Burton (1986). *Lucifer: The Devil in the Middle Ages* (Ithaca, Cornell).

Ryan, William F., S.J. (1963). 'The Teaching of St Thomas in the *Summa* concerning the Baptismal Character', *American Ecclesiastical Review*, 149, pp. 361–85.

Sabean, David Warren (1984). *Power in the Blood: Popular Culture and Village Discourse*

(Cambridge, CUP).

Saga of Gisli, The (1973). Ed. Peter Foote and George Johnston (London, Everyman).

Said, Edward W. (1985). *Orientalism* (Harmondsworth, Penguin).

Saintyves, P. (1910). 'Ceintures magiques et processions enveloppantes', *Revue des Traditions Populaires*, 15, pp. 113–23.

Saintyves, P. (1911). 'Les résurrections d'enfants mort-nés et les sanctuaires à"répit" ', *Revue d'Ethnographie et de Sociologie*, 2, pp. 65–74.

Saintyves, P. (1922). 'Le tour et la ceinture de l'église', *Revue Archéologique*, 5th series, 15, pp. 79–113.

Saintyves, P. (1935). 'Le folklore des eaux dans le Roussillon, le département de l'Ariège, la Haute-Garonne, les Hautes-Pyrénées, les Basses-Pyrénées', *L'Ethnographie*, 30/31, pp. 3–64.

Salet, François (1948). *La Madeleine de Vézelay* (Melun).

Sallmann, Jean-Michel (1979). 'Image et fonction du saint dans la région de Naples à la fin du XVIIe et au début du XVIIIe siècle', *Mélanges de l'Ecole Française de Rome*, 91, pp. 827–74.

Salomone-Marino, Salvatore (1981). *Customs and Habits of the Sicilian Peasants*, ed. Rosalie N. Norris (Rutherford, Fairleigh Dickinson; original edn, 1897).

Sand, George (1926). *La Petite Fadette* (Paris, Calmann-Lévy; original edn, 1848).

Saravelli-Retali, F. (1976). *La Vie en Corse à travers proverbes et dictons*.

Sautman, Francesca (1990). 'Saint Anne in Folk Tradition: Late Medieval France', in Kathleen Ashley and Pamela Sheingorn (eds.), *Interpreting Cultural Symbols: Saint Anne in Late Medieval Society* (Athens, University of Georgia), pp. 69–94.

Sauzet, Robert (1965). 'Pèlerinage panique et pèlerinage de dévotion: Notre-Dame de Rochefort au XVIIe siècle, *Annales du Midi*, 77, pp. 375–97.

Sauzet, Robert (no date). *Contre-réforme et réforme catholique en Bas-Languedoc: le diocèse de Nîmes au XVIIe siècle* (Paris and Brussels, Publications de la Sorbonne), Series, N.S. Recherches, 30.

Schama, Simon (1987). *The Embarrassment of Riches: An Interpretation of Dutch Culture in the Golden Age* (London, Collins).

Schmitt, Jean-Claude (1981). 'Les traditions folkloriques dans la culture médiévale: quelques refléxions de méthode', *Archives de Sciences Sociales des Religions*, 52, pp. 5–20.

Schneid, Hayyim (1973). *Popular History of Jewish Civilization, Family* (New York, Leon Amiel).

Schneider, Peter and Jane (1973–4). 'Sicilian Harvest Song', *Journal of Peasant Studies*, 1, pp. 390–5.

Schnucker, R.V. (1974). 'The English Puritans and Pregnancy, Delivery and Breast Feeding', *History of Childhood Quarterly*, 1, pp. 637–58.

Scot, Reginald (1973). *The Discoverie of Witchcraft* (1584) (Wakefield).

Scott, Sir Walter (1884). *Letters on Demonology and Witchcraft* (London, Routledge; original edn, 1830).

Scott, Sir Walter (1860). *Rob Roy* (Edinburgh, Black) 2 vols; original edn, 1817.

Scribner, R.W. (1987). *Popular Culture and Popular Movements in Reformation Germany* (London, Hambledon Press).

Sebald, Hans (1980). 'Franconian Witchcraft: The Demise of a Folk Magic', *Anthropological Quarterly*, 53, pp. 173–87.

Sébillot, Paul (1899a). 'Notes sur le culte des arbres'. *Revue des Traditions Populaires*, 14, pp. 449–58.

Sébillot, Paul (1899b). 'Le culte des fontaines', *Revue des Traditions Populaires*, 14, pp. 593–607.

Sébillot, Paul (1899c). 'La mer et les eaux: le baptême', *Revue des Traditions Populaires*, 14, pp. 390–7.

Sébillot, Paul (1906a), 'Les ex-voto', *Revue des Traditions Populaires*, 21, pp. 161–4.

Sébillot, Paul (1906b), 'Le tour de l'église', *Revue des Traditions Populaires*, 21, pp. 164–5.

Sébillot, Paul (1968). *Le Folk-lore de France* (Paris: Maisonneuve, 4 vols. Original edn, 1904–7).

Sedgwick, Anne Douglas (1919). *A Childhood in Brittany Eighty Years Ago* (London, Edward Arnold).

Segalen, Martine (1975). 'Rituels funéraires en Normandie et attitudes vis-à-vis de la mort', *Archives de Sciences Sociales des Religions*, 39, pp. 79–88.

Segalen, Martine (1983). *Love and Power in the Peasant Family: Rural France in the Nineteenth Century* (Oxford, Blackwell).

Seneca (1986). *Three Tragedies: Trojan Women, Medea, Phaedra*, ed. Frederick Ahl (Ithaca, Cornell).

Senior, Nancy (1982–3). 'Aspects of Infant Feeding in Eighteenth-Century France' *Eighteenth-Century Studies*, 16, pp. 367–88.

Sévigné, Madame de (1955). *Letters*, ed. Violet Hammersley (London, Secker and Warburg).

Seznec, Jean (1972). *The Survival of the Pagan Gods: The Mythological Tradition and its Place in Renaissance Humanism and Art* (Princeton), Bollingen Series, 38. Original edn. 1939.

Shahar, Shulamith (1990). *Childhood in the Middle Ages* (London, Routledge).

Shakespeare, William. The Arden edition (London, Methuen) of the individual plays has been used.

Sharpe, C.K. (1972). *A Historical Account of the Belief in Witchcraft in Scotland* (Wakefield; original edn, 1884).

Shaw, William A. (ed.). (1891). *Minutes of the Manchester Presbyterian Classis, 1646–1660*, Chetham Society, 20, 22, and 24.

Sherwood, Joan (1988). *Poverty in Eighteenth-Century Spain: The Women and Children of the Inclusa* (Toronto).

Sigal, Pierre-André (1969). 'Maladie, pèlerinage et guérison au XIIe siècle: les miracles de Saint Gibrien à Reims', *Annales*, 24, pp. 1522–39.

Simon, Marcel (1981). *Le Christianisme antique et son contexte religieux: Scripta varia*, I. (Tübingen, Mohr), Wissenschaftliche Untersuchungen zum Neuen Testament, 23.

Simpson, Jacqueline (1976). *The Folklore of the Welsh Border* (London, Batsford).

Sinanoglou, Leah (1973). 'The Christ Child as Sacrifice: A Medieval Tradition and the Corpus Christi Plays', *Speculum*, 48, pp. 491–509.

Sinclar, George (1871). *Satan's Invisible World Discovered* (1685) (Edinburgh).

Sisson, C.J. (1958). 'The Magic of Prospero', *Shakespeare Survey*, 11, pp. 70–7.

Slack, Paul A. (1987). 'Vagrants and Vagrancy in England, 1598–1664', in Peter Clark and David Souden (eds), *Migration and Society in Early Modern England* (London, Hutchinson), ch. 2.

Slater, Miriam (1984). *Family Life in the Seventeenth Century: The Verneys of Claydon House* (London, Routledge).

Smollett, Tobias (1943). *The Expedition of Humphry Clinker* (London, Everyman; original edn, 1771).

Solnon, Jean-François (1987). *La Cour de France* (Paris, Fayard).

Song of Roland, The (1990). Ed. Guy Burgess (Harmondsworth, Penguin).

Sophocles (1947). *The Theban Plays* (Harmondsworth, Penguin).

Southwell Colucci, Edith (1933). *Canti popolari corsi* (Leghorn).

Spence, Jonathan D. (1988). *The Memory Palace of Matteo Ricci* (London, Faber).

Spenser, Edmund (1952). *The Poetical Works*, eds. J.C. Smith and E. de Selincourt (Oxford, OUP).

Spranger, J.A. (1922). 'The Festival of San Zopito and the Ox at Loreto Aprutino', *Journal of the Royal Anthropological Institute of Great Britain*, 52, pp. 306–19.

Stahl, Paul-Henri (1973). 'L'organisation magique du territoire villageois roumain', *L'Homme*, 13, pp. 150–62.

Stannard, David E. (1979). *The Puritan Way of Death: A Study in Religion, Culture, and Social Change* (New York, OUP).

Steer, John (1989). *Venetian Painting: A Concise History* (London: Thames and Hudson).

Stendhal (1953). *Mémoires d'un touriste* (Paris, Calmann-Lévy), 2 vols.

Stenton, F.M. (1943). *Anglo-Saxon England* (Oxford, Clarendon Press).

Sterne, Laurence (1951). *The Life and Opinions of Tristram Shandy Gentleman* (Oxford, OUP, World's Classics; original edn, 1759–67).

Stevens, Catrin (1986). *Iorwerth C. Peate* (Cardiff, University of Wales).

Stevenson, Kenneth (1983). *Nuptial Blessing: A Study of Christian Marriage Rites* (New York, OUP).

Stopp, Elisabeth (1962). *Madame de Chantal: Portrait of a Saint* (London, Faber).

Storms, G. (1948). *Anglo-Saxon Magic* (The Hague, Nijhoff).

Story, William W. (1863). *Roba di Roma* (London), 2 vols.

Stow, John (1893). *A Survey of London: Written in the Year 1598* (London, Routledge).

Strauss, Gerald (1975). 'Success and Failure in the German Reformation', *Past and Present*, 67, pp. 30–63.

Strauss, Walter L. (ed.) (1981). *The Intaglio Prints of Albrecht Dürer* (New York).

Stuart, H. (1976). 'The Anglo-Saxon Elf', *Studia Neophilologica*, 48, pp. 313–20.

Suetonius (1957). *The Twelve Caesars*, trans. Robert Graves (Harmondsworth, Penguin).

Sussman, George D. (1982). *Selling Mothers' Milk: The Wet-Nursing Business in France, 1715–1914* (Urbana, University of Illinois).

Swann, J.M. (1969). 'Shoes Concealed in Buildings', *Northampton Museums and Art Gallery Journal*, 6, pp. 8–9.

Swift, Jonathan (1948). *Journal to Stella*, ed. Harold Williams (Oxford, Clarendon Press), 2 vols.

Sydow, Carl Wilhelm von (1948). *Selected Papers on Folklore* (Copenhagen).

Synge, J.M. (1979). *The Aran Islands*, ed. Robin Skelton (Oxford, OUP; original edn, 1907).

Tacitus (1956). *The Annals of Imperial Rome*, ed. Michael Grant (Harmondsworth, Penguin).

Talbot, C.H. (ed.) (1954). *The Anglo-Saxon Missionaries in Germany* (London, Sheed and Ward).

Tavenor-Perry, J. (1905). 'Dragons and Monsters beneath Baptismal Fonts', *Reliquary*, 3rd Series, 11, pp. 189–95.

Tax Freeman, Susan (1979). *The Pasiegos: Spaniards in No Man's Land* (Chicago).

Taylor, Archer (1932). 'The Pertinacious Cobold', *Journal of English and Germanic Philology*, 31, pp. 1–9.

Tebbenhoff, Edward H. (1984–5). 'Tacit Rules and Hidden Family Structures: Naming Practices and Godparenting in Schenectady, New York, 1680–1800', *Journal of Social History*, 18, pp. 567–85.

Tennyson, Lady (1981). *Journal*, ed. James O. Hoge (Charlottesville, University of Virginia).

Teresa of Jesus (of Ávila), St (1916). *The Life*, ed. Benedict Zimmerman, O.C.D. (London, Thomas Baker).

Theis, Laurent (1976). 'Saints sans famille? Quelques remarques sur la famille dans le monde franc à travers les sources hagiographiques', *Revue Historique*, 255, pp. 3–20.

Thiriat, X. (1878). 'Croyances, superstitions, préjugés, usages et coutumes dans le département des Vosges', *Mélusine*, 1, pp. 453–8, 478–9 and 498–502.

Thomas, Keith (1973). *Religion and the Decline of Magic: Studies in Popular Beliefs in Sixteenth- and Seventeenth-Century England* (Harmondsworth, Penguin).

Thomas, Keith (1984). *Man and the Natural World: Changing Attitudes in England, 1500–1800* (Harmondsworth, Penguin).

Thompson, Flora (1973). *Lark Rise to Candleford* (Harmondsworth, Penguin; original edns, 1939–45).

Thompson, Stith (1977). *The Folktale* (Berkeley, University of California).

Thompson, T.W. (1925). 'English Gypsy Folk-Medicine', *Journal of the Gypsy Lore Society*, 4, pp. 159–72.

Thorpe, Lewis (ed.) (1969). *Einhard and Notker the Stammerer: Two Lives of Charlemagne* (Harmondsworth, Penguin).

Thrupp, Sylvia L. (1962). *The Merchant Class of Medieval London, 1300–1500* (Ann Arbor, University of Michigan).

Thuillier, Guy (1977). *Pour une histoire du quotidien au XIXe siècle en Nivernais* (The Hague, Mouton).

Thun, Nils (1969). 'The Malignant Elves: Notes on Anglo-Saxon Magic and Germanic Myth', *Studia Neophilologica*, 41, pp. 378–96.

Thurston, Herbert, S.J., (1906). *The Stations of the Cross: An Account of their History and Devotional Purpose* (London, Burns and Oates).

Tibullus (1924). In Catullus, Tibullus and *Pervigilium Veneris* (London, Heinemann, and New York, Putnam) Loeb.

Tilly, Louise A. and Scott, Joan W. (1989). *Women, Work, and the Family* (London and New York, Routledge).

Tomasi, Xavier (no date). *Les Chansons de Cyrnus: anthologie de la chanson populaire de l'île de Corse* (Marseille).

Tommaséo, Niccoló (1855). *Canti popolari corsi* (Bastia, Cesare Fabiani; 2nd edn).

Toubert, Pierre (1973). *Les Structures du Latium médiéval: le Latium méridional et la Sabine du IXe siècle à la fin du XIIe siècle* (Rome, Ecole Française).

Traimond, Bernard (1988). *Le Pouvoir de la maladie: magie et politique dans les Landes de Gascogne, 1750–1826* (Bordeaux, Presses Universitaires), Mémoires des Cahiers ethnologiques, 2.

Trevelyan, Raleigh (1960). *A Hermit Disclosed* (London, Longmans).

Trexler, Richard C. (1972). 'Florentine Religious Experience: The Sacred Image', *Studies in the Renaissance*, 19, pp. 7–41.

Trexler, Richard C. (1973–4). 'The Foundlings of Florence, 1395–1455', *History of Childhood Quarterly*, 1, pp. 259–84.

Trexler, Richard C. (1974). 'Ritual in Florence: Adolescence and Salvation in the

Renaissance', in Charles Trinkaus and Heiko A. Oberman (eds.), *The Pursuit of Holiness in Late Medieval and Renaissance Religion* (Leiden, Brill), ch. 3.

Trigg, E.B. (1975). *Gypsy Demons and Divinities: The Magical and Supernatural Practices of the Gypsies* (London, Sheldon Press).

Turgenev, Ivan (1959). *A Sportsman's Notebook* (London, The Book Society; original edn, 1852).

Tusser, Thomas (1984). *Five Hundred Points of Good Husbandry* (Oxford, OUP).

Tyack, Rev G.S. (1895). 'Holy Day Customs', in William Andrews (ed.), *Curious Church Customs* (Hull, William Andrews), pp. 21–32.

Usher, Roland G. (ed.) (1905). *The Presbyterian Movement in the Reign of Queen Elizabeth as Illustrated by the Minute Book of the Dedham Classis, 1582–1589* (London, Royal Historical Society).

Vacandard, E. (1912). *Etudes de critique et d'histoire religieuse*, troisième série (Paris, Victor Lecoffe/Gabalda).

Valéry, Paul (1968). 'Descartes' (1925), in Valéry, *Masters and Friends* (Princeton), Bollingen Series, 45/9.

Vandenbroucke, D.F., O.S.B., (1947). 'La profession, second baptême', *La Vie Spirituelle*, 315, pp. 250–63.

Varagnac, André (1948). *Civilisation traditionnelle et genres de vie* (Paris, Albin Michel).

Vasari, Giorgio (1987). *Lives of the Artists*, I, ed. George Bull (Harmondsworth, Penguin).

Vauchez, André (1966). 'La religion populaire dans la France méridionale au XIVe siècle, d'après les procès de canonisation', *Cahiers de Fanjeaux*, 11, pp. 92–107.

Vauchez, André (1988). *La Sainteté en Occident aux derniers siècles du moyen âge* (Rome, Ecole Française).

Vaughan, Henry (1891). *Sacred Poems and Pious Ejaculations* (London, Bell; original edn, 1655).

Venard, Marc (1977). 'Itinéraires de processions dans la ville d'Avignon', *Ethnologie Française*, 7, pp. 55–62.

Verga, Giovanni (1985). *I Malavoglia* (London, Dedalus; original edn, 1881).

Vespasiano da Bisticci (1926). *Memoirs: Lives of Illustrious Men of the XVth Century* (London, Routledge).

Vicaire, M.-H., O.P. (1964). *Saint Dominic and his Times* (London, Darton, Longman and Todd).

Villari, Pasquale (1923). *Life and Times of Girolamo Savonarola* (London, Fisher Unwin).

Villette, P. (1961). 'La sorcellerie à Douai', *Mélanges de Science Religieuse*, 18, pp. 123–73.

Villette, P. (1976). *La Sorcellerie et sa répression dans le Nord de la France* (Paris).

Vincent Ferrer, St (1954). *A Christology from the Sermons* (London, Blackfriars).

Virgil (1950 and 1974). Ed. H.R Fairclough (London: Heinemann, and Cambridge, Mass., Harvard) Loeb, 2 vols.

Vita Sanctae Coletae (1381–1447) (1982). Ed. C. Van Corstanje (Tielt and Leiden).

Vloberg, Maurice (1936). *Les Fêtes de la France: coutumes religieuses et populaires* (Grenoble, Arthaud).

Vloberg, Maurice (1960). 'Les réanimations d'enfants mort-nés dans les sanctuaires, dits "à répit", de la Vierge', *Sanctuaires et Pèlerinages*, 18/1, pp. 17–32.

Vogler, Bernard (1972). 'La Réforme et le concept de miracle au XVIe siècle', *Revue d'Histoire de la Spiritualité*, 48, pp. 145–9.

Voigts, Linde E. (1979). 'Anglo-Saxon Plant Remedies and the Anglo-Saxons', *Isis*, 70, pp. 250–68.

Voltaire (1877). *Oeuvres complètes*, X (Paris, Garnier).

Vries, Jan de (1958). 'L'aspect magique de la religion celtique', *Ogam*, 10, pp. 273–84.

Vuillier, Gaston (1896). *The Forgotten Isles: Impressions of Travel in the Balearic Isles, Corsica and Sardinia* (London).

Walker, Susan (1985). *Memorials to the Roman Dead* (London, British Museum Publications).

Walle, Etienne and Francine van de (1972). 'Allaitement, stérilité et contraception: les opinions jusqu' au XIXe siècle', *Population*, 27, pp. 685–700.

Ward, Benedicta (1987). *Miracles and the Medieval Mind: Theory, Record and Event* (London, Wildwood House).

Ward, Donald J. (1970). 'The Separate Functions of the Indo-European Divine Twins', in Jaan Puhvel (ed.), *Myth and Law among the Indo-Europeans* (Berkeley, University of California), pp. 193–202.

Warren, W.L. (1990). *King John* (London, Methuen).

Wear, Andrew (1985). 'Puritan Perceptions of Illness in Seventeenth-Century England', in Roy Porter (ed.), *Patients and Practitioners*, ch. 3.

Webb, J.F. (ed.) (1965). *Lives of the Saints: The Voyage of St Brendan; Bede, Life of Cuthbert; Eddius Stephanus, Life of Wilfrid* (Harmondsworth, Penguin).

Webb, Geoffrey and Walker, Adrian (eds.). (1960). *St Bernard of Clairvaux: The Vita Prima Bernardi* (London, Mowbray).

Weibust, Knut (1972). 'Ritual Coparenthood in Peasant Societies', *Ethnologica Scandinavica*, pp. 101–14.

Whale, J.S. (1955). *The Protestant Tradition: An Essay in Interpretation* (Cambridge, CUP).

Whitaker, E.C. (1960). *Documents of the Baptismal Liturgy* (London, SPCK).

White, Gilbert (No date). *The Natural History of Selborne* (London, Walter Scott; original edn, 1789).

Wickersheimer, Ernest (1922). 'Les guérisons miraculeuses du Cardinal Pierre de Luxembourg (1387–1390)', *Comptes rendus du deuxième congrès international de l'histoire de médecine*, 2, pp. 371–89.

Wiesner, Merry E. (1986). 'Early Modern Midwifery: A Case Study', in Barbara A. Hanawalt (ed.), *Women and Work in Preindustrial Europe* (Bloomington, University of Indiana), ch. 6.

Wilson, Adrian (1985). 'Participant or Patient? Seventeenth-Century Childbirth from the Mother's Point of View', in Roy Porter (ed.), *Patients and Practitioners*, ch. 5.

Wilson, C. Anne (1976). *Food and Drink in Britain from the Stone Age to Recent Times* (Harmondsworth, Penguin).

Wilson, Francesca (1970). *Muscovy: Russia through Foreign Eyes, 1553–1900* (London).

Wilson, J. Dover (1925). *Life in Shakespeare's England: A Book of Elizabethan Prose* (Cambridge, CUP).

Wilson, Stephen (1988). *Feuding, Conflict and Banditry in Nineteenth-Century Corsica* (Cambridge, CUP).

Wilson, Stephen (1998). *The Means of Naming: A Social and Cultural History of Personal Naming in Western Europe* (London, UCL Press).

Wilson, Thomas (1964). *The Diaries, 1731–37 and 1750*, ed. C.L.S. Linnell (London, SPCK).

Wood, Andy (1999). *The Politics of Social Conflict: The Peak Country, 1520–1770* (Cambridge, CUP).

Wood, Charles T. (1981). 'The Doctor's Dilemma: Sin, Salvation, and the Menstrual Cycle in Medieval Thought', *Speculum*, 56, pp. 710–27.

Woodforde, James (1978). *The Diary of a Country Parson, 1758–1802*, ed. John Beresford (Oxford, OUP).

Wrightson, Keith (1975). 'Infanticide in Earlier Seventeenth-Century England', *Local Population Studies*, 15, pp. 10–22.

Wyatt-Brown, Bertram (1983). *Southern Honor: Ethics and Behavior in the Old South* (New York, OUP).

Yerkes, Royden Keith (1953). *Sacrifice in Greek and Roman Religions and Early Judaism* (London, Black).

Young, Michael and Willmott, Peter (1957). *Family and Kinship in East London* (Harmondsworth, Penguin).

Youngson, A.J. (ed.) (1974). *Beyond the Highland Line: Three Journals of Travel in Eighteenth-Century Scotland* (London, Collins).

Zguta, Russell (1977a). 'The Ordeal by Water (Swimming of Witches) in the East Slavic World', *Slavic Review*, 36, pp. 220–30.

Zguta, Russell (1977b). 'Witchcraft Trials in Seventeenth-Century Russia', *American Historical Review*, 82, pp. 1187–1207.

Zguta, Russell (1978). 'Witchcraft and Medicine in Pre-Petrine Russia', *Russian Review*, 37, pp. 438–48.

Zika, Charles (1988). 'Hosts, Processions and Pilgrimages: Controlling the Sacred in Fifteenth-Century Germany', *Past and Present*, 118, pp. 25–64.

Zmigrodzki, Michel de (1890). 'La mère et l'enfant', *Revue des Traditions Populaires*, 5, pp. 385–91.

Zonabend, Françoise (1973). 'Les morts et les vivants: le cimetière de Minot en Chatillonnais', *Etudes Rurales*, 52, pp. 7–23.

Zonabend, Françoise (1978). 'La parenté baptismale à Minot (Côte-d'Or)', *Annales*, 33, pp. 656–76.

Zonabend, Françoise (1980). *La Mémoire longue: temps et histoires au village* (Paris, PUF).

Zuccarelli, Charles (no date). *En glanant quelques souvenirs* (Toulon, SNIP).

Zwingli, Ulrich (1972). *Selected Works*, ed. S.M. Jackson and E. Peters (Philadelphia, University of Pennsylvania).

Index